The Columbia World Dictionary of Islamism

French Edition

EDITORS

Olivier Roy: Research supervisor at the National Center for Scientific Research (CNRS), Paris. Olivier Roy is the author of many books, including *The New Central Asia* (New York University Press, 2000) and *Globalized Islam* (Columbia University Press, 2004).

Antoine Sfeir: Journalist, Editor-in-Chief of *Cahiers d'Orient*, director of the Center for Study and Reflection on the Middle East (CERPO), Paris. Antoine Sfeir's numerous publications include *Islam* (Marabout, 1991) and *Les Réseaux d'Allah – les filières islamistes en France et en Europe* (Plon, 1997).

CONTRIBUTORS

Khattar Abou Diab: Political scientist and researcher in international relations and strategic studies. Khattar Abou Diab was a contributor to *Clés pour l'Islam*, ed. Andrée Gérard (GRIP, 1993) and has made frequent contributors to magazines including *Arabies, Les Cahiers d'Orient, Géopolitique*, and *Rive*.

Patrick Karam: Political scientist, specialist in geopolitics. Patrick Karam is the author of *Les guerres du Caucase* (Perrin, 1995), *Le retour de l'Islam dans l'ex-Empire russe* (L'Harmattan, 1996), and *Asie centrale, le nouveau grand jeu* (L'Harmattan, 2002).

Richard Labevière: Editor-in-Chief at Radio France Internationale (RFI). Richard Labevière has published *Dollars for Terror* (Algora Publishing, 2000) and (with Pierre Péan) *Bethléem en Palestine* (Fayard, 1999).

Julien Lariège (editorial coordination): Political scientist and researcher in association with the Center for Advanced Study on Modern Africa and Asia (CHEAM) and CERPO.

With the assistance of:

Ali Rastebeen: Director of the International Institute for Strategic Studies (Paris) and the Avicenna Cultural Institute; **François Constantini:** Consultant and researcher; **Clément Piault:** Researcher; and **Staff and Contributors of *Cahiers d'Orient*.**

English Edition

EDITOR AND TRANSLATOR *(responsible for updating and additional material)*

John King: Journalist, editor, researcher and translator. Formerly executive producer, BBC Arabic Service, BBC World Service, BBC Radio 4; former Research Fellow, Centre for Research in Ethnic Relations (CRER), University of Warwick; Leverhulme Research Fellow, Paris; Research Fellow, St. Antony's College, Oxford; and Lecturer in political science, University of Khartoum, Sudan. Author of *Three Asian Associations* (CRER, University of Warwick, 1994) and *Handshake in Washington: the beginning of Middle East peace?* (Ithaca Press, 1994).

The
COLUMBIA
WORLD
DICTIONARY
of
ISLAMISM

Olivier Roy and Antoine Sfeir

EDITORS

English edition translated, edited, and adapted by
John King

Columbia University Press   *New York*

Columbia University Press

Publishers Since 1893

New York, Chichester, West Sussex

Copyright © 2007 Columbia University Press

Library of Congress Cataloging-in-Publication Data

Dictionnaire mondial de l'islamisme. English

The Columbia world dictionary of Islamism / Olivier Roy and Antoine Sfeir,
editors ; translated by John King.

p. cm.

Includes index.

ISBN-13: 978-0-231-13130-8 (alk. paper)

ISBN-10: 0-231-13130-5 (alk. paper)

1. Islam—Dictionaries. 2. Islam and politics—Dictionaries.
I. Roy, Olivier, 1949- II. Sfeir, Antoine. III. Title.

BP40.D5313 2007

320.5′5703—dc22

2007030191

Contents

Introduction

ANTOINE SFEIR

The day after September 11, 2001, the world became aware of an Islam whose existence it had scarcely suspected. At once, misunderstandings began to gain currency. It was supposed that all Arabs are Muslims, forgetting that there are some fifteen million who are not. Again it was presumed that all Muslims are Islamists, though Islamists are only a minority in the Muslim world. Finally, all Islamists were taken to be terrorists, although terrorism has been practiced by only a handful of individuals dreaming of Islamic conquest. Islamism is a broad intellectual, religious, and political school within contemporary Islam whose adherents cling to the doctrine that the faith is indivisible, and base their actions on its fundamental principles. Islamists fear modernity, which they regard as a threat to the integrity of their faith.

Is the Islamist Phenomenon New?

Islamism is as old as the Islamic faith, but its modern version had its origin in the beginning of the twentieth century, in reaction to a movement to promote an Arab renaissance, which advocated that Islam should be adapted to modern circumstances. It was in that sense a kind of counter-reformation, against the reformist school of thought inaugurated by the Persian thinker Sayyid Jamal ad-Din al-Afghani (1838–1897). Jamal ad-Din al-Afghani advocated a critical reinterpretation of the Quran in the light of history, philology, and archaeology. His disciple, the Egyptian scholar Muhammad Abduh (1849–1905), took his line of argument further, calling for the secularization of Muslim society. The reaction against these ideas came initially from the Syrian Rashid Rida (1865–1935), one of Abduh's pupils, who presented himself as the herald of the restoration of a mythical golden age of Islam.

In 1928, the Muslim Brotherhood was founded in the Egyptian town of Ismailia. The Brotherhood, whose slogan was "The Quran is our constitution," was in many ways the origin of today's Islamist movement. It militated for the complete Islamization of the state and the imposition of the Shari'a as the basis of law, together with the expulsion of all alien cultural accretions from Islam. By definition, women and foreigners were of a lesser status. As the traditions of Islam, as expressed in the Quran and the Sunna, were universally and eternally valid, the Islamist movement condemned any modernist approach to the Quran as sacrilege.

Who are the Islamists?

All who seek to Islamize their environment, whether in relation to their lives in society, their family circumstances, or the workplace, may be described as Islamists. Some progress from proselytization to violent action. These are the terrorists who are today sought and hunted down by the intelligence services of the West. Others present a human and friendly face and are willing to coexist with the societies in which they live. They accept the laws and regulations of their host countries, while nonetheless insisting on respect for their Islamic identity and specificity. In contrast to the terrorists, they win the confidence of the police and the legal authorities, who often seek them out as useful interlocutors. Nevertheless, political analysts and sociologists should be concerned, because, slowly but surely, the Islamists are constructing social structures of their own, which in practice reject assimilation, on the fringe of the national societies of their countries of residence. For the countries of the West, there are two threats here: a security threat linked to terrorism and an existential threat arising from the possibility that host societies may be undermined.

Many questions may be asked. Are the events of September 11, 2001, in any way justified by the Quran? What has been the role of the United States and the U.S. intelligence services in the growth of Islamism? How is Islam to be contained in the secular societies of the West? *The Columbia World Dictionary of Islamism* seeks to answer all these questions. It gives an account of organizations, individuals, historical contexts, and the interconnections and alliances of the Islamists between themselves, both in a global context and as they manifest themselves in individual countries. The authors have chosen to offer some discussions of concepts related to the Islamic faith, but relate their analyses to the concept of Islamism. We believe that Islamism is today a phenomenon with which every Western country has to deal. The coverage offered by *The Columbia World Dictionary of Islamism* therefore extends not only to geopolitical issues but also to other fields, including, for example, the global economy, where oil-related questions connected to the conflict in Afghanistan are examined.

Methodology

For reasons just mentioned, the authors have judged it appropriate to deal first with the fundamental principles of Islam, a better way to grasp the ideas of Islamism, as a prelude to a discussion of Islam's historical origins and an examination of Islam's various theological and juridical schools of thought, seeking to clarify the extent to which contemporary Islamism is a novel departure. The book goes on to review movements round the world that proclaim their allegiance to Islam, and to identify those individuals who have wider ambitions.

There is today a multiplicity of Islamic organizations, in every country, which are both numerous and diverse. Some, as we shall see, have crossed frontiers. Basing themselves on specific and well-known schools of doctrine, they have clear historical roots. *The Columbia World Dictionary of Islamism* devotes much space to these foundations to provide a clear explanation of the desire of the Islamists to return to the ways of their ancestors—the *Salaf.* There are also many notable individuals. The media has made us aware of some leaders, such as Bin Laden, Mullah Omar, and Hassan al-Turabi. But there are also hordes of men in the middle rank—aides, fighting men, administrators— of whom we know little. We have attempted to turn our spotlight on some of these people, and not only on those who have already been identified and sometimes placed under arrest but also on those who continue to work behind the scenes as they did thirty years ago.

Is There an International Islamist Organization?

As authors of *The Columbia World Dictionary of Islamism*, we attempt to answer the question of whether there is an international Islamist organization, throwing light on a new development in recent years: the growth of contact across frontiers between the various leading Islamist figures and schools of thought, as well as between different movements and organizations. These interconnections are a nightmare for the Western intelligence services. How can the struggle be sustained against this plague afflicting modern societies without adding to the suffering of the world's Muslims? How can the confusion between Islam and Islamism be avoided? And how can concepts and ideas

that seem at first sight complex and even incomprehensible be simply explained?

The Columbia World Dictionary of Islamism analyzes the following issues: the concepts, the tendencies, the participants (both major and minor), and the organizations, as well as economic and financial networks and both public and private institutions. A team of specialists, centered on *Les Cahiers de l'Orient* and its writing team, has developed each entry in the dictionary. Our task has been to illuminate, in terms of current events and also on the basis of geopolitics, history, and sociology, the significance of Islamist ideas and their influence, both on the development of Muslim countries and within the Western societies where Muslim communities continue to increase in size.

The Columbia World Dictionary of Islamism is not merely a working tool, it is also intended to draw back the curtain and throw new light on the causes of recent events. Its objective is to raise the level of understanding and leave its readers better prepared for developments to come. For *Les Cahiers de l'Orient*, Plon, and Columbia University Press, this ambitious project breaks new ground in France and in the United States. It has been conceived in the conviction that the Muslim countries, especially those friendly to the West, will play a significant part in our future.

The Columbia World Dictionary of Islamism

ABU HAMZA AL-MASRI (UNITED KINGDOM)

Abu Hamza al-Masri, whose birth name is Mustafa Kamil Mustafa, is an Egyptian citizen who was born in Alexandria in 1958. He first came to London in 1979, to study as an engineer, and acquired British citizenship in 1986 after marriage to a British woman. In 1991, he went to fight against the Soviets in Afghanistan. In 1993, he was seriously wounded, losing both hands and an eye. He sometimes wears a hook on one amputated hand. On his return to London he set up the Ansar al-Shari'a al-Islamiyya (The Supporters of the Islamic Shari'a). This group has close links with the Islamic Army of Aden Abyan and the Algerian GIA (Armed Islamic Groups). In 1995, he went to Bosnia. London's Finsbury Park mosque, where Abu Hamza officiated from 1997, became a rendezvous for veterans of the Afghan war. In 1999, he was arrested on suspicion of connection with an incident in Yemen when four Western tourists were killed. In April 2002, the British authorities forbade him from preaching for a year. In 2003, the authorities closed the Finsbury Park Mosque and he began to preach in the street. In 2004, he was arrested on a U.S. extradition warrant and was later charged under British law with soliciting murder. In February 2006, he was convicted of soliciting murder and was sentenced to prison for seven years.

ABU MUS'AB (aka OMAR ABDUL HAKIM AL-SURI)

Syrian by origin, Abu Mus'ab is also known as Omar Abdul Hakim al-Suri and as Mustafa Setmariam Nasar, which is apparently his childhood nickname (Sitt-Mariam was the name of his grandmother). He was born in Aleppo. In Syria he was a radical member of the Muslim Brotherhood and wrote a text entitled "The Islamic Revolutionary Struggle in Syria." He left Syria after the regime's violent suppression of the Muslim Brotherhood in Hama in 1982. Later in the 1980s, he based himself in London and in Spain, where he married a Spanish citizen and came into contact with Algerian Islamists. He frequented mosques in London and then went to Afghanistan where he took charge of training camps near Khost, in the east of the country. In Afghanistan, he is said to have become a responsible official within Al-Qa'ida. Between 1992 and 1998, he was once more in Europe. In 1998 he returned to Afghanistan, where he pledged allegiance to Mullah Omar and worked at the Arabic section of Kabul radio. The U.S. State Department believes he was in fact an explosives expert. In July 2000, persistent reports said he had attempted to lead a split within Al-Qa'ida. With the alleged support of sixty senior Arab combatants from Algeria, Jordan, Saudi Arabia, Egypt, and Syria he apparently attempted to bring about a closer merger among the 1,200 Arab fighters in Afghanistan and the Taliban. This was a period when Bin Laden's position in Afghanistan seemed insecure, as the Afghan government took steps to take closer control of Al-Qa'ida's activities, close down Bin Laden's camps, and cut off his communications. At the same time, however, the Taliban maintained their links with Abu Mus'ab's faction. There were reports that Pakistan had decided to withdraw support for Bin Laden, handing him over to the United States. It was alleged that Abu Mus'ab had been asked to carry out this plan. In an interview with Al-Jazeera television in August 2000, Abu Musab denied these reports. After September 11, 2001, he pledged his allegiance to Osama Bin Laden. He was named in Spain in 2003 as a trainer of Al-Qa'ida agents and was suspected of implication in the Madrid train bombings of March 11, 2004. He has written about the jihad and is regarded as a theorist of Islamist action. He appears to have been captured by Pakistani intelligence in Pakistan in November 2005 and handed over to U.S. agents. He is apparently now held in custody at an unknown location. He appears to have been an objective of the U.S. rendition program, under which terrorist suspects are apprehended by U.S. agents and transferred to undisclosed locations in third countries.

ABU QATADA (UNITED KINGDOM)

Abu Qatada is a political fugitive of Palestinian origin, now based in London, who was born in 1960 in Bethlehem and was brought up in Jordan. His birth name was Omar Mahmoud Muhammad Othman, and he is also known as Abu Omar. According to some accounts, he is said to be the spiritual leader of Al-Qa'ida in Europe. He denies ever having met Osama Bin Laden. His name was mentioned in published

investigations in Paris and Madrid in the wake of September 11, 2001. He seems to have been the ideological role model for the two Frenchmen Zacarias Moussaoui and Djamel Beghal, as well as for the British citizen Richard Reid, who hid explosives in his shoes to blow up a flight from Paris to Miami on December 22, 2001. These three were all typical products of London's Islamist circles. Videos of Abu Qatada's sermons were found in Hamburg, in a flat used by some of those responsible for the attacks of September 11, 2001.

Abu Qatada's career displayed the classic route into terrorism taken by an Islamic radical. He was a naturalized Jordanian and fought in Afghanistan during the 1990s, where he ran a training camp. In 1988, he returned to Amman to head "Al-Islah wa-l Tahadi," a group accused of terrorist threats. In 1989, he was obliged to flee from Jordan and took refuge in Pakistan, moving from there to London in 1993. In London, he acquired the status of a political refugee and began to preach in mosques in London. Between 1993 and 1996, Abu Qatada drafted fatwas for issue by the GIA in Algeria as well as acted as one of the editors of the GIA's London publication, *Al Ansar*. In 1999, he was condemned to death in absentia in Jordan for his contribution to the financing of "Jaish Muhammad," a group implicated in planning attacks at Jordanian tourist sites intended to take place during the millennium celebrations in 2000. Despite his denials, he has been described by other Islamists as "the representative of Bin Laden in Europe and one of the six members of Al-Qa'ida's fatwa committee."

Under pressure from the Jordanians, the British authorities agreed to curtail his activities, and he was forbidden to preach at the Regent's Park Mosque. He continued to operate, however, from a sporting club that was transformed into a prayer room (the Fourth Feather, which is very close to the Regent's Park Mosque), as well as from his home in Acton, a down-at-heel London suburb. Abu Qatada disappeared in early 2002, on the eve of the implementation of British legislation providing for virtually unlimited detention without trial for any suspected terrorist of foreign nationality who cannot be deported. He was traced in October 2002 and placed in detention in London's Belmarsh high-security prison. He was freed on bail in March 2005, subject to severe restrictions on his movements. The British government rearrested him in August 2005 and sought his deportation to Jordan. In August 2006, Britain reached an agreement with Jordan intended to facilitate his deportation. Jordan agreed that he would be exempt from the death penalty and immune from torture. Lawyers for Abu Qatada challenged the deal, saying that Jordan was unlikely to adhere to its terms. He is still in a high-security prison in the United Kingdom, where he has challenged the legal basis for his deportation. At an appeal in October 2006, his legal team argued he would be at risk in Jordan.

ADALAT (UZBEKISTAN)

The Adalat (justice) movement is also known as Islam Lashkari (the Soldiers of Islam), but initially it was not a religious movement. It was set up by members of the Party of the Islamic Renaissance within the former Soviet Union as a "popular force against criminality and criminal groups," and was initially aimed at the restoration of public order and justice. It was not until October 1990 that it gravitated toward Islam under the influence of a Wahhabi group, which at their initial encounter encouraged Adalat to act in the name of Islam and to make itself known in the mosques, placing a Mullah in a position of authority.

Adalat understood the advantage of declaring itself an Islamic organization. Many Mullahs would support action in the name of Islam, which would give Adalat the ideological basis that it lacked. The movement thrived in the Namangan region, where it attracted twelve thousand militants of all ages and walks of life, later expanding into Ferghana, Indigan, and Tashkent. In essence, it conceived of itself as a moral movement. Its slogan was the struggle against hooliganism, theft, corruption, drugs, drink, and adultery. It practiced summary justice, and its Islamic courts supplanted the power of the state courts to try and punish offenders.

Adalat never proclaimed the intention of setting up an Islamic republic, but the direction taken by its activities led it to openly dispute the regional administrative and political procedures. Its operations appeared as a real challenge to political authority. For example, it took control of the national repositories of food products, selling off or even giving away the stocks to the public and also set prices in the markets to prevent speculation. In March 1992, following a visit by the president of the republic, Islam Karimov, to the offices of the regional administration, Adalat occupied the building and flew an Islamic flag.

Accusing Adalat of racketeering, among other transgressions, the government sent shock troops into the towns of Namangan, Indigan, Ferghana, and Chortok. More than seven hundred people were arrested, according to the Islamists, and the movement was decapitated. This took place after Karimov's participation at a meeting of the OSCE (Organization for Security and Cooperation in Europe) where he denounced Islamic fundamentalism as the ultimate menace and undertook to prevent its spread. The government also acted to suppress other Islamist movements and organizations to prevent them from mounting a challenge to Karimov's legitimacy.

AFGHANISTAN

There is no question that one of the consequences of the invasion of Afghanistan by Soviet troops in 1979 was the radical political re-Islamization of the population as a whole. It was under the banner of Islam that the mujahidin threw themselves into the resistance against the Red Army. In the space of a few years, this country, which had been open and tolerant, fell under the shadow of an Islamism formed by the Wahhabi school.

Afghanistan stands at the crossroads of great trade routes and civilizations, and it has never ceased to arouse the greed of conquerors who have one after another invaded its territory. Wars and internal divisions preceded the creation of the modern state in the nineteenth century, founded on the Pushtun tribes and their ethnicity. The founder of the Kingdom was Ahmed Shah, but his ambition was thwarted on the one hand by the Russian push toward the south and the warm water oceans and on the other hand by Britain's desire to reinforce the western flank of its Indian empire.

Afghanistan became a buffer state, at the heart of the "great game" played by the two European empires. The romantic legend of the bravery and wildness of Afghanistan's warriors dates from this era and from the misfortunes of the British who attempted to subdue them. The British expeditionary force sent to Kabul in 1839 did not dream that a handful of ragged fighters would even attempt to resist them. Two years later, obliged to fall back to Jalalabad, the sixteen thousand British solders were massacred on the road; all but one who lived to report the disaster. Anglo-Russian rivalry turned in Britain's favor with the Granville-Gorchakoff agreement of 1872, which allowed the British to impose their protectorate.

In 1879, Kabul was obliged to sign a treaty giving London control over its foreign policy and to accept the presence of an ambassador who was empowered to exercise plenipotentiary authority. The British envoy and all his staff were massacred some months later. On this occasion, having learned its lesson from the indomitability of the Afghan people, Britain chose to exercise its influence at a distance, protecting the frontiers defined by the Durand line. (This frontier included what are today the tribal zones of Pakistan, which are probably being used by Osama Bin Laden and Mullah Omar as a refuge from the American search for them.) Britain also joined with Russia to define the northern frontiers.

A rebellion provoked by the Bolshevik Revolution obtained full sovereignty for the Afghans. The scene was set for the long conflict between Russia and the West for hegemony in Afghanistan. In 1921, a treaty of friendship with Moscow guaranteed Afghanistan an annual grant of half a million dollars from the Soviet Union. The nonaggression pact signed in 1926 was regularly renewed. In 1929, a new King, Nadir Khan, overthrew King Amanullah, whose stated aim had been to modernize and laicize his country. Muhammad Zaher Shah succeeded his father as king in 1933, at the age of nineteen, inaugurating a long period of relative stability. In 1963, he asked his cousin and brother-in-law, General Sardar Ahmad Daoud, to step down as prime minister and appointed a new government that was free of members of the royal family, which brought in a new constitution embodying modern political freedoms. In 1973, however, Daoud overthrew the king and proclaimed Afghanistan a republic. Daoud had the backing of the Soviet Union, but once in power he made approaches for support to the West as well as to Iran, Saudi Arabia, and Japan. He also appealed to Islam and to the nonaligned movement. This was too much for the Soviet Union. On April 27, 1978, Marxist-progressive officers carried out a military coup, and Daoud was assassinated. On May 1, Nur Muhammad Taraki became president of Afghanistan and renamed the country the Democratic Republic of Afghanistan. He planned a close alliance with the Soviet Union, which he hoped would help him stamp out Islamist influence; a perilous undertaking at the moment when the events leading to the Islamic Revolution were already well under way in Iran. The ruling coalition rapidly disintegrated, and Taraki purged the followers of one of its former members, Babrak Karmal. In July 1978, the first Islamist insurrection broke out. Agrarian reform and reforms such as the literacy campaign and the introduction of women to public life were put on hold. The rebellion spread toward the northeast. The west of the country fell to the Islamists after attacks in Herat in March 1979 when tens of thousands of civilians died. Within the army, there were many desertions, and the administration was paralyzed. In September 1979, Moscow advised Taraki to rid himself of his close collaborator Hafizullah Amin. Amin, however, got wind of the plot and killed Taraki and his entourage on September 14, taking the position of president for himself. Between December 11 and 15, the Soviets massed troops on the north bank of the river Amu Daria, which forms the frontier between Uzbekistan and Afghanistan. On December 25, an air lift, Operation "Squall 333," began, supposedly at the request of the Afghans. On December 27, Hafizullah Amin was brutally assassinated in his palace and Babrak Karmal became president.

The United States took advantage of the mounting chaos in Afghanistan to back a candidate unsettle the communists by backing the opposition. They armed and financed the Islamists, with the help of the Saudis and the Chinese. Throughout the Arab world, in the name of Islam, the United States connived at the recruitment of combatants who were then housed and trained in Pakistan. Stinger ground-to-air missiles, deployed from 1986, were provided to threaten the Soviet forces. On May 4, 1986, Babrak Karmal resigned and Muhammad Najibullah, the head of the Afghan intelligence services, came to power. The Kabul government toughened its resistance to the Islamists, but to little effect. In 1989, with Soviet power crumbling at home, Gorbachev withdrew his troops, acknowledging that the Soviet intervention had been a mistake. Evidently, the Soviets had concluded that a satellite regime in Kabul could not be sustained. The toll had been dreadful: fifteen thousand Soviet troops had died, along with a million Afghans, while there were 5 million refugees. The story did not end there, however. Hardly had the Soviets left when the Afghan Islamist opposition split over the composition of the Shura, the council responsible for installing a provisional government. On April 16, 1992, after sustained pressure form the United Front, Muhammad Najibullah's regime fell. Najibullah took refuge in the United Nations compound.

The civilian population hoped peace might come at last. Unfortunately, however, the initial victors, the leaders of the United Islamic Front for the Salvation of Afghanistan, were incapable of agreement on an equitable division of power. To break the deadlock, they installed a rotating presidency at the head of a provisional council. Sibghatullah Mujaddidi took the presidency first. Forces loyal to Burhanuddin Rabbani, the leader of Jamiyet-e Islami, under the military command of Ahmed Massoud, entered Kabul on April 25, and expelled the forces of Gulbuddin Hekmatyar from key points. Mujaddidi served as president for two months. Friction with Hekmatyar continued. In June, Burhanuddin Rabbani, the leader of Jamiyet-e Islami, succeeded him, with Ahmed Massoud as his defense minister and military strongman. Rabbani, however, did not stick to the agreed rules. Instead, he convened an assembly to confirm his legitimacy and declared himself president of the Islamic State of Afghanistan.

Civil war succeeded the war against colonial domination, which was every bit as savage and murderous for the innocent population. Throughout the country, and even inside the capital, bitter fighting sporadically broke out. The pattern of conflicts and alliances followed the country's ethnic and tribal distribution. The Muslim faith, shared by all Afghans, was unable to unite them. Most of the ethnic communities extended over the frontiers with neighboring states, except for the Hazara Shi'ites concentrated in the center of the country. The most recent census dated from 1974, and in the absence of any recent enumeration, demographic statistics were manipulated for political ends, with each community tending to overestimate its size.

Applying the proportions that prevailed in 1974 to the present population of 26 million, the **Pushtuns** make up 40 percent. Distributed in a semicircle from the east to the south, it was they who first created Afghanistan and they expect to wield power.

The Persian-speaking **Tajiks** make up 27 percent of the population in the neighborhood of Herat in the west and in the mountains of the northeast.

The **Hazaras,** who make up 17 percent to the population, enjoy the support of Iran and participate in the struggle for power. They have always been excluded by their allegiance to Shi'ism, viewed as heretical by the Sunnis, which has inclined them toward separatist ambitions. They ally themselves with the Northern Alliance against the Taliban extremists, who oppress them because of their religion.

The Turkish-speaking **Uzbeks** represent about 6 percent, distributed between the west and the north.

Other minorities play a minor political role. The Turkish-speaking **Turkmens,** of whom there are between 300,000 and a million, in common with the Khirgiz, are not politically organized. Some 750,000 semi-nomadic Aymaks live between Hazarajat and the mountains of Herat. They are less rigid in their customs, their women going unveiled while the men drink wine.

The **Baluchis** and the **Brawis** represent several hundred thousand people distributed to the south of Qandahar and along the frontier with the Baluchi area of Pakistan. There are 3 million Baluchis in Pakistan and 1.2 million in Iran.

Finally, the **Nuristanis,** another small minority, live in the mountains to the northeast of Kabul. The Nuristanis were formerly known as "kafirin" (unbelievers) and were forcibly converted to Islam in the nineteenth century.

To each of these ethnic communities there corresponds one or more military-political formations. Solidarity is at the ethnic and tribal levels, rather than at the level of the nation, which accounts for the prevalence of interethnic conflict. Alliances in Afghanistan are dizzyingly unstable. From 1992, Burhanuddin Rabbani continued to stand out against the Pushtun bid for supremacy. Rabbani had links with the militia of the Uzbek General Rashid Dostum, who aligned himself with the communist authorities in Dushanbe and received assistance from Uzbekistan. Gulbuddin Hekmatyar was largely able to rely on military support from the Islamists of Tajikistan. Rabbani's presidential mandate was extended until mid-1995, while Hekmatyar became prime minister. In early 1994, Dostum deserted Rabbani and joined up with Hekmatyar.

Political divisions in the Afghan opposition also reflected to some extent the lines of quarrels between Tajiks and ethnic Uzbeks in Tajikistan. The ethnic and political splits south of Afghanistan's northern frontier

along the Amu-Daria River reflected those to the north. Tajiks, who were especially in the majority in the east, were supported by the Islamic resistance parties, while the west was controlled by Jumbesh, basically made up of communists, which was identified with General Abdul Rashid Dostum's militias. Tajik Islamist groups were identified with Afghan parties fighting inside Afghanistan. The various Tajik military groups, nominally unified under the aegis of a government in exile, were linked to three Afghan parties that played a key role in supporting them and controlled their access to the frontiers of Tajikistan. To help them achieve this end, they were in receipt of a substantial level of financial support from Saudi Arabia. These three parties were as follows:

Jamiyat. This aided the Tajiks out of ethnic solidarity. This contrasted with the positions taken officially by Jamiyat's leaders— ex-president Rabbani and Ahmed Shah Massoud, the hero of the anti-Soviet resistance— who prioritized the reconstruction of the Afghan State and placed emphasis on respect for frontiers and for international law. Massoud, however, it should be noted, had for some years been lending surreptitious support to various Islamic groups, providing them with military training at his own training camps. From 1991 to 1992, Massoud attempted to construct a political base for himself in Tajikistan by distributing widely his movement's militant literature. He maintained close links with Abdullah Nuri, the president of the Tajik Islamic Movement in exile in Afghanistan, and he attempted to extend his influence over the refugees as well as over the Tajik opposition to whom he was giving training as well as ideological education. His actions were aimed at exercising control over this ethnic group in order to give himself bargaining points in negotiations with Tajikistan, Uzbekistan, and Russia.

Ettehad. This was the most influential and wealthiest party in the Kunduz region, basically professed Islamic solidarity with the Tajiks because of the substantial Arab financial support this brought. Nevertheless Ettehad is basically a Pushtun party and has no local solidarity with the Tajiks. In the short term, it opted to send groups of commandos into Tajikistan, which it armed and financed in proportion to the foreign aid it received.

Hezb-i Islami. This was the party of the former prime minister Gulbuddin Hekmatyar, was financed both by the Arabs and the Pakistanis. Its strategy at the outset of the Tajik conflict was resolute support for the Tajik Islamists, of whom trained groups were infiltrated from the Kabul region to the Tajik frontier.

In the context of the regional conflict, the Uzbek leaders had at their disposal between 1.3 and 2 million Uzbeks living in the north of Afghanistan, whose principal leader, General Dostum, maintained close links with Tashkent. The refugees in the camps controlled by Jumbesh had been disarmed and politically neutralized. A large part of the frontier lay under Dostum's control, which the Uzbeks as well as the Russians saw as the best guarantee for the stability of northern Afghanistan.

Tashkent provided logistic support and arms to Dostum, and the Uzbek air force had no compunction over bombing Rabbani's camps. Uzbekistan feared the spread of destabilization from Afghanistan, where there were Tajik exiles who had fled from the regions of Samarkand, Bukhara, and Andigan after the revolution of 1917. In the summer of 1993, after a visit by Dostum to Karimov, the Uzbek general used his troops against the Tajik opposition forces entrenched in northern Afghanistan in a large-scale offensive, which, nevertheless, failed to subdue the Tajiks. Afghanistan

was crucial to Uzbekistan's economic prospects, potentially providing access to the Indian Ocean by way of Pakistan for Uzbekistan's oil exports, as well as access to the Gulf via Iran. In 1993, Karimov said, "we should do everything to settle the Afghan problem."

Russia strove to normalize the situation in the country, which it saw as liable to bring about a reinforcement of the Tajik front. Moscow feared that the ultra-fundamentalism of the Taliban—Islamic militia educated in the Quranic schools of Pakistan—might spread throughout Central Asia. Russian support for Rabbani, who exercised a strong influence over the Tajik Islamists, enabled Moscow to avoid appearing as the aggressor and to preserve its role as a mediator. Rabbani's concern over the deployment of twenty-five thousand troops of the Community of Independent States (ex-Soviet Union) on Afghanistan's northern frontier obliged him to compromise, due to the threat of Russian reprisals, including bombing raids after breaches of the frontier. Rabbani was also faced by destabilization resulting from the rise of the Taliban. On December 22, 1993, after the first Afghan-Tajik summit in Kabul from August 28 to 30, 1993, Rabbani signed an agreement with Tajikistan providing for the return of Tajik refugees as well as for frontier normalization. He also offered his services as a mediator between the Tajik government and the opposition. On May 16, 1995, his efforts bore fruit in the shape of three meetings between President Rakhmonov and Abdullah Nuri, the leader of the armed opposition.

The good intentions of the Afghan president fell on sympathetic ears in Dushanbe, where, from January 1996, daily flights carried arms to Kabul to help him against the Taliban. A further realignment of the factions resulted from the irresistible rise to power of the Taliban in the Pushtun regions of the south in the autumn of 1994 and the spring of 1995. Another factor was the military

defeat of Hekmatyar, who was driven from his base at Sharyasab to the south of Kabul in February 1995. Hekmatyar, abandoned by his Pakistani protectors in favor of the Taliban, and now viewed with suspicion by the Americans, was obliged to make his peace with Rabbani.

In spite of this last minute agreement, the situation changed radically in September 1996, when the Taliban captured Kabul and set up an Islamic regime under the leadership of Mullah Omar. On 27 September, Najibullah was dragged from the United compound, where he had taken refuge, and brutally murdered. The deposed government fled to the north of the country and invited other factions, including that of the Uzbek General Dostum to rejoin the coalition with the objective of defeating the Taliban. The strategy was to open several fronts to occupy the Taliban and prevent them from massing for a final assault. However, a lack of confidence between the warlords prevented the formulation of an effective military strategy. After a successful counterattack, Massoud once more reached the gates of the capital toward the end of 1996, and in the spring of 1997, after an attempt to capture Mazar-i Sharif, the Taliban were driven back by Dostum's militia. The respite, however, was short, and the Taliban regained their advantage on the ground.

The victorious Taliban movement was from top to bottom a Pakistani creation, aimed at regaining control of an Afghanistan, which, having lost some of its Pushtun territories to Pakistan at the hands of the British, had been hostile to that country's creation since its foundation in 1947. Islamabad also aimed to undercut the separatist tendencies of its own Pushtun minority, the Pathans, by installing in Kabul Pushtuns loyal to itself, while also unsettling Afghanistan's traditional ally India, which was apprehensive of a conflagration in Kashmir. The Taliban were largely financed by Saudi

Arabia, while the United States saw them as a bulwark against the influence of Iran, whose ascendancy had become more marked under the Rabbani government.

In 1996, the "students of religion" were welcomed with relief by the majority of the population, who were weary of ceaseless political maneuvering and the trail of killings, deprivation, and refugees. The religious police, who enforced the strict rules of conduct, soon came to be detested for the abuses and their tyrannical behavior. However, the benefits of peace outweighed the problems, and anything would be better than the forty thousand dead and 2 million displaced persons, which had resulted from the settlement of accounts between the mujahidin. Reluctant Afghans soon learned to accommodate the rules, respecting them in public only to subvert them all the more within the privacy of their homes. In fact, the measures introduced by the Taliban met with the assent of a majority of the population, which continue to be deeply conservative and traditional. Setting aside Kabul and a few other large towns, day-to-day life did not change for inhabitants of the provinces who were very much in rhythm with decrees, which simply reflected their everyday existence.

The Taliban's assumption of power was centered round a single theme: the pacification of the country in its entirety. It should be pointed out that in the more sparsely populated north, 60 percent of the country's agricultural resources were concentrated, together with 80 percent of its potential resources in the fields of industry, mining, and gas extraction. The objective of the Taliban was certainly achieved in 80 percent of the territory, but the process of government was another story. Their martial and religious inclinations were no preparation for the administration of a stricken country of which every aspect required reconstruction, including the administration itself. Their ideology, which prioritized faith and ethnic solidarity over

efficiency, was out of tune with the construction of a modern state. Each ministry was packed with the minister's family and associates, members of his clan and tribe. These rustics, with their background in the Quranic schools, were extremely wary of the urban intelligentsia, who were seen as in league with an educational system corrupted either by the West or by the Soviets. They continued to be strongly marked by their rural origins and by their mistrust of the world outside. The founders of the movement either died in the fighting or perished from disease, as in the case of the number two in the regime, Mullah Muhammad Rabbani. The new recruits who replaced them had joined up with the Taliban only after they took power and were not necessarily as rigid in their attitudes as the founding fathers.

There was a strange amalgam of extreme centralization and organized anarchy. For the discussion of all issues deemed important by men who were obsessed by their "divine mission," their leader, Mullah Omar, was able to summon an expanded Shura, or consultative council, of the Ulema (religious scholars). The Shura, as at the time of the Prophet, was meant to guarantee the agreement of all believers and to ensure respect for all sensitivities. Debates were liable to continue throughout the night, and all participants, including the simple fighting men, were entitled to take part. What seemed to be an organized hierarchy, at whose head stood Mullah Omar, concealed an improvisational and disorganized style of day-to-day government. The ministers worked badly together. Not infrequently, different ministers made contradictory decisions on the same subject. In any case, ministerial instructions were not enforced and were frequently contradicted by the Shura of Qandahar. This city, where Mullah Omar had his residence, was doubly symbolic for the Pushtuns and for the Taliban. The council of ministers frequently had to clear even its

most trivial decisions with Qandahar, which was a cause of inefficiency and waste of time. In provinces where the Pushtuns were in a minority, power lay in practice in the hands of local notables. Occasional government appointments were made in the case of key positions, but the Pushtun appointees had no real power over those whom they administered. For instance, in Kabul and in Herat, the governor, the mayor, police chiefs, and senior officials were Pushtuns from Qandahar. They were unable to make themselves understood, since they did not speak Dari, the principal language of the country. In order to prevent them from establishing local clans, a likely outcome in a disintegrating country, governors were strictly controlled, often silenced, and sometimes sent to fight at the front.

The aim of Russia, which was nervous of the Taliban, was to avoid a renewal of the Tajik confrontation. Russia's fear was the destabilization of Central Asia by Taliban hordes, who might brush past Russia's frontier posts and push onward into the plains of Siberia or at least initiate a conflict on the borders. On October 4, 1996, at a special summit meeting at the Kazakh capital Almaty, Russia, Kazakhstan, Kirghizstan, Uzbekistan, and Tajikistan warned the Taliban against any extension of the Afghan conflict. Turkmenistan, sticking to its own doctrine, once more set itself apart, as President Niazov, the Turkmen leader, attempted to negotiate with Pakistan and the Taliban regime over a gas pipeline from Turkmenistan to the Indian Ocean. This discreet support for the Taliban irritated Russia, which blocked exports of Turkmen gas via Gazprom. Russia at this point abandoned the tacit Russian-American agreement of the spring of 1996, which placed an embargo on arms deliveries to all parties in Afghanistan. General Massoud's troops were authorized by the Russians to use Tajik territory as a base, to the great annoyance of Uzbekistan, which feared

the development of ethnic antagonism inside Tajikistan in which Tashkent might become incidentally involved. However, Tashkent had no choice. A coincidence of circumstances brought together former enemies and the Northern Alliance was formed, which to a great extent united the Tajiks, the Uzbeks, and the Shi'ite Hazaras. In January 1998, Pakistan, Turkmenistan, the Taliban, and a group of U.S. investors signed an agreement on funding for a gas pipeline. This decision was taken in spite of the evident instability of Afghanistan, the refusal of international organizations to support the plan, and the opposition of American feminists who were shocked by the position to which women in Kabul were relegated.

The Taliban were initially involved in the narcotics trade, which brought them substantial returns in foreign currency. They later changed their position, to the point where they must be given credit for playing a part in the fight against drugs. Cannabis has always been grown in Central Asia. For a considerable time, the opium poppy has also been cultivated. It is consumed in food and sweets, taken as a medicine, and is smoked. The endemic production of opium, which the Soviet authorities were never able to stamp out completely, once more exploded after the disengagement of the Soviets. The incentives to produce high-profit crops appeared irresistible in a situation of impunity due to neglect and complicity on the part of state and local authorities, to the war, and lastly to the critical economic circumstances in which all social classes, including the peasants, had become impoverished. The cultivation of the poppy, and the local preparation of derivatives, by means of both purification and treatment, and the transport of large quantities by the most up-to-date methods—containers or even airplanes—threatened to render Central Asia a new giant of the drugs trade. In the Chou valley, in the southeast of Kazakhstan, it was

estimated that the area planted with cannabis was 138,000 hectares, while there were 60,000 hectares in Kirghizstan. In Uzbekistan, crops were increased tenfold during 1992. The role of Tajikistan was significant owing to its instability and the permeability of its frontiers with Afghanistan. A major proportion of the Afghan traffic that fed western Europe and the United States went by way of Tajik Pamir and Osh in Kirghizstan, then by two routes via Kazakhstan or Uzbekistan to destinations in Russia, principally Moscow, St. Petersburg, and the Baltic countries. The profit from this trade went mainly to the warring Afghan parties and to the criminal organizations of Southeast Asia.

Afghanistan first began to produce drugs on a large scale during the struggle against the Soviets. The trucks of the ISI (the Pakistani secret services) that delivered arms to the Afghan mujahidin returned full of opium. The Americans turned a blind eye or even lent active encouragement to the trade. After the Soviet defeat, the profits from drugs financed the Islamists in Kashmir, dissidents in India, and the Sikhs in the Punjab. In 1994, Afghanistan became the world's leading producer of drugs, with an output of 2,800 tonnes of opium, far ahead of Burma. Four-fifths of Europe's opium came from Golden Crescent of Afghanistan and Pakistan. In 1999, production reached a new record of 4,600 tonnes, and 3,276 tonnes were produced in 2000. The religious regime profited from the trade, on which, as with other crops, the obligatory charitable "zakat" tax was raised at a level of 10 percent of the sale price. The Islamic Movement of Uzbekistan, led by Jouma Namangani, an ally of Osama Bin Laden, played an important part in the trade, from which it derived a substantial income. In July 2000, Mullah Omar declared a total ban on the cultivation of the opium poppy. Production fell dramatically: in 2001 only 185 tonnes were produced, with the effect of cutting world

output by 75 percent. In the regions under Taliban control the eradication was almost complete.

The province of Helmand, which had been the leading producer within the Taliban's territory, with 42,000 hectares devoted to the poppy, now produced nothing. In 1997, of the 7,606 hectares of poppies counted by the UNDCP (United Nations International Drugs Control Program), as against 82,172 the previous year, 83 percent were in the province of Badakhshan, under the control of the United Front, allied to the United States. In an unexpected development, the amount of land devoted to poppy cultivation in 2001 once more increased by more than twofold, since Mullah Omar's ban was not observed after the American bombing. Planting resumed from mid-October to mid-November 2001. Though Commander Massoud carried on an antidrugs campaign and opposed those local commanders of the United Front in Badakhshan who actively participated in the traffic, his ally General Dostum derived significant funding from it.

In March 2001, Commander Massoud made a secret trip to Moscow where he took part in a meeting attended by representatives of the ministries of defense and the security organizations of Russia, Tajikistan, Uzbekistan, Iran, and India whose agenda was to plan a counterattack against the Taliban. At this meeting, the opposition to the Taliban took shape; according to some sources, a further meeting soon followed. In April, General Dostum returned from his exile in Turkey and some time afterward Ismail Khan brought to a close his period of exile in Iran. However, the Afghan opposition began to suspect that Moscow and Teheran might be playing a double game when they saw that the level of military aid they were being given was insufficient to ensure them victory, though they were able to avoid compete defeat. Divisions and instability enabled Moscow and Teheran to maintain their influence. In the struggle with the Taliban, the Russians helped their old ally Massoud, allied to the communist Dostum, as well as to the Shi'ites, who were supported by Iran and Uzbekistan.

On the other hand, Russia's excessively blatant support for the opposition and Moscow's role as an arms supplier, together with the involvement of former communist officers, prompted some defections from the opposition camp. Further factors were universal war-weariness, felt by both the fighters on the ground and the highest officers, together with financial inducements from the Taliban. The Taliban also targeted the opposition abroad. On July 3, 2001, when the German police closed an unofficial Taliban consulate in Frankfurt, they came across a letter from Mullah Omar written in Pushtu under the letterhead of the "Service of the Secretariat of the Emirate." This exhorted Taliban supporters to eliminate any antagonists who "either in Afghanistan or elsewhere oppose the Islamic Emirate and, with the assistance of foreign countries, or of atheist communist forces, attempt to destroy our Islamic institutions." The letter authorized action against opposition figures to be carried out as soon as was practicable, and it contained a list of 106 names of opposition figures of all tendencies resident outside Afghanistan. In the period following the date of the letter, ten of those named had already met their deaths.

After the arrival of Osama Bin Laden in Qandahar in 1996, to take personal charge of the Arab volunteer forces, he gradually began to impose his own shape on the conflict. His relations with the Taliban leadership, and in particular with Mullah Omar, progressively improved, and the Al-Qa'ida leader gradually won his partners round to his own position. Finally, the Taliban regime was to sacrifice its national interests to pseudo-religious and supranational

objectives. As part of Bin Laden's bid for ascendancy, Massoud was assassinated on September 9, 2001. Meanwhile the Taliban launched an attack near Farkhur and at the foot of the Panjshir valley. Wild with fury at the treacherous attack against Massoud, while also believing he was still alive, the fighters of the United Front pushed them back. After Massoud's death, Yunus Qanuni became the political leader of the opposition and Muhammad Fahim took over the military leadership. Dr. Abdullah Abdullah played a purely diplomatic role. However, the United Front was united only in name, with continuing disagreements even within the parties making it up.

On September 11, 2001, the unthinkable happened when a handful of fanatics armed with knives flew airliners into the Twin Towers of the World Trade Center in New York and the Pentagon in Washington. It soon became evident that Bin Laden was behind the attacks. The American response was predictable. However, their hope of acting through a proxy against Bin Laden and Mullah Omar was hampered by Massoud's death, as Bin Laden had intended. With the United Front decapitated, the Taliban's hope was that no remaining force would be able to carry out land operations against them. The Americans were obliged to resort to relatively ineffectual bombing raids in their effort to overthrow the Taliban government, which now extended over the whole of Afghanistan. A further problem was that the instability created by the new situation could infect the Muslim states of the former Soviet Union and spark off a conflagration in the entire region, to the further profit of the Taliban.

The Americans, nevertheless, decided to deploy their vast fleet of bombers in order to destroy the defensive ability of the enemy. Their objective was to neutralize Osama Bin Laden, dismantle his network and his camps, and to eliminate the Taliban as a military force. The initial American demand that Bin Laden be handed over was ignored. The bombing began to have some effect, however, and at the end of October 2001 Mullah Wakil Ahmad Mutawakkil, speaking on behalf of the Taliban, asked Pakistan to open negotiations with the United States on the extradition of Bin Laden and his principal lieutenants. This was a little too late. The United States had already deployed forces on the ground and evidently meant to destroy the terrorist camps by its own efforts.

American strategies encountered the kind of difficulties illustrated by the Soviet experience. Bombing alone was insufficient in an extensive and mountainous country. Before the Americans came, the Soviet air force had bombed indefatigably for ten years, disregarding the welfare of the civilian population. The Americans, in contrast, attempted to spare civilians, but without success. For their part, the rebels simply waited in their caves for the end of the air attacks. A further difficulty for the Americans was that the Taliban were able to mingle with the civilian population. They were in control of the towns, the villages, and the mountains. In Iraq in 1991, the coalition faced a static and organized army, but in Afghanistan it was a matter of guerrilla warfare. In Iraq and in Yugoslavia, the destruction of bases and communication networks had disorganized the enemy forces. In Afghanistan, carrier pigeons and basic radio transceivers took the place of networks, and every cave was a potential base. Satellite surveillance could be countered merely by shifting a few stones.

The Russian command had already learned that the deployment of special forces alone could not bring victory. The Soviets sent such units into action to attempt the destruction of the Taliban's logistic columns, with relatively nugatory results in practice. However, the advantage enjoyed by the Red Army was the military bases it had established throughout the country, with a division in Kabul and a brigade at Jalalabad, together with regiments based at Mazar-i Sharif, Qandahar, and Herat. They were also able to call on the Afghan army, which was well equipped and numbered 100,000 men. On the other hand, the forces allied within the United Front, for their part, controlled only northern Afghanistan, and they did not have the advantage of a joint headquarters. The Taliban's opponents were inferior in numbers, while the Taliban enjoyed a degree of legitimacy in the eyes of the civilian population, who had not forgotten the bloody internecine fighting of the United Front's mujahidin. The deleterious effects of this fighting constituted another factor bringing into being a degree of unity behind the Taliban. A handful of Taliban fighters in the hills were able to halt an entire battalion. The Taliban also had the use of ground-to-air missiles, which were brought to them on horseback and which one man alone could fire. This meant that air support could not be brought in, while bombing had to be carried out from high altitudes, without the precision and efficiency necessary to fly missions in support of ground operations.

The remoteness of the field of operations also complicated the U.S. bombing campaign. In contrast to the Gulf conflict or Kosovo, where planes flew from nearby bases, the heavy B-52, B-1, and B-2 bombers took off from Diego Garcia in the Indian Ocean or even from bases in the Pacific or the domestic United States. Other planes and the helicopters used in special forces operations took off from carriers in the Arabian Sea or from bases in Uzbekistan. The distances involved necessitated in-flight refueling by aircraft flying in from Germany. The American command also deployed unmanned spy planes for reconnaissance. The most effective of these planes, the Global Hawk, was based in Germany, which lengthened its reaction time to operational requests.

The Western press reported on these issues to a public becoming increasingly skeptical. A further difficulty was presented by Pakistan in its attempt to contrive the participation of the so-called moderate Taliban in a political solution. The principle of dialogue with certain Taliban representatives was agreed by the United States, which had an interest in dividing the Taliban and were sympathetic to Islamabad's interests. In October 2001, it was in this context that Jalaluddin Haqqani, the Taliban minister for frontiers and tribes, held talks with Pakistani government on "the feasibility, prospects and likelihood of a representative government." From the moment when the United States went to war against the Taliban as a consequence of the events of September 2001, Gulbuddin Hekmatyar made peace with his enemies and provided them with arms supplies.

There was no undisputed leader within any of the ethnic minorities. The Tajiks were divided. President Rabbani, whose legitimacy was derived from the United Nations and who was also the nominal leader of the United Front, aimed to reestablish his authority but had no forces. As Massoud's replacement, Fahim had no charisma and did not enjoy the uncontested respect accorded to his predecessor. Nothing distinguished him from other commanders and his hasty selection as makeshift leader was insufficient to lend him the authority he needed to impose his will.

The Tajik leader Ismail Khan and the Uzbek chief Rashid Dostum ruled as absolute masters of their territories and had no intention of sharing their power, which they did not owe to Muhammad Fahim. Fahim's communist past in any case rendered him suspect in the eyes of the fundamentalist Abdul Rasul Sayyaf, who rejected all cooperation with the ex-communist officers recruited by Massoud. He had strained relations with Dostum, who had made the pilgrimage to Mecca to efface his commu-

nist past and his loose morals. Abdul Rasul Sayyaf's loyalty was suspect, and various rumors circulated after the death of Massoud at the hands of the two false journalists for whom Sayyaf had vouched.

There was mutual detestation between the two Uzbek leaders, General Dostum, the former communist, and General Abdul Malik, whose treachery had at one point led to the loss of Mazar-i Sharif, and the Shi'ite leader Muhaqqiq was able to challenge Dostum's supremacy in Mazar-i Sharif. Another Uzbek leader, Piram Qul from the province of Takhar, claimed to be in control of the northeast of the country, on the Tajik frontier.

The Shi'ite Hazaras, for their part, were also divided between Karim Khalili and Muhammad Muhaqqiq, who were enemies. Said Hussein Anwari, with seven hundred men, was able to challenge Khalili's control of Bamyan. In short, the divisions of the United Front threatened a return of the anarchy that prevailed from 1992 to 1996.

Jalaluddin Haqqani, who had in his day been invited to the White House by Ronald Reagan, was in command of the strategic region of Khost, on the Pakistani frontier. However, there had been widespread hostility from the moment the word "Taliban" was first heard, leading to a change in the language of the Pakistanis, who began to speak of "moderate Pushtuns." The United States had long been reluctant to open the road to Kabul to the opposition. The Americans needed to be tactful with regard to their Pakistani ally, whose support for the military operation was vital. They were apprehensive lest the United Front establish itself in Kabul, whence it would be impossible to dislodge in favor of a government broadly representative of the country's ethnic mosaic. This would entail the attendant risk of hardening the lines of an ethnic conflict grouping the Pushtuns around the Taliban and their leader.

The solution favored by the West involved power-sharing between the United Front and Pushtun representatives or tribal chiefs who could be brought to change sides. In early October 2001 at a meeting in Rome, the opposition decided to form a "Supreme Council for the Unity of Afghanistan." Made up of 120 members, this council proclaimed itself open to all elements within Afghan society. It paved the way for a Loya Jirga (or Great Council) whose task would be to "elect a head of State and a transitional government." If such a gathering could not be held, the council would itself designate the executive authority.

The unifying role of Mullah Omar and his relations with Bin Laden provide an explanation of their commitment to the Taliban. For some time, the American intelligence services believed that consistent pressure on the Taliban would lead to a rebellion when they came to feel that the alliance with Bin Laden was costing them too dearly. Further, U.S. intelligence concluded that Saudi interests and those of the Taliban, as economically deprived nationalists, did not necessarily coincide. Bin Laden wanted to drive the "crusaders and the Jews" from the Middle East, while from the outset the objectives of the Taliban were entirely limited to Afghanistan. The attack on Massoud and the shooting of commander Abdul Haq were blamed by the Pushtun opposition on Bin Laden's "Arabs," as the members of Al-Qa'ida were pejoratively known, whether they were in fact Arabs, Pakistanis, or others. There was an urge to differentiate between what the Taliban were responsible for and what was Bin Laden's doing.

Most Afghans condemned the attacks of September 11, 2001, and the popular support from which the Taliban had for a while benefited began to crumble. They were especially criticized for their alliance with Bin Laden and his fighters, who were highly unpopular. The Arabs were the most hated of the foreign Islamists. They came from Algeria, Saudi Arabia, and other countries in the Arabian Peninsula and the Middle East, as well as from North Africa. The Arabs committed undoubted excesses in the name of a version of Islam even more rigorous than that of the Taliban, and they also interfered in many ways in the daily life of the population, treating them almost as wayward children, which provoked resentment. In combat, the Arabs were given the task of breaking through enemy fronts or of recapturing lost positions. They would then give way to the Afghans and retire to the third line behind the Pakistanis, killing on the spot any who attempted to flee. They were at once feared and envied by the badly paid Taliban, who did not enjoy the same attractive remuneration or the same privileged living conditions.

As their reward, Mullah Omar gave his Arab allies lands in the Qandahar region, arousing the anger of the local Pushtun tribes: a reaction not reported to the elite leadership group. The immediate circle surrounding the Taliban's leadership came mainly from the three regions of Qandahar, Helmand, and Uruzgan. This small group of men, who had studied in the Pakistani Quranic schools, took part from the beginning in military action and was unwaveringly committed to Mullah Omar. On the other hand, the later arrivals, opportunists who joined the newly victorious movement between 1994 and 1996, were kept at a marked distance from the supreme leader. Though some held minor positions in the government, in local administrations, or at the front line, they had in common an instinctive rejection of the foreign fighters and were in favor of a more liberal government.

The death in April 2001 of Mullah Muhammad Kabbani, whose power base was the town of Jalalabad, robbed the reformist movement of its unchallenged leader. At one point, Western policymakers pinned their hopes on the Afghan foreign minister, Wakil Ahmad Mutawakkil. They failed to take into account, however, his closeness to Mullah Omar. He was Mullah Omar's personal secretary, chauffeur, food-taster, and confidant, and having studied in the same madrasa as Mullah Omar, he was committed to obedience and respect to the Taliban leader: a state of psychological dependence that ruled out open dissidence. In addition, Mutawakkil's influence in the circles of power was in reality limited. The fear Mullah Omar was able to inspire was a strong disincentive to all dissidence. At the moment of the American strikes, the Taliban arrested many commanders suspected of conspiring against the regime, some of whom were tortured and summarily executed.

Several thousand foreign combatants, both Pushtun Pakistanis and Arab volunteers attempted to join the Taliban before the American attack. Those who were not halted at the frontier found themselves facing the misgivings of the Taliban who feared the presence among the volunteers of unreliable elements who might pass information to the enemy. They were also faced with the hostility of the Afghans, who saw the foreigners as responsible for their misfortunes.

On October 7, 2001, as the first air strikes took place, the United States missed a major opportunity when an unmanned CIA plane equipped with two antitank missiles targeted a convoy that included Mullah Omar. The central command in Florida refused to give the CIA permission to fire, which angered the U.S. defense secretary. Mullah Omar's hiding places were always a priority target, and American special forces engaged on the ground would later search one of his houses. Mullah Omar, who continued to run the country, was an easier target than Bin Laden. He made telephone calls, moved from place to place, met his military and civilian officials, and contacted them by radio so that intelligence services could more easily detect his activities.

As the situation developed, the United States failed to win the Pushtun tribal chiefs over to their side, failing even to provide effective assistance to those who might have started a movement favorable to the American cause. The prestigious commander Abdul Haq, an exiled Pushtun mujahid, who won his spurs against the Soviets, agreed to undertake a tour of the mountainous regions to exhort the Pushtun tribes to join an anti-Taliban coalition. The announcement of his return to Afghanistan was enough to arouse emotions. The press presented him as the potential catalyst of an early rebellion of the Pushtun tribes against the Taliban. However, no sooner had he arrived in Afghan territory than he was caught in an ambush, and, surrounded, he used his satellite phone to ask for help. Robert McFarlane—President Reagan's former national security counselor—contacted the CIA. More than four hours after the call, two American planes vainly attacked a convoy of vehicles, but Abdul Haq was captured and executed by the Taliban.

The question was asked, how had the Taliban located Abdul Haq in the wilderness of the Afghan mountains, and who had passed the information to them? It has been suggested that the Pakistani secret services were responsible for such leaks, as on the occasion in 1999 when unknown armed men entered Abdul Haq's house in Peshawar and killed his wife and his son of eleven. Abdul Haq commented that "at that time someone wished to punish me for wishing to bring together the moderate opponents of the Taliban." This "someone" was in his view either the Pakistani secret services or the Taliban themselves.

This resounding setback underlined the Americans' inability to help their potential allies and to make use of anti-Taliban sentiment for their own purposes. It was a resounding warning to all those who were inclined to follow Abdul Haq's example: the most prestigious of the commanders supported by the United States had been captured without offering any resistance. In a country obsessed by myths and rumors, the message was clear and served to strengthen the Taliban: God was with them and would protect them.

Food rations, pamphlets dropped from the air, and radio broadcasts aimed at the Afghans were another variety of warfare. The Americans publicized their efforts to limit collateral damage to civilians to the point of deliberate disinformation, while at the same time the Taliban issued a daily casualty count, which did not shrink from manipulation of the figures. Humanitarian aid was also an issue of concern. On September 27, the UN Secretary-General Kofi Annan issued an appeal for $584 million. However, aid reached those who needed it only with difficulty, across closed frontiers and along the precipitous roads.

In military terms, the Americans moved into higher gear. Up to this point they had targeted strategic objectives in the south while exempting the Taliban forces in the north. However, in a wide-ranging clandestine operation, the Taliban had been able to regroup their forces, which up to then were dispersed. Now, by targeting the Taliban far away from their bases in the south—where they would have been more dangerous—the Americans hoped to entrap the most effective Taliban units.

There was a double objective. By inflicting sufficient losses on the Taliban the Americans forestalled stronger resistance from them on their home territory. At the same time, the Americans hoped that the Pushtun tribes and military allies of the fundamentalist regime would switch their allegiance when they had been militarily defeated.

With the approach of Ramadan and also of winter, which would be a hindrance to ground operations, the American leadership—conscious that the public in the United States expected results—decided to step up the campaign. To this end, they used local allies, with American officers who acted in conjunction with American special forces, who carried out intelligence missions, as well as guiding air strikes, and giving strategic assistance to coalition troops. Intensive bombing of the Taliban front line enabled the United Front to score its first success. The fall of Mazar-i Sharif on November 9 confused the Taliban forces and signaled a series of defeats, retreats, and shifting allegiances that opened the way for the opposition to march onto Kabul. On November 10, President Bush had called on the Front not to enter Kabul. However, the United Front's promise as to not to move onto the Afghan capital was not kept. The following day, Defense Secretary Donald Rumsfeld qualified the president's position, accepting that the northern coalition could act as it wished, while hoping that their reprisals would be limited. The U.S. Vice President Dick Cheney confirmed that the United Front would behave "in a responsible manner" as they took Kabul. The Taliban abandoned the capital on November 12. The conquerors moved in without incident, in an initial atmosphere of fear, which then developed into a somewhat strained show of jubilation.

Black turbans, the symbol of the Taliban, disappeared from the streets of Kabul. Together with the reappearance of music, the shaving of beards, and the license given to women to return to work, these were all phenomena that testified to the end of the Taliban dictatorship. What the future held, however, remained uncertain. The inhabitants of Kabul wanted an international force that would serve as a guarantee of their security. Wary after their experience in 1992, the people were apprehensive of the potential consequences of dissent among the city's new masters.

The Taliban had paid the price for the mistake of not having organized soon enough their strategic response, which got under way only a few days before the attack.

Harried by infantry at the same time as by American air power, whole battalions had dispersed in utter chaos. On November 13, Mullah Omar made a radio broadcast, ordering his men to "obey implicitly the orders of your commanders. . . . Do not run right and left like headless chickens who will end up dead in a ditch. . . . Regroup, resist, and fight. Do not listen to opposition propaganda. I am in Qandahar and I have gone nowhere. This is a battle for Islam."

The Arab fighters executed all who negotiated or tried to flee, but their efforts were wasted. The additional deaths only served further to enrage the Afghans. The domino effect trapped large Taliban formations and their Al-Qa'ida allies in the Kunduz region. Since the Taliban custom was not to waste effort defending towns where the balance of forces against them was unfavorable, they withdrew to the mountains and bided their time. On this occasion, however, they also took casualties while losing ground.

Such apparently easy victories could not have been achieved solely by the frontal assault carried out by the American troops. The Taliban Pushtuns were in hostile territory. The local people rose up against them, and volunteers among them deserted. The Taliban had never been at home in the northern provinces, whose inhabitants were drawn from other ethnic minorities of Afghanistan. When they were able to retreat, the Taliban opted for the safer Pushtun regions in the south of the country around Qandahar.

As was always the case in Afghanistan, local guerrilla leaders, in this case those allied to the Taliban, switched their allegiances in order to maintain their control over the regions, towns, or even villages that they held. Local commanders on the two sides were always in touch with each other, exchanging information and wheeling and dealing over allegiances after any successful attack. The myth of forces motivated by ideology

alone, rather than by ethnic considerations, had always been hard to sustain. Even senior Taliban figures changed sides without much soul searching. This was what happened, for example, in the case of Mullah Muhammad Khaksar, the head of the Taliban intelligence services, later a deputy minister, a Pushtun from Qandahar. On November 24, 2001, at a press conference in Kabul, he explained that he had quarreled with Mullah Omar to whom, he said, he had frequently emphasized that "the foreigners should long ago have left our country, which they are bringing to ruin."

Conquests were accompanied by massacres, to which the Americans turned a blind eye. The victims were the foreign Al-Qa'ida fighters and the Pakistanis. On November 19, the American Defense Secretary Donald Rumsfeld warned that "the United States is not inclined to negotiate surrender terms, and neither are we, in view of our small numbers on the ground, in a position to take prisoners."

The following day Rumsfeld said at the Pentagon that it would be "most unfortunate if the foreign fighters of Al-Qa'ida at Kunduz were left at liberty and allowed to reach other countries where they could take part in similar terrorist acts." This encouragement to murder met with the general approval of the Afghans. The commander of the United Front, Muhammad Ustaz Atta, made no secret of his view when he announced on November 20 that "we cannot guarantee the safety of foreign combatants as they have been the cause of a humanitarian catastrophe in Afghanistan."

The alleged mutiny of eight hundred Al-Qa'ida militiamen taken prisoner by Dostum's troops at the time of the fall of Kunduz had a bloody outcome thanks to intense air attacks on the prisoners. With this episode as witness to what awaited them should they surrender, the foreign fighters resisted to the last on other fronts.

Meanwhile Pushtun Taliban fighters, who had long been without pay, deserted en masse and simply went back to their villages. Some ten thousand religious fighters rallied round Mullah Omar in Qandahar, where several thousand Pakistani volunteers attempted to continue the combat. Occasionally, Taliban units stayed together, aiming to carrying on guerrilla warfare in the mountains or in far-flung regions where caves had long been prepared as refuges.

Attention was primarily focused, however, on the Al-Qa'ida forces. These were obliged to fight to the last man. They could not surrender, since they would have been executed, but as foreigners they could not take refuge in the mountain villages. They sought refuge in the networks of tunnels and caves, which then became the objective of intense bombing. Unable to speak the local languages, however, they were rejected by the Pushtun population, who made them the scapegoat for all their misfortunes.

The United Front's thirty thousand fighters were insufficient both to press on with military operations, while at the same time securing all the liberated areas. They were unable to guarantee a strong enough military presence to ensure that regional strongholds did not once more emerge under the leadership of their former commanders. To this uncertainty was added dissension arising out of conflicting territorial claims between the warlords. However, the United Front was unwilling to cooperate with the British or French troops brought in under the auspices of the UN, as they did not want to see their victory taken from them. The Americans, who did not want to lose their free hand over their own military operations, tacitly backed their stand.

On November 19, speaking in Teheran, President Rabbani said he rejected "the presence of foreign troops, and foreign interference." The arrival at Bagram air base of the British Royal Marines caused an out-

cry. General Fahim, the minister of defense, warned that "the British forces may have made a deal with the United Nations, but not with us." Yunus Qanuni, the minister of the interior, went further: "We want no further foreign troops. We do not see the need."

Such clashes of view did not arise solely from a stance of rigid nationalism on the part of the United Front. The demand of the victorious commanders to remain the undisputed masters of the country had a more practical aim. They wanted to put themselves in a strong position at the negotiations over Afghanistan's national future, which were about to open at the German city of Bonn. The aim of each commander was to strengthen his personal position. Since the Taliban had now effectively been defeated, there was no need, as the commanders saw it, to overcome by force those who remained. In the view of the commanders, any attack would entail the loss of men, which would in consequence put each of them in a weaker position with respect to today's allies, who might yet be tomorrow's enemies. All stood to benefit from negotiations with Taliban military leaders on changes of allegiance that might prompt them to change sides, bringing with them their arms and men.

In Kunduz, the last pocket of Taliban resistance in the north, whole columns of tanks and trucks left the Taliban's ranks to place themselves under Dostum's or Daoud's command. According to the United Front, some foreign combatants were evacuated and captured Pakistani officers were flown out by their government in planes or by helicopter. In this situation, such operations had the blessing of the United States, which controlled the Afghan skies. On November 25, once the Afghan and Pakistani defenders of Kunduz had left, the town was finally captured.

The Pushtuns, threatened by the local ethnic communities, regrouped in order to repel their attackers. In order to maintain the influence of their own community, the Taliban handed over regions from which they had withdrawn to commanders of Pushtun ethnicity. Mullah Omar ordered his forces to withdraw from the eastern provinces and retire to the province of Qandahar. Four commanders disputed control of the province of Ghazni. The Taliban entrusted the province of Nangarhar to the eighty-year-old Yunus Khales, a legendary figure of the anti-Soviet resistance. His party, which had split off from Hekmatyar's Hezb-i Islami, had been the breeding ground of the "students of religion." It was anti-Western and had maintained good relations with the Arab commanders. Yunus Khales appointed Awa Gul as his chief in Jalalabad, who was immediately challenged by Haji Qadir, the brother of Abdul Haq, who had been executed by the Taliban, as well as by Haji Muhammad Zaman, an ally of another of Abdul Haq's brothers, and by Hazrat Ali.

On the ground, the coalition of non-Pushtun ethnicities secured its hold on the north. The south and the east remained in the hands of the Pushtuns. The Americans attempted to organize opposition to the Taliban within the Pushtun tribes, a kind of southern alliance, going as far as to provide substantial finance. They rejected any exchange of the lives and freedom of the defenders for the surrender of Taliban strongholds, especially if any of these were members of Al-Qa'ida. On November 25, 2001, they underlined their determination to crush Al-Qa'ida by deploying thousands of Marines to the south of Qandahar with the aim of flushing out Bin Laden's network. They also aimed to control the movements of remaining Taliban groups, while preventing them from reaching the mountainous regions. The operation was also intended to stiffen the resolve of anti-Taliban Pushtun forces, who could not achieve victory over the Taliban unaided. The intention was to

enhance the balance of forces on the ground while reinforcing the anti-Taliban position in future negotiations on power sharing.

Real anxiety continued to be felt, lest either the Taliban or Bin Laden's supporters should prove capable of organizing a guerrilla force which might operate out of the Pakistani tribal zones. The issue was how could any such force be pursued on the ground or attacked from the air without destabilizing America's already vulnerable Pakistani ally. Islamabad moved more troops up to its frontiers, but the configuration of the mountains made it impossible to seal the border perfectly. In a further complication, old quarrels between the Pushtun tribes obliged the Americans to open talks with other ethnic communities.

Haji Qadeer held Jalalabad while Dostum took control of Mazar-i Sharif. Kabul was controlled by Tajiks from Panjshir, who were Massoud's successors. America's other allies protested. The Hazaras despatched several hundred fighters to secure their own position. However, real power was held by the Tajik troika: Yunus Qanuni, minister of the interior, Dr. Abdullah Abdullah, minister of foreign affairs, and Muhammad Fahim, minister of defense. Meanwhile, on the ground, the long-standing rivalry between the Uzbeks and the Tajiks once more broke out, with the difference that now the Uzbeks were led by American commandos, while the Tajiks coordinated their activities with Russian special forces.

Twenty-five million dollars were offered for the capture of Bin Laden, in the hope that greed would lead to treachery, thus enabling his capture, "dead or alive." On November 14, with this in view, President Bush signed an order enabling him to specify which prisoners were liable to trial by special military tribunals. Those targeted were foreigners suspected of committing terrorist acts or of harboring terrorists. Such military tribunals, which were empowered to inflict the death penalty, would be able to convene abroad. The prosecutor John Ashcroft explained: "We may apprehend terrorists in places like Afghanistan … and not find it necessary to bring them back to the United States to face justice."

Osama Bin Laden was reported to have said to a Pakistani journalist, "I love death as much as you love life." This met with the approval of Donald Rumsfeld, who said that—as far as he was concerned—he would "rather Bin Laden was killed than taken prisoner." To try Bin Laden would serve only to provide a gratuitous platform for terrorist views and would, therefore, run the risk of encouraging others.

The fall of the Taliban offered a turning point at which Afghanistan could have availed itself of the opportunity to take a new direction, and it was toward this goal that the endeavors of the United Nations were aimed. November 26 saw the opening of a meeting at Schloss Petersberg in Bonn that brought together thirty Afghan delegates grouped into four delegations. These were the United Front (also known as the Northern Alliance), the Council of Understanding and National Unity of Afghanistan (also known as Peshawar group), the Cyprus Process, and the Rome Process. Some individual tribal leaders also attended the meeting. Yunus Qanuni, officially minister of the interior, led the United Front delegation. The Tajiks, the Shi'ite Hazaras, the Uzbeks, and the Pushtuns were all represented. In contrast with the situation in 1992, the idea of a multi-ethnic government was accepted by all sides.

Three Afghan exile groups were the principal representatives of the Pushtuns. One of these consisted of the supporters of the king, Zahir Shah, who was currently in exile in Rome. Their leader was the former minister of justice, Abdul Sattar Sirat. Another was the Peshawar group, which favored the return of Zahir Shah. This group was led by Sayyedun Ahmed Gaylani, a Pushtun in his seventies who was the son of Pir Gaylani, the descendant of Sufi dignitaries of the Qadiriyya order, who had assembled several hundred Pushtun representatives to oppose the Taliban. The third Pushtun group was the Cyprus group, supported by Teheran, which was made up of those exiles opposed to the Rome group.

The former Prime Minister Gulbuddin Hekmatyar, who continued to advocate "national unity," including the Taliban, against the United States, denounced the Bonn meeting as "an American conference, not a United Nations conference." Nevertheless, his son-in-law Humayin Jarir was the leader of the Tajik delegation. Humayun Jarir, from the Panjshir Valley, was on very poor terms with the United Front, which accused him of giving assistance to Hekmatyar while he was the object of attacks between 1992 and 1996. At that time, Massoud had felt it necessary to arrest Jarir.

Lakhdar Brahimi, the United Nations special representative subsequently invited the Afghan delegates to an inter-Afghan conference whose aim was to facilitate preliminary discussions aimed at the formation of a representative government. Brahimi's aim was to set up a conference that could take place free of interference by neighboring countries. Nonetheless, foreign diplomats were able to attend, and the Americans, the Russians, the British, the French, and the Pakistanis took advantage of the opportunity to voice their positions. The Russians and the French argued for a key role for the United Front, which would exclude the Pushtuns. However the Pakistanis demanded representation for the Pushtuns in proportion to their demographic representation within Afghanistan.

The international community agreed to spend ten billion dollars in Afghanistan over a ten-year period on condition that the Afghan factions agreed on the future of their country. Such assistance was vital in a country in which 70 percent of the population was malnourished, only 13 percent had access to drinkable water, and only a third of the children went to school.

On December 4, in the face of ex-president Rabbani's opposition, agreement was reached on interim institutions. There was to be a cabinet of twenty-nine members and a special commission of twenty-one members, whose task would be to settle current issues and to prepare urgently for the meeting of a Loya Jirga in the spring of 2002.

The head of the new government that emerged from this process was Hamid Karzai, a Pushtun aristocrat, born in 1957 and a member of the small Popolzai clan. He had studied law in India and then in the United States. However, he could claim no military legitimacy as he had not participated in the fight against the Soviets. Nevertheless, he became deputy minister for foreign affairs in Rabbani's government. General Fahim, Massoud's intelligence chief, later had him arrested on suspicion of collusion with Pakistan. In 1994, he escaped during an attack on Kabul, joining the Taliban. He hoped to become the Taliban representative at the United Nations, but his ambition was disappointed. He subsequently settled in the Pakistani town of Quetta, where he became a consultant to the petroleum company "Unocal," which was planning the Afghan oil pipeline. He turned down the opportunity to join his two brothers in the United States, where both were successful restaurateurs, preferring to stay with his father, until the latter was murdered in Quetta in obscure circumstances in 1999. He traveled secretly to Afghanistan in early October 2001 with the aim of raising a rebellion of southern Pushtun tribes against the Taliban regime. Surrounded by the Taliban, he escaped thanks to his rescue by an American helicopter. He subsequently led an offensive against the Taliban in Qandahar with the

assistance of American forces and negotiated their surrender on December 7, 2001.

After Karzai's appointment as the head of the government, a Pakistani journalist Kamran Khan, in an article published on December 6, 2001, described him as "for years the man of the CIA and the ISI. The appointment of this moderate English-speaking Muslim, seldom seen praying, is the doing of the Americans, but also that of the Pakistanis, because of his long-standing links with them and his knowledge of the Urdu language. He has spent more time in Pakistan than in Afghanistan."

His most serious challenger, Rahim Wardak, a Pushtun soldier close to Zahir Shah, was awarded only the ministry of tourism and air transport. Before his appointment, Wardak had attempted to raise an army by recruiting former officers and soldiers in Islamabad and Peshawar. Another issue was that women were meant to form part of Karzai's government. Proportionality between the communities appeared to be respected, at least on paper. On the eve of Karzai's appointment as head of state, the Pushtuns held eleven ministries, the Tajiks eiggt, and the Hazaras five, while the Uzbeks had three and the other ethnic minorities shared three portfolios among them. The United Front held sixteeen ministries out of thirty. In practice, the Tajiks were the big winners. They retained the key defense ministry, with Muhammad Fahim as minister, holding also the interior ministry, with Yunus Qanuni, and the ministry of foreign affairs, which was held by Dr. Abdullah Abdullah.

Karzai's major disadvantage, however, as Afghanistan's new leader was that as he enjoyed no status as a warlord he held little real sway within his own ethnic community. Mullah Naqib and the former governor of Qandahar, Gul Agha, soon challenged him for control of Qandahar. The warlords, who had returned to their former fiefs, or at least were in contention for them, were blatantly omitted from the provisional government. The challenge to the regional autonomy of the warlords was rejected by the strongest among them. These included the Uzbek leader, Abdul Rahim Dostum, once more ensconced in his domain at Mazar-i Sharif; the Tajik Ismail Khan at Herat; the Pushtun strongman Abdul Rasul Sayyaf at Paghman, at the gates of Kabul; and another Pushtun, Haji Qadir at Jalalabad.

On the issue of security, the United Nations representative Lakhdar Brahimi put forward the idea of a multinational force under the mandate of the Security Council. The United Front opposed this and demanded a purely Afghan solution. Ex-president Rabbani cautioned the Westerners: "The Afghan people will not agree to the installation on Afghan soil of a foreign force, of no matter what kind, and demands that all foreign forces leave Afghanistan."

The United States viewed favorably the solution of an Afghan force, which would provide tribal chiefs with the means to equip and maintain units whose task would be to maintain order. The agreement, nevertheless, provided for an international security force under UN mandate that would "give assistance in maintaining order in Kabul and its environs." The minister of defense, General Fahim, expressed his preference for a force of limited size whose brief would be "to protect government buildings."

The surrender of Qandahar, negotiated by Hamid Karzai in exchange for an amnesty, was the occasion for a severe warning issued by the Americans. The United States threatened to withdraw its backing both for the government and for the United Front if any amnesty were to be extended to Mullah Omar or if he were helped to flee. Bin Laden, for his part, though trapped in the Tora Bora area, which was being massively bombed by the Americans, succeeded in making his escape with the help of an Afghan tribal chief, finding refuge in the tribal zone on the Pakistani frontier. The warlords were eventually driven to seek a compromise as the result of various factors, including both the war-weariness of the fighters and the suffering of the civilian population. A further factor was international pressure of various kinds, together with the conditions attached to the foreign aid provided for the reconstruction of the country, which was accompanied by a veritable financial bonanza. The Afghans had learned the lessons of the years spent tearing each other apart, and they now yearned for a more comfortable and peaceful life. The Taliban had collapsed, and the basis of Al-Qa'ida's support system had been destroyed while its fleeing leaders were cut off from communication with the outside world.

All these positive factors, however, had their disadvantages, carrying with them the potential to unleash once more the cycle of violence. As concerns Afghanistan's neighbors, there was the issue of how the interests of Russia, Iran, and Pakistan were to be reconciled. There was also the problem of the imposition of a compromise solution on the local chieftains, as well as the growing difficulty of reconciling all the various factions within the United Front.

General Dostum, one of the United Front's big hitters, had rejected the Bonn accord. Meanwhile, Ismail Khan, the governor of Herat, refused to forgive his betrayal in 1999 by another of the United Front's commanders, Abdul Malik Pawlawan, which had cost him his fief and put him in prison. The adherence of the warlords as well as the small local commanders, neglected by the Bonn accord, was indispensable for the reestablishment of security. However, enmities were perpetuated as warlords large and small vied with increasing determination for influence, position, and cash. The West, in an attempt to defuse local tensions, was obliged to offer generous subventions in order to avert the defection of fighters, always ready to re-embark on a campaign against the foreign presence in order to boost their influence and power.

The Loya Jirga met on June 12, 2002, to appoint a new government and a parliament, which would in turn have two years to prepare a new constitution. Hamid Karzai was elected as head of state after he won the backing of the king, Zahir Shah, who refused to accept a mandate for himself. Hamid Karzai thus became the first elected head of state in the postwar period. However, on the ground, all the ingredients of instability were more than ever in evidence. Power was fragmented and divided, the warlords reemerged, and security became a real problem. The military ineptitude of the Americans aroused the anger of the Afghan population. There were a number of occasions when American attacks inflicted civilian casualties including the deaths of children, which were hard for the public to accept. Meanwhile, there appeared to be a resurgence of Taliban activity in the south of the country near the Pakistani border, while purported messages from Osama Bin Laden continued to appear, mainly in the Arabic media.

Nonetheless, the international community seemed determined not to permit history to repeat itself and, in particular, not to allow the reenactment of the fragmentation and chaos that had followed the defeat of communism in Afghanistan after the Russian withdrawal. Western plans for Afghanistan's future as an independent and democratic nation continued to be implemented. NATO took over responsibility for security in Afghanistan in August 2003. In December 2003, a further Loya Jirga was convened to adopt a constitution, but the meeting dragged on into January 2004 before an agreement could be reached. Presidential elections were eventually scheduled for June 2004, but were postponed until October 9, 2004. In these elections, Hamid Karzai won a convincing victory, with more than 55 percent of the vote and was elected for a five-year term. Parliamentary elections were held in September 2005 and the new

Afghan parliament held its inaugural session in December 2005.

A continuing problem for Afghanistan, however, has been the resurgence of the Taliban. By the early summer of 2006, the new Taliban commander Mullah Dadullah claimed to have twelve thousand men under arms and to be in control of areas in the southern provinces of the country. Later in 2006, the NATO forces, which were now in charge of maintaining security, had begun to face fierce opposition in Helmand and elsewhere. In January 2007, a senior NATO commander, Britain's General David Richards, suggested that a further year's effort would be required on the part of the NATO forces to quell the Taliban resurgence. As to the whereabouts of the former protagonists, some analysts have claimed that Osama Bin Laden is in the tribal areas on the northern part of the frontier of Afghanistan and Pakistan. The former Taliban and Al-Qa'ida leadership is evidently fragmented, as Bin Laden's former lieutenant Ayman al-Zawahiri said in late 2006 that he had no idea of Bin Laden's whereabouts. Mullah Omar was reported in January 2007 to be in Quetta, in the central region of the Pakistan-Afghanistan frontier, where he moves constantly from one safe house to another, though the captured Taliban spokesman who gave this information may have intended deliberately to mislead.

Actors in the Afghan Conflict

The United Front. The United Front came into existence as a coalition of convenience against the Taliban, which was composed basically of non-Pushtun elements. Its underlying coherence is a matter of doubt. Ethnic rivalry and personal quarrels have stood in the way of the formation of a unified and effective command. The leading personalities within the front were Dostum, Hekmatyar, and Massoud (each of whom has a separate entry in this dictionary).

Other United Front figures are listed below:

Dr. Abdullah Abdullah. Dr. Abdullah was a medical doctor. His father was a Pushtun from Qandahar and his mother was a Tajik from Panjshir. Between 1992 and 1996, Dr. Abdullah was Massoud's spokesman before becoming the United Front's minister of foreign affairs.

Burhanuddin Rabbani. Rabbani became president of the Islamic state of Afghanistan in 1992. The Islamic state was recognized by the United Nations until June 13, 2002, the date when the Loya Jirga, which brought together some 1,500 delegates in Kabul, elected Hamid Karzai as head of state. Rabbani was a Tajik, born in Faizabad in the province of Badakhshan in 1940 and studied theology at the celebrated University of Al-Azhar in Cairo before teaching at the University of Kabul. He began his political career as an opponent of the communists within the Islamic anti-communist movement. He energetically repudiated Zahir Shah's modest reform measures, behind which he saw the hand of the commnists. Jamiyat-i Islami, of which he was in charge in 1971, became the spearhead of the struggle against the communist regime. The overthrow of the king in 1973 meant that in 1974 Rabbani was obliged to go into exile in Pakistan in order to escape retribution at the hands of General Daud's regime. As a fundamentalist Islamist, he led the struggle against the Soviets from Peshawar, relying on the exceptional abilities of two of his lieutenants, Ismail Khan and Ahmad Shah Massoud. By the end of the jihad, he had under his command some twenty thousand fighters. He became president of the Islamic state of Afghanistan as the result of a coup, and he governed according to the Quran and the Shari'a. After his defeat at the hands of the Taliban, he fled to his native village. Rabbani had hitherto maintained political control through the skillful exploitation of the recognition accorded to him by the United Nations and the divisions that existed among the commanders. However, though General Massoud, his minister of defense in 1992, enjoyed immense popularity and a degree of legitimacy derived from his military achievements, Rabbani himself was unable, because of his difficult relationship with Massoud, to turn this to his own advantage.

Muhammad Fahim. Muhammad Fahim was born in 1958. He was the son of a Tajik "mawlawi," an Islamic scholar, from Panjshir and became head of the security services of the Northern Alliance. Fahim was an opportunist whose self-interest led him to move from one end to the other of the political spectrum. He was Muhammad Najibullah's deputy in the pro-communist regime in Kabul. He rose through the ranks of the intelligence services.

Karim Khalili. Khalili was a Shi'ite who was the leader of the major branch of Hezb-i Wahdat (Party of Unity) in 1995. Khalili's sworn enemy Muhammad Muhaqqiq led the other branch. Supported by Iran, he waged war against the Taliban in the center of the country, in the region of Bamyan. He suffered the loss of his personal fief, the village of Bamyan, on February 17, 2001.

Muhammad Yunis Qanuni. Qanuni was a Tajik from the town of Rukha, the intellectual center of the Panjshir valley. He was a recognized representative of the mujahidin in Pakistan at the time of the anti-Soviet jihad and became deputy minister of defense for Rabbani in 1992, who was then minister of the interior. He was a close associate of Massoud. He bears the scars of an ambush for which Hekmatyar is regarded as responsible.

Ismail Khan. Ismail Khan was a Tajik career soldier. He began his jihad in 1979 with the massacre of 350 Soviet advisers and their families. The reprisals for this act, carried out with extreme violence, prompted the first mutinies in the ranks of the Red Army. He was a member of Jamiyat-i Islami and gained his status as a commander through his bravery at the front. In 1990, he imposed himself as governor of Herat and five provinces in western Afghanistan. Though from a family of poor peasants, he built himself a palace and lived luxuriously until the arrival of the Taliban in 1995. He was betrayed and handed over to the Taliban by Abdul Malik, an Uzbek general who was an associate of Dostum. He escaped in 2000, and in the spring of 2001 returned to Afghanistan with several hundred men armed by Iran.

Abdul Rasul Sayyaf. Sayyaf is a Pushtun, who led the movement Ittihad-i Islami, which he founded in 1982. He was educated in Cairo at the Al-Azhar University, where he studied theology. By 1980, he was the spokesman of the mujahidin in Peshawar. He was associated with the Wahhabi movement and was generously funded by the Gulf monarchies and, in particular, by the Saudi royal family. He became deputy prime minister in the Rabbani government. His personal fief was Gulbahar, at the foot of the Panjshir valley. Sayyaf and Massoud were in general wary of each other.

AHBASH, AL- (LEBANON)

Al-Ahbash (literally "the Ethiopians") is the name of an Islamic benevolent society, the "Association for Islamic Benevolent Works," which has been active in Lebanon since the mid-1980s. It was inspired by the ideas of Sheikh Abdallah al-Hariri, who was originally from Ethiopia (in Arabic, Al-Habash). It claims to base its ideas on "authentic" Islam and on the schools of jurisprudence, especially the Shafi'i school, which dates back to 1,200 years ago. It presents itself as doctrinally opposed to the thirteenth century theologian Ibn Taymiyya, and of the Wahhabis, and regards the Muslim Brotherhood and the Islamic Liberation Party as "extremist groups divorced from the inheritance of the sunna."

Abdel Nasser Tamim, one of the founders of the association in 1991 in Paris, stresses the respect of the Ahbash for the "Tariqa al-Rifa'iyya" (one of the Sufi "turuq" (plural of "tariqa") or mystical brotherhoods),

whose name refers to Imam Ibn Ahmad al-Rifa'i, whose tomb is near Baghdad. According to the association's literature, its style of personal proselytization, with its mystical element, is intended as an alternative to the philosophy of "Takfir wa-l Hijra"—excommunication and withdrawal—practiced by the Muslim Brotherhood and its disciples.

Al-Ahbash originated in the Beirut suburb of Bourj Abu Haidar, and thence spread through West Beirut, the northern city of Tripoli, Akkar, and Iqlim al-Kharrub, setting up a number of religious and educational centres. On the model of its sworn enemy, the Muslim Brotherhood, al-Ahbash made use of its charitable presence as a means of establishing itself on the political scene. Its alignment with Syrian policy and its close cooperation with the Lebanese intelligence services prepared the way for its entry into parliament in 1992, in the shape of its representative Adnan Trabulsi, elected as deputy for a Beirut constituency.

However, al-Ahbash's ideological differences with both the Salafis and the Muslim Brotherhood led to clashes and, in particular, to the assassination on August 31, 1995, of the organization's president, Nizar Halabi, a crime for which certain radical Islamists from northern Lebanon were convicted and subsequently executed. Nizar Halabi was succeeded by Hussam Qaraqira, acting under the aegis of Sheikh Abdallah Al-Harari, who is resident in both Lebanon and in Lausanne. Qaraqira directs Al-Ahbash together with the former deputy Adnan Trabulsi, assisted also by Taha Naji (a veteran of the Afghan war based in Tripoli), as well as the two Sheikhs Samir al-Qadi and Usama al-Sayyed.

Al-Ahbash has been active in France since 1991: in Paris in particular, where it has two centers, as well as in Montpellier, Narbonne, Dizier, and St. Etienne. The organization claims to have adherents throughout France.

Walid Dabbous, a professor of information technology, became its leader in France in 2002. Sheikh Khaled al-Zanat is the imam of the principal al-Ahbash mosque in France, in Montpellier. Every year Al-Ahbash organizes a major festival in Saint-Denis on the occasion of "Mawlid an-Nabi" (the birthday of the prophet), a festival not observed by strict Sunnis such as the Wahhabis of Saudi Arabia. The particular constituency it targets is the new generation of French citizens of Maghrebi origin. Al-Ahbash also has a presence in Switzerland, Denmark, and Sweden, as well as in the Muslim republics of the former Soviet Union, Ukraine, and the United States.

One of the salient characteristics of al-Ahbash is its abstention from political and militant propaganda. Its adoption of an apparently moderate stance—expressed through its condemnation of terrorism in Egypt and Algeria—appears to dissimulate its true intention, namely to achieve domination in the field of Islamism and subsequently to impose a strict and pure fundamentalism, together with a determined opposition to modernity.

AHL-I HADITH (PEOPLE OF THE PROPHET'S WORD) (INDIA AND PAKISTAN)

The Ahl-i Hadith was initially a strictly religious movement, founded in northern India in the mid-nineteenth century. It advocated radical religious reform more radical than that of the Deobandi school, rejecting everything introduced into Islam after the earliest times, that is to say after the Quran, the Sunna, and the Hadith, from which it derives its name. In practice, it does not greatly differ from Saudi Wahhabism and is frequently characterized as "Wahhabi" in both Pakistan and India. In particular, it repudiates the tradition of schools of Islamic jurisprudence, which sets it in opposition to the Islamic tradition dominant in the Indian subcontinent and in Afghanistan, which subscribes to the Hanafi school. Ahl-i Hadith places particular emphasis on teaching, and is somewhat elitist, recruiting from the higher castes and among the "sayyids" or descendants of the prophet. It is, therefore, a minor movement in relation to the other principal Pakistani and Indian religious tendencies—the Deobandis and the Barelvis among the majority Sunni community and the minority Shi'ites.

Ahl-i Hadith was founded in 1930 in India as a small political party and became increasingly active in Pakistan from the 1970s onward, under the impetus of its leader Allama Ehsan Elahi Zaheer, who was assassinated in 1987. Ahl-i Hadith supported the Jihad against the Soviets in Afghanistan and then backed the Taliban. In the context of Pakistani politics it has taken a radical stance, particularly in its opposition to the Shi'ites. This politicization culminated in the creation of "Markaz Da'wat wa-l Irshad," the preaching and educational branch of the movement, which split off from the parent organization. In the 1970s, the Ahl-i Hadith also gained a foothold in Afghanistan through the activity of mullahs educated in its schools, who waged a struggle to establish Wahhabism in some areas. Such figures included Jamil-ar-Rahman in the Pech valley and Mullah Afzal in Upper Nuristan. The Ahl-i Hadith controls a network of mosques and madrasas as well as two student organizations: "Ahl-i Hadith Students Federation" and "Ahl-i Hadith Ittehad Council."

ALBANIA

Islamism is a very recent phenomenon in Albania, a country better known for its obdurate nationalism than for its religious

problems. The population of Albania consists of 70 percent Muslims and 30 percent
Christians. The Muslims are two-thirds
Sunni, with the remainder belonging to religious orders such as the Turkey-based Bektashis, who have Shi'ite connections. Of the
Christians, 25 percent of the total population is Orthodox and 5 percent is Catholic.

A north-south division also exists in Albania on the two sides of the river Shkumbi.
The north is mainly Muslim and tribal, following customary law, while the south tends
rather to be Christian, with a greater open-
ness to the outside world and more observant of contemporary legislation. For the
majority of Albanians, the Muslim faith is
an important statement of identity, but one
that takes its place alongside others, namely
nationalism, language, and culture. Thanks
to these factors, the Albanians were able
clearly to distinguish themselves from the
Ottoman Empire, of which Albania formed
a part until 1912, as well as from neighboring
Greece. In 1941, Albanian nationalism paved
the way for the move by Nazi Germany during World War II to set up a Greater Albania, with the subsequent creation in April
1944 of the Skanderberg division of the SS,
named after the Albanian hero of the fif-
teenth century.

When Enver Hodja's communists took
power after World War II, Albania shut itself
off from the outside world. On December 27,
1967, it officially became a nonreligious state
and 2,200 religious buildings were looted or
destroyed. In 1991, Hodja's successor, Ramiz
Alia, attempted to bolster his power through
the reintroduction of religious liberties and
the restoration to the Islamic community of
a number of mosques, of which 1,700 had
been destroyed since 1946.

In 1991, the Communist Party, now
transformed into a socialist party, won the
country's first free elections. In further elections held in March 1992, the winner was the
Democratic Party, which had been set up in

November 1991. It was under the Democratic
Party that Islamism took root in Albania. At
the time of the fall of the communist regime
in 1992 the structures of the state had virtually disintegrated. The fact that the majority
of Albania's population was Muslim, albeit
nonpracticing, meant that Albania presented
an attractive target for Islamist activists and
Islamic NGOs. In the circumstances, they
saw an opportunity to revive the Muslim
faith in what was the only Muslim-majority
European country (except for the anoma-
lous case of Turkey). The prevailing political
chaos led also to Albania becoming a refuge
for a number of radical Islamists, mainly of
Egyptian origin, who were able to draw on
the support of Wahhabi NGOs both to meet
the costs of their initial establishment and to
provide them with an ongoing income.

The new president, Sali Berisha, was a
Sunni Muslim. He ruled in an authoritarian style, making the maintenance of his
own power his first priority. To this end, he
allied himself with Islam, which he introduced into the Albanian political scene.
On December 2, 1992, he took Albania into
the Organization of the Islamic Conference
(OIC). In addition to looking to Turkey for
military assistance, he turned to Saudi Arabia for financial support. This policy led to
a reconstruction of Albanian Islam on the
model of the practice of the Gulf countries.
This new Islam brought with it a new out-
look. Henceforth, the Muslim faith was an
essential feature of Albanian identity, and
it was with the Islamic world that Albania's
relations were closest. The architect of the
Islamic transformation of the country was
Bashkim Gazidede, one of Berisha's advisers, who became head of the secret services
in 1992 and maintained special relationships
with his Arab and Iranian counterparts. The
socialists and the Christians expressed concern over these developments and accused
Berisha of aiming at the establishment of
an Islamic state in Albania. The Albanian

regime, however, came increasingly to rely on its support in the Muslim north of the country, thus casting into doubt the traditional consensus among Albanians of different faiths.

Among the first foreign Islamists to come to Albania was Muhammad al Zawahiri, the brother of Ayman al Zawahiri, the leader of the Egyptian Islamic Jihad movement and Osama Bin Laden's key lieutenant. Muhammad al-Zawahiri arrived in Albania as an accountant for the International Islamic Relief Organization (IIRO), a Saudi NGO secretly charged with the task of helping other members of Islamic Jihad to find positions in Albania within "charitable organizations building mosques, orphanages and clinics."

This conspiracy was later exposed during the investigation carried out by the American and Albanian secret services, which led to the dismantling of the IIRO in July 1998. In January 1993, Muhammad al-Zawahiri brought the architect Muhammad Hassan Tita, a member of Islamic Jihad in Egypt, to work for the IIRO, assigning him the task of collecting 20 percent of the salaries earned by Islamic Jihad members employed by NGOs. By the mid-1980s, the Tirana cell of Islamic Jihad numbered sixteen members. Tita arranged for the Islamic NGOs to find a place for Shawki Salama Attiya, a former instructor in the Afghan camps in the 1980s, who specialized in false identity documents. He came to Albania under the pseudonym of Majed Mustafa, obtaining a job in an Albanian orphanage at a salary of U.S.$700 per month. Another of Tita's recruits was Ahmed Osman Saleh, who was wanted by the Egyptian authorities on suspicion of involvement in the attempted assassination of Egypt's Prime Minister Atef Sidqi in 1993, whose official reason for coming to Albania was to teach the Quran and to manage an orphanage. Finally, in 1997, Ahmed Ibrahim Naggar came to Tirana to take up a post in the NGO Al-Haramein. Naggar was to

become Attiya's principal assistant. Both men maintained direct links with Ayman al-Zawahiri, who had by now joined Bin Laden in Afghanistan. At the same period, many mujahidin from Algeria, Sudan, and Afghanistan passed through Albania. The intelligence services of numerous Muslim countries were also strongly represented in the country. Finally, the Albanian nexus was one of the sources of funding for the Kosovo Liberation Army (UCK).

Saudi Arabia's assistance strengthened Berisha in his plan to re-Islamize the country, an organized project undertaken by preachers and Islamic NGOs. The preachers' approach was to expunge indigenous Albanian ideas about Islam, before replacing it with a version of the faith more in conformity with the Wahhabi model. As part of the process, the teaching of Arabic was intensified, thanks to generous levels of funding. Islam in its most radical form was taught as the only true faith, while tolerance was seen as an indication of weakness. The preachers imposed the vision of the "umma"—the world Muslim community—on a country hitherto marked by national pride. Hatred of the West was raised to the status of a creed.

In Albania, the Islamic NGOs vied with each other. They built mosques—some two hundred in the case of the Saudi NGOs—and were active in the humanitarian, economic, and social fields. King Fahd of Saudi Arabia donated a million copies of an Albanian language version of the Quran. Thirty NGOs and Islamic associations worked toward an undisguised goal, namely the re-Islamization of the country. Thirteen of these organizations formed a "Coordination Council of Arab Foundations." The most radical maintained close links with Libya and Sudan. Saudi Arabia sponsored "Al Haramein" and "Muwafaq" (which were based in Britain). Iran operated by means of the "Jihad for Reconstruction" and the "Saadi

Shirazi Foundation." The Turkish state undertook only political and military activity, but Necmettin Erbakan's "Refah Partisi" ran its own NGO. The common thread was the instrumentalization of humanitarian aid as a means of proselytization and of bringing pressure to bear for the establishment of an Islamic society based principally on Wahhabism. At the same time, the influence of Iran was reinforced by the Bektashis, who reformed their dogma to bring themselves into line with Iranian Shi'ite Islam. Bektashi clerics thus became the principal vector of Iranian influence in the country. This was a visible reaction to the Islamic upsurge. The Greek right wing, supported by the Orthodox clergy, vigorously supported the southern part of Albania, which was regarded by the Greeks as a northern extension of the Greek province of Epirus.

In February 1998, Albania's economic situation deteriorated. The pyramid fundraising organizations, which had financed the president and his party, collapsed. Severe disturbances broke out in the south, which were crushed by heavily armed reprisals. Peace was restored by international intervention. In April 1997, Italy, Greece, and France interceded in the framework of "Operation Alba." Elections were held during the summer, which resulted in victory for the Socialist Party. Rexhep Meidani became president and the prime ministership went to Fatos Nano, an Orthodox Christian who had been imprisoned under Berisha.

Once in power, the socialists embarked on a reexamination of the place of Islam in Albanian society. Their view was that Muslim identity, as redefined by the Islamists, was incompatible with a European identity. Islam was, therefore, excluded from social life as far as was feasible. The financial regime imposed by the International Monetary Fund, together with Europe's oversight in security matters, helped to minimize the influence of the Islamists. Socialists and nonreligious intellectuals began to speak about an "Islamic plot" in which both Berisha and the Arab countries were implicated. In the event, in June 1998, the Albanian secret services and the CIA arrested three Egyptian Islamists accused of terrorist activities. Further arrests took place in September 1998, following the attacks in August 1998 against the U.S. embassies in Nairobi and Dar es-Salaam.

When war broke out in Kosovo, a province of neighboring Yugoslavia, destabilization seemed at first to be a possibility. The Democratic Party insisted on its strong concern over events in Kosovo, and though the Socialist Party insisted that the war was not Albania's affair, the unity of the Albanian people came under threat. In July 1998, the Democratic Party withdrew from parliament, and attempted a coup d'état after the assassination of one of its deputies. It also rejected the constitution adopted by the referendum of November 22, 1998. In March 1999, NATO intervened in Kosovo, using Albania as its base of operations, thus averting a further crisis in the country. The influx of Kosovar refugees, amounting to 450,000 in 1999, did not significantly affect Albania's internal situation.

The "Islamic menace" was contained, in spite of the efforts of the Islamists, though thanks to Berisha, the Islamists gained an important foothold and will continue to present a serious problem for the maintenance of the country's unity. However, stability should continue to prevail as long as the Socialist Party remains in power and while the West continues to be represented in Albania. The Democratic Party returned to politics and further elections were held in June 2001, when the Socialist Party retained power and Fatos Nano returned as prime minister. At the end of President Meidani's mandate, the national assembly elected Alfred Moisiu as a consensus candidate for the presidency on June 24, 2002.

ALGERIA

Historically, the first appearance of a political current embodying Islamic values dates back to the 1930s, with the emergence of the "Parti du Peuple Algérien" (Algerian People's Party) (PPA) and Ben Badis's "Association of Ulema." The latter group merged with the National Liberation Front (FLN) in 1956. Many former independence fighters adhered to the Association of Ulema's ideas as Algeria's new ruling elite took shape. At independence in 1962, even though most members of the new regime were secular and leftist, the Muslim and Arab aspects of the new nation were allowed to stand alongside its socialist philosophy.

Throughout the 1970s, the place and significance of Islam in Algeria were strengthened by a series of major legislative measures. For example, Friday was declared to be the obligatory day of rest and the sale of alcoholic drinks was banned, together with the production of pork. The National Charter of 1976 declared that "Islam is the religion of the State." There were, however, local particularities. Various rites and schools of Islamic jurisprudence were practiced, including the Maliki school, and the Hanafi school, introduced by the former Turkish regime. Ibadism (a Kharijite sect) was practiced almost exclusively in the Mzab region of southern Algeria.

The state exercised close control over religious activity through the agency of the Ministry of Religious Affairs, and a "High Islamic Council." Imams became state officials, and their activities were rigorously supervised. Successive ministers of religious affairs (Tawfik el-Madani, Mouloud Kacim, and Abderrahmane Chibane) encouraged the prolific building of mosques and importing preachers from the Middle East—mainly from Egypt, Syria, and Saudi Arabia—many of whom were sympathetic to the Muslim Brotherhood. A religious association "Al Qiyam" ("Values"), whose establishment was authorized in 1964, adopted not only the ideas of Salafi thinkers such as Mohammed Abduh and Rashid Ridha, but also those of Hassan al-Banna and Sayyed Qutb, the leaders of the Muslim Brotherhood in Egypt. Al Qiyam disseminated its views by way of the *Revue de l'Education Musulmane* (*Journal of Muslim Education*). However, its opinions on sensitive issues, such as the execution in Egypt of Sayyed Qutb, aroused the hostility of the authorities. On March 17, 1970, both Al Qiyam and another organization, "Junud Allah" ("The Soldiers of God"), were dissolved by a decree issued by the Ministry of the Interior.

On December 3, 1971, the Ministry of the Interior issued a further decree establishing extremely strict controls over the formation of such associations. In the case of organizations whose activities were religious, it was laid down that approval should be obtained from the Ministry of the Interior as well as from the Ministry of Religious Affairs. In these circumstances, many organizations were set up clandestinely, propagating Islamist values in secret. During the 1970s, a number of notable personalities began to condemn the decadence, corruption, and the pernicious influence of the West. One of these was Sheikh Soltani, the author of a book entitled "Mazdaqism is the Source of Socialism" ("Mazdaq" was a sixth century Iranian figure who advocated egalitarianism). Others were the preacher Mohammed Sahnoun and Mohammed Salah Abed, the imam of Constantine and the president of the "Association for Moral and Social Reform." Each of these two charismatic figures had considerable followings.

Following President Chadli Benjedid's accession to power in 1979, the atmosphere was relatively liberal, and the distribution of a wide variety of publications was permitted. Mosques were built without legal authorization, often in centers of population and became the preferred vantage points for Islamists who expounded views strongly critical of the authorities. The radicalization of some militants contributed to the informal establishment of groups, some of which resorted to violent methods, especially within the universities.

In 1982, the first armed group came into existence. Its moving spirit was Mustafa Bouyali, an employee of the national electricity company and a former member of the FLN, who became the leader of the "Mouvement Islamique Algérien" (Algerian Islamic Movement). This was finally to be broken up by the authorities in February 1987. On October 4, 1988, while the country was in the grip of a serious social crisis, and as strikes were taking place in industrial plants, violent confrontations took place in Algiers during demonstrations over the shortages and rising prices of basic commodities. Riots erupted in several large towns, and the army opened fire on the demonstrators. These disturbances, an indication of deepening popular disillusion, were to lead to profound political changes.

A new constitution was adopted on February 23, 1989, and some months later a law governing "associations of a political nature" formalized the end of the one-party system, offering an opportunity for Islamic militants to take part without hindrance in political activity. Building on the profound distrust of the citizens of Algeria toward the establishment and its representatives, the Islamic Salvation Front (FIS), the principal Islamic group, took up politics and twice showed itself to be the country's most popular party, in June 1990 and December 1991.

In January 1992, following the FIS victory in the first round of legislative elections, the army put an end to the "democratic experiment," demanding President Chadli Benjedid's resignation. The military leadership set up provisional constitutional arrangements, and supreme power was vested in a five-member High Committee of State (HCS) headed by a former FLN veteran, Mohammed Boudiaf. Another member of the HCS was the minister of defense in the outgoing government, General Khaled Nezzar, the army leader, widely seen as the éminence grise behind developments in Algeria. A powerful High Council for Security also came into being, which was chaired by General Nezzar. Thousands of militant Islamists opted for armed struggle, inaugurating a long civil war.

With the exception of the FIS, dissolved in March 1992, religious parties were not banned by the various Algerian regimes that succeeded after the departure of President Chadli Benjedid and the onset of terrorism. On the contrary, they were assimilated into the political process, and provision was made for the expression of dissident views. The aim was to bring under control a current of political opinion whose popularity had been demonstrated by the FIS's electoral success. However, when a new constitution was drafted in 1996, an article relating to the establishment of political parties was included, which appeared to mark a change of attitude. Article 42 stipulated that: "The right to establish political parties is recognized and guaranteed. ... While observing the provisions of the present constitution, parties may not be established on the basis of religion, language, race, sex, occupation or region."

In the event, however, the introduction of prescriptive regulations did not result in radical change. Hamas, for example, as the principal Islamist movement that had continued to be recognized, merely changed its name to become the "Social Movement for Peace" (Mouvement de la Société pour la Paix) (MSP), without modifying either its program or its strategy for obtaining power. The normalization of political Islam was effectively completed at the presidential election of 1995, when Hamas, under the leadership of Mahfoud Nahnah became part of the governing coalition. By thus integrating the Islamist movement into the political process, the Algerian regime displayed the ability to create and sustain new élites, drawn from the country's middle classes. The groups linked with this political tendency played a part in the process of economic privatization, which they furthered through their ministerial portfolios, including those of the Ministry for Small and Medium Business and the Ministry of Labor.

On April 15, 1999, the election of Abdelaziz Bouteflika as head of state, with a program of civil reconciliation, set the scene for an at least partially successful program to bring armed Islamist dissidence to an end. One aspect of this was the dismantling of the Islamic Salvation Army ("Armée Islamique du Salut") (AIS), the armed wing of the FIS, which had continued to exist as a guerrilla organization after the dissolution of the FIS itself. The members of the AIS were persuaded individually to abandon their campaign. However, in the absence of a comprehensive amnesty covering the entire spectrum of the armed opposition, the outcome was disappointing, so that civil strife in Algeria was not totally eradicated. Terrorism continued to affect in varying degrees more than thirty of Algeria's "Wilayas" (administrative regions). Most attacks took place in rural or mountainous areas close to the upland forests, which serve as havens for the armed movements. The reemergence in 2000 of bomb attacks in a number of built-up areas, including Algiers itself, which had been relatively spared for some years previously, has been an illustration of the persistence of the terrorist phenomenon. Nevertheless, the activities of the armed groups declined in comparison with the early years of the conflict. This was due in part to a further success on the part of the government: the collapse of the Armed Islamic Group (Groupe Islamique Armé) (GIA), a group outside the AIS that had been the principal clandestine opposition faction in the period from 1993 to 1999. Only the extremist GSPC (Group Salafite pour la Prédication et le Combat) has continued to

fight. The GSPC has links outside Algeria, through the personal trajectories of many of its members, with extremist organizations in Europe and terrorist groups in the Middle East and beyond. It might be said that as distinct from the FIS and its offshoot the GIA, whose motivations lay in Algerian politics, the GSPC's modus operandi was connected with international terrorist goals.

Meanwhile, Algeria's officially recognized Islamist movements that had continued to operate within the law after 1991 appear to have benefited from political maneuvering connected with the Kabyle crisis. In December 1999, with military approval, President Bouteflika set up a governing coalition in which all political elements in the country were represented. However, the bloody riots that began in April 2001 led to the withdrawal of some of the coalition partners, including the Kabyle-based Assembly for Culture and Democracy (RCD) (Rassemblement pour la Culture et la Démocratie). In the context of the power struggle, the various vying factions found themselves obliged to solicit the support of the officially recognized Islamist groups. This inevitably strengthened the Islamists. However, the electoral decline of the Islamist parties in the legislative elections of May 2002 seemed to vindicate those of the other parties opposed to permanent agreements with such factions. President Bouteflika sought to diminish the influence of Islamist factions in the run-up to the presidential election of 2004. In September 2005, Algerian voters gave their approval in a referendum to President Bouteflika's proposed "Charter for Peace and National Reconciliation," which was intended to bring terrorism to an end. By the end of 2006, however, Amnesty International said no real attempt seemed to have been made to implement the charter. A few hundred Islamist militants are said to be still at large in the country.

Much of Algeria is now broadly secure, and terrorism has little impact on day-to-day life. Foreigners are once again able to visit the country with a reasonable degree of security, both to work and even as tourists. Low-level violence, nevertheless, rumbles on. In September 2006, the GSPC claimed it was henceforth to be regarded as affiliated to Al-Qa'ida. In December 2006, the GSPC claimed responsibility for an attack on foreign oil workers as they traveled between Al-Achour and Staoueli. On January 8, a GSPC leader, Abu Musan Abdul Wadud, called for attacks on Algerian government targets and on French interests. On January 12, Algerian security forces reported that they had killed six militants hiding out near Skikda in eastern Algeria. Incidents in Tunisia in December 2006 and January 2007 appear to have been cause by GSPC-linked groups crossing into Tunisia from Algeria. A reason why this low-level conflict does not seem likely to be brought entirely to a halt in the short or medium term is the prevalence of unemployment and deprivation among Algerian young people, which aggravates popular dissatisfaction with the government.

Breakdown of Algerian Islamist Groups (Legal and Nonlegal)

Islamist parties forming part of the governmental coalition:

- Social Movement for Peace (MSP) (*Mouvement de la Société pour la Paix*); the leader is Abu Jarrah Sultani (replacing the veteran Islamist leader Mohammed Nahnah, who died in 2003).
- Al-Nahda; the leader is Lahbib Adami

Other recognized opposition parties represented in the National Assembly:

- Al-Islah (Mouvement de la Réforme Nationale); the leader is Abdallah Saad Djaballah

Non-recognized groups:

- Groups related to Al-Wafa and led by Ahmed Taleb Ibrahimi
- Groups related to the FIS

Clandestine groups:

- GSPC (Groupe Salafite pour la Prédication et le Combat): a guerrilla group motivated by terrorism
- GIA (Groupe Islamique Armé): a revolutionary guerrilla group responsible for massacres, with political goals
- Takfir w'al-Hijra: a sectarian religious group prepared to undertake violence.

Algerianism (Al-Jaz'ara)

"Algerianism" is a political and religious tendency bringing together those Algerian Islamists who reject links with international movements and organizations. The ideas of Algerianism are integral to the turbulent history of the series of movements, often clandestine, whose ultimate aim has is the overthrow of the present order in Algeria. The contention of such movements is that Algeria's successive governments have not truly broken their links with the colonial heritage of France and that they are undermining Islamic values. The Algerianist school of thought is linked to the "Association of Ulema" founded by Abdelhamid Ben Badis and with the Francophone writer and thinker Malek Bennabi, who was Algeria's director of higher education until his death in 1973.

In 1972, the founders and early activists of Algerianism held the inaugural conference at Beni Yaala, a small town in Kabylie, of their earliest organization, the "Jama'a Islamiya," which was initially organized as a secret society violently antagonistic to the "oriental" influence of the Muslim Brotherhood. It was one of the most entrenched opponents of the Muslim Brotherhood, Mahmud Nahnah who was responsible for naming it Al-Jaz'ara (from the Arabic name of Algeria, Al-Jaza'ir), in order to emphasize its Algerian character. Its most influential members were university teachers from a scientific background, such as Anwar Haddam, a nuclear scientist from Tlemcen with a doctorate in physics, whose aspiration, in common with that of the group's other members, was to give embodiment to a "new elite."

Some of the Algerianists were members of the "League for Da'wa and Jihad," and they claimed intellectual links with Sheikh Ahmed Sahnoun, who is noted for his combination of theological erudition with his hatred of the regime. As individuals, they later became members of the "Islamic Salvation Front" (FIS), which was at the time of its formation in 1989 a coalition of several different tendencies. One of the leading figures of "Jama'a Islamiya," Mohammed Said, claimed membership of the FIS in October 1990. This was risky to say the least, since in the summer of 1990 a "rejection front" had come into being within the FIS to oppose—unsuccessfully—the infiltration of the movement by the Algerianists. This front consisted of nine prominent personalities—Qamreddine Kerbane, Bachir Fikh, Said Guechi, Mohammed al-Imam, Mohammed Kerrar, Said Mekhloufi, Ahmed Merrani, Benazouz Zebda, and Al-Hachemi Sahnouni—who strove constantly to reduce the influence of Al-Jaz'ara.

On November 12, 1990, in parallel with their clandestine activities, the Algerianists set up an official organization called "The Islamic Association for Civilizational Enlightenment." In the course of the conference held by the FIS at Batna on July 23, 1991, shortly after the arrests of Abassi Madani and Ali Belhadj, the Algerianists were able to strengthen their influence. As yet, however, they were unable to take complete control of the FIS's political structure. Abdelkader Hachani, a petrochemical engineer who shared Al-Jaz'ara's theoretical position and tactical approach without formally being a member of the group, became president of the FIS's provisional executive bureau. The Algerianists at this point opted to work within the limitations of the law and pursued this policy even after the wave of arrests that took place in June 1991.

Some months later, the results of the legislative elections of December 1991 gave a new mandate to the FIS when it won 188 of the parliamentary seats in the first round. Many of the FIS candidates were members of Al-Jaz'ara. After the annulment of the elections, and the ousting of President Chadli Benjedid, together with numerous arrests, many Algerianist militant members of the FIS went underground. Some Algerianist leaders, however, in the face of dissent, continued to seek compromise with the regime. Following the arrest and imprisonment of Abdelkader Hachani, Mohammed Said took on the mantle of the intellectual leadership of the Algerianists, attempting to put in place reliable and disciplined clandestine structures. An early organization thus created was the Islamic Front for the Armed Jihad (FIDA) (Front Islamique pour le Djihad Armé), which was presented as the armed wing of Al-Jaz'ara. Claiming links with the FIS, FIDA nevertheless failed to establish an operational framework throughout the country. In 1994, prompted by this setback, Mohammed Said opted for wholesale integration into the "Armed Islamic Group" (GIA), aiming to take it over in the longer run.

At the same time, however, the Algerianists continued not to rule out the possibility of a negotiated solution. Anwar Haddam, a representative of Al-Jaz'ara, affiliated to the GIA, was to take part in the meetings in Rome that culminated in January 1995 with the signature of a pact by the majority of the groups opposing the current regime. Later, dissent between factions within the GIA intensified, and the GIA national leader Jamil Zitouni, suspecting the Algerianists of being soft on the issue of compromise with the regime, carried out a purge. Summary sentences were passed and executions carried out by impromptu Islamic tribunals, with the particular support of the members of Takfir wa-l Hijra.

In November 1995, Mohammed Said was killed in the mountains near Medea, while the FIDA leader Abdelwahab Lamara was kidnapped and killed by a GIA guerrilla group. The political branch of FIDA, together with fighters who had made good their escape, forged largely expedient alliances with other groups and attempted to set up new organizations, such as the "Mouvement Islamique pour la Prédication et le Djihad" (Islamic Movement for Preaching and Jihad) (MIPD).

GIA propagandists accused the Algerianists of every possible crime. For example, in September 1996 the editorial view of the magazine *Al-Jama'a* was that "they have attempted to use the jihad as a way to induce the apostate Taghout (literally "the idol," i.e. the Algerian state) to return to the path of democracy and elections." In fact, the majority of the fighters within Algeria who adhered to the Algerianist faction agreed in principle to the cease-fire declared at the end of 1997 and later accepted President Bouteflika's plan for "civil concord," though those in exile outside the country continued to oppose it. In reaction to the proposal on the part of the IEFE (Instance Exécutive du FIS à l'Etranger) (Executive Authority of the FIS Abroad), led by Rabah Kebir, to normalize relations with the regime, the Algerianists in exile in the West continued to take a radical stand. They maintained this position even after Madani Mezrag, who spoke for the Islamic Salvation Army (Armeé Islamique du Salut) (AIS), declared a unilateral cease-fire.

In October 1997, Al-Jaz'ara was responsible for setting up a new exile organization, the "Conseil de Coordination du Front Islamique du Salut" (CCFIS) (Coordination Council of the Islamic Salvation Front), bringing together former members of the GIA who had favored Mohammed Said's planned takeover. A significant network continued to operate in Switzerland led by such figures as the spokesman Mourad Dhina and Mustafa Brahimi, the editor of "El Minbar" (The Pulpit). From the outset, the CCFIS stressed its rejection of the cease-fire and of any kind of agreement with the "military junta." However, consistent with their strategy, those identified with the Algerianist faction expressed their support for any peaceful solution consistent with the restoration of power to the people. They leveled accusations against the GIA, which they now stigmatized as "Groupes Infiltrés de l'Armée" ("Groups Infiltrated by the Army"), which they now regarded as entirely responsible for the massacres perpetrated in Algeria.

Hoping to win acceptance in Europe, the exiled Algerianists proclaimed their respect for human rights. At the same time, however, they maintained their contacts with the militants of the "Groupe Salafite pour la Prédication et le Combat" (Salafi Group for Preaching and Combat) (GSPC), the principal armed Islamist movement in Algeria. The suspicious death of Abdelkader Hachani, formerly a member of the FIS leadership, and the marginalization of Ahmed Taleb Ibrahimi, a candidate in the presidential election of 1999 identified with the IEFE, reinforced the determination of those Al-Djaz'ara diehards who believed that no compromise was possible with the "military junta."

Al-Baqun 'Ala al-Ahd
(The Keepers of the Oath)

This clandestine organization made its first claims of militant action in February 1992.

Led by Slimane Maherzi, also known as Abderrahmane Abou Djamil, it was based in Algiers and its outskirts during the earliest years of the conflict in Algeria, but undertook few operations. However, the massive defection of detainees from the prison at Tazoult in January 1994 brought it new recruits.

In Europe, its representative was an official of the FIS (Islamic Salvation Front), Qamereddine Kherbane, who was notorious for having worked as an instructor in an Islamist training camp in Peshawar, in Pakistan. Kherbane, who claimed to be a former Algerian air force pilot and had directed an Islamic NGO, "Human Concern International," was the ideologue of the Baqun. In 1997, the organization rejected the idea of a truce suggested by the AIS. However, it also condemned the terrorist strategy advocated by the GIA leader Antar Zouabri. In two of its publications that were circulated in Europe, *Saut al-Jibha* and *Nur al-Misbah,* it claimed to have undertaken a number of targeted attacks. It was supposed to be responsible for the murder of the director of the weekly magazine *Ash-Shuruk.* Later, it encouraged its fighters to join the "Groupe Salafite pour la Prédication et Combat" (Salafi Group for Preaching and Combat) (GSPC), the principal armed Islamist movement in Algeria after the AIS truce, but kept a small number of fighters of its own. It shared the strategic and political philosophy of the Hassan Hattab organization.

AIS (Armee Islamique de Salvation (Islamic Salvation Army) (Algeria)

The Islamic Salvation Army, known as the AIS (Armée Islamique de Salvation), came into existence in 1994, shortly after various influential figures within the Islamic Salvation Front (FIS) such as Mohammed Said and Said Mekhloufi had thrown in their lot with the GIA (Islamic Armed Group). The AIS acknowledged the authority of Abassi Madani and Ali Belhadj. According to its founders, it was based on the idea of "recourse to the jihad" and to the installation of "an Islamic state in Algeria, in preparation for the establishment of a rightly guided Caliphate according to the precepts of the Prophet." The establishment of the AIS was announced in a communiqué issued on July 18, 1994 by its "emirs" (leaders) Madani Mezrag and Ahmed Benaicha. However, in the absence of uncontested spiritual leadership, and without the adherence of significant networks operating in the region of Algiers, the organization, which styled itself the "armed wing" of the FIS, appeared to suffer from a lack of legitimacy in comparison to the GIA.

It drew its inspiration from the strategies developed by the ALN, the "Armée de la Libération Nationale" (National Liberation Army) during Algeria's war of independence and directed its attacks mainly at the various security services. The AIS had an official presence in Europe, the IEFE (Instance Executive du FIS à l'Etranger), (FIS Executive Authority Abroad), directed by Rabah Kebir in Germany. It also maintained propaganda publications distributed both in Algeria and from 1994 in various foreign capitals. These included *Al-Jaish* (*The Army*), *Al-Shahid* (*The Martyr*), *Al-Furqan* (*The Proof*), *Al-Hujjat Al-Balighat* (*The Irrefutable Contention*), and *Al-Ribat* (*The Link*). In addition, it benefited from support networks, which moved arms and cash to where they were needed, and also undertook recruiting. At the same time, while maintaining contact with Abassi Madani's political leadership, talks were opened with emissaries from the president and with high-ranking Algerian army officers in the search for a negotiated solution.

In January 1995, a formula was announced in Rome proposing a "way out of the crisis"

predicated on a process of national reconciliation. The Rome-based Christian community of Sant'Egidio (a Catholic organization
dedicated to the process of mediation) provided the facilities for holding the meeting
that led to this formula, which was signed
by a number of opposition groups. Nothing resulted from it, however, since the
Algerian authorities refused to recognize its
validity on the grounds that it represented
foreign interference in Algerian affairs.
Madani Mezrag, alias Abu al-Haitham, a
thirty-eight-year-old former middle-ranking
official of the FIS from Djidjel, in Kabylia
became the national "amir" or leader of the
AIS in March 1995. As time went on, Algerian military leaders ceased to negotiate with
the political wing of the organization, the
FIS and, in particular, with its leader Abassi
Madani, preferring to communicate with
Mezrag, who was known to favor dialogue.

The AIS controlled a number of substantial sections of the countryside, such
as the Ouarsenis hills, but was subject to
constant attacks by the GIA, which resulted
in numerous casualties. In its publications,
the GIA accused the AIS of "exploiting the
armed struggle as a means of exercising pressure to recover its own holdings, including
seats in parliament." In order to appear as
a "responsible interlocutor," the leadership
of the AIS refrained from large-scale campaigns destructive to state property. Madani
Mezrag was convinced that without the
unification of all the armed groups the
regime could not be overthrown by armed
insurrection. He therefore sought to reopen
negotiations, with the government, the
political parties, and the population at large.
He also attempted to obtain guarantees for
the safety of his men in the event of a comprehensive agreement. The authorities sent
intermediaries to open negotiations, including General Boughaba, responsible for the
fifth military district, and Othman Aissani,
formerly a founder member of the FIS.

Madani Mezrag ordered a halt to all
military operations as of October 1, 1997
and also made an appeal to the other factions to abandon the jihad. At this time,
a very limited number of fighters opted
for surrender, giving up their arms. These
included the LIDD ("Ligue Islamique pour
le Da'wa et le Djihad") (Islamic League for
Da'wa and Jihad), which declared its support for the truce. Certain diehards, however, chose to transfer their allegiance to
the GIA. The option of active collaboration
between the AIS and the security forces to
fight the GIA was considered, but rejected.
Madani Mezrag's ultimate aim was to get
an amnesty for all his fighters, together with
the parallel rehabilitation of the FIS. Recurrent problems among his lieutenants, passed
on by political activists, generated a climate
of suspicion and undermined the possibility of a final and comprehensive agreement.
In several regions, AIS fighters were held in
camps under the surveillance of the security forces, in order to ensure that the truce
agreed by Madani Mezrag was observed.
This took place in Blida, Chelf, Jijel, and
Skikda.

The resignation of President Zeroual, as
the result of "amicable pressure," after discussion within the military leadership on the
details of a plan based on national reconciliation, proved to be the precursor of new
political arrangements. Abdelaziz Bouteflika, a professed advocate of civil coexistence, was selected by the military strongmen
as the most suitable person to bring the new
accord to fruition. Some 2,500 imprisoned
Islamists were freed even before the presidential ballot was held. In April 1999, some
days after his election, Zeroual, as the new
head of state, announced that he would
"consider the credentials of the AIS in order
to endow it with political and juridical status." On June 6, 1999, a communiqué signed
by Madani Mezrag announced "the definitive end of the armed struggle."

Despite the death in suspicious circumstances on November 22 of Abdelkader Hachani, of one of the most respected leaders of the FIS, the 2,800 fighters of the AIS laid down their weapons in accordance with the agreement signed by their leader. They were later granted an amnesty, while measures were taken by the authorities to assist them to resume their place in civil society. However, Madani Mezrag's initiative to obtain the rehabilitation of the FIS was unsuccessful. In some departments there were defections, for example in Skikda, when diehard combatants rejoined clandestine groups that continued to opt for armed struggle.

FIDA (Front Islamique pour le Djihad Armé) (Islamic Front for Armed Jihad)

The Islamic Front for Armed Jihad (FIDA: "Front Islamique pour le Djihad Armé") was established by "Algerianist" members of the FIS ("Front Islamiqe du Salut"— Islamic Salvation Front) and carried out its first attacks at the end of 1992. The movement's "emir" was Abdelwahab Lamara. Its program was to carry out attacks on the political and cultural elite that supported the regime. In March 1993, this group was responsible for the death of the director of the Ecole des Beaux Arts in Algeria. Over the next year, it assassinated a number of other prominent figures: the writer Tahar Djaout, Djillali Lyabes, head of the National Institute for studies in Global Strategy, and the playwright Abdelkader Alloula. Its claims of responsibility for these murders were published in the Islamist publication Al-Fida'i. FIDA's armed groups were active in the Algerian capital, Algiers, from 1993 to 1996, and its supporters in Europe set up propaganda channels to publicize its cause. Various publications, officially claiming affiliation to the FIS but actually attached to the FIDA, for example "The Cause," published in Switzerland, publicized the views of the political wing of the movement based abroad.

On May 13, 1994, the Armed Islamic Groups (GIA) published a manifesto under the title "Unity and Jihad: respect for the Book and the Tradition." After this, the FIDA declared its adherence to the GIA. The Algerianist tendency was also represented within the GIA, notably by Mohammed Said, who made attempts to gain control of the organization. FIDA's ideology was somewhat contradictory, since its theorists went against the GIA line in supporting the Sant'Egidio agreement signed in Rome in January 1995. This was a declaration by a number of legal and proscribed Algerian opposition groups, intended to offer the basis for "a peaceful solution by political means to the Algerian crisis." One of those who signed on behalf of the FIS was Anouar Haddam, who was part of the Algerianist tendency within the GIA. FIDA members were a very troublesome element within GIA. In November 1995, Djamel Zitouni, emir of the GIA, ordered a purge within the organization to stamp out as far as possible the Algerianists, in the course of which Mohammed Said and other FIDA fighters were killed by their supposed comrades in arms. Disturbances continued, and some weeks later, Abdelwahab Lamara was kidnapped by guerrillas and executed. His successor was one of his deputies, Mohammed Brahimi, a former doctor who had edited the Islamist publication Al-Tadhkir. At this point, there was a complete split between the FIDA and the GIA. Some months later, the main FIDA group operating in Algiers was uncovered and destroyed by a security forces operation in the Said Hamdine quarter. Brahimi was killed along with a number of his lieutenants.

The new leadership was well aware of the extent of the damage inflicted on its armed organization in Algeria. In consultation with the political wing of the movement in Europe it therefore looked for new alliances. In 1996, FIDA put out feelers to Mustafa Katali, who was operating in the Larbaa region, as well as to Ali Ben Hadjar and Mahfoud Ramani. It also participated in the formations of at least two new organizations that subscribed to Algerianist ideas: the Islamic Movement for Preaching and Jihad and the Islamic League for Da'wa and Jihad. Nothing came of these initiatives, and FIDA's fighters on the ground began to fear for their own safety. They started to distance themselves from the movement's political theorists, whose reluctance to enter into compromises was all the more entrenched as they were based outside Algeria and lived in relative safety. On October 15, 1997, FIDA in Algeria announced what it said was the "cessation of all activities within the national territory," thus associating itself with the truce proclaimed by the AIS. FIDA subsequently opened negotiations to obtain guarantees for its members in the framework of surrender with honor. At the end of the period laid down by the civil accord of July 13, 1999, the FIDA fighters, confined to camps controlled by the security forces, surrendered their arms in order to benefit from the terms of the amnesty.

The movement's political circles in Europe refused to give their approval to either the truce or the surrender and began to look for new alliances. A number of subsequent assassinations were attributed to the FIDA. These included the deaths of General Ali Bouthigane, Colonel Zerdani Salah, Lieutenant Colonel Abdenour Boumezrag, as well as two former ministers of the interior, Abou bakr Belkaid and Mohammed Hardi, and two professors, Said Messai and Mahfoud Boucebi. FIDA was also apparently responsible for the murder of the president of the Algerian Football League, Rachid Harraigue. However, certain sources, trustworthy to varying degrees, claim that some of these killings, blamed on FIDA, were actually the work of other clandestine groups. For example, sources within the group of dissidents known as the Algerian Free Officers Movement give different accounts of the murders of high-ranking military officers, claiming that these were actually purges and the settling of scores carried out within the machinery of the state.

FIS (Front Islamique du Salut) (Islamic Salvation Front)

The FIS grew out of the Al-Sunna Mosque in Bab el Oued, in Algiers. Its establishment can be traced to a conference on March 18, 1989, as troubles arising out of popular discontent with the government of President Chadli Benjedid beset Algeria. The FIS included numerous militants as members who had previously been more or less active members of more structured organizations. These included the Da'wa League, Al-Amr bi-l Ma'ruf wa'l Nahi 'an al-Munkar (The Ordinance of Right and the Proscription of Evil), the Umma Party, the People of the Vanguard, and Jama'at al-Tabligh. Various well-known figures were involved in the negotiations that led to the foundation of the FIS, some of whom refused to attend the movement's founding conference. These included Mahfoud Nahnah, Sheikh Sahnoun, and Djaballah. Abbasi Madani was appointed president and spokesman for the FIS. He was assisted by Al Belhadj, the imam of the Sunna Mosque. The vice president was Bannazouz Zebda, also an imam, who was a former fighter in the Algerian War of Independence. Others who took positions in the newly formed FIS were Othman Aissani, Mokhtar Brahimi, Ahsin Dhaoui, Ali Djeddi, Kamel Guemmazi, Abdallah Hammouche, Mohammed Kerrar, Mohammed Larbi Mariche, Said Mekhloufi, Ahmed Merani, Ashhour Rebihi, and Abderrazaq Redjam. From the outset the aim of the

FIS was the creation of an Islamic state, and it was a party of popular appeal that drew upon nationalist sentiments. It endorsed the struggle against all forms of neocolonialism and set itself to achieve the objectives of those who fought in the War of Independence. It took up part of the principles and doctrine of the old PPA (Algerian Popular Party), the widely based party led by Messali Hadj, which had aimed at independence, and advocated a return to authentic Islamic values.

Though it initially brought together various currents of opinion, the FIS fell after a few months under the influence of the "Salafis," who insisted on a return to the earliest sources of Islam and the rejection of all reform. The leading figure in Algerian Salafism (Al-Salafiya) was Ali Hachemi Sahnouni, the imam of a mosque in Belcourt. He exercised a degree of charisma over the young militants and held administrative responsibility in the Executive Office of the FIS, which gave him considerable influence. Sheikh Sahnouni was arrested in 1982, having publicly spoken out against the decadence of Algerian society. The FIS was undoubtedly a religious movement that preached the installation of Shari'a law. However, from late 1989 it began to take on the shape of a regular political party. An analysis of its structure shows the fundamental part played by two structures, each of which exercised significant power. These were the Executive Office, which was made up of eleven members, and the Consultative Council, with thirty-five members. The leadership soon succeeded in establishing an operational structure spanning many towns and villages and trained its militants in the techniques of political propaganda. The FIS brought together a spectrum of movements representing various political and social points of view. Its most enthusiastic adherents came from among Algeria's disadvantaged youth, the unemployed, and from students seeking social status. It also attracted the support of small tradesmen who felt they had experienced no benefit from economic liberalization.

Torn between the desire for respectability and the radical aspirations of its membership, the leaders of the FIS presented themselves in one light to Algeria's senior military hierarchy, the determinant force in the country, and in quite a different way to their own militants. Internal tensions among the various factions were strong, and the movement's social ideas, as portrayed by the movement's publication *Al-Munqidh* (*The Savior*) were extremely fluid. The FIS set up and carried on a significant chain of charitable associations, financed principally by generous donors from the Gulf monarchies. It also began to draw support from within Algeria's industrial base, after the establishment of the Islamic Workers' Union (SIT—Syndicat Islamique du Travail), run by the Salafi adherent, Said Mekhloufi.

On June 12, 1990, in the first free election held in Algeria since independence, the Algerian public voted for the administrations of local authorities and the assemblies of the "Wilayas" (regions). The FIS obtained 54.2 percent of the votes cast (4,331,472 votes) and took control of 856 local authorities. In some areas, the FIS's showing was even stronger. These included Algiers, Oran, and Constantine. In Medea, more than 90 percent of the electorate opted for the FIS. Of the towns with populations larger than 100,000, only two were not taken by the FIS: Tizi-Ouzou and Bejaia. The elections for the assemblies in the Wilayas (the regions) went in the same direction. The vote for the FIS was only low in the south of the country, in Kabylie, and in a handful of FLN strongholds in the east of the country, such as Tebessa and El-Tarf. In those areas where the FIS leadership took control, stress was soon laid on puritanism and the imposition of new rules of conduct on the population, in order to counter all manifestations of deviant behavior. Impromptu squads of vigilantes rooted out delinquents, while merchants who sold alcoholic beverages were invited to turn over a new leaf and satellite dishes, with the tacit approval of local administrators, were destroyed unless their owners succeeded in spiriting them away. Women were subjected to pressure to conform to Islamic dress codes. The FIS militants took it upon themselves to enforce this new moral order. However, in the absence of either the legal framework or the financial resources to implement the FIS's more basic policies platform, these actions were sufficient to satisfy various sections of the population, including the shopkeepers, unhappy because of the lack of security.

In the spring of 1990, serious tensions began to appear within the FIS when the movement began to look at the idea of including Islamists of the Algerianist tendency. Nine leading members attempted to block the move, but without success. Decision-making processes within the organization theoretically embodied two principles: that of consensus together with priority in case of a disagreement for the Consultative Council (Shura). In practice, a predominant role was given to the FIS's two leading figures, Abassi Madani and Ali Belhadj. The ideas of Madani and Belhadj were not identical, but each was able, as time passed, to establish for himself a position of firmly founded influence. During the Gulf War, after some hesitation, the FIS took up a stance of unconditional support for the Iraqi regime. It called for the establishment of international Islamic brigades and castigated the policies of the Algerian authorities, whom it dismissed as timid.

In April 1991, the Algerian National Assembly adopted a new electoral law. This instituted majority voting for single member constituencies in two stages, together with a redistribution of constituency boundaries calculated to favor the FLN and a ban on campaigning through the mosques. In the wake of this, the FIS decided on head-on confrontation with the authorities. FIS made its continued participation in the electoral process conditional on the satisfaction of five demands. These were (1) the abandonment of the proposed changes relating to constituency boundaries and the modalities of the parliamentary elections; (2) the holding of planned presidential elections; (3) arrangements to subject the process of voting to adequate scrutiny; (4) a guarantee of noninterference by the government and the National Assembly in the electoral process; (5) equal television coverage for all political parties. Abassi Madani let it be known that if these conditions were not met, the next step would be a general strike.

When the authorities failed to respond, demonstrations were organized in a number of towns. On May 23, 1991, The FIS leadership, confident of the support of its trade union and the participation of its militants, declared a countrywide strike. At the same time, Abassi Madani embarked on talks with the speaker of the National Assembly, Abdelaziz Belkhadem, in search of a compromise. On May 26, however, the first casualties of the confrontation lost their lives, during violent clashes between the demonstrators and the government's riot police. On June 4, as the situation became increasingly tense, the government proclaimed a state of siege for four months, which gave it special powers. The Hamrouche government resigned, and the electoral process was suspended with plans to hold parliamentary elections temporarily abandoned. Meanwhile, large-scale demonstrations and disturbances took place in Algeria's heartland, around the capital. The FIS were not successful in spreading their action throughout the country, however, and in a number of major towns only minor demonstrations were seen. Within a number of manufacturing establishments, the UGTA (Union Générale des Travailleurs Algériens)—the country's major trade union, which reflected official views—was able to restrict the occupation of premises and the resulting confrontations. A brief respite followed a meeting between Abassi Madani and Ali Belhadj and the new prime minister, Sid Ahmed Ghozali. On June 21, however, clashes were renewed after the military high command decided to remove signs that read "Islamic Municipality," which the FIS had placed on the town halls of the districts they controlled.

On June 30, 1991, seven members of the FIS leadership were arrested, including Abassi Madani and Ali Belhadj. The FIS had to revise and adjust its strategy to respond to the regime's repressive policy. Abdelkader Hachani, who had become vice president of the FIS within a temporary leadership, held a conference at Batna on July 25 and 26, 1991, at which the administration of the FIS was fundamentally reorganized. Hachani turned to local strongmen, to his old colleagues in eastern Algeria, and to the Algerianists, increasing the size of the Consultative Council and getting rid of some members who might have mounted a challenge to him. Hachani was himself briefly arrested in October 1991. The new leadership opted for a "legalist" strategy and voted to take part in the parliamentary elections, where the first round was now rescheduled for December 26, 1991. In these elections, despite the continuing detention of its principal leaders, the FIS took 46.27 percent of the vote (with 3,260,222 of the votes cast) and held 188 of the 430 seats in the National Assembly. The announcement of the results led to grave misgivings within the senior ranks of the military hierarchy in Algeria. On January 11, 1992, President Chadli Benjedid was obliged to resign, after pressure from the military élite. Two days later, the elections were suspended. A period of transition was declared and a High Council of State was

proclaimed, at the instance of the military, to fill the vacuum of power. The president of this body was Mohammed Boudiaf, a former member of the FLN during the war of independence, who returned from abroad to take up the position.

Some days later, Abdelkader Hachani was arrested and imprisoned. A full state of emergency was proclaimed and FIS officials were placed under arrest. On March 4, 1992, the FIS was officially dissolved by a decision of the high court in Algiers. The new regime set up seven detention centers in central Algeria, at Ain M'gule, Ain Salah, Bordj Omar Driss, El Homr, Ouargla, and Tsabit. Within a few weeks some seven thousand FIS members were accommodated in tented camps at these locations. Thousands of other activists went underground to escape being rounded up by government forces. Some fled abroad, while others initiated an armed struggle against the authorities. Some months later, attempts were made by FIS officials in exile to set up new political and military structures on the basis of networks situated abroad. Rabah Kebir, together with others, established a FIS executive body in exile (IEFE—"Instance Exécutive du FIS à l'Etranger"). Rabah Kebir was a former spokesman in charge of relations with the press, who had succeeded in reaching Germany in September 1992. Anouar Haddam, an Algerianist sympathizer who had been elected as a member of the National Assembly in December 1991, also decided to go into exile and fled to the United States, where he set up another body, the "Parliamentary Delegation of FIS Abroad." Internal disagreements began to make their appearance between these two structures, based both on personality clashes and arising from policy and strategic differences. In 1994, inside Algeria, the Islamic Salvation Army was set up, while certain FIS leaders and some of the membership went over to the Armed Islamic Groups (GIA), which also stirred up disagreements. From 1993 to 1998, as the troubles in Algeria continued, up to 100,000 civilians may have lost their lives, but most of the slaughter had been perpetrated by the GIA.

While the IEFE favored the search for a political solution, the Parliamentary Delegation, which had branches in a number of European capitals, preferred to escalate the situation, activating dormant GIA cells in Europe. At the Sant'Egidio meeting in Rome, both of these movements took part, together with various other legal and banned opposition organizations, including the FFS, FLN, MDA, and al-Nahda. At this gathering, they helped to draft what was described as a "platform for a peaceful resolution of the Algerian Crisis," which was signed on January 13, 1995. This accord demanded the freeing of the FIS leaders held in Algiers and the reversal of the dissolution of the FIS by the government. As the Algerian military and the presidency of the republic refused to recognize the platform, it was never the subject of any meaningful negotiations. The Algerian authorities, meanwhile, took care of their own interests in promoting internal dissent within the Islamist movement. In the presidential elections in Algeria in 1995, Liamine Zeroual, already president of the High Council of State, was confirmed as president of the republic. This was followed by the brief appearance of another supposed FIS office that was set up in Turkey, under the title of the Official Office of the Islamic Front Abroad. This, however, was blatantly the creation of the Algerian security services.

The FIS abroad was able to benefit from the prevailing atmosphere of freedom existing in the West. In Germany, Rabah Kebir was accepted as a political figure, and Anouar Haddam, at least at the start of his sojourn in the United States, was accorded substantial facilities. When contacts were renewed between representatives of the Algerian presidency and the AIS in 1995, IEFE played

a part. The AIS was represented by the imprisoned leadership (Abassi Madani, Ali Belhadj, and Abdelkader Hachani) and by its current leaders Ali Djeddi and Abdelkader Boukhamkham, who actually contacted the government's spokesmen, while the military leader Madani Mezrag and IEFE also had an input. Meanwhile, the parliamentary delegation issued statements that condemned the compromises that it alleged the IEFE proposed to make with the regime and called for the overthrow of what it called the "apostate government."

In 1996, President Zeroual launched a crackdown on the FIS and the GIA. After purges and internal conflicts within the GIA, a new body made its appearance in March 1997. This was the "Group of 40," which was an explicitly Salafi organization that claimed to maintain the line laid down by the FIS. Its leaders were Qamreddine Kherbane and Nadir Remli, who were linked to the armed group known as Al-Baqun 'Ala al-Ahd (Faithful to the Oath). However, Rabah Kebir and other IEFE figures such as Ould Adda Abdelkrim and Ghemati Abdelkrim believed that if the desired military victory could not be gained, the preferable course was to negotiate with the regime so that the FIS could be rehabilitated and reassume its place in Algerian political life. In parliamentary elections in Algeria in June 1997, pro-government parties won a stunning victory. In September 1997, Madani Mezrag, the leader of the AIS, declared a unilateral truce. This led the Algerianist group to establish a new structure, which they called the FIS Coordination Council (CCFIS) to oppose any agreement with the government, which in their view would be contrary to the interests of the FIS.

In the presidential elections of 1999, the IEFE supported the candidacy of Ahmed Taleb Ibrahimi, the son of Sheikh Bashir Ibrahimi, who had several times served as a minister under the presidencies of

Boumedienne and Chadli Benjedid and was favorable to the concept of national reconciliation. The intention was to promote new alliances and to favor the reemergence of the FIS onto the political scene and the FIS had followed the lead of the AIS by declaring a truce. However, after the election of Abdelaziz Bouteflika as president, the strategy appeared to have come to nothing. Bouteflika's administration appeared to have no intention of permitting the FIS to return to political life, though he did offer an amnesty to those former FIS members who did not have "blood on their hands." The FIS leader Abdelkader Hachani, who continued to favor compromise, was murdered in November 1999, presumably by militants. Nevertheless, the FIS formally dissolved itself in January 2000, though Abassi Madani and Ali Belhadj continued to be detained, by now under a regime of house arrest. The Al Wafa Party, led by Ahmed Taleb Ibrahimi, which was meant to be a vehicle for former FIS activists and militants, remained unrecognized by the authorities. Meanwhile, the leaders of the CCFIS, who stuck to their call for the overthrow of the regime, attempted to reorganize outside the country. However, the atmosphere of suspicion in Western countries toward any Islamist organization after the events of September 11, 2001 in the United States made any such project almost impossible to realize. In the twenty-first century, small-scale violence has continued in Algeria, largely perpetrated by groups that have emerged from the GIA, but the FIS's original plan to bring about political reform in Algeria on Islamic lines is now in abeyance.

GIA (Groupe Islamique Armé) (Armed Islamic Group)

Much remains unknown regarding the establishment of the GIA—the Armed Islamic Group. It apparently took shape over the course of several years. Both outside observers and successive leaders of the organization are in agreement that its first recognized "emir" (leader) was Abdelhaq Layada, a former metal worker from Algiers. He took control of a fighting unit based in the Léveille and Eucalyptus regions of the capital and then brought together a number of small groups. The acronym GIA made its appearance on a number of leaflets in the second half of 1992. Abdelhaq Layada, whose nom de guerre was Abu Adlan, left the Algiers region and assigned organizational titles and duties to several of his associates. He kept his distance, however, from Islamist figures such as Said Mekhloufi and from the Algerianists. On January 13, 1993, he published a statement that presented itself as a "warning to the mercenary press." From 1993, the official organ of the GIA was "Al-Shehada," which set out the movement's doctrine and strategy. Specific reference was made to the Afghan heritage, and the authority of the FIS was explicitly repudiated. The GIA declared that its objectives were to overthrow the "apostate" regime and restore the Caliphate, both of which were to be achieved by Jihad.

Many attacks, especially in the region of Algiers, were attributed to the GIA by the authorities. In June 1993, Abdelhaq Layada was arrested in Morocco while trying to set up an arms supply chain. After being extradited to Algeria, he was held in the Serkaji prison. In September 1993, the name of his successor was proclaimed in another of the GIA's publications, *Al-Ansar*. This was Mourad Sid Ahmed, also known as Jaafar al-Afghani, who had fought against the Soviets in Afghanistan. At this time the GIA began to issue its statements bearing a seal whose design was formed of swords and a lectern bearing a Quran that was consciously reminiscent of the symbol of Gulbuddin Hekmatyar's Hizb-i Islami in Afghanistan. The design included Verse 39 of the Quranic Sura "Al-Anfal," which was the GIA's watchword.

"Fight them until there is no more discord, and the faith belongs entirely to God." The new emir benefited from the backing of supporters in Europe, and especially in London, including Palestinians, Syrians, and Egyptians as well as Algerians.

In Algeria, the GIA began to target foreigners. On September 21, 1993, two French surveyors were killed by an armed group in the neighborhood of Sidi-Bel-Abbès. The GIA condemned France as the "source of all evil" and pronounced a sentence of death on all intellectuals who had cooperated with the regime or exalted Western values. Terrorists claiming to be attached to the GIA assassinated journalists and prominent cultural and political figures, especially in the Algiers region. Jaafar al-Afghani was killed by the Algerian security forces in March 1994. His successor was Chérif Gousmi, known as Abu Abdallah Ahmed, who from the outset attempted to exert tighter control over the GIA and to systematize its operations. He divided the country into nine regions, corresponding to internal administrative divisions in the organization. Regional "emirs" were appointed to control operations in each zone, though some of these became involved in rivalry with each other. Chérif Gousmi also lost no time in initiating a dialogue with prominent Islamist figures in order to bring all the armed groups under his control. On May 13, 1994, the GIA published a declaration under the title "On Unity and the Jihad, and concerning respect for the Sunna and the Book." This was signed by Said Mekhloufi of the "Movement for an Islamic State" and by Aberrazaq Redjam, founder member of the FIS, who represented the Algerianists. This proclaimed that "The Jihad should serve to establish the Caliphate according to the practice of the Prophet," and that "The GIA is the sole vehicle of the Jihad in Algeria." This declaration confirmed the GIA's dominance of the armed Islamist movement.

Though the GIA's dynamic was ultraradical and sectarian, it was still prey to rival ideological and religious currents, each of which was equally determined to gain complete control of the organization. In early October 1994, Chérif Gousmi lost his life in the course of a military operation. The question of who was to succeed him gave rise to repeated factional struggles. His successor was initially an Algerianist, Mahfoud Tajine, also known as Abou Khalil Mahfouz, who was then replaced by a Salafi, Djamel Zitouni, known as Abou Abderrahman Amin. This new emir, who had strong support in Europe, had the ambition to extend the conflict beyond Algeria. In December 1994, the GIA made an unsuccessful attempt to carry out a spectacular operation on French soil by commandeering an Air France flight from Algiers with the intention of crashing the aircraft into the Eiffel Tower in Paris. The flight was diverted to Marseille, however, and the attempt was foiled by the French anti-terrorist unit known as the GIGN (Groupe d'Intervention de la Gendarmerie Nationale). Some days later, Zitouni commissioned and organized the assassination of the White Fathers at Tizi-Ouzou. The four missionaries were killed at their residence on December 27, 1994. Between June and October 1995, small groups linked to the GIA were responsible for a number of lethal attacks in France, but their organization in France was quickly broken up.

At this stage, apparently with the help of a faction linked to Takfir wa-l Hijra, Zitouni mounted a purge of Algerianists within the GIA. In the fall of 1995, the purge had set in train an apparently irreversible process that led to a series of splits within the organization and a collapse in the level of support it received from abroad. Mahfoud Tajine, and another important figure, Mohammed Said, were killed at the orders of the GIA's own leadership, together with others. These included Abderrazaq Redjam, Nasseredine

Turkman (formerly head of the FIS in Medea), Azzedine Baa (formerly FIS representative in Blida), and Nasser Tetraoui (FIS representative in Ouargla). Sectarian divisions in the GIA continued to multiply. Those loyal to the leader, who called themselves Jihadist Salafis, appeared to be no longer more than a small community, which continually ostracized other groups. The abduction and execution of the Trappist monks of the monastery at Tibhirine at Zitouni's orders left the movement further isolated. The publication *Al-Ansar* ceased to appear because of the level of hostility between the various Islamist figures.

On July 17, 1996, Zitouni was himself killed, in uncertain circumstances, having been described as an "agent of military security" by Algerianist fighters, and a new succession struggle ensued. Habibi Miloud, "emir" of the sixth region, was the first to emerge as leader, but was thrust aside by the supporters of another official of the movement, Antar Zouabri, known as Abou Talha. In 1997, Zouabri published a tract entitled the "The Cutting Sword" in London, after which his supporters in London remained for some time relatively quiescent. This inaugurated a policy of terror, with repeated collective massacres against the population, mainly in the countryside. Many observers noted the lack of response on the part of the security forces. New splits in the movement took place after the GSPC (The Salafi Group for Preaching and War—Groupe Salafite pour la Prédication et Combat) came into existence in September 1998. Burgeoning splits in the GIA owing to the inability of the national leader to maintain control led to a total disintegration of the political and military structure of the GIA.

Zouabri found himself relatively isolated and was threatened by the forces of the dissident leader in the Medea region, Abdel Kader Souane, known as Abou Thoumana, who had been responsible for many operations.

Zouabri was forced to take refuge with his immediate supporters, known as the "Green Brigade," in a mountainous region close to Blida, where he remained, unable to communicate with other groups that still recognized his authority. During 2001, he made repeated attempts to rebuild his support in the Mitidja. On February 8, during a visit to his native village of Boufarik, he was killed by the Algerian security forces. The former commander of his "Green Brigade," Abou Tourab, became emir and continued Zouabri's ideological line and military strategy. At the same time, the GIA name began to be used by small criminal groups, sometimes linked to political factions, that were pursuing financial gain or settling personal scores. For this reason, many acts of sabotage, the burning of factories and workshops and some assassinations were wrongly attributed to the GIA.

GSPC (Group Salafite pour la Predication et le Combat) (Salafi Group for Preaching and Combat)

The GSPC was formally established in September 1998 at a conference of twenty-one armed fighters held in a secluded location in Kabylia. It was originally a splinter group of the GIA started by Hassan Hattab, the "emir" of the GIA zone covering the Kabyle region east of Algiers. In its initial statement, Hattab spoke out against the successive purges mounted by the GIA leadership from 1995 onward. It was especially antagonistic to the activists of Takfir wa-l Hijra who were accused of being particularly involved in this process of political and military extermination. The moment was propitious for the new group to occupy a vacant space in the political and military landscape, given the radicalism of the GIA on the one hand and the truce declared by the AIS in October 1997.

From the outset, the GSPC was made up of a series of tightly knit units known as "phalanges" operating in the Wilayas of Jijel, Sétif, Batna, El Oued, and Tebessa. Some sections of the GIA based in southern Algeria also joined up with the new structure. The Baqun 'Ala al-Had also allied themselves in principle with the GSPC, with the aim of "fighting more effectively the apostate regime." This agreement was crucial for Hassan Hattab, who thus acquired important support networks in Europe and particularly in the United Kingdom. From late 1998, exiled activists were in contact with Qamereddine Kherbane, the leading figure in Baqun 'Ala al-Had and also appear to have made contact with people connected with the Bin Laden nexus. In London, funds were raised and new sympathisers were recruited, especially at the Regent's Park Mosque and the mosque at Finsbury Park. The policy of civil reconciliation initiated by President Bouteflika at the beginning of his presidency tended to thin out the armed Islamist movement, which in fact benefited the GSPC. Not only did the GSPC itself remain unaffected by the government's initiative; it also benefited from the adherence of an appreciable number of new fighters from dissolved units. Soldiers and police who had quit their units were also a significant element within the GSPC, even in its decision-making circles. The best known of these deserters were Abi Abdelaziz, also known as Okacha, who was a former para from the special forces unit of the Algerian Army based in Biskra, and Saifi Lamari, also known as Abderrazaq "El Para," a former sergeant major from Tebessa. Persistent rumors hinted at attempts at subversion.

Like the GIA, the GSPC divided the territory of Algeria into administrative regions. For instance, the GSPC's Zone 6, run by Mokhtar Belmokhtar, corresponded to two Wilayas in the south and east of the country. The basic unit was the cell, with between seven and fifteen fighters, and the "phalange" with three or four cells. A "company" comprised a number of phalanges. This theoretical plan was more or less followed by the "emirs" of the various regions. The GSPC maintained a presence in many Wilayas, and its operational groups were especially concentrated in Kabylie, Batna, Jijal, and Tebessa. In December 2001, Algerian press reports spoke of 1,500 armed combatants in Kabylia alone. Most of the units operated out of remote and isolated wooded areas where the fighters could take refuge if need be.

Significantly, the GSPC was a more disciplined organization than the other armed groups that had emerged in Algeria and was less prone to internal dissent. In contrast to the GIA, the GSPC did not carry out random attacks in urban areas. Its operations were always carefully targeted. In 1998, the year in which the GSPC declared itself to have begun its operations, in the Wilaya of Tizi-Ouzou, where only the GSPC was active, forty-eight of the sixty-eight victims of attacks reported by the press were members of the security forces, including soldiers, policemen, and security guards. Anyone working for the state was a target. On October 3, 2001, in the Wilays of Bejaia, a state prosecutor and a local government official were killed by a GSPC unit under the command of Hassan Hattab. Since then, similar tactics have been employed in the activities of all GSPC units, wherever based. Nevertheless, civilians have also been seriously threatened. There has been blackmail, the exaction of taxes from traders, and roadblocks that seemed to indicate that threats might be put into practice. However, deaths of civilians as the result of GSPC terrorist actions tended to be unusual and exemplary.

The GSPC financed itself in a wide variety of ways. In addition to voluntary contributions and extortion, the GSPC has also acquired lands, houses, and commercial premises, especially in the Algiers region. Businesses, which were subject only to loose control, were able to donate part of their profits to the Jihad. The GSPC set up smuggling operations between Algeria and Tunisia, particularly in the Tebessa region, with the help of powerful local tribal leaders with political connections. In southern Algeria, the GSPC also established an arms trade run by smugglers operating on the roads through Tamanrasset and Bordj Badji Mokhtar.

Under Hassan Hattab, the GSPC adopted differing strategies in different regions, in response to local conditions and to the structure and extent of existing local networks. Sometime, the GSPC emirs set up their own criminal structures, but for the most part they struck up pragmatic local alliances with well-established smugglers, who were sometimes in collaboration with unscrupulous local officials.

The GSPC's Contacts in Europe

It seems clear from the conclusions of a number of inquiries in Europe relating to the GSPC that—in Europe at least—the GSPC—received help and cooperation to differing degrees from groups with connections of some kind with the Bin Laden nexus. As a quid pro quo, members of the GSPC who were dormant in Europe would be available to undertake missions in various countries in Europe. According to allegations carried in certain Algerian newspapers in 2001, the confessions of captured GSPC combatants have indicated that the group was set up with Osama Bin Laden's collaboration. The arrest in Europe of various GSPC sympathizers and militants who have been shown to have links with lieutenants of Osama Bin Laden would seem to give credence to this hypothesis.

In 1998, secret GSPC cells were established in Europe and supporters of Hassan Hattab were sighted in a number of countries, particularly in Belgium, Spain, Italy, France, and the United Kingdom. In December 2000, four Algerians suspected of intending to commit terrorist acts were interrogated in the German city of Frankfurt. Two months later, in London, more GSPC agents were arrested. On April 4, 2001, in Milan, the Italian police dismantled an Islamist ring that was planning a chemical arms attack in France. According to Italian police sources, the members of this group were both GSPC activists and operatives for Bin Laden's supposed organization. In each of these cases, police sources said that contacts with Bin Laden had been found to exist. In the words of the U.S. State Department, from the year 2000, the spread and growth of the clandestine cells of the Algerian Islamist movement had become "a potential threat." On September 15, 2002, after Al-Qa'ida had been officially implicated in the September 11 attacks in New York and Washington, Hassan Hattab put out a statement in which he threatened to strike at "European and especially U.S. interests" in Algeria. Some day later, President Bush froze the assets, in the United States, of a number of organizations suspected of links with Bin Laden, including the GSPC.

The published conclusions of an inquiry linked to the arrest of six GSPC activists in Spain on September 26, 2001 threw light to some extent on the activities of these kinds of clandestine cells in Europe, as well as their connections with other groups sharing the same objectives. In the words of the Spanish interior minister, the dismantled network "supported individuals intending to carry out suicide attacks on U.S. targets." He also said the group "was particularly engaged in the acquisition of optical devices, as well as telecommunications, electronic and electromagnetic equipment, intending to send this material on to Algeria." This Spanish police operation also disclosed the links between the GSPC and another Algerian

Salafi movement, Takfir wa-l Hijra. Though rivals in Algeria, these two groups had set up joint operations in Europe. Investigators were able to assess the kinds of contacts regularly maintained between the Spanish group and Islamists belonging to the Franco-Algerian activist, Dhamel Beghal, who was a member of Takfir al-Hijra and had strong ties to Al-Qa'ida. Al-Qa'ida appeared to be a loosely organized federation of groups in various countries, including Algeria, Egypt, Yemen, and other countries as far afield as India and China. The GSPC consequently gave a double role to its external units. Their task was not only to provide logistic support and finance for armed groups operating in Algeria, but also to take part as appropriate in large-scale operations against Western interests, including those run by other organizations.

In fact, some of the external groups were not solely made up of Algerians but also included operatives of other nationalities, such as the group dismantled in Milan in April 2001, which was led by a Tunisian national, Essid Sami Ben Khemais. Another foreign GSPC member was the Hervé Djamel Loiseau, who was killed fighting for the Taliban in Afghanistan in December 2001; he had been convicted in a French court in December 2000 after another GSPC group was exposed and dismantled. Hassan Hattab appointed a European coordinator, whose role was to transmit his instructions, in order to keep control of GSPC brigades stationed outside Algeria that might have been tempted by their internationalist inclinations to take unilateral action. The GSPC's stance on Algerian political affairs contrasted with the terrorist inclination of its international links, which could have led it into involvement in "spectacular" operations in the West. The GSPC has continued to fight on in Algeria, even after the GIA broadly surrendered its arms in response to President Bouteflika's overtures. In September 2006, the GSCP overtly declared its affiliation to Al-Qa'ida, though in practice this probably signifies little except an expression of sympathy for Al-Qa'ida's stated goals.

Hamas (Algeria)

Hamas in Algeria is a political party that was officially recognized on December 5, 1990. It was founded by Sheikh Mahfoud Nahnah on the basis of Algeria's most influential charitable organization, "Al-Irshad wa-l-Islah" ("Guidance and Reform"), which aids the poor and preaches a return to the Islamic faith. This organization is linked to the Muslim Brotherhood, sharing its goals of operating within the law, and advocates the adoption of a moderate attitude toward the existing Algerian regime. It advocates a political system based on the Islamic concept of "Shura" or consultation, which recognizes the principle of the public expression of differing views and rejects despotism.

Hamas organized itself as a political party after the unprecedented success of the FIS (Islamic Salvation Front) in local elections. But despite its heavy support in many areas of the country, Mahfoudf Nahnah's creation failed to make any impression on the support gained by FIS in the first round of the parliamentary elections in December 1991. On that occasion, Hamas's share of the votes came to little more than 5 percent of the ballots cast, just 368,697 votes. It was, nevertheless, the fourth political movement in the country, after the FIS, the FLN (the old National Liberation Front), and the FFS ("Front des Forces Socialistes"—Socialist Forces Front, largely supported by the Berber element of the population). After the outbreak of terrorism in Algeria, Hamas opted for a policy of integrating itself into the state, when it refused to join the "Rejection Front" formed by the FFS and the FLN, together with the Movement for Democracy in Algeria (MDA) and the En-Nahda movement. These groups then proceeded to draw up what they called a "platform for peace." Mahfoud Nahnah's plea was for talks between the military Chiefs of Staff and the imprisoned leaders of the FIS, Abassi Madani and Ali Belhadj.

Nahnah was regarded as a traitor by those who saw the way to achieve their goals in armed confrontation with the regime, and his conciliatory policy toward the "junta" was strongly opposed by the armed groups. In 1993, Mohammed Bouslimani, who led Al-Irshad wa-l-Islah, and had been a close associate of Sheikh Nahnah for a number of years, was kidnapped near Blida and then murdered. However, by opting for a political approach, Hamas attracted much support from the middle class and especially among small businessmen, who were alarmed by the mounting climate of violence and attracted by Hamas's reformist rhetoric and puritanical tone. The Hamas leadership was aware of the growing isolation of the regime, which no longer had even the support it traditionally drew from the FLN and supported the constitutional reforms proposed by the government. The main opposition parties, on the other hand, called for a boycott of the presidential election of November 1995. Sheikh Nahnah, however, decided to stand as a candidate, with the intention of taking part in what saw as a return to republican legitimacy after a number of "transitional" years. Due partly to the boycott of the polls by the FIS, the Sheikh took 25 percent of the vote. This election effectively endorsed President Zeroual as leader of the country, but also inaugurated a rearrangement of the political landscape in Algeria and the formation of a new tendency that could be described as "conservative Islamist."

With the approval of the military high command, Hamas became part of the government and in January 1996 was given two ministerial portfolios, including the trade ministry, a post taken by Rida Hamiani.

The Algerian government's policy of privatization was endorsed by Mahfoud Nahnah, as it acted to the benefit of Hamas's constituency in the country. At the same period, Hamas attempted to use its activists to take control of the trades unions, as well as various quasi-governmental organizations and charitable foundations. Following the adoption of the constitutional amendments in a referendum, Hamas changed its name and on November 28, 1996 became the MSP (Social Movement for Peace—"Mouvement de la Société pour la Paix").

LIDD (Ligue Islamique pour Da'wa et Djihad) (Islamic League for Da'wa and Jihad)

LIDD was an organization that took its inspiration from the Algerianist movement. It was founded on February 5, 1997 by two members of the FIS (Front Islamique du Salut), Ali Ben Hadjar and Sheikh Mahfoud Rahmani. A third former member of the officially dissolved FIS, Yousef Boubras, was listed as a founding member of LIDD in the declaration announcing the movement's establishment. LIDD's fighters were for the most part former members of the GIA who had repudiated the GIA's more bloodthirsty excesses. They appear to have left the Islamic Movement for Preaching and Jihad after internal disputes.

Sheikh Ali Ben Hadjar became the national leader and declared his adherence to the philosophy of Abassi Madani, Ali Belhadj, and Mohammed Said. LIDD allied itself with FIDA (the Islamic Front for Armed Jihad), another clandestine movement linked to "Algerianism." It was able to operate only a few small-scale armed groups in the region of Algiers and the Wilaya of Blida. After negotiations, LIDD decided to join the truce declared by Madani Mezrag in October 1997. Its fighting men went into the government's camps, pending an overall political agreement. In a statement published in January 2000, Sheikh Ben Hadjar announced the dissolution of the organization. Its members benefited from the government amnesty and received the same terms for their reintegration into society offered by the authorities to the AIS.

MEI (Mouvement pour L'état Islamique) (Movement for the Islamic State)

The MEI—Movement for an Islamic State—was set up in 1991 by Said Mekhloufi, a former member of the FIS. Mekhloufi was of Kabyle origin and edited the publication *Al-Munqidh* from 1989 to 1991. He also wrote a tract entitled "Civil Disobedience," which had been widely distributed before the annulment of the elections. He was accused of involvement in an armed attack at Algiers airport in August 1992 and was sentenced to death in absentia in 1993. The MEI operated in the Algiers region, in Kabylie, and in a number of departments in the west of the country. Mekhloufi's aim was to attract support in the most deprived areas of the country. Many army deserters also joined him. Nevertheless, when the predominance of the GIA (Armed Islamic Group) could no longer be ignored, the MEI leadership decided to join it. Mekhloufi announced the merger on May 13, 1994 when his tract on "Unity in the Jihad and respect for the Sunna" was published. The MEI membership was marginalized within the GIA, which at that time contained other groups—Algerianists and Takfiris—who had ambitions to become the GIA's leadership. From November 1995, the national "emir" of the GIA, Djamel Zitouni, launched a bloody purge with the murder of several dozen fighters and in particular the Algerianists. The MEI refused to endorse the purge and decided some months later once more to operate entirely on its own. The organization by now had only a few fighters, deployed in the region near the Moroccan border and the hills of Ouarsenis. It was virtually wiped out in a series of military actions against it and Mekhloufi was apparently killed by GIA guerrillas in 1997 near the town of Béchar. Lacking a successor of sufficient stature, the MEI inevitably disintegrated. After 1998, it was apparently no longer active.

MIA (Mouvement Islamique Armé) (Armed Islamic Movement)

The founders of the MIA were rejectionists who refused to accept the decision to operate within the law adopted by the new leadership of the FIS after the events of June 1991 and the arrests of Abassi Madani and Ali Belhadj. From the outset, the MIA was run by supporters of Mustafa Bouyali. The leading figure, Abdelkader Chebouti, had been a peripatetic trader. He was one of Bouyali's deputies and participated in the attack on the police college at Soumaa on August 27, 1985. He was sentenced to death, but was pardoned in 1990 in an act of leniency by the government. In April 1992, Chebouti was appointed as military leader of the organization at a secret meeting of a number of influential "emirs" operating in the central region of the country. A few months later, Ali Belhadj and Rabah Kebir accepted him as the head of the MIA, which was effectively the armed wing of the FIS.

Rival movements made their appearance, however, for a number of reasons. A particular difficulty was that the MIA operated strict entry criteria for its activists and refused to recruit young men from the criminal fringes of society. This favored the expansion of the rival GIA (Groupe Islamique Armé) (the Armed Islamic Group). The MIA deployed its principal forces in the Blida hills and also maintained networks in Algiers as well as in the deprived outskirts of the capital. For a while, it benefited from the charisma earned by Chebouti, who was nicknamed the "Lion of the Mountain." Chebouti's supporters tried to set up what they called "liberated zones." The MIA's ambition had been to create a stable coalition of the various armed factions. In this, however, it failed. When a number of influential figures including Mohammed Said and Said Mekhloufi announced in May 1994 that they intended to join the GIA, the MIA vanished from the political and military scene. Many of its members joined the newly formed organization, the AIS (Armée Islamique du Salut) (Islamic Salvation Army).

MNA (Mouvement de la Nahda Islamique) (Movement of the Islamic Renaissance) (Algeria)

The MNI, known as Al-Nahda, was recognized as a political party on October 3, 1990. Later, it became part of the governing coalition, after Abdelaziz Bouteflika became president of Algeria in 1999. It was first established in the early 1980s. In its initial form, it was connected with the activities of a militant Islamist group led by Sheikh Adballah Djaballah, who was active in the region of Constantine. Djaballah was born on March 2, 1956, in Bouchtata in the Wilaya of Skikda and was one of the founding members of Rabitat ad-Da'wa. He studied law at the University of Constantine in the 1970s and was a disciple of Abdellatif Soltani, Mohammed Salah, and Mohammed Sahnoun. These three embodied to varying degrees the rebirth of Islamic thought in Algeria at the time and became popular figures. Together with other students, Abdallah Djaballah set up a secret association named Al-Jama'a al-Islamiya, which aimed to lay the foundations for a political organization in the spirit of the teaching of the Quran.

In 1987, Djaballah fell out with various other members of the organization, who became leading figures in the FIS. These included Abdelkader Hachani, Rabah Kebir, and Ali Djeddi. In 1988, Djaballah founded and became the leader of what he called Al-Nahda, which he conceived as a national association of a social and cultural nature. Shortly after the victory of the FIS in the municipal and Wilaya elections of June 1990, he took the decision, with the support of some of his former colleagues in Al-Jama'a al-Islamiya, to set up his own political organization, under a name reflecting that of the existing association. He became the founding president of the "Mouvement de la Nahda Islamique" and campaigned in the parliamentary elections of December 1991. Though he had networks of supporters in the eastern part of Algeria, the new party's results in the election were disappointing. It attracted only some 150,000 votes, just over 2 percent of the votes cast. In the event, since the MNI's platform differed from that of the FIS only in a few minor points, the electorate had chosen for the most part to support the movement led by Abassi Madani and Abdelkader Hachani.

After the effective coup of January 1992, and following the onset of terrorist activities, the MNI welcomed former FIS members who wished to continue in the path of militant activity but had also rejected the option of armed conflict. The MNI joined a rejectionist front that also comprised the FLN (National Liberation Front), the FFS (the Socialist Forces Front), the Workers Party, and the supporters of Ben Bella. These groups set the seal on their union with the publication on January 13 of what they called the "platform for a political and peaceful resolution of the Algerian crisis," signed in Rome. This, however, failed to gain the approval of the military high command, and therefore nothing came of it, despite various high-level international interventions. MNI representatives were, nevertheless, active in attempting to establish and maintain a dialogue between the Algerian government and the AIS (Islamic Salvation Army).

Over time, the MNI set up offices in most of Algeria's Wilayas, and in the parliamentary elections of June 1997, it won 34 seats, taking the opportunity to demonstrate the extent of its support at the national level. It won further electoral success at the local elections of October 1997. Shortly afterward, however, disagreements became evident within the MNI over its historic tactics. A significant part of the movement, represented within the party's leadership by Lahbib Adami, favored the MNI taking any opportunity that might present itself to become part of the governing coalition. Abdallah Djaballah refused to accept any compromise with the military authorities and together with some of the party's activists announced the formation of a new organization, the MRN (Mouvement de la Réforme Nationale), of which he became leader. Meanwhile, in the presidential elections of 1999, the MNI supported the candidacy of Abdelaziz Bouteflika. Subsequently, the MNI took the decision to support the policies of the new president, who deiced to assemble a coalition government including parties of what he called the "revolutionary family." These included the FLN, the RND (Rassemblement National Démocratique) (National Democratic Assembly), and two Islamist movements, the MSP (Mouvement de la Société pour la Paix) (Social Movement for Peace) and the MNI. Also included were groups claiming to belong to the "democratic camp," such as the RCD (Rassemblement pour la Culture et la Démocratie) (Assembly for Culture and Democracy), the Kabyle-based movement. Weakened by the departure of many militants identified with the charismatic figure of Abdallah Djaballah, the MNI came eventually to play a minor role in the Algerian political scene. Djaballah criticized his former colleagues as opportunists in search of high office. At the parliamentary elections of May 30, 2002, the MNI won only one seat in the National Popular Assembly.

(Mouvement Islamique Algérien) (Algerian Islamic Movement)

The Mouvement Islamique Algérien was an Islamist group founded long before the troubles in Algeria of 1991. Its aim was the immediate application of the Shari'a law. It initially brought together a number of religiously inspired small groups that dreamed of armed action, such as the "Association for Struggle against Illegality" and the "Injunction of Good and Expulsion of Evil." Mustafa Bouyali, a former fighter in Algeria's War of Independence, who had become an employee of Algeria's national electricity company, joined the resistance organized by Ait Ahmed in 1963 and then became leader of the Mouvement Islamique Algérien. He was a family man and the father of seven children, and was not particularly schooled in Islam, but proved to be an effective strategist who paid little attention to political theory. From 1983 to 1987, the movement committed itself to armed struggle, especially in the Mitidja.

On August 27, 1985, the Mouvement Islamique Algérien attacked the police college at Soumaa and killed a member of the security forces. The ferocity of its fighters shocked the authorities. The Mouvement Islamique Algérien was finally crushed after the death of Bouyali, who was killed in an ambush by the security forces on February 3, 1987. When the members of the organization were put on trial, they admitted to plans to murder the prime minister and to kidnap one of the leaders of the FLN, Sherif Messadia. The State Security Court handed down stern punishments. Seven members were condemned to death in a trial in which two verdicts were handed down, one in 1985 and the other in 1987. However, this small group of Islamic combatants was in the end set at liberty after judicial indecision and secret negotiations. Two of Bouyali's loyal lieutenants, Abdelkader Chebouti and Mansouri Meliani, were first condemned to death, then pardoned and freed. They then set up two new Islamist organizations dedicated to the overthrow of the state, which proved to be key organizations in the continuation of the Islamist struggle: the MIA (Movement Islamique Armé) (Armed Islamic Movement) and the GIA (Armed Islamic Group).

MRN (Mouvement de la Réforme Nationale) (Movement for National Reform)

The MRN or the "Harakat al-Islah al-Watani" was recognized as a party in 1999 and is generally known by its Arabic name Al-Islah. It is a group that broke off from the MNI (Al-Nahda). In opposition in parliament, it is led by the former leader of the MNI, Sheikh Abdallah Djaballah. It frequently declares its solidarity with the "oppressed Muslim nations" and adopts a pan-Islamic stance in alignment with that of the Muslim Brotherhood. The MRN gains support from students and from middle class voters such as government officials and small tradesmen. Taking note of the failure of the violent excesses of political Islamism, and of the bitter divisions within Algerian society, the MRN has come down in favor of social and political action within an institutional framework. Though Abdallah Djaballa is opposed to any compromise with Algeria's behind-the-scenes military decision makers, he, nevertheless, ran as a presidential candidate in 1999, before joining other candidates in a denunciation of what they called the "electoral charade." The MRN has worked to construct alliances with the other recognized Islamist groups that sit in parliament, as well as with the more conservative wing of the FLN. Its strategy is to bring pressure to bear on what it regards as crucial issues such as the reform of family law, the teaching of foreign languages, and the administration of justice.

Since the establishment of the MRN in 1999, its policy has borne fruit. A number of pieces of legislation potentially damaging to the ideas of the Islamists have been dropped, thanks to the MRN's alliances and in the absence of any widely based political consensus behind them. Because of its oppositional stance, the MRN has been able to mobilize a substantial section of the electorate. By winning forty-three seats in the parliamentary elections of May 30, 2002, Abdallah Djaballah's party has become the first Algerian Islamist organization to be represented in the National Popular Assembly.

MSP (Movement de la Société pour la Paix) (Social Movement for Peace)

The MSP is the new title adopted by Hamas, originally founded by Sheikh Mahfoud Nahnah. Following the adoption of new regulations governing the activities of political parties embodied in the constitution of 1996, the MSP has readopted the doctrinal and strategic principles laid down by its leadership in the aftermath of the annulment of the electoral process in 1992. At the parliamentary elections of June 7, 1997, it became the second largest political grouping in the country, with sixty-nine seats. With bases in all Algerian regions, except Kabylie and some of the relatively unpopulated southern Wilayas, the MSP has at its disposal a solid network of disciplined supporters. Its electorate is largely made up of blue collar voters, such as government employees, small tradesmen, and workers, who are attracted by its moderate conservative political line. It favors the plan for civil reconciliation put forward by President Bouteflika. It has also taken on board the principle of participation in a government of national unity, even though parties flatly hostile to the Islamist project such as the RCD also form part of the governing coalition. Any relative loss of influence was compensated by its acquisition of a key government post by one of MSP's increasingly high-profile members, Bouguerra Soltani, who became minister for work and professional training.

Following the political upheaval prompted by the suppression of the uprisings in Kabylie in the spring of 2001, Sheikh Nahnah's party consolidated its position within the governing coalition. After the resignation of the two RCD ministers who had held office since December 1999, the government had taken on a more Islamist and conservative character. In order to effectively counter proposals it opposed in the fields of family law, education, and justice, the MSP had struck up over a period of years alliances with figures from the FLN and the RND, which were also parties within the government. The MSP thus demonstrated that it was able to set up effectively pressure groups. Following the lead of the Muslim Brotherhood, the MSP alternates between collaboration with the military decision makers and playing to its militant power base. In the political context of violent disturbances and mounting social discontent, however, Mahfoud Nahnah's political pragmatism apparently met with the disapproval of the electorate. In the parliamentary elections of May 30, 2002, the MSP won only thirty-eight seats as against the sixty-nine they had held in the previous National Assembly.

PPS (Protectors of Salafite Preaching)

This group, also known in Algeria by the Arabic name "Katibat al-Ahwal" (Brigade of Strength), is an armed militant group that emerged from a split in the GIA. The GIA's leader in what the organization called Zone 4 was Kada Benchiha, also known as Abderrahim Larbi, a former barber born in 1963 in Sidi Bel-Abbès. Zone 4, in western Algeria, comprised the Wilayas of Mascara, Oran, Ain Temouchent, and Tlemcen. In September 1995, Kada Benchiha quarrelled with the national leader of the GIA, Djamel Zitouni, when he claimed possession of a weapons store. Zitouni sentenced him to death, whereupon he set up his own secret organization known as the PPS. However, he continued to carry out his terrorist operations under the GIA's name. As leader, he appointed his own commanders to various fighting units in the various Wilayas of western Algeria. On September 26, 1995, he was taken prisoner by a rival group under the GIA's command. He died in unknown circumstances some weeks later. His military adviser, Tayeb Djeriri, took over his organization, whose members acclaimed him as their leader. Djeriri declared his affiliation to the Salafi position and his commitment to jihad, on the lines of the doctrine disseminated by the GIA's publication *Al-Ansar,* and kept up a strategy of terror. Numerous collective massacres carried out in the Wilayas of Chlef and Ain Defla were laid at his door. He was never able to extend his influence outside his original region and never succeeded in transforming the group into a nation-wide organization.

Takfir wa-l-Hijra (Excommunication and Exodus) (Algeria)

Takfir wa-l-Hijra in Algeria was inspired by the example of its eponymous Egyptian antecedent. It was established by former fighters back from Afghanistan who claimed for most part to be disciples of Sheikh Sahnouni, the leading light of Salafism in Algeria. Its leading figures were Ahmed Boumara and Noureddin Seddiki. Takfir operated as a secret society, whose members eschewed attendance at public prayers and held aloof from all manifestations of the government. Takfir was fundamentally antagonistic to the FIS's attempts to operate within the law. On November 28, 1990, some weeks before the parliamentary elections, the organization mounted its first large-scale armed operation at the frontier post at Guemmar. Takfir's view was that it was legitimate to take the lives of Muslims who were in a state of impiety and who failed to serve the jihad, arguing that such people, through their inaction, were effectively helping to sustain the regime in power. Takfir merged with the GIA and entered a pragmatic alliance with the emir, Djamel Zitouni, in 1995 in order to participate in the sweeping purge within the GIA's ranks.

From 1997, Takfir's leadership justified the execution of collective massacres in various rural areas of Algeria on the grounds that authentic Islam was no longer practiced in Algeria. Such actions were frequently carried out under the banner of the GIA. A number of small groups attached to Takfir operated in the Dahra hills, in the Wilaya of Ain Defla. The precise structure and characteristics of Takfir are still obscure. Certain European cells attached to Takfir, entirely made up of Algerians, seem to have established links with Al-Qa'ida and made attempts to become involved in armed actions against American targets. These groups cooperated with members of the GSPC. The leader of one of these groups, Djamel Beghal, who was of French nationality and Algerian origin, was arrested in Dubai in July 2001. In the context of a broad inquiry into the attempted attack on the U.S. Embassy in Paris, other Takfiris were later arrested in the Paris region. So far, Takfir and the GSPC have been the sole organizations capable of extending their recruitment and propaganda efforts into multiple European states.

ALI, MUHAMMAD

Muhammad Ali was the name adopted by the American heavyweight boxer Cassius Marcellus Clay on his conversion to Islam. Cassius Clay was born in 1942 in Louisville, Kentucky, and boxed from the age of twelve. He turned professional in 1960, and on February 25, 1964, at the age of twenty-two, became heavyweight champion of the world when he took the world heavyweight title from Sonny Liston.

After his victory, he declared his adherence to the "Nation of Islam" and announced his new name. Clay, now Muhammad Ali, had for some time been strongly influenced by the Nation of Islam's leader, Malcolm X, with whom he allied himself during the "long, hot summer" of 1964, the first summer of rioting in the black ghettos of inner city America. As he said at that time: "Cassius Clay is a slave name. I did not choose and I didn't want it. I am Muhammad Ali, a free name—it means beloved of God—and I insist people use it when speaking to me and of me."

From this point on, Ali's career and his charisma were at the service of the Black Muslim cause, and he took up Malcolm X's confrontational style, associating himself with the attack on the "myths created by white society." In 1967, he refused to serve in Vietnam, was stripped of his heavyweight title, and faced prosecution. The U.S. Supreme Court exonerated him in 1971 and he returned to boxing, regaining his title on October 30, 1974 in the famous "Rumble in the Jungle" in Kinshasa, the capital of Zaire (today the Democratic Republic of Congo), when he fought and knocked out George Foreman in front of television cameras and a crowd of sixty thousand enthusiastic supporters.

He retired from boxing in 1981 and has continued to be involved in the cause of Islam in America, which he sees as no contradiction to his patriotism. At the opening of

Olympic Games in Atlanta in 1996 he carried the Olympic flame, under the American flag. He had earlier offered himself as a mediator between Iraq and Iran and visited Baghdad on a number of occasions. Muhammad Ali presently lives in Chicago, which is regarded a center of Islamist activities in the United States. In 2002, Mohammed Ali made a visit to Kabul, as he put it, "to raise awareness of the plight of the Afghan people."

AMAL (LEBANON)

The Amal Movement (Harakat al-Amal) is a Lebanese Shi'ite organization founded in 1974 by Musa Sadr, an Iranian Shi'ite religious dignitary who came to Lebanon in 1959. The word "Amal" means "hope" in Arabic and is also an acronym for the full name of the movement, "Afwaj al-Muqawama al-Lubnaniyya" (The Regiments of the Lebanese Resistance). Musa Sadr progressively laid claim to the position of political spokesman for Shi'ism, which as a faith community had effectively been excluded from political power by the Lebanese "National Pact" between the Maronite Christians and the Sunnis.

Shi'ite youths from the underprivileged classes had been increasingly drawn to the ideology of left-wing parties such as the Lebanese Communist Party, the Organization for Communist Action and the Ba'ath Party, in both its Syrian and Iraqi tendencies. Musa Sadr set himself to change the situation, setting up the Superior Shi'ite Council, which came to eclipse the influence of the Sunni religious establishment, inaugurating a political project to shake up the Shi'ite political scene at the expense both of the feudal Shi'ite politicians and the leftist parties. His plans, however, were disrupted by the outbreak of armed clashes in Lebanon. He was able to exercise little influence over the combatants, giving his approval and

in the end his encouragement to the Syrian intervention of 1975–1976.

However, Musa Sadr's ambiguous attitude toward the Palestinians and other regional factions augured badly for his future. In August 1978, Musa Sadr disappeared in mysterious circumstances during a visit to Libya. His followers accused Colonel Gaddafi of kidnapping him, together with his two traveling companions. His disappearance had a powerful symbolic significance for the Shi'ites of Lebanon, and his supporters still anticipate his return, regarding him as having been "occulted," like the Hidden Imam for whose return pious Shi'ites wait in anticipation of the end of days. After Musa Sadr's disappearance, the presidency of the Higher Shi'ite Council was assumed by Sheikh Mohammed Shamseddin, hitherto the council's vice president.

Nevertheless, by the end of the 1970s, the Amal Movement, bolstered by Syrian support, was able to entrench its position. After the Israeli invasion of 1982 it became a leading force in Lebanese politics. The parliamentary deputy Hussein al-Husseini had briefly headed the movement, but from April 1980 Amal's leader was Nabih Berri, a young lawyer. Thanks to his unswerving loyalty to the Syrians, he has since 1992 been speaker of Lebanon's parliament and an indispensable member of the trio of senior figures in Lebanese politics, together with the president (always a Maronite Christian under the terms of the National Pact) and the prime minister (always a Sunni Muslim). Between 1982 and 1991, the Amal militia was among the most active of those who divided Lebanon up into their respective spheres of influence. It was still, however, plagued by splits, which led to the formation of Hussein Moussawi's "Islamic Amal" and of the present Hizbollah movement. Islamic Amal—which came under suspicion over the attacks on the French and American forces in Beirut in 1983—was predicated on closer cooperation with Shi'ite Iran. It was based mainly at Baalbek in the Bekaa valley, under the strict supervision of the Syrian intelligence services.

The Taif accords of 1989 put the Amal movement in a favorable position, enabling it to introduce thousands of its supporters into the machinery of state. From 1992, Nabim Berri led the largest parliamentary group, known as the "Liberation Group," which by 2002 had the support of some twenty members of parliament. With its Shi'ite confessional makeup, and its strong basis in southern Lebanon, Amal has many thousands of members and supporters. Among its demands are the abolition of Lebanon's confessional system of government. Among its political leadership are a number of ministers and former ministers, including Mohammed Beydun, Ayyub Umayyad, and Mohammed Abu Hamdan. However, following Shamseddin's demise on January 10, 2001, at the age of sixty-eight, splits appeared within the religious leadership of the Shi'ite community. Shekih Abdel Amir Qabalan was confirmed as the Higher Shi'ite Council's interim leader, retaining the position of vice president.

ASIA, CENTRAL

A Regional School of Islam

The collapse of the Soviet Union in December 1991 was followed by rapid changes in the spiritual, moral, and mental landscape of the societies of Central Asia. Islam reassumed its position in the public sphere. The terminology of "Islamic Republics," and the insistence on "forgotten Muslims," gave place in much of the journalistic coverage to the concept of a "broad regional Muslim identity" to the south of Russia that would coalesce around their common faith. The practice of Islam, however, was not uniform.

The multifarious religious reality attached to the various nationalities can be grasped only by speaking of different "Islams."

In the Uzbek and Tajik region, where religious feeling is at its highest, there has been a sharp increase in the number of mosques. By 2002, there were some five thousand in Uzbekistan and half that figure in Tajikistan, for a much smaller population. Religious figures are greatly respected. The ancient region of Transoxania, historically settled and devout, has provided Islam with great theologians such as Bukhari, one of the great compilers of Hadith (Islamic traditions deriving from the life of the Prophet). Transoxania was also fertile ground for the great Sufi movements, for example Naqshabandiyya order, founded in Bukhara by Baha'uddin Naqshband, a Persian speaker. This movement gives expression to a mystical form of moderate Islamic fundamentalism, and its membership spans the social classes. It became increasingly radical during the Tsarist era and the Soviet period.

On the other hand, Kazakhstan, Kirghizstan, and Turkmenistan display features in common: Islam is relatively less strong there, except in the frontier regions inhabited by Uzbek minorities. The increase in the number of mosques has been less rapid in Kazakhstan, with five hundred mosques, and in Turkmenistan, where there are two hundred mosques of significant size. The picture differs, however, in Kirghizstan, where there are two thousand mosques and also the number of mosques is larger in proportion to the population. These mosques are less frequented, however, and there is also a dearth of religious personnel, who are undereducated and poorly regarded.

Meanwhile, the Turkmens, Kirghiz, and Kazakhs, nomadic peoples who have relatively recently been Islamized and sedentarized, practice "shamanic" traditions, together with the Sufi Islam of the Yassawiyya brotherhood, founded by Ahmed Yassawi, a Turkic speaker. This brotherhood, less orthodox than the Naqshbandiyya, and influenced by non-Islamic beliefs, has members among the nomads and the urban population. Proverbs mocking the Quran and the mullahs are an indication of the low level of religiousness. Not all Islamic officials speak Arabic, so that few can read the Quran, and are relatively uneducated.

There is also a generational split. The Islamic faithful are for the most part men over sixty and, in some cases, their grand-children. The generation born in the decade after 1960 is apparently absent. As one cleric explained: "They grew up in the age of com-munism, and, especially in the towns, they have fallen under the influence of commu-nist ideology." The spread of education has been a further factor tending toward aliena-tion from Islam.

Central Asian Islam displays character-istic features based on local traditions. The strength of local tradition was one of the reasons why religious practices persisted through the Soviet era. Some such customs and traditions mingle national and religious aspects very closely, and it is difficult to distinguish one aspect from the other. For example, it is a little known fact that the Islamic veil, known locally as the "farandja" in Tajikistan, was introduced into the Mid-dle East in the twelfth century by female Christian companions of the Crusaders. "Farandja" is the feminine form of an adjec-tive "faranji"or Frankish, a word signifying a Westerner at the time of the Crusades.

The women are more emancipated than in other Muslim countries, studying at the same schools and universities as the men, living active working lives and seldom wearing the "chadra." Their faces are most often uncovered. The Islamic headscarf is found most frequently in Uzbekistan and Tajikistan. The women who tragically burned themselves to death in Central Asia during the period of "perestroika" were seen by Russian journalists as a rejection of the tyranny of Muslim tradition. Local observ-ers, however, saw the deaths as a protest against the intolerable circumstances of their lives, especially in the cotton planta-tions, which had nothing to do with Islam.

Polygamy, though legally banned, persists, but to an extent difficult to determine in the absence of statistics. Local sociologists esti-mate that in Kirghizstan more than 10 percent of households are involved. This is a figure apparently higher than that for Uzbekistan or Tajikistan. Alcohol, which is outlawed by Islam, is more sought after by Kazakhs and Kirghiz than by Tajiks or Uzbeks.

One specific characteristic of Islam in Central Asia relates to the significance of the Sufi movements, which date from the Middle Ages and have always played a major political role. Religious leaders have always sought legitimacy from the practice of Suf-ism, which served as the means by which Islam spread, and as the basis on which it was sustained, under the communist regime. Suf-ism pervades the education of the mullahs. Sufi movements, though placing their emphasis on spirituality and contemplation, have hurled themselves into recent political controversies. Sufi sheikhs have taken part in demonstrations in the Chechen capital Gro-zny and in anticommunist demonstrations at Dushanbe, in Tajikistan.

Some Islamic sects represented in Cen-tral Asia, such as wahhabism, have their origin in the strict Islam of Saudi Arabia. The Saudi government, however, does not officially support these movements, prefer-ring to fund other tendencies. Nevertheless, this Sufi practice often involves former emi-grants from the Gulf countries, who return to their countries of origin imbued with an Islam that professes to represent a return to the source, thus making a contribution to its propagation. The wahhabis advocate the practice of an Islam purged of local influences and denounce close ties between religion and

popular tradition. For instance, they condemn funeral practices, reject pilgrimages to
the tombs of "holy men," and burn certain
religious texts, such as the "Chahar Kitab,"
which is found in some mosques. Wahhabism, frequently characterized as "fundamentalist," aims at the re-Islamization of the
masses, eschewing involvement with politics. Attempts are made to suppress it by the
official clergy, whose authority it frequently
refuses to accept. An Indo-Pakistani association, Jamaat al-Tabligh (also known as
Tablighi Jamaat) is also making efforts to
extend its influence in Central Asia. Jamaat
al-Tabligh places stress on re-Islamization to
the greatest extent possible, and on the strict
practice of religious ritual, to the exclusion of both theology and mysticism, and
is making efforts to develop its presence in
Central Asia.

Central Asia and the Islamic Bomb

At the time of independence in 1991, Khaza-
khstan officially held some 1,400 nuclear
warheads. Nuclear issues were a source of
concern to the West, since the use and the
maintenance of these "Soviet" weapons were
outside the control of the Kazakh authorities, even though Kazakhstan believed it was
capable of preventing the launch of nuclear
weapons from its soil. Kazakhstan did not
conceal its intention to make use of nuclear
issues as a bargaining counter in its relations
with Russia, aiming to oblige Russia to share
out the heritage of the Soviet Union. A further aim was to persuade Moscow to take
a generous stand on economic exchanges,
including compensation for the damage
done by the nuclear testing center at Semipalatinsk, and from the use of the space
center at Baikonur.

Kazakhstan aroused American fears on
account of the intercontinental nuclear missiles based in its territory, to greater extent

than in the case of Russia itself, or the two
other "nuclear" republics that emerged from
the disintegration of the Soviet Union,
namely Ukraine and Byelorussia. Only tactical nuclear weapons targeted at the European
theater were sited in Ukraine. However, the
START I Treaty, signed between the United
States and the Soviet Union in 1991, was ratified by Kazakhstan in July 1992, before the
other three "nuclear" republics of the former
Soviet Union.

President Nazarbaev committed himself
to eliminate all nuclear weapons from his
country, by returning them to Russia, in the
course of a seven-year period as laid down
by the START Treaty. This, however, stipulated the dismantling of only half the weapons. In return, he obtained most-favored
nation status from the United States, which
brought with it preferential treatment for
his country's products in the American market. As early as July 1992, the entire tactical
nuclear arsenal of Kazakhstan was dismantled and sent to Russia. In December 1993,
the Kazakh parliament ratified the Nuclear
Non-Proliferation Treaty (NPT) of July 1,
1968, agreeing to denuclearize the country
in accordance with the Lisbon Protocol,
signed on May 26, 1992. This was completed
by April 1995.

As regards the position of the tactical
arsenal in 1991, it was spread throughout all
the Central Asian republics, with 75 missiles in Tajikistan, 75 in Kirgizstan, 105 in
Uzbekistan, and 125 in Turkmenistan. By
their nature, these were weapons that were
more widely distributed than the strategic weapons, and some—the warheads on
anti-aircraft missiles—were extremely light,
amounting only to 100 or 150 kilograms
(220 to 330 pounds). The risk that a war-
head might "disappear" was not negligible.
Further, even if a weapon with its detona-
tor removed was not operational, the plu-
tonium it contained could be of interest to
powers desiring to acquire nuclear weapons.

The withdrawal of these tactical weapons from the Muslim republics did not rule out possible "losses." Though the nuclear weapons were repatriated from Turkmenistan, the nuclear launch facilities were still there, together with their equipment.

On August 27, 1991, the president of Kazakhstan ordered the closure of the center at Semipalatinsk, 18,500 square kilometers in extent (7,250 square miles), which formerly served as the Red Army's principal nuclear testing facility. Public opinion was alerted to the issue by a film made by the renowned poet Oljas Suleimanov. The country continues to suffer human and ecological damage from the effects of 467 nuclear tests carried out since 1948, of which 124 were atmospheric and 343 underground. The center was finally closed down on July 29, 2000, when the last tunnels built for underground tests were destroyed.

Nonetheless, Kazakhstan and other Central Asian republics continue to have at their disposal certain elements of the nuclear chain. There are still trained personnel, some of local origin, as well as uranium extraction sites and processing facilities, including those at Shalovsk, in Tajikistan. Tajikistan, which was the source of the uranium for the construction of the first Soviet atomic bomb, has denied persistent rumors that it has sold uranium to Iran and to Libya, claiming that its mines are exhausted and that it does not possess the necessary facilities for uranium enrichment. Uzbekistan also has substantial uranium deposits. In the Kirgizstan region of Jalalabad, there is an opencast uranium mine next to the town of Malisov. The departure of Russian experts from this site threatens an ecological catastrophe, since mudslides that result from rainfall carry unrefined uranium ore into the rivers. Each year Kazakhstan produces hundreds of tons of uranium extracted from seven mines. It also maintains two factories for the production of uranium oxide and another for the

manufacture of nuclear fuel for reactors of the VVK and RMBK types. At Mangishlak, there is a nuclear power station used in water desalinization that utilizes a Bin 350 reactor. The enriched uranium needed for the operation of this reactor is currently imported from Russia.

Scientific literature currently in the public domain could facilitate the construction of nuclear devices. For terrorist use, prior testing would not be necessary, and nuclear material is stable and easily transportable, unlike chemical and biological agents. The theft of nuclear technology or material would certainly be feasible, since the former Soviet countries have low average incomes, opening the door to corruption. Within the CIS, there are ten nuclear sites, at which thousands of scientists and technicians have undergone a sharp fall in their standard of living since the disappearance of the Soviet Union. The guards who protect the perimeters of these sites earn only U.S.$200 per month. It is therefore understandable that in a difficult economic situation, it could be difficult to resist the blandishments of foreign agents offering plentiful hard cash.

The perpetrators of the attacks against the Americans in 1998 claimed that Osama Bin Laden has attempted to procure nuclear material from the CIS. Alternative radioactive sources, such as caesium 137 and cobalt 60, used in medicine, industry, and agriculture, are easily accessible. Used in conjunction with a conventional explosive, their contaminating effect would be catastrophic.

The "Umma Tameer-i Nau," a Pakistani NGO, has both military officers and former Pakistani government nuclear scientists as members. The organization is affiliated to the Al-Rasheed trust and is banned because of its links with Bin Laden. It operates in the region of Qandahar, Mullah Omar's home territory. Certain of its members are suspected of having sold secrets, and even nuclear material, to Al-Qa'ida militants.

The terrorist danger is being taken seriously. In the case of Pakistan, it is rumored that the American security services have prepared a plan to secure the 245 nuclear warheads the country possesses, in the event of the overthrow of President Musharraf.

ASSOCIATION FOR THE DEFENCE OF THE VALUES OF THE ISLAMIC REVOLUTION (IRAN)

ASSOCIATION OF MILITANT CLERGY (JAMIYAT RUHANIYAT MOBAREZ: JRM) (IRAN)

ASSOCIATION OF ISLAMIC YOUTH (ASSOCIATION DE LA JEUNESSE ISLAMIQUE: AJI) (MOROCCO)

AZZAM, ABDULLAH

Abdullah Azzam was born near Jenin in Palestine in 1941 and migrated to Jordan after the war of 1967. He was the prime mover of the "Islamic Legion" of the volunteers who came from all over the Middle East to fight at the side of the Afghan mujahidin against the Soviets in the 1980s. He was originally a schoolteacher and studied Islamic theology in Damascus, later obtaining a qualification in Islamic Law at Cairo's Al-Azhar university in 1973. In Egypt, he joined the Muslim Brotherhood and always kept his distance from the PLO, which he regarded as too nationalistic and secular. At the end of his studies he moved to Saudi Arabia, where he taught at King Abdulaziz University in Jeddah. Osama Bin Laden attended some of his courses.

In 1980, after the invasion of Afghanistan by Soviet troops, he went to Pakistan. At the time, he was at the time the only Islamist to give higher priority to the jihad against the Soviets than to the struggle against the Americans. Other Islamists, and above all the Iranians, saw the United States as the principal adversary, regarding the Soviets, if not as friends, then at least as pragmatic and temporary allies in their battle against American imperialism. Azzam elicited a favorable response from the Pakistani government, as well as from the Saudis, who were keen to mobilize Islam against communism, both to enhance its legitimacy and also to deflect the hostility of radical factions in the Middle East toward a more distant target. In the first instance, Azzam was appointed as a teacher at the Islamic University in Islamabad, which had often served as a cover for the recruitment of Islamic volunteers.

With the assistance of the Pakistani secret intelligence services (ISI), Azzam set up in Peshawar the Maktab al-Khidmat (Service Office), also known as the Beit al-Ansar (House of the Assistants). The role of this organization was to shelter and channel international militants and then to send them on to Afghanistan, assigning them to various mujahidin commanders identified for the most part by the ISI. The volunteers were first transported from their countries of origin to Jeddah in Saudi Arabia and then provided with travel documents; they were sent first to the Pakistani port of Karachi and then to Lahore.

Thousands of foreign volunteers, mainly Arabs (for the most part Algerians, Saudis, and Egyptians), spent periods of months this way in Afghanistan, developing the "jihadi" spirit and at the same time establishing close personal relationships. These would later serve as the basis of international networks. In 1987, Azzam was joined by Osama Bin Laden. Abdallah Anas (Boudjemaa Bounawas), one of the founders of the FIS in Algeria, became Azzam's brother-in-law.

Abdallah Azzam was widely respected in Afghanistan, and the role of a mediator among the Afghan factions came naturally to him, especially after the announcement of the Soviet withdrawal in February 1988.

Azzam had close links with the Pakistani Jamaat-i Islami, and with its Afghan counterpart, Hizb-i Islami, and in the spring of 1988 he undertook a journey into the Panjshir Valley to meet Commander Massoud for the first time. No doubt it was this that led to his death: he was killed on November 24, 1988 by a remote-controlled bomb along with his two sons. Against the will of Abdallah Anas, Osama Bin Laden took Azzam's place at the head of the Maktab al-Khidmat. In addition to his activities as a militant, Abdullah Azzam developed a theory of jihad as an obligation for Muslims. He ran the magazine *Jihad,* and after his death the Web site in his name developed ideas that were more radical than its founder's position.

AZERBAIJAN

Azerbaijan, with 8 million inhabitants, is basically a Shi'ite country. Its language and culture are Turkic. It became independent in 1991 after the fall of the Soviet Union. Public religious observance had been virtually suppressed during the Soviet period, with fewer than twenty mosques operating openly. The Soviet authorities set up a Spiritual Board of Muslims for the Caucasus to control Islam in Azerbaijan and other Muslim regions. There were, however, thousands of unofficial prayer rooms and clandestine Islamic groups. Over 90 percent of the population is Muslim. Seventy percent of these are Shi'ites and the rest are Sunnis. The Sunni Muslims are mainly Dagestanis, in the north of Azerbaijan. The post-Soviet history of Azerbaijan has been turbulent, with internal troubles and a persistent war with neighboring Armenia over the enclave of Nagorno-Karabakh. Azerbaijan has attracted Western attention because of its oil reserves. Since 2003, Azerbaijan's political leader has been President Ilham Aliyev, the son of the independent country's first president, Heydar Aliyev, a former Soviet politician.

Islamist movements have not until recently played much part in Azerbaijan, thanks to the suppression of all forms of dissent by the government. In 1997, the government suppressed the Islamic Party of Azerbaijan. In 2000, action was taken to crush a group that had taken the name of Jaishullah (The Army of God), which aimed to attack Western targets, including reportedly the U.S. Embassy. In June 2001, Haydar Aliyev set up a State Committee on Religious Affairs. Nevertheless, Islamist activity continued to increase. There were riots in June 2002 in Nardaran, which is regarded as a Shi'ite holy city thanks to the burial there of the wife of the seventh Imam. The ringleader, Alikaram Aliyev, was sentenced to six years in prison. In December 2003, there were further troubles when the government tried to close down a mosque where radical tendencies had been preached by a fiery local Shi'ite cleric, Ilqar Ibrahimoglu, whom some had called the Azeri Khomeini. In 2005, known associates of the Islamic Party were still banned from becoming election candidates.

There are also Sunni Islamist movements in Azerbaijan, which adopt a predictably Wahhabi and Salafi tone. Wahhabism has been evident in Chechnya, Dagestan, and northern Azerbaijan for a decade. Many profess to be followers of movements based abroad, and there is some suggestion of funds for Wahhabi institutions from Saudi Arabia. The first Salafi preachers came to Azerbaijan from other states in the Caucasus in the mid-1990s. They initially met with hostile attitudes among the local Sunni population that limited their appeal. Azerbaijan has strong Turkic links, and a school of Sunni Islam identified with a version of pan-Turkic nationalism had become popular. This movement, known as Nurcular and found by Said Nursi, an Islamic scholar who died aged eighty-four in 1960, is carefully monitored by the government.

In 1999, however, with the Chechen war beginning to expand, the Salafis gained more ground, though extremely few of their adherents were mainstream ethnic Azeris. An important factor was the arrival of Chechen refugees in Azerbaijan. Arab missionaries from the Gulf also began to make inroads, and the activities of Arab Muslim NGOs based in Saudi Arabia and the Gulf increased. In early 2001, the authorities arrested a number of Azerbaijan citizens who planned to go to fight in Chechnya. In 2002, an Azeri minister alleged that organizations in the Gulf countries had plans to expand Sunni Islamist activities in Azerbaijan. By 2003, there were said to be sixty-five new mosques under the control of the Salafis. A major mosque in Baku, the Abu Bakr mosque, funded by Kuwait and opened in 1997, has in recent years become highly popular, attracting worshippers in the thousands.

The Salafis make no secret of their political ambitions in Azerbaijan and the large-scale oil pipeline projects currently under construction may be subject to threat. International Sunni Islamist terrorist groups have threatened violent action, and Azerbaijan may be an easy target for those who wish indirectly to disrupt the Western economy. On the other hand, the country's Shi'ite identity is unshaken and the Salafis are numerically small. Though the authorities are vigilant, the likelihood is remote that the Salafis could cause more than short-lived disruption through terrorism.

Afghan Mujahidin in Azerbaijan

The arrival of Mujahidin from Afghanistan was an odd phenomenon. They first came in the latter part of 1993. Most were Sunni Tajiks loyal to Gulbuddin Hekmatyar. They ostensibly sought to fight for Azerbaijan in the war with Armenia. Their numbers have fluctuated between 500 and 2,500. Their journey was never easy: Iran refused them transit, seeking to limit the influence of Afghanistan on Muslim states to the west. They also appeared to be pursuing other goals. Some seemed to have come to settle scores with Azeris and other Afghans who had fought on the Soviet side in Afghanistan. They were in any case a disruptive influence. Thanks to American largesse, they were disproportionately well paid in a relatively poor country and this caused economic and social disruption. Communication was difficult as Tajiks speak Dari, a Persian dialect, and they were seen as poor fighters, with no stomach for continued battle. It was scarcely surprising that there was friction between them and the local people. Only in the case of an outright civil conflict in Azerbaijan between Sunnis and Shi'ites—an unlikely event—could they have gained any political foothold in the country.

Islamic Party (Azerbaijan)

By 1994 there were forty-five registered political parties in Afghanistan and fifteen others had applied for recognition. Only five of these were in fact properly constituted as political parties, and of these the Islamic Party, first registered in 1991, was one of the best organized. The power base of the party was within the Shi'ite community. The party was banned in 1997 and three of its leaders were sent to prison on charges of spying for Iran. These were Alikaram Aliyev, Vagif Gasymov, and Hajiaga Nuriyev. All were pardoned in 2000. The Islamic Party currently claims a membership of around ten thousand. In 2000, it formed an electoral bloc to contest elections, but a ban on electoral participation was imposed on former known members of the Islamic Party. The ban on Nuriyev was still in force in 2005. In 2006, Nuriyev spoke out against what he said were scurrilous comments made about the Islamic Party by the government and blamed them on the influence of the United

States. He also complained that the authorities were attempting to link the Islamic Party with the Salafi Wahhabis and had alleged that his organization was unpatriotic. The Islamic Party also continues to reject all suggestions that it represents Shi'ite Iran, though party officials acknowledge that they recognize the spiritual authority of the Iranian Ayatollahs.

Tawbah (Repentance) (Azerbaijan)

The "Tawbah Society" was established in 1985 by Hajji Abdul Islami. It was a predecessor of the Islamic Party and many of the figures associated with the Islamic Party had previously been members of it. It made very ambitious claims regarding the size of its membership. It was largely nonpolitical, demanding observance of the basic principles of Islam from the relatively lax population of Azerbaijan. It perceived its role as the reinforcement of morality and the proselytization of Muslims to join its ranks. It claimed to be tolerant of non-Muslims and in 1992, after Azerbaijan's independence, Abdul Islami was imprisoned for having supported the communists. Freed in 1993, he went to Moscow for medical treatment. On his return, he attempted without success to rebuild the movement. On May 9, 1994, the Sheikh ul-Islam (the official head and government appointed leader of the Islamic faith in Azerbaijan) installed Abdul Islami as imam of the Hussein Mosque in Baku. Though he claimed to recognize the spiritual authority of the Iranian Ayatollahs, he demanded the reunification of Azerbaijan with the Azeri part of Iran, which earned him the hostility of Iran. In due course more ideological members of the Tawbah Society mainly joined the Islamic Party.

BAHRAIN

Bahrain is unique among the Gulf states in its confessional makeup. Shi'ites make up at least 60 percent of the island's population, and possibly as much as 75 percent. It is also unusual because of its transformation in February 2002 into a kingdom under the sovereignty of Sheikh Hamad Bin Issa Al Khalifa, who succeeded his father in 1999. Reforms and political liberalization have been intended to lead to the return of parliamentary activity, and the government attempted to conciliate the Shi'ite community. In May 2000, successful municipal elections gave the credibility of the authorities a boost, when Shi'ite Islamist groups took twenty-three seats out of fifty, while Sunni Islamists took twenty seats, seven seats remaining in the hands of independents with links to the ruler. The left wing, the Arab nationalists, and women took no seats.

However, the credibility of the democratic process was put to a further test with the parliamentary elections of October 2002 when the Shi'ite opposition boycotted the election. Of the forty members of Parliament elected on this occasion, only twelve were Shi'ites, all businessmen who stood as independents. No women were elected, though Sheikh Hamad appointed four women to the advisory shura council. A planned opposition conference in February 2004 was aborted when the authorities banned most participants from entering the country.

Shi'ite Islamism has traditionally been linked with dissidence in Bahrain, where the Shi'ite population has waged a campaign of opposition to the Al Khalifa dynasty. In 1977, the Islamic Front for the Liberation of Bahrain set up in London by Hadi al-Madrasi—who was of Iranian origin—began to militate for an Islamic state on the model devised by the Iranian mullahs. Other activist parties such as Hezbollah backed this idea, as well as Al-Dawa al-Islamiyya, a Shi'ite organization formed in Iraq.

In 1982, Abdul Jamri, a prominent Shi'ite dignitary and a former member of the parliament in 1975, launched the Bahrain Freedom Movement (BFM) to advocate a more moderate and community-oriented style of political action. Sheikh Jamri was detained from 1993 because of his activities, and there are allegations that he was maltreated in prison. He was released in 1999 after the succession of Sheikh Hamad to the throne. Opposition political activity in Bahrain has centered round this religious leader and his son Mansur, the spokesman of the BFM in London.

Between 1994 and 1998, the emirate was the scene of violent disturbances when dozens of people were killed and wounded, and many were imprisoned for political reasons. However, the death of Sheikh

Issa in 1999 and the succession to power of Sheikh Hamad saw the start of a process of liberalization, notable for the adoption of a "National Action Charter." Sheikh Hamad initiated what he hoped would be a process of reconciliation between the regime and the Shi'ite opposition.

In the context of the new political situation, and since the activity of political parties in Bahrain was now in theory subject to no legal restraint, the opposition set up political organizations. Shi'ite Islam was represented by the "Association for National Reconciliation" under the leadership of Sheikh Jamri; among its influential members were Abdul Wahhab Hussein and Hassan Mushami. Nevertheless, the London-based diehards of the "Bahrain Freedom Movement" continued to criticize and condemn the authorities.

Sunni Islamism in Bahrain is linked to the Muslim Brotherhood. Two groups represent this tendency: the "National Islamic Forum" and the "Association for Islamic Education." One of the latter's leaders is Sheikh Mohammed Khaled. Meanwhile, the Arab Nationalists and the former pro-Iraqi Baathists gravitate toward the "Forum" of the Arab nationalist community, whose leaders are Abdul Rahman al-Naimi, and Rasul Jashi.

Bahrain, which is connected to mainland Saudi Arabia by a causeway, takes a more liberal attitude than does the Saudi Kingdom to expatriate Westerners. Alcohol is permitted under certain restrictions, and women are permitted to wear Western dress. It has served as a retreat for expatriates from the strict Saudi system. However, following the attacks on Westerners in Saudi Arabia in 2004, Bahrain also began to appear to some extent unsafe. Suspected Islamic militants were arrested in June 2004 and accused of planning attacks on Western-related targets, but they were released for lack of evidence. Bahrain serves as the base for the U.S. Fifth Fleet, which in July 2004 evacuated more

than a thousand dependents and nonessential staff. The United States also advised civilians to leave.

BALKAN ISLAM

The Balkan states are a mosaic of diverse religious communities. Islam, the Orthodox Churches, and Roman Catholicism are the principal confessions, together with handfuls of Armenian Christians, Protestants, and Jews. The Ottoman Turkish conquest began in the fourteenth century, but it was not until the seventeenth century that substantial Muslim populations first made their appearance in Albania, Macedonia, and Bulgaria. Because of the solidarity of the religious communities in the Balkans, the Muslims effectively came to be a nationality of their own. The post-World War II communist regime in Yugoslavia still described one of its nationalities as the "Muslims of Bosnia."

Balkan Muslims became a substantial part of the population, living among or in proximity to their Christian neighbors. Since the Ottoman conquest, the population of Bosnia-Herzegovina had consisted of a land owning class of Slavs converted to Islam, who were collaborators of the occupying power, and a Serbian Orthodox peasantry. Islamization had taken some time to take root, but had already persisted for several centuries. Albania had become predominantly Muslim in Ottoman times, with 70 percent Muslims, 20 percent Orthodox, and 10 percent Catholic. In neighboring Kosovo, the geographical heart of Serbian culture, the figures are even more striking. Ninety percent of the population is Muslim, according to figures just before the outbreak of the war. Finally, in Macedonia, Muslim Albanians make up almost a quarter of the population.

Though the Muslims may have in a sense become a nationality in the Balkans, religion became a factor in the wars in Bosnia, Kosovo, and Albania after the break up of Yugoslavia and the onset of communal competition for resources. Osama Bin Laden's Afghans offered their services on a number of occasions both to the Albanians and to the Kosovars of the independence movement, the UCK, who declined the offer. In 2001, Egyptian Islamists also came to Tirana to put their experience as "mujahidin" at the disposal of the Islamist cause. Other Islamists have individually become involved as fighters or as operatives for the Muslim NGOs who came to strengthen the Muslim community. Middle Eastern Islamist saw the Balkan Muslims as falling away form the faith and made efforts to re-Islamize the population. Their involvement rendered all the more bitter the intercommunal conflict in which the peoples of the Balkans had become embroiled thanks to the breakdown of earlier political arrangements.

BANGLADESH

Bangladesh became an independent state after the War of Independence of 1971, when India assisted what had been the eastern part of Pakistan to become an independent state. Pakistan ceased hostilities on December 16, 1971 and Sheikh Mujib Rahman, the head of the Awami League, led the country to independence in 1972. Sheikh Mujib and his family were murdered in an army coup in 1975. His daughter, Sheikh Hasina Wajed, was by chance abroad and survived. She was still in 2007 the head of the Awami League, which remains in opposition. Bangladesh's first military leader was General Ziaur Rahman (universally known as Zia). He was assassinated in 1981. His successor was General Hussein Ershad. Ershad's most controversial act was to push through a constitutional amendment in 1988 making Islam the official religion of Bangladesh. He

resigned in 1990. In 1991, he was imprisoned. In 1991, the Bangladesh National Party came to power in the country's first real election, led by Begum Khalida Zia, the widow of General Zia. In 1994, a Bangladeshi woman writer, Taslima Nasreen, was threatened with death by Islamists after extremist clerics pronounced a "fatwa" against her because of the supposedly anti-Islamic contents of her book "Lajja" (Shame), published in 1993. Chatra Shibir, the student wing of Jamaat-i Islami, was especially active against her and she went into exile for her own safety.

From 1991, Sheikh Hasina and Begum Khalida Zia at the head of their respective political formations, contested the political leadership of Bangladesh. The feud between the country's two female leaders was bitter and personal. Meanwhile, General Ershad was provisionally released in 1997. His Jatiya Party continued to contest elections, but split into several factions and included some candidates identified with the Islamic National Unity Front. In February 2001, in the run up to the elections of February 27, the caretaker government launched a crackdown on the Islamists. Maulana Azizul Haq and Mufti Fazlul Haq Amini, leading figures in a hard line Islamic group, and Islami Oikya Jote were arrested. Violence between the police and Islamists had followed a government decree banning the issue of "fatwas" or Islamic edicts. After September 11, 2001, there were anti-American demonstrations in Dhaka, and expressions of support for Osama Bin Laden.

Numerous incidents followed, including some assassinations, many of which appeared to be linked to Chatra Shibir, the student wing of Jamaat-i Islami. On August 17, 2005, almost five hundred small bomb attacks were carried out across Bangladesh within the space of half an hour, including some at Dhaka's international airport. Other attacks were on government buildings and major hotels. The devices were small and few deaths were caused. Jamaatul Mujahideen Bangladesh was apparently responsible. This formation had been officially banned since February 2005 along with another Islamist group, Jagarat Muslim Bangladesh, after attacks on NGOs operating in the country. The clear intention appeared to be to discredit the democratic system in Bangladesh and to make the strength of the Islamist dissidents clear. The strategy of the Islamists appears to have been to operate simultaneously within the legal political system, while also launching terrorist attacks. Prime Minister Khalida Zia was reluctant to admit to the existence of violent Islamists in Bangladesh, but the concerted attacks of 2005 obliged her to recognize the phenomenon. Some observers believe the flight of Islamists from Afghanistan after 2003 contributed to the heightening of tension in Sough Asian countries, including Bangladesh.

The mainstream politics of Bangladesh have in any case always been turbulent. In 2007, as a new election was awaited, the Bangladesh Nationalist Party (BNP), which formed the last government, and the opposition Awami League found it difficult to agree on fair conditions in which the election could be held. In the meantime, Islamist politics continued to play a marginal but potentially significant electoral role. In the 2001 elections, each of the two major parties won over 22 million votes, with the BNP scoring a slight majority. Jamaat-i Islami Bangladesh is the major legal Islamic party, but in 2001 took only 2.4 million votes. For the 2007 elections, Sheikh Hasina went into an electoral pact with another Islamic party, Khelafat Majlis, and also made an agreement with General Ershad's Jatiya faction. There were claims that Khelafat Majlis had links with international Islamist terror organizations including Al-Qa'ida, and some of its activists were said to have been in Afghanistan. A newly significant component of Bangladesh's Islamist scene is Harkat-ul Jihihad al-Islami, known as "Hujib." Hujib has expressed sympathy with the Taliban and apparently aspired to become linked more closely with Al-Qa'ida. Other Islamist groups resort to local action to enforce compliance with so-called Islamic standards in dress and behavior. Though electoral results have tended to indicate that support for Islamism is numerically small, its adherents are making every effort to impose their views.

Jamaat-e Islami (Bangladesh)

Jamaati-i Islami is an Islamist formation that functions as a political party in Bangladesh and holds seats in Parliament. It is an offshoot of Pakistan's Jamaat-i Islami, which was set up in 1941 by Abu Ala Mawdudi (1903–1979). Mawdudi sought the establishment of an Islamic state and in any case rejected the idea of bringing into existence any new state that could be "an obstacle to the development of the Islamic Umma." After the declaration of Bangladeshi independence in March 1971, the local wing of Jamaat-i Islami was banned and its leading figure, Golam Azam, was stripped of his nationality. He subsequently went went into exile in Pakistan, also visiting Britain and a number of Arab countries. He stayed in Pakistan until 1978 when General Zia allowed him to return to Bangladesh. Though for a time it was constrained to operate in secret, Jamaat-i Islami had been officially recognized in 1976. It adopted a policy of operating within the political system and took part in the 1979 elections, calling itself the Democratic Islamic Alliance.

Golam Azam's Bangladeshi nationality was restored in 1994, and he resumed his official role and functions as head of Jamaat-i Islami. After the resignation of Ershad, he played a significant political role in the parliamentary elections of 1991. During the period from 1991 to 1996, when the Bangladesh National Party (BNP) was in power,

Azam and the Jamaat again faced legal problems. The movement's highly active student wing, Chatra Shibir, played a leading part in the campaign against Taslima Nasreen, the Bengali woman writer and intellectual, who was accused of hurting the religious sensibilities of the population. After a poor performance in the elections of 1996, Jamaat-i Islami went into alliances with other factions, including the BNP. In the elections of 2001, it won eighteen seats and appeared to be making an appeal to a new constituency at a time of political turbulence when there was endemic violence, with particular threats to the country's Hindu minority.

BANNA, HASSAN AL- (EGYPT)

Hassan al-Banna was born in 1906 in the small town of Mahmudiyya in the Nile Delta. His father, a prayer leader at the local mosque, had studied at Al-Azhar. From the age of sixteen Hassan al-Banna studied at the famous Dar-al-Ulum Islamic college in Cairo, which was set up under the Egyptian monarchy to train qualified religious teachers from backgrounds different from the products of the Quranic schools. At the Dar al-Ulum, Banna read the works of the Egyptian Salafi movement, including Muhammad Abduh, who combined Salafism with social reformism. He was also influenced by the Syrian Islamic thinker, Rashid Rida, who edited an influential magazine, *Al-Manar* (*The Minaret*), published in Cairo until 1935. In 1927, at the age of twenty-one, Banna became an elementary school teacher in Ismailiya, on the Suez Canal. Just a year later, in 1928, he set up the Muslim Brotherhood, whose aim was to apply Islamic law and to work for the institution of a government that would be governed by Quranic precepts.

Hassan al-Banna was a charismatic leader and a gifted orator and as a mentor was both obeyed and respected. In 1945, each active member of the Brotherhood swore the following oath: "I promise before God the Highest and Greatest to follow strictly the message of the Muslim Brotherhood, to fight for it, to live according to the rules of its members, to have total confidence in its leader and to obey implicitly at all times, in good times and in bad." Under Hassan Banna's leadership, the Muslim Brotherhood initially confined itself to the dissemination of the good word and to charitable acts. During the first two decades of the Brotherhood's existence, from 1928 to 1948, it underwent headlong expansion and untrammeled growth.

The war of 1948 in Palestine brought to a head the division between King Farouk and the Muslim Brotherhood, many of whose militants fought in the conflict. The Brotherhood agitated for Egypt's full mobilization on the side of the Palestinians. At this historic moment, Banna lost the sympathy of the government, which announced a ban on his organization in December 1948. The Brotherhood's clandestine faction assassinated Nuqrashi Pasha, the Egyptian prime minister of the day, on whose orders the organization had been banned. Banna was later the target of reprisals and was in turn murdered on February 12, 1948, putatively by a government agent. Banna's death, however, brought no more than a pause in the development of the organization, which spread throughout the Arab world and elsewhere, and was in time to become the first real international Islamist organization.

The Fifty Principles of Hassan al-Banna's Program

(The Arabic text appears in *Memoirs of the Imam Shahid Hassan al-Banna*, 2nd edition, no place of publication, 1386/1966.)

These precepts are a starting point for the consideration of specialists in the fields concerned, and are not intended to encompass all the needs of the Umma, or all the factors which may contribute to the Renaissance (Nahda). Some of these issues may in practice encounter great obstacles, and will require patience, wisdom and perseverance. Collectively, they constitute an ideal for the aspirations of the Muslim Brothers.

SECTION 1: The Field of Politics and Law

1. Overcome political divisions and direct the political impetus of the *umma* toward a single objective.
2. Reform the law in conformity with Islamic law, particularly as regards infractions and penalties.
3. Strengthen the army and increase the numbers of youth groups, educating them to wage the holy war.
4. Strengthen the links between all Muslim states, and particularly between the Arab countries, to lay the foundation for a real and practical approach to the lost caliphate.
5. Disseminate the Islamic ideas in administrative circles, so that citizens as a whole feel themselves called to apply the principles of Islam.
6. Examine the personal behavior of officials, drawing no distinction between their public and private roles.
7. Schedule the operations of the administration, in summer and in winter, so that the hours of religious observance are respected, putting an end to nocturnal laxity.
8. Abolish the needs for gratuities and incentives, and ensure that the basis should be efficiency and the application of the law.
9. Activities should be subjected to the values and precepts of Islam; the management of hospitals and prisons should not contradict these principles; working hours should be arranged to respect the hours of prayer and official ceremonies should also respect Islamic principles.
10. Certain military and administrative positions should be entrusted to graduates of Al-Azhar.

SECTION 2: The Social and Scientific Field

1. Introduce the population to respect for morals and to make public the requirements of the law, showing firmness in the application of penal sanctions in relation to moral issues.
2. Examine the question of women, bringing into play both modernity and authenticity in pursuit of the principles of Islam. This question, the most important social issue, must not be relinquished to mere publicists or ill-intentioned opinion.
3. Suppress prostitution in both its discreet and overt forms, and to view fornication, whatever its circumstances, as a serious crime requiring legal sanction.
4. Abolish games of chance of all kinds.
5. Combat the consumption of alcohol and drugs, forbidding them and preserving the Umma from their serious consequences.
6. Deprecate exhibitionism of all kinds, demanding that women should behave respectably, in particular teachers, schoolgirls and students, doctors, and so on.
7. Reexamine the way in which girls are taught, paying attention to the need to differentiate between how girls are taught from the methods employed in the case of boys at all levels of instruction.
8. Forbid the coeducation of boys and girls, regarding all close contact as a crime liable to be punished.
9. Encourage in every way marriage and procreation, providing legislation that safeguards the family and the couple and which conduces to the overcoming of obstacles to marriage.
10. Close dance-halls, which are places of licentiousness, forbidding dancing and all physical contact between men and women.
11. Supervise closely the theater and the cinema, selecting plays fit to be performed and films fit to be shown.
12. Rigorously examine and filter popular songs before they are allowed to be heard.

13. Restrict carefully what is broadcast on the radio, scrutinizing carefully the content of talks and subjects under discussion. Radio should be used as means to promote civic and moral education.

14. Ban sensational novels, as well as books that cast doubt on the faith and pervert the soul. Forbid also all publications tending to corrupt morals that may excite improper desires.

15. Take control of places of leisure, ending the uncontrolled behavior and immorality that prevail within them.

16. Set opening and closing hours for cafés, exercising vigilance over those who work in them and those who frequent them. Their customers should be guided toward more useful activities by discouraging them from wasting their time.

17. Make use of cafés as place to teach reading and writing: the more devout teachers and students will be of great help in attaining this objective.

18. Militate against practices detrimental to the economy at rituals connected with birth, marriage, and death, attempting to reform common practices in the general interest. The government should set an example.

19. Revive the role of the "hisba" [the moral police], punishing those who fail to respect the precepts of Islam, as well as those who fail to observe its requirements, such as the fasting month of Ramadan and the prayers, and also those who insult the faith.

20. Establish a link within the villages between the public schools and the mosques, in order to initiate the young into the habit of prayer and to encourage the old to take up the pursuit of knowledge.

21. Make religious teaching compulsory at all stages of education, including the university.

22. Encourage the teaching of the Quran in public and private schools, instituting a system whereby knowledge of the Quran in its entirety should be an obligatory condition for the granting of a qualification in religious

and literary studies. In other disciplines, a partial knowledge of the Quran will suffice.

23. Institute a consistent educational policy, aimed at the raising the level of education by bringing together all its branches, while taking into account the varying cultures present within the Umma, and devoting the primary level to the consolidation of civic and moral education.

24. Lay stress on the importance of the Arabic language at all stages of education. Primary education must be conducted in Arabic.

25. Emphasize the history and civilization of Islam and the history of the nation.

26. Take thought concerning the most effective means toward the progressive harmonization of styles of dress throughout the entire Umma.

27. Expunge foreign influence [i.e., Western influence] within households, especially as regards language, customs, and usages, and in the recruitment of teachers and nursemaids. Prefer Egyptianization in all its aspects, especially in the houses of the wealthier classes.

28. Direct the press toward the theme of virtue, encouraging authors and writers to discuss specifically Oriental Islamic issues.

29. Pay great attention to public health by means of the dissemination of health-oriented and preventive information. Increase the number of hospitals, doctors, and peripatetic clinics in order to facilitate access to care.

30. Pay special attention to the small villages, especially in relation to their amenities, their sanitation, and the purification of their water supplies. Pay attention also to culture and leisure activities.

SECTION 3: The Economic Field

1. Organize the collection and expenditure of the "zakat" [obligatory charitable giving] according to the rules of Islamic law, so that charitable organizations such as retirement homes and orphanages reap the benefit, as well as financing the armed forces.

2. Prohibit usury and take control of the activity of the banks. Call upon the government to set an example by renouncing interest deriving from its own activities, such as lending institutions, industrial banks, or others.

3. Initiate more economic schemes in order to provide work for unemployed citizens, while nationalizing foreign businesses.

4. Offer protection to the population from exploitation by businesses, which should be prohibited from the infringement of the rights of citizens. Obtain the greatest possible concession from business in the interests of the people.

5. Improve the economic situation of minor officials by increasing their salaries and paying bonuses in full, while reducing the salaries of senior officials.

6. Cut down the number of officials, restricting them to the most necessary areas. Work should be allotted equitably to officials, whose responsibilities should be precisely defined.

7. Promote a professional attitude in the fields of agriculture and industry, inculcating in farmers and workers the spirit of productivity.

8. Provide skills training to workers, improving their basic living conditions.

9. Exploit natural resources such as land lying fallow and abandoned mines.

10. Prioritize essential projects over those whose importance is secondary or less.

Source: General information office of the Muslim Brotherhood in Cairo

BASAYEV, SHAMIL

Shamil Basayev was born in 1965 in the village of Tsa-Vedeno, in Chechnya. In August 1991, he fought in Moscow in the defense of the Russian parliament against the instigators of the conservative coup. After carrying out his first armed operation, when he hijacked a transport plane to Turkey, he returned to the Caucasus in 1992 and joined the Azeri conflict with the Armenians in Nagorny Karabakh, and then took arms alongside the Abkhazian secessionists against the Republic of Georgia. After military training in Afghanistan in 1994, he returned to Chechnya, joining Dudaiev's struggle against the Russian-backed armed opposition. In 1996, he became the military leader of the Chechen forces. He enjoyed considerable popularity, and stood in the presidential elections of 1997 against Aslan Maskhadov. Maskhadov became president, however, with Basayev winning only 22.7 percent of the votes. A disagreement between Basayev and Maskhadov led him to leave the government and to side with the opposition.

In 1998, he set up the Council of Commanders, a collegiate body, and became president of the Islamist Congress in Chechnya and Daghestan. In August 1999, he and Commander Khattab allied themselves in a joint jihad, launching an armed raid into Daghestan. This attack precipitated the second Russian-Chechen war. On January 31, 2000, during the retreat from Grozny amid savage fighting, his right leg was amputated. Though viewed as a hero and a militant by many of his compatriots, Shamil Basayev is primarily an agitator, as witnessed by his 1999 Daghestan incursion. The Russian government disposed of Dzhokar Dudayev by using a missile that homed in on his mobile phone, but was unsuccessful in eliminating Basayev.

Basayev became one of the leading protagonists of Wahhabism in his region. He came from humble origins as a shepherd in the Caucasus mountains, but was a complex and apparently cultured figure who also claimed to be a devotee of poetry. He was responsible for a long series of terrorist attacks from 1999 onward in Moscow, elsewhere in Russia, and in the countries of the Caucasus, including

Chechnya. These included bomb attacks on apartment blocks in Moscow and other Russian cities in September 1999 (200 deaths), guerrilla attacks on Russian bases in Chechen in July 2000, the Moscow theater siege of October 2002 (129 deaths of hostages), a suicide bombing at Znamenskoe in Chechnya on May 2003 (59 deaths), a suicide bombing at Mozdork, in North Ossetia, in August 2003 (50 deaths), and suicide bombing on a Moscow subway train in February 2004 (at least 40 deaths). Since Beslan, he has claimed to be involved in other incidents in Chechnya and elsewhere in the Caucasus. He was apparently killed in an accidental explosion in Ingushetia in July 2006; an incident for which Russian forces claimed responsibility.

BEGHAL, DJAMEL

Djamel Beghal, a French national, was the putative head of an Islamist network suspected of planning attacks against U.S. interests in Paris. He was arrested at the end of July 2001 in the UAE city of Dubai and then extradited to France where he was imprisoned on October 1, 2001. His coconspirator Nizar Trabelsi, a Tunisian national and ex-soccer player, was apprehended in Belgium. Trabelsi, according to the charges leveled against him, had been delegated by Beghal to blow up the U.S. Embassy in Paris. The other members of Beghal's group, later identified by the French judicial authorities, were Kamel Daoudi, a computer specialist who was arrested in the British city of Leicester on September 25, 2001, Nabil Bounour, Yohan Bonté, and Jean-Marc Grandvizir.

BELGIUM

In Belgium, after the same pattern as France, Islam and Islamism took root in three stages. Initially, unqualified workers came to Belgium in the 1960s, intending only to remit money to their countries of origin to support their families. Religious observance was kept within the private sphere and went virtually unseen. In the second phase, from the mid-1970s, the second generation embarked on a process of social and economic integration through the establishment of small businesses. However, a situation of economic crisis and the emergence of unemployment led to withdrawal from economic life and the onset of a process of return to religion. This retreat to an identity centered round the issue of religion was simultaneously subjected to the influence of proselytizing movements from abroad that presented themselves as nonpolitical. The most meaningful and effective of these was Jamaat al-Tabligh, known in Belgium as "Faith and Practice." Though this movement denied all connection with political Islam, it was to bring about the re-Islamization of the Muslim community and its visibility. Tabligh was a challenge to the Islamic Center in Brussels, which it referred to as the seat of "government Islam," which was under the control of the Saudis. Tabligh brought about the early recognition of Islam by the Belgian government, which took place in 1974. This recognition related fundamentally to two issues. The first of these was the question of places of worship, together with the acceptance by the state of the payment of salaries and pensions for ministers of religion. The second issue was that of education, where the educational structure in force at the time in Belgium provided for government assistance to private religious schools, to which subventions were granted for the payment of teachers.

The third phase followed the completion of the process of re-Islamization. From the mid-1990s, politics took over the mosques and prayer rooms. Movements that adopted increasingly political interpretations of Islam quietly began to acquire more influence, under the pretext of introducing the language of morality into places of worship. Chief among these was the Muslim Brotherhood, especially its Syrian branch, led by Issam al-Attar, which had taken refuge at Aix-la-Chapelle after the Syrian government's suppression of the Muslim Brotherhood at Hama. Issam al-Attar was responsible for the establishment of a major prayer center in Brussels. The organization known as "Al-Tali'a al-Islamiya" (The Islamic Vanguard) employed the usual Muslim Brotherhood techniques, working through the intermediary of a group of social and political associations to encourage radicalism. Other associations were set up by the Egyptian Muslim Brotherhood, among Muslim workers and students, the Islamic assistance league, a humanitarian association for youth activities, Muslim Aid, and so on. The Muslim Brotherhood was careful to exclude all mention of violence from its language.

In the 1980s, the Islamic Revolution in Iran became a model for Muslims in Belgium. Other influences on Muslims with radical tendencies included the Afghan War and developments in Algeria, which stirred up emotions. The Afghan Services Office for the Mujahidin was well entrenched in Brussels. This was an offshoot of Hezb-i Islami, led by Gulbuddin Hekmatyar. As regards Algeria, what was at issue was no longer support for the families of martyrs, or the rhetoric of encouragement, but real systems of logistic support, or even the establishment of groups whose goal was to strike at Western countries that supported the Algerian government. After 1992, when the FIS (Islamic Salvation Front) was dissolved in Algiers, the front's leading publication, *Al-Munqidh* (*The Savior*), was published in Belgium, in a semi-clandestine way. A group known as the "Zaoui network," after Ahmed Zaoui, who was arrested in Belgium, was broken up in 1995. Zaoui was released under the supervision of the courts, but contrived to make his escape to Switzerland, where he was not pursued. The names of persons with links to the Zaoui network came up in connection with attacks carried out in the summer of that year in France.

Algeria, followed by Bosnia and Chechnya, gave fresh impetus to the Islamization of young Muslims in search of an identity. From 1998, this tendency led to the training camps of Afghanistan, by way of the leadership offered to the young by various Muslim associations and NGOs, which took place with some level of connivance on the part of the Taliban government and the Pakistani intelligence services (ISI). Those who answered the call were recruited in their countries of origin and were sent on through channels linked to the Muslim NGOs, often after a period in the United Kingdom, Malaysia, the United Arab Emirates, or Saudi Arabia. At Afghanistan's frontier with Pakistan, they were sent either to military training camps or to more sophisticated centers, where they were trained in explosives techniques or guerrilla warfare. Some went to the battlefront, where they fought alongside the Taliban, or to Chechnya. Others were sent back to Europe to become "sleepers."

The international nature of the networks of individuals who had returned from Afghanistan was revealed by the dismantling in 1998 of the network around Farid Mellouk. Mellouk was under investigation by the French police, but was arrested on March 5 in Belgium. He had undergone explosives training at a camp at Darunta in Afghanistan linked to Al-Qa'ida. Darunta was known to give a two-month course in the manufacture of explosives for terrorist attacks. Individuals of various nationalities were implicated, including Algerian, Tunisian, Moroccan, and French. The network specialized in the supply of false documents and was laying the groundwork for an armed Islamist movement to be known as "Al-Jama'a al-Islamiya al-Mujahida fi-l-Maghrib" (The Combatant

Islamic Group in the Maghreb). Explosives in the course of manufacture were discovered by the investigators and Mellouk was extradited to France. The Mellouk network was linked to the Algerian GSPC as well as to the Tunisian Islamists. Before its demise, it was very well established in Belgium and was directly in contact with Al-Qa'ida, especially through its leader, Sayf Allah Ben Hassine.

These transnational networks universally had links stretching throughout Europe. All were linked to Afghanistan by way of structures based in London, under the inevitable aegis of Abu Qatada. In the last report, what was unique in the development of Islamism in Belgium was its relationship with organized crime, a link intensified by the presence in Belgian prisons of hard-line Islamists who devoted themselves to preaching and recruitment.

BELHADJ, ALI (ALGERIA)

Ali Belhadj, whose family was originally from the Algerian administrative district (the Wilaya) of Béchar, was born in a refugee camp in Tunisia on December 16, 1956. He was the son of a fighter who died in Algeria's war of national liberation against France and was raised by his maternal grandfather. He spent his early years in Tunisia, after which his family moved to the quarter of Kouba in Algiers. His education did not proceed smoothly, but he eventually qualified as a teacher in 1979.

While completing his religious education, he met and then became a disciple of Sheikh Al Hachemi Sahnouni, the imam of the Salaheddine al-Ayoubi mosque in the Belcourt region of Algiers. It was at this point that he became a member of the group associated with Salafism in Algeria. As a preacher in the Al-Achour mosque, he also became acquainted with the circle around

Mustafa Bouyali and publicly declared allegiance to the jihad. He was arrested in 1983, tried, and sentenced to imprisonment by the State Security Court. In 1987, he was freed and placed for some months under house arrest at Ouargla. On his return to the capital, he once more made contact with Sheikh Sahnouni and, resuming his position as a preacher, built up a large following among Algeria's youth, thanks to his oratorical gifts that blended popular language with religious vocabulary.

During the disturbances of October 1988, Ali Belhadj on several occasions exhorted the population to rebel, and then took upon himself the role of negotiator, voicing the grievances of those rioters who were affiliated to the Islamic movement. Thanks to his charisma, and despite accusations both on the part of the authorities and from some Islamic leaders that he was indirectly responsible for the deaths of many of the rioters, he participated in the efforts that preceded the formation of the Islamic Salvation Front (FIS) [Front Islamique du Salut], then becoming a member of the leadership of the new organization. As a respected exponent of the tenets of Salafism, he became the editor of the weekly magazine *El-Hidaya,* established by Sheikh Sahnouni.

As the second in command of the organization, Belhadj was viewed by Algeria's military oligarchy as a figure unlikely to compromise: he never abandoned his opposition to democratic practices and accepted only with difficulty the option that the party might operate within the law. During the Gulf War of 1990–1991, with the agreement of some of the other leaders, Ali Belhadj laid down an anti-American line, accepting the risk of alienating the party from the support of its Saudi paymasters. A significant decision he took was the dispatch of three hundred Algerian volunteers to fight with the Iraqi forces. At other times during this brief period he appeared to be sizing up the "military" abilities of his organization, when on two occasions in January 1991 he called out his supporters to demonstrate. Nevertheless, Ali Belhadj took part in negotiations on a number of occasions during the strike of May/June 1991. Though initially he accepted the principle of compromise following a meeting on June 7 with the prime minister, he issued a call to revolt only days later, in the belief that the regime could be overthrown.

On June 30, 1991, he was arrested together with Abassi Madani and five other members of the Consultative Council. He was imprisoned and on July 5, 1992, he was sentenced by the military tribunal at Blida to serve twelve years imprisonment. However Ali Belhadj, who is in any case seriously ill, has since his imprisonment played only a marginal political role. Apparently as a result of the policy of national reconciliation inaugurated by President Bouteflika, he was released on July 2, 2003. He and his fellow detainee Abassi Madani, who was allowed to leave prison in 1997 due to ill health and has since been under house arrest, are subject to restrictions amounting to a complete ban on all political activity or participation in public life.

BESLAN

On September 1, 2004, Islamist terrorists opposed to the government of Russia occupied a school in the town of Beslan in North Ossetia, a southern republic that forms part of Russia. On September 4, the incident came to an end with an appalling massacre as the security forces stormed the school, taking 1,200 people hostage. More than three hundred died, including children, parents, and teachers, and hundreds more were injured. The population of North Ossetia is mixed, with 40 percent Muslims and 60 percent Christians. Beslan is a relatively new settlement, with an unusually high Muslim population of 70 percent and just 30 percent of Christians. North Ossetia has been a loyal part of Russia and has not suffered the troubles of other states in the Caucasus. The appalling upheavals of neighboring Chechnya, where Muslim separatists have been struggling against Russia for independence since 1991, have been constantly in the public eye. There have also been less publicized disturbances in neighboring Ingushetia.

On September 17, responsibility for the school siege was claimed by Shamil Basayev, the Chechen rebel leader. He said the demand of the hostage takers was an end to the Chechen conflict, with the withdrawal of Russian forces from Chechnya. Basayev said that if Russia had fulfilled this condition, Chechnya would have remained part of the Russian sphere of influence. He also demanded the resignation of President Putin. Basayev denied that Chechen rebels were receiving money from Al-Qa'ida. He said the cost of the operation had been just over ten thousand dollars, and that no Al-Qa'ida support had been necessary. Initial reports of the involvement of Arabs and other foreign nationals seem to have been misplaced, however. The only surviving terrorist was Nurpasha Kulayev, a Chechen builder, who was sentenced to life imprisonment. His testimony indicates that the terrorist base was in Ingushetia and that he was aware only of the involvement of nationals of regional countries.

Basayev has been responsible for a sustained campaign of terrorism in Moscow, elsewhere in Russia, and in the neighboring state of the Caucasus as well as in Chechnya itself. While speaking about Beslan, he also claimed responsibility for a suicide bombing in Moscow on August 31 and the downing of two Russian passenger aircraft on August 24. Chechen terrorists have carried out a range of other incidents both in Moscow and in the Caucasus. Forty died in a suicide attack in a Moscow subway train in February 2004, and in August 2003, fifty-four were killed in an attack in North Ossetia when a bomb-packed truck was driven into a military hospital. The most spectacular Chechen attack in Moscow had been the siege of a theater in Moscow in October 2002, where 700 were held hostage for three days and 170 people (including 41 terrorists) died. The previous occurrence that bore the greatest resemblance to Beslan was a siege led by Basayev in person in the south Russian town of Budyonnovsk in 1995, where 166 hostages were killed as Russian security forces stormed the building.

Since the attacks, authorities have brought Muslim activity in North Ossetia under official state control with the institution of a Muslim Spiritual Directorate, headed by a ex-police official. The incident was a blow to the government of President Putin, which found itself widely criticized in Russia for what was seen as bad handling of the incident that caused so many deaths.

BIN LADEN, OSAMA

Osama Bin Laden was born in Riyadh in 1957. His father, Mohammed bin Laden, was an engineer of Yemeni origin who had made his fortune working for the Saudi royal family. Mohammed bin Laden was the father of some fifty children by a number of mothers. Osama, his brother Ahmed, and a sister who died in 2000 were the children of a Syrian woman from the Alawi community. He lived a life normal for the scion of a wealthy family. He attended an exclusive private school in Jeddah, and from 1976 to 1978 he studied business management and economics at King Abdulaziz University in Jeddah. His interest in Islam had already begun to take shape at school, and at university he met Abdullah Azzam, a Palestinian associated with the Muslim Brotherhood, who

was to become the leading foreign ideologist of the jihad in Afghanistan. Bin Laden attended some of Azzam's courses in Islamic law.

In 1980, after Bin Laden had completed his studies, he set up an organization known as the the Beit al-Ansar ("The House of the Companions": a reference to the companions of the Prophet). The organization recruited volunteers to fight in Afghanistan; these volunteers came from a number of countries including Saudi Arabia, Egypt, Turkey, Yemen, Algeria, and Lebanon. He used his own funds, since he had by now received a family inheritance that gave him substantial wealth, but also benefited from help from the governments of Saudi Arabia and Pakistan.

In 1979, the United States wished to set up a discreet channel for the transfer of arms to the Afghan resistance against the country's communist government, and Bin Laden was contacted for this purpose by Saudi Arabia's Prince Turki bin Faisal. The two met in Istanbul in 1982. Bin Laden was entrusted with the task of purchasing arms and delivering them to the Afghan mujahidin, which he did through the intermediary of a number of organizations he established, which were either purely or virtually intended to serve as a cover for his operations. Arms purchases, funded both by Washington and by Riyadh, reached the level of $1.2 billion a year. The arms were sent by way of Sudan, Bosnia, and Turkey. The U.S. aim was to of course to expel the Soviets from Afghanistan, but Washington also wanted to control the routes of future oil and gas pipelines between Central Asia and the Indian Ocean. By now trusted by his paymasters, Bin Laden went in person to Afghanistan to divide up the petrodollar bounty between the anti-communist Afghan factions, who were often also the rivals of each other. The friendship he struck up at this time with Gulbudding Hekmatyar was a fruitful one. The Afghan warlord exercised sole control over the poppy crops of Helmand province. Bin Laden set up a branch of the opium trade to supply the West. In addition, he used his own civil engineering companies to build up the infrastructure in Afghanistan, including roads, hospitals, and underground shelters, which won him much local kudos. In 1980, Abdullah Azzam set up the Maktab al-Khidamat (Services Office) in the Pakistani city of Peshawar to organize the operations of the foreign mujahidin. Bin Laden was one of its main financial backers and ran the logistics side of the office's operations between 1982 and 1984. Between 1984 and 1986 he traveled widely in the Arab world, raising funds.

A new phase began in 1986 when Bin Laden went to fight in person in Afghanistan, apparently for the first time. He took part in battles at Jaji in 1986 and at Shaban in 1987. However, what principally contributed to the founding myth of the future Al-Qa'ida was the battle of the "Lion's Den" (Masadah) when a group of Arab fighters, including Bin Laden, held off a Soviet offensive for seven days before withdrawing. The legend of Bin Laden's prowess dates from that day. Al-Qa'ida, literally "The Base," which was to become the natural focus for the Arab mujahidin, was established in November 1987. That was also the date when Bin Laden first made contact with other Islamic movements in the Arab world, in Egypt, Palestine, Algeria, and Yemen. Those who were to become his close associates also began to emerge at this time, including the Palestinian Abdullah Azzam, whose responsibility was religious training, and the Iraqi engineer Mohammed Saad, who was responsible for logistics.

However, it was from the ranks of the Egyptian movement that Bin Laden was to find many of his comrades in arms, who were drawn from the Gama'a Islamiyya and Islamic Jihad. Foremost among them was Ayman al Zawahiri, who, after the Gulf War, was to develop the military wing of Islamic Jihad, setting up the Talai' al-Fath (Vanguard of Victory) and would later reemerge in Iraq. Zawahiri, who had been implicated in the assassination of the Egyptian President Anwar Sadat, was a member of Bin Laden's inner circle and was a former member of the Gama'a Islamiyya. He had been trained as a doctor. Other close associates of Bin Laden were Ahmed Ibrahim al-Najjar, Osman Khaled Samaan, Ahmed Mustafa Nawa'a, Osman Ali Ayyub, Mustafa Hamza, Hussein Shmeit, Adel Said Abdel Quds, Yasser Tawfiq al-Sirri, and Osama Rushdi al-Khalifa, who was later to marry a daughter of the Algerian Islamist leader, Abassi Madani.

Bin Laden took over the operational direction of the Maktab al-Khidamat after Abdullah Azzam's death in 1989. This was a moment when activity was at a low ebb, since the mujahidin were disheartened by their failure to overthrow Najibullah's communist regime in Kabul, even after the withdrawal of the Soviet troops from Afghanistan. During the occupation of Kuwait by the Iraqis in 1990 and 1991, Bin Laden went to Saudi Arabia, offering to put his Islamic militants at King Fahd's disposal to drive the Iraqis out. He also pleaded in vain that Western troops should not be brought in. His vehement opposition to the West dates from this era.

The Saudi authorities watched him carefully and banned him from leaving the country. At the same time, however, they encouraged him to pursue the jihad by supporting the Islamists of North Yemen against South Yemen's communist regime. From his temporary base in Saudi Arabia, he helped set up a jihadist group in South Yemen, which was later run by Tariq al-Fadhli. Bin Laden eventually left Saudi Arabia in 1991 for Sudan, which was at that time under the de facto control of Hassan al-Turabi, a charismatic Islamist leader. There he set up his import-export company, Wadi al-Aqiq, which served as an umbrella for his business enterprises, and also established a construction company, "Al-Hijra for Construction and Development," in partnership with Sudan's ruling National Islamic Front party. In Khartoum, he briefly enjoyed a virtual monopoly over construction and was in particular responsible for the construction of both a new airport at Port Sudan and a 750-mile highway from Port Sudan to Khartoum. He also ran the Taba investment company and the Al-Shamal Islamic Bank, as well as built up a major agricultural project near Khartoum. No doubt his activities also included the raising of funds, and he also watched closely the U.S. intervention in Somalia in 1992, where he is said to have played a part in the organization of attacks against the American forces.

In February 1993, a number of his associates were implicated in the first attack on the World Trade Center in New York, when six people were killed. It was at this stage that Bin Laden first began to be viewed as a terrorist by the Americans. In 1994, his attacks on Saudi Arabia escalated to a level where he was stripped of his Saudi nationality and was—at least officially—disowned by his family. It was at this time that Bin Laden set up the Committee for Advice and Reform (see below). A year later, Bin Laden took part in the Arabic and Islamic People's Conference in Khartoum, where he contacted the leading figures in Islamist movements, foremost among which were the Palestinian movements, Hamas, and Islamic Jihad.

In 1996, in an effort to improve relations with the West, Sudan decided to rid itself of various radical elements resident in its territory. The terrorist "Carlos" was handed over to the French. On two separate occasions, the Sudanese offered to hand Bin Laden over to the Americans, but each time Washington responded that he should be deported to Saudi Arabia. In the end, in the spring of 1996, Bin Laden left the country and returned to Afghanistan. He and his close entourage were flown to Jalalabad, which was then under the control of Hajji Qader, who was an associate of Massud. There, relying once more on Bin Laden's financial resources, they set up a residential compound outside the town. These events were probably the spark for Bin Laden's antipathy toward Muslim regimes, even those such as Saudi Arabia and Sudan, who proclaimed themselves to be Islamic. Bin Laden concluded that such states would always prioritize their national interests above the interests of the Muslim community, the umma. Bin Laden also maintained his links with the Saudi Wahhabi Sheikhs opposed to the Saudi government, including such opposition figures such as Hawali and Auda as well as members of the Saudi religious establishment.

In September 1996, when the Taliban captured Kabul, Bin Laden rapidly established contact with Mullah Omar, the Taliban leader, striking up a good relationship with him from the start. Mullah Omar gave Bin Laden responsibility for the organization of all the foreign volunteers on Afghan soil, with only the Pakistanis retaining their autonomy. The Arabs lived in residential compounds and camps apart from the Afghan population, with whom there was a degree of friction. At this stage, Bin Laden began to develop more fully Al-Qa'ida's organizational structure, and relationships between fighters were transformed into personal relationships, for example with the marriage of a son of Bin Laden to the daughter of his lieutenant Mohammed Atef.

His influence over the Taliban appeared strong, though the nature of his personal relationship with them remains obscure. His links were closest with Mullah Omar. One of Mullah Omar's sons married a daughter of Bin Laden, while Bin Laden himself married Mullah Omar's daughter.

Bin Laden also brought the Uzbek Islamic Movement into Al-Qa'ida and pressed for the radicalization of the Taliban movement. Backed by his Arab "Afghans," he continued to run networks that he had set up. According to the then director of the CIA, the budding terrorist already had at his disposal "a secret army of ten thousand men trained in his camps," of which a dozen were in the region of Qandahar. As the financial backer of the jihad, he ran a group of organizations and NGOs, of which some had their bases in the Pakistani city of Peshawar. He used the ramifications of these organizations to sustain the Sunni Islamic revolution around the world. His influence extended to Algeria, where he had links with the GIA (Armed Islamic Group), and Anwar Hattab's Salafi Group for Preaching and Combat (GSPC). In Egypt, his networks were linked to the Gama'a Islamiyya and the Islamic Jihad. In addition, he also had influence in a number of Asian countries, such as Indonesia, Malaysia, the Philippines, and Thailand. Links between the Middle East and the separatist Muslim movements in Southeast Asia had long existed, but after the Afghan war against communism, and with the resurgence of the mujahidin, the Islamization of Southeast Asian societies underwent an acceleration. From the beginning of the 1990s, the stamp of Bin Laden was evident on the mode of action of the Asian "Afghans."

There was also an alteration at this time in Bin Laden's comportment and his pronouncements. He began to attribute directly to the United States the blame for the predicament Saudi Arabia found itself in. He directed his ire against his former Saudi patrons, whom he reproached for having allowed the infidel Americans to desecrate the sacred soil of Saudi Arabia, as he saw it, and for permitting them to station their troops there after the Gulf War. His attitude toward Saddam Hussein, hitherto implacably hostile, became more conciliatory. He continued to finance Yemeni and Egyptian Islamist groups, waging his war against the American "Satan" in all parts of the globe. In 1995, suspicion was directed toward him in relation to attacks against American nationals, and in 1996 he was also suspected of involvement in the Khobar attack, which left twenty-four dead at an American military residential facility. He was also suspected of being connected with the slaughter of tourists by Egyptian terrorists at Luxor in 1997.

On August 23, 1996, from his base in Afghanistan, Bin Laden launched his "Declaration of War" on the Americans, whom he accused of occupying Islam's "Holy Places." This declaration was a document of a dozen pages in length that appealed for armed struggle against the American military presence in Saudi Arabia. Gradually, however, he transformed his struggle against the Americans from one limited to Saudi Arabia into a global confrontation. This development was clearly set out in the fatwa he issued on February 23, 1998 (see below), which enlarged the scope of the struggle inaugurated by the fatwa of 1996.

Later in 1998, Bin Laden was also accused of implication in the attacks on August 7, 1998, against the U.S. embassies in Nairobi and Dar es-Salaam, which caused the deaths of 224 mainly local people and left more than 4,000 wounded. At this point, the FBI declared him "public enemy number one." Nevertheless, his responsibility as the direct instigator or paymaster for these attacks has never been proved. However, the actual perpetrators, in their claim of responsibility, mentioned Bin Laden by name and referred to the fatwa of February 13, 1998, thus claiming Bin Laden as their ideological inspiration. The names given by the perpetrators to both these attacks indicated their Islamic connections. The Dar es-Salaam operation was designated "Operation Aqsa Mosque" and the Nairobi operation was called "Holy

Kaaba." The claim of responsibility contained the following: "The Islamic Army for the Liberation of the Two Holy Places makes clear its intention of driving out the American forces and of striking against American interests wherever they may be, until the following demands have been met: the withdrawal of American and western forces from Islamic countries in general and from the Arabian Peninsula in particular. This also applies to American citizens." From this point onward, American agencies actively hunted Bin Laden. In June 1999, his name was put on the list of the ten persons most wanted by the FBI, and a reward of $5 million was offered for his capture.

There ensued many terrorist attacks or attempted attacks that were directly or indirectly attributed to Bin Laden. These included "Operation Millennium," the name given to attacks planned in Jordan and in the United States. These attacks were allegedly forestalled with the arrest of a group of Islamists in Jordan and of the Algerian Ahmed Ressam on the frontier between Canada and the United States in December 1999. Bin Laden was also supposed to be connected with the attack on the USS Cole in the port of Aden on October 12, 2000. Other incidents supposedly planned included an attack on the cathedral at Strasbourg; a planned attack against the U.S. Embassy in Paris, which it was claimed was halted by the arrest of Djamel Beghal in Dubai in July 2001 and the exposure of his European contacts. Bin Laden was also linked to the destruction of the World Trade Center in New York on September 11, 2001, by hijacked aircraft and the similar attack on the Pentagon in Washington, DC. He made a call for total war against American interests in a video cassette on December 26, 2001; many other appeals for war against the Americans were made by way of the many Internet sites controlled by Bin Laden. Many of these, which were physically based in Italy, Sweden, the United Kingdom, Poland, Malaysia, Singapore, and Saudi Arabia, were closed after the dissemination of threatening messages from Bin Laden in March 2002 and from various of his lieutenants on April 9, 24, and 26, 2002.

All threats by Islamic groups against the United States are now automatically linked with Bin Laden. The question that must be answered is: Are his networks a myth that springs from the joint paranoia of journalists and officials? Or are they truly a reality? The fear of the intelligence services is that the latter is true. However, the menace may in fact be even more insidious if there were a global network of autonomous anti-Western Islamic activists, any of whom may initiate attacks. As far as can be discerned, beyond Bin Laden's inner circle and his close associates, to the extent that this circle still exists in whatever circumstances Bin Laden now finds himself, the members of the movement associated with him are organized into "sleeping" networks. For the most part, these are made up of former "Afghans," disposed throughout their countries of origin, whether in Europe or in North America. They lead an apparently peaceful life, made up of work, family life, and leisure, until the moment comes for them to act.

Bin Laden's preparation for the World Trade Center attacks of September 11 had been lengthy, and he was no doubt well aware that there would be an American counterattack. Immediately before September 11, Bin Laden took steps to make Afghanistan a safe haven for himself by eliminating Massud, who was now his adversary. The death of Massud was intended to open the way for the liquidation of the last anti-Taliban stronghold in Afghanistan. Massud was killed by a suicide mission on September 9, 2001, but in the event it was already too late to destroy the Northern Alliance. It may be that Bin Laden thought he had more time before the date set for the attacks in the United States, of which he may have been unaware. On September 12, Massud's successors made immediate contact with the United States and Bin Laden's stratagem to destroy the Northern Alliance failed. With help from the United States, the Northern Alliance successfully attacked the Taliban. Mullah Omar was unwilling to give Bin Laden up and as a result faced unrelenting hostility from the United States, culminating in the collapse of the Taliban regime. Bin Laden fled, at first apparently to the mountainous Tora Bora area, which was bombed by the Americans. He seems to have escaped with the aid of Pushtun tribes sympathetic to the Taliban and may have found refuge in the tribal zone on the Pakistani frontier. The best guess is that he continues to be in this area. He has since issued a number of videotaped and audio statements threatening the Americans and commenting on current developments. In January 2006, in an apparently authentic message from his hiding place, he offered a truce to the United States in exchange for the withdrawal of American troops from Iraq and Afghanistan, an offer dismissed by President Bush. Failing this, Bin Laden threatened that there would be further attacks in the United States.

The extent to which Bin Laden is today a threat is debatable. His principal role appears to be as the moral inspiration of Islamic terrorist action and of violent Islamic insurgence, in Iraq in particular. Ayman al-Zawahiri called his movement "Al-Qa'ida in Iraq," more as a declaration of ideological affiliation than of any actual connection with Bin Laden. Looking back on Bin Laden's career, it is worthy of note that he did not at first make any explicit demands beyond the withdrawal of the United States from Saudi Arabia, though he has also referred to the liberation of Jerusalem. His present threats against the United States are of a more general nature, however. Bin Laden's movement initially appealed to young Arab graduates and especially technologists and scientists. These were the disaffected group who were disillusioned with secular Arab governments and were increasingly drawn to Islamic extremism as the remedy for their ills.

In the first instance, Bin Laden had the benefit of his own substantial wealth. He also showed great skill at marshaling human, logistic, and military resources and used his own money to raise more resources. But more important than this, his success in the Muslim world came through his ability to transcend national differences and to appeal to young Muslims of a particular cast of mind wherever they might be in the world. Today, Muslims as far afield as Indonesia and Africa claim affiliation with Al-Qa'ida, though this seems more to be affiliation to an idea than to an actual organization. Bin Laden's greatest victory was to revitalize across frontiers the idea of the "umma," the community of the faithful. His own ideas evolved from their origins in the Arabian idea of Wahhabism toward salafism, a more universal idea of a return to the basics of Islam. During his Saudi period, he contented himself with the demand for a regime in Saudi Arabia that would apply the rules of the Shari'a. In his later pronouncements, however, he began to think on a world scale and to ask for the restoration of the Caliphate. Finally, it seems that the followers that Bin Laden has attracted to his banner over the last quarter of a century are both active and dormant at the same time. A few of these knew Bin Laden himself or those closely connected with him. Others had some contact with his organization. The allegiance of many of those who claim to be his supporters today, however, seems more to be to an idea than to a man or to an organization that has any real existence. The threat to the West today, it seems, is not so much Bin Laden as the idea of Bin Laden.

None of the intelligence agencies that seek him so actively had, by the end of 2006, the slightest idea of his whereabouts.

Osama Bin Laden's Saudi Operations: The Committee for Advice and Reform

In contrast to Salman Al Auda or Safar al Hawali, whose goal was to protect Muslims from Western influence, Osama Bin Laden advocated "preventive" actions, going as far as violence, to dissuade the West from imposing its values on Muslims. The Committee for Advice and Reform (CAR) provided an informal forum for different radical Islamist groups in Saudi Arabia from the 1980s. Several of its members undertook military training in Afghanistan at that time. The CAR ceased to be a clandestine organization only in April 1994, some months after the creation of Mohammed Mas'ari's Committee for the Defense of Legitimate Rights (CDLR). The principal difference between the CDLR and the CAR was that the former believed the Saudi regime was capable of change by way of a process of reform, while the latter took the view that the regime, which it regarded as anti-Islamic, ought to be overthrown by force in favor of a theocratic government.

The CAR described itself as "an all-embracing organisation aiming to apply God's teaching in every aspect of life. Its approach to political and social change was based on a strict interpretation of the Quran and of the Sunna as it was laid down by our Sunni predecessors." On this last point, Osama Bin Laden claimed to be heir to the tradition of the founder of Wahhabism, Muhammad Ibn Abd el-Wahhab. The CAR had four objectives. These were: first, to set up an authentically Islamic system of justice; second, to reform the Saudi political system, purging it of corruption and injustice; third, to enable citizens to criticize the senior figures within the state; and the fourth was

that the senior figures should be guided by the teaching of the great ulema.

On August 3, 1995, Bin Laden published an "Open Letter to His Majesty the King," in which he charged the regime with neglect of the teaching of Ibn Abd el-Wahhab. He also accused them of inability to defend the nation and said they had brought in unbelievers to defend the nation, a task that they were themselves apparently incapable of. Finally, he alleged that the regime was managing the nation's finances badly and was wasting Saudi Arabia's oil income. He concluded his letter by asking King Fahd to step down from the throne. It is noteworthy that the then crown prince Abdullah, now king of Saudi Arabia, offered no response to Bin Laden's strictures.

Bin Laden also attacked Saudi Arabia's senior ulema and criticized their fatwas, especially those that had justified the call for foreign troops during the Gulf crisis and those that advocated reconciliation between Arabs and Israelis. His view of the world at that time was based on the idea that Muslim culture in its weakness was subject to threat by hostile Western actions and that it therefore needed to be protected. His idea of the "jihad" as a combat against the non-Muslims took center stage, reinforced by the Muslim struggle against atheism in Afghanistan, which would in due course be extended to the "crusaders" and the Jews. After its official establishment, the CAR opened an office in London, run by Khaled al-Fawwaz. The arrest of Al-Fawaaz in 1998, in the context of the enquiry into the attacks in Nairobi and Dar es-Salaam, was what in fact caused the demise of the CAR.

Fatwa (Issued by Bin Laden) February 23, 1998

(This communiqué proclaimed the creation of the Global Islamic Front for Jihad against the Jews and the Crusaders.)

A CALL TO JIHAD FOR THE LIBERATION OF THE MUSLIM HOLY PLACES.

"Praise by to God, who revealed the Book, who scatters the clouds and defeats our enemies." Since God created the Arabian Peninsula, with its deserts and seas, it has never been subjected to a trial such as that which it suffers at the present time at the hands of the crusader forces. They spread throughout its territories like a plague of locusts, devouring its riches and its produce. This comes at a moment when there is an alliance of many nations against the Muslims, like those who squabble over a plate of food. Given the gravity of the situation, and our lack of aid, we must look together at the meaning of present events, in order to reach an understanding on how to assess them, and react to them.

None today disputes the existence of three demonstrable facts. We shall present them one by one, so that all may be aware of them, both those who live and those who die, may be aware of these truths.

O ye, our Muslim Nation:

First: The United States occupies the most holy place within the land of Islam, namely the Arabian Peninsula. The United States pillages the Peninsula's riches, dictates to its leaders how to rule, humiliates its inhabitants and terrorizes its neighbours. It is transforming its bases in the Peninsula into an iron spear to fight the neighboring Muslim peoples. Formerly, some denied the reality of this occupation. Today, however, all the inhabitants of the Arabian Peninsula recognize its existence. This unanimity was demonstrated when the Americans persisted in their aggression against the Iraqi people from the Arabian Peninsula. Though its leaders had rejected the use of their territory for this purpose, they were obliged to acquiesce.

Second: In spite of the widespread devastation inflicted on the Iraqi people by the Crusader-Zionist alliance and the large number of dead, which exceeds a million, the Americans have proceeded once more to attempt the commission of hideous massacres. It appears that they are no longer content with the protracted sanctions which have succeeded the violence of war, nor with the destruction and dismemberment of the country. They are preparing to complete the genocide of what remains of the people, and to humiliate Iraq's Muslim neighbors.

Third: Though the objectives of the Americans for these wars are religious and economic, they also distract attention from the occupation of Jerusalem and from the slaughter of Muslims by Israel. The actions of the Americans demonstrate their wish to destroy Iraq, and to reduce all the States of the region, including Iraq, Saudi Arabia, Egypt and Sudan, to mini-States, weak and disunited. Their intention is to guarantee the survival of Israel and to render permanent the execrable occupation of the Peninsula by the Crusaders.

O ye, our Muslim nation:

All these crimes and depredations committed by the Americans constitute an open declaration of war against God, his Prophet and the Muslims. All past ulema across all the ages of Islam are in agreement that jihad is an obligation if the enemy attacks the lands of the Muslims, which is the sixth pillar of Islam.

O ye, our Muslim nation:

Consequently, and in accordance with the commandments of God, we promulgate this fatwa, addressed to all Muslims. "To kill the Americans and their civil and military allies is an individual duty for every Muslim in a position to do so, until the Aqsa Mosque and the Holy Mosque in Mecca are freed from their domination. Drive their armies out of the lands of Islam, conquered, humiliated and no longer capable of menacing any Muslim. ... We call on the Muslim ulema, on loyal Muslim rulers, on the young and on the soldiers of the faithful to launch their attacks on the soldiers of

Satan, the Americans and their allies, Satan's agents. ..."

February 23, 1998
Signed by:
Sheikh Osama Bin Mohammed Bin Laden
Dr Ayman al-Zawahiri (Emir of the Jihad in Egypt)
Sheikh Abu Yasser Rifai Ahmed Taha (from the leadership of the Gamaa Islamiyya, Egypt)
Maulana Mir Hamza (Secretary of the Association of Ulema of Pakistan)
Maulana Fazl al-Rahman Khalil (Emir of the Ansar Movement of Pakistan)
Sheikh Abdel Salam Mohammed (Emir of the Johan Movement of Bangladesh)

BIN LADEN, YISLAM

Yislam Bin Laden, the president of the finance house known as the Saudi Investment Company (SICO), is one of Osama Bin Laden's half brothers and the full brother of Bakr Bin Laden, the head of the family. Since September 2001, he has been under suspicion of some degree of involvement in Osama's activities, though nothing has been proved against him. Having obtained Swiss nationality in 2001, he says he has not seen his half brother Osama for twenty years. On September 13, 2001, Yislam told a Swiss reporter: "The last time I saw my half-brother Osama was in 1981, in Saudi Arabia." SICO was set up in May 1980 and is based in Geneva. Its role is to manage a portion of the equity of the family corporation, the Saudi Binladin Group (SBG). The description of its corporate activity is: "Fund management, shareholding and investment services."

Yislam Bin Laden is also the principal shareholder of another company named SICO based in Curaçao, which owns property round the world, and is also involved in various ways in other Bin Laden companies. He is also one of the principal shareholders in a private airline operating between Switzerland, Britain, and Saudi Arabia. None of this activity in itself suggests criminal activity, but the network of companies in which Yislam Bin Laden is involved is complex and makes full use of commercial and banking confidentiality. The financial resources involved are legitimate, but the attention of both the U.S. and European legal systems has been directed at Yislam Bin Laden. Since December 2001, French fiscal investigators have taken an interest in his activities. In March 2002, financial inspectors seized documents from Yislam Bin Laden's villa in Cannes for inspection in connection with the suspected transfer of millions of dollars to Pakistan, which could conceivably have been made available to Osama Bin Laden. In 2004, the scope of the investigation was widened and Yislam Bin Laden agreed that he and Osama had both been among the signatories of a Bin Laden family bank account in Switzerland from 1990 to 1997.

When asked by a journalist in 2004 if he would give up Osama Bin Laden to the authorities if he knew his whereabouts, he said that he would not, commenting: "Would you give up your brother?" In July 2005, he said that if Osama were ever captured, he would pay for his defense, though he also said that what Osama had done had damaged the Bin Laden family. In an interview with *Time* magazine, Yislam said: "Every person is responsible for his acts. If somebody has done something that is illegal, nobody on earth will help him or stand by him. The family will not be responsible for the acts of one of its members." In an interview for Al-Arabiyya television Yislam said he did not believe Osama was dead. Yislam Bin Laden has spoken out against terrorism and condemned the London bomb blasts of July 2005.

BIRRI, KHALED AL-

Khaled al-Birri, a reformed Egyptian Islamist, born in Assiut in Upper Egypt, came from a good family background. From his teenage days he was involved with the Gama'a Islamiyya and quickly rose to be an "emir," or leader, highly respected by the younger members. In 2002, however, he published a book entitled "Earth is more beautiful than heaven," which gives a groundbreaking account of his experience in the Gama'a Islamiyya and explains the factors that impelled him to leave it and helped him make his escape.

BOSNIA HERZEGOVINA

Militant Islam made its first appearance in Bosnia Herzegovina before World War II, at the time of the emergence of the Kingdom of the Serbs, Croatians, and Slovenes in 1918. In 1920, Bosnia Herzegovina became part of the kingdom, which was renamed the Kingdom of Yugoslavia. Two problems quickly emerged. One of these concerned the political representation of the Bosnian Muslims within an entity that blatantly viewed them as unimportant. The other, at a more profound level, arose from the challenge to the identity of a community whose territory was partitioned into regions described as "Serb" or "Croat" according to the ethnicity of the majority of their Christian populations. Faced with these frustrations, the Muslim Bosnians sought whatever assistance they could find. They sent delegates to the pan-Islamic conference in Jerusalem in 1931 and to a similar conference held in Geneva in 1935. They made contact with the Muslim Brotherhood in the Middle East, as well as with other Islamist groups, and in early 1941 the indigenous organization known as the "Young Muslims" (Mladi Muslimani) was established. The German invasion of Yugoslavia and the "Ustashe" Croat state led the Bosnian Muslims to believe that the road to the creation of a Muslim state lay in active collaboration with the Third Reich. In 1943, at the initiative of Hajj Amin al-Husseini, the grand mufti of Jerusalem (who was regarded as an "honorary Aryan" according to a document given to him by Hitler), the Bosnian SS Division known as "Handzar" (The Fist) was set up. This unit was implicated in crimes of the worst kind, perpetrated on a large scale, against the Jewish and Orthodox Serb populations.

In 1945, Bosnia Herzegovina became one of the six republics that constituted communist Yugoslavia. The identity problem, however, remained unresolved, since the Muslims were not the majority of the population of the new entity, but only the largest minority: a situation that has persisted up to recent times. In 1991, the population consisted of 43.3 percent of Muslims, 31.4 percent of Serbs, and 17.3 percent Croats. The government of President Tito was opposed to any form of confessionally based political representation, and though the Yugoslav Muslims formed an official body, known as the "Islamic Community," they were denied official representation. From 1947, Muslim courts were banned, the "waqf" (Muslim charitable endowments) was nationalized, and religious schools were closed.

In 1968, however, the existence of a "Muslim nationality" was proclaimed in communist Yugoslavia as a designation for Bosnian Muslims who did not identify themselves as either Croats or Serbs. This "Muslim nationality," however, was an ethnic designation and a citizen who opted for it did imply active adhesion to the Muslim faith. In the 1970s, a Muslim resurgence took hold, within which the theme of pan-Islamism again arose. Communally based parties were first formed, however, only with the free elections of 1990. Three such parties then came into existence: the Muslim SDA—the "Democratic Action Party" or "Stranka Demokratske Akcije"—the Serbian SDS, and the Croatian HDZ. In December 1990, Alija Izetbegovic, the leader of the SDA, which represented the predominant Muslim community, became president of Bosnia Herzegovina. On October 15, 1991, he proclaimed the sovereignty of the new state and declared its independence in March 1992.

On April 6, 1992, the Bosnian war began. The Serbs and Croats took steps to strengthen their position in the regions where they were in the majority, while the SDA became the sole source of authority in the Muslim remainder of Bosnia. The Islamists, and especially the Muslim Brothers, saw the Bosnian war as an extension of the Afghan conflict against the Soviets. The start of the war in 1992 coincided with the fall of the communist regime in Kabul. Since the mid-1980s, the Islamic leaders had issued warnings over the threat of Serbian nationalism. In August 1991, one of the leaders of the Islamic community of Yugoslavia, Jakub Selimovski, who was the leader of the ulema, formulated the fears of the Muslims in a memorandum addressed to "all the world's Islamic organizations and institutions," asking for the assistance of the "umma." As he put it, "The protection of the faith, of life, of honour and of possessions is a religious duty, and the responsibility for our fate falls upon the entire Muslim umma."

Henceforth, the struggle for national liberation was presented as a jihad in which every Muslim should participate. The SDA, as the principal Muslim party, threw itself into the mobilization of the community as a whole. One of the founders of the SDA, alongside Alija Izetbegovic, was Mustafa Ceric, the imam of the Zagreb Mosque. In September 1992, he organized a conference on the "protection of human rights" in Bosnia, which brought together representatives from thirty Muslim countries. These included the Egyptian Yusuf al-Qaradawi, a theoretician in the field of Islamic economics and a sympathizer with the Muslim Brotherhood, as well as Khurshid Ahmed, the head of the Islamic Foundation in London. Another attendee was Yusuf Islam,

as the former popular singer Cat Stephens was now known, who had become the president of Muslim Aid, a society set up in 1984 by an Egyptian medical student, Hani al-Banna. Both Khurshid Ahmed and Yusuf Islam followed the line of the Pakistani Jam'at-i Islami. The conference passed resolutions that declared without ambiguity that the aim of the conflict was the extermination of Bosnia's Muslims.

These efforts at mobilization bore fruit. In 1991, the "International Islamic Relief Organization" (IIRO) set up an Islamic Council for Eastern Europe, which Jakub Selimoski headed. Meanwhile, "Islamic Relief," which was based in Birmingham (United Kingdom) and had branches throughout western Europe, helped to found a charitable organization known as "Merhamet," under the auspices of the SDA. "Islamic Relief" also produced a videocassette entitled "Yugoslavia: the crimes of our age," which depicted the Serbs as criminals and the Muslims as victims. Mobilization also had its drawbacks, however. The economic, financial, and voluntary networks of Islamic states competed with each other, particularly those of Saudi Arabia, Iran, Sudan, and Turkey. The Egyptian Islamists, meanwhile, made use of the Bosnia Herzegovina issue in their domestic strategy of questioning the legitimacy of their own government. The most committed were the Islamic organizations in western Europe, who nevertheless made use of the Bosnian crisis to improve their standing among the Muslim populations of Europe, especially in Great Britain, and also to raise their profile with the authorities in the western European countries.

In the long term, Muslim mobilization took on a military aspect, as numbers of foreign fighters came to Bosnia to participate in the jihad against the "infidel." In addition to the Arab "Afghans" (returned fighters from that conflict), and the armed Sunni groups and volunteers from the Middle

East and elsewhere, it should be noted that there were also pro-Iranian fighters. This was an indication of Teheran's commitment and also accounts for the links between Alija Izetbegovic and the Iranian religious establishment. In 1994, the Western media reported arms sales and the dispatch of volunteers from Iran, and in 1996 this was taken note of by the U.S. Congress. The Clinton administration's reaction to this was one of benevolent neutrality. An airlift from Iran to Croatia, via Turkey, delivered to the Bosnian army, giving 30 percent to Croatia in return for its clandestine participation. It may therefore be said with truth that the Islamist movements had the blessing of the United States in their diplomatic and political efforts to promote the new state of Bosnia within part of the territory of the former Yugoslavia.

The exigencies of the war led the SDA to exploit all possible channels of humanitarian aid for Bosnia, whether through the humanitarian NGOs working directly on the ground, or through the "Organization for Aid to the Muslims of Bosnia-Herzegovina," which was set up in 1994. The financial assistance the SDA received allowed it to control the army, to undermine the influence of Jakub Selimoski's "Islamic Community"—less committed than was the SDA itself to the politicization of Islam and pan-Islamism—and to counteract the influence of the secular Bosnian parties. The SDA brought Muslim religious instruction into the schools, opened up prayer rooms, and used the leverage of its distribution of aid to pressurize the population to adopt Muslim names, to wear the veil, and grow beards. It also strictly prohibited drinking alcohol or eating pork. In terms of politics, the SDA's objectives became clearer. It aimed to establish a Muslim state in the Balkans by bringing together the Muslims of Bosnia with those of the Sanjak of Novi Pazar, a historic region in the north of Montenegro

and the southwest of Serbia where the population was 51 percent Muslim. The balance of power on the ground, however, obliged it to moderate its ambitions.

The Bosnian war was a prominent instance of the utilization of Islamic NGOs for military and terrorist purposes. From 1992, the Islamist volunteers who went to Bosnia to fight the Serbs passed through Croatia, principally through Zagreb and Split, thanks to the professional identity cards issued by the NGOs. A list of the NGOs involved includes the following:

- The Society for the Renewal of the Heritage of Islam (Kuwait)
- The International Islamic Relief Organization (Saudi Arabia)
- The Saudi High Commission for Relief (Saudi Arabia)
- Third World Relief Agency (Sudan)
- The Egyptian Humanitarian Relief Agency (Egypt)
- The Muwaffaq Foundations (Saudi Arabia) (which had good relations with the Bosnian army)

In Zagreb, the nerve center for the transit of Muslim volunteers was the Mosque run by Imam Hassan Cengic. Cengic later became a member of the SDA, led by President Alija Izetbegovic, and was later a general in the Bosnian army, where he founded the "Mujahidin Battalion," which was personally commissioned by President Izetbegovic and set up on August 13, 1993. It leader was an Algerian, Abou al-Maali, formerly a member of the Algerian GIA. It was the best equipped and most aggressive formation in the Bosnian army and was directly responsible to the president.

The signing of the Dayton Accords on December 14, 1995, brought the war to an end. The Dayton Accords provided for the continued theoretical existence of an undivided Bosnia Herzegovina, while in practice bringing into existence two separate entities. These were the Federation of Bosnia Herzegovina (made up of Croats and Muslims and occupying 51 percent of the territory) and the Serbian Republic (with a Serbian population and 49 percent of the territory). A joint three-man presidency with Muslim, Serb, and Croat members was set up, as well as a joint parliamentary assembly.

There was also an international dimension. Following Dayton, Bosnia Herzegovina was placed first under the aegis of the United Nations and then of NATO, when the international force already established in 1992 under the designation UNPROFOR was replaced in 1995 by IFOR, still with a strong U.S. element. In 1996, a smaller, NATO-led Stabilization Force (SFOR) was set up to succeed IFOR, with the remit of deterring renewed hostilities. European Union peacekeeping troops (EUFOR) replaced SFOR in December 2004. Their role is to maintain peace and stability throughout the country. The Western presence also had a nonmilitary dimension. A high representative was appointed, exercising in practice the powers of the joint presidency over the two areas, despite the reluctance of both the Serbs and the Croats.

The presence of outside forces in Bosnia certainly succeeded in putting an end to the war, though it was unable to facilitate the return of the refugees to their homes. They also had the effect of undermining seriously the SDA. The SDA was no longer taken seriously by Teheran and was no longer able to exercise control over the volunteers and the Muslim NGOs. In addition, the lay parties increased their strength at the expense of the Islamists, whose excesses during the war had tarnished their appeal. Many Muslim volunteers remained in Bosnia, however, especially in the Zenica region, where they worked for the Bosnian army or for private companies, having obtained Bosnian identity papers as the result of their military

service. In the elections of September 1997, the SDA's share of the vote fell by 5 percent to 34.9 percent and the Islamic movement began to split apart. Its swift disintegration prompted the SDA leadership to an attempt to rely on the prestige of President Izetbegovic, asking him to stand for reelection in 1998, even though he had difficulties with his health. He alone was in a position to maintain the party's cohesion, and he was able to use his great personal popularity to restore its standing.

The events of September 11, 2001, introduced a new atmosphere. On September 26, four individuals connected with the Saudi High Commission for Relief were interrogated by SFOR on suspicion of implication in support for terrorism. All four were released, but the mere fact that they were questioned clearly shows that the Islamic NGOs were henceforth regarded by the Western intelligence services as objects of suspicion. In May 2002, five other suspects were arrested and handed over to the United States. Nevertheless, the NGOs continued their efforts to "re-Islamize" Bosnia Herzegovina, using the leverage of their resources to impose Islamic conduct and behavior on the public. They began systematically dismantling Bosnia's secular artistic and cultural heritage and replacing it with the construction of mosques and other Islamic edifices in accordance with their vision of Islam. Bosnian Islam, like that of the Ottoman Empire in general, adhered to the Hanafi "madhhab" (school of jurisprudence), which was the most liberal of the four schools in Sunni Islam. The Islamic NGOs in Bosnia, however, were all under the influence of the Wahhabi doctrine, itself aligned with the Hanbali "madhhab," prevalent in Saudi Arabia, which is the most conservative of all the interpretative traditions.

There were questions implicit in the imposition of order by NATO forces, including the issue of how long it was meant to continue and of how effective it would be in repairing the damage done by the war. There were also issues about the SDA's utilization of Islam. The question remains open whether Islam can continue to serve as a rallying point for all Bosnian Muslims, or if, alternatively, in future it may become a source of conflict between secular Bosnians and Islamists.

BRITAIN

Great Britain plays a central role in the spread of Islamism in Europe. British law places no obstacle in the way of communities seeking to establish their own institutions and this is much exploited by the Islamists. They are subject to legal sanctions only if their actions endanger public order. Even if they are sought by other European legal authorities, as in the case of Rachid Ramda, who was suspected of implication in the attacks at the Saint-Michel Métro station, the extradition procedure is long and meticulous. Unfortunately, the events of September 11, 2001, have not resulted in a change in the attitudes of the British authorities.

Islam in Britain presents a complex pattern. Nonetheless, it may be said that numerically by far the largest proportion of Britain's Muslim population of over 1.5 million comes from the Indian subcontinent, including Pakistan, India, and Bangladesh. Other Muslims of South Asian origin have come to Britain from families previously resident in East and South Africa. There are two main schools within the Pakistani and Indian community:

1. The first of these is the Barelvi movement. This has its roots in India, but is today very much linked with Pakistan. Its name derives from that of its founder, Ahmad Riza Khan of Bareilly. Barelvi Islam has directly descended from the original Islam of the Indian subcontinent in the nineteenth century, as distinct from the reformist construction of Deoband. For many Pakistani Muslims, Barelvi practices are the Islam of the family, the "biraderi" (a group of Pakistani men bound by family links to support and help each other), and of society. It may be said to be folk Islam. Barelvis observe the cult of shrines and venerate saints, whom they believe are able to intercede on their behalf. They keep feast days and use music as part of their religious practice. Barelvis particularly venerate the Prophet Muhammad as well as Ali, his son-in-law and cousin, though they are in no sense Shi'ites. They are often referred to as Sufi, because of their mystic practices, but have little in common with the Sufism of the classical Islamic mystics.

2. The other division of subcontinental Islam is the Deobandi movement. The sect derives its name from the Indian religious seminary at Deoband, not far from Delhi. Its historical root was the attempt by Muslims to reform their faith in the nineteenth century after the Indian rebellion known as the mutiny. Deoband preaches the strict observance of Sunni Islam together with meticulous observance of the Shari'a. It is strongly anti-Shi'ite and deprecates what are said to be the uncanonical additions to Islam made by Barelvis. Deoband restricts Sufi practices to the most basic observances, rejecting all veneration of saints or intercession with God by human agency. Today, the school at Deoband is widely regarded as the most important world center of Islamic learning after Al-Azhar in Cairo. In Britain, as elsewhere, the Deobandis represent a stronghold of conservative Sunni othodoxy. In the context of Islamism, Deoband is not far removed from Salafi and Wahhabi practice, and Deobandi orthodoxy provided the soil in which the Taliban movement took root and grew in northern Pakistan and southern Afghanistan.

In addition to the two great schools of subcontinental Islam there are two major movements, each more inclined toward the Deobandi community:

1. Tablighi Jamaat, referred to in Arabic as Jamaat al-Tabligh. This movement had its origin in India in the 1920s, but is today equally connected to Pakistan. In Pakistani circles it is also sometimes called the "Tahrik-i Iman"—the Faith Movement. Tabligh, as it is familiarly known, is a proselytizing movement that seeks to re-Islamize Muslims who have fallen away from proper observance of the faith. Each adherent is supposed to spend part of his time on the task of proselytization. Tabligh has spread throughout the world and is today represented in at least a hundred countries, where local branches are independent and autonomous. It is a Sunni movement that is strict in its interpretation of Islam and is linked in practice to the Deobandi network of mosques. Its British headquarters is at Dewsbury, in Yorkshire; there is a mosque and a madrasa, with accommodation for visiting Tablighis passing through on what are now the global journeys of preaching undertaken by some devotees. This serves as Tabligh's center in Europe. As a global movement, Tabligh uses the English language to a great extent, and at Dewsbury Gujarati is also a social language, reflecting the origins of many of the members. The languages of instruction are Urdu and Arabic. There is no doubt that many Muslims inclined toward Islamism, and sometimes to extremism, have passed through Tabligh. Two of the bombers involved in the July 2005 bombings are known to have visited Dewsbury. This does not imply that the movement itself has any propensity toward violence. Tabligh proclaims itself to be not merely nonviolent but also nonpolitical. This could be contrasted with Tabligh's activities in North Africa, where the movement does appear to have become implicated in politics.

2. Jamaat-i Islami. This is also a strict Sunni movement, based on the teachings of the Pakistani theologian Sayyid Abul Alal Mawdudi, and was founded in 1941. It is organized in a formal and hierarchical manner, unlike Tabligh. It shares much in its approach with the Muslim Brotherhood. In Pakistan, it has operated as a political party, which has wielded an influence disproportionate to its relatively limited electoral support. In the 1990s, allegations were made in a U.S. congressional report that Jamaat-i Islami was linked to a terrorist group active in Kashmir known as Hizbul Mujahideen. Outside Pakistan, Jamaat-i Islami branches have sprung up following the lines of Pakistani emigration to South Africa, Mauritius, and Britain. Jamaat-i Islami within Pakistan sought to play a part in organizing the resistance across Pakistan's northern frontier to the Soviet occupation of Afghanistan. It had links in terms of common interest and shared membership with Gulbuddin Hekmatyar's Hizb-i Islami.

There were five hundred mosques in Britain in 1993. By 2006, the total was over 1,500, together with other unofficial places of prayer. There were also around one hundred Muslim schools. The influence of Islamists is felt to a greater or lesser extent in many of these, though some voices are raised in favor of social integration. The United Kingdom does not restrict the activities of either Muslim refugees or of other members of resident Muslim communities, on condition that their legal status in the country is in order. Of course, like any other citizen or resident, they must not commit acts of violence or break the law and must not threaten the security of the country. The authorities regard Muslim migrants simply as ethnic groups, without taking into consideration their religious affiliation. The Anglican church is the official religion of the United Kingdom. Other religious confessions fall under the general umbrella of the law, which more or less reflects Christian values. Religious institutions do not benefit, as they do elsewhere in Europe, from financial support from the state, apart from subventions for approved faith schools. They are, however, able to take advantage of registration as charities, which gives them fiscal benefits. Only 329 mosques had registered in this way by 2002. Otherwise, in order to build or occupy a place of worship, Islamic organizations are obliged to approach the local authorities. Such applications will be judged in accordance with the exigencies of particular local circumstances. Factors including local planning exigencies, the environment, the external appearance of the buildings, including towers, the use of loudspeakers, and so on would be considered. Britain's Muslims are in general concentrated in urban centers, especially London and Birmingham. There is, however, a substantial concentration in the northwest of England and in Yorkshire, in such towns as Bradford, Dewsbury, Blackburn, and Bolton, and also a considerable Muslim population in Scotland, particularly in the Glasgow region. In recent years, the Muslim population in Britain has increased sharply as a result of demographic growth, rather than further migration.

This subcontinental Islam, with its own characteristics, has in general shown a will to integrate and to participate in British public life, despite the activities of Islamists. An Islamic political party, established in September 1989 by a British convert, attracted several thousand adherents. More importantly, there were by 2007 two Muslim Members of Parliament in Britain, representing the Labor Party, together with one member of the European parliament. Others have been appointed to the House of Lords, the British Upper Chamber, whose role is to examine legislation before it is passed into law. There are also many Muslim elected representatives in local government in Britain. Most

Muslims of the first generation of migrants were in any case British citizens. Until 1948, any person born in any British territory had the unlimited right to entry and residence in Britain itself as British citizens. After 1948, as British territories began to achieve independence, citizens of Commonwealth countries were easily able to gain British citizenship. Most of Britain's Muslims were from Commonwealth countries. The Commonwealth Immigration Act of 1961 placed restrictions on the right of Commonwealth citizens to reside in Britain, though those who gained entry could still become British by a simple act of registration. A further Act in 1968 restricted the right of British passport holders from the Commonwealth countries to come to Britain. The British Nationality Act of 1981 placed Commonwealth citizens on an equal footing with other non-British nationals, requiring them to seek naturalization, rather than being able simply to register to obtain British citizenship.

Muslims certainly benefit from the particularities of British society. British society has hitherto always been characterized by a toleration of the presence of diverse cultural communities, which facilitates their relations with the state. The ethnic diversity of the Muslim community has had the result that individual Muslims communicate with each other in English, and even the sermons in the mosques are given in English, by virtue of which they are accessible to all members of the community. Muslims are seldom subjected to constraints relating to their dress if they choose to wear what the Muslim community regards as conventional Muslim dress. Even in schools (in contrast to France) Muslim girls are normally allowed to wear hair coverings of whatever kind they choose, while adaptations such as longer skirts or trousers are in general permitted in schools where school uniform is the rule. There are many Muslim success stories in

Britain. Muslims have become university professors, doctors, lawyers, engineers, and entrepreneurs, to add to the stock professions of restaurant proprietor or small-shop owner.

On the other hand, for the Muslim population of Britain as a whole, there are downsides. Muslims are more liable in Britain to unemployment, with an unemployment rate of 15 percent in 2004—three times the national average. For young Muslims under twenty-five, the rate doubles, with 30 percent unemployed. Apparently rebuffed by British society, the younger generation of Muslims in Britain appears to have returned to the Islamic faith as a consequence of their disillusionment with secular society as a basis for personal values and family relationships. For those Muslims born in the United Kingdom, the overall environment of uncompromising secularity, the exclusive nature of Western culture, together with international events characterized by Islamophobia, all have an effect. Recent events, including September 11, 2001 in the United States and Britain's own suicide bombings of July 7, 2005, have, however, driven a wedge between the Muslim community and British society, with many British people regarding Muslims with a growing degree of suspicion. The result has been to drive young Muslims into an emotional response, rediscovering their Islamic faith as both a religious and a cultural identity.

All the above considerations apply in particular to the subcontinental community. However, Muslims whose origins lie in zones other than the Indian subcontinent also have a part to play in Britain, albeit a minor one. Perhaps, the earliest Muslim community in Britain was that of the Yemenis. They arrived as seafaring men a hundred years ago, and many stayed to form communities in the ports, such as Cardiff in Wales and the port of South Shields in the northeast of England. In more recent times, there has been immigration by Arabs of Middle Eastern origin, for example from Lebanon, Syria, and Jordan, as well as by Palestinians. There are also Gulf citizens from Kuwait and the other Gulf States, as well as Saudi Arabia. The Egyptian community is of significant size. There has also been immigration from North Africa, with Algerians and especially Moroccans arriving in significant numbers. There is also a Turkish community and significant numbers of Iranians. There are also African and Southeast Asian Muslims from such countries as Malaysia. However, the overall numbers are not great in comparison to the subcontinental community.

A key moment in the radicalization of the British Muslim community was the campaign against the book *The Satanic Verses* by the British writer Salman Rushdie, of Indian Muslim descent, published in 1988. Rushdie was a prizewinning novelist and a prominent literary figure in Britain. The book was seen as offensive to Muslims because of its disrespect to Prophet Muhammad. In January 1989, copies of the book were burned at a demonstration in Bradford and Muslims from the north of England traveled to London for a mass demonstration against the book, asking for government action to ban it and to change the blasphemy laws. In February 1989, a British Muslim intellectual, Dr. Kalim Siddiqui, the founder of a British Muslim think tank known as the Muslim Institute, traveled to Iran. At the end of his visit there, Ayatollah Khomeini pronounced a fatwa ruling that the blasphemy contained in the "Satanic Verses" justified the murder of its author. Rushdie has lived under protection ever since. British Muslims of all communities were aroused against Rushdie and saw the defensive reaction of the British intellectual and political community as a symptom of hostility toward Islam. Siddiqui moved ahead to create the organization he called the Muslim Parliament, which he claimed was a representative institution for British Muslims. Siddiqui died in 1996, leaving the parliament to be run by his successor, Muhammad Ghaysuddin. The Muslim Parliament continues to exist, but is challenged by other institutions that also vie for the leadership of the Muslim community.

The establishment of organizations to represent the Muslim population of Britain began in the relatively early days of the Muslim community, when it was still a very small and on the whole invisible minority. An organization that called itself the Jamiat al-Muslimeen was set up in 1934, with branches in Birmingham, Manchester, Newcastle, and Glasgow. In 1962, Muslim students assembled in Birmingham for the foundation meeting of FOSIS—the Federation of Student Islamic Societies, which now has ninety affiliated student groups. In the early days of the establishment of the Muslim community, some group or other contrived to establish a Muslim community center in each urban location where a sufficient concentration of Muslims was found. This would serve as a venue for prayer and a place for teaching and education. Such a center would solicit gifts and subventions. Those centers that adhered to strict Wahhabi doctrines tended to receive—more or less discreetly—donations from Saudi Arabia, Kuwait, and Pakistan. A society of Muslim doctors was formed in 1968, and the Muslim Educational Trust published its first book on Islam for children in 1969. The Union of Muslim Organizations (UMO) was set up in 1970. This is still active under the direction of Syed Hossein Pasha, but is regarded by Muslims as out of touch with the grassroots. A British "Ulema" society— for scholars of religion and clerics—was set up in 1971. Important initiatives were taken in centers outside London. In the northern city of Bradford in 1981, the municipality helped to fund the Bradford Council of Mosques. This had the unexpected effect of marginalizing nonreligious representation for Muslims, making the mosques and their leaders the spokesmen for the community. There are also Shi'ite institutions set up at much the same time, for example the federation of Kkhja Shi'a communities, known as the KSMIC, and the Al-Khoei cultural center in west London.

The multiculturalism that was brought into being by such initiatives as that in Bradford did not create radical Islamism, but it helped to foster it by strengthening the position of conservative leaders and by giving Muslims the idea of themselves as a separate "tribe" within the nation. The development threw up significant leaders such as Sher Azzam, who was prominent in the Rushdie affair. The Rushdie affair also led to the establishment of the UK Action Committee on Islamic Affairs in 1988 and in due course to the Muslim Parliament. The Muslim Council of Britain was the outcome of a consultation committee in 1996 in Bradford, in which the Bradford Council of Mosques played a leading part. The MCB came into existence in 1998. Its general secretary until 2006 was Iqbal Sacranie, who was honored by the queen in 2005 when he was granted a knighthood and became Sir Iqbal Sacranie. Inayat Bunglawala succeeded Sacranie as general secretary in 2006.

After the foundation of the MCB in 1998, however, its initial denunciation of Salman Rushdie was followed by overtures to Osama Bin Laden and other indications that it favored radical and Salafi activity. There was increasing criticism in political circles in Britain that the MCB represented Deobandi Islam and Tablighi Jamat and was even attracted to radical Salafite and Wahhabi tendencies. In July 2006, with the encouragement of the British government, a new body came into being known as the Sufi Muslim Council (SMC), which claimed to represent abroad the spread of Muslims, but seemed primarily to be identified with the Barelvi Pakistani community. The Communities Minister, Ruth Kelly, was present at the inaugural meeting. The SMC claimed to have made an alliance with a group of some 300 Barelvi mosques in the north of England that called itself the British Muslim Forum.

Finally, mention should be made of what might be regarded as an early attempt to establish an official Islam in the United Kingdom. The London Central Mosque, otherwise known as the Regents Park Mosque, was set up in Regent's Park on a site allocated by Britain's Prime Minister Winston Churchill in 1940, during World War II. The foundation of the mosque and its associated Islamic Cultural Center were intended as an acknowledgment of the substantial Muslim population of the British Empire and the part it had played in the war. The Cultural Center was opened in 1944. The mosque, however, was not finally competed until 1977. It has a large golden dome and a minaret over forty meters high. Today, the trustees of the mosque are the ambassadors of Muslim countries accredited to the United Kingdom. The mosque is widely regarded as being under the influence of Saudi Arabia and is seen as a manifestation of Arab Islam, rather than that of the Indian subcontinent. The mosque came under sharp criticism at the end of 2006 when it was revealed that radical Muslim literature and videos were being sold in the shop. It has been for some time the practice of radical Muslim groups, and especially Hizb ut-Tahrir and the Muhajirun, to set up stalls outside the mosque and attempt to attract the attention of worshippers leaving the Friday prayers.

Hizb ut-Tahrir, founded in the Middle East in 1953 and banned in many countries, works for the reestablishment of the caliphate—the secular and religious authority that would in theory govern the entire Muslim community. The membership of Hizb ut-Tahrir in Britain is small, but it appears well organized. Many of its adherents are students, who seem often to leave the organization when they complete their studies. The group's leadership tends to be Arab, while the members are predominantly Pakistani, Indian, or Bangladeshi. Hizb ut-Tahrir has spread from Britain to Pakistan, where it is a cause for concern for the authorities. In August 2003, after the invasion of Iraq, a Hizb ut-Tahrir spokesman said Britain should be wary of bomb attacks. The National Union of Students has banned Hizb ut-Tahrir from activity in British Universities. In December 2005, Hizb ut-Tahrir staged a march in London, protesting against the government's stated intention to ban the organization. The initial leader of Hizb ut-Tahrir in Britain was Omar Bakri Mohammed, a Syrian, who founded the London branch in 1985. He became a legal resident of Britain and applied in 1996 for British citizenship for himself and his Lebanese wife. At the high point of his influence, he preached in a number of different London mosques. He split off from the movement in 1996 and founded his own equally extremist organization known as the Muhajirun, which explicitly advocated violent attacks on Western targets. Omar Bakri Mohammed is now in exile in Lebanon.

Britain was brought face to face with the possible consequences of indigenous Islamic extremism when bombs were exploded on the London transport system on July 7, 2005. Four young Muslims from Yorkshire came to London and committed suicide attacks, three on underground trains and the fourth on a bus. Why would young British citizens commit such attacks? From video evidence left behind by the bombers, it would appear that they had become profoundly alienated from British society by what they regarded as British participation in a worldwide assault on Muslims. Events in Iraq and in Palestine were cited as a justification for regarding the British state as the enemy. The British government, for its own reasons, rejected this interpretation while failing to present any convincing alternative rationale. The attacks were carried out with homemade bombs, which had not cost a great deal to produce, and suggestions of links with international organizations such as Al-Qa'ida have been largely discounted, except that Al-Qa'ida and other international organizations may have provided the inspiration for the attacks. Palestinian Hamas, which has also promoted suicide bombing in its campaign against what it regards as Israel's illegal occupation of Palestinian territory, may also have been an example. Two weeks later in London, a further set of would-be Muslim suicide bombers provided themselves with ineffective weapons and were brought to trial in January 2007. These six were London residents, some of whom were of African origin.

A survey published in Britain in January 2007 concluded that young Muslims have become more interested in radical idea. Of young Muslims surveyed, 12 percent expressed admiration for such groups as Al-Qa'ida that are prepared to fight the West. Others said they would like to live under Shari'a law, and a majority said that women should wear the veil. British foreign policy looms large, with almost 60 percent blaming what was described as "Western arrogance" for world problems. However, the same survey revealed a considerable level of ignorance of world affairs among the Muslims who were surveyed. According to one of the Muslim authors of the report, "there is clearly a conflict within British Islam between a moderate majority that accepts the norms of British democracy and a growing minority that does not." At the same time, another Muslim sociologist said that greater participation in British society would resolve the problems faced by British Muslims.

In November 2006, the British internal intelligence service, MI5, said there were around 1,600 terrorists in Britain of whom most were British-born and most claimed to have connections with Al-Qa'ida. There were as many as two hundred separate groups, of whom some thirty appeared to be engaged in developing serious terrorist plots.

CHECHNYA

The Chechens are a people who have long lived in the Caucasus. Chechnya is bordered by Daghestan in the east, Russia to the north, and Georgia to the south. To the west lie Ingushetia and then North Ossetia, part of which has ancestrally been Chechen territory. From the sixteenth century, the Chechens have been trapped among three imperial powers, Russia, Persia, and the Ottoman Empire. The Chechen barons only kept their independence by playing one off against the others. In the late eighteenth century, Sunni Islam became the faith of the region, with strong influence from the Sufi religious brotherhoods. The earliest missionaries came from Daghestan. Once established, they soon succeeded in spreading Islam as the way of life and drove out the old ways. They also introduced Arabic script as the standard way of writing the local language.

Islam became a unifying force and the spearhead against the Russians, whose policies had been overtly colonialist since the days of Peter the Great. In the eighteenth century, the Russians annexed Ossetia and attempted to do the same with Chechnya, but came up against popular resistance. They founded the city of Grozny (the Stronghold) as a base for their military deployment. In 1795, Sheikh Mansur, a Chechen imam, fought against

Russia. He attempted to unify the Muslims in an Islamic state. His plan was brought to fruition by a member of the Avar people of Daghestan, the legendary Imam Shamil, who unified the Sufi sects of the Caucasus into a single order, the "Muridiya," which was the backbone of his imamate. Shamil's war against Russia, from 1834 to 1859, ended with the capture of Shamil and his exile into captivity in Russia. Nonetheless, troubles continued in Chechnya, and the Russians were obliged to suppress revolts severely in 1860–1861, 1864, and 1877–1878. The impact on Chechnya was catastrophic. The population fell from 200,000 to 100,000 over the course of twenty years.

Chechen resistance went underground, led by spiritual leaders of Sufi inspiration. The two Sufi brotherhoods that predominated in the region were the Naqshbandiya, of Central Asian origin, and the Qadiriya, founded in Baghdad. Religious sentiment in the Caucasus was not in general of a militant nature, with the exception of the Chechens and the Ingush. However, the Chechens sought and found inspiration in religion for their struggle against Russia. The Bolshevik Revolution in Russia initially promised autonomy and control over the land to the Chechens and was therefore greeted with enthusiasm. Before long the imperialist ambitions of Lenin's successors became evident and the struggle began afresh. At first, there were moves to root out Islam, with the closure and destruction of mosques, followed by attempts at assimilation. The Russians replaced the Arab script with the Roman and then the Cyrillic alphabet. The aim was to cut the Chechens off both from their fellow Muslims and from their own past. Anti-religious propaganda, of a kind widespread in the USSR, was applied in Chechnya with especial vigor.

While the practice of Islam was permitted in Central Asia, albeit under strict control, in Chechnya the Soviet authorities set about stamping it out entirely. Neither mosques nor officially recognized Islamic clergy were allowed to remain in the land. In February 1944, during World War II, a crackdown on Muslims and Chechen nationalists was accompanied by the mass deportation of Chechens to Siberia and Kazakhstan, removing a third of the Chechen population. In parallel, a plan systematically to eradicate the memory of the population was under way. Archives were destroyed, together with documents relating to the history and literature of Chechnya and the study of its people. All were burned on great bonfires in Lenin Square in Grozny. In the 1950s, however, the process of de-Stalinization resulted in an attempt to make amends for these crimes, and the Chechens were rehabilitated. Those who had been deported were permitted to go home. In January 1957, an autonomous Soviet Socialist Republic was created for the Chechens and the Ingush.

In June 1991, as the Soviet Union fell, the National Congress, set up by General Dzhokar Dudayev, the former hero of Afghanistan, who claimed to speak both for the nationalist movement and the former communist authorities, proclaimed the country's independence. Dudayev declared the abolition of the Supreme Soviet and all the other Soviet institutions in the country. On the ground, however, nothing changed. Russia's President Boris Yeltsin sent a high-level delegation to open talks with Dudayev and the National Congress. They proposed a deal: Dudayev would be recognized as head of the autonomous republic if he would in turn recognize Yeltsin as the head of state. This however, was a misreading of the stubborn Chechen general. Dudayev meant to make the most of the opportunity presented by an unstable situation in Moscow, in which governmental authority in Moscow was in dispute between Yeltsin and Gorbachev. His aim was to secure a Chechnya independent of Russia, in which his own power would be all the greater.

Dudayev therefore turned down Yeltsin's proposal. The Russian delegation declared that he was acting without constitutional authority and that his government was therefore without a legal basis. Dudayev went on, nevertheless, to organize elections, and on October 29, 1991, he was elected president of an independent Chechnya. His first act as Chechen head of state was to declare Chechnya an independent republic. Yeltsin saw this as a challenge to his authority, and on November 7, 1991 he declared a state of emergency. In an outburst of patriotism, the Chechen people—for once with one mind—set aside their political differences and mobilized en masse against the Russian invader, who had been responsible for their deportation during World War II. Over 300,000 people packed Lenin Square, where the old men wore the same warlike garb that had been worn during the Caucasian wars of their ancestors.

Dudayev laid siege to the military airfield and stopped the Russian helicopters from landing. The Russian garrison of two thousand men was first taken hostage and then sent overland to North Ossetia on November 10. Yeltsin's humiliation was compounded a few days later when the Russian parliament rejected his declaration of a state of emergency and annulled it. On July 6, 1992, all Russian troops were forced to quit the territory of Chechnya. Russia canceled all aid to Chechnya forthwith, and put in place a military blockade of Chechnya accompanied by an economic and financial embargo and the freezing of all Chechen assets in Russian banks.

In the context of this confrontation with Moscow, unity was a prerequisite for the new state of Chechnya to achieve real independence. Chechnya's powerful neighbor—Russia—continued to stir up internal disputes and incited frontier tensions, all aimed to serve as an excuse for Russian intervention. Dudayev failed to attract the necessary unanimity for himself and soon faced opposition. A dissident pro-Russian movement on the ground quickly made its appearance, and he also found himself pitted against the former Soviet political establishment, who constituted an entrenched opposition to all his policies. Though Dudayev's regime was secular, he turned to Islam to reinforce the country's unity and consolidate opposition to the Russian presence. He sought the backing of the Sufi brotherhoods and approached other Muslim countries for support to aid his tiny and isolated republic. Dudayev also cultivated the other faiths. He arranged for the reopening of the synagogues and underwrote the rebuilding of the Orthodox churches.

The call to prayer, which was in Arabic according to the custom, was broadcast five times a day on the state radio. On television, religious broadcasts were transmitted twice each week. The dates of weekly days of rest were adjusted so that the weekend consisted of Friday and Saturday, whereas the Muslim former republics of the USSR for the most part stuck to the former system. According to official pronouncements, Islam was intended to bring about the "spiritual regeneration of the people." The state encouraged and supported the establishment of Islamic organizations, especially those with roots in society. Dudayev's aim was to consoli-

date his position in the country and build support.

Dudayev decided to finance and institutionalize the renewal of Islam to bring it under control. He also worked through the so-called Idarat, which ran the mosques and took responsibility for relations with other Muslim countries. The "Idarat" also ran the Islamic courts, which had jurisdiction over matters concerning divorce and inheritance, though their rulings were not obligatory as they operated in parallel with civil courts. When Dudayev seized power, the current Mufti, Mohammed Bashir Hajji, attempted to draw a line between religion and politics by refusing to give his support to the new Chechen president. Though his competence as a religious leader was not in question, he was replaced before the end of 1992. His successor, Garkev Mahmoud Hajji, was also sacked after major opposition demonstrations in the spring of 1993. After this, many of the local "ulema" (known locally as "hakim") refused ostentatiously to take part in the election of a new Mufti. The next Mufti, Mohammed Hossein Hajji, effectively a puppet of Dudayev, was backed by some chapters of the Qadiriya, but much of the Naqshbandiya was hostile to him and mounted a challenge to the government.

Dudayev's government founded and financed the Islamic University with its various faculties. The aim of this institution was to unify religious sciences with other disciplines, such as economics, technical subjects, and even medicine. The idea was to employ Islam in the restoration of moral values and Chechen traditions. Between 1989 and 1994, more than seven hundred mosques were opened. Each town—even each village—had its central mosque and district mosques. Unofficial financial aid came from various Islamic foundations in Saudi Arabia, Kuwait, and Jordan. The Soviet period, however, had left its mark. For the younger generation, Islam was observed only in a formal way.

The prohibitions on alcohol and pork generally went unobserved. A stroll through Grozny would have been enough to see that dress codes and sexual mores were relatively unconstrained. The war put religious concerns on the back burner. Religion became a weapon against the Russians. Arab so-called Afghans lined up together with Chechens to wage war on the Russians. The most notorious of these was "Commander" Amir Khattab, a Saudi citizen who fought with and helped to finance the Islamic opposition to Russia.

In the summer of 1994, Russia stepped up its campaign against Dudayev, supporting various opposition groups. A Russian-backed armed insurrection broke out in September 1994, though it had no impact on Dudayev's government. On November 26, an armed opposition movement launched a major offensive, making a bid to take Grozny, with the backing of Russian "volunteers." This was a total failure. Yeltsin issued an ultimatum on November 29, threatening to invade within forty-eight hours. On December 10, what has become known as the First Chechen War began when Russian forces entered Chechnya expecting a walkover. This did not happen. The Russian troops were quickly bogged down and suffered heavy losses. The Russian army took its revenge on the population, with massacres and looting, pillage, and rape. This marked the beginning of a bloody war. In December 1994 and January 1995, the Russian army bombed and shelled Grozny, resulting in heavy loss of life. Hundreds of thousands of civilians were forced to flee. To keep the Islamic clergy on his side, Dudayev proclaimed the Shari'a law, while maintaining the civil courts for Chechnya's non-Muslim inhabitants. Dudayev and his government fled Grozny for the historic Chechen capital of Vedeno, in the south of the country. Chechen guerrilla fighters conducted operations throughout the country,

inflicting serious losses to the Soviet forces. The Mufti of Ichkeria, Ahmad Kadyrov, declared a Jihad against Russia, and foreign Islamist fighters from neighboring republics and further afield began to arrive.

As the conflict proceeded, Dudayev found support in surprising places, including elements within the Russian military-industrial complex. Those who sought to restore the old USSR, and therefore opposed Yeltsin, supported Dudayev's regime in Grozny in order to weaken the Russian leader by supporting the Chechens against him. In addition, Chechnya—in an anarchic condition—had become a channel for the arms traffic, enabling profits to be made from the export of armaments. Russian interests were also involved in oil smuggling and sharing the profits with the smugglers. The Chechen Republic was perceived for all these reason as a danger to Russian unity and also a risk to the stability of the entire North Caucasus region. Other states there feared the spread of instability from their Chechen neighbor.

Earlier in 1994, Russia had succeeded in bringing another dissident republic, Tatarstan, back into the fold with concessions and incentives that had led to the signature of a treaty. However, negotiations with Chechnya that were aimed at securing its reintegration with Russia were not successful, and Russia, henceforth, had little choice. It was virtually impossible to seal the frontiers effectively, without committing huge resources. An independent Chechnya, were it to prosper, could set a highly dangerous precedent for the region, especially as Moscow's hold over the neighboring republics was less than complete, except perhaps for North Ossetia. There was also the issue of the security of the various oil transit routes that passed through Chechnya. Russia needed to win. However, in June 1995, Shamil Bassayev, with a handful of fighters, launched a raid into Russia, where he took hostages at Budionnovsk. This startling operation was enough to bring about a fragile cease-fire and to get negotiations started. On July 30, 1995, Dudayev's forces agreed to a military cease-fire, under whose terms the Russians would withdraw if the rebels disbanded. This was never really implemented. Later in 1995, the Russians announced that elections would be held in December for the pro-Russian puppet government it had installed in Grozny after the departure of General Dudayev. These were held on December 17, but were deemed invalid by international monitors. Dudayev was killed in action on April 21, 1996. He was hit by air-to-ground missiles after his position was detected by tracking his mobile phone. His successor was Zelimkhan Yandarbiyev, who was replaced by Maskhadov in January 1997.

After Yeltsin's reelection on June 3, 1996, fighting broke out once more. On August 6, 1996, the Chechen forces launched an all-out attack on Grozny, retaking the city in a few days. On August 12, Yeltsin sent General Lebed to negotiate with Aslan Maskhadov, the chief of staff of the Chechen military. An agreement signed at Khasavyurt on August 31, 1996, ended the conflict, but deferred until a later date the all-important issue of Chechen independence, thus failing to resolve the conflict. The toll taken by the war had been catastrophic. The country had been destroyed, and warlords were in charge. In two years, more than seventy thousand civilians had died—10 percent of the population. Thousands more had fled Chechnya forever. More than five thousand Chechen fighters had died and six thousand remained, under the command of various warlords. In January 1997, Maskhadov was elected president, but the country continued to slide into anarchy and economic crisis. Maskhadov's government was powerless to crush the warlords and was constantly threatened by civil war. Though Chechnya's independence was still not agreed, Maskhadov went to Moscow where on May 12, 1997, he signed

a peace treaty with Boris Yeltisn. Kidnappings, terrorism, and organized crime prevailed and the situation in Chechnya continued to be chaotic. Maskhadov confirmed the introduction of Islamic law, though he failed in an attempt to counter the spread of Wahabbi Salafist movements. These were supported by Basayev, and the result was a split in the Chechen ranks between nationalists and Islamists.

What has been described as the second Chechen War broke out on August 7, 1999, when a raid across the frontier into Daghestan by Chechen Islamists, led by Basayev and Khattab, unleashed a new cycle of violence. Just two days later, Vladimir Putin became prime minister of Russia with the mandate of expunging the Chechen "gangrene," as the Russians had begun to call it. At the end of August 1999, Putin launched devastating air attacks on Chechnya. By the end of September, the telephone and broadcasting system had been destroyed, bridges and roads had been cut, and electricity supplies no longer functioned. Hundreds of civilians died and perhaps a hundred thousand fled in a new wave of refugees, many of them to Ingushetia. On October 1, Putin declared Maskhadov's regime in Chechnya illegal and Russian troops once more invaded Chechnya. Military operations continued on a large scale over the following months and the number of refugees reached a quarter of a million, most seeking to enter neighboring countries. In Russia, Yeltsin unexpectedly resigned on December 31, and Putin became acting president. He was confirmed as president in the Russian election of March 2000, after the Russian forces had once more seized Grozny on February 2, 2000. Meanwhile, Maskhadov made his peace with the Islamists, and in October 1999 set up a "Committee for National Defense," one of whose members was Basayev. Maskhadov saw that he could not confront the Russians on the ground and opted for guerrilla resistance against the continuing Russian occupation.

Since then the conflict has rumbled on. Russia has tried to normalize the situation, but Chechen resistance has continued. A number of different organizations have emerged within the broad thrust of Islamist activity, driven to some extent not only by differing goals, but also by the ambition of various leaders. The organization Shamil Basayev headed until his death was called variously the United Forces of the Caucasian Mujahideen or the Supreme Military Majlis al-Shura. The role of this structure was to attempt to maintain a level of coordination among the activities of the various Salafist groups. The late "commander" Khattab's organization was known as the Islamic International Brigade, and it was toward this group that Arab and other foreign fighters gravitated. If there were links with Al-Qa'ida, it would be through connections maintained by members of this group. The so-called Special Purposes Islamic regiment specialized in attacks on Russian military units. "Riyad al-Salihin" was a group dedicated to the development of suicide operations and seems to have been involved in the Beslan affair. There were also linked operations in Daghestan and Ingushetia.

In May 2000, President Putin declared direct rule over Chechnya by Moscow. In April, he appointed Ahmad Kadyrov as head of a provisional government. On March 20, 2002, the Russians scored a small success when "Commander" Khattab was assassinated, apparently by Russian secret agents. In March 2003, a referendum held in Chechnya under Russian auspices ratified a new constitution that gave the country a degree of local autonomy while preserving its link with Russia. Many Chechens, including those who supported the resistance, boycotted the referendum. Kadyrov was assassinated on May 9, 2004. Chechen resistance tactics have included targeted assassinations of pro-Russian figures and suicide attacks on government institutions. On February 2,

2005, Maskhadov called for a cease-fire, but on March 8 he was killed by Russian security forces. The Chechen resistance leadership announced that Maskhadov's successor was Abdul Karim Sadulayev. This was approved by Shamil Basayev. Sadulayev was killed in June 2006 and was succeeded by another guerrilla leader, Doku Umarov, who said that the resistance would continue. The result of the continued guerrilla warfare against the Russians and the elimination of resistance leaders has been to further radicalize the resistance. Rebel spokesmen now speak of the need to expel Russia from the whole North Caucasus and to establish an Islamic State.

COURTAILLER, DAVID AND JEROME

The Courtailler brothers were born in the French town of Bonneville in the French Alps. Their father was a respected local figure and a butcher by trade. The two boys were popular at school, but less than successful and slipped into bad company. David Courtailler, born in 1975, converted to Islam in Britain in 1996, and then went to Afghanistan where he attended mujahidin training camps. He returned to France in 1998 and came to the attention of the French police in 1999. In 2000, the French police detained him. In May 2004, he was sentenced to two years imprisonment because of his links with Islamic militants. He was accused of giving assistance to a terrorist group planning a bomb attack. Jerome Courtailler, born in 1973, also converted to Islam. He was convicted in absentia by a Dutch court of implication in planning a terrorist attack on the French Embassy in Paris and turned himself over to the police in the Netherlands. He was sentenced in September 2004 to six years' confinement. They are seen in France as a part of an increasing trend of converts to Islam to become involved in militant activity.

DAR AL-MAL AL-ISLAMI TRUST (DMI)

In 1981, during the Islamic summit in the Saudi city of Ta'if, Prince Mohammed Ibn Faisal Al Saud, a son of the late King Faisal, organized a meeting of major investors in the Kingdom of Saudi Arabia and in the Emirates to set up a private Islamic bank. The bank was to be known as the Dar al-Mal al-Islami (DMI): literally the Islamic Finance House. The bank is incorporated in the Bahamas, which is also the company address of al-Taqwa, the bank run by the Muslim Brotherhood. The Sudanese Islamist leader Hassan al-Turabi was involved in its foundation. A year later, King Fahd asked his brother-in-law to found another private Islamic bank, the Dallah al-Baraka.

Thus, a new source of finance came into being in Saudi Arabia, which was available for Islamism—but not for terrorism. Through these two banks, countless Islamic NGOs were funded, which served as instruments of the Saudi family's "Islamic diplomacy." The former public relations director of the DMI, Mouaouia Mokhtari—an Algerian citizen—expressed the official line: "DMI and its associates arrived in the market before the advent of fundamentalism and associated themselves with a moderate Islamic tendency." While Mokhtari spoke for the DMI, its director, Ali Omar Abdi—a

leading specialist in Islamic finance from Somalia—never appeared in public and gave no interviews.

The DMI was a consortium of investors from a range of economic and financial interests, such as Faisal Finance, the Gulf Islamic Investment Corporation, and others. Its head office was in Geneva close to Cointrin international airport, and it maintained branches in various countries, including Bahrain, Pakistan, Turkey, Denmark, Guinea, Senegal, Niger, and Luxembourg. The King Faisal Foundation, based in Riyadh, was one of its main shareholders. This foundation had been established by the Saudi royal family and was well known for its links with religious proselytization, particularly through the financing of Quranic schools, Islamic cultural centres, and mosques. The DMI was also a shareholder in Al-Taqwa, the bank run by the Egyptian Muslim Brothers.

The DMI's financial policy, in line with Islamic doctrine, was to rule out profit-based interest from loans. The bank therefore invested in revenue producing activities. Investors purchased shares with a nominal value of $100,000, which they could augment in steps of $20,000. By 2002, DMI managed funds of $3.5 billion, as against an initial value of $852 million in 1982. Profits made by DMI's investment managers were shared in the proportion of 80 percent for the investors and 20 percent for the bank, which also took a 0.1 percent management fee on the cash entrusted to it for investment. Finally, the investors undertook to pay annually from their own funds the "zakat"—the religious tax destined for charitable purposes—as prescribed by Islamic law.

It was this provision that placed the DMI in a central role in the financing of a multiplicity of Islamic activities in Europe and in the world at large. Its report for 1999 records more than 2 million dollars of "zakat," but gives no indication of who the beneficiaries may have been or what use was made of these funds, on which no report was made to the bank. According to financial experts, this religious tax was the principal source of funds for Islamic organizations whose official remit was to undertake religious and humanitarian activities. In the 1990s, the DMI suffered significant losses for a number of reasons. These included unwise speculation in gold and foreign exchange, a rise in interest rates that eroded the profit margins on which its management was based, the repatriation of funds by a number of Saudi investors after the Gulf War of 1990–1991, and a fall in oil profits. Because of all these difficulties the DMI undertook a major restructuring in early 1994 and dismissed dozens of executives and employees. The bank also decided to spread is investor base more widely and took the decision at a general meeting of its eighteen-man management board to seek investors in the Maghreb, Syria, and Lebanon and in non-Arab Muslim countries such as Pakistan, Indonesia, and Malaysia.

In 1997, though as an Islamic bank the DMI continued to practice noninterest bearing investment, its branches began to undertake portfolio investment. For example, Dallah al Baraka launched the Al-Safwa International Equity Fund, an investment fund worth 2 billion dollars. The DMI claims that its principle of not profiting from interest has not been compromised, and that it chooses investments on this basis. In a move to associate itself with partners with a track record in this market, the Saudi bank took investment advice from "Rolls & Ross Asset Management," an American concern that specialized in company evaluation. This new development, which came some twenty years after the foundation of the first Islamic banks, was prompted by the globalization of financial institutions and by the Bank's desire to establish a place for itself within the traditional financial system. The DMI continues to operate, in contrast to Al-Taqwa, whose assets were frozen in November 2001. In 2005, Dar al-Mal al-Islami was described as flourishing, along with a group of other banks such as the Al-Mal-Al-Islami Trust, Islamic Development Bank, Al Rajhi Banking and Investment Corp, Al Baraka Group, and the Kuwait Finance House.

DENMARK

From as early as the late 1960s, Muslims came to Denmark from Turkey, Pakistan, Morocco, and the former Yugoslavia. Most were economic migrants in search of work. By the 1980s and 1990s, however, the majority of new immigrants were refugees. They came from various countries, including Iran, Iraq, Somalia, and Bosnia, though the majority of Muslims in the country continued to be of Turkish origin. From 1985 onward, foreigners resident in Denmark for more than three years were permitted to participate in local elections as voters and candidates. Denmark also guaranteed full and equal religious freedom for all communities. However, housing and employment have been a concern for Muslims in Denmark. By 2006, the Muslim population totaled 200,000—5 percent in a country of 5.4 million inhabitants. Most are concentrated in Copenhagen and in Aarhus, many in such ethnically diverse neighborhoods as Norrebro in the capital and the Gellerup suburb of Aarhus. Danish citizenship has been granted only to a minority of Denmark's Muslim residents. However, Denmark's attitude toward migrants has become much stricter, with controls on further migration and an emphasis on integration.

A cultural center and a mosque, which by 2000 were run by followers of Necmettin Erbakan, have continued to provide a focus for the Turkish community. Others have their own social centers. The Shi'a mosque known as the Islamic Jaffaria Center attracts mainly Pakistani Shi'ite Muslims and claims to be nonpolitical. One leading imam, Ahmed Abu Laban, has attempted to unify the various ethnic groups. However, Abu Laban is seen as a hard-liner by the Danish media, because of the stress he places on the primacy for Muslims of their loyalty to Islam as against other cultural or nationalistic factors. Among Islamist influences, the Muslim Brotherhood was able to gain a firm footing. As regards more radical groups, the Egyptian Gama'a Islamiya, led by Fouad Tala'at Mohammed attracted a wide spread of migrants from the various Maghreb countries. In addition, the Algerian GSPC and the Algerian version of Takfir wa'l Hijra have been active in Denmark and have gained a foothold among Denmark's Muslim immigrants. In 2004, in the atmosphere of increasing tension that followed September 11, 2001, the U.S.-led invasion of Iraq in March 2003, and the Madrid train bombings in March 2004, the Danish police made approaches to Muslim community leaders in Copenhagen, asking for their cooperation in maintaining security.

In September 2005, however, a difficult chapter in the history of Muslims in Denmark began with the publication of cartoons critical of Islam and the Prophet Muhammad in the Danish newspaper *Jyllands-Posten*. The self-declared aim of the newspaper's cultural editor, Flemming Rose,

was to protest against what he said was self-censorship in the European press following the assassination of the Dutch filmmaker Theo Van Gogh in 2004 after the release of a film critical of the treatment of women in Islam. *Jyllands-Posten* had already conducted a campaign against two Salafist imams of Lebanese origin, Raed Hlayhel and Ahmed Akkari. These two aroused local and international reactions to the cartoons. Ahmed Abu Laban said the aim of the cartoons was to provoke Muslims and was a deliberate attempt by right-wing politicians in Denmark to antagonize the population against the Muslim community. Two delegations of Danish Muslims traveled abroad to drum up reaction to the incident. In the end, the result was the radicalization of the Danish Muslim community and a widespread international reaction. In February 2006, the Danish embassies in Lebanon and Syria were attacked and there were anti-Danish riots as far afield as Kashmir and Indonesia.

DOSTUM, ABDUL RASHID

Abdul Rashid Dostum, leader of the Jombesh-i Melli Islami movement in Afghanistan, is an ethnic Uzbek by origin. He was born in 1954 into a family of landless peasant farmers and learned to read late. He received military training in the 1980s in the Soviet Union and first came to notice in 1991 during the struggle against the Mujahidin, when he led a mainly Uzbek militia of 20,000 men. He was a capable and ruthless chieftain and did not shrink from rape, pillage, and assassination in order to make himself feared. He was appointed a Hero of the Afghan Republic and was a member of the Central Committee of the Afghan Communist Party.

In February 1992, Dostum—ever an opportunist—abandoned the communist leader Najibullah two months before his fall to join the Mujahidin. He made approached the militia leader Ahmed Shah Massoud and helped defend Kabul against the approaching forces of Gulbuddin Hekmatyar. Kabul was virtually destroyed in the fighting. In the subsequent political arrangement between the Mujahidin militia leaders, Massoud and Hekmatyar uneasily cooperated in a new government. Amidst the ever-shifting alliances among Afghanistan's commanders, Dostum later drew closer to Hekmatyar.

Dostum, who had amassed perhaps the strongest single force in Afghanistan, later retired to his old stronghold at Mazar-i Sharif, which became virtually a state within a state. He had his own army and his own aircraft, flew his own flag, and issued his own currency. Aid from countries unhappy about the rise of the Taliban ("Students of Religion") helped him to hold them back. Dostum was betrayed by one of his lieutenants, Abdul Malik Pahlawan, with the result that in 1997 he was obliged to quit Mazar-i Sharif, which was captured by the Taliban. His former ally then turned against the Taliban, who lost a major battle. In September 1997, Dostum retook Mazar-i Sharif and held out there until August 1998, when the support he had from Uzbekistan, which now sought to reach its own accord with the Taliban, was withdrawn. He went into exile in Turkey, but returned to the Northern Alliance camp in 2001, when he was able to reach another agreement with Massoud. After the fall of the Taliban, he became deputy minister of defense in the provisional government of Hamid Karzai.

EGYPT

Gamaa Islamiya (GI—The Islamic Group)

Dating from 1976, this was a legitimate student group whose origins lay in university circles in Cairo. It shared much of its ideology with Egyptian Islamic Jihad and Takfir wa-l-Hijra, as well as with the Muslim Brotherhood, from which many of its members came. In its early years, it was tolerated by the administration of President Sadat, who was in difficulties with the Nasserists and the left wing. From 1981 onward, however, after Sadat's murder at the hands of Takfir wa-l Hijra, it went underground and began to adopt violent tactics.

The movement's leader in its early years was Sheikh Omar Abdel Rahman, born in 1938, who was a graduate of Al-Azhar and an outspoken critic of Egypt's secularism. The Sheikh's inspirations were Sayyed Qutb and the medieval Islamic philosopher Ibn Taymiya. Charismatic despite having been blind from his early childhood, the Sheikh exercised a strong control over his followers. After Sadat's murder, he spent three years in prison, accused of justifying the assassination with a fatwa. He was acquitted, but was expelled from Egypt. In the mid-1980s, he made his way to Afghanistan where he made contact with Abdullah Azzam and met Osama bin Laden. He cooperated with

the United States to recruit Egyptian fighters to join the Jihad against the Afghan communists and their Soviet backers. In the early 1990s, he moved to the United States to coordinate the recruitment effort there. In 1993, he issued fatwas justifying violence against American targets. He was accused by the U.S. security authorities of planning the first bombing of the World Trade Center, and in 1995 he was convicted of seditious conspiracy and was given a life sentence. The Sheikh's conversion to anti-Americanism was similar to that of his contemporaries who broke with Washington after the Gulf War and the establishment of the Americans in the Arabian Peninsula.

Once the Afghan Jihad was over, the Gamaa Islamiya began to advocate the violent overthrow of the regime in Egypt. Returning fighters from Afghanistan, who had received various degrees of combat training, made the organization more formidable. From 1989 onward, tourists, lay intellectuals, political figures, and Copts became the targets for a relentless terrorist campaign. At the same time, the Egyptian security forces mounted a systematic program to stamp out terrorist activities, especially in Cairo and its suburbs and in upper Egypt. At the same time, members of the GI began to move abroad. Some went to Afghanistan, where the factional struggle that brought the Taliban to power was raging. Others went to Pakistan, to Yemen, to Kenya, or even farther afield, to Europe or the Americas.

The most ambitious action carried out by the GI was the attempted assassination in June 1995 of the Egyptian leader President Husni Mubarak in Addis Ababa, the capital of Ethiopia, as he arrived to attend an Organization of African Unity meeting. Otherwise, the most flagrant atrocity committed by the group was the massacre of foreign tourists at Luxor in November 1997, where sixty-seven non-Egyptians were killed and dozens wounded. The instigator of these two actions was Mustafa Hamza, the head of the GI's Shura (Consultative) Council, who later fled to Sudan and then to Afghanistan, where he remained until 1999. He was the most senior GI leader to have eluded capture by the Egyptian authorities. Rifa'i Taha, his colleague, was handed over to the Egyptians after 9/11 following his expulsion from Sudan to Syria. In February 1998, Taha had participated together with Bin Laden and Ayman al-Zawahiri in the creation of the "World Islamic Front Against the Crusaders and the Jews." However, the GI drew a line—at least in public—between itself and Al-Qa'ida after the operations of August 1998 in East Africa, when the U.S. embassies in Kenya and Tanzania were attacked. The revision of the GI's military strategy in October 1999 and the call for cessation of armed actions were issued by a number of GI leaders and officials imprisoned in Egypt.

In the post–9/11 period, the faction that wanted a halt to violence gained strength. The move was not supported, however, by GI leaders abroad. These included Omar Abdel Rahman, who was in prison in the United States. Other exiled leaders who remained silent included Osama Rushdy, who was in London; Hana Siba'i, who was imprisoned in Afghanistan after the plot against Massud; and Adel Abdul Majid, who was held in Britain and wanted by the United States. Other GI officials who had remained in Egypt, including Ala' Abderrazak and Rif'at Zaydan, supported the new policy and in particular condemned the attacks on tourists. Their aim was political rehabilitation. Some even favored the establishment of a political party and supported the move by a journalist close to the GI, Jamal Sultan, who planned the establishment of some kind of reformist party within which former militants could participate in politics. In March 2002, the historic leadership of the group in Egypt under Mustafa Hamza renounced violence, and in 2003 the government release almost one thousand former GI activists from prison.

Islamic Jihad

Islamic Jihad in Egypt is a clandestine organization that appeared in the latter half of the 1970s. In 1977, a group that included Lieutenant Colonel Abboud el-Zomor, backed by a secretive Shura Council (consultative council), set up "Al-Jihad al-Islami." Its aim from the outset was nothing less than the establishment of an Islamic state. Later, an essential part of its platform was the overthrow of the "impious" Egyptian government, which had signed a peace treaty with Israel.

On October 6, 1981, four Islamic Jihad militants, including Lt. Khaled Slambouli, assassinated Egypt's President Sadat at a military parade to celebrate the anniversary of the crossing of the Suez Canal by Egyptian troops in 1973. Slambouli was tried and executed in 1982. His brother, Mohammed Shawki Slambouli, went to Pakistan and Afghanistan, where he joined forces with Ayman al-Zawahri, an associate of Osama bin Laden. After the assassination, Islamic Jihad attempted to stir up a revolt in the Egyptian town of Assiut, in upper Egypt, a town with a large Coptic Christian minority, where the Muslim Brotherhood and other Muslim militant groups were active among the Muslim population. Hundreds of adherents of the Islamic Jihad and other groups were arrested.

Jihad's members, who are organized into compartmentalized cells, specialize in assassinations. In 1993, they attempted to murder Egypt's prime minister and interior minister. They were also responsible for the attack on the Egyptian Embassy in the Pakistani capital Islamabad, in which seventeen were killed and fifty-nine wounded. As from February 1998, Ayman al-Zawahiri, the effective head of the Egyptian Islamic Jihad, took the organization into an alliance with Osama bin Laden. He did not have unanimous support for this move, especially among the eleven Jihad leaders imprisoned in Egypt. In July 2000, they put their signatures to a declaration calling for a halt to armed operations and in particular to attacks on civilians. The signatories included Ismail Nasreddin and Amr Abdul Moneim, both presumed members of Jihad's Shura Council. However, the most influential of Jihad's leaders stayed loyal to Zawahiri. These included the organization's security chief, Tharwat Salah Shehata, as well as Osama Siddiq Ayyub and Mohammed Mekkawi, the head of Jihad's armed wing Tali'at al Fath (The Vanguard of Conquest).

After Zawahiri's flight from Afghanistan, the "prison leadership" has regained some influence. Proponents of the school that advocated "jihad at all costs" seem to have been sidelined. However, Jihad's extremist ideology could lead to a relapse into violence. It should be noted that in practical terms, the Egyptian Islamic Jihad has no connection with the Lebanese and Palestinian groups that bear the same name.

ERBAKAN, NECMETTIN

Necmettin Erbakan was born in 1926 in the town of Sinop, in northern Turkey, into a pious Islamic family. His father had been a "cadi" (an Islamic judge). He studied at the Technical University in Istanbul, and then continued his studies in Germany. He returned to Turkey with a doctorate in mechanical engineering and made his career in teaching and technical enterprises. He joined Suleyman Demirel's Justice Party, which was committed to the support of Islamic ideas, and also achieved a responsible position in Turkey's national organization of Chambers of Commerce. However, his ideas began to diverge from the Justice Party and he founded the Islamic ideological movement known as Milli Görüs or "National View." This lay behind all the subsequent political parties Erbakan and his followers established and also became active in the Turkish community in Europe, particularly Germany. Erbakan stood for parliament as an independent in the elections of 1969 for the constituency of Konya, a city known as a bastion of Islamic conservatism, on a platform embodying the philosophy of Milli Görüs. Konya was subsequently to become his power base. He won election to parliament and, with the support of some of the Islamic brotherhoods, he set up his own political organization, the National Order Party (Milli Nizam), in February 1970. A year later, after the military coup of May 1971, Erbakan explicitly challenged some elements of the principles of secular Kemalist ideology, thus attracting the unfavorable attention of Turkey's military establishment, which regards itself as the guardian of the country's secular and republican constitution. Since the military government in Turkey in 1960, the General Staff has occupied key seats on the so-called National Security Council, together with senior civilian political figures, which gives rulings on constitutional issues. Erbakan was obliged temporarily to leave Turkey, spending two years in Switzerland.

After his return in 1973, he joined the National Salvation Party, set up a year earlier, within which he rapidly rose to become leader. He always had the facility to make compromises and to form alliances with political rivals who did not share his ideas. After the elections of 1973, in which his party won impressive results, he went into a coalition government with Bulent Ecevit's Republican People's Party. Standing on a pan-Islamic and patriotic platform, he spoke out for traditional values and took a belligerent position at the time of the Turkish army's invasion of Cyprus in 1974. With the support of other Islamist ministers, his aim was to put militants into key positions in the administration, for example in religious affairs and education. In the governments led by Sulyeman Demirel, who was elected in March 1975 and January 1978, he served as deputy prime minister. However, the country continued to be racked by violent conflicts. Multiplying political factions following radically different ideological directions—nationalists, Maoists, and Islamists—were opposed each other violently, up to and including armed conflict. A second military coup in September 1980 led to the suspension of political activities. In common with other well-known figures, Erbakan was banned from political activity and from making any public statement.

In 1983, the stage seemed set for his return to public life. The former leaders of the National Salvation Party reassembled to form the Refah Party (the Party of Prosperity), which espoused the Milli Görüs philosophy. As Erbakan was still prohibited from active politics, the party's temporary leader was Ali Turkmen. After an amnesty in 1985, Necmettin Erbakan was once more allowed to take part in politics. He reassumed control of the Refah Party and worked to transform it into a mass movement with Islamic sympathies. He based his platform on the fight against corruption and on social issues. However, he was unable to make headway against Turgut Ozal's party, the Mother-

land Party (ANAP), which also advocated a return to moral values, and consequently the Refah Party had difficulty in expanding its appeal. Necmettin Erbakan, therefore, took the Refah Party into a pragmatic electoral alliance with the extreme right wing supporters of Colonel Türkes. The resulting joint lists took 17 percent of the seats in the parliamentary elections of 1991, obtaining forty seats in the parliament under Turkey's proportional representation system.

In the elections of 1994 and 1995, Erbakan attracted much support. During the conflicts in Bosnia and Nagorny-Karabagh, he frequently spoke out against the West. He opted to compromise by going into coalition with Tansu Çiller's Justice Party in order to hold on to power. Erbakan became prime minister in July 1996, but immediately came under pressure from many directions. On August 26, he signed a cooperation agreement with Israel, at the insistence of the general staff of the army. The resulting military maneuvers damaged Erbakan's stature as Turkey's leading Islamist thinker, with the result that Arab countries castigated him as a dupe of Zionism. In addition, Turkey was rocked by a series of financial scandals. Erbakan made sweeping changes in the upper echelons of Turkey's administration, but his period in office came to an end in July 1997 after a further crisis between the Islamic government and the Turkish military authorities led to a threat of the breakup of the governing coalition.

Shortly before leaving office, however, Erbakan succeeded in setting up the D8 group of nations—an Islamic organization that concentrates on trade and welfare. In addition to Turkey, D8 includes Bangladesh, Egypt, Indonesia, Iran, Malaysia, Nigeria, and Pakistan. Its stated aim is to improve the position of the developing countries in the world economy and to improve the standards of living of their citizens. Erbakan regarded the creation of the D8 group as his major international achievement during his period in office. At its meeting in Bali in June 2006, it asserted the right of the Islamic nations to the peaceful use of nuclear energy.

Once Erbakan was out of office, the military took steps against him and his party. In January 1998, following accusations by the military general staff that the Refah Party was engaging in "anti-secular activities," Necmettin Erbakan was banned from political activity for five years, and on February 28—in what was referred to as a "soft" coup d'état—the Refah Party was dissolved. His personal attempt to accommodate his politics to the constraints imposed by Turkish constitutional conventions came to an end. However, former members of the Refah Party and Milli Görüs sympathizers formed the new Fazilet Party (Virtue Party) to take its place. The new FP was keen on dialogue with the European Union, closer association with which it hoped might lead to restrictions on the role of the military in Turkish politics. In 2001, however, the FP was dissolved after the Turkish constitutional court ruled that it had acted unconstitutionally in defending the right of Turkish women state employees and students to wear the Islamic headscarf. It was succeeded by yet another party based on the ideas of Milli Görüs, the Saadet Party (Felicity Party). However, a younger group led by Tayep Erdogan set up the AKP (Justice and Development Party), which has achieved the reputation of a moderate Islamist party.

On March 2, 2002, Necmettin Erbakan, then aged seventy-six, who was still the principal leader of the Islamist movement, was sentenced to two years and four months imprisonment in relation to a fraud concerning the former Refah Party's finances. After Refah was dissolved in 1998, the court had demanded the return of funds Refah had received from the Turkish state as a legitimate political party. Erbakan was alleged to

have disbursed the money in cash to party branch chairmen in order to safeguard it for the party. Erbakan appealed against his sentence, which was deferred five times. In June 2006 it was finally agreed that Erbakan, now over eighty, could serve his sentence as a period of house arrest. However, the conviction put an end to his political career.

ERITREA

Eritrea is a state situated in the Horn of Africa with a population of 4.4 million, divided virtually equally into Muslims (46 percent) and Christians (45.2 percent), who mainly adhere to the Eritrean church, which split off from the Ethiopian church in 1998. Since achieving independence from Ethiopia in 1993, the local Islamic movement has risen to prominence. A key factor is that Eritrean independence is supported by Islamist states such as Iran, Saudi Arabia, and Sudan. The Eritrean Islamic Jihad Movement, led by Mohammed Ismail Abduh, is the most significant Eritrean Islamist movement. It changed its name in 1998 to the Islamic Liberation Movement. It initially backed the Eritrean Liberation Front, but later opposed the new government established in Asmara. In the early months of independence, fighters based in Sudanese territory embarked on guerrilla activity in the north of the country, assisted by the Sudanese government, which viewed the Eritrean government as "impious," due to its Christian component. Saudi Arabia also takes a hand in Eritrean affairs. Its aim is to promote the Islamization of the country in the long term through the infiltration of Islamists into the government. The conflict resulted in the breaking off of diplomatic relations between Khartoum and Asmara and meant that Eritrea has become a proxy for the United States in its effort to contain militant Islamism. Moves toward the settlement of the border conflict with

Ethiopia, which facilitated the deployment of the regular army against the Islamist guerrillas, undermined their position. The Islamists also appear to have lost the protection of Sudan. However, an unsettled situation in Eritrea could allow the threat to reemerge.

ETHIOPIA

As in Eritrea, the population of Ethiopia is made of approximately equal numbers of Christians and Muslims, though most sources put the Christians in a slight majority. The Christians belong mainly to the autonomous Ethiopian Church. Within the country's ethnic diversity, the various Islamic movements have for the most part aligned themselves with tribal and other factional tendencies.

In the late 1960s, the Oromo Islamic Liberation Front made its appearance in southern Ethiopia. The Oromo people have their own national ambitions, and Sunni Islam has historical roots in the region. On the other hand, the secular Oromo Liberation Front, with a broadly Christian leadership, in fact took a more central role in the struggle of the Oromo minority against Ethiopia, rallying many Oromo Muslims to its banner. Under Mengistu's Marxist and pro-Soviet regime, the leaders of the Oromo Islamic Liberation Front, some of whom had

Wahhabi sympathies, took refuge in Saudi Arabia. After the fall of Mengistu in 1991, the Oromo Islamic Liberation Front received the backing of the Islamist regime in Khartoum and recovered some of its impetus. It appears never to have been an especially effective movement on the ground, though it scored some military successes against the Ethiopian forces. However, action by the Ethiopian army and the involuntary retirement in 2001 of Sudan's Islamic figurehead Hassan al-Turabi deprived the Islamic Front of support. By 2002, it had lost its way.

Other Islamic movements emerged among the Somali ethnic community, in the Ogaden region in the southwest of the country. These challenged the leadership of the Ogaden National Liberation Front. The principal Somali Islamist movement—Al-Ittihad al-Islami—was established in the early 1990s, with the goal of creating a "Greater Somalia." In 1994, the Ethiopian government launched a comprehensive attack on the Islamists, who withdrew most of their force into neighboring Somalia. In 1996, Al-Ittihad al-Islami began a campaign of terrorism against the members of the Ethiopian government. It has considerable support from some circles within the Sudanese and Saudi governments. By 2002, some of the movement's members had rallied to the support of the transitional government in Somalia.

FARRAKHAN, LOUIS

Louis Farrakhan is the leader of the U.S.-based movement known as the Nation of Islam. He was born in 1933, as Louis Wolcott, and until he met Malcolm X in the early 1950s, his ambition was to be a musician. He became the imam of the Nation of Islam's "Temple" in Boston, where he wrote his anthem, "A white man's heaven is a black man's hell." When Malcolm X was expelled from the Nation of Islam, Farrakhan did not follow him. Instead, he became the imam of the Harlem Temple, a key position in the organization. Afterward, he disassociated himself from the reformist doctrine preached by Wallace Muhammad, the son of the movement's founder Elijah Muhammad, who moved away from the heterodox beliefs of the Nation of Islam and transformed it into the American Muslim Mission, a movement more aligned with Sunni Islam. In February 1981, Louis Farrakhan refounded the Nation of Islam.

Under the presidency of Ronald Reagan, the United States embarked on a policy of "integration from above," encouraging the rise of such black figures as Colin Powell, Michael Jackson, Eddie Murphy, and Carl Lewis in public life, in spheres including politics, sport, cinema, and media. Meanwhile, Farrakhan wanted to see the gangs in the ghettos merge themselves into an "Army of Allah," thus enabling young blacks to escape the evils caused, according to him, by the white community, such as drugs, crime, prostitution, and the lack of education.

In politics, Farrakhan several times committed his movement to the support of the Democrat Jesse Jackson, a black minister of religion who openly rejected all efforts at integration and took subventions from the Libyan leader Colonel Gaddafi. The Reverend Jackson did not hesitate to compare the situation of American blacks with that of the Palestinians. He aroused the active hostility of American Jews when he called New York "Hymietown." In 1984, Farrakhan made his own contribution when he described Israel as an illegal state, which resulted in a unanimous Senate vote condemning his statement as anti-Semitic.

The anti-Semitic tone he adopted strengthened the emotional links between the black American community and the Arab and Islamic world. For example, from the mid-1980s, Libyan funds began to swell the coffers of the Nation of Islam. In 1985, Farrakhan made a pilgrimage to Mecca in the company of Abdullah Omar Nasif, the secretary-general of the World Islamic League, whose role was to act as a conduit for the political and religious influence of Saudi Arabia toward the Islamic world. In 1990–1991, Farrakhan came out in opposition to Saddam Hussein, with the approval of the U.S. leadership.

In October 1996, Farrakhan organized the so-called million man march in Washington, DC, while the Nation of Islam once more took a higher profile.

At the time of the "million man march," Farrakhan developed his "separatist" plan, proposing a political and social separation between the blacks and other Americans. His model was for a kind of equitable apartheid, under which the five states of the southeastern United States, the majority of whose population was black, would gain total independence, forming the "black American State." Farrakhan has continued to be regarded as an important leader by many black people in America. Over the decade up to 2006, he continued to make a series of hostile statements about white Americans. He vocally criticized the handling by the U.S. authorities of the crisis that followed Hurricane Katrina in 2005, claiming that there had been a deliberate attack on America's black population. In September 2006, Farrakhan announced that he was seriously ill, but asked his followers to carry on his movement. In October 1996, the Nation of Islam marked the tenth anniversary of the million man march with another major demonstration in Washington, DC.

FRANCE

The Islamist militants of Europe are dispersed into a complex pattern of associations, mosques, and economic organizations. This is so especially in France, where there were by 2007 some 6 million Muslim residents. A third of these live in the Paris region. As to their origins, just over a third come from Algeria and a similar number from Morocco. However, only 40 percent say that they are Muslim believers, though 70 percent fast during Ramadan. For the Islamists, the European Union has been an unanticipated windfall. Building in various ways on

the different forms of social organization in Europe, the Islamists have had no difficulty in emphasizing their European identity. The Islamist associations in Europe have all been influenced by one or other of the movements on the world scene. In France and Belgium, for example, the Muslim Brotherhood has made a bid to control the Muslim associations. Their rivalry with the Turks has been fierce. Germany has a large Turkish population, but the Turks have also been strongly represented in France since the 1980s. Other contenders for influence in France are the India–Pakistan-based Tablighi Jamaat and the Saudi Salafis, who are in practice allied with those supported by the Moroccan government. Young Muslims confused over their identity constitute the obvious target of all these groups. These are clearly a fertile field for rapid re-Islamization, before being dragooned into a system of associations and other institutions.

In France, certainly, all the Islamist groups mentioned above have targeted young Muslims of North African origin of the third generation—those whose parents were born in France. To understand the inroads made by Islamic fundamentalists in France, it should be recalled that in the early 1960s, on the threshold of the Evian agreement, which ended the Algerian War of Independence, the French manufacturing industry thirsted for unskilled labor. This brought the first generation of Muslims to France. These new arrivals practiced Islam discreetly and almost apologetically at their places of work. From 1965, prayer rooms were often made available to them, for example at the Renault factory at Billancourt.

The legislation on family reunification put on the statute book in 1971 and implemented in 1974 led rapidly to the arrival of the spouses of the immigrants and to the appearance of a second generation of Muslims in France. These Muslim French men and women sought to integrate themselves into French society and the French economy. At this stage, many small businesses made their appearance, most visibly shops and restaurants. Up to this stage, Islam in France had maintained strong links with the countries of origin. The next generation to appear—the third generation: the children of those born in France—emerged in the early years of the 1980s, at a time of upheaval in the Muslim world, following the Islamic Revolution in Iran in 1979, and the Soviet invasion of Afghanistan in the same year. At the same time, in a development crucial for the evolution of the situation in France, changes in the law on the formation of associations permitted Muslims to sever the link with their countries of origin and set the scene for the multiplication of new Muslim associations.

What young Muslims born in France want above all is the right to be what they are. As they discover their Islamicity, their first rebellion is against their father and grandfathers, who rejected or abandoned their religion. Subsequently, their search for an identity impelled them to rediscover both their unknown countries of origin and an Islam of which they knew nothing. This frequently led to strife within the family. Patriarchal authority, traditionally the kernel of the family unit, ceded its place to authority derived from knowledge, which for the young Muslim was often the prerogative of his sister, who did well at school and then at university and was able to find work. The first masculine authority he was obliged to confront was that of the policeman or the magistrate. Many young Muslims resorted to the reassertion of their self-respect through the acquisition of money, which only too often led to delinquency. The alternative route toward "becoming somebody" lay through adherence to one of the Muslim groups.

In France, the Muslim Brotherhood was the driving force behind two distinct groups, the Association of Islamic Students in France

("Association des Etudiants Islamiques en France") (AEIF) and the Union of Islamic Organizations in France ("Union des Organisations Islamiques en France") (UOIF). The latter controlled a number of major mosques, including the principal mosque in Lille, where there is a substantial Muslim population. The UOIF also ran a number of satellite organizations such as the Young Muslims of France ("Jeunes musulmans de France") (JMF) and the Muslim Students of France ("Etudiants musulmans de France") (EMF). Tablighi Jamaat—in Arabic Jamaat at-Tabligh (The Societies of the Message)—has also been a major factor in the re-Islamization of young people. It is especially well represented in the Parisian region and in the northern part of France, as well as in Marseille, Dreux, and Alsace.

Another factor is the so-called Salafi groups. This is what strict Wahhabi Muslims like to call themselves. They claim to derive their doctrine directly from the Quran and the Sunna, rejecting the codified interpretations of the four traditional schools of religious law and the carefully tabulated doctrine of conventional conservative Muslims. In Europe, certain Salafis made an iconic figure of Abu Hamza al-Masri, the erstwhile imam of the Finsbury Park Mosque in north London to which many young French Muslims made their way. By 2006, Abdelhadi Doudi, the imam of the celebrated Salafi Mosque on the Boulevard National in Marseille, was seen as a leading Salafi. He was what had by now come to be called in France a "Sheikhist" Salafi. This expression referred to those who adhered strictly to edicts issued by the Saudi religious authorities and concentrated on spiritual and personal issues, rejecting involvement in politics or radical stances on world affairs. The Salafis, with their claim to Islamic purity, have great appeal to young Muslims and have succeeded in recruiting from the Tablighi mosques as well as from the Muslim Brotherhood.

In 1989, when the state first clashed with Muslims over the issue of women wearing Muslim head coverings, the government set up a body known as CORIF ("Working Council on Islam in France") to attempt to settle issues relating to the status of Muslims and to avert radicalism. Six well-known imams were appointed to the council, who co-opted nine other members. CORIF was clearly the creation of the French state and held its meetings at the Interior Ministry. In 1996, a socialist government in France widened the membership of CORIF to produce a more representative council. Finally, a consultation committee held in December 2002 set the scene for the next move.

By 2003, with the Muslim population beginning to approach 5 million, there were already 1,500 places of worship for Muslims. The French government was beginning to feel the need to negotiate with the Muslim community as a whole and decided to promote the formation of a single body to represent the entire community. This was in itself a new departure for France, where since 1905 strict legislation on secularism (known in French as "laïcité") has barred the state from giving financial support to any religion. "Laïcité" has become a key principle of French politics, and political leaders of all persuasions see any move to accord recognition to any religious group as a move toward "community" based politics, a misdemeanor they believe that is prevalent in the Anglo-Saxon world.

On April 13, 2003, the "Conseil français du culte musulman" (CFCM) (French Council for Muslim Worship), together with twenty-five regional councils, was elected to represent French Muslims by four thousand representatives of the various Muslim bodies in the country. Among the organizations represented on the CFCM were the UOIF and the FNMF (National Federation of French Muslims), supported by Morocco. The Paris Mosque was also represented, as an institu-

tion that already supported cooperation with the French Republic and its legal rules. The Paris Mosque, under its rector, Dalil Boubakeur, is financed by Algeria. It controls about a hundred small mosques, mainly in the region of Paris. According to Nicolas Sarkozy, who as France's interior minister was responsible for setting up the CFCM, its role was to be a "recognized forum for dialogue" over issues concerning the place of Muslims in French society. Though the UOIF took the majority of the seats, closely followed by the FNMF, Dalil Boubakeur was chosen as president of the council. He was reappointed to the position after further elections in 2005, following legal challenges and internal difficulties.

In 2004, the French government clashed with Muslims over the issue of whether head coverings could be worn by girls in school. The government ruled that conspicuous religious symbols, including the headscarf, could not be worn. There was much public controversy, and a number of demonstrations by Muslims, but in the end the headscarf disappeared from French schools with relatively little fuss. The government concluded that its move had undermined support for extremist Islam in French schools and in the projects where the families of many Muslim pupils lived. There is, however, little evidence relating to the extent of support for Jihadist Islam in France, either before or after the government crackdown on the wearing of Islamic dress. The riots of 2005 appear to have had no real link with Islam; indeed, such organizations at the UOIF attempted without success to bring them to a halt.

Nonetheless, there is some evidence of radicalism in France. The French government has over the last decade expelled a considerable number of Muslim clerics who preach violence in their Friday sermons, and there have been violent incidents, beginning with bombs in Paris in 1995 and an apparent attempt to derail a train in the same year. In 2002, a plan to conduct a chemical attack in Paris was uncovered, for which two men from central France, both radical Muslims, were convicted in 2004. The alleged twentieth man from the September 11 plot, Zacarias Moussaoui, is from Narbonne in southern France, and at least two French prisoners are held at Guantanamo Bay by the Americans. In January 2007, the GSPC, the Algerian Salafi group, called for attacks on French citizens in Algeria, whom it described as crusaders. (In September 2006, Ayman al-Zawahiri, the second in command of Al-Qa'ida announced the establishment of a link with the GSPC.)

Federation Nationale des Musulmans de France (FNMF)

The FNMF was established in 1985 with the aim of representing the Muslims of France. At the outset, French converts to Islam played a significant role within it. Its founding president was Jacques Yakoub Roty. One of its initial aims was to challenge the Algerian-dominated Grand Mosque in Paris for the leadership of France's Muslim community. In 1989, the FNMF attracted the attention of the wider public when the issue of the Islamic headscarf first made its appearance. It spoke out against the arguments of those who advocated laicity in schools, and its then president, Daniel Youssef Leclerc, also one of the FNMF's founding members, was especially vocal.

Dalil Boubakeur's appointment to the rectorate of the Grand Mosque in 1989 coincided with a realignment of views within the FNMF, which concluded that it wished to present itself as more amenable to French republican ideas. In 1993, Mohamed Béchari took over as president, with support from Morocco, and the FNMF's links with Morocco became close. It was said at the time to enjoy the support of Morocco's

powerful interior minister, Driss Basri. The FNMF embarked on a process of reconciliation with the Grand Mosque, and in 1993 the FNMF and the Mosque established the "Coordination Nationale des Musulmans en France" (National Coordination of French Muslims). After only three months, the period of newfound cooperation came to an end when the FNMF broke away from the venture and resumed its virulent criticism of the rector. In a communiqué issued on June 21, 1993, the FNFM declared its position as follows: "The FNMF has observed with regret that after a number of meetings, it has become clear that the personal and political ambitions of Dr. Dalil Boubakeur are wholly incompatible with the goals initially laid down at the time of the original establishment of the Coordination. The FNMF is unable to associate itself with such efforts to exploit the Muslim community of France."

From the early 1990s, however, the FNMF had begun to experience problems. In 1991, Daniel Youssef Leclerc left the organization to take up a position with the World Islamic League, and his successor as president, Mustapha Dogan, later took the Turkish supporters of Milli Görüs out of the FNMF when he left the organization. At the same time, the alternative grouping, the UOIF (Union des Organisations Islamiques en France), began to gain strength. When Mohamed Bechari became president in 1993, he claimed that the FNMF organization incorporated some five hundred groups, though this was challenged by some. In 2003, when elections were held within the Muslim community under the auspices of the French government for the Conseil Français du Culte Musulman (CFCM) (Council for the Muslim Faith), the FNMF won eighteen seats out of a total of forty-one. The UOIF gained thirteen seats and the Grand Mosque secured six, while Turkish and independent candidates took four. After the elections, Béchari became vice president of the CFCM. In September 2004, however, Mohamed Béchari met Abassi Madani, the former leader of Algeria's dissolved Islamic Salvation Front, which alarmed the other members of the CFCM. In October 2005, Béchari was suspended from his CFCM and FNMF positions after allegations of administrative and financial irregularities in the FNMF. Within the FNMF, he was challenged by his deputy, Abdellah Boussouf, who now benefited from the support from Morocco that Béchari had formerly enjoyed. All the charges of irregularity were dismissed by a French judge in June 2006, and Béchari announced he would resume his position in the CFCM. Nevertheless, in September 2006, after the Grand Mosque and the UOIF withdrew their support for Béchari, the CFCM elected a new council and Béchari was replaced by Abdellah Boussouf as CFCM vice president. Within the FNMF, however, Béchari continued to hold on to his position as president.

The FNMF is a Sunni organization, with links with the World Islamic League, sponsored by Saudi Arabia. It has a number of major mosques in the outskirts of Paris, including Evry, Mantes la Jolie, and Asnières. The funds for the fine mosque at Evry were obtained from the Saudis by FNMF activist Khalil Meroun. The FNMF recognizes that there are members of radical Islamist movements including Jamaat at-Tabligh (Tablighi Jamaat) within its ranks. However, it has barred members of the Moroccan radical movement Adl wa-l Ihsan, which challenges the Moroccan state. The FNMF publishes an internal journal *Lumière*.

UJM Union des Jeunes Musulmans (Union of Young Muslims)

This group was set up in 1987 in Les Minguettes, a working class suburb of Lyon, by a group of young third-generation Maghrebi citizens. One of the leading figures was Yamin Makri, the proprietor of the bookshop "Al Tawhid" and a cousin of the Algerian Islamist Mahfoud Nahnah. Makri put forward a new political program, demanding recognition of "the rights of Muslims as French citizens in a secular Republic." In the controversy over such matters as the Rushdie affair and the controversy of the wearing of Islamic dress, the UJM presented itself as the advocate of a neo-Islamist position. Its stated goal was reconciliation between Islam and the official French position of "laïcité" (secularism), in what it called a "French society hostile to visible Islam."

The UJM claimed to have a growing membership and coordinated its activity with the youth organizations linked to the UOIF, such as the "Association des Etudiants Musulmans de France" (EMF) (Association of Muslim Students in France). This was based in Besançon but was also active in other towns and achieved as much as 20 percent of the vote in elections for interuniversity student bodies. Tariq Ramadan used the UJM as a vehicle for the propagation of his ideas in France. Tariq Ramadan's books were published and distributed by Yamin Makri's "Al-Tawhid," and his speaking tours of France were organized in Lyon.

UOIF (Union des Organisations Islamiques de France) (Union of Islamic Organizations in France)

The UOIF is a confederation of organizations set up in 1983. Its original nucleus was the GIF (Groupement Islamique de France) (Islamic Grouping in France), which already comprised some ten separate associations. The GIF's head at the time was Ahmed Nashat, an Egyptian, and its spiritual leader was the Lebanese Sheikh Faisal al-Nawlawi. It was run by two Moroccans: Thami Breze and Fouad Allaoui, an accomplished media spokesman who lived in Bordeaux. By 2006, the UOIF had given well over two hundred groups in

France the status of member or associate. The UOIF has fifty-two appointed officials and five hundred volunteers. Notable constituent groups include the JMF (Young Muslims of France), the Institute Européen des Sciences Humaines (European Institute of Human Sciences), which trains imams, the Avicenna Medical Association, and the Euro-Media company, which produces and distributes books, videos, and audiocassettes. The UOIF holds its annual conference at Le Bourget, attracting tens of thousands of participants. It has been building new offices at La Corneuve, in the outskirts of Paris, paid for largely by donations from the Gulf countries.

In ideological terms, the UOIF follows the line of the Muslim Brotherhood. It bases its position on the view of Sheikh Mawlawi and of the Egyptian theologian Yusuf al-Qaradawi. However, it is also attempting to develop a theoretical framework for the particular case of the position of Islam in France. With strong territorial bases and impressive leaders, the UOIF benefited from the reshuffle of institutions after the disappearance of CORIF (Conseil de Réflexion sur l'Islam en France) (Council for Reflection on Islam in France). Its current goal is to establish itself as the government's natural interlocutor in the Muslim community.

GHANNOUCHI, RASHID (TUNISIA)

Rashid Ghannouchi was born in 1941 in the district of Gabès in southern Tunisia into a large family. Thanks to family support, he was able to go to Tunis at the age of eighteen to study Islamic subjects at the az-Zaytuna school from 1959 to 1962. On graduation from az-Zaytuna he briefly worked as a primary school teacher, but inspired by the ideas of Arab nationalism and Nasserism, and unhappy with his circumstances in Tunisia, he went to Cairo. In 1964, he enrolled at the faculty of agriculture at Cairo University, but was expelled from Egypt after a few months as a dissident as the result of an agreement between the Egyptian government and Egypt's President Bourguiba. Ghannouchi fled to Syria and began to study philosophy and social sciences. In Damascus he fell under the influence of Islamist thinkers from the Muslim Brotherhood. He was strongly influenced by the writings of Hassan al-Banna and Sayyed Qutb and was at the same time passionately interested in politics and determined to take his religious studies to a high level, taking part in advanced discussion groups at the mosques. In 1965, he spent a period in Europe, traveling to Germany by way of Turkey, Yugoslavia, and Bulgaria, and then spending time in Germany, France, Belgium, and the Netherlands. He was appalled by what he saw as Western decadence, and began to lose his faith in Arab nationalism. By 1966, Ghannouchi was proclaiming his adherence to Islam and began to move in salafi circles. He graduated in Damascus in 1968 and went to Paris, where he enrolled as an MA student in philosophy and encountered activists from Tablighi Jamaat and became general secretary of a student Islamic society.

In late 1969, he returned to Tunisia, where he embarked on a career as a teacher. In Tunis, he met fundamentalist Muslims who, like him, rejected the current ascendancy of the socialist intellectuals. He took up journalism and joined an Islamist magazine, *Al-Ma'rifa*. As a religious commentator propagating the ideals of the Muslim Brotherhood, he criticized the collapse of morals in the West and advocated the Islamization of Tunisian society. He dealt with political themes whilst avoiding head-on clashes with the political authorities. From 1977, he was editor of the publication and also moved in university circles in Tunis, seeking to counter the influence of Marxist student groups. Together with other Islamists, he began to set up a political network, "Islamic Action." In August 1979, Islamic Action set up a new publication, *Al-Mujtama'*. Rashid Ghannouchi and his colleagues now saw the transition to politics as a realistic objective. At a time when the Iranian Revolution was creating waves in several Arab states, this magazine was banned after a few months. Ghannouchi was arrested on December 21, 1979, accused of spreading false information and encouraging subversion. He was imprisoned, but was set free a few days later on January 5, 1980. However, this decided him to change his way of life, and after some travel abroad he returned to Tunisia to set up his Islamist organization, the MTI— "Mouvement de la Tendance Islamique" (Movement of the Islamic Tendency). A founding conference was held, at which he was appointed "emir" of the organization, for which he tried in vain to find a place in the field of official politics. A request for recognition was turned down.

In July 1981, the regime set in train a campaign of arrests. Rashid Ghannouchi was arrested, together with most of the other members of the MTI's leadership. He was arrested, tried, and sentenced to eleven years imprisonment on a number of charges, including belonging to an unrecognized organization. He was held at Bordj Erroumi and then transferred to a prison in Tunis. On August 31, 1984, he was set free as the result of an amnesty, from which the other MTI leaders also benefited. Once more installed as "emir" of the MTI, he rebuilt the organization's clandestine networks and opened negotiations with Tunisia's prime minister, Mohammed Mzali. In 1985, a student branch was set up in addition to the movement's other wings. This was the UGTE—the "Union Générale Tunisienne des Etudiants."

Ghannouchi was still seen as a leading opponent of the regime and was arrested again on March 13, 1987. At a group trial of a large number of MTI militants and officials, he was sentenced to life imprisonment. However, the fall of President Bourguiba on November 7, 1987 opened the way for a new policy of reconciliation on the part of President Ben Ali. In May 1988, Ghannouchi was pardoned, and he adopted a highly conciliatory attitude toward the new regime, agreeing to participate on behalf of his organization in talks on the proposed "national pact." At the parliamentary elections of April 2, 1989, Islamist candidates were permitted to stand as independents. As a result of the vote, the movement, which had by now adopted its new title, En-Nahda (Rebirth), appeared to be the only opposition group that had any real following in the country. However, fearing a new wave of repression, following public discussion of what status Islamists should be allowed to occupy in Tunisian politics, Rashid Ghannouchi decided to leave the country.

Ghannouchi had reliable support networks in Europe and had good relations with the Islamic Republic in Iran. However, he went to Sudan, where he stayed for a while, with a friendly welcome from Hassan al-Turabi. During the Gulf War of 1990–1991, he took a belligerent stand, calling for a Jihad against the coalition forces in Iraq. With a Sudanese passport, he traveled to London in 1991 with the agreement of the British authorities. President Ben Ali's conciliatory mood did not persist, and in 1992, as the result of his activities and statements abroad, Ghannouchi was sentenced to death in absentia in Tunisia for plotting to overthrow the government. In 1993, he was granted political asylum in Britain. From London, he set up European links and wielded considerable religious and political influence over the Muslim community in Britain. He has been a skilled practitioner of the art of justifying the use of violence as a means of political action, whilst in other contexts elevating the principles of democracy and human rights. Always the pragmatist, Ghannouchi established connections with Tunisian opposition groups whose views diverged from his own and took care not to compromise himself by being seen to have links with radical groups practicing violence in the West. However, he has largely concentrated on theoretical and abstract studies of Islam in politics. In international affairs, he has taken a strongly anti-American stand and has condemned the Middle East peace process as one of surrender to Israel. He won damages in 2003 in the British courts against publications that claimed he had links with Al-Qa'ida. He has since taken a relatively high profile in the United Kingdom, taking part in conferences and lecturing at reputable academic institutions. In February 2006, President Ben Ali pardoned and released some seventy-five En-Nahda activists still imprisoned in Tunisia, though no pardon has been extended to Ghannouchi, whose sentence of life imprisonment still stands.

HAMA, MASSACRE (SYRIA)

The destruction of Hama and the massacres that took place there between February 2 and 26, 1982, marked the final phase of the confrontation between Syria's President Hafez al-Assad and the Muslim Brotherhood. Assad, born in 1930, an adherent of the Ba'th Party, and Syria's president from 1971, came from the minority Alawi community in Syria, which was a mystical splinter sect associate with the Shi'ite wing of the Islamic faith. His relations with Islamist groups were ambiguous. Internally, he adopted a repressive stance; externally, he was not reluctant to make use of Islamist groups.

From the mid 1970s, both the Alawi authorities and the Ba'th Party, each despised as impious by the Islamists, were the object of murderous attacks by Islamist groups. More than three hundred such attacks are on record between 1979 and 1981. President Assad himself barely escaped an assassination attempt in June 1980. Between 1976 and 1982, the political and ideological clash between President Assad's regime and the Muslim Brotherhood developed into a bloody and merciless confrontation. The anti-Alawi challenge was concealed behind slogans calling for Jihad against neocolonialism. The struggle was couched in religious terms, with the Islamists calling on the population to make their choice between Islam and the Ba'th Party. The Islamists drew support from such antagonists of the Syrian Ba'th as the Iraqi Ba'thists, the Jordanian monarchy, and even part of the Palestinian Fatah movement. In 1979, the Muslim Brotherhood assassinated a number of Alawi figures identified with the regime. The conflict reached its apex in the two great Sunni cities of Aleppo and Hama. In June 1979, Muslim Brothers killed thirty-two Alawi cadets and officers at the artillery school in Aleppo. In 1980, the regime struck back, with the arrest of 1,500 Muslim Brotherhood sympathizers, hundreds of whom were killed in prison. However, it was Hama that came to symbolize this savage episode in the history of Syria when an insurrection by the Muslim Brothers was met with a bloodbath. For a while, mass demonstrations and strikes by Sunnis threatened the stability of the state. Then, a Syrian Army patrol attacked the headquarters of the Brotherhood's leader in Hama, Omar Jawaa, also known as Abu Bakr, and was repulsed with severe losses. From February 3 to 26, 1982, Alawi special forces led by President Assad's brother Rifaat occupied the town and systematically razed its old quarters. Sources estimate the number of deaths at between ten thousand and thirty thousand. The Hama massacre, which was not revealed to the outside world until April 1982, was the last convulsion of a tragedy that for the time being put an end to the threat from the Muslim Brotherhood in Syria.

In terms of external relations, the situation was quite different. Hafez al-Assad frequently found occasion to make use of armed Islamist movements to realize his plans and used armed Islamist movements against the Christians in Lebanon, as well as against the Palestinians and the Israeli occupying forces. The exception was the support he gave to Alawi and Ba'thist militias in the Lebanese city of Tripoli against Harakat al-Tawhid al-Islami ("The Movement of Islamic Unity"). The Syrian secret services even came under suspicion on several occasions of giving covert help to Islamist movements that were acting in effect as a destabilizing influence in Iraq and even in Turkey.

Starting in 1994, amnesty was granted to imprisoned members of the Muslim Brotherhood. Sheikh Abdel Fattah Abou Ghudda, seen as a leading Islamist figure, was allowed to return to Syria, having fled during the disturbances.

In 1996, an exiled Syrian Brother, Ali Sadreddine al-Bayanouni, based in Amman, became the Syrian Brotherhood's "General Supervisor" ("Al-Muraqib al-Am") and continued the search for an accommodation with the regime. When Bashar al-Assad became president of Syria in June 2000, the regime's policy toward the Islamists remained unaltered. Islamists who had fled to Germany to join the exiled leader Issam al-Attar were allowed to return only on an individual basis, and having sworn an oath of loyalty to the regime, after negotiations with the army intelligence service. There was to be no recognition of the Muslim Brotherhood in Syria and no permission for them to resume their activities. In 2000, Bayanouni was expelled from Jordan and took up residence in London. In October 2005, the Syrian Muslim Brotherhood joined other Syrian opposition groups by

signing the so-called Damascus Declaration, calling for the establishment of democracy in Syria. In February 2006, the brotherhood made contact with the former Syrian vice president, Abdel Halim Khaddam, now living abroad, who opposes the Syrian regime. Low-level persecution of those connected to the Muslim Brotherhood in Syria apparently continues.

HAMAS (PALESTINE)

The name of the Islamic resistance movement Hamas is an acronym derived from the phrase "Harakat al-Muqawama al-Islamiya" (Movement of the Islamic Resistance) and also means "zeal." The name was conceived at the meeting of Muslim Brotherhood leaders in Palestine who decided in the immediate aftermath of the outbreak of the Palestinian Intifada on December 8, 1987 to establish a new militant Islamist entity. The founding date of Hamas is commonly taken to be December 14, 1987, when the first communiqué was issued in the name of the organization. Its first leader was Sheikh Ahmed Yassin. The Muslim Brotherhood in Palestine was closely linked to the movement's wing in Jordan, and both were linked to the mother organization in Egypt.

Historically, the Muslim Brotherhood had played a part in the great Palestinian revolt led by Sheikh Izzedine al-Qassam in 1935 against the British mandatory occupation of Palestine and what were regarded by the Arabs as the pro-Zionist policies of the British. It also had contacts with Hajj Amin al-Hussseini, the mufti of Jerusalem. Hajj Amin was in practice the leader of the Palestinian national movement at the time of the Nakba (the "Catastrophe") of 1948, the first war between Israel and the Arabs, which was regarded by the Palestinians as the embodiment of their misfortunes. The Muslim Brotherhood had a presence in several towns in Palestine as early as 1936 in the shape of individual members of the Egyptian organization, but there had been no move to set up a separate Palestinian national organization. The philosophy of the Muslim Brotherhood had been to make no distinction between the Egyptians and Palestinians who shared the same religion and had the same objectives: the brotherhood was seen as being attached to the Islamic "Umma" as a whole and not to any particular nationality.

This lies at the origin of its hostility to the Fatah movement, even though the founders of Fatah had been closely linked to the Islamic movement during their student years and their early days as activists in Egypt from 1952 to 1959. Yasser Arafat himself had links to the Islamic movement, as did Salah Khalaf—known as Abu Iyad, who was murdered by Israeli agents in Tunis in 1991—and Khalil al-Wazir (Abu Jihad), who was killed by Israel in 1988. Nevertheless, the earliest Palestinian guerrilla actions in occupied Gaza, between 1952 and 1959, were organized by the Muslim Brotherhood and Khalil al-Wazir is given credit for leading them.

In the 1950s and 1960s, the Muslim Brotherhood allied itself with Hashemite Jordan against President Nasser. The liberation of Palestine had never been its first priority. After the 1967 War, Fatah and the PLO (Palestine Liberation Organization) dominated the Arab political landscape, with its nationalist and Marxist rhetoric. From the early 1980s, the circumstances changed, with the advent of the Islamic Revolution in Iran and the expulsion of the PLO from Lebanon in 1982. This opened the way for the rise of a new Islamist Palestinian movement. The first to take the center stage was Islamic Jihad, which had actually been set up in 1980, and then Hamas in 1987.

From his base in Gaza, Sheikh Yassin, the blind teacher and scholar who was the spiritual leader of Palestine's Islamists, took charge of the new movement, which he had played a key role in initiating. In justification of the choice by the brotherhood of this particular moment to launch Hamas, thus embarking on political action in Palestine, his saying was, "When all doors close, God's doors open." Later, Hamas would draw further strength from the blow struck at Fatah by the murder of Abu Jihad, who was in effect Fatah's administrator for the historic territory of Palestine and the coordinator of the Intifada. It would also benefit from Israel's policy, which tended to prefer the Islamists to the PLO, on which it put the blame for all terrorist actions.

In due course, Hamas, given confidence by its militancy in the First Intifada, rejected compromise solutions and began to demand "the recovery of Palestine, from the river to the sea." At the same time, it insisted that the entire territory of Palestine was an Islamic "Waqf" (a charitable legacy whose circumstances are defined by the provisions of Shari'a law), because of the presence in Jerusalem of Islam's third holiest shrine. While it struggled against Israel, Hamas also came into conflict with the PLO leadership and was instrumental in bringing about the failure of the Oslo accords. It began to undertake suicide operations in 1996 in reprisal for the murder by Israeli agents of one of its leading figures, Yahya Ayash, known as "The Engineer," who was a technical expert and one of the founding figures of its armed wing.

After Sheikh Yassin, the most influential Hamas leaders were Abdelaziz al-Rantisi and Mahmud al-Zahar. Outside Palestine, and especially in Jordan, Hamas developed rapidly and a parallel leadership emerged including such figures as Ibrahim Ghosheh—a former Muslim Brotherhood activist—and Khaled Mish'al, the senior Hamas leader outside Palestine. In 1997, Mish'al narrowly escaped death at the hands of Israeli agents who attacked him near his office in Amman. In the aftermath of this incident, King

Hussein obtained from an embarrassed Israeli government the release of Sheikh Yassin, who had been imprisoned for his activities in Gaza. Other leading figures of Hamas outside Palestine included Musa Abu Marzouq, Mohammed Nazal, and Ima al-Alami. Despite its external relationships, for example with Saudi Arabia and Iran, Hamas maintained a very large measure of independence and represented an alternative face of Palestinian nationalism to that presented by Fatah.

In the Second Intifada, Hamas did not play a leading part. However, its spectacular suicide bombings—"martyrdom operations," as it prefers to call them—in which national militancy and religious faith combined led down the path toward increasing violence and radicalism. A new phenomenon in 2000–2002 was the creation of ties between Hamas and the Islamic movement inside Israel. After September 11, 2001, the movement's position became more sensitive, especially after the United States declared it a terrorist organization. The European Union went no farther than to put the Izzedin al-Qassam Brigades—the title given to Hamas's military wing—on its own list of terrorist organizations. It should be recalled that from 1988 to 1991 there was a dialog between the United States and Hamas, at a time when Washington saw advantages in giving encouragement to political Islamism.

Hamas also gained ground owing to its social and benevolent action. It runs schools, mosques, medical clinics, sports clubs, and welfare organizations of other kinds. Such functions tend to be neglected by the Palestinian Authority. It has adopted a pragmatic political attitude that enabled it to work with the Palestinian Authority when the PA was under Fatah's control. It was also averse to inter-Palestinian conflict and its leadership always held back from outright clashes with other Palestinian factions. Israel has targeted its leadership, and Sheikh Yassin was killed in an Israeli air attack directed at him in March 2004. A month later, Abdel Aziz Rantisi was killed in a similar action. Israel's action was intended to weaken Hamas, but had little effect. New leaders arose to replace those who had died, and the organization's popularity was not diminished. It held back from participation in the Palestinian electoral process until 2006, when it won the Palestinian legislative elections. Since then it has coexisted with difficulty with the president of the Palestinian Authority, a post still held by Mahmoud Abbas, a member of Fatah and a close associate of the late Yasser Arafat. It has faced a difficult situation, with international donors withholding funds, and Israel refusing to pass to the Palestinian Authority funds needed for it to carry on its administration of the Palestinian territories. After an attack by Israel in November 2006, which resulted in the deaths of many civilians, Hamas declared that a unilateral truce to which it had adhered, which suspended suicide bombings, was at an end.

HATTAB, HASSAN (ALGERIA)

Hassan Hattab was born on December 19, 1967 at Rouiba, some fifteen kilometers from Algiers. He came from a religious family and excelled in sport and the martial arts. In 1989, after his military service, he became a founder member of the FIS ("Front Islamique de Salvation"—"Islamic Salvation Front"). He became the head of the FIS office near his residence in Bordj el-Kiffan, and in 1991, after the dissolution of the FIS, he went into hiding to avoid arrest. Like many others, including his brother Toufik and his uncle Abdelkader Hattab, an Afghan veteran known as Mouloud, Hassan Hattab joined an armed group, attaching himself to Said Mekhloufi's Movement for an Islamic State (MEI), operating in the eastern part of Algiers.

After the assassination of the prime minister of Algeria, Kasdi Merbah, on August 22, 1993, the authorities launched a search for Hassan Hattab, who was by now the head of the FIS's military security operation, as well as for his uncle. Hassan Hattab was also a suspect in the murder of the head of Algerian TV, Mustapha Abada, on October 14, 2003. Hattab fled into the mountains of Kabylia to escape capture. In May 1994, Said Mekhloufi took his organization into the GIA. As a local leader of some notoriety, Hassan Hattab took charge of a GIA phalange comprising some one hundred fighters. In July 1994, his uncle was killed, apparently by the security forces, but some rumors insisted that Hassan Hattab may have had a hand in his uncle's death. In May 1995, the army mounted a large-scale operation led by a senior officer, General Said Bey, in the hills around Khemis al-Khechna, which was intended to destroy Hattab's group. While his positions were being shelled, Hattab succeeded in making his escape by slipping between the perimeter guards around his location. In October 1995, Ait Ziane, was killed in action. Ziane had been the "emir" of the region the GIA had designated as Zone 2—the eastern side of the capital and Kabylia, Ouzou. Hassan Hattab took charge of the reorganization of the GIA units in Zone 2 and set up his headquarters to the west of Tizi-Ouzou. He rejected the offer of a truce by the government.

The GIA was wracked by bloody purges for a period beginning in November 1995, in which it is hard to be sure what part was played by Hattab. On the orders of Djamel Zitouni, various leading Islamist figures who were suspected of preparing a coup against the leadership were killed, including Mohammed Said. Said Mekhloufi condemned the internal purges and announced that he was quitting the GIA. Hassan Hattab, however, stood firm. He did not fall victim to the settling of accounts, presumably after declaring his loyalty to those behind the purges. When Zitouni was killed, on December 17, 1996, Hattab backed Habbi Miloud, known as Abou al-Walid, who was a member of the national leadership and ran a group in the hinterland of Algiers known as Al-Muhajirun. Abou al-Walid was declared leader, but was swiftly pushed aside by Antar Zouabri.

Hassan Hattab, who was not a supporter of Zouabri and was unhappy with the strategy of promoting terror through indiscriminate massacres, decided secretly to defect. He began to organize a new group that proclaimed its adherence to Salafist ideology. Before announcing his decision to secede, he took steps to reinforce his authority by attracting as many supporters as he was able to, to guard against reprisals. On May 8, 1998, in an open letter, he repudiated both the truce declared by the national leadership of the AIS and the massacres perpetrated by Antar Zouabri. He was conscious of the GIA's increasing isolation, as well as of the effects of the spread of self-defense groups in Kabylia and, therefore, reverted to a more conventional military strategy, based on direct attacks on the security forces. He also took care to eliminate rival groups and in December 1997 was responsible for the death of a rival "emir" operating in the Algiers region.

Now confident of his strength, he convened a founding conference in the village of Takhoukht, in the Wilaya of Tizi-Ouzou, where he gathered together twenty-one GIA fighters representing various zones of the country, especially from eastern Algeria (including Tebessa, El Oued, and Batna) and from the south of the country. In a declaration issued on September 14, 1998, the establishment of the GSPC (Groupe Salafite pour la Prédication et le Combat) was announced. Hassan Hattab, appointed the movement's national leader, justified his actions with a condemnation of the successive purges in the GIA, which he blamed on Takfir wa-l-Hijra. Allegedly with the help of funds from Osama bin Laden, the GSPC quickly established itself as the only armed movement with a military and political structure that was operational across much of Algeria. Hattab was assisted by the adherence of a number of smaller groups aligned with his political and military doctrine.

In April 1999, in a confused process that has not been satisfactorily explained, Hassan Hattab was ousted from his position of leadership by a former FIS activist, Ahmed Dichou, who was the former imam of the mosque at Bordj-Menaiel, in the Wilaya of Boumerdès. For a further period of several weeks, however, at a time when intense controversy reigned over the government's proposal of "civil reconciliation," Hattab continued to occupy the position of a regional commander. In August 1999, the death of Abdelmajid Dichou was announced: he had evidently lost his life in an operation by the security forces two months earlier. However, the circumstances of his death have not been fully clarified and rumors persist that he was the victim of an internal settling of scores. In any case, Hassan Hattab was restored to the position of national leader of the GSPC. When the government made contact with him with regard to President Bouteflika's laws proposing civil reconciliation, Hattab stuck to his strategic and political policy and rejected the idea of a truce and a fortiori of surrender. His statements always embodies what he called his three "nos"—no dialogue, no truce, and no reconciliation. According to some accounts of this period, however, Hattab would not necessarily have been opposed to a truce that would have allowed his men to give up the struggle with honor and which would have given him personally some recognition.

Following the events of September 11, 2001 in the United States, the GSPC was declared by the Americans to be an organization affiliated to Bin Laden's "network." The GSPC responded with a statement signed by Hassan Hattab, threatening the United States and Europe in the event of any action against it. Hassan Hattab, with resources at his disposal that had a substantial capacity for action, appeared by this stage to be the leading figure within the armed Islamist movement in Algeria. Nevertheless, he is said to have engaged in deeply secret exchanges with the authorities, which continued until 2002. Hassan Hattab was apparently ousted in the late summer of 2003, apparently by rivals within his own organization, but was still claiming in 2004 to be head of the GSPC. On February 9, 2005, the GSPC announced that he was to be permanently excluded from the organization on the grounds that he had abandoned the Jihad and had submitted to the "tyranny" of the government.

HEKMATYAR, GULBUDDIN (AFGHANISTAN)

Gulbduddin Hekmatyar, born in 1947, is an Afghan Pushtun from Imam Saheb in northern Afghanistan, in the province of Kunduz. He is a member of the Kharuti tribe, which is part of the Ghilzai confederation. By upbringing, he is a strict Sunni Muslim. He attended the Sher Khan High School in Kunduz, where in 1968 he caught the eye of his tribal chieftain, Gholam Serwar Nasher, who sent him to the Mahtab Qala military college. His early political affiliation was apparently to the People's Democratic Part of Afghanistan (PDPA), the Afghan communist movement, though his supporters deny this. He was asked to leave military school after two years because of his political activities and transferred in 1970 to the Faculty of Engineering at the University of Kabul where he studied for two years but did not graduate. As an engineering student at the university he came under the influence of Islamists and he joined a movement known as Muslim Youth (Nahzat-e Jawanan Musalman), where he came under the influence of such radical Sunni leaders as Burhanuddin Rabbani and Qazi Muhammad Amin Waqad. In 1972, he was imprisoned on suspicion of complicity in the murder of a Maoist political rival. In 1973, King Zahir was overthrown in a coup mounted by his cousin, Muhammad Daoud, and in 1974 Hekmatyar was released, subsequently fleeing to Peshawar in Pakistan, as did many other Islamists.

In 1975, as the Muslim Youth movement broke up, Hekmatyar set up his own party in Pakistan, known as Hezb-e Islami Afghanistan. Like the leaders of other exiled factions, he was opposed to the Daoud regime and set himself to oust Daoud after the failed Islamist coup in Afghanistan in 1975. Hekmatyar positioned himself as the favored client of the Pakistan intelligence services, the ISI (Inter Services Intelligence), and received substantial assistance from Pakistan. He broke with former colleagues and rival leaders to consolidate the power of his own faction. He apparently also received help from Saudi Arabia, and from the United States, though he never acknowledged any relationship with the Americans. In 1979, the communists took over in Kabul with Soviet support, after which the struggle between anti-communist factions and the communist regime began. Hekmatyar's ability to rally strength on the ground in Afghanistan made him a significant figure. After the Soviet withdrawal in 1989, and the fall of the pro-communist regime of Muhammad Najibullah, Hekmatyar precipitated the struggle between the Islamist factions in Afghanistan, in which Rabbani and Massoud were also important participants. Hekmatyar, Rabbani, and Massoud fought for supremacy in a civil war, which laid waste the country and devastated Kabul. Ultimately, however, they joined forces in an attempt to exclude the Taliban, who were by now the preferred candidates of Pakistan

for power in Afghanistan. In May 1986, Hekmatyar briefly became prime minister, but had to flee Kabul after three months, taking refuge in Iran as the Taliban took power in Afghanistan.

In exile, he continued to head Hezb-e Islami Afghanistan, but was tolerated in Shi'ite Iran, where he lived quietly in the capital, Teheran. After September 11, 2001, however, Hekmatyar was outspoken in his support for Osama Bin Laden and his opposition to the plans of the United States for a new government in Afghanistan, as well as to Hamid Karzai, the preferred candidate of the Americans to be Afghanistan's new leader. In February 2002, Hekmatyar was expelled from Iran and apparently returned to Afghanistan. Subsequently, little has been known about his whereabouts. In May 2002, the CIA reported that he had been sighted and that an unsuccessful attempt had been made to kill him. In December 2002, he distributed a defiant message to the Afghan population. This said, "Hezb-e Islami will fight our Jihad until foreign troops are gone from Afghanistan and the Afghan people have established an Islamic government." In September 2003, he denied that he was interested in any form of alliance with the Taliban, but expressed his approval for attacks on American and international forces. He sent a video to Al-Jazeera television in May 2006 in which he expressed his continuing antagonism to the United States and his ambition to see an independent Islamist state in Afghanistan.

HIZB AL-ADL W-AL- INMA' ("JUSTICE AND DEVELOPMENT PARTY"—"PARTI DE LA JUSTICE ET DU DEVELOPMENT"—PJD) (MOROCCO)

The PJD originated as a previous political party, the Popular, Democratic and

Constitutional Movement (PDCM), which adopted a new name at an extraordinary meeting on October 4, 1998. The PDCM had a number of members of the Moroccan parliament and represented the Islamist movement on Morocco's official political scene. The PJD was led by Dr. Abdelkrim Al-Khatib (a former PDCM official) and by Abdelilah Benkirane, a former official of Al-Islah wa-l-Tajdid (Reform and Renewal). The organization promoted what it called the application of the Shari'a in a progressive and adapted version, taking its inspiration from the Muslim Brotherhood. Its line was to back what it regarded as constructive policies and take a pragmatic approach. In February 1998, when Abderrahmane Youssoufi of the socialist USFP (Union Socialiste des Forces Populaires) formed a government, the PJD agreed to participate.

However, the PJD was unable to support the USFP's plan to liberalize the law in Morocco relating to individual rights and in particular to improve the rights of women. In November 1999, the PJD set up a pressure group it called as the "National Defense Committee for the Moroccan Family" to militate against change. In 2000, large-scale demonstrations were held in Rabat and Casablanca to express opposition to the proposed reforms. The PJD returned to the opposition benches in 2001. At a general meeting called on October 13, 2001, the party decided to table a motion of censure against the government.

On the social front, the PJD has followed the successful policy of Islamist movements elsewhere by promoting charitable organizations spread throughout the country and run by members of the party. These come under the umbrella of the supervisory organization, the Movement for Unity and Reform, responsible for finance and overall direction, which was led by a PJD official Ahmed Raissouni. This organization attracts PJD figures who aim at a career in politics,

who deplore Western influence in Morocco, whilst being careful not to make any explicit challenge to the monarchy. Mustafa Ramid, a Casablanca-based lawyer, is responsible for relations between the PJD and Islamist organizations abroad. After the beginning of the campaign in Afghanistan by the U.S.-led coalition forces in 2001, the authorities banned a demonstration in Rabat planned by the PJD.

The PJD's popularity has not waned. In new elections in September 2002, the PJD tripled its representation, winning 43 seats out of 325. The party had run candidates in only fifty-six of Morocco's ninety-one multimember constituencies. Abdelilah Benkirane said this was deliberate restraint, since too aggressive a stance on the part of the Islamists could have brought a reaction from the monarchy like that in Algeria, which had led to the dissolution of the FIS after its election victory in 1991. In 2003, just four months after the terrorist attacks in Morocco, which were blamed on Islamists, the PJD had a similar success in local elections, though one again limited by its participation in only some of the seats contested. The PJD continued to gain ground in the elections of September 2006.

HIZB-I ISLAMI (AFGHANISTAN)

Hizb-i Islami in Afghanistan was the political party set up by Gulbuddin Hekmatyar in Peshawar in the 1970s. Its membership came from a faction of the Young Muslims movement and from Jamiat-i Islami. Very much under the control of its charismatic leader, it was highly centralized. It took its ideological basis from the Muslim Brotherhood and the Pakistani ideologue Abu al Ala al-Mawdudi. Hizb-i Islami was a Pushtun movement, which drew members from urban and educated Pushtun circles, especially among science and technology students and graduates. It had small military units strategically dispersed throughout the country, and during the war against the Russians tended to present more of a problem to the other mujahidin than to the enemy. Up to 1994, it had a good relationship with the Pakistani intelligence services and received more arms than was justified by its strength on the ground.

In April 1992, when the Northern Coalition under the command of Massoud took Kabul, Hizb-i Islami—prompted by the Pakistanis—shelled and largely destroyed the capital. In September 1996, it was in its turn driven out by the Taliban. Many of its local commanders joined the Taliban, both out of ideological sympathy and for reason of tribal solidarity. Hizb-i Islami always took a very anti-Western position. In 1990–1991, it gave its endorsement to Saddam Hussein after the invasion of Kuwait, though this cost it the support it had received from Saudi Arabia. In October 1991, it condemned the American intervention in Afghanistan and called for the American forces to be driven out. Having lost external support, the remainder of Hizb-i Islami merged into Al-Qa'ida and the Taliban.

HIZB-I WAHDAT (AFGHANISTAN)

Hizb-i Wahdat (The Party of Unity) was an Afghan Shi'ite party set up in June 1990 with Iranian support to formalize the alliance that had hitherto existed among the country's Shi'ite groups. The party was led by Abdul Ali Mazari until his murder by the Taliban in September 1995. Its membership was largely made up of former adherents of the Nasr Party or of the Afghan Sepah-i Pasdaran. These were radical pro-Iranians who had fought in the brief civil war amongst Afghanistan's Shi'ites from 1982 to 1984, in which the pro-Iranian Islamists had emerged victorious. The price of that

victory, however, had been to deprive them of support, both within Afghanistan and internationally, and to exclude them from the internal deals that accompanied the Soviet withdrawal in 1989. Though the leadership of Hizb-i Wahdat consisted of young clerics who had studied in Iran, it became effectively an Afghan ethnic movement, representing the Shi'ite Hazara minority. Its ideological aspect was outweighed by its Hazara ethnic identity. After 1995, and the death of its original leaders, the party split into a number of factions. The principal one of these, based in Bamyan and led by Karim Khalili, joined the Northern Alliance under Massoud. By 2000, Hizb-i Wahdfat's goal was the recognition of the Shi'ite community as a political identity and for the autonomy of Hazarajat, the homeland of the Hazaras. The party's relations with Iran deteriorated to the point where it warmly welcomed the arrival of the American forces in October 2001.

THE HOJJATIEH MAHDAVIEH SOCIETY (IRAN)

The word Hojjatieh derives from the Persian word Hojja (the proof), which relates to the concept of the return of the Hidden Imam. Literally, "Hojjatiyeh" signifies the society of those who await the return of the Hidden Imam, who will return as the Mahdi. The tradition dates back to the Imam Mohammed al-Mahdi, the twelfth Imam of the orthodox Shi'ite tradition, which holds that there were twelve Caliphs after the Prophet Mohammed. According to tradition, Mohammed al-Mahdi disappeared in the year 920 C.E. in the city of Samarra, in Iraq.

The Hojjatiyeh was founded in Teheran in 1953 by Sheikh Mahmoud Halabi, a preacher from Mashhad, who was violently opposed to the Bahai faith. Bahaism was a sect that had made its appearance in Iran in the early nineteenth century, which was regarded as heretical by orthodox Shi'ite Muslims and was, therefore, subject to severe persecution. The then ruler of Iran, the Shah, encouraged the anti-Bahai activities of the Hojjatiyyeh. The society's full name was "Anjoman-i Khayriyeh-yi Hojjaiteh Mahdavieh." It purported to be an Islamic discussion and study group whose aim was solely to promote the purity and orthodoxy of Iran's Shi'ite Islam. However, over time, under the direction of Ayatollah Khashani, the Hojjatiyyeh developed into a secret organization strongly concerned with politics, with significant financial, commercial, and property interests.

The Hojjatiyeh at its high point claimed that more than 20 percent of Iran's clergy were among its members. Its ideological foundations were puritanical and unyielding, demanding a literal and unselective interpretation of the Quran and the Hadith. These included the severest "Hadd" penalties—stoning, beating, and the severing of hands—and did not contemplate any social reform. Over the thirty years of its existence, the Hojjatiyeh was at the heart of political evolution in Iran. Mahmoud Halabi, its founder, was an associate of Dr. Mossadegh, but in 1953 it opposed him and sided with the CIA-organized coup d'état against him. This was led by General Zahedi, whose son was married to the daughter of the Shah. It took the Shah's side in 1964 and 1970, during the action taken by Savak (the Shah's secret police) against the Islamic leadership, including the Ayatollahs Khomeini, Taleghani, and Saidi. Then, however, it opposed the Shah when Abbas Hoveyda—who was rumored to be a secret Bahai—became prime minister. Finally, it backed Khomeini

in the uprising of February 12, 1979, which brought the Ayatollah to power. Until 1984, the new regime tolerated the activities of the Hojjatiyeh, but the authorities then decided it was subversive. Ayatollah Khalkhali spoke out against it in Parliament and it was attacked in a book by the commander of the Pasdaran (Revolutionary Guards); it was then obliged to dissolve itself. The Pasdaran chief, Moshen Razai, went as far as to call it the Hezb-i Shaitan (The Devil's Party).

Hojjatiyeh appears since to have maintained a secret existence, and prominent individuals connected with it were very discreet about their activities. These included Moussavi Ardabili, a former minister of justice, and Abdollah Nouri, formerly minister of interior. Hojjatiyeh seems to have been able to maintain a degree of influence. As supreme leader in succession to Khomeini, Ayatollah Khamenei is thought by some to have encouraged conservative groups such as Hojjatiyeh on which he could rely for support. In the presidential election of 2001, when the reformist Mohammed Khatami was reelected, one of his opponents, Mohammed Kashani—the son of Ayatollah Kashani—was known to be a member of Hojjatiyeh. The presidential election of 2005 saw the victory of President Ahmedinejad, who appeared to sympathize with the ideas of Hojjatiyeh. The ousted President Khatami warned that Hojjatiyeh might return, and pro-reform clerics also expressed alarm. President Ahmedinejad's reference to the awaited return of the Twelfth Iman in his speech to the United Nations in September 2005 aroused critical attention and a spokesman found it necessary to deny any connection between the president and the now-banned society.

IBDA-C (İSLAMI BÜYÜKDOĞU AKINCILAR CEPHESI) (GREAT EASTERN ISLAMIC RAIDERS FRONT) (TURKEY)

IBDA-C made its appearance in Turkey in the 1970s as a violent splinter group that broke off from the Islamic Salvation Party led by Necmettin Erbakan. Its current leader is Salih Izzet Erdis, also known as Sali Mirzabeyoglu. Its spirit was that of Salafism, and its platform was a return to the original sources of Islam and its pure form, which it combined with left-wing social ideas. Its ideology was derived from the "Great East" movement, originated by Necip Fazil Kisakurek, a Turkish writer and Islamic theorist. Its stated long-term goal is the creation of a Sunni Islamic federal state in the Middle East and a return to the caliphate. IBDA-C is hostile to Shi'ites and other Muslim minorities and is violently anti-Christian and anti-Jewish. Its membership is thought to be small in numbers.

In the 1990s, it embarked on a program of violent action, and in 1994 alone was responsible for over ninety bomb attacks. It has made secular intellectuals a particular target. It is thought to have been responsible for the killings of the journalists Cetin Emeç and Ugur Muncu, and the lawyer Muanmer Aksoy. It appears to have little formal structure and its activists plan and commit their violent actions alone or in small groups. Salih

Izzet Erdis was arrested in December 1998 on charges of attempting to overthrow the government, along with other members of the organization. They continued to attempt to stir up trouble in prison and were responsible for at least one prison riot. In April 2001, Erdis was condemned to death by the State Security Court in Istanbul, which was commuted to life imprisonment the following year when Turkey abolished the death penalty. He is presumed to continue to lead IBDA-C from prison.

The group has claimed responsibility for attacks on a number of Christian and Jewish places of worship, as well as TV stations, publishers, and individual journalists. It has defaced statues of Kemal Ataturk, Turkey's secular founding father, and attacked such impious institutions as bars, shops where alcohol is sold, and banks. In February 2000, nineteen people were killed when it bombed a hotel in Sivas, in eastern Turkey. However, the most spectacular recent operations it has claimed have been the bombing of synagogues in Istanbul on November 15, 2003, in which twenty-four people died, and the later attack on the HSBC Bank and the British Consulate in Istanbul. The Turkish authorities launched a major operation against IBDA-C in May 2006, and a number of suspected members have been arrested. It is still regarded as a security threat by the Turkish government.

Its ideology aligns it with Al-Qa'ida, and its goals are compatible. However, there is not thought to be any real connection between the two organizations. In 2005, known members of IBDA-C began to publish a Turkish magazine entitled *Kaide,* whose editor, however, denied anything other than "emotional" ties with Osama Bin Laden's organization. Nonetheless, the journal praised such events as the beheading of prisoners in Iraq and the resurgence of the Taliban in Afghanistan.

IBN TAYMIYYA

Ibn Taymiyya, who lived from 1263 to 1328, was a major Islamic philosopher. His ideas are held in high esteem by Sunni Islamists today. He was born in the town of Harran in northern Syria (a location that now lies within the territory of Turkey), at a time of great political turbulence. The Abbasid Empire had fallen to the Mongols, and Ibn Taymiyya's family fled from the advancing Mongol invasion to take refuge in Damascus, where he was brought up. Syria itself had fallen under the rule of the Mamluk sultans, and the crusaders had not been entirely expelled from Palestine. At the same time, the Sufi orders were spreading unorthodox ideas in the Muslim world. Against this background of unrest, Ibn Taymiyya studied and formed his views.

He became a theologian and a renowned jurist of the Hanbali school of law, though his mature view was that reliance should not be placed exclusively on any school of interpretation. The thrust of his opinions was the refutation of what he regarded as unacceptable philosophical and mystical views, especially those of the Sufis, and a reliance on the true sources of the faith, the Quran and the Sunna. His lack of inhibition in expressing his views made enemies and attracted hostility toward himself. In particular, in his views of the attributes of God, he was accused of attaching to God some of the qualities of man: the fallacy of anthropomorphism. He was led to this view by his determination to read the Quran literally. He spent substantial periods in prison as the result of the animosity of various Muslim rulers to his theological ideas, and in his lifetime his fortunes rose and fell periodically. He issued a large number of fatwas, or legal rulings, some of which were regarded by officialdom as difficult to accept. Despite the controversy that he aroused, he was hostile to innovation and was rigidly conservative in most of his thinking.

His ideas were studied by the eighteenth-century founders of the Wahhabi tradition in the Arabian Peninsula, who had links with Hanbali jurists in Damascus, and are highly regarded by today's Wahhabi theologians in Saudi Arabia. Wahhabi tracts quoting a digest of the pronouncements of Ibn Taymiyya have been widely disseminated and were influential in the formation of fundamentalist Islamic ideas. He is also a claimed as a point of reference for today's Wahhabi-Salafi Islamist activists, who make a point of mentioning him, though it would be an anachronism to claim Ibn Taymiyya himself was a Salafi. In particular, Ibn Taymiyya applied the expression "Jahiliyya" (ignorance)—which applies to the state in which men lived before Islam—to modern circumstances, theorizing that misguided rulers were in a condition of Jahiliyya. Modern Islamists have made free use of this idea, considering states and rulers to be open to hostility from Muslims if they were deemed to have deviated from the correct interpretation of Islam. This lies behind the philosophy of such groups as Takfir wa-l Hijra (literally "Repudiation and Departure"), which assassinated President Sadat of Egypt in 1981. Ibn Taymiyya himself declared that a Sunni Muslim ruler should apply the Shari'a in his domains or be repudiated as an apostate. The Pakistani theologian Mawdudi also made use of Ibn Taymiyya's ideas. The Algerian Islamists who in 1996 assassinated members of Christian monastic orders serving at missions in Algeria also claimed to justify themselves on the basis of Ibn Taymiyya.

IMAM JOMAA (IRAN)

The Imam Jomaa is the senior Iranian cleric who organizes the Friday prayer throughout the country. In comparison with the Sunni tradition, the emphasis placed on the particular virtue of the collective Friday prayer is less, though of course in practice Friday prayers at the mosque are as much the custom in Shi'ite as in Sunni Islamic societies. There is a certain amount of theoretical debate among the Shi'ite Ayatollahs as to whether the Friday prayer is theologically necessary in the absence of the Hidden Twelfth Imam, whose return is theoretically awaited by Shi'ites. This has given rise to a false supposition in some Sunni circles that Shi'ites do not follow the custom of Friday prayer, which is somewhat at variance with observable reality.

From the earliest establishment of the Islamic Republic, Ayatollah Khomeini, the Republic's supreme leader and spiritual guide, in fact placed great stress on the importance of Friday prayer. He established a structure to supervise the organization and management of Friday prayers, which reported directly to his own office, under the control of a single imam to be known as the Imam Jomaa, who was to be directly appointed by the Supreme Leader. All Friday prayer leaders are appointed by the state, and any dissidence or deviance on the part of clerics with responsibility for the control of popular worship would be severely viewed. In the last resort, punishment could be imposed by the Special Court for the Clergy, which exercises wide powers of punishment. The role of the Friday Imamate is to ensure that the organization of the prayers and the content of sermons continue to serve the purposes

of the leadership of the Islamic Republic. Khomeini also insisted that prayers should be held on university campuses, in order to underline the authority of the clergy over the universities and the students.

The imams in charge of Friday prayers throughout the country enjoy influence and administrative powers based on their status as direct representatives of the Supreme Leader. This group of clerics is in general both ambitious and influential, and its members play significant political and social roles. In general, local political authorities are obliged to pay heed to their views and to implement their wishes. An indication of the importance of the position of Imam Jomaa was the decision of Ayatollah Khomeini's successor, Ayatollah Khamenei, to retain it for himself, while delegating its responsibilities to deputies. Given the crucial political role the regional imams play in implementing the administrative system established in Iran by the Islamic Republic, it is scarcely a surprise that they have sometimes faced violent opposition that has placed them in danger. The Ayatollahs Madani, Dastgheb, Ashrafi Esfahani, and Sadoghi Yazdi were all murdered and were accorded the status of martyrs for their faith.

Clearly, no analysis of the structure of the Islamic regime in Iran and of the status of the Supreme Leader can neglect the role of the imams who are placed in charge of Friday prayer throughout the country. The influence of these imams substantially restricts the freedom of action of other clerics who are technically independent of the state in various parts of the country.

INDIA

The population of the Republic of India was estimated in July 2006 to be just over a billion people, of which 14 percent, according to official statistics, are Muslims, mainly of the Sunni faith. India's faith communities include Hindus, Muslims, Sikhs, and Christians, among others. Their coexistence within the country's federal state is guaranteed by the country's secular constitution, but its stability has been threatened by the increasing vehemence of regional conflicts, notably in Punjab, where Sikh separatism has been a problem, and in Kashmir. An atmosphere of political instability has contributed to the problem, which has been further complicated by the rise of Hindu nationalism. Challenges from neighboring powers such as Pakistan, China, and Bangladesh helped to perpetuate a climate of violence punctuated, especially during the 1990s, by periodical crises.

In 1992, the Babri Mosque at Ayodhya, in the state of Uttar Pradesh, was destroyed by Hindu nationalists, sparking off violent disturbances in which two thousand people lost their lives across the country. The reason was a clash between the Muslim community and Hindus who insisted that the mosque, built in 1528, had been constructed on top of the birthplace of the Hindu deity Lord Rama. A number of Hindu organizations were identified of having been responsible for the violence, such as Rashtriya Swayamsevak (The Association of National Volunteers). In 2002, on the tenth anniversary of the original riots, between one thousand and two thousand people, mainly Muslims, died in Gujarat after an attack on Hindus traveling on a train in the province. In July 2005, Islamic militants attacked the site of the former mosque with explosives, hoping to frustrate Hindu plans to build a temple. Other outbreaks of violence were directed at the Christian community. In Gujarat, converts to Christianity and Christian priests were singled out for attack by small militant groups.

Instability was fostered by an electoral system in which unstable coalitions tended to take power, enabling Hindu nationalists to strengthen their hold on power in India.

Meanwhile Islamists relying on outside support continued to promote the struggle to liberate Kashmir entirely from Indian rule. However, India and Pakistan appeared to take the decision to try to defuse the conflict. In July 2001, Prime Minister Vajpayee met the Pakistani President Pervez Musharraf in the first summit meeting between the two sides in over two years. The talks achieved little, and during 2001 tension mounted between India and Pakistan. In December 2001, Muslim militants attacked the Indian parliament building in New Delhi. The Pakistani militant organization Lashkar-i Taiba was identified as responsible. For a while in 2002, it appeared as if war might break out between the two sides, with the added fear of a nuclear conflict.

In 2003, a ceasefire over Kashmir was declared by Pakistan, reciprocated by India. In 2004, the Indian Congress Party took power in general elections, marking the first reverse for the Hindu nationalists for some years. From the declaration of the ceasefire, on the other hand, militant Muslims seemed determined to create renewed tension. In Mumbai, fifty-three people were killed by car bombs in 2003, and in October 2005, bombs in the Indian capital New Delhi killed sixty-two. Responsibility was claimed by a Muslim group identifying itself with the issue of Kashmir, and on July 11, 2006, 180 people died in attacks on rush-hour trains in Mumbai. In December 2006, President Musharraf of Pakistan proposed that India and Pakistan should work together to allow Kashmir to become self-governing.

INDONESIA

Aceh Sumatra National Liberation Front

The Aceh Sumatra National Liberation Front—ASNLF—was founded on December 4, 1976, with just 150 members. It is popularly known as the GAM ("Gerakan Aceh Merdeka"—the Free Aceh Movement). Its founder was the Indonesian opposition leader Hassan Di Tiro, a descendant of Aceh's former rulers, who went into exile in Sweden in 1979. It grew into an armed secessionist organization, and according to an estimate in early 2005 it had three thousand or more members. According to some commentators GAM is not a militant Islamic movement and would be better described as an independence movement whose membership happens to be composed of Muslims. GAM claims to be committed to the defense of both the cultural identity and the economic interests of the island of Sumatra, a part of Indonesia rich in oil resources.

Indonesia has faced challenges from Islamic opposition movements from the earliest days of the Indonesian Republic, whose existence as an independent state was declared in 1945 as the country embarked on its struggle to free itself from Dutch rule. The country's first leader, President Sukarno, drew his support from a secular political movement. Underground guerrilla organizations were set up in the 1950s in Java, in the Celebes. The argument put forward by separatists in the province of Aceh was that Aceh should never have been incorporated in the republic, as it had never been under Dutch rule. In the 1950s, a movement known as Dar ul Islam attempted to free the province of Aceh as a separate Islamic state. The ASNLF based itself in part on the teachings and strategy of the rebel Dar ul Islam movement and founded its support on the hostility of the population toward the central government. Its early tactics were to set up stable and highly mobile fighting units. These units launched attacks not only on the military, but also on civilians suspected of supporting the government. The organizational long-term aim was to create an independent state under local Muslim rule, but in the short term they had

little success in establishing local "liberated" regions because of the presence in force of the Indonesian military.

In the 1990s, while Suharto was still president, the government decided to attempt to put a definitive end to the local insurgency in Aceh. The movement was subjected to draconian military repression, and summary executions were frequent. However, after the fall of Sukarno in 1998 as the result of a spectacular financial crisis, the new Indonesian regime made offers of peace including a large measure of autonomy. Due to the intransigence of the rebels, these came to nothing. The ASNLF was financed by the profits of illicit trade, including cannabis smuggling. It had begun to be riven by internal divisions, and no leader was able to exercise control over all its armed factions. In 1999, a branch under local leadership indicated that it wished to take a tougher line against the Indonesian government. Activists trained in Libya called for a more aggressive approach.

GAM's activities had their effects on the Indonesian economy. In 2001, the American oil company Exxon Mobil, under contract to the Indonesian government to exploit the country's oil resources, suspended its activities. Such developments were partially what influenced the Indonesian government to seek further accommodation with GAM. A plan was devised offering limited autonomy to Aceh, with the right to keep 70 percent of the oil revenues. GAM's fighters were supposed to disarm in exchange for the withdrawal of Indonesian troops. Neither side kept its side of the bargain. In 2003, negotiations broke down and the Indonesian government launched a large-scale military operation against the Acehnese rebels. After the Asian tsunami of December 26, 2004, aid workers were allowed in for the first time, and a ceasefire was declared. However, Islamic NGOs also took the opportunity to infiltrate the territory, offering help to local militant Muslim groups. Attempts to radicalize the conflict in Aceh appear, however, to have been unsuccessful. The territory remained relatively free of militant violence, however, and by mid-2005 exiled GAM leaders had begun to return, in anticipation of elections for a local assembly to be held in December 2006 after a new peace agreement reached at a meeting in Helsinki.

IRAN

Historical Overview

From the geopolitical and strategic standpoint, Iran is a country of great significance. With a population of almost 69 million people and a land area of 1,648 million square kilometers, Iran has been a point of contact for many peoples and civilizations. At various times, it has been the scene for successive empires of substantial weight in terms of world history. Its natural resources in the energy field and its geographical position, on the edge of the Middle East and at the gateway to Central Asia, give it substantial geopolitical importance.

The name *Iran* dates from the Aryan people who lived in the territory of Iran from 3 millennia B.C. In classical and medieval times the country was known as Persia and was renamed Iran in 1935 by Reza Shah. The Aryans mixed with local people and toward the middle of the last millennium B.C. Iran developed into the great Persian Empire of antiquity, after the conquests of Cyrus, Cambyses, and Darius. It was finally overthrown by Alexander the Great in 332 B.C. In 250 B.C. Persian rulers again reassumed control. Five hundred years later, the great dynasty of the Sassanids came to power.

In 633, a new factor made its appearance, when the newly expansionist Arabs launched their first attack on Persian territory as they spread out from the Arabian peninsula, driven by the enthusiasm of their freshly minted proselytizing religion. The Sassanid dynasty was overthrown in A.D. 651, eighteen years later. However, the Arabs took several centuries to consolidate their hold in Persia. Arab tribes and colonies brought new customs and altered the social fabric of the country. Nevertheless, though Arabic loan words made their appearance, the Persian language broadly resisted and preserved its essential structure, in contrast to other countries the Arabs had invaded. Persia's cultural resistance made it the country it is today—Muslim, but also separate from the Arab world and individual in its character.

Prophet Muhammad's cousin and son-in-law Ali, who reigned as Caliph from 656 to 661, was challenged by Mu'awiyah, who became Caliph after his death. The martyrdom of Ali's two sons Hassan (allegedly murdered in 669) and Hussein (killed in battle in 680) led to the formation of the Shi'a, the faction of Ali's supporters who never accepted the rule of the Sunni Muslim caliphs. The Persians played a part in the divisions that developed within the Muslim lands. Their support was crucial to the rise of the Abbasid Caliphate, which ruled in Baghdad from 750 to 1258. However, at the same time, the Persians were also associated with a number of uprisings against the discriminatory social and religious practices of the caliphs. The first Persian political entity of the Islamic era was carved out of the lands to the east of the Abbasid Caliphate by the Tahirid dynasty of Khorasan, whose capital was in Nishapur. The founder was Tahir ibn Hussein, a Sunni general in the caliph's service. This was followed by the Samanid dynasty in Khorasan, the Saffarids in Sistan, the Ziyarids in southern and central Iran, and the Shi'ite Bouyids, who actually dominated the caliphate in Baghdad while continuing ostensibly to serve the caliph as his military governors.

From 976, a new element was introduced into the region when ethnic Turkic warlords from the east first began to turn their attention to the lands that lay to their west, conquering them on their way westward to what would eventually become modern day Turkey. Henceforth, Persia would be overcome by one warlike newcomer after another, though many remained to become bastions of civilization. The arrival of the Turkish tribes on Persian territory was first signaled by the appearance of the Ghaznevid dynasty, Sunni Muslims whose capital was in the eastern city of Ghazni. The first Ghaznevid ruler was Saboktakin, a former Turkish slave from the court of the Samanids. The second Ghaznevid ruler, Mahmoud, controlled most of eastern and central Iran and assisted the caliph in Baghdad by taking action against hostile religious factions. On this principle, it attacked towns in central Persia, such as Rey and Isfahan, which were the seats of various Shi'ite sects. Mahmoud crushed the Bouyids. However, his growing power began to alarm the caliph, who encouraged yet another Turkish element, the Seljuks, to cross Persia's eastern frontier. In 1037, the Seljuks under their ruler Tugrul Beg sacked the Ghaznevid capital and began to establish a new dynasty.

The Seljuks, who continued faithfully to support the caliphate, extended their domains as far as Baghdad itself, strengthening the Sunni political entity and building a great empire in Persia and Asia Minor. Differences quickly made themselves felt, however, between them and the caliph. The Seljuk Turks governed Persia from 1037 to 1157, but failed to maintain a unified political entity. After the death of the great Seljuk Sultan MalikShah, separate Seljuk rulers governed various parts of Persia. By 1200, other Turkish warlords drove the Seljuks out of the territory of Persia, though Seljuk rulers held on to Anatolia and effectively founded what became modern Turkey.

The new rulers in Khorassan were known as the Khwarezmshah. The last of these, Sultan Muhammad, extended this control over much of Iran and even challenged the authority of the caliph in Baghdad. In 1226, however, he fled before the Mongols of Genghis Khan, who extended their power over Persia.

In 1258, a Mongol army under Hulagu, Genghis Khan's grandson, swept out of the East to conquer Baghdad and kill the last Abassid caliph, Al-Musta'sim. The Mongols ruled their new conquests from Asia, and their successors held Iran until the fourteenth century. In 1295, the Mongol ruler Ghazan converted to Sunni Islam. Persia recovered some of its prosperity with the rise of cities such as Isfahan, Shiraz, and Tabriz. A century later, however, under Timur, a further wave of Turkic invaders from the east took the country. They began their attack on Iran in 1383 and made good their hold over it by 1390. After Timur's death in 1405, his successors vied for power in Persia with local dynasties until the end of the sixteenth century. In 1502, Ismail, the first Safavid ruler, who was a Shi'ite Muslim, was named shah. He made Shi'ism the official faith in Persia and brought Shi'ite clerics from Arab countries to help establish it. The Safavid dynasty lasted for two hundred years, but in secular terms relied heavily on the support of a number of local tribes, who inevitably vied among each other. The last Safavid shah was deposed in 1722 and murdered in 1729.

After a period of rivalry and internal strife, the leaders of one of these tribes, the Qajars, were to provide the next dynasty. The Qajar Shahs were also Shi'ites, but also made much of their supposed descent from Genghis Khan. In 1779, the Qajar leader Agha Muhammad Khan embarked on a campaign to reunify Persia. By 1794, he had overcome all his rivals and was crowned shah in 1796. He established his capital at Teheran, then nothing but a small market town. The following year, 1797, he was succeeded by his nephew, Fath Ali Shah. The Qajars were provincial and remained relatively ignorant both of the outside world and of Persia's heritage. Under their rule, which lacked clear vision and administrative flair, Persia became weak and unable to defend itself.

Fatefully for Persia, a new picture was soon to emerge. Non-Muslim powers, Russia to the north and Great Britain to the west and south, in the shape of its Indian dominion and its client states in the Middle East, became Persia's new neighbors. Colonialism began to gestate its schemes for the future of Persia, while internally the country was weakened by quarrels, violence, and feudalism. Europe took advantage of the naivety of the Qajar court. Meanwhile, Russia launched incursions into Persia, and by occupying Georgia and Armenia prepared the ground for the extension of its colonialist influence over Persia.

Inside Persia, conflict between religious factions was beginning to take shape, in which the "Usulis" (fundamentalists) confronted the "Akhbaris" (traditionalists). The Usulis contended that in the absence of the Hidden Imam, the most learned Muslim should be followed. This laid the foundation for the idea of "emulation" of senior ayatollahs that prevails in Iran today. "Akhbaris" were essentially Salafis who believed that each man should attempt to reach his own interpretation of the original meaning of the Quran with no intermediary. After Persian forces were humiliated by a defeat at the hands of the Russians, new sects emerged. "Sheikhism" was a heterodox Islam that rejected a number of basic tenets, and "Babisme" had mystical aspects. The "Usulis" put forward the idea of Velayat-i Faqih, which eventually became the basis of the Islamic Republic, placing the most senior cleric in ultimate control of the country. The Shi'ite clerics became a power to be reckoned with, and under the fourth Qajar Shah they became a factor on the political scene, aligning themselves with the interests of the merchant class and challenging the authority of the fourth Qajar sovereign, Nasreddin.

Many factors predisposed Persia under the Qajars to a political upheaval. These included the Qajars' failure to offer effective opposition to the colonial powers, the individual despotism of the rulers, and the commercial preponderance of the foreign powers. The collapse of local industry and commerce in the face of foreign competition was another cause of social stress that set the scene for a popular rising demanding a change of government. The assassination of Nasreddin in 1896 was the signal for revolution. Under his successor, Muzzafareddin, the demand was for justice and freedom. The clerics again took a hand and participated in the negotiations that led to the signature of a new constitution that embodied the principle of the Velayat-i Faqih. From 1906, Iran became a constitutional monarchy. Nonetheless, confrontation reached a peak between clerics and conservatives on the one hand and reformers and revolutionaries on the other.

In World War I, Persia took on great geopolitical significance. Both the Russians and the British saw great advantage in holding influence in Iran. However, the October Revolution in Russia in 1917 effectively removed it from contention. Once peace was signed, Britain was the only foreign power with influence in Persia. The military coup of February 21, 1921, ended the Qajar monarchy. The new military regime dreamed of a republic like the new state in Turkey. The clerics, however, who were also aware of developments in Turkey, were opposed to the idea, fearing that Persia might also move toward secularization following the Turkish model. The leader of the military resolved the confrontation by placing himself on the throne of Persia as shah in December 1925, as Reza Shah Pahlavi.

This at once rendered irrelevant the conflict within Persia between reformers and conservatives. Both factions were left high and dry by the installation of the new regime. Reza Shah's reforms, however, were not far-reaching. However, one step he did take was to forbid the interference of the clerics in spheres not related to religion, especially in politics. In August 1941, Iran, as the country was now once more called, was occupied by the Western Allies, and Reza, who was accused of partiality toward the Germans, was obliged to abdicate. His son, Mohammed Reza Shah—the last shah of Iran—succeeded him. The clerics returned to the political scene and allied themselves with conservative politicians, much to the disgust of modernizers and intellectuals. One reformist figure in particular, Ahmed Kasravi, a legal scholar and intellectual, opposed the clerical establishment, with the result that in 1945 he was murdered. A group called the "Fedayin of Islam" was formed under the leadership of a young theologian, Navab Safavi, who killed him inside Iran's High Court. One of the many publications that had called for his death was a journal published by Ruhollah Khomeini, later Iran's Faqih and supreme leader under the Islamic Republic.

Anarchy broke out in the country, and acts of terror and killings became commonplace. The reticence of the government on what was taking place, together with the support of the religious establishment and the commercial class, raised the Fedayin of Islam to the level of a political faction. They also had the support of an important ayatollah, Abolghassem Kachani. The periodical *The People's Fight* (*Nabard-i Melli*) became the Fedayin's mouthpiece and bore the slogan "Islam before All." A series of political assassinations followed, including those of Prime Minister General Razmara, Abdolhossein Hagir, a former prime minister, and Dr. Zangini, minister of culture and dean of the faculty of law at Teheran University. All these were the responsibility of the Fedayin of Islam, whose leader, Navab Safavi, had by this time visited Egypt and made contact with the Muslim Brotherhood.

As the nationalist movement in Iran reached its height, with the rise to power of Prime Minister Mohammed Mossadegh, differences emerged between the Navab Safavi group and Ayatollah Kachani. The "Navab" group wanted to assassinate both Mossadegh and the Foreign Minister Hassan Fatemi, but neither plan succeeded. After the coup of 1953 against Dr. Mossadegh, orchestrated by the American CIA, in which the Shi'ite clerical establishment played a significant role, the Fedayin's star began to wane. A failed attempt to assassinate the new prime minister, Hossein Ala, led to the arrest, trial, and execution of a number of members of the "Navab" group. Later, however, with the murder of another prime minister, Hassan Ali Mansour, and an attempt on the life of the shah, the reputation of the Fedayin began to be reestablished.

At this time, the agrarian reform program initiated by Prime Minister Ali Amini was starting to make a real social impact in Iran. The clerics were opposed to it and also opposed the findings of a commission set up to examine the issue of women's rights. For the first time, the name of Ruhollah Khomeini began to appear on publications intended to arouse popular feeling. This resulted in the developments of 1963, when Khomeini was arrested. He was elevated by the religious establishment to the rank of ayatollah, which probably saved his life, He was sent instead into exile in Turkey. These events were at the origin of the new religious opposition movement to the regime of the shah. The anti-monarchists continued to agitate until 1979, when the monarchy was overthrown and the old dream of the establishment of a theocratic regime in Iran was at last realized.

The Contemporary Scene

Iran's population of 70 million consists for the most part of Persian speaking Shi'ites, but there are both religious and ethnic minorities within the state. Ten percent of the population is made up of Sunni Muslims, of which eight percent are Kurdish Sunnis close to the border with Iraq and the rest Baluchis, living in the south east of the country. The Arabic-speaking minority of 4 million in the southwest of the country are Shi'ites. There are a perhaps 100,000 Christians, mainly of various eastern rites, and a dwindling Jewish minority of probably less than 10,000.

After February 11, 1979, the great division within Iran has been that between the state, on the one hand, and the Revolution, on the other. Paradoxically, each of these two institutions derived its legitimacy in the first instance from the person of Ayatollah Khomeini and drew their strength from a separate but overlapping clientele. Each was essentially concerned to lead and develop the population through the intermediary of a multiplicity of institutions: Islamic councils, groups, networks, committees, and associations. All these made their contribution to the consolidation of Khomeini's administration in the face of whatever internal opposition to it might remain. At first, these popular foundations helped to preserve the new system against the many internal and external challenges it faced. Today, however, they are in danger of leading to a collapse from within. Without internal enemies, the various elements of the Islamic Republic launch attacks on each other, and allow their conflicts to become visible, where previously they were able to avoid confrontation thanks to the arbitration of the imam, who settled any major dispute. The legitimacy of the regime rests on the Revolution, but the state, once established, has acquired substantial powers, so that the division of responsibility between the two was the object of constant vigilance by the Imam.

To understand the Islamic Revolution in Iran, a historical perspective is necessary. In particular, the part played by the Shi'ite clergy during the uprisings in Iraq in the 1920s was significant. In the face of severe repression on the part of the British, the most militant of the Iraqi Shi'ite clerics were driven into exile in Iran. Forty years later, this upsurge of Shi'ite revolutionary spirit reemerged with the beginnings of an organized movement. In the Shi'ite holy cities in Iraq, Najaf, Karbala, and Qadhimiya, a new generation of Shi'ite clerics prepared themselves to face the key questions on the future of Islam and the direction to be taken by the revolutionary struggle. In Najaf, in the 1960s, the political theory of Shi'ite Islam was being developed by Mohammed Baqr al-Sadr, who inspired the present Iranian constitution. His principle was to provide a more coherent and solid system than that which could be derived from isolated fatwas, for the benefit of an impoverished and rebellious younger generation disillusioned with communism. His associates were the spiritual leader of the Lebanese Shi'ites, Mohammed Hussein Fadlallah, as well as Mohammed Mehid Shamseddin, vice president of the Lebanese Supreme Shi'ite Council. He also made contact with Khomeini, the hero of the Shi'ite resistance in Iran in 1963, who was taking refuge from the shah's relentless suppression.

Najaf, in the 1960s, saw the development of the theory of the political leadership of the Faqih, which became the cornerstone of Shi'ite political theory. It was then that Khomeini, taking his inspiration from the ideas of Baqr al-Sadr, gave his first public lectures on what an Islamic government should be. At the same period, Baqr al-Sadr's earliest works appeared. These were "Falsafatuna" (Our Philosophy) and "Iqtisaduna" (Our Economics), which presented a real Islamic alternative to the political theories of capitalism and socialism. Here, for the first time, the various options of an Islamic government based on the concept of Velayet-i Faqih were developed. By 1969, Baqr al-Sadr had already concluded that society was divided into those who could lead and those who needed to be led. There were also distinctions within the clergy. Only those Ayatollahs whose level of Islamic scholarship had raised them to the level of "Mujtahid"—those capable of deriving independently new meanings from the scriptures—would be capable of giving leadership to the community.

The Islamic Revolution succeeded in mobilizing a clergy that had not always seen eye to eye on such issues. This was all the more an achievement, since by no means all agreed with Khomeini's acceptance of the principle of the Velayet-i Faqih. The ostensible unanimity of the clergy in 1979 and its support for the Revolution appeared to be a reaction against the growing marginalization of which it had been the object under the shah. Though strongly politicized since the nineteenth century, however, the clergy were not the only social force from which the "Khomeinist" movement derived support. Secular militants also participated in the revolutionary movement. These included the merchant class and the so-called Mostazafin—the underclass, which had been left behind by economic development. In addition, the clergy as a whole were wary of identifying themselves with the state, even though the state, and especially parliament, seemed in the early days to consist entirely of clergy. In any case, the clergy were far from being wholly identified with the Islamic Revolution—they were there before it and will be there long after the Revolution has worked itself out. Individual clerics were to be found in all the political groupings, organizations, and institutions that arose from the Revolution.

The aspect where the unity of the clergy is more than superficial, and where clerics all agree, is on the fundamental values of society, including morality and respect for the Islamic way of life. The Iranian clergy aims above all to safeguard its leading position through the maintenance of its control over society and the economy. This appears to be why, in the last resort, the clerics support the Revolution rather than the state, though without necessarily seeking, within the state, a greater role for themselves.

In many ways, a critical moment for the Islamic Revolution was the death in 1989 of Ayatollah Khomeini, the first Supreme Leader, who embodied the Revolution's values. His successor as Supreme Leader and Faqih was Ayatollah Ali Khamenei, who was duly elected by the Assembly of Experts. The issue was whether the doctrine of Velayat-e Faqih could survive the disappearance from the scene of Khomeini, whose immense prestige was such that none found it incongruous that he had been placed in a position where his judgments were regarded as infallible. Khamenei had not achieved the position of "marja'" when he was elected—an authority accepted by the consensus of clerics as fit to be emulated without question—but was quickly elected to the rank by a group of senior ayatollahs, though this was disputed by others. He vigorously defended the position and the role of the Faqih, but has to some extent saved himself from criticism by refraining from making excessive number of pronouncements. He has, however, taken a number of steps to strengthen the conservative tendency, especially since the election as president in 1997 of the reformist candidate Mohammed Khatami, who took 70 percent of the vote in a contest with the conservative champion Ali Akbar Nateq-Nuri. Numerous newspapers have been shut down, closing off a channel by which liberal ideas are disseminated, and the Council of Guardians disqualified many liberal candidates in the

2004 elections. Politics in Iran could be seen as a struggle for power between the Supreme Leader and the president, though it was not seen as surprising that Khatami lost no opportunity to express his loyalty. Since 2005, Ayatollah Khamenei has given vocal support to the new government of President Mahmoud Ahmedinejad and has condemned those who oppose him as traitors.

Tendencies Within the Islamic Republic

In the first days of the Islamic Republic, two great currents of thought took shape. One of these was the "Islamic" tendency, generally referred to by the name "Hezbollah," together with the Nezhat-i Azadi (Movement for Democracy). The other was the "Nationalist" tendency, identified with the Jebhe Melli (National Front). The "Organization of the Mujahidin of the Islamic Revolution of Iran" distinguishes, in a publication entitled "The political tendencies within Iran today," four main groups, which it characterizes as (1) "Traditional Right," (2) "Modernizing Right," (3) "Modernizing Left," and (4) "Left." In practice, these correspond to four political options, as follows:

1. The "Traditional Right" seeks less of the Revolution and more of the state. They seek the preeminence of the state and the absorption of the revolutionary institutions into it, while also moderating its interference in the economic and social life.
2. The "Modernizing Right" advocates that both revolution and state should be reduced. They want the revolutionary process to end and its institutions to be taken over, but they also want to limit the intervention of the state in economic and social affairs.
3. The "Modernizing Left" seeks more of the Revolution and less of the state, in other words the domination of the state by the revolutionary institutions, the submission of the state to the Shari'a, and nonintervention by the state in the economic and social life.
4. Finally, the "Left" seeks both more of the Revolution and more of the state, that is to say, the preeminence of the state and also the commitment of the state to a kind of permanent revolution. This state, after taking over the revolutionary institutions, would be interventionist in all fields and at all levels of social activity.

These divisions are manifested within the Party of the Islamic Republic, on the one hand, over agrarian reform, labor law, and the definition of the Velayat-i Faqih, and on the other hand within parliament, around issues relating to economic planning, and the free market. The political parties disagree over the interpretation of Article 44 of the constitution, which defines the Iranian economic system as being made up of three sectors, the public, the cooperative, and the private. They also disagree over the activities of the private sector, the nationalization of foreign trade, and the law concerning the nationalization of industry. These divergences are exacerbated by the state's assumption of control over the economy and the distribution of goods. From 1982, these distinctions were known within the government as the "Right" and the "Left."

Following a split within the Association of Militant Clergy and the consequent formation of the left-wing Assembly of Militant Clerics, the existence of the two tendencies was officially recognized within the government. Ayatollah Khomeini himself approved of the split, and the left wing, including the Assembly of Militant Clerics, received his support. At the time, the right wing, supported by the religious conservatives, was opposed to an absolute Velayet-i Faqih, which it considered could only be exercised by to the original twelve Imams of the Shi'ite faith and could not exist in modern times. It called instead for the application of the fundamental precepts of Islam, which it understood as immutable divine rules. The left wing, in contrast, supported the absolute nature of the Velayat-i Faqih and accepted the principle of "secondary rules," in other words of precepts laid down by the clergy in response to present needs and which serve in the place of the fundamental precepts for as long as the conditions that led to their promulgation persist. After Khomeini's death, the right wing began to support the Velayet-i Faqih, while the left wing stressed its conditional nature. Both the left and the right, however, took an identical economic approach. The merchants and the religious conservatives backed the traditional economy against the technocrats, those who sought industrial development, those who supported a state-run economy, and the religious modernizers.

The right wing included a broad spectrum of factions, grouped around the Association of Militant Clergy. These included such groups as the Association of Preachers, the Association of Professional Bodies and Merchants, the Women's Association, the Students' and University Teachers' Organizations, the Engineers' Professional Association, and the Ansar Hezbollah. On the left wing, the associated groups are of a broadly intellectual and Islamic nature. These include the Association of Teachers at the Theological School of Qom, the Organization of the Mujahidin of the Islamic Revolution, the Islamic Association of University Teachers, the Islamic Students' Association, the Office for Consolidation and Unity, the Participation Front for Islamic Iran, and the Islamic Association of engineers.

It should also be mentioned that a group of Islamic intellectuals exists that attempts to reconcile the ideas of the various currents of opinion with the dominant ideology. Their concern is to bring about evolutionary change in the current situation. The leading exponent is the philosopher Abdolkarim Soroush, who returned to Iran in July 2004 after years of exile to continue his work on the theory of Islam and democracy. He is regarded as Iran's foremost liberal thinker in the field of religion and politics.

Recent Events

In the presidential elections of June 24, 2005, a conservative religious candidate, the former mayor of Teheran Mahmoud Ahmedinejad, defeated the former President Ali Akbar Hashemi Rafsanjani to become president of Iran in succession to President Khatami. President Ahmedinejad was a well-known figure as the result of his years at the head of the municipality of Teheran and was popular with right-wing factions. He represented a movement known as the Abadgaran ("The Alliance of the Builders of Islamic Iran"). The leaders of this faction were of a younger generation than the clergy who formed the current political leadership of both the conventional conservative and reformist factions. The Abadgaran seems to have been formed in 2003, and it is made up broadly of figures under the age of fifty, who are nonclerics, but believe strongly in the principles initially laid down for the Islamic Republic by Khomeini in 1979. Commentators have noted that they tend to dress in the new uniform of the nonclerical Iranian elite, in dark suits, beards, and tieless shirts. Many members of the Abadgaran have seen service in the Revolutionary Guard, or have emerged from other militia groups such as the Basij, and some are veterans of the Iran–Iraq War. Few have a long political track record. Their support comes massively from the poorer people of Iran, especially the slums of South Teheran where support for Islamic militias has always been strong. The primary aim of the Abadgaran has been to crush the reformists as a political force; a process they began by reducing President Khatami to the status of a lame duck in his last year of office.

The Abadgaran, itself an alliance of conservative factions, won most of the seats in the municipal elections of 2003 and followed that up with a massive victory in the parliamentary election of 2004, so Ahmedinejad's victory in the 2005 presidential election should not have come as a shock. They have been described as Iran's neoconservatives. Even before Ahmedinejad's election, they passed laws in parliament that hampered foreign investment and foreign trade. Though they primarily oppose the reformists, the Abadgaran has also unsettled the conservative establishment of the Association of Militant Clergy, whose press organs have drawn attention to what they have called dangerous radicalism and extremism. The Abadgaran makes no secret of their fierce belief in the utopian principles of the Islamic Revolution, with its theocratic and authoritarian structure, combined with and egalitarian public-sector economy and a proselytizing approach to foreign policy. They believe that the clerics should step back to the supervisory positions provided by the constitution to oversee Iran's adherence to Islamic principles, such as the Council of Guardians, the Assembly of Experts, and the Expediency Council, while the executive positions should fall to laymen such as themselves with a technocratic approach. On the other hand, they are strongly committed to the principle of the Velayat-e Faqih and appear in some sense to have formed an alliance with Ayatollah Khamenei as supreme leader over the heads of the conservative clerics. Ayatollah Khamenei has probably not forgotten the opposition from some clerical conservatives to his elevation to the status of "Marja'."

Ahmedinejad's election as president in 2005 could be said to have brought to an end a long period of factional infighting in Iran that followed the death of Khomeini. His supporters are now firmly entrenched in all important posts. There were initial suggestions that they were ideologues who would be incompetent to govern, but this did not prove to be the case at first. On the other hand, by January 2007, the electorate seemed to have become disillusioned with him. Serious losses in the municipal elections indicated that the public had lost its enthusiasm for Ahmedinejad's ideological certainties, as rampant price inflation of basic foodstuffs was causing concern. However, he has stood firm over Iran's right to develop peaceful nuclear power as laid down by the Nuclear Nonproliferation Treaty, which Iran has signed, which has earned him wide popularity at home. He has also shocked international opinion by his hostility to Israel and his apparent Holocaust-denial, which have also gained him approval from extremist Islamists in Iran. Meanwhile, his firm opposition to corruption has stood him in good stead. He has also dipped into Iran's reserves to make direct contributions to the improvement of the standard of living of Iran's poorest. Nonetheless, in December 2006, there were somewhat surprising indications in the municipal elections in Teheran and elsewhere, and in elections for the Assembly of Experts, that the ascendancy of President Ahmedinejad and the Abadgaran was on the wane when he lost the majority of local government seats in Teheran.

Ansar-e Hezbollah

The groups referred to by this name date from the first days of the Islamic Revolution, though at this early stage they were not organized. "Ansar," in Arabic, simply means "supporters." Those who have disapproved of the Ansar's activities have called them thugs. The members of the groups make up a semi-official and quasi-clandestine organization of a paramilitary character that performs vigilante duties, pulling up citizens who behave in a supposedly un-Islamic way, and keeps particular vigilance over the comportment of women, in a sometimes aggressive way.

The regime also uses them to quell any hostile demonstrations. Some are ex-military and others are members of the Basij militia. In general terms, their remit is to defend the values of the Revolution. With little formal structure, they give those who wish to support the Islamic Revolution an opportunity to play a part in spreading and maintaining the spirit of the revolution in Iran. In the early days of the Islamic Republic, they operated under the umbrella of the so-called Party of the Islamic Republic, formed by Ayatollah Ruholla Khomeini in 1979 to give a formal structure to the prerevolutionary groups formed in Iran before 1979 under the general title of Hezbollah. The Party of the Islamic Republic was dissolved in 1988, but the Ansar continued to exist, doing the bidding of the more conservative elements of Iran's Islamic establishment and especially answering to the Supreme Leader, Ayatollah Khamenei, Ayatollah Khomeini's successor, or those who claim to represent him.

The degree of organization within the Ansar increased after the end of the Iran–Iraq War in 1988, when the concern was to channel the energy of the young soldiers who had returned from the front into directions acceptable to the regime at a time when there were considerable social and economic difficulties. The activists of Iran's Hezbollah—fundamentally the supporters of the line of Ayatollah Khomenei—orchestrated the demobilization of the young combatants and directed their zeal into a struggle against corruption, social misdemeanors, and the encroachments of Western culture. The Ansar set up what were essentially combat units, who demonstrated in the streets and imposed their own version of civil order. The two principal organizers of the movement were Hadji Karadji and Hossein Allah Karam. The views of Hezbollah found expression in the monthly magazine *Sobh* and the daily newspaper *Keyan*. Hezbollah also had a monthly

journal of its own, *Shalamsheh*, whose editor Massoud Dehnamaki wrote as follows about the Ansar: "Up to 1990, the Ansar operated simply under the name of Hezbollah. This was the case up to 1993, when the name Ansar-e Hezbollah first made its appearance. Their aim was to promote desirable goals, and suppress anything illicit."

In an interview in 1998, Hossein Allah Karam said, "When we heard the leader declare the principle of fighting for good and against evil, we rediscovered the impetus we had lost. This was when the Ansar brought into politics a faction of religious scholars who represented their views, and went under the name of Ansar-e Hezbollah. Today, the Ansar themselves continue to operate under a variety of names, such as 'Ansar-e Velayet,' 'Hezbollah Students,' and 'Fighters of the Army of Islam.' Their philosophy is that all who are not with the Hezbollah are our sworn enemies.' They preach the need for permanent revolution. In foreign policy, they are partisans of export of the Revolution. They are diametrically opposed to anything that smacks of the West and reject all relationships with the West. In economic terms, they are opposed to any investments or loans from abroad and also oppose privatization. Their ideal is a traditional agricultural economy, in which the old structure of society is preserved. In politics, they seek the election of conservative clergy, whom they deem capable of maintaining the old traditions without relying on the government.

The Ansar-e Hezbollah became more prominent in 1999 after troubles during which it attacked the student dormitories of Teheran University. The attack came in response to what the students claimed was a peaceful protest on July 8 after the government imposed new restrictions on the freedom of the press. The police joined Ansar-e Hezbollah members in pursuing the students back to their dormitories. Two students died and a score were hospitalized. Protests spread throughout Iran when the brutality of the Ansar attack was publicized in Iran and abroad. This was a clear instance where the Islamic government chose to use the semiofficial instrument represented by the Ansar to suppress dissent, rather than turning out uniformed forces against the students, which could have led to a hardening of battle lines in the confrontation. With the departure of President Khatami after the elections of June 2005 and his replacement by President Ahmedinejad, conservative Islam has triumphed in Iran. Nonetheless, such social forces as Hezbollah and the Ansar stand ready in the wings to defend the conservative position if need be.

Association of Militant Clergy

The Association of Militant Clergy (JRM) (Jame'-e Ruhaniyat-e Mobarez) was established in Tehran in 1978, before the overthrow of the shah, by the supporters of Ayatollah Khomeini. The association organized religious and political demonstrations in the mosques, which continued throughout the revolutionary period in collaboration with the "teaching body of the theological school of Qom." The ideology of the JRM, which is highly conservative, derives from the directives of Ayatollah Khomeini regarding the struggle against the regime of the shah and the exclusion of Marxists from the revolutionary movement.

The central council of the association includes Ayatollah Murtada Mottahari, Ayatollah Seyed Mohammad Beheshti, Hojatulislam Mohammad Jaffar Bahunar, and Ayatollah Moffatah. The association's spokesman is Hojatulislam Falsafi, one of the heroes of the occupation of the Bahai temple in 1953, while Ayatollah Mahdavi Kani, one of its founders, is responsible for the general oversight of its revolutionary

committees while also holding the position of general director of the police.

Despite its significance in the provisional government of Bani Sadr, the JRM remained a minority movement. However, in elections to Iran's fourth majlis (parliament) on April 10, 1992, it obtained a parliamentary majority, giving its support to Rafsanjani. Its victory enabled it to occupy key posts in government, confirming its influence in the legislature, the executive, and the judiciary. It held the Ministry of Guidance, the Ministry of the Interior, and the Ministry of Information, as well as a position in the Council of Guardians and in the Revolutionary Guard (the Pasdaran).

From 1982 onward, the choice between a free and a planned economy was first the cause of a split within the government and then between the Party of the Islamic Republic and the parliament. This cemented the opposition between an economic right wing favoring a market economy and a left wing that advocated economic planning. The JRM abstained from taking sides in this controversy for some time. However, after the dissolution of the Party of the Islamic Republic in 1987, some of this party's former members, supporters of a free economy, joined the JRM. This led to a split within the party and to the formation of the more leftist Assembly of Militant Clergy (Majm'a-i Ruhaniyun-i Mobarez) in 1988. This split, which was unopposed by Ayatollah Khomeini, contributed to the ideological purification of the JRM and strengthened its role in the government and in parliament.

A further disagreement arose concerning the question whether the JRM should remain as a religious movement or transform itself into a political party. Ayatollah Mahdavi, at the head of the religious faction, who found himself in the minority, resigned his position as secretary in favor of Ayatollah Ali Akbar Nategh Nuri, the leader of the political tendency. At the elections for the fifth majlis (National Assembly), the JRM ran candidates throughout the country, but was comprehensively defeated. Ayatollah Nategh Nuri, who at the time was also the speaker of the majlis, resigned as head of the JRM and a council took his place. At the termination of the fifth majlis, Nuri became one of the advisers of the "faqih" (the leader, at the time Ayatollah Khomeini).

The JRM exercises control over the centers of religious education, such as that in Qom, of which Ayatollah Madvavi Kani was rector, and which was the university of Imam Sadegh, among others. The JRM also maintains a presence in all political bodies and professional organizations, at all levels and in every field. Despite its low standing in public opinion, it controls the majority of offices of the state and dominates religious and cultural propaganda. It is also to some extent in control of the economy.

The varying positions of the JRM on the issue of the primary role of the theologian in Islamic society (the concept of "velayet-i faqih": see separate entry) are summarized in the following extract from its literature:

The "velayet-i faqih is a divine relationship in Islamic society deriving its legitimacy not from the people but by virtue of its link with the universal and divine "velayet" (authority). ... All criticisms regarding the progressive and revolutionary theory of the absolute "velayet" of the faqih, which reduces its position to that of a mandate or limits it to a restricted or pre-determined field would divest both the political system and Islam of their real power. ... In no case does the "velayet" derive its legitimacy from the people, who have little role to play in its nature. In an Islamic system, in the absence of the Imam (see separate entry), the last word lies with the "velayet-i faqih" ... The Islamic parliament should serve as the executive arm of the "velayet" in the administration of the country and should exert its efforts to achieve the velayet's objectives. ... The only concern of the parliament should be fully and compliantly to put into practice the will of the Leader. ... The legality of parliament arises from its legitimacy, which flows from the "velayet." We regard as legal any government which observes divine precepts, even if it is rejected by the population. On the contrary, however, we regard as illegitimate any government which fails to conform to such precepts, even were it to enjoy the approval of the entire population. The institution of any government not inspired by the clergy, together with any move tending to exclude the authentic clergy from government, are a grave derogation from the will of the Imam.

On the issue of freedom, acceptable from the liberal standpoint, the JRM takes the view that it is "a deviation from Islamic principles. ... The participation of the people in political life is not a right, but rather a religious duty, in regard to which no latitude can be allowed." The newspaper *Resalat* offers the following definition of freedom of the press: "certainly there are principles, but there are also limits which may be transgressed, especially in regard to anything concerning the 'velayet-i faqih,' the personality of the Leader (the Imam), or the clergy."

On the issue of the exportation of the revolution: "The responsibility of the President of the Republic is an onerous one. In addition to the duties he must fulfil in respect of the 70 million Iranians, he also bears other responsibilities in relation to the billion Muslims throughout the world for whom Iran represents the ideal state."

On external politics, the JRM professes itself favorable to a liberal and open policy: "We shall maintain reciprocal relations based on mutual interests with all countries which do not aim at domination over Iran." However, the JRM excludes any relationship, direct or indirect, with the United States.

In the field of economics, the JRM gives primacy to the private sector and characterizes public ownership of the economy as one of society's grave economic ills: "We do not believe that everything should be concentrated in the hands of the state. Our duty is to encourage the people to participate in the economy of the country and to move in the direction of privatization."

In relation to economic growth and social equality: "Social equality is the primordial objective to be achieved. Justice is primary and progress is a means by which it may be achieved.... The pursuit of ideals and the improvement of the lot of the oppressed are the imperative."

In relation to the direction to be taken by the economy, and the use of foreign resources in the field of investment, the JRM makes the following statement: "We do not consider that our industry and agriculture will alone suffice for the needs of our country. On the contrary, we have important resources to offer in the fields of international commerce and trade, and we are able to play the role of a bridge between many countries.... Iran is in no way suited to a policy of closed doors in the field of economics, and indeed views such a policy as inimical. No restrictions are envisaged on either national or international investors in the fields of energy, gas, oil, petrochemicals, mines metals, transport, tourism and manufacturing industry."

Finally, as regards cultural affairs, the JRM rejects the concept of cultural exchanges, which it regards as a danger to the country.

Association for the Defense of the Values of the Islamic Revolution

The Association for the Defense of the Values of the Islamic Republic (Jame'-e Defa'-e Az Arzesha-ye Enqelab-e Eslami) was founded in 1996 by Hojjatuleslam Rayshahri, before the elections of March and April of that year.

The movement was established in opposition to President Rafsanjani. Rayshahri, who became the association's secretary-general, had been a feared revolutionary prosecutor in the years after the Islamic Revolution, before becoming minister of information in 1984. He was then state prosecutor from 1989 to 1991, before taking responsibility for the Hajj in 1991.

Rayshahri is said to be close to Ayatollah Khamenei and has expressed his philosophy relating to the leadership of Iran as follows: "The Vali Faqih is chosen by God without any part being played by the people in his appointment.... The Velayat-i Faqih is in reality the extension of the reign of the chosen prophets.... Islam requires that the individual should support these values and apply them to his individual, family and social life, even when the majority may be opposed to such values." Ahmad Purnijati, a founder member of the association, affirms: "In particular and necessary circumstances the Vali Faqih may act outside the power accorded to him by article 110 of the constitution."

In relation to politics, the Association for the Defense of the Values of the Islamic Revolution accepted the multiplicity of parties on the condition that all should lie within the framework of the "Party of God." Rayshahri says: "The political party, as such, has its role in other societies but not in our Islamic society.... Within Islam, there exists only one true party, the Party of God (Hezbollah), and the principles of the divine party are unique and inalterable. The Quran considers all parties, other than the Party of God, as parties of the devil."

The association supported a policy of supervised freedom for the press. In the field of foreign policy, it advocates the exportation of the Revolution and stresses the necessity of transformation in the global order: "Flexibility in political negotiations, intended to attract the approval of foreigners, constitutes treason to our ideals and values. ... We cannot trust in western governments to establish reliable and durable relations. ... The objective of the Islamic Revolution is the destruction of the aggressive American regime ..." In the economic field, the association is opposed to state control of the economy, but, nonetheless, opposes the concentration of corporations in the hands of overpowerful private groups: its preference is for a cooperative system. It advocates economic self-sufficiency, and Rayshahri has declared that "there is no value in dependency on western industry: Islamic society should rely on its own resources." In the cultural sphere, the association advocates proactive censorship and is intensely concerned by the invasion of foreign culture.

The association suspended its activities in November 1998 because of its relative failure to establish itself politically and after disagreement among its leaders. It had been representative of a radical current within Iranian society and continued to exercise some influence through those of its former members who held important official positions.

Assembly of Militant Clerics (Majma'-e Ruhaniyun-e Mobarez, MRM)

The Assembly of Militant Clerics (MRM), of which President Khatami was a founding member, was established in 1988, with the authorization of Ayatollah Khomeini, following a split with the Association of Militant Clergy led by Seyyed Mahmoud Doa'i, Jalali Khomeini, and Mehdi Karroubi. After the split, the majority of parliamentarians joined the MRM. The government, however, remained committed to the Association of Militant Clergy (JRM), which was comprehensively defeated at the legislative elections in 1988 and found itself in a minority. At these elections, the Council of Guardians disallowed the candidature of eighty MRM members. Within the MRM,

with the exception of such figures as Hojjatuleslam Sadegh Khalkhali and Ayatollah Moussavi Ardabili, there were revolutionary activists who were close to Ayatollah Khomeini's close circle and occupied important posts. These included Mohammed Khatami, Abdullah Nuri, Ali Akbar Mohtashemi (who was responsible for Palestine and Lebanon), Hojjatuleslam Karrubi, who was the MRM's secretary-general and the speaker of parliament, Moussavi Khoiniha, Seyyed Mahmoud Doa'i, and Jalali Khomeini. In May 1997, another split in the MRM gave rise to a further group, the Line of the Imam (Khat-e Imami). Many of those who joined this group had been ardent supporters of Ayatollah Khomeini in the early days of the Revolution, and it included many members of the student organization of the same name, which seized the hostages at the U.S. Embassy in Tehran in 1979. Their views are similar to those of the MRM, and they are seen as leftist in Iranian terms.

A number of other organizations are associated with the MRM. The "Islamic Teachers' Association," originating from a split within the MRM, was set up by Mohammed Ali Raja'i just before the elections for the third Majlis. Another group of organizations is known as the "Unified Groups of the Line of the Imam." This consists of the Islamic Workers Association, the Islamic Employees Association, the Islamic Students Association, the Islamic Teachers Association, and the Organization of the Mujahidin of the Islamic Revolution. Together with the MRM they constitute the leftist or reformist group within the spectrum of Iranian Islamic parties.

Philosophically, the MRM argues that the powers of the Vali Faqih are limited to those laid down in the constitution. The periodical Asr-e Ma, run by the Khat-e Imami but expressing views in line with those of the MRM, puts the position as follows: "Absolute Velayet is a term which belongs to the conceptual rather than the personal realm, in the sense that the Islamic government has the power to intervene in all matters within the country. At the same time, however, such absolute power must not stand in the way of a logical separation between various authorities. ... We view the Islamic Republic as an active society, with Islamic legislation, in which each of the members of society, irrespective of his material or moral standing, may play a part equal to that played by others, and may by virtue of the part he plays determine his own destiny. For this reason the leaders of such a society, in addition to their divine responsibility, are responsible to those who form part of such a society; and further, the political structure of the Islamic state is not fixed, but must respond to the needs of the times and of society."

The MRM and other groups that follow a similar line lay stress on the role of the political parties, regarding them as a guarantee against the introduction of a despotic system. The MRM's secretary-general puts it thus: "The emergence of political parties further reinforces parliament, makes the electoral process more meaningful, strengthens the system and arouses the enthusiasm of the people." The MRM also gives its approval to freedom of expression. The daily newspaper *Salam,* its mouthpiece and spokesman, is supported by "The Islamic World," a body led by Hadi Khamenei, the brother of Ayatollah Khomeini's successor, the leader Ali Khamenei. The MRM and its allies are seen as accomplished practitioners of the exportation of the Revolution: "The national interests of Iran oblige us to assist people subject to domination, especially Muslim peoples, so that they may achieve independence and freedom, while countering the effects of global imperialism." In the field of economics, the MRM and organizations affiliated to it opposed the widespread privatization of the means of production,

which they accepted only to a limited and conditional extent.

Ali Akbar Mohtashemi affirms that the exportation of the Revolution is a fundamental principle of Islam: "Many verses in the Quran confirm that the Prophet has been chosen for all peoples, and that his revolution and his thought are of universal application." The "Khordad 2 Front," the name given to the group of political parties that supports President Khatami, named after the (Iranian) date of their electoral victory in 1997, places no faith in the United Nations and its subsidiary organizations, regarding them as "an integral part of the U.S. State Department." In its official program, the Organization of the Mujahidin of the Islamic Revolution (Sazman-e Mojahedin-e Enqelab-e Eslami), which follows a similar line, sets out in its program a number of objectives:

- The creation of autonomous blocs of Muslim states within international organizations and assemblies.
- The reinforcement of anti-Zionist and anti-imperialist positions within such organizations and assemblies.
- The deployment of the widest efforts to curb the dependence of Muslim peoples and countries on the United States and other dominant powers.

The establishment of the nucleus of a principled alliance among Muslim countries.

In the sphere of international relations, the Khordad 2 Front favors a policy of the extension of Iran's relations with Western powers other than the United States. On the other hand, it rejects all relations with the United States, which it views as "the central and strategic enemy of the Revolution and of the Islamic Republic." However, after the election of President Khatami, the Khordad 2 Front modified its foreign policy to accept the principle of the normalization of relations between Iran and the United States, at least as a theoretical goal.

The election of President Khatami not only inaugurated a new era for the Islamic Republic, but also exacerbated the struggle between the two political wings: those seen by the West as conservatives and reformers. The result was violence. The JRM, the conservative wing, believed that its hold over public opinion was dropping and that the balance of power was not favorable to it. It therefore went on the offensive, embarking on violent action, which included political assassinations, tough action against the opposition press, attacks by volunteers and revolutionary guards on demonstrations, meetings, and lectures at mosques and universities, and assaults on student hostels in Tehran and Tabriz, which caused deaths and injuries. It interfered with the judiciary in the interests of the conservatives, a move that resulted in the condemnation and imprisonment of religious modernists. The JRM, with the acquiescence of the leader, initiated the prosecution of Abdullah Nuri, the minister of education in the Khatami government, and the condemnation of others by the "Special Religious Tribunal."

The Khordad 2 Front, which had support in the media and from senior members of the university faculties, took up increasingly more defensive positions in the face of the growing virulence of the attacks launched on them by their adversaries, a process that resulted in the paralysis of parliamentary activity. In consequence, the reformers have not succeeded in putting place or bringing to completion any substantive reforms. The determining factor in this struggle has been the position of the leader, whose absolute authority gave him all the necessary powers to reinforce the conservatives in their contest with the reformist front. He controlled a spread of bodies, all of which wielded power of various kinds: the judiciary, the Council of Guardians of the Constitution, the Distinguished Council for the Interests of the Regime, the Assembly of the Wise, the Friday Imams, the Army of the Guardians, and the Bassiji (the volunteers).

From 1997, the government has been unable to put into practice any of its decisions in the military and security fields, while the judicial authorities have been unable to promulgate new laws without the approval of the leader, the Vali Faqih. Though President Khatami was reelected in 2001, the situation has reached stalemate. The parliamentary elections of 2004, when the Council of Guardians disqualified large numbers of reformist candidates, resulted in a parliament with a conservative majority. This merely underlined the situation in which the legislature and the executive are paralyzed by the restrictions imposed by the higher nonelected authorities. Since the election of President Mahmoud Ahmedinejad on June 25, 2005, there has been less tension between the executive and the Supreme Leader. Observers believe the change in the direction of politics in Iran arose because of popular discontent at the relative lack of achievement under President Khatami, which was partly caused by the extent to which he was hampered by the conservative regulatory bodies.

Buniad Mostazefine (Foundation for the Expropriated)

Khomeini set up this organization after the Islamic Revolution in Iran specifically to take control of the funds of the Pahlavi Foundation. Its remit was to manage and make use of the expropriated resources of exiles and collaborators of the former regime. It therefore took charge, where appropriate, of companies, industrial plants, real estate, and investments.

Buniad Shahid (Martyrs' Foundation)

This organization was created by Ayatollah Khomeini to assist the families of militants who had fallen on the field of battle for the Islamic cause. It shared its funds with the Foundation for the Expropriated. It was originally run by the office of the Faqih. Its first director was Khomeini's personal representative, Mehdi Kharroubi.

Coalition of Islamic Societies (Iran) (Hay'atha-ye Mo'talafe-ye Eslami)

The Coalition of Islamic Societies began to take shape in 1962 at the initiative of Ayatollah Khomeini, as his initial confrontation with the shah of Iran began to harden. Its founding members were bazaar merchants, members of the bazaar guilds who had formed their own religious societies. An important founder member was Habibollah Asgar Ouladi, who became minister of trade following the Islamic Revolution. On of its leading figures is Hajji Araghi. The alliance crystallized on the eve of the rising against the shah known as the events of Khordad 15 (June 5), 1963, following which Khomeini was imprisoned and then transferred to the Shi'ite shrine city of Najaf, in Iraq.

Following Khordad 15, many from both religious and nonreligious backgrounds were imprisoned in Tehran and in Qom. Most of the members of the coalition who remained in prison were freed in 1977–1978, on the eve of the Islamic Revolution. After the Revolution, the association merged with the Party of the Islamic Republic. In 1988–1989, it resumed its independent activity, and in recent years it has followed the line of the JRM (Association of Militant Clergy). The Unified Islamic Association is identified with the Ministry of Commerce, and as a result of its activities and its origins it has been called the "Bazaar Party." It is linked to the Chamber of Commerce and most ministers of commerce appointed since the Revolution have belonged to it. It has also set up a credit organization for traders and is active within the executive committee for elections as well as other organizations.

The Unified Islamic Organization is the only Iranian party closely identified with a particular social base, as a result of its continuing connections with bazaar merchants and with a section of their professional organizations. During the Revolution, the association served as one of Ayatollah Khomeini's power bases. It took part in the training of young men abroad for guerrilla operations, giving financial aid to combatants and controlling a nucleus of guerrilla fighters. In April 1979, Hajji Araghi, together with Ayatollah Lahouti, headed the two training centers for the Pasdaran (Revolutionary Guards) at Ali Abad.

Its philosophical standpoint is expressed in a statement of its principles. "The duty of jihad and rebellion under the leadership of the rightly-guided Vali Faqih is incumbent upon all who recognize the sovereignty of Islam, so that oppressed believers may save the world from injustice, and may play the representative role which the Merciful has conferred upon them. This is valid at any moment and during all time up to the Revolution, since every day is an Ashura (see entry on Shi'ism) and every land is a Qarbala (see entry on Shi'ism)."

The coalition is also able to call on the loyalty of student groups, which it encourages through holding conferences and giving support to theological schools and training centers, where political and scientific personalities are invited to lecture. Similarly, seminars are held in many Iranian cities and abroad, especially in Lebanon and Syria. The coalition's members also include women, whose activities are mainly in the social and cultural fields, where the coalition organizes meetings, encourages scientific and artistic education, holds exhibitions and other events, as well as subsidizes magazines. Since 1991, the coalition has also trained young people in sports and foreign languages. Benefiting from its connections with the country's economic institutions, the association has been able to exercise considerable influence, as part of the right-wing faction within the regime.

Council of Guardians

In order to avoid contradictions between the decisions of the Iranian parliament (the Islamic Consultative Assembly) and the Islamic principles of the constitution, a Council of Guardians was set up, consisting of twelve members who serve for a period of six years. Its composition is as follows:

- Six doctors of Islamic Law (Mujtahids) are appointed by the leader or the Leadership Council (composed of the president, the head of the Judiciary and a member of the existing Council of Guardians, which governs in the event that no leader is in office). They should be reputed for their impartiality and their concern with current problems and exigencies.
- Six jurists specialized in various fields of law, elected by parliament from a list put before them by the Higher Judicial Council.

Without the Council of Guardians, the parliament has no power, except to approve the appointment of its members and to elect the six jurists to the council. All measures taken by the parliament must be submitted to it, and it must within ten days rule on their conformity with the principles of Islam and the constitution. If contradictions emerge, the council's duty is to refer parliament's decisions back to it for revision. If the council approves the parliament's actions, they then have the force of law.

The interpretation of the constitution also falls within the competence of the Council of Guardians, whose decisions in this respect must be taken by a majority of three-quarters. It also supervises the election of the president of the Islamic Republic, parliamentary elections, and any referenda that may be held. In the case of an irresolvable disagreement between parliament and the Council of Guardians, the power to resolve the dispute rests with a further body, the Expediency Council, instituted by Ayatollah Khomeini in February 1988.

Hezbollah

From February 11, 1979, the date when Ayatollah Khomeini secured power in Iran for the Islamic Republic, the great dichotomy in Iran has been the permanent antithesis between the state and the Revolution. Hezbollah, which means literally the Party of God, is a conservative faction identified with the Revolution, rather than with the state. Its position was never formalized, though it was represented in the Revolution's earlier years by the Islamic Liberation Movement, ILM. Its members come from the great groundswell of ordinary Iranians who supported the Revolution and brought the Islamic Republic into existence. It was a shadowy institution that sprang into active existence, when required, and still exists today. Its grassroots members, the Ansar-i Hezbollah (Ansar means "supporters"), can still be called upon by conservatives to come into the streets to demonstrate and, if necessary, fight against anything the conservative leadership identifies as contrary to Islam.

Hezbollah's activists believe they fight for nothing less than the survival of Islam. Their veneration for Khomeini led them to a passionate belief in the system of Velayet-e Faqih, in which the senior cleric stands above the administration and, as the Supreme Leader, gives the final ruling on all issues.

Only in this way will the Islamic Revolution be preserved. The Faqih is chosen by God, and elections are a means for the people to demonstrate their readiness to follow his leadership. As Hezbollah sources put it: "The wise men to not choose the Faqih: on the contrary, thanks to their wisdom, they find him." Meanwhile, the ordinary people, unqualified in religious matters, should have no say in the choice of the Faqih.

Hezbollah also operates outside Iran. From the earliest days, the exportation of the values of the Revolution has been a goal of the Iranian leadership. In practice, this has been achieved by means of a multiplicity of organizations, such as the International Brigades of the Guardians of the Revolution, as well as by Hezbollah groups in Iran and abroad. Linked to Hezbollah are the Iranian terrorist organizations that operated abroad and were set up by ruthless young men, including Sayed Mehdi Hashemi and Mohammed Montazeri, the son of Ayatollah Montazeri, who had been designated as Khomeini's deputy. The main aim of the terrorist organizations was to eliminate the opponents of the regime. The Islamic Liberation Movement (ILM), which the two established in 1979, had financial autonomy, giving it considerable independence from the Iranian state. This enabled it to set up training camps that produced thousands of Hezbollah militants. A struggle between the adherents of the ILM and the supporters of Ali Akbar Hashemi Rafsanjani, the standard-bearer of the supremacy of the state, ended with the partial dismantling of the ILM in 1987 and the execution of some of its organizers. Mehdi Hashemi was shot for treason in 1987 after confessing to the bombing of the Islamic Republican Party's headquarters in an incident in which many died. Mohammed Montazeri had already died in an explosion in Teheran in 1981.

Despite the official disbandment of the movement, the supporters of the ILM remained well organized, and the members of Iranian Hezbollah continued to have access to arms and to be very active within the various Islamic revolutionary institutions in Iran and also to turn their attention abroad. They frequently operated under the aegis of a section of the Pasdaran or Revolutionary Guard. In 1984, Lebanese Hezbollah was formally constituted as a Shi'ite resistance movement in the context of the Israeli occupation of the southern part of the country, and though it was never a subsidiary of any movement in Iran, it, nonetheless, maintained contact with the Iranian Hezbollah, whose members gave collective and individual help. In Iraq, meanwhile, in the early days of the Iran–Iraq War, the Pasdaran took charge of the Iraqi movements opposed to Saddam Hussein. However, those Iranian leaders who hoped for a Shi'ite revolution in Iraq were disappointed, due to the strength of nationalist feeling in the Iraqi Shi'ite community. Another department of the ILM was responsible for intelligence and coordinated their action with the Pasdaran. It carried out thorough analyses of Islamist movements in the Philippines, Afghanistan, Iraq, Erythrea, and Lebanon, as well as studies of the organization of the Muslim Brotherhood and of the Irish movement, the IRA. In 1982, this section even developed an interest as far afield as New Caledonia, inviting the leadership of the United Front for Kanak Liberation to visit Teheran.

In Lebanon, the ILM encouraged the Islamic political activists of the Amal movement, led by Hussein al-Moussawi (also known as Abu Hisham). It helped to establish various Lebanese Hezbollah groups, led by such figures as Abbas al-Moussawi, Sobhi al-Tufaili, Hussein al-Khalil, Afif an-Nabulsi, and Ibrahim al-Amin. It also organized an armed group known as Jundullah (God's Army) led by Sheikh Karim Shamseddine and the Lebanese Shi'ite clerical organization known as the Association of Fighting Clergy with Sheikh Mohammed Hussein Fadlallah and Maher al-Hammoud. A training and instruction section gave instruction to selected Muslim recruits in guerrilla warfare. Finally, a cultural section carried out the instructions of the ILM leadership. Lebanese Hezbollah formally came into existence in 1984.

Hezbollah's aim was to identify Islamist groups and associations and encourage them to put their Islamism into practice. Their aid was not only practical, but also included intensive spiritual education with a strong Shi'ite flavor. Recruits were found in Iraq and Lebanon, as well as in other Arab countries. For instance, in Oman, the Islamic Organization for the Liberation of Oman was led by Salim Ali Azizi, and a similar organization in Bahrain, where there is a large Shi'ite population, was headed by Hodjatuleslam Hadi Mudarissi. There were groups also in Kuwait, Saudi Arabia, and, beyond the Arab sphere, Turkey. The condition was laid down, however, that such groups ceased to draw inspiration from the sources of Sunni Muslim culture, such as Al Azhar University in Cairo, or maintain links with such Sunni organizations as the Muslim Brotherhood. On two occasions, in 1994 and 1996, the Iranians brought together in Teheran factions who opposed the continuation of the Middle East "Peace Process." More than fifty extremist organizations attended these meetings, constituting a kind of Islamist international.

Outside the Muslim world, in the United States, in South America, and in Europe, the Iranians have attempted to sow the seeds of militant Islamist groups by working through local Islamist organizations, often remaining reticent that the funding came from a Shi'ite source where the local population was predominantly Sunni. The priority was to promote Iran's particular standpoint, rather than a general Islamic position. There was no attempt to set up Islamic republics in such states, as is distinct from the plans drawn up for Muslim-majority countries. Everywhere, however, equal emphasis was laid on the identification, surveillance, and elimination of Iranian dissidents hostile to the regime in Teheran. When circumstances were appropriate, specifically Shi'ite organizations were set up, such as the Ahl al-Bayt (The People of the House), but Western intelligence has been swift to monitor such groups and counter their influence where necessary. In 1986, the French intelligence services identified Shi'ite groups backed by Iran in French cities such as Lyon, Strasbourg, Marseille, Toulouse, Montpellier, and the Paris suburb of Kremlin-Bicêtre.

Iran's revolutionary proselytism continues unabated in the twenty-first century, now under the supervision of the highest institutions of state. In particular, the Higher Council for National Security gathers together various services responsible for exporting Iranian revolutionary ideas and lays down targets to be achieved. The department within the Pasdaran that looks after Palestinian and Lebanese affairs is known as the Quds Force. In 2006, Iran continued to press forward with its plans to extend its influence in the Arab world and elsewhere. In the southern Shi'ite areas of Lebanon, posters of Ayatollah Khomeini are seen everywhere, and Iranian money funds not only militia forces, but also widespread charitable work. In the region at large, Iran has identified areas of Shi'ite population to create an archipelago of zones of influence, in which Shi'ites are no longer content to remain in their traditional position of subservience to Sunni political authorities.

Islamic Revolutionary Council

This was an institution of the Iranian revolutionary movement prior to the establishment of the Islamic Republic, which continued to play a part in the transitional period before the institutions of the Islamic Republic were fully established. On October 7, 1978, Ayatollah Khomeini arrived in Paris. Soon afterward, his advisers and associates set up a leadership structure and established links with revolutionary circles inside Iran. In December, Khomeini, in consultation with Ayatollah Motahari, selected the membership of the Islamic Revolutionary Council. Its clerical members were Ayatollah Taleghani, Ayatollah Montazeri, Ayatollah Mohammed Beheshti, Hojatuleslam Hashemi Rafsanjani, Ayatollah Mahdavi Keni, Hojatuleslam Bahonar, Ayatollah Mussavi Ardabili, and Ayatollah Seyyed Abufazel Nussavi Zanjani. To these were added, as lay and military representatives, Dr. Mehdi Bazarghan, Dr. Yadolah Sahabi, Dr. Yzdi, Ahmed Sadr Hajj Seyyed Javadi; Dr. Katirai, Dr. Shibani, General Dr. Ezatollah Sahabi, General Gharani and General Massoudi. Some of these were members of Iran's Hezbollah (the Party of God—not organically connected with the Hezbollah movements in Arab various countries), some were members of the Movement for the Liberation of Iran, and others belonged to the National Front.

The Council met secretly each week or more often when events so dictated. On February 4, Mehdi Bazarghan set up his provisional government and selected his ministers from the members of the Islamic Revolutionary Council, whose ranks were replenished by the entry of new members, including Hojatuleslam Khamenei (later Khomeini's successor as leader). Other new members were Abolhassan Bani Sadr and Sadegh Ghotbzadeh (who was later disgraced and shot). General Massoudi left the council and General Gharani became the chief of staff of the army. With Khamenei's arrival, the clergy, who were also members of Hezbollah, became a majority in the council. After Bazarghan's provisional government was established, the council did duty as parliament, and after the ratification of the constitution it undertook the duties of the presidency of the republic and of the prime minister until a president was elected and a prime minister was designated. The council's role came to an end once the new institutions of the Islamic Republic came into full operation.

Office for the Consolidation of Unity

The Office for the Consolidation of Unity is a Students' Union that emerged from the cultural revolution launched by the students who backed the "Line of the Imam," in the form of the "Students' Islamic Committee." Its aim is the consolidation of unity between the university and the theological establishment, and it is for this reason that it took the name "Office for the Consolidation of Unity." The group's relations with other factions have undergone successive changes. The constitution of the union laid down the following definition. "The Union may conduct its activities within the Associations of students, teachers, staff members of the national educational system, graduates, workers and salary earners. An Islamic Committee may be set up within each of these bodies, and may take the name of the members of that body."

After 1983, changes took place within the union, which split apart as a result. In 1997, though the union supported the principle of the absolute Velayat, General Tabarzade made the following statement: "The powers of the Vali Faqih are limited by the articles of the Constitution." The union insisted that it must be within the law for the parties to engage in political activity, that the people should be allowed to engage in political activity, and that the limits of freedom within society should be set only by "national security and Islamic values." The union supported the concept of the exportation of the Islamic Revolution, and took the view that the slogan

"A Developed Iran" was pro-Western. It demanded the adoption of a revolutionary attitude toward the United States.

From 1997, in fact, Tabarzadi declared that his present position was that "action in the field of foreign politics should be undertaken in a spirit of realism toward international developments." A similar change was to be seen in attitudes toward the United States. "The President of the Republic must lay down the conditions for the establishment of relations with other states. In these circumstances, we could also have relations with the United States."

In the field of economics, the union's position is close to that of the Organization of Mujahidin of the Islamic Revolution. It advocates popular participation in economic activities, supports state intervention in the economy and subsidies for consumer goods, while it rejects foreign investment and advocates public action in the interests of social justice. In cultural affairs, the union regards the ownership of satellite dishes as a private matter in which the government should not interfere. Its stand is similar over dress conventions. Tabardzadi rejects the "violent approach" regarding women's adoption of the Islamic veil. The union presents itself as a movement belonging to the "modernist left." After the demonstrations of July 9, 1997, the attitude of the state toward the universities became more radical. As a result, the traditional right, including the Basij (youthful Islamic volunteers) and the Pasdaran (Revolutionary Guards), became more hostile to Tabardzadi, as well as to the union and its student committees.

Organization of the Mujahidin of the Islamic Revolution

This was an organization formed on April 5, 1979, when Ayatollah Khomeini and Ayatollah Motahari ordered seven separate Islamic groups committed to armed struggle against the regime of the shah to unify. In May 1979, internal clashes broke out within the organization's council. Khomeini appointed Hossein Rasti Kashani to rule on religious issues and Ayatollah Moytahari to resolve political differences. Ayatollah Motahari was assassinated on May 2, leaving Rasti Kashani as Khomeini's sole representative. His conservative view led to a difference of opinion with the modernizing members of the organization.

On April 4, 1982, Rasti Kashani dissolved the council and appointed a replacement. Khomeini wrote a letter offering council members the alternative of cooperation with his representative or resignation. Thirty-seven members resigned, but the organization's problems remained unresolved, and in September 1986 the organization was again dissolved and did not resume its activities until September 23, 1991. The organization is left wing in its position and takes a line similar to that of the Assembly of Militant Clerics. Its position includes the following points:

1. restriction of powers of the Supreme Leader
2. equal weight for the republican and Islamic aspects of the regime
3. greater flexibility in the Islamic regime
4. freedom of action for political parties
5. widening political participation
6. the export of the Revolution
7. development of Iran's relations in the Middle East
8. unity with other countries
9. resistance to the United States

The organization also advocated for state intervention in economic affairs and opposed the privatization of heavy industry and electricity supply, as well as the maintenance of major agricultural and construction projects in state hands. The organization prioritized its social and economic aims as follows:

1. social equality and economic development
2. access to the ownership of property

3. popular participation in investment
4. expansion of the cooperative program
5. higher taxes on the rich
6. lower taxes on the poor
7. allowances from the state
8. universal medical insurance
9. improvements in the banking system
10. unemployment insurance
11. encouragement of a mixed economy and investment abroad.

The organization also placed stress on the maintenance of Iran's national culture and encouraged cultural exchanges.

Party of the Islamic Republic (PIR)

During his exile in Iraq at the Shi'ite holy city of Najaf, Ayatollah Khomeini instructed his disciples and supporters in Iran and abroad to build a "Party of God" (Hezbollah) in order to counterbalance the other parties and political organizations in Iran. Up to February 1978, in competition with other groups opposed to the shah's regime, the "Partisans of God" (Hezbollahis) attempted to take control and run all revolutionary activity and to keep them out of the hands of others, especially the students and university staff. They sometimes took violent action, notably at the protest over the murder of Dr. Nijatollahi. After the referendum of March 3, 1979, in favor of the establishment of the Islamic Republic, certain religious figures from Ayatollah Khomeini's entourage and the Revolutionary Council proclaimed the foundation of the "Party of the Islamic Republic," and as instructed all factions of Hezbollah merged themselves at once into the new party.

The founding members were virtually all disciples and faithful friends of Khomeini. Among them were Hojatoleslam Ali Khamenei (now Khomeni's successor as Supreme Leader), Hojatoleslam Hashemi Rafsanjani (larter President of Iran), Hojatoleslam Bahonar, Ayatollah Musavi Ardabili, and Ayatollah Beheshti, who served as the first party secretary. According to its founding members, the aim of the party was "the protection of the achievements of the Revolution, the struggle against counter-Revolutionary elements and the encouragement of the Iranian people to make constructive use of the results of its struggle against the oppression of the Pahlavi dynasty."

In practice, the principal role of the PIR was to give Hezbollah a new ideological and political leadership, which enabled it to continue its struggle more effectively against such rival formations as the National Front, the clandestine extreme left-wing groups, the communist Tudeh Party, and President Bani Sadr's secular Movement for the Liberation of Iran. The PIR represented the position of the new regime, and was the mechanism by which all factions loyal to the Supreme Leader were marshaled. The PIR included an international wing, a workers' branch, a university branch, and the party's representations within the various aspects of civil society. Permission was granted to Ali Khamenei to publish the party's official publications. In the first instance, the party published a monthly magazine, *Urual Wasghi,* intended for students and university teachers. These were a group whose increasingly active participation in the country's political affairs had been a major factor behind the Islamic Revolution that the new government wished to encourage.

In parallel to the PIR, the supporters of Ayatollah Shariat Madari also embarked on the establishment of a party, to be known as the Party of the Muslim People. This supported Ayatollah Khomeini in his efforts to maintain control over the institutions of government, a struggle in which the PIR found itself opposed to others among Khomeini's early allies. President Bani Sadr's faction and his allies in the nationalist opposition movement, the Muhjahidin Khalq, were swiftly pushed aside, and the PIR took total control of the government. Bani Sadr's dismissal and departure from the country were a major victory for the PIR. On June 28, 1988, an attack on the headquarters of the PIR was attributed to Bani Sadr's allies in the Mujahidin Khalq, though this may not have been true. Ayatollah Beheshti and seventy others died in the explosion, including Sheikh Montazeri, the eldest son of Ayatollah Montazeri.

Following this disaster, Ali Hashemi Rafsanjani went as far as to say in a television broadcast that "the very existence of the Islamic Republic is under threat." After the arrival of several thousand Pasdaran (Revolutionary Guards) from Najafabad, where Ayatollah Montazeri was in control, the leadership's confidence was restored. However, the PIR was never again able to serve as a mechanism for the organization of the membership of Hezbollah—that is to say of the popular Islamist factions who backed Ayatollah Khomeini and shared his political viewpoint. The Party of the Muslim People was dissolved and Ayatollah Shariat Madari was put under house arrest, but shortly afterward the PIR was also dismantled. However, its publication, *The Islamic Republic,* continues to appear and is still regarded as the voice of Ali Khamenei, Khomeini's successor as Supreme Leader of the Islamic Revolution.

The Pasdaran (Sepah-e Pasdaran-e Enghelab-e Eslami) (Army of the Guardians of the Islamic Revolution)

The Sepah-e Pasdaran, commonly known as the Revolutionary Guards, was set up by the provisional government and the Revolutionary Council in February 1979, and took the place of a number of other armed groups.

Those who took the initiative were Ibrahim Yazdi, Sadegh Ghtobzadeh, General Massoudi, and Ayatollah Lahoudi, who acted as Khomeini's representative. The Organization of the Mujahidin of the Revolution merged with the Pasdaran and became their nucleus. The present commander in chief of the Pasdaran is General Yahya Rahim Safavi. Safavi is highly vocal on Iran's right to self-defence and has repeatedly warned that any American attack on Iran will be responded to. The Pasdaran plays an important part in the repression of dissidents inside Iran and the consolidation of the authority of the Supreme Leader. It is able to continue the extension of its power thanks to the substantial support it receives from the government. It is active outside Iran as well as at home. Pasdaran has been active in Bosnia, Afghanistan, and Lebanon and in eliminating those who oppose the Iranian Islamic regime in Europe and the United States. They cooperate with the Ministry of Information (which controls Iran's intelligence services) and runs various groups based in Africa and Asia in the interests of the Iranian regime.

During the Iran–Iraq War, the Pasdaran suffered heavy losses. The current president of Iran, Mahmoud Ahmedinejad, served in the Pasdaran during this period. Today, they are very well armed and have at their disposal conventional land, sea, and air forces. As the organization developed, it recruited large numbers of civilians with diverse skills, including engineers, doctors, teachers, translators, and other officials. This transformed the Sebah-e Pasdaran into a wide-scale political and military organization. A number of subsidiary organizations run by the Pasdaran play a significant role in its operations. Functions performed by such organizations include the training of teachers, political and ideological indoctrination, support for combatants and the families of martyrs, and public relations.

Recalling that their organization was set up in early days of the Islamic Revolution, the Pasdaran regards itself as the "Guardians of the Revolution," and takes upon itself the task of safeguarding the Revolution and its achievements. The limits of their duties and responsibilities are defined within a framework of law.

The Servants of Construction (Kargozaran-e Sazandegi)

The "Kargozaran," or as they are sometimes known "Fansalaran," is a group of technocrats that came into existence under the presidency of Hashemi Rafsanjani from 1989 to 1997 and took part in the two governments that served under him. Atollah Mohajerani had this to say about its establishment: "It was from the start a politically active movement, motivated by our sense that the country's political landscape was tending towards a monopoly of power." For seven years, the Kargozaran had no official independent existence and was affiliated to no particular group, being seen as part of the traditional right. In the fifth parliamentary elections held in March and April 1996, however, they abandoned the traditional right, identifying themselves with the slogan "Islamic pride and the development of Iran." In the presidential elections of 1996, the Kargozaran opposed the candidate of the Association of Militant Clergy, which attracted certain repressive measures, including the arrest of one of its leading figures, the then mayor of Teheran, Gholam Hossein Karbashi, as well as the group's secretary-general. The Kargozaran initially supported the reelection of Rafsanjani, but in the end they backed Seyyed Mohammed Khatami. During the fifth parliament, the Kargozaran came together with the Supporters of the Line of the Imam to form the Parliamentary Party of God (Hezbollah-e Mejlis).

In economic terms, the goal of the Kargozaran was development and economic progress, which they saw as prerequisite for the reconstruction of the country. They took the view that economic freedom was fundamentally linked to cultural and political freedom, but that it should not be allowed to conflict with development. The Kargozaran embraced modernity, as well as the evolution of traditions and change in the socioreligious aspects of society, with a progressive reduction of the role played by religion. They envisaged the creation of a liberal culture, within the framework of tolerance and liberty created by a technocratic administration. They placed great emphasis on modern and efficient management of the country. According to Ataollah Mohajerani, "technocracy is not of itself contrary to moral values: it means in fact giving priority to technical issues over religion, nothing more." The Kargozaran place their faith in the effectiveness of the market, in privatization, and in the restriction of the economic role of the state. They do not oppose foreign investment. The economic model to which they aspire is that of the countries of Southeast Asia.

As regards the structure of the state, they take the view that in the Islamic Republic of Iran the source of legitimacy is the Vilayat-e Faqih and they lay stress on the following issues. They insist that political activity should take place within the framework of the political parties and not by violent means, and that popular participation in politics is crucial to the guarantee of fundamental rights to the people. They also believe that there should be scope for the expression of varying opinions within society, and that no restrictions should be put on the press. In terms of foreign politics, the Kargozaran favors the establishment of economic relations with the United States in a manner profitable to Iran, while, nevertheless, continuing the political struggle. Members of the Kargozaran, benefiting from their new political alliance with the Islamic left wing, have in previous governments held various ministerial posts. In the sixth parliamentary elections, however, they broke this link and associated themselves with Hashemi Rafsanjani, afterward becoming less active as a political group. The party was refounded in August 1999 under the auspices of ex-President Rafsanjani, whose brother and one daughter were members of it. They endorsed Rafsanjani's support for Khatami in the 2001 presidential elections. In 2005, they backed Rafsanjani's campaign for reelection to a third term and, therefore, joined the opposition to the fundamentalist regime of President Ahmadinejad.

IRAQ

Prior to the American-led invasion of Iraq in 2003, Islamists played little or no role in Iraq. The regime of Saddam Hussein was resolutely secular, though he had prudently added the Islamic slogan "Allahu Akbar" (God is the greatest) to the Iraqi flag. All institutions other than those explicitly approved by the Ba'th party were prohibited. This applied to all manifestations of Islam other than those in the official mosques. Islamist ideas had no currency in society. There was little restriction on social life in Iraq. Cafés and restaurants were full, alcoholic drink was available, music and theater were performed, there was little restriction on what was seen on television, and wealthy Iraqis and foreigners made full use of the capital's international hotels. Women were able to work and play a full part in work, education, and society. Above all, Saddam Hussein would have been extremely wary of giving assistance to Islamic terror groups because he was aware that their weapons would be turned first of all against him. After the invasion, the situation changed.

First of all, the various Iraqi Shi'ite movements in exile began to renew their interest in the politics of Iraq. Some Shi'ite politicians sought involvement in the new process of government in Iraq instituted by the occupying powers, while others opted for independence and militancy. Prime Minister Nuri al-Maliki was a member of the Al-Da'wa Party, founded by Ayatollah Mohammed Baqr al-Sadr, while Baqr al-Sadr's nephew, Moqtada al-Sadr, is the leader of the militant Mahdi Army. Other Shi'ite leaders are involved in diverse political and social activities. The most senior Iraqi Shi'ite leader, the Grand Ayatollah Ali al-Sistani, born in 1930, is widely seen as the most influential Shi'ite figure in modern day Iraq and takes a close interest in developments without himself taking any direct part in politics. He stressed the importance of voting for the Iraqi people in the election of January 2005 and had urged Iraqi Shi'ites not to respond in kind to what he had called Sunni Salafi attacks on their community. The leader who above all represented the Shi'ite community in exile during the Saddam Hussein years was Ayatollah Muhammad Baqr al-Hakim, the leader of SCIRI (Supreme Council for the Islamic Revolution in Iraq), based in Iran. He was killed after his return to Iraq in a massive car bombing perpetrated by Sunni militants in Najaf in August 2003.

The Sunni militants in Iraq, meanwhile, are composed of a number of elements. First, there are hard-line nonreligious Ba'thists who would simply like to see the return of something resembling the old regime, even after the execution of Saddam Hussein in January 2007. Second, there are nationalists who detest the fact that Iraq has been invaded by a foreign power and wish to drive the invading forces out. These include many individuals who have been prompted to take action against the invading troops and the new Iraqi government out of a spirit of revenge for perceived injustices against themselves and their families. Third, there are those Sunnis who have seized with both hands the opportunity to inflict losses on the Shi'ite community, who they see as effectively having taken power in the country with the help of the occupying forces. Fourth, however, there are the Islamists.

The Sunni Islamists in Iraq are for the most part Salafi militants who seek to inflict damage on the United States and other occupying forces. It should be said that rather than wishing to achieve a defined political objective in Iraq, their intention is simply to use the theater of war in Iraq as an opportunity to attack the United States forces at close quarters. They have also become involved in anti-Shi'ite actions. Some of these fighters are Iraqis, while others are foreigners, mainly Arabs, who have come to join the struggle. In January 2007, the leader seen as second-in command of Al-Qa'ida, Ayman al-Zawahiri, who is in hiding probably somewhere in Afghanistan or Pakistan, said in a video message that the American forces in Iraq should be annihilated. The structure of the Salafi groups in Iraq is shadowy. However, in September 2004, the Salafi Islamist leader from Jordan, Abu Musab al-Zarqawi, the leader of an Islamist guerrilla group that had originally called itself Jama'at al-Tawhid wal-Jihad, renamed his organization Al-Qa'ida in Iraq. This was probably a declaration of sympathy with the aims of Al-Qa'ida than any real structural link, since the Al-Qa'ida leaders, in hiding, apparently have little contact with each other, let alone with small groups in third countries. Zarqawi was killed in an American air strike on June 7, 2006, and the new Salafi leader has been named as Abu Hamza al-Muhajir. (It should be noted that names of this form that begin with Abu and end with an adjectival form such as al-Zawahiri and al-Muhajir are invariably pseudonyms.)

Hizb Al-Da'wa (Iraq)

Some 60 percent of the population of Iraq consists of Shi'ites. However, before the fall of Saddam Hussein's regime in 2003, the Shi'ites played only a subsidiary role in the workings of a state dominated by the minority Sunni community. Despite this, Iraq is also the site of the holiest places of Shi'ism—Najaf and Kerbala—and the Shi'ite clergy always represented a challenge to the authorities in Baghdad. One of these was the Grand Ayatollah Mohammed Baqr al-Sadr. Baqr al-Sadr was arrested in 1977 after an uprising in Iraq by the supporters of Khomeini. In 1980, he was rearrested and executed by the Ba'thists in 1980 for writing in support of Ayatollah Khomeini. The present prime minister of Iraq, Nuri al-Maliki, was also an activist in Al-Da'wa at the time. After fleeing the country in 1980, Maliki was also sentenced to death in absentia by Saddam Hussein's government. Ayatollah Baqr al-Sadr was the uncle of the leader of Moqtada al-Sadr, the present day militant leader, who leads the Sadr Group (Jamaat al-Sadr al-Thani) based in Najaf, which opposes the conservative Shi'ite Ayatollahs and calls for more radical action. Moqtada also heads the so-called Mahdi Army, with its power base in the Shi'ite slum area of Sadr City, in Baghdad.

The Grand Ayatollah Baqr al-Sadr was a respected exponent of the ideas of the Islamic Revolution and a theorist of Muslim economics. As a Shi'ite cleric, he was recognized as a "Marja'"—an authority to be emulated. He founded the Al-Da'wa party as long ago as 1956, when he was in exile in Egypt. At that time, it was the first Shi'ite movement in the Arab world, and part of its platform was the establishment of an Islamic society in Iraq. His earliest supporters were drawn from the students of the "Hawza" of Najaf—the Islamic theological school—and he also gained support in Syria. After Sadr's death, Al-Da'wa was led by Mahdi al-Asifi and Abdul Hamid Kachani. Mohammed Hossein Nasrallah, later to become the head of Lebanese Hezbollah, was just one of the many influential Shi'ites who started out as members of the party.

From 1980, Al-Da'wa constituted the principal opposition force in Iraq. It survived successive attempts by the authorities to stamp it out. Its alliance with Iran did not reduce it to the status of a pawn in the hands of the Iranian religious establishment. Neither was it subservient to Iranian Islam, like other Iraqi Shi'ite groups such as SCIRI (The Supreme Council for the Islamic Revolution in Iraq), whose leader, Mohammed Baqr al-Hakim, was based in Iran, with an armed wing, the Badr Brigades, deployed on the southern frontier with Iraq. Another important Shi'ite figure was Mohammed Bahr ul-Ulum, who was an ally of the Iraqi National Congress, the exiled opposition movement led by Mohammed Shalabi backed by the Clinton administration. Another Shi'ite institution was "Al-Amal al-Islami" (Islamic Action) led by Mohammed Taki Mudarrissi, who was based in Damascus.

In contrast to the Shi'ite forces that operated under the aegis of Teheran, Al-Da'wa's policies were autonomously formed. In May 2002, soon before the U.S.-led invasion of Iraq, his political leadership, established in secret inside Iraq with three regional organizations and a central administration, condemned the American plans for regime change in Baghdad. In a document published in October 2002, Al-Da'wa committed itself to "respect the choice of the people as expressed through universal suffrage, even if this choice is not an Islamic one." After the American-led invasion in March 2003, Al-Da'wa opted for participation in democratic politics, though the historically linked faction owing allegiance to Moqtada al-Sadr has kept open the option of taking part in

mainstream politics while also appearing to threaten direct action.

Supreme Council for the Islamic Revolution in Iraq (SCIRI)

SCIRI, also known as the Supreme Assembly for the Islamic Revolution in Iraq, was established in 1982 as a Shi'ite-led coalition opposed to the regime in Iraq. SCIRI also claimed to represent Sunni Muslims. It was set up by the Iraqi Shi'ite leader Ayatollah Mohammed Baqir al-Hakim, who was in exile in Iran, under Teheran's auspices. SCIRI was in the first instance the outcome of a strategic and political alliance concluded by two armed Shi'ite movements, namely Al-Da'wa, led by Sheikh Mohammed Mahdi al-Asifi, set up in the late 1950s, and Islamic Action in Iraq, headed by Ayatollah Mohammed Taqi Mudarrisi, based in Iran. Following the Gulf War of 1990–1991, SCIRI assembled both Islamic and lay movements. In addition to al-Da'wa and Islamic Action, SCIRI brought together both Kurdish and smaller Islamic movements. The Kurdish groups included the Socialist Party of Kurdistan (PSK), the Democratic People's Party of Kurdistan, and the Iraqi Kurdish Islamic movement. The Islamist groups included the Junud al-Islam, the Iraqi Islamic Assembly, the Jamaat al-Ulema al Mujahidin, and the Iraqi Islamic Movement. SCIRI was also able to put in place alliances with other groups with that it had little in common with except their opposition to Saddam Hussein, such as the major Kurdish parties, the KDP and the PUK, as well as the small Assyrian Democratic Movement. SCIRI soon organized its armed wing, the so-called "Badr Brigade," with several thousand fighters. SCIRI also had the help of Iraqi officers who had fled to Iran. Militias were banned in September 2003 and the Badr Brigade was renamed the Badr Organization. By 2005, its strength was some ten thousand. SCIRI claims that its goal, as well as participation in politics, is the maintenance of security and stability in Iraq.

From its first appearance, SCIRI enjoyed the good will of the United States, which had just set up the no-fly zone that protected the predominantly Shi'ite regions of southern Iraq from air attack by Iraqi government forces. It established secret cells throughout Iraq and still maintains this clandestine structure in parallel to its overt political activities. During 1997, there was a large-scale Iraqi military incursion into southern Iraq, with attacks on the civilian population and summary executions, resulting in an exodus of population that partially depopulated the Shi'ite region. SCIRI lost many fighters, especially during violent clashes in the marshes, near Basra. SCIRI distanced itself from the United States, so as not to attract the hostility of the population that was gravely damaged by the United Nations sanctions backed by the American administration. Its relations with Iran also deteriorated at this period, however, following internal dissension.

Under the news dispensation in Iraq, SCIRI has consistently given broad support to the American-prompted political process, though it has not shrunk from criticizing Washington for not handing more power sooner to Iraq leaders. The United States for its part has viewed SCIRI warily because of its closeness to the Iranian regime. In May 2003, two months after the American-led invasion, Mohammed Baqr al-Hakim returned to Iraq. However, in August 2003, six months later, in what was a serious blow to the SCIRI leadership, he was killed in a huge car bombing in the Shi'ite holy city of Najaf. His brother, Abdel Aziz al-Hakim, now heads SCIRI and was a member of the transitional governing council, but has not been included in government. In 2004, a senior SCIRI official became minister of finance. SCIRI forms part of the Uniefd Iraqi

Alliance, the party that took power at the head of the governing coalition in January 2005. SCIRI still has at its disposal an armed wing, now known as the Badr Organization, armed and financed by Iran, which has not played a major role so far.

Moqtada Al-Sadr's Group

The group headed by Moqtada al-Sadr, which is known as the Sadrists (Jamaat al-Sadr al-Thani) (The Second Sadr Group), together with his armed organization, the Mehdi Army (Jaish al-Mahdi), represents a radical force in Shi'ite politics in Iraq. Al-Sadr's Shi'ite antecedents are impeccable. His uncle and father-in-law was the Grand Ayatollah Baqr al-Sadr, who was executed in 1980 by Saddam Hussein for expressing support for Ayatollah Khomeini and the Islamic Revolution in Iran. His father was the Grand Ayatollah Mohammed Sadiq al-Sadr, Baqr al-Sadr's cousin, who was assassinated in 1999 allegedly by agents of Saddam Hussein. Moqtada, who was born in 1973, holds only the rank of Hojatoleslam, a much more lowly religious position. However, his youth is an attraction for many, he is personable, and he commands a growing popular following.

After the invasion of Iraq and the fall of Saddam Hussein's regime, Moqtada al-Sadr lost no time in establishing a power base. His popularity lay among younger Iraqis and the poor. This has led some to make the mistake of dismissing him as little more than the leader of a criminal band. The Coalition Provisional Authority installed by the Americans in 2003 made the mistake of thinking he had little appeal. His relations with other Shi'a groups are intermittently hostile. His organization is thought to have been responsible for the murder of Imam Abdul Majid al-Khoei, the son of Grand Ayatollah Abdul Qasim al-Khoei, who was killed in Iraq in April 2003 while visiting the country. Khoei's father had also been murdered by Saddam Hussein. By 2004, he was in undisputed control of Sadr City in Baghdad, a slum area where many Shi'ites live, and provided services for the population. In March 2004, his forces became involved in clashes in Najaf and Basra as well as in Sadr City. The Americans attempted to eliminate him, but were unable to do so, and in June 2004 he agreed to a truce. He then decided to participate in the political process. In July 2004, he refused to attend a national conference on the future of Iraq. By August 2004, the Iraqi government, backed by the United States, had once more decided to crush his forces and attempted to kill him. Extraordinary scenes followed, when his house was surrounded by troops on August 3, 2004, which failed to apprehend him. As August wore on, very serious fighting took place in Najaf between the Mehdi Army and the U.S. and Iraqi forces. A truce was achieved through the intervention of Ayatollah Sistani, but fighting continued in Sadr City. Nevertheless, candidates representing Moqtada al-Sadr's interests eventually stood in the January 2005 election. He backed the nominally independent "National Independent Cadres and Élites Party."

Intermittent violence between Moqtada's supporters and the authorities continued through 2006, though full-scale conflict was avoided, apparently due to the influence of the Iraqi government. Nuri al-Maliki, also a Shi'ite and with a shared background of links to the old Da'wa party, was seemingly reluctant to move against a Shi'ite ally whose support had been useful to him. On March 25, a mortar attack on Moqtada's home failed to harm him. In October 2006, fighting broke out when the Mehdi Army took control of Amarah, in southern Iraq, though this may have been without the specific instructions of Moqtada. Small-scale clashes took place elsewhere. However, the Iraqi Prime Minister Nuri al-Maliki seems

to have gone out of his way to indicate that he did not back any attempt to eliminate Moqtada al-Sadr. In October 2006, Nuri al-Maliki met Moqtada at his house in Najaf. By January 2007, however, al-Maliki was beginning to speak critically about Moqtada and, on January 19, Moqtada was reported to have sent his family into hiding, anticipating a further attempt to arrest or kill him by the United States. The relationship between Nuri-Malki and Moqtada al-Sadr had become very hard to read.

Al-Qa'ida in Iraq

On the Sunni side of the fence, the mainly foreign Islamist militants who came to Iraq to take the opportunity presented by the chaotic situation that followed the collapse of Saddam Hussein's regime organized themselves under their former leader Abu Musab al-Zarqawi into an organization known as Jamaat al-Tawhid wal-Jihad (JTJ) (The Group for Monotheism and Holy War). Zarqawi was a Jordanian national whose birth name was Ahmad Fadil al-Nazal al-Khalayleh. He was a former fighter in Afghanistan, who had been imprisoned for conspiracy against the government after his return in Jordan. He returned to Afghanistan on his release, where he claimed to have ingratiated himself with Osama bin Laden. When the U.S. invasion of Iraq began, he traveled to Iraq to set up his organization to fight the Americans. Under Zarqawi's leadership, JTJ began to specialize in suicide bombings. Its goal was to inflict damage on the U.S. forces and to overthrow the Iraqi government. At some point before October 2004, Zarqawi renamed his group "Tanzim Qa'ida al-Jihad fi Bilad ar-Rafidain" (The Organization of the Base of Jihad in the Land of the two Rivers), commonly called Al-Qa'ida in Iraq. The group was prolific in its assaults on the Iraqi government, Shi'ite and American targets. Zarqawi was killed in an American air strike on June 7, 2006. An announcement was made shortly afterward that Abu Hamza al-Muhajir, an Egyptian militant, was to succeed him.

Sunni Groups in Iraq

It should be noted that there is also a spectrum of Iraqi Sunni Islamist groups that claim to pursue a similar Salafi agenda. All these operate in the strictest clandestine conditions, generally emerging intermittently in the shape of communiqués or claims of responsibility. Names that have been observed include Jaish Ta'ifa al-Mansura (Army of the Victorious Sect), Kata'ib Ansar al-Tawhid (Brigades of the Supporters of Monotheism), Saray al-Jihad (Command of the Jihad), Kata'ib al-Ghuraba (Foreign Brigades), Kata'ib al-Ahwal (Brigades of Power), Jaish al-Islam fi-l Iraq (Army of Islam in Iraq), Muqawama al-Islamiya al-Wataniya (Islamic National Opposition), Al-Jabha al-Islamiya li-l Muqawama al-Iraqiya (Islamic Front for Opposition in Iraq), Jaish al-Mujahidin (Army of the Mujahidin), Kata'ib Mujahidin al-Jamaat al-Salafiya fi-l Iraq (Brigades of the Mujahidin of the Salafi Group of Mujahidin in Iraq). All such names have a certain repetitive quality of variation on a limited range of vocabulary, and it is to be supposed that the membership and existence of such groups are very fluid. At any given time, it may be supposed that the number of active Salafi fighters numbers only a few thousand, at most.

ISLAMISM

The use of such terms as "fundamentalism" and "Islamism" is fraught with controversy. The word "islamisme" began to be used by French authors in around 1980 to signify the belief among radical Muslims that political and social action should be based on Islam. More recently, "Islamism" has been used by British and American authors in a similar sense. In some contexts, the word carries negative connotations and may be an unsuitable vehicle for dispassionate analysis. In the case of Muslim fundamentalist movements, the problems are most severe. The French word "islamisme" has become a synonym for "fundamentalism" and even—though not legitimately—for "terrorism." However, such alternatives as "religious militancy," "traditionalism," or "orthodoxy" are also inadequate. Not all fundamentalist movements are militant, let alone terrorist. Many self-styled radicals have little real knowledge of Islam, and others are far from orthodox. Not all traditional Muslims are fundamentalist. Not all conservative Muslims are radical. Broadly, in reference to the crudest of Western ideas about Islamic fundamentalism, it should be obvious that no link can be made between the depth or sincerity of religious feeling and a propensity to violence.

In more specific terms, Islamism is a political and religious ideology that aims to establish an Islamic state under the Shari'a law and to reunify the Muslim Umma (i.e. the Islamic community). Behind this relatively simple definition lies a complex picture where the situation varies in different countries, or as interpreted by different ideological movements, such as the Sunni Muslim Brotherhood and the radical Shi'ites. A growing Sunni phenomenon is that of the Salafis (the word is derived from an Arabic term meaning "ancestors," and it refers to those who immediately followed the Prophet Muhammad). They contend that all accretions to Islam that have developed over fourteen centuries must be swept away, and a good Muslim must refer only to the Quran and what is known about the Prophet's own practice. In addition, Islamist movements vary between the ambition to maintain literal fidelity to the tradition on the one hand and the desire for change on the other, whether achieved through reform or revolution.

Nonetheless, there is a phenomenon to be studied. It remains the case that a substantial number of Muslims have concluded, across a broad range of situations, that violence or extremism is a legitimate mean to the achievement of desirable goals. Such Muslims have shown the ability to form organizations and societies, to communicate with each other across national frontiers, to travel widely in the interests of achieving their goals, and to risk their lives when necessary. The study of Islamism is the investigation of what the objectives of such action might be, what precise methods are used, what philosophical rationale is adduced, and what may be the level of threat to established societies both in the West and in the Muslim states.

The Algerian Islamist Networks

Currents of thought within the Muslim world transcend national and ethnic divisions. However, the movements whose activities regularly make the headlines in the media and that claim responsibility for terrorist attacks in Europe, Israel, or Palestine are not driven by ideas, but are essentially Islamo-nationalist organizations. Though most such movements have their thinkers, their role is to provide a rationale for action. The primary motives of the militants are political. Such movements include the FIS and the GIA in Algeria, Hamas and Islamic Jihad in Palestine, and various movements in Pakistan. Many other movements across the entire extent of the Islamic world are struggling to overthrow regimes seen as impious, treacherous, corrupt, or devalued.

The FIS was initially as much attracted by the idea of nationalist Arab solidarity, rather than religious solidarity from the Muslim world. In the early phase, there was an internal struggle within the FIS between the Algerianist nationalist tendency, led by Mohammed Said, and the Salafis, inspired by Ali Belhadj. The Salafis, who were implacably opposed to a non-Muslim state and sought the return of the caliphate, were strongly inspired by the Muslim Brotherhood and the ideas of Sayed al-Qutb. Despite foreign influences, however, the demands of the proliferating Islamic movements, associations, and groups in Algeria were aimed at specific changes within Algerian society and had nothing to do with the Muslim Umma.

Whether Algerian, Palestinian, or Pakistani, such movements were primarily nationalist in the sense that their ambitions were confined to the limits of a single nation. Islam was essentially no more than a vehicle for their ambitions, and, therefore, they were properly to be seen as Islamo-nationalist movements and not universal Islamists, as envisaged in the Islamist theories. When the local population was receptive to their religious rhetoric, this was more indicative of ignorance of Islam among the population than of their adherence to Islamist theories. Such movements were too far divorced from the Islamist theories from which they, nevertheless, sought inspiration. The objective to which they devoted their efforts was not to re-Islamize society, but to seize power. Their strategy was not to transform the everyday lives of individual Muslims, but to use terror to destabilize the regime and the existing administration with the intention of installing an alternative.

The GIA, when it carried out attacks in Algiers or Paris, became a terrorist organization like any other, whose tactics were susceptible to police action or judicial measures. In Algeria, from 1992 onward, GIA units developed their ability to get operatives into Europe. Once they arrived, they would be met by "sleepers," whose lives in Europe had long been, on the surface, above suspicion. They then became part of various systems of support for the fighters on the ground in Algeria. False documents were obtained in Europe, so that the militants could move about in safety; cash was raised through the drug trade; and finally arms were bought with the profits made from drugs. Switzerland and Belgium were the usual channels for these operations. Arms purchases by expatriate Algerians in France, Italy, Spain, and Belgium to supply the Algerian fighters in Algeria were of course illegal and attracted the attention of European security services.

The Islamist theorists, to whom the guerrillas made constant reference, did not themselves, of course, have any link with such activities. Fundamentalist Islamic thinkers did not become involved in criminality and maintained a clear distinction between what was legal and what was not. Their goal was to improve the situation of the Muslims in their everyday lives in Europe. Their activities gave them a positive image in the eyes of the European authorities, while also gaining the approval of their communities. In the long term, however, the ideologists may in truth have been more dangerous. They rejected integration into European society, and they have made efforts to take control of the mosques, the Muslim religious institutions, and the Islamic associations that they found. They have thus gained access to funds and have been able to present themselves as the representatives of the Muslim communities. In this way they obtained a measure of recognition on the part of the authorities in European countries.

Islamism and the United States

Relations between the United States and Islam, and particularly with Islamism, go back to the early twentieth century. The first interlocutors for the Americans in the Middle East were the Saudis, the new masters of Arabia. The relationship sprang up in the context of oil prospecting by American companies in Arabia in the 1920s and 1930s and the emergence of the United States as the new great world power after World War II. A historical view is essential for an understanding of this strong but ill-defined relationship.

In modern times, the supremacy of the United States in the Middle East has flowed from the ill-judged Suez venture, when Britain and France invaded the Suez Canal Zone in collusion with Israel, which simultaneously attacked the Sinai Peninsula. Under joint pressure from the United States and the Soviet Union, the victorious invaders were obliged to withdraw from Egypt's territory, with the result that Britain and France lost the remnants of their hegemonic standing in the Middle East to the new nuclear superpowers. In effect, the United States and the Soviet Union became the new arbiters of the Arab and Muslim Middle East. The Arab world emerged from the experience severed into two parts. On the one hand, the countries that regarded themselves as progressive regrouped around the leadership of Nasser, while the conservatives lined up behind Saudi Arabia.

The decision of the United States to sponsor the petroleum monarchies was not an accident. The United States, as the British had done before, prioritized their own interest in controlling the oil and gas fields, exploitation, refineries, and transportation. It was scarcely surprising in that light that Saudi Arabia became a key element of American strategy, in preference to Egypt, not an oil power, whose ruler had shown an arrogant hostility toward the West. Arabia was not the only interlocutor to be singled out in this way. Iran, despite the internal troubles that threatened its vast oil reserves, was also targeted by the United States. Meanwhile, for strategic reasons, Turkey—a redoubtable bulwark against the

Soviets—and, after 1967, Israel also joined the American bloc.

At the same time, the United States also shrank from relationships with organized groups of states, though the Arab countries had formed themselves into a coherent group under the umbrella of the Arab League. Washington wanted only bilateral relations, and its aim was to prize the Arab League apart, following the maxim "Divide and rule." This was how Americans preferred to operate. The change of direction in July 1972 by Egypt's President Anwar Sadat, who sent home some eighteen thousand Soviet advisers, provided U.S. diplomacy with a unique occasion to reconstruct the balance of power in the region. From then on, Washington's economic priorities were in harmony with its strategic interests in the region. To win Egypt over to the Western camp was all the easier since the West presented itself as the sponsor of peace in the region.

The strategy of Henry Kissinger had four main objectives. These were:

1. The fragmentation of the Middle East.
2. U.S. involvement in all regional problems, where the United States would present itself as an interlocutor impossible to ignore.
3. The control of oil and other major economic sectors, including air transport, telecommunications, and IT industries.
4. The suppression of all manifestations of Arab unity, which in Washington's view could only be hostile.

To achieve these objectives, three principle strategies were brought to bear. These were:

1. Weakening and undermining hostile regimes.
2. Making use of Islam and Islamism.
3. Management by proxy of a fluid and unstable region.

The Lebanese War, usually referred to as a "civil war," was a focus for all the contradictions and paradoxes of the Middle East. From 1975 to 1983, during the first eight years of the conflict, foreign actors were involved in every aspect of the Lebanese War, including Palestinians, Syrians, Libyans, Sudanese, and Israelis. Only in September 1983 did the war become truly a "civil" conflict for the first time when the Christians found themselves in conflict with the Druzes. It should be observed that from the moment the first shot was fired in Lebanon, there were no further conflicts, coups, or revolutions elsewhere in the Arab world. Seen thus, the Lebanon War appeared to be the first success of the Kissinger strategy. The Camp David Accords, which were agreed in 1978, and the subsequent peace treaty between Egypt and Israel, seemed to be a further manifestation. Henceforth, the Arab world would lack Egypt's leadership. All the hyperbole of the "Rejectionist Front" countries and any acts of terrorism they might instigate were to be of little avail. The Arab world was henceforth powerless.

There then ensued the Islamic Revolution in Iran and its consequences, including the seizure of the U.S. Embassy in Tehran and the holding of its diplomatic staff hostage. However, the Iranian Islamic Revolution did not represent a threat for the United States alone. It was perhaps an even greater threat to Saudi Arabia, America's leading ally in the region. Iran was a Shi'ite country in a Sunni world and a lone Persian state with a population of some 40 million at that time among an Arab population of hundreds of millions. It was in a sense a natural frontier between Arab and non-Arab Islam. It was also the powerful overseer of the Persian Gulf and therefore of the transit route for 35 percent of the oil supplies of the West. The emergence of a newly powerful Iran looked like a new threat to the United States. However, Iran's immediate Arab neighbor was Iraq, which had itself become a source of concern owing to its military power, its industrial development, its growing economy, and its belligerent attitude. Iraq represented a serious challenge to Saudi Arabia. But Saddam Hussein and his armed forces believed themselves to have been entrusted with a new mission—that of defending the West against the follies and excesses of Iran's ayatollahs.

On September 22, 1980, as the Soviets were moving into Afghanistan, Saddam Hussein invaded Iran. The resulting war was to last eight years, weakening both countries and in the end bringing no change on the ground. Only Saudi Arabia benefited from the temporary distraction of its two regional rivals. Iraq, however, continued to challenge Saudi Arabia's regional preeminence, and Saddam Hussein demanded the spoils of his country's "sacrifice." His casus belli was Iraq's access to the Gulf. In 1990, he revived the Iraqi demand that Kuwait cede the islands of Bubiyan and Warbah, which would provide Iraq with a shoreline, but Kuwait refused. In July 1990, when Saddam held his last talk with the American ambassador in Iraq, April Glaspie, she said that the United States had "no opinion on the Arab–Arab conflicts, like Iraq's border dispute with Kuwait." This may have given the Iraqi leader the impression that Washington would not object to any moves against Kuwait he might choose to make.

However, when Iraqi forces occupied Kuwait on August 2, 1990, the response was the U.S.-led operation known as "Desert Storm." Iraq's action was taken for a number of reasons. The old Iraqi claim that Kuwait was rightfully part of Iraq's territory was resuscitated, and Iraq not only wished to escape repayment of the debt Kuwait claimed it owed for assistance rendered during the Iran–Iraq War, but also to avail itself of Kuwait's oil resources for the future. Twenty-nine countries from around the

world came together under the leadership of the elder President George Bush to eject the Iraqi invaders. These included Arab states such as Syria and Morocco. The outcome was the destruction of the Iraqi army, purported by the Americans at the time to have been the fourth strongest armed force in the world. Saudi Arabia had every reason to believe itself restored to security. However, many unpredictable consequences flowed from President Bush's "crusade" against Iraq.

First, there was the resultant fragmentation of the Arab world. From this time on, each state was obliged to rely solely on its own resources and its alliances with states beyond the region. This had the detrimental effect that each country was able to help itself only at the expense of others. Another consequence was that the ideological victory of Islamism over the secular concept of Arabism was complete. Policies primarily motivated by security concerns supplanted any unifying sentiment of solidarity and prevailed over Arab nationalism. These new concerns were reflected in the policies of the Arab states toward outside powers. The objective was to achieve recognition as a regional power through establishing a relationship with a power outside the region, thus aiding the outside power to dominate others.

The second consequence was the risk that Iraq might fall apart, thus setting a precedent for frontier change in the region as a whole. The outcome was that Syria, Iran, and Turkey were all henceforth on their guard against any move that might result in alterations in the frontiers of Iraq.

The third consequence of the crisis was the emergence of a third non-Arab power as a major player in the region. In addition to Iran and Turkey, Israel took its place on the stage. A number of elements combined to mitigate the threat to Israel from the Arabs and to reinforce its position. Such considerations included Iraq's disappearance as a factor in the regional scene, the American decision to restrain Iran, the prevalence of inter-Arab splits, the financial crisis of the oil monarchies, and the collapse of the Soviet Union, which happened to take place immediately after the Gulf War. Israel's superiority manifested itself in the fields of security, military strength, economics, and technology.

Finally, the modalities of U.S. relations with the Arab and Muslim countries accentuated the divisions among regional states. The United States identified particular powers to act on their behalf in each region. These were Saudi Arabia for the Arabian Peninsula, Egypt for the Nile Valley, and Israel for the Levant. In North Africa, the United States believed it could work through Algeria. Algeria is a state that had fought against France and that was in possession of vast oil and gas resources. Before becoming a client of the United States, which put its weight unobtrusively behind the Algerian authorities, it was threatened with destabilization following the rise of an Islamist movement whose goal was to overthrow the government.

In the closing years of the twentieth century, the Arab world was still politically disunited and technologically backward, with economic disparities such that wealth served only to highlight the problems of backwardness rather than to ameliorate them. In this situation of disarray, the region lay broadly under American tutelage, with U.S. bases in the Gulf and in ten Arab states, including Egypt and Saudi Arabia. Those Arab states that rejected American hegemony were subjected to international opprobrium and were characterized as pariah states or states that supported terrorism. The first group contained Iraq, Libya, and Sudan, though the threat from Iraq was countered by the U.S.-led invasion in 2003 and Libya took the decision to ingratiate itself with the

United States. The most prominent member of the second group was Syria, accused by the United States of sponsoring terrorist activities.

In the situation faced by the Middle East, the Islamists took the lead in the denunciation of the region's decline. In the mosques and madrasas across the region, the Islamist viewpoint became dominant, and the United States seized the chance to make use of it, allowing those states that did not align themselves with American policy to face the threat of destabilization. The part played by the United States in the expansion of Islamism was part of a widespread strategy that operated in Central Asia and the Indian subcontinent, as well as in the Middle East. In 1977, the ambition of the Saudis and their new ally, Pakistan, under the leadership of Zia ul-Haq, was to establish a Sunni Muslim entity among the Soviet Union, India, and Iran. This was almost realized on three occasions, after the invasion of Afghanistan by the Soviet Union, when the Islamic Revolution took place in Iran, and when the United States succeeded in its efforts to undermine the Soviet Union.

It should be said that on occasions the destabilization of existing regimes by Wahhabi Islamists suited the purposes of the United States, as for example in Afghanistan where it served them as a weapon against the communists. Pakistan and Saudi Arabia operated in close collaboration in the 1980s in Central Asia and in Afghanistan. Their goal was the spread of re-Islamization, which they believed would bring to power conservative Muslim regimes. Saudi Arabia was backed by the United States, which saw it as a counterbalance to Iranian influence, and had great wealth at its disposal. Its role was to provide finance, through private or semipublic channels, for Islamic projects. These included the construction of mosques, the distribution of copies of the Quran, the endowment of scholarships, and the provision of religious teachers. In Uzbekistan in 1992 and 1993, however, there was a setback due to the hostility of the religious teaching staff to the local version of Shi'ism, which was matched by the antagonism toward them of the local Shi'ite Mullahs. As regards the Afghan conflict, the United States became more directly involved. According to a congressional report, the CIA financed the Afghan mujahidin to the extent of between $150 million and $300 million a year, paid through accounts run by the Pakistani secret services (the ISI).

Until September 11, 2001, it did not occur to the Americans that Wahhabi-Salafi Islam could be a danger to the United States itself, on its own soil. After September 11, 2001, FBI investigators began to uncover the origins of the personal fortune of Osama bin Laden, who had received a considerable sum as part of his share of the family fortune. His father, Mohammed Awad bin Laden, who died in 1967, was the founder of the civil engineering conglomerate, the Saudi Bin Laden Group (SBLG). With financial subsidiaries in Europe and the United States, the family business bought a stake in the Carlyle Group, an American investment management company of which the elder President George Bush was a prominent shareholder, though this was later sold. The SBLG also took substantial holdings in other American funds. At Mohammed Awad bin Laden's death in 1967, when the group was worth an estimated $2 billion, control of the SBLG passed to Salem bin Laden, the eldest son, who pursued the goal of establishing close relations with American business leaders. There appears, in particular, to have been a concentration on the family of President Bush and his associates. Osama bin Laden's personal fortune, however, was apparently based on a personal inheritance settled on him at the time of his father's death and did not depend on the family firm. In the 1970s, Osama bin Laden progressively distanced

himself from his family and became a radical Islamist. During the 1979–1989 Afghan War against the Soviets and their allies in Afghanistan, he raised money and provided engineering services for the Islamists. He also became directly involved in the fighting. At this stage, he continued to receive help from the United States through various channels.

In 1991, Osama bin Laden broke with the United States. He had returned to Saudi Arabia, but was obliged by the Saudi authorities to leave the country after the Gulf War because of his criticism of the Saudi regime and his anti-American statements. In 1994, he was stripped of his Saudi nationality. In 1997, he said the continued presence of American troops in Arabia amounted to an occupation of the Muslim holy places. The strain that developed between Bin Laden and the United States during the 1990s exemplified the gradual divorce between American policy and radical Islamism. On August 20, 1998, the breach became overt, when President Clinton ordered an air strike on Bin Laden's training camps in Afghanistan in retaliation for the attacks on the U.S. embassies in Kenya and Tanzania. It was not until a year later that the United States imposed sanctions on the Taliban. The United Nations brought in its own sanctions a year later, in December 2000. Until this time, however, the United States carefully refrained from questioning the assistance given by the Pakistani ISI and Saudi Arabia to the Taliban and to Bin Laden's "Afghans."

By 1998, the United States had seen that complete victory for the Taliban would for various reasons be prevented by Russia, Iran, and India. They then began to bring pressure to bear on the sponsors of the various Afghan factions to ensure an agreement among all the parties involved. The United States demanded that the Taliban should extradite Bin Laden and come to an agreement with the Northern Alliance, their principal internal enemies. In return, the United States would recognize the Taliban regime and would ensure that it received international aid, as well as completing the outstanding gas pipeline project planned by Unocal from Central Asia through Afghanistan to Pakistan. In order to bring pressure to bear on the regime, the United States sponsored the UN Security Council resolution 1267, passed on October 15, 1999, which imposed sanctions on the Taliban regime. At the same time, it set up the negotiating group known as the 6 plus 2, which comprised the six states bordering on Afghanistan, together with Russia and the United States.

President George W. Bush's electoral victory in 2000 led to the re-opening of a relationship between the United States and the Taliban. Like Bush himself, most of his staff had links to the oil companies. His closest collaborator, the National Security Advisor, Condoleezza Rice, who had advised his father on Soviet affairs, had been since 1991 a member of the Board of Directors of Chevron Oil and had advised the Board on Central Asia. Her adviser on Afghanistan was Zalmay Khalilzad—later U.S. ambassador to post-conflict Iraq and then the United Nations—who between 1995 and 1998 negotiated the line of the Unocal oil pipeline with the Taliban. Many other members of the Bush administration had links with oil companies, not the least Vice President Dick Cheney, former CEO of Halliburton, the leading company providing services to the oil industry. Throughout 2001, the Bush administration attempted to persuade the Taliban to hold a "Loya Jirga," (a grand council of tribes and factions). The Bush administration judged this an authentic and moderate Muslim procedure, which was also the option favored by President Bush's adviser on Afghanistan, who was still negotiating with the Taliban over the expulsion of Bin Laden.

The Bush administration also refrained from giving support to the Northern Alliance, which renamed itself the United Front in the beginning of 2001. The Northern Alliance had at its disposal five thousand men loyal to Massoud and Sayyaf in the northwest of the country, with fifteen thousand others who could be called on, as well as Rashid Dostum's force, which was at most five thousand men, and an indeterminate number of Shi'ite Hazaras. They were vastly outnumbered by the Taliban and their allies, who had fifteen thousand men and another seventy thousand who could be summoned from the tribal hinterland. The Taliban also had the support of the five thousand or so Arab "Afghans" loyal to Bin Laden who could be called on to fight, which gave them a substantial advantage. The main advantage enjoyed by the Taliban, however, was the Northern Alliance's lack of unity. The overall strategy of the Americans was dictated by oil interests in the region. Hitherto, the Caspian countries had been obliged to use the Russian oil pipelines to transport their oil and gas output with the payment of large premiums.

American interests have continued to dictate developments in the oil sector. In spite of the events of September 11, 2001, and their consequences, the United States continued to protect Saudi Arabia and 100 billion barrels of proven reserves. American attacks against Islamists have continued to respond selectively to circumstances. The Bush administration has apparently chosen to deal with Islamists who serve their interests and combat those who are hostile to the United States. One thing which is certain, however, is that the events of September 11 have encouraged and assisted the United States to extend the "Americanization" of the entire the Middle East and Central Asia, begun at the time of the Gulf War in 1991.

Nonetheless, the attitude of the United States to Islamism in the post-September 11 period has been paradoxical. First, the United States continues to be in close alliance with Saudi Arabia, an explicitly Wahhabi power whose links to Islamism are ambiguous in the extreme. Though the Saudi regime itself comes under attack from Salafi factions that believe it has deviated from the true path of Islam, the contradiction inherent in U.S.–Saudi relations remains evident. Second, the United States chose to identify as a part of the Islamist threat the regime of Saddam Hussein in Iraq, which seems extremely likely to have had no connection with Islamic extremism. Third, the United States has been extremely anxious to promote a campaign to win over hearts and minds in the Middle East. However, the security measures targeted at Arabs and Muslims, together with social and political attitudes toward them in the United States and on the part of Americans abroad, have alienated Muslims. The result has been increasingly to drive a wedge between the United States on the one hand and the Arab world and Muslim Umma on the other.

IVORY COAST

In 1999, an army coup in Ivory Coast mounted by General Guei overthrew President Bedié, the legitimate successor of President Houphouet Boigny. This was followed by the elections of 2000, which brought Laurent Gbagbo to power after General Guei withdrew his candidacy. A leading opponent of Gbagbo was Alassane Ouattara, a Muslim from the north of the country, who had been prime minister under Houphouet Boigny from 1990 to 1993. Gbagbo barred Ouattara from standing as a candidate on the alleged grounds that both his parents were born in Burkina Faso, which meant his Ivorian nationality was open to question and that in any case he lacked roots in the country, or what has been called "Ivority."

The slight to Ouattar appears to have been a factor leading to the emergence of a militant Islamic movement in a country, where the Muslim population exceeds 40 percent and is mainly concentrated in the north. Until more recent revisions, the Ivorian constitution as developed under Bedié and Gbagbo continued to exclude those with foreign connections from citizenship and insisted on the importance of "Ivority." Most of the country's migrant workers are from neighboring Muslim states.

Since the events of 2000, the Supreme Council of Imams (known as COSIM), headed by Koudous Idriss Koné, has taken upon itself the task of speaking for the Muslim community. Its spokesman, Aboubacar Fofana, has taken every opportunity to condemn what he has described as an "ethno-religious war directed against the Muslims of Ivory Coast and orchestrated by the Catholic Church." COSIM has sought to swell the Muslim population with the arrival of migrants from neighboring Muslim countries, such as Burkina Faso. Meanwhile another Muslim institution, the National Islamic Council (CNI) has drawn strength from its links with the embassies of Islamic countries, issuing documents that it claimed contained proof of the prejudice faced by the Ivorian Muslims. In the words of one such statement, "If we look at history, we quickly see that in every society there have been massacres of men and women, the first response has been to single out a particular community and to present it as responsible for all social problems. The full power of the state has then been brought to bear to attribute blame to the selected community."

Clearly, the increasingly political Islamist movement was attaching blame to the regime. The Islamists were increasingly identified with certain ethnic groups, such as the Malinké and the Douala. Aboubacar Fofana also regularly launched attacks on France in his excitable speeches, accusing France of historical responsibility for the demarcation of the frontiers that separated Ivory Coast from its immediate Muslim neighbors, Mali and Burkina Faso. The Ivorian Islamic movement began to call into question the Ivorian constitution's definition of citizenship in favor of considerations that could conduce to the reinforcement of Islamic solidarity. As Aboubacar Fofana put it, "the issue of 'Ivority' has seen off Bédié and Gueï. Gbagbo should therefore think carefully before taking that road." A military coup in 2002 failed to displace President Gbagbo, but by January 2003 rebels effectively controlled the Muslim north of the country. Under a reconciliation agreement, rebels were given positions in the government. Nonetheless, the government has no effective control over the north of the country. In January 2006, with the position over his nationality resolved, Alassane Ouattara returned to the country after three years of voluntary exile in France, and again announced that he would be a candidate for the presidency as the head of the RDR (Rassemblement des Républicains). The elections were due to take place in October 2006, but were abandoned due to the generalized unrest. In December 2006, Ouattara reaffirmed his commitment to a United Nations peace plan for Cote d'Ivoire, wracked by recurring rebellious movements.

IZETBEGOVIC, ALIJA

Izetbegovic was born in Bosnia on August 8, 1925, at the town of Bosanski Samac in northern Bosnia. As a young man he soon began to take part in political life and was an early member of the militant Islamist movement in Yugoslavia. He was never attached to the Yugoslav Communist Party. He joined the nationalist group known as the "Young Muslims" (Mladi Muslimani) and at the age of twenty he was arrested for his membership in this movement. He was released in 1949 and graduated from university in 1956 as a lawyer, which became his profession. In 1970, he wrote a book, *The Islamic Declaration,* in which he argued for the establishment of a fundamentalist Islamic State and rejected any coexistence among communities based on equal rights. In 1980, he published his major work, Islam between East and West. Both books were cited in evidence when he was tried for seditious activity in 1983, when he was sentenced to fourteen years in prison. He was pardoned and released in 1988, as the communist regime began to crumble.

In March 1990 he founded the "Democratic Action Party" (Stranka Demokratske Akcije—SDA) that presented itself as the representative of the Bosnian Muslim community. In its manifesto the party included typically Muslim measures, such as the observance of Muslim festivals and the reconstruction of mosques. In December 1990, Izetbegovic was elected President of Bosnia in the first multiparty elections held in the former Yugoslavia, and was regarded as a hero throughout the Muslim countries—in 1993 he was given an Islamic award by King Fahd for his efforts on behalf of the jihad. In 1991, he declared Bosnia's sovereignty and in March 1992 its independence. As soon as he took power, he embarked on a policy of establishing closer relations with Islamic countries and with Islamists. In February 1991, he visited Libya and he visited Iran in April 1991. He inaugurated close ties between the SDA and Iran, which would lead to significant Iranian aid and the presence of a number of Iranian fighters during the Bosnian War.

Thanks to his cultivation of a favorable image in Europe and the United States he was able to establish good political links with the West. The Bosnian War, which broke out in 1992, allowed him to assert his uncontested authority. Thanks to the SDA and to the aid he controlled, he was able to exert his authority over every aspect of the Bosnian state. Bosnia became gradually more and more Islamized, and the Shari'a was progressively introduced into the courts. Mixed marriages were deprecated and Izetbegovic even expressed sympathy for some who advocated the suppression of Christmas and New Year celebrations. After the departure of the Serbs and the Croats, Sarajevo, which had traditionally been a multicommunal city, became exclusively Muslim, where evidence of the influence of Islamism became more ostentatious. Izetbegovic welcomed the most extreme Islamic movements into the country and sought aid from the principal paymasters of Islamism. He was militarily unable, however, to carry out on the ground what had been his original plan, to unite the Muslims of Bosnia and those of the Sanjak of Novi Pazar.

Izetbegovic was in a way a victim of his own efforts to save Bosnia. He signed the Dayton Accords on December 14, 1995, which ended the war but installed Western supervision of the country. Bosnia's secular parties and personalities, who rejected his policies because they were too closely allied to Islamism, were then able to undermine his authority. In the event, support for the SDA fell at the elections of 1997. Disillusionment was profound among large sections of the Bosnian public after the rapid and authoritarian Islamization of the country favored by the SDA, which was possible thanks to the assistance given by the Saudi NGOs, among others. The United Front that existed during the war soon fractured. This was a great relief to the West, which was reluctant to see Iranian influence take hold in Bosnia, or, after September 11, 2001, to accept the presence of radical Islamic groups.

The SDA emerged weakened from the parallel competition it underwent from both secular and Islamic groups. It was unable to identify a universally acceptable candidate for the 1998 elections and asked Izetbegovic to stand once more in order to preserve the unity and popularity of the party. In 2000, however, Izetbegovic's health obliged him to stand down. He died on October 19, 2003.

JAZEERA, AL-

Al-Jazeera is a twenty-four-hour TV news station broadcasting in Arabic. Al-Jazeera means "The Island," and refers to the expression "Jazeera al-Arab," which means "The Arabian Peninsula." It is based in Doha, the capital of Qatar, and was set up in November 1996 at the initiative of Emir Hamad bin Khalifa Al Thani, the ruler of Qatar. It enjoys the services of experienced journalists, many of whom formerly worked for the Arabic Service of the BBC and for the short-lived BBC Arabic TV station. Its talent for breaking exclusive stories and its freedom of expression—unusual in the Middle East—have made it the channel most watched in the region. Its nickname has been the "Arabic CNN." It claims to be objective and covers all developments. For example, it has given full coverage to the political protests of the Lebanese Christian community. After the attacks on the American embassies in Nairobi and Dar es-Salaam in 1999, Osama bin Laden gave an unprecedented and exclusive interview to Al-Jazeera at his Afghan headquarters in which he gave an account of the rationale behind his struggle against the United States. Al-Jazeera presents itself foremost as a news channel and its aim is to take precedence over CNN on Arab and Islamic issues.

After September 11, 2001, it was the only news agency accredited by the Taliban and became the only outlet to carry news from Kabul. Al-Jazeera pays special attention to the role of Islam in the contemporary world. Its broadcasts by the theologian Yusuf al-Qaradawi, the distinguished Egyptian Islamic scholar who is identified with the views of the Muslim Brotherhood, have achieved very large viewing figures. Al-Jazeera makes great efforts to achieve visibility in Western countries such as the United States, Britain, and France, where there are significant Muslim communities. In the live broadcasts presented by the Syrian-born journalist Faisal Qasim, who previously worked for the BBC and holds British nationality, local listeners criticize American policy in the region as well as attack the policies of Arab states on various issues.

Al-Jazeera has frequently been involved in controversies. Many in the West regard it as, in some sense, the mouthpiece for Islamist views. Al-Jazeera draws attention to what it says is its undeniable objectivity and insists that it may appear as a mouth piece for Islamic radicals simply because Western TV stations refuse to broadcast such views at all. It has on a number of occasions served as the means of delivery for messages contained in video tapes sent to the station by Osama bin Laden and other Al-Qaida figures, but makes these tapes available to other TV stations. It has never broadcast terrorist videos of beheadings and the like and demands retractions when such allegations are made. The allegation was made by Donald Rumsfeld on June 2, 2005, and has been carried by Fox News as recently as November 15, 2006, the launch day of Al-Jazeera's English-language channel. Western journalists, who find increasing difficulty in reporting from conflict zones in Iraq and Afghanistan, frequently turn to Al-Jazeera for the basic facts they need in order not to depend entirely on Western military sources.

Al-Jazeera has been in conflict with a number of Arab states. The station says the Qatari foreign ministry has received more than four hundred complaints about its activities. For instance, Algeria banned the station's correspondent in 2004, apparently as retribution for a hostile report. The station's correspondents were banned from Bahrain in 2002 for allegedly unwarranted criticism. The Al-Jazeera office in Jordan was closed down in 2002, for similar reasons. In late 2002, Kuwait closed down Al-Jazeera's office there, which remained shut until May 2005. No Al-Jazeera correspondent is based permanently in Saudi Arabia, which allows the station's journalists in only to cover special events. The Egyptian government has sponsored campaigns against what it calls Al-Jazeera's bias in its own state-controlled media. In February 2007, a producer for the station was prosecuted in Egypt for planning a documentary on torture in Egypt's police stations. The Palestinian presidency is less than pleased by the coverage given to Hamas by Al-Jazeera, though the station is monitored constantly in the presidential offices as it is in government offices throughout the entire Arab world. In February 2005, Al-Jazeera was prevented from gathering news in Iran and the ban was not lifted until June 2006.

In Iraq, the U.S. authorities have been constantly concerned by the activities of Al-Jazeera. In the early weeks of the U.S.-led invasion, one of the station's correspondents, Tayseer Allouni, was expelled, and Diyar al-Omari's accreditation was withdrawn. Al-Jazeera announced on April 2, 2003, that it was suspending its coverage of Iraq. In May 2003, the CIA alleged that Al-Jazeera had been infiltrated by agents hostile to the United States. In August 2004, the Iraqi government of Iyad Allawi closed down Al-Jazeera's operation in Iraq.

U.S. hostility to Al-Jazeera has occasionally lurched into physical aggression. American missiles hit the station's Kabul bureau on November 13, 2001. U.S. sources claimed this was an accident. An Al-Jazeera cameraman of Sudanese nationality named Sami al-Hajj was arrested in December 2001 and has been detained in Guantanamo Bay. According to Al-Hajj's lawyer speaking in 2005, he has been repeatedly questioned on whether Al-Jazeera is a front for Al-Qaida. Al-Jazeera's Baghdad office was hit by a U.S. missile on April 8, 2003, killing a reporter, Tareq Ayyoub. On January 30, 2005, *The New York Times* reported that the station would be sold. This has proved ill-founded. In November 2005, rumors surfaced that President George W. Bush had considered bombing Al-Jazeera's headquarters in Doha. This would have been difficult to reconcile with the prevailing friendly relationship between the United States and Qatar, where the American fleet in the Gulf has a major base.

In 2006, Al-Jazeera launched a major expansion into the field of international broadcasting with the inauguration of an English-language service, Al-Jazeera International. It also moved into Southeast Asia, with broadcasts of its Arabic channel including some translated material into Malaysia and Indonesia.

JIHAD

"Jihad" is a word at the mercy of the vagaries of current events. Its definition in the modern world is fraught with difficulty. The root meaning of the word is a struggle toward a goal. Some Muslims today maintain that according to the letter of Islamic doctrine, Jihad is primarily a struggle against oneself and one's impulses, instincts, and temptations. According to the *Encyclopedia of Islam,* "Certain writers … qualify this Jihad as 'spiritual Jihad' and as the 'greater Jihad' in opposition to the 'lesser Jihad.'" This idea is based on a Hadith, where the Prophet, returning from battle to the quotidian existence of the Muslim community, is reported to have said, "We return from the small Jihad to the greater Jihad." Armed conflict is therefore regarded as a "lesser Jihad." Nevertheless, armed struggle is the sense of the word that is much more prevalent. Jihad is armed conflict, originally in the interests of extending the area of submission to Islam or of defending its existing scope. By its nature Jihad is offensive, but can also be defensive.

Jihad is the sole form of warfare authorized by Islam and the doctrine forbids all conflict among Muslims. Today, however, the Islamists sometimes seek to justify Jihad against Muslim regimes. Such an interpretation was first suggested by the thirteenth-century theologian Ibn Taymiya, much admired by the Salafis, who sought to justify attacks by Muslims on Mongol sovereigns who had technically converted to Islam. Hassan Turabi, the Sudanese lawyer and Islamic thinker seen as an authority on contemporary Islamism put the position as follows: "Muslims should not seek to provoke antagonism and violent confrontation for as long as the political authority refrains from so acting, in the interests of its own authority and power. Only in such cases should Muslims respond with Jihad, which should be directed and controlled according in the light of piety and discipline, whilst ensuring that clashes embarked upon in anger do not affect those not involved and innocent parties."

Not all are as careful in their formulation as was Turabi. The meaning of Jihad has evolved. Such figures as Osama bin Laden have waged an offensive Jihad against Muslim authorities who are accused of governing badly. Jihad is invoked to justify what might otherwise be seen as mere "Fitna," rebellion that is seen as undesirable within the Muslim community. However, Jihad is also still a war by Muslims against Western states and non-Muslims in general. Grievances felt by Muslims against the West that justify Jihad include the memory of colonial exploitation and the appropriation and misuse by the West of resources perceived as properly belonging to the Muslims, such as oil. Other sources of anger are the presence of Westerners in lands seen as sacrosanct, such as Saudi Arabia, and neocolonial endeavors to undermine the Muslim countries. The Muslims also resent what they see as the deception practiced on them by the West, the West's efforts to restrict their practice of what they see as proper Islam. All this is part of what militant Muslims see ultimately as an effort by the West to destroy the basis of Islam, as it should be.

Jihad is not one of the pillars of Islam. However, it is an obligation upon Muslims to be seen primarily as a duty of the Muslim community as a whole. The use of force against non-Muslims has always been acceptable within Islam, but was never an obligation on the individual. It is a duty that will continue until Islam has achieved universal domination. The recent predominance of this idea is in part an explanation for the reemergence of the idea of Jihad. Jihad has served a banner at a time of decolonization and as independence movements emerged. Today it has appeared once more, not only in opposition to the imposition of external authority, but also against internal enemies. At its origins, Jihad was a means of effecting the conversion of non-Muslims or their submission to the authority of Islam and such considerations also find a place in contemporary Islamist statements.

The idea of Jihad as a war waged by the Islamists against Western countries, or other non-Muslims whoever they may be, has come to predominate in the West. The events of September 11, 2001, have come to symbolize, in Western eyes, the meaning of Jihad and the threat it represents. On this issue, the Quran enjoins Muslims as follows: "Do not submit yourselves to the unbelievers, but struggle against them by force, by means of the Quran" (Quran: Sura 25, Verse 52). Distinguished theologians have promoted the idea of Jihad in the twentieth century. The Pakistani fundamentalist Mawdudi, in the context of British colonialism in the Indian subcontinent, called for all to engage in Jihad against the colonial power. In Egypt, the Muslim Brotherhood ideologue, Sayyed Qutb, said Muslims should emulate Mohammed's flight from Mecca and his subsequent Jihad against the unconverted. (This was the thinking that lay behind those groups that called themselves Takfir wa-l-Hijra.) By the twenty-first century, calls for Jihad have become almost commonplace among Salafi groups, whose belief that they are in touch with the original sources of the faith gives them a strong sense of their own rectitude.

In theory, Islam should constitute a unitary community under a single authority. This authority would be empowered to declare Jihad. Islamists contend that the obligation to Jihad will continue for as long as Islam has not become the universal religion. While awaiting the arrival of the caliphate, the ability legitimately to declare Jihad has been seen by some Muslim political theorists as a characteristic of sovereignty, not unlike the Western concept of the state's monopoly of force. Any declaration of Jihad is a claim to authority. For the Salafis, in consequence, the declaration of Jihad constitutes among other things a challenge to the sovereignty of governments regarded by them as illegitimate.

JORDAN

Jordan is an anomaly in the Middle East. It is a monarchy without roots. The Jordanian state was invented by Britain in 1921 when Britain's colonial secretary, Winston Churchill, agreed to appoint the Hashemite Emir Abdullah as leader of a separate political entity to be known as Transjordan. This consisted of that part of the territory entrusted to British administration under the Palestine mandate that lay to the east of the River Jordan. The Hashemites were an aristocratic family from Mecca in Saudi Arabia who had supported the British against the Germans and Turks in World War II. King Hussein, Abdullah's grandson, became king in 1952 (after his father Talal abdicated due to mental incapacity). King Abdullah II, whose mother was British, became king in 1999. Iraq had also been a Hashemite kingdom, but there the monarchy was overthrown in 1958. With a great deal of support from the West and a good deal of luck, however, the Jordanian monarchy survived. It is in theory a constitutional monarchy, but under the constitution the king retains a great deal of executive power. Democracy was suspended by royal decree in Jordan in 1967 after the Israeli annexation of the West Bank. New elections were not held until 1989.

The Muslim Brotherhood has long been a legal organization in Jordan. Under its leader, Abdul Latif Abu Qurah, it obtained the status of a charitable society in January 1945. Islamist ideas found early favor in Jordan. In July 1940, King Abdullah asked his prime minister to issue an order banning women from leaving their homes without the veil and modest Islamic dress. In November 1945, King Abdullah presided over the opening of the Brotherhood's offices in Amman.

King Hussein also carefully balanced his approach to the Muslim Brotherhood and was well aware that a good relationship with the Brotherhood would be of service to him in the maintenance of stability in Jordan. In 1953, Mohammed Abdul Rahman Khalifah succeeded Abu Qurah as leader and the Brotherhood widened the basis of its legal status. It now became a recognized society permitted to preach and take part in political activity. Indeed, after King Hussein's dissolution of the political parties in Jordan in 1957, its continued existence as a charity meant it remained the only legal political organization. In the 1960s and 1970s, it served as a counterweight to the more radical groups such as Hizb al-Tahrir.

By the time new elections were held in Jordan in 1989, the Brotherhood had been able to prepare itself for political contestation and had infiltrated its members into positions of responsibility throughout the country. The result was that its members, standing as independents, won a substantial number of seats. In 1989, they won twenty-one out of eighty seats, with thirteen other Islamist candidates sympathetic to their view also elected. In 1992, a new law on political parties was promulgated, and a group of Muslim Brothers set up a new political party to fight future elections, known as the Islamic Action Front (IAF). The IAF claims it is not simply the political wing of the Muslim Brotherhood, but the degree of identification between the two was strong. From 1998 to 2006, the leader of the Muslim Brotherhood in Jordan was Abdul Majeed Thuneibat, who was seen as a moderate. In 2006, he was succeeded by Salem Falahat. Over the years, the party's share of the vote has declined, and in 2003, out of 110 seats in a reformed and expanded Jordanian parliament, the IAF took only sixteen seats—its lowest score since 1989.

At the same time, Islamic extremism has manifested itself in Jordan outside the Muslim Brotherhood. The erstwhile leader of the Islamist faction in Iraq claiming affiliation to Al-Qaida was a Jordanian, Abu Mus'ab al-Zarqawi, apparently killed in June 2006. Followers of Zarqawi are presumed to have been responsible for the bombing of hotels in Amman in November 2005 in which fifty-seven people were killed.

Abdullah II, King of Jordan (Position on Islamism)

King Abdullah II came to the throne of Jordan in February 1999 after the death of his father, King Hussein, from cancer. He is the late king's eldest son. His mother was Princess Muna, who was originally of British origin. He was educated largely in Britain and the United States. Like King Hussein he has been careful in his dealing with the Muslim Brotherhood and has tried to avoid confrontation. In a speech he gave in December 2005, shortly after the Amman hotel bombings, he stressed the pacific side of Islam. "Anyone who claims that Islam is founded on a violent ideology must answer to the innocent Muslims, men women and children, who have been killed because they did not subscribe to the corrupt ideology of a deviant minority." He referred in his speech to the official adoption of Jordan of a position expressed in what is referred to as the "Amman Message," issued by an international conference of "Ulema" summoned by Jordan in 2004. The document lays emphasis on the importance of tolerance and condemns terrorism in unambiguous terms. "Such despotic attacks on human life transgress the law of God and we denounce them." The conference that produced the Amman Message included scholars from forty-five Muslim countries. It also laid down the conditions for the issue of legitimate Fatwas, so that King Abdullah was able to say, "Muslims can now assert without doubt or hesitation that a purported Fatwa calling for the killing of innocent civilians, whether Muslim or non-Muslim, violates the most fundamental principles of Islam."

Hizb al-Tahrir (Liberation Party) (Jordan)

This movement was established in Amman in 1953 by Sheikh Taqieddine Nabhani, who died in 1977. Nabhani was a member of the Muslim Brotherhood, but was dissatisfied with what he saw as the Brotherhood's inadequate support for the Palestinians. The "Tahrir" of the movement's name was intended to be liberation of Palestine. In fact, the movement developed during the 1970s in an unusual direction. It advocated the restoration of the caliphate, whose authority should cover the entire Muslim world, and insisted that it was a religious duty upon all Muslims to work for its establishment. The movement also took the original view that the caliphate should not be identified with any specific geographical location, and that it should have no link with any state or Islamist movement. The idea was that through the process of Da'wa, a sufficient number of militants unidentified with any national or ethnic specificity would come together to found the caliphate and that even Western peoples would agree to live under its authority.

The movement gradually lost its connection with Palestine. Though its spiritual leader, Sheikh Abdelkader Zulum, lived in Beirut, it eventually based itself in London. There, it established close ties with the Muhajirun, led by the Syrian Omar Bakri, which also sought the reestablishment of the caliphate. Hizb al-Tahrir had a solid basis in Britain and had also spread in northern Europe among young Muslims of the second generation. What attracted such young people was the internationalism of the movement and the fact that the Muslims of the West were its key membership. It has since spread further afield, with members in the United States, Turkey, and Pakistan. It has a substantial presence in Uzbekistan, from where it has spread to Tajikistan and Kirghizstan. It is a separatist movement that eschews ties with other radical Islamic movements, and its rhetoric is virulent. However, it refrains from terrorist action and escaped mention in the lists of terrorist organizations set up by the Americans and the British in 2001. Nevertheless, it has attracted unfavorable attention on the campuses of British universities and is banned by many student unions because of its exclusive nature and the kind of hostile attitude it promotes.

Islamic Action Front (IAF)

The Islamic Action front, an Islamist Jordanian political party set up in 1982, represents the Muslim Brotherhood in the field of politics. However, it denies that it is simply the political wing of the Brotherhood and claims that the only link between the two is that many Muslim Brothers are members of the IAF. The IAF now says that the Brotherhood's role lies entirely in religion and charitable work and that politics is the IAF's preserve. The IAF has given Muslim Brothers greater flexibility and freedom in the political arena, since matters of policy no longer need to be referred back to the Brotherhood. However, its foundation has also been a political stratagem that has, by separating the political organization from the Brotherhood itself, been able to ensure that any political move to ban the IAF would leave the Brotherhood unscathed. The IAF has also been able to incorporate members of other Islamist political tendencies in Jordan who were not members of the Muslim Brotherhood.

The IAF's published platform includes a number of points, of which the following are central:

1. The resumption of Islamic life and the application of Islamic Shari'a in all fields.

2. The preparation of the nation for armed conflict against Zionism and imperialism.

3. The achievement of national unity, based on democracy and the Shari'a.

The organization also commits itself to political pluralism and dialogue, as well as freedom of expression. The party also wants an egalitarian economy based on Islamic principles and an end to corruption and the promotion of Islamic culture.

In 2002, the IAF's Shura Council elected as leader Hamzeh Mansour, a teacher and educationist who has been a member of the Jordanian parliament. In the elections of 2003, the party took seventeen seats in Jordan's parliament, with at least six other independent Islamists loosely in support. In February 2006, the post of secretary-general was taken by Zaki Irshaid, a laboratory technician who was a member of the Shura Council for Zarqa. In February 2007, Irshaid said that the party rejects further government restrictions on press freedom and other encroachments on what he called Jordan's democratic freedom. He added that the IAF had every right to form the next government if it achieved a parliamentary majority. He refused to accept that the influence of the United States was a factor in the region, adding that Jordan's political destiny should be decided by the country's own people.

Jaish Mohammed (Army of Mohammed)

Jaish Mohammed in Jordan is an Islamist group that came into existence in the early 1990s, in pursuit of the philosophy of Takfir wa-l-Hijra, where any compromise with non-Muslim ideas is totally rejected and all contemporary Muslim states are condemned as un-Islamic. Its originator went by the name of Khader Abu Ghoshar, an Arab veteran of the fighting in Afghanistan who was trained in the use of explosives. Abu Ghoshar had been jailed in Jordan in 1993, but was released under a general royal amnesty. In 1994, after Jordan's signature of a peace treaty with Israel, the group took a violent turn, threatening to attack Israeli and American targets. It was violently opposed to any contact with Israel. It resumed its activities in 1998, with bomb attacks on tourist sites in Jordan, by which time it was said to have links with Al-Qaida.

In December 1999, the Jordanian authorities arrested fourteen militants from Jaish Mohammed; they included twelve Jordanians, an Algerian, and an Iraqi. All had experience in Afghanistan, and the group allegedly received encouragement from Osama bin Laden. One of the arrestees, Khalil Deek, was a Jordanian citizen with a U.S. passport, who had been arrested in the Pakistani city of Peshawar. Financial backing was said to have been coming from Omar Abu Omar, a Jordanian, also known as Abu Qatada, who was resident in London. Abu Qatada had already been sentenced to death in absentia in Jordan for his involvement in other terrorist incidents linked with a group known as "Islah wa Tahaddi" (Reform and Confrontation).

According to the Jordanian authorities, planned targets for the group's attacks in 1999 had in common a non-Muslim character. These included the supposed site where St. John the Baptist baptized Jesus in the Jordan River, Mount Nebo near Madaba, Jerash (a Roman site), and Petra (the location of spectacular pre-Roman Nabatean antiquities). These are also major tourist attractions. Attacks on Christians and supposedly apostate Muslims would be characteristic of the ideas of Takfir. The Jordanian security authorities said the entire network had been dismantled, and the group's plans to carry out further attacks had been completely frustrated.

Shubeilat, Laith

Laith Shubeilat, born in 1942, is a prominent Jordanian Islamist. He is a member of a distinguished family from Tafila, in southern Jordan. His father was a senior official at the Royal Court under King Hussein and was a minister in the 1950s. He is a member of an influential tribal group. As a student of civil engineering at the American University of Beirut (AUB) he began to become interested in Islam and by his own account this distanced him from his circle of friends. He continues to contribute to the AUB as an alumnus. He went on to take a master's degree at Georgetown University in the United States. Like Sayyed Qotb, the influential Egyptian Islamist, his time in the United States convinced him that Western society is decadent and corrupt. He also takes the view that the United States and Israel are engaged in a conspiracy to weaken and humiliate the Arab world. On his return to Jordan in 1968, he joined a Sufi order, where the rituals and contact with senior members helped him to practice his faith whilst pursuing his professional life.

In 1982, he became president of the Jordanian Engineers Association and also accepted an invitation in 1982 from King Hussein to become a member of the National Consultative Council (Majlis al-Watani al-Istishari). This body helped lay the foundations for the resumption of parliamentary life in 1984, when the old parliament was recalled and special elections were held to fill vacant seats. Shubeilat was elected as an independent Islamist. In the election of 1989 he won a seat in central Amman. In 1991, at the time of the first Gulf War to expel Saddam Hussein's Iraqi invading forces from Kuwait, he agitated for arms to be given out to the Jordanian population so that they could defend themselves, if necessary, against Israeli or American attack. In parliament, he headed a judicial committee that pursued investigations into corruption until 1993 when powerful enemies arranged his own detention for an alleged coup plot. He was sentenced to twenty years imprisonment, but was pardoned by King Hussein two days later. He then left politics, disillusioned with the political process. In March 1993, he established the Association Against Zionism and Racism (AZAR), through which he expresses his political opposition to Israel.

He returned to the Engineers Association and served for two more terms, as well as ran his successful engineering firm, Shubeilat Badran associates, where his partner was Rasem Badran, a Palestinian from Ramallah. Shubeilat Badran undertook commissions all over the Middle East and particularly in Lebanon, where Shubeilat took the chance to make contact with local Islamists including the Shi'ite community. The firm was renamed Dar al-Omran in 2001. Since the peace treaty between Jordan and Israel in 1994, he has been influential in promoting the stand of the Engineers Association and other professional bodies against normalization with Israel. He was arrested in December 1995 for public criticism of King Hussein, who pardoned him in November 1996. The king, keen to encourage better relations with the Islamists, came personally to the prison and drove Shubeilat back to Amman in order to have time to discuss matters with him. In February 1998, he was again imprisoned, this time sentenced to nine months for inciting an illegal demonstration in the course of an address he gave at a mosque in Ma'an, in southern Jordan, where there had been antigovernment disturbances. He was held until October 1998.

He was undeterred and continued to speak out against the activities of the regime in Jordan. In 1999, he made it clear that while he was not opposed to the monarchy as such, he demanded a constitutional monarchy and that the king should be subject to the law. After the events of September 11, 2001, Shubeilat spoke out against the attacks. "Most Islamists are against such attacks." The Jordanian authorities continued to monitor him carefully. In February 2002, the offices of

(AZAR) were ransacked, and in November 2002 Shubeilat was detained for questioning, having been asked to travel from his home in Tafilah to meet the governor of Amman.

In 2003, however, Shubeilat came out strongly against the U.S.-led invasion of Iraq. He called Jordan's policy of backing the Americans "stupid and short-sighted." He believes King Abdullah has chosen a dangerous path. "Why doesn't he denounce the war"? He said, "doesn't he have the courage to say it is a war of aggression? The government is dragging Jordan very close to what people think is treason." He also helped draft an open letter to the king, asking him to condemn the invasion, signed by many public figures in Jordan including four former prime ministers. He also became involved in the controversy over the anti-Islamic cartoons published in Denmark in 2003, with an open letter addressed to the Danish prime minister asking Denmark not to abandon its traditions of tolerance. In 2004, in a televised debate, he argued that the state needs guidance from religion. He is now retired from full-time activity as an engineer, but consults for his former firm, leaving him more time for his public activities.

KAPLAN, METIN

Metin Kaplan, imprisoned in Turkey since 2005, is the leader of an Islamist organization based in Germany known in Turkish as Hilafet Devleti (caliphate state), which is also known as the Union of Islamic Associations and Communities. This organization, based in the German city of Köln, was estimated at its high point to have 800 to 1,300 members, mainly in Nordrhein-Westfalen, but it was believed to have wider influence in the Turkish Muslim community in Germany. The founder of the organization, originally set up in the 1980s, was Kalan's father, Cemaleddin Kaplan, whose birth name was Cemaleddin Hacaoglu. Its members were sympathizers of Milli Görüs, the Islamic group initiated by Necmettin Erbakan. Cemaleddin Kaplan came to Germany claiming asylum in 1983 after being sentenced to death in Turkey. Hilafet Devleti advocated the reestablishment of the Islamic caliphate, based in Istanbul, which until it lapsed with the fall of the Turkish Ottoman Empire theoretically ruled all Muslims. Cemaleddin Kaplan established an Islamic center in Köln, which was closed by the authorities in 1987. He also ran two publications, Teblig and Ummet.

Metin Kaplan, born in 1952, took over the leadership after his father's death in 1995. He was alleged to have advocated violent methods, sending his followers for military and ideological training in Afghanistan and was kept under constant police surveillance. He was accused of implication in the death of a rival for the leadership of the organization, Ibrahim Sofu, and in 2000 was sentenced to four years imprisonment in Germany for incitement to murder. Hilafat Devleti was banned in Germany in 2001, as a threat to the German state. Metin Kaplan's extradition to Turkey was ordered in 2004. He was flown to Istanbul by private jet and handed over to the Turkish police. At his extradition hearing it was claimed that he had sent funds to Muslim insurgents in Afghanistan, Bosnia, and Chechnya. He was accused of planning attacks on targets in Turkey in 1998. He was sentenced to life imprisonment in June 2005. His erstwhile followers in Germany are said to regard him as a martyr to their cause. German legal officials commented that Kaplan was a figure with whom Islamic extremists could identify, and Otto Schily, the interior minister, said that he should leave Germany because of his opposition to the German political system.

KARIMOV, ISLAM (UZBEKISTAN)

Islam Karimov was born in January 1938 and was brought up in a Soviet orphanage. He studied engineering and economics in Tashkent. His patron within the Uzbek communist party was Sharaf Rashidov, who led Uzbekistan in the 1970s and 1980s. Under his aegis, Karimov headed the Planning Committee from 1966 to 1983. He stood out against reform during the days of "Perestroika" in the 1980s. In 1991, he opposed the attempted coup when hard-line communists attempted to displace Gorbachev, but supported Boris Yeltsin as Gorbachev's successor.

He had become first secretary of the Communist Party in Uzbekistan in 1989, and in 1990, he was elected president of the Uzbek Soviet Socialist Republic. In 1991, he became president of independent Uzbekistan by an overwhelming margin, taking 86 percent of the votes cast to beat his opponent, Mohammed Salik of the "Democratic Party." He has been in power continuously since then, though he has rigged elections and referendums in order to do so. On January 9, 2002, he was reelected for a further five-year term by a margin of almost 92 percent against a puppet opponent, Khafiz Izhalalov, who took only 4 percent of the vote. His mandate was extended by parliament to December 2007 when the next elections were scheduled.

Karimov, as his career demonstrates, has never allowed himself to be troubled by democratic scruples. Opportunism has been his watchword. He has presented himself as a communist, a nationalist, and a Muslim according to the exigencies of the moment and has no hesitation in contradicting his former position when his interests demand. For example, when he was electioneering in 1991, Karimov was besieged by Islamist demonstrators to whom he was obliged to make a number of promises, including an undertaking to swear his oath of office on the Quran. Adolat created an Islamic parallel state in Namangan, clamping down on what they regarded as moral turpitude such as music, alcohol, and prostitution. Once Karimov was reinstalled in office, however,

he took action against the Adolat Islamists in the Ferghana Valley and elsewhere, frustrating their ambitions. Part of the leadership of Adolat went into exile in Tajikistan and Afghanistan.

Under the Soviets, Islam had been reduced to a formal remnant in Uzbekistan as elsewhere in the former Soviet Union. In 1989, there were only eighty-seven mosques in Uzbekistan (by 1997 that had increased to some 3,000). In 1989, Muslims successfully demonstrated in Tashkent to demand the resignation of a Soviet-appointed mufti, Shamsuddin Babakahan. President Karimov already regarded all Islamist movements as potential terrorists and was determined not to give way. In 1992, he banned all opposition parties. This gave rise to student unrest and in fact promoted the development of Islamism. By 1998 and 1999, there was a vigorous underground Islamist movement. A number of parties emerged. These included parties under familiar names, such as Tawba (Repentance), Hizbollah, and Hizb al-Tahrir, whose ideology of Islamic unity and purification struck a sympathetic chord.

In 1998, various groups came together to form the Islamic Movement of Uzbekistan (IMU). The IMU appears to have been behind bomb attacks on February 16, 1999, that killed sixteen people and injured a hundred. The IMU mounted other attacks in 1999 and 2000. Hizb al-Tahrir stayed out of this alliance, and in line with its philosophy of supplanting existing states in order to establish a renewed caliphate, Hizb al-Tahrir aimed to fuse the existing Central Asian state into a single Islamic entity. Some members of the IMU's armed groups appear to have been trained in Afghanistan.

In 2005, Karimov ruthlessly suppressed demonstrations in the city of Andijan, not far from Namangana. On May 13, 2005, hundreds of people died when security forces attacked a demonstration demanding the release of a number of people charged with religious extremism. Some claim the casualty toll was in the thousands. Karimov blamed what he called "extremist Islamist groups" for the events. Many tried to flee to neighboring Kyrgyzstan. Western governments censured Karimov for the ferocity of his response.

KARZAI, HAMID

The president of Afghanistan, Hamid Karzai, was born in Kandahar on December 24, 1957. He is a member of a prominent family of the Popolzai Pushtun clan, linked to the former king of Afghanistan, Zaher Shah. His grandfather and his father had each played modest a role in Afghan politics. His grandfather was deputy speaker of the Senate, and his father, Abdul Ahad Karzai, was a member of Afghanistan's national parliament in the 1960s. After schooling in Kabul, Hamid Karzai was educated in India, where he studied political science at the University of Himachal Pradesh. He graduated in 1983. Since the Soviet-backed regime was in power in Kabul, he went to Pakistan, rather than returning home.

In Quetta, he worked with Professor Sebghatullah Mujaddidi as deputy director of information in the political office of the Afghan National Liberation Front. He became the front's director of information in 1985 and joined its political department in 1987. He was involved in the process of supporting and supplying anti-Soviet Mujahidin fighters, at a time when the United States was helping to fund the anti-Soviet resistance. In 1989, he became director of the foreign relations unit in the office of the president of the interim government. He is said to have developed relations with the Pakistani intelligence services, the ISI, who later supported the Taliban. After his return to Afghanistan, he was deputy foreign minister in the Mujahidin government

of Burhanuddin Rabbani from 1992 to 1994. He resigned this position when the internal struggle between the Mujahidin groups began. In the mid-1990s, he coexisted with the Taliban, which is essentially a Pushtun movement. At this period, he was retained as a consultant for the U.S. oil company Unocal, which was interested in building a pipeline across Afghanistan to take Uzbek oil into Pakistan and to the sea. This was known as the CentGas project.

He was reportedly concerned about the extent to which the Taliban regime was controlled by the Pakistani ISI and Osama bin Laden's Arab fighters, and in the mid-1990s his relationship with the Taliban leadership became more distant. In 1996, he refused the Taliban's request that he serve as their ambassador to the United Nations, and his position in Afghanistan became untenable. In 1997, he returned to Quetta. Efforts to bring the CentGas project to fruition were reportedly abandoned in 1998. In 1999, any remaining links Hamid Karzai may have had with the Taliban were severed when his father was murdered in the street in Quetta, apparently by Taliban agents.

In 2001, soon after the events of September 11, Karzai organized a militia to fight the Taliban. In October 2001, after the start of the U.S. bombing of Taliban targets, he led his men into Afghanistan, but had to be rescued by American helicopter. The boldness of his initiative impressed the Americans, and on December 22, 2001, at a meeting of distinguished Afghan exiles in the German city of Bonn, he was sworn in, with backing from the United States, as head of a provisional administration in Afghanistan. On June 19, 2002, at a Loya Jirga (grand gathering) of the Afghan notability, he was elected president of the Afghan Transitional Authority, with the agreement of the former king Zaher. In the election of October 9, 2004, he became Afghanistan's first post-Taliban elected president. At a speech at the United

Nations General Assembly on September 20, 2006, he drew attention to the resurgence of Taliban attacks in Afghanistan. Taliban operations were by this time causing much concern to the NATO peacekeeping force in the country. President Karzai said that those who were concerned about Islamist terrorism should look to what he described as the international networks that offer support and backing to terrorists.

KASHMIR

Kashmir is a zone of crisis, where all the regional powers have their own conflicting agendas. It has become the principal regional theater for operations by the armed Islamic movements. Historically, the state, known as Jammu and Kashmir, was a princely state in the northwest of India, where, prior to partition, a Hindu sovereign reigned with the support of a Hindu administration over a state whose population was two-thirds Muslim. The modern dispute over the status of Indian Kashmir began after the independence of Pakistan in 1947, when Pakistan laid claim to the whole of Kashmir. The ruler of Jammu and Kashmir, Maharajah Hari Singh, himself a Hindu, hesitated between whether to join India or Pakistan. In the autumn of 1947, India offered him the independence of Kashmir under Indian protection and Indian troops moved in to help the ruler repel Pakistani incursions.

After some months of instability, an agreement was reached under the auspices of the United Nations, which allocated two-thirds of the territory provisionally to India, something less than a third to Pakistan, and a narrow strip to China. The border between the Indian- and Pakistani administered sectors is known as the Line of Control. A referendum to be held by India, which was intended to determine the future of the territory, was never held, in spite of reiterated demands on the part of the Muslim population. In 1965, there was a further armed clash when a trivial incident between an Indian and a Pakistani patrol degenerated into outright fighting. In 1971, there were further increases of tension on the frontier between India and Pakistan when India backed the Bengali separatists in Pakistan's eastern wing, inflicting a severe military defeat on the Pakistani forces, which resulted in the independence of Bangladesh.

The population of Kashmir was most recently estimated, in 1999, at some 13 million. Of these, more than 4 million live in the part of Kashmir administered by Pakistan and around 9 million in the Indian-administered remainder of the old state of Jammu and Kashmir. The population of Pakistani Kashmir is almost entirely Muslim. The population of Indian-administered Jammu and Kashmir is 64 percent Muslim: around 6 million people. Thirty-three percent are Hindus and 3 percent are Buddhists and other religions (Sikhs and Christians). Eighty-five percent of these Muslims live in the part of Jammu and Kashmir known as the Kashmir Valley, which has just over half the population and a population that is over 90 percent Muslim. Of these 6 million Muslims, most are Sunni Muslims, but up to a million are Shi'ites. The situation of the Muslims in India is ambiguous. In principle, the Indian state is secular and all citizens are equal. In practice, the history of intercommunal relations in India has been marked by frequent conflict. In addition, Muslim society is rigidly stratified and subject to the caste system characteristic of Hindu society.

The appearance of armed movements in Kashmir goes back to the war of 1965. This was when the National Liberation Front made its first appearance, apparently with the connivance of the Pakistani authorities. However, it was not until the 1970s that there appeared the first organization that had genuine popular support and which was therefore easily able to assemble a substantial number of combatants. One of its principal founders was Amanullah Khan, a former member of the security forces, who had spent some time in Britain. The Jammu and Kashmir Liberation Front (JKLF) officially came into existence in 1977. It has not been regarded as an Islamist movement, thought many of its activists and organizers adopt ideological and religious positions that could be described as Islamist. The ultimate objective of the JKLF was the reunification of Kashmir. Its armed wing, the Kashmir Liberation Army (KLA), undertook frequent terrorist actions, especially in 1988–1999, during a particularly savage campaign.

Following the hanging of its leader, Maqbool Butt, Javed Ahmed Mir became the leader of the organization on the Indian side. The movement was concerned to underline its independence from Pakistan, and its position on Azad Kashmir (the Pakistani-held portion of Kashmir) and its potential reunification with Indian Kashmir angered the government in Islamabad. For this reason, it did not receive substantial backing from the Pakistani intelligence services (ISI) until some years after its establishment. In response to repeated attacks by the JKLF, as well as to the activities of Sikh separatists and Maoist movements in West Bengal, India brought in a significant battery of emergency legislation. This included the National Security Act, the Jammu and Kashmir Public Safety Act, and the Terrorist and Disruptive Activities Act.

In 1994, the JKLF opened talks with the government and declared a unilateral ceasefire. The organization split into two: that led by Yassin Malik, who had succeeded Javed Ahmed Mir, and that led by Amanullah Khan, who was now based in Azad Kashmir. The latter continued to carry out sporadic terrorist acts when it had the opportunity to enter Indian territory. The Indian authorities also faced terrorism from other revolutionary movements claiming to be inspired by Islamism. The first such small group, Al Badr, made its appearance in 1971, though it was relatively ineffectual. Numerous other groups were set up by former JKLF activists who opposed the establishment of an independent Kashmir and sought unification with Pakistan. The group that seems so far to have been able to muster the most manpower and resources appears to be the Hizb ul-Mujahidin, set up in 1989 by Ahsan Dar, a former schoolteacher. This organization was established simultaneously in both Pakistan and India and has political and operational links with the Jamiat Ulema Islam. With some 1,500 fighters, the group has clashed not only with the various security forces, but also with Kashmiri paramilitary groups financed by the Indian authorities. There are persistent tensions within this group between two factions, one based in Pakistan and financed by the ISI and another that seeks greater independence from Islamabad.

Pakistan's security forces support Islamists in Kashmir to further their own regional interests. Continuing the practice of his predecessors, Pakistan's President Pervez Musharraf, a former artillery general, also pays lip service to the idea of Jihad in Kashmir. The Pakistani National Pact makes the claim to Kashmir part of its political platform. Any deviation from this policy, a part of Pakistan's founding mythology, to which Pakistan has adhered since its foundation, would lead to a revolt. On October 1, 2001, the group known as Jaish-i-Mohammed, which had close ties to the ISI, claimed responsibility for a car bomb attack on the provincial parliament building in Srinagar, Kashmir's summer capital, in which thirty-four people were killed. Later in October, responsibility for bomb explosions in New Delhi was claimed by Kashmiri militants. On December 13, 2001, an attack on the parliament building in the Indian capital New Delhi was blamed on Jaish-i-Mohammed. The attack on the parliament caused a number of casualties, but failed in its apparent objective of the destruction of the parliament buildings. It seemed to be linked to an escalation of Muslim militancy in Kashmir and sparked a sharp increase of tension between India and Pakistan, both nuclear powers.

President Musharraf, though unable to take effective action, could not ignore the fact that Pakistan's relations with India and the United States were endangered by extremist movements such as these, operating in Kashmir, which had links with the Pakistani military. Subsequently, the deployment of medium-range nuclear missiles and the mobilization of troops on the frontiers, accompanied by bellicose proclamations on both sides, brought with them the threat of a high-level conflict. In recent years, both India and Pakistan have made efforts to calm the frontier tension between the two countries, but the problem of Kashmir remains unresolved.

By 2003, energetic diplomacy between India and Pakistan appears to have resulted in a new determination to resolve the Kashmir conflict at the level of relations between the two neighboring countries. Within Kashmir, however, Islamist militants seemed determined to keep up the tension. In October 2003, militants attacked the residence of the chief minister of Indian Kashmir, Mohammed Sayeed. Despite this, a ceasefire and confidence-building measures were agreed between the two countries. Low-level violence has continued in Kashmir. However, the earthquake of October 8, 2005, with its disastrous consequences for Kashmir, had led to cooperation between India and Kashmir and seemed to be likely to make a peaceful resolution of the Kashmir conflict more likely. On October 29, 2005, the Pakistani group Lashkar-i-Tayba, which has been especially active in Kashmir, seems to have been responsible for bombings that killed fifty-nine people in the Indian capital.

The evident aim was to continue to sour the atmosphere and prevent further diplomatic progress.

KHALIFA, MUHAMMAD JAMAL

Muhammad Jamal Khalifa, who was found dead in Madagascar on January 31, 2007, was typical of the wealthy Saudi private citizens who have supported both Islamic NGOs and have been close to Jihadist activity. He was born in 1958 and met Osama bin Laden when both were students in Jeddah. In 1985, he went to Afghanistan to involve himself in the struggle against the Soviets there. He married one of bin Laden's sisters. However, his friendship with bin Laden is supposed to have ended, reputedly over bin Laden's decision to establish Al-Qaida and promote global Jihad instead of confining himself to the Afghan conflict.

He then transferred his activities to the Philippines, where he contributed to and dispensed funds for Islamic charitable activity, funding the construction of schools and mosques. Some who have monitored his activity, however, believe he supports terrorist organizations such as the Abu Sayyaf group. He established a series of what were allegedly front organizations for the support of terror groups called the Benevolence International Corporation, the Islamic Benevolence Committee, and the Benevolence Foundation. Whilst in the Philippines he married Jamila Yabo, who was a sister of a Filipino Islamist. He set up a number of locally based businesses, which were also supposed by intelligence agents to be fronts for the transfer of money. He also ran an international NGO himself in the Philippines, known as the International Relations and Information Center.

On December 14, 1994, Khalifa was arrested in California on suspicion of involvement in the abortive 1993 plot to attack the World Trade Center. He was found to be in possession of terrorist literature and had contact numbers for known terrorists. Meanwhile, he was given a death sentence in absentia in Jordan for allegedly supporting terrorist activity. On May 5, he was deported to Jordan, but was acquitted by the Jordanian courts. After this, he appears to have returned to legitimate business activities in Saudi Arabia, where he was briefly arrested after the events of September 11, 2001. The Saudi authorities quickly released him, but imposed a travel ban that hampered his activities. He was also still monitored by U.S. intelligence agencies. When the Saudi travel ban was lifted, he decided to visit Madagascar to investigate a precious-stones mine he owned, which was being worked by squatters. It was there that Khalifa met his death.

KHATTAB, EMIR IBN (CHECHNYA)

The so-called Commander Khattab, whose birth name was Samir Saleh Abdullah al-Suwailem, played a marginal but high-profile role in the Chechen conflict. Born in 1969, he was of Saudi origin. He was apparently born in the northern Saudi town of Arar, close to the Jordanian frontier, though there is some confusion about his origins to which he seems deliberately to have contributed. He allowed it to be supposed that his mother was of Central Asian origin and he maintained a level of vagueness about whether he was in fact born in Jordan. He is said to have accepted the nickname Ibn Khattab because of his admiration for the Caliph Umar, the second leader of the Islamic community after the death of the Prophet Muhammad, whose full name was Umar ibn Al-Khattab. He was murdered in 2002 by the Russian Federal Security Service, which arranged for him to open a letter steeped in poison.

He was an intelligent school student and took an early interest in Islamic matters. He went to the war in Afghanistan in 1987, when he was still only seventeen years of age. Though his father attempted to persuade him to come home to the family home in Al-Khobar, he continued to fight in various conflicts in Central Asia, returning for visits only twice before his death. In 1992, he went to Azerbaijan as a Chechen volunteer to fight in Nagorny Karabakh. From 1993 to 1995, he was with Islamist groups in Tajikistan. He was prompted to go to Chechnya by TV reports that showed groups of Chechen fighters, which inspired him to go there to join the Jihad in 1995. He was evidently able to tap sources of finance in Saudi Arabia, which gave him a degree of leverage unavailable to the ordinary Arab combatants who came to join the Chechen struggle. He gained the confidence of the Chechen rebel leader Shamil Basayev. Over the years, he was wounded four times, including once by a grenade that blew off part of his hand.

His reputation in Russia, where he was regarded as a major adversary and a destabilizing factor in Chechnya, dated from his ambush of a Russian unit in the southern Chechen mountains, an engagement in which official Russian sources concede that at least fifty-three Russians died. When the First Chechen War ended, with the signing of the Khasayvurt Treaty in 1996, Khattab became a warlord in his own right and set up the "Islamic Regiment," made up of Arab and other foreign fighters. He established military training camps and accepted volunteers from all over the region. On December 22, 1997, despite the peace treaty, his men raided a Russian base. In 1998, he and Basayev set up the so-called Islamic Peacekeeping Army, which effectively started the Second Chechen War in 1999. Khattab hurled himself into conflict with the Russians wherever the opportunity presented itself until his death. The Russian public greeted his disappearance with some relief. His successor as the conduit for Saudi funds to the Chechen conflict was a figure known by the name of Amir Abu al-Walid, also reported to have been killed in 2004.

As he was not a Chechen, he was unable to take the lead in the conflict on the ground and came under the authority of Basayev. The facts demonstrate that he actually enjoyed full autonomy, on a level with Basayev himself. His popularity among the Chechen fighters, who called him "The Black Arab," lay in the training he offered. From him, they learned guerrilla techniques and, in particular, how to attack the Russian tanks. His style was to mount spectacular operations, both inside Chechnya and in neighboring countries.

KENYA

At least 10 percent of Kenya's population of over 34 million people are Muslims. The Muslim population is not a homogenous community. The main body is in coastal Kenya, where the Muslims comprise half the population. These are for the most part Swahili speakers with an admixture of ethnic Arabs. Many of the small Arab population are the descendants of merchants and seafarers from the Arabian Peninsula, many originally from Oman, who are known as the "old" Arabs. There are also a certain number of Persian merchant families. Together with Shi'ite traders from Lebanon these introduce a Shi'ite element. Other Muslims are scattered around the country, including a good number in the capital Nairobi. There are also Muslim migrants from the Indian subcontinent who arrived during the colonial period as merchants, who have refrained on the whole from any involvement with politics, though the Tablighi Jamaat movement is active. Finally, there is a small Somali contingent in the north of the country and a number of Muslim refugees.

Sufi orders have been widely prevalent, including the Qadiriya and, among the Arabs, the Ibadiya (an order characteristically linked with Oman). For the most part, the Muslim consists of orthodox Sunnis of the Shafi'i school, with groups of Hanafis, the mainstream Muslim persuasion of the Arab world and the Indian subcontinent. The various Shi'ite groups are also represented, though most of the Shi'ites are orthodox "twelvers" of the Ja'afari school. Finally, there is a minority of adherents of the Ahmadiya, who are regarded as heretical by most Muslims and have been condemned as apostates by some authorities, who regard them as "Kafirun" (unbelievers). The Ahmadis have translated the Quran into Swahili, which is in itself a dubious enterprise in the eyes of many Muslims since the Quran is meant to exist only in the shape of the Arabic text revealed to the Prophet Muhammad.

Since 1968, the Kenyan government has made attempts to organize the Muslim community. A body called the National Union of Kenya Muslims (NUKEM) was set up in 1968. In 1973, this was superseded by another government-sponsored body, the Supreme Council of Kenyan Muslims (SUPKEM). By 1996, this organization had 50 branches and 150 affiliated Muslim organizations. Other organizations have included the Muslim Consultative Council, the Association for Reform in Islam, and various Muslim students and welfare associations. However, the Muslims have been frustrated by the constitutional ban on a Muslim political party. In 1992, a formation calling itself the Islamic Party of Kenya (IPK) was set up in 1992, but was not allowed to play a political role, though it did succeed in calling attention to Muslim grievances. Under its leader Sheikh Khaled Balala, it took a radical turn. The government's response was to promote an alternative grouping known as the United Muslims of Africa (UMA) under the leadership of Rashid Sajjad, a rich Shi'ite businessman who was a former director of the Kenya Ports Authority and close to the government. Meanwhile, the Saudi religious NGOs and private Saudi beneficence have overseen the increasing construction of mosques and the inauguration of Islamic schools, which some believe has led to increasing radicalism.

There have been a number of disturbances in Kenya that have originated with the Muslim population. In 1992, the IPK was responsible for unrest in Mombasa after a number if its militants and several imams were arrested. For a year after this, the supporters of the IPK clashed with the UMA. Strikes and arson attacks continued despite the efforts of the government-controlled SUPKEM to mediate. In 1994, there were disturbances of an Islamist nature in various parts of coastal Kenya. These were conjecture to have been inspired by supporters of the Tabligh movement. Matters took a more serious turn in 1997, when there was extensive violence in the coastal region of Kenya. In a variety of incidents, at least one hundred people are said to have been killed. Both government militias and semi-criminal groups appear to have been involved in a period of communal strife whose complexities are difficult fully to understand.

In 1998, there was a devastating bomb attack on the U.S. Embassy in Nairobi simultaneously with a similar attack in Tanzania. Responsibility was claimed by a hitherto unheard of group calling itself the Islamic Liberation Army of the People of Kenya (ILAPK). It has been assumed that there were links between this organization and Osama bin Laden's Al-Qaida, which may have helped to plan and finance the attack. The fact that it was coordinated with the Tanzanian attacks certainly argues for some outside influence. This may be said to be evidence that radicalization in Kenya has reached a pitch where those among Kenya's Islamists who are inclined to violent gestures are capable of giving substantial support to international terrorism. Islamists are thought to base themselves in the north of the country among the Somali population, close to the insecure border with Somalia. In the wake of the 1998 action, the government of President Moi clamped down on a wide spread of Islamic organizations, many of them ostensibly charitable. Kenya is not widely regarded as a country where radicalism has swept up the majority of the Muslim population, but it is seen as a place where extremist groups can operate. With a long coastline and a diverse population, Kenya is difficult to secure.

In December 2001, an agreement was signed in Nairobi between the British Defense Minister Geoff Hoon and President Moi. The Kenyan leader agreed that Kenya would serve as a base for actions against Islamist radicals in Somalia when necessary. In recompense, Britain and the United States were to increase their aid to Kenya. In 2002, two attacks were launched against targets in the leisure industry in Kenya that were seen as linked to Israel. Such attacks are, nevertheless, not thought to represent the opinions or preferences of the majority of Kenya's Muslims. Kenya has received American support in upgrading its security and surveillance services. This has no doubt accounted for the willing complicity of Kenya in the action against the Somali Union of Islamic Courts in December 2006 and January 2007.

KHOMEINI, AYATOLLAH RUHOLLAH

Ruhollah Khomeini, later to be the spiritual leader of Iran and the originator of Iran's Islamic Revolution, was born in 1902 in the small town of Khomein in central Iran. He was the son of Ayatollah Seyyed Mostafa, whose father was Seyyed Ahmad Musavi Hindi, who was born in Kintur, near Lucknow in India. Ruhollah Khomeini is therefore a Musavi Seyyed, descended from the Prophet through the seventh Imam of the Shi'ite dynasty, Musa al-Kazem. Seyyed Ahmad had left India in 1830 to perform a pilgrimage to the Shi'ite holy city of Najaf in Iraq and never returned to the subcontinent. He settled instead in Persia, where he bought a substantial house and grounds in Khomein. He later purchased more land in and around Khomein. The property remained in the family up to modern times.

Ruhollah Khomeini's father was killed in a mysterious shooting incident just a year after his birth. Looked after by relatives, he began his theological studies at the age of seventeen in nearby Arak with Ayatollah Hajj Sheikh Abdolkarim Ha'eri, a distinguished graduate of the school of theological studies in Najaf. In 1922, Khomeini went to the holy city of Qom to continue his studies with Ha'eri, who had transferred there and was setting up a prestigious school. Khomeini also studied "Fiqh"—effectively Islamic case law, enabling the student to reach judgments in actual situations of no matter what kind—with Ayatollah Ali Yasrebi-Kashani. By 1929, Khomeini had begun to teach on his own account, and by 1936, he had achieved from his peers his license to practice "Ijtihad," the independent interpretation of the fundamentals of Islam, which entitled him to be known as Hojateleslam.

By World War II, Khomeini was already beginning to cross over from theology into politics. In 1943, he published anonymously a short book entitled *Kash al-Asrar* (The Revelation of Secrets) in which he opposed the monarchical principal and condemned secularism. This was the first indication of his ideas on the theory of Vilayet-i Faqih—the primacy of the theologian and Islamic jurist within Muslim society—which would

underlie the constitution of the Islamic Republic. In the 1950s, he became an adviser to the recognized senior Grand Ayatollah Borujerdi, who died in 1961. No longer obliged to defer to Borujerdi, Khomeini believed the moment had come to step boldly out into the political arena.

In 1962, he spoke out against the shah's "White Revolution," which was a package of reformist measures intended by the shah to combat unrest. In particular, he opposed agrarian reform—the clergy were great landowners—and the participation of women in political life. The Iranian secret police, known as SAVAK, clamped down on all political and religious opposition, and Khomeini was imprisoned for some months. On June 3, 1963, Khomeini delivered a much-anticipated sermon that attacked the shah to a vast crowd. The result was that he was arrested. At this stage, Ayatollah Shariatmadari proposed that he should be elevated to the rank of ayatollah, to ensure his personal safety. He was held under house arrest until early 1964. He continued his campaign against the shah, however, and after another inflammatory sermon in October 1964 he was sent into exile.

He went first to Turkey, where he was kept under house arrest for a year in Bursa, but then moved on to the Iraqi Shi'ite shrine at Najaf, where he set up his own seminary. This soon made its mark in Iran and elsewhere, especially while the ban on political party activity in Iran left the Shi'ite clergy as the only channel through which the grievances of the Iranian people could be expressed. His influence grew to the point where larger and larger demonstrations were held in his support in Iran. Under pressure from the Iranian authorities, Iraq asked him to leave the country. In October 1978, he went to France, where he set up residence at Neauphle-le-Château, in the outskirts of Paris.

Political pressure on the shah in Iran, meanwhile, mounted to the point where he felt that he could no longer sustain his regime. The people were against him and he seemed to have no power base left to which he could turn. His international allies were also deserting him. On February 1, 1979, after the shah's precipitate departure on January 16, Khomeini returned to the country. He was welcomed by 3 million people in the streets of Teheran. He found himself at the head of a very broad political coalition of those who had struggled to overthrow the imperial regime. Having to deal with the nonreligious parties and the Tudeh communist party, he imposed his own ideas and later in 1979 he installed a new constitution that embodied the concept of "Velayet-i Faqih," which he had first begun to develop so many years before. Meanwhile the U.S. hostage crisis, the detention of U.S. diplomats inside their own embassy by so-called Revolutionary Guards, and the wave of anti-American feeling it provoked also rallied the nation behind him.

The war unleashed on Iran by the Iraqi attack of September 22, 1980, rallied all factions in Iran behind Ayatollah Khomeini and gave him the opportunity to eliminate his unwanted allies and to consolidate his undisputed hold on power. After the end of the war in 1988, Iran's economic and political problems came once more to the fore, but did not loosen the political grip of his new order. Shortly before his death, he provoked a crisis between Iran and the West when he pronounced a Fatwa concerning the British writer Salman Rushdie in which he ruled that it was legal to kill Rushdie because of the disrespect for the Prophet Muhammad in his book *The Satanic Verses*. The crisis persisted after Khomeini's departure and became an ongoing thorn in the flesh of relations between Iran and the West. In May 1989, Khomeini was hospitalized and died on June 3 that year. Khomeini's career has had a profound effect on contemporary life, since he not only created an entirely novel revolutionary theocracy, but also gave Muslim states an example to follow and an alternative to the abandoned concept of nonalignment in international politics.

KOSOVO

Kosovo (Kosovo and Metohija, to give it its full name), with its capital Pristina, has been since the dismemberment of the former Yugoslavia an autonomous province of the Republic of Serbia. By 2007, its future status was in the hands of an international process supervised by the United Nations. It has some 2 million inhabitants in a mere 11,000 square kilometers, bordering Serbia, Macedonia, Montenegro, and Albania. Over 80 percent of its inhabitants are ethnic Albanians. In terms of the successor states of the former Yugoslavia, its case is very different from that of Bosnia-Herzegovina. The Muslim Bosnians speak Serbo-Croat and differ from their Serb neighbors only in their religion. Kosovo differ from the Serbs in its language, its culture, and its social traditions. The Albanian national identity verges on dominance over the Muslim religious identity. The Albanian Muslim community in Kosovo is represented by a body known as the Islamic Community of Kosovo (BIK) (Bashkësia Islame e Kosovës), headed by the mufti of Kosovo.

Within the former Yugoslavia, the use of the Albanian language in education, and the creation of the University of Pristina in 1970, intensified the ambition of the Kosovars to see Kosovo accorded the status of a constituent republic within the federal state. However, the Yugoslav constitution promulgated in 1974 accorded it only a substantial measure of autonomy. The Kosovars had been keen to see their national identity reinforced, rather than their religion, where they already enjoyed the status of Muslim "nationality." After the death of Marshal

Tito in 1980, dialog between the Kosovars and the Yugoslav state, in any case, came to an end. Riots broke out in 1981 and 1982 in Pristina and the Serb population flooded out of Kosovo. Some 30,000 left in the space of only a few years. The conclusion seemed to be that it was not Albanian nationalism alone that was the driving force behind an increasingly radicalized activism. Religious considerations also seemed to have played their part.

The rise to power of Slobodan Milosevic in Belgrade stiffened the attitude of Yugoslavia toward the disturbances in Kosovo. On October 20, 1988, the Serbs mounted a demonstration against the progressive "Albanization" of Kosovo at Krovo Polje—the "Field of Blackbirds"—the site where Ottoman Turkish troops vanquished a Serb army on June 28, 1389. This incident, six hundred years in the past, is enormously important for the Serbs, for whom the defeat and the defiance it caused constitute a defining element of Serb national feeling. This marked the beginning of a sterner Serbian position on Kosovo and its pretensions to independence.

On June 26, 1990, Kosovo's local institutions were suspended by the federal government. The response of the Kosovo regional parliament was to declare Kosovo's independence. Kosovo's parliament was dissolved on July 5 as the result of a referendum that ratified Milosevic's constitutional changes. Belgrade embarked on a policy of compulsory "Serbianization" of Kosovo, covering the public services, education, and the media. In September 1991, an unofficial referendum organized by the Kosovar resistance, despite widespread harassment by the Serbian force, gave a 98 percent majority for the establishment of an independent Republic of Kosovo. On May 24, 1992, after a period of confusion, Ibrahim Rugova, the founder of the Democratic League for Kosovo, was elected president of the country in

elections that were not recognized by the federal state. At this stage, two interpretations of the events were possible. In the view of Ibrahim Rugova and of a contingent of Kosovar intellectuals, the struggle was for independence. However, for the Islamists, it was clear that what was taking place was a religious confrontation. The Albanian Muslim community in Kosovo established a body to be entitled "The Islamic Community in Kosovo" (KBI). At that date there were 607 mosques.

The Dayton conference in December 1995 on the future relations between the state of the former Yugoslavia did not examine the claims of Kosovo. This intensified Kosovar radicalism, with the effect that attacks against the Serbs increased in number and the Kosovo Liberation Army (UCK) made no secret of its activities. A tough Serb reaction halted the UCK's operations in the summer of 1998, but the use of disproportional violence drew the international community into the conflict. In October 1998, NATO put in place an observer mission supervised by the OSCE (Organization for the Security and Cooperation in Europe). Violence, nevertheless, flared up again, and talks held in Rambouillet and Paris in February and March 1999 were inconclusive. On March 24, NATO began a bombing campaign against the Serbs that lasted until June 3. Despite the war, the Islamists were able to continue their exploitation and to expand their constituency. The Rifa'iya religious brotherhood continued to be well represented. The Muslim press and Muslim publishing also expanded during the conflict.

Various religious groups made a bid to challenge the dominance of the BIK (Islamic Community of Kosovo) over religious affairs. However there were relatively few Wahhabi sympathizers and Salafis and only a very small group of Shi'ites. Some pan-Islamic movements, including Bosnian elements, had recently attempted to operate in Kosovo, through the agency of young Ulema trained in Sarajevo, but had little influence. Muslim volunteers, who came to fight in Kosovo—at little personal risk, it must be said—were absorbed into the ranks of the UCK. Islamist NGOs also operated, though were unable to wield much influence thanks to the Western presence. Nonetheless, they attracted a good deal of suspicion. On April 3, 2000, KFOR (the Kosovo intervention force) seized the offices of a Saudi NGO, the Saudi Joint Relief Committee (SJRC), as certain members of its staff were suspected of planning terrorist attacks. Two former officials of the SJRC, Wa'el Hamza Juleidan (the former director) and Mohammed Sadiq bin Kazem, were later identified by Western intelligence services as "associated" with Osama bin Laden. Wa'el Juleidan was accused of assisting bin Laden in the transfer of personnel and funds to and from the Balkans.

In reality, NATO's dominant position in the conflict obstructed the Kosovars themselves from taking either the military or the political initiative. This enabled traditional Islam in Kosovo, as represented by the BIK, to be the benchmark for Kosovo's less than dominant Islamic identity. By 2002, two problems remained unsolved. The first problem was the clash between two political objectives: on the one hand, the United Nations' plan to enable the Serbs of Kosovo to return to their homes and, on the other hand, the Kosovar ambition to achieve independence. The second problem was the insistence of the Islamic countries on coming to the aid of their brothers in religion, despite the absence of Islamic movements on the ground, and in the face of the strength of Albanian nationalism. Preachers from Egypt and the Gulf were already making their appearance in small numbers by this time.

The United Nations, however, came to realize that Kosovo's desire for independ-ence was too strong to ignore. By 2005, the UN was planning talks on Kosovo's status. Secretary General Kofi Annan entrusted the task of mediating between the Serbs and the Kosovars to an experienced intermediary, the former Finnish foreign minister Martti Ahtisaari, who had already been instrumental in brokering the cease-fire between NATO and Serbia in 1999. By 2007, Mr. Ahtisaari had produced a plan that not only did not explicitly mention Kosovar independence, but also stopped short of referring to Ser-bian sovereignty. The level of autonomy in the plans to be exercised under some outside supervision seemed likely to disappoint Kos-ovar nationalists, but would also be seen as undesirable by the Serbs. The Islamists may recognize a Kosovo free from Serb domina-tion as a field within which they can consoli-date a more radical Islam.

KURDISTAN

The Islamist movement in Iraqi Kurdistan has a complex history. It is composed of Sunni Muslims, and the principal group was originally the Islamic Movement of Kurdis-tan, whose ideology was modeled on that of the Muslim Brotherhood. The IMK was set up in 1987 by Sheikh Uthman Abdul Aziz on the basis of various preexisting movements and developed an armed militia several hundred strong. Its base was in Halabjah, the town attacked by chemical weapons by Saddam Hussein during the Anfal campaign in 1988. It was a broad movement including a number of tendencies and had pragmatic links both with Iran and the secular Kurd-ish movements. After splits and reunions it reformed with the same name in 2001. Another significant movement is the Kurdis-tan Islamic Union, known as Yekgirtu, led by Salahadin Mohammed Bahaedin. This was established in 1994. The major Kurdish Islamic movements have found it difficult to coexist with Kurdistan's principal secular parties, Massoud Barzani's KDP and Jalal Talabani's PUK.

There are also smaller Islamist groups. The Kurdistan Islamic group, led by Maulana Ali Bapir, is based in the region of Soran, in the border territory close to Iran. It has had armed confrontations with the KDP, one of the two main Kurdish secular parties. Its operational leader is Abdullah Al-Shafi. It merged in 1999 with a number of other small groups such as Islamic Jihad, the Peshmerga of Soran, and Al-Tawhid. In 2001, these small groups merged under the name Jund al-Islam (Soldiers of Islam). They took a puritanical stance and carried out attacks on women's hair salons and alcoholic liquor shops. Notoriously, it carried out the assassination in 2001 of a senior KDP figure of Assyrian Christian origin, FranÁois Hariri. The Kurdish authorities of the KDP and the PUK announced that Jund al-Islam was linked to Al-Qaida. It merged with a splinter group from the IMK in 2001 to form Ansar al-Islam (Companions of Islam). In November 2001, there was fighting between the Jund and the PUK. The accusations that the organization had links with Al-Qaida continued, as it included a number of figures such as Maulana Krekar who had been to Afghanistan. There seems no reason to suppose that Al-Qaida directs the operations of the Kurdish Islamists, but on an individual level many Islamists in Kurdistan have connections with Afghanistan and Al-Qaida figures.

In March 2003, after the beginning of the U.S.-led invasion of Iraq, U.S. bombers attacked Ansar al-Islam positions in northeast Iraq. The American administration appeared to believe they might have some kind of connection with Saddam Hussein's regime. In August 2003, a number of Islamic groups merged into a new formation, Ansar al-Sunna. As with its predecessors, this was a strict Sunni group, of Salafi inclination, opposed to the American-led occupation of Iraq. Its goal is to conduct Jihad against what it regards as a collaborationist Iraqi government that is in fact implementing an American political agenda. The group has claimed responsibility for a number of attacks against foreign targets and PUK targets. It describes Iraq's Kurdish president, Jalal Talabani, as a traitor.

KUWAIT

The Kuwaiti branch of the Muslim Brotherhood was formed in 1952 as the "Islamic Guidance Society," but was soon suppressed. It reemerged after Kuwait's independence in 1961 under the name "Social Reform Society." It has always played a significant part in Kuwaiti politics. In the July 2003 elections, the Islamic group in parliament held twenty-one of the fifty elected seats. This number reduced to seventeen in the elections of June 2006. The Islamic Constitutional Movement is a group linked to the Muslim Brotherhood in parliament, and there are at least two separate Salafi groups.

Political parties were proscribed in the November 1962 constitution in Kuwait, following its independence from British tutelage in 1961. Members of the country's National Assembly were obliged to sit as independents. However, groups and tendencies soon formed of which the Islamic factions were prominent. It should be stressed that Kuwait is not a democracy. It is ruled by the emir, to whom the prime minister is responsible. Until recently, it was customary for the crown prince to be prime minister, but in 2003 the post was given to a nephew of the emir. The key cabinet posts are also customarily taken by members of the ruling family. However, the assembly can propose legislation and is empowered to subject government policy to scrutiny. Parliament was suspended in 1976 and restored in 1980.

Palriament was again suspended in 1986 and was once more restored in 1990 and, after the Gulf War and the departure of the invading Iraqi forces from Kuwait, new elections were held in 1992. Parliament was again briefly suspended in 1999.

Individual members of the Muslim Brotherhood held a few seats in the National Assembly for the start, and in 1976 a Muslim Brotherhood sympathizer accepted a post in the cabinet appointed by the emir during parliament's suspension. The Social Reform Society as a group held aloof from politics, but concentrated on charitable activities and educational ventures. In 1981, Brotherhood candidates again won parliamentary sets. In 1990, however, with the Iraqi occupation of Kuwait, a new phase began. The Brotherhood in Kuwait repudiated the position taken by the international Muslim Brotherhood of reaching an accommodation with Iraq and set about organizing resistance inside Kuwait. Younger activists that had remained in Kuwait during the invasion took the leadership. In 1991, with the restoration of the status quo in Kuwait, the Islamic Constitutional Movement (ICM) ("Al-Haraka al-Islamiya al-Dusturiya") was formed. Links were not restored with the international Muslim Brotherhood until 1998. As a political movement, the ICM advocated the introduction of Shari'a law and a generally conservative agenda. In 1999, they were instrumental in the parliamentary confrontation with the monarchy over women's voting rights. Leading members of the ICM are Mubarak al-Duwaila and Ismail Khidr al-Shati. The group's spokesman is Mohammed Abdel Alim.

In 2006, the ICM played a prominent part in the controversy over the succession to the Kuwaiti monarchy. After the death on January 15, 2006, of the old emir, Jaber Al Ahmed Al Sabah, his successor was Saad Al Abdullah Al Sabah. The Emir Saad, who was seventy-six and seriously ill, was apparently not up to the job, but refused to abdicate. Parliament ousted him at the request of the cabinet—as it had the constitutional power to do—in favor of his cousin Sheikh Sabah Al Ahmad Al Sabah who had been prime minister and de facto ruler of Kuwait for some years. Sheikh Sabah dissolved parliament early in May 2006 in order to hold early elections. Kuwait politics continues to display the paradox of confrontation between a reforming monarchy and a more conservative parliament where the attitude is colored by its Islamist members.

There have recently been two visible Salafi groups in Kuwait. One of these, the "Popular Islamic Assembly" (PIA) ("Al-Tajammu al-Islami al-Shaabi"), came under American scrutiny in 2001 as a possible financial backer of terrorism, even though it was represented by two members of parliament. The PIA's stated goal is the installation of the Shari'a and the re-Islamization of Kuwait. Leading figures of this group include Khaled Sultan, the leader of its small parliamentary group. Fahd al-Khanna, Ahmad Baqir, and Mafraj Nihad al-Mitari are also attached to this formation. An Egyptian cleric resident in Kuwait, Abdel Rahman Abdul Khaleq, is also attached to the PIA. The other group is the Scientific Salafi Movement (SSM) ("Al-Haraka al-Salafiya al-Ilmiya"). The members of this latter group are predominantly of the younger generation. The secretary-general of the SSM is Sheikh Hamad Al Ali and one parliamentarian is sympathetic to its ideas, Walid Tabtabai.

In 2004, a small group of Salafi attached to the SSM—Hakim al-Mutairi, Hussain al-Saeed, and Sajjid al-Abdouli—proposed the installation of party politics in Kuwait and the establishment of a new political party, which they proposed calling the "Umma" Party. They declared their opposition to the continued presence of American forces in the region, but also asked for multi-party democracy in Kuwait and enhanced personal freedom. Hostile commentators suggested that this group was linked to those who had supported Saddam Hussein in 1990–1991. Such extremists are presumed to have little popular support. The Salafis are said to be badly organized, with little or no control over who is attached to their organizations, and some have the shadow of suspicion attached to them because they sympathize with Al-Qaida or terror groups. Other radical Sunni movements active in Kuwait but based outside the country include Tablighi Jamaat and Hizb al-Tahrir.

Finally, the National Alliance (Al-I'tilaf al-Islami al-Watani) represents the Shi'ites of Kuwait, about 30 percent of the population as a whole. The Shi'ites are underrepresented in the Kuwait parliament. Six members represented the Shi'ites in the 1999 parliament; among them were Sayyed al-Qallaf, Dr. Hassan al-Joha, and Adnan Abdel Samad, a former minister. Very few

Kuwaiti Shi'ites are attracted by the revolutionary principles advanced by the Islamic Republic of Iran. On the other hand, certain Shi'ite activists in Kuwait, the other Gulf states, and Saudi Arabia regard themselves as linked to a shadowy "Hizbollah" movement in the Gulf.

A number of charitable institutions are run by self-confessed Islamists. These include the official Beit al-Zakat, run by the government, and the Islamic World Welfare Organization, which collects money in Kuwait and has been active in Afghanistan, Chechnya, and Bosnia. In January 2002, the U.S. Treasury Secretary Paul O'Neill, during a visit to Kuwait, persuaded the government to close down the collection of money for Islamic charitable causes, much of which—the United States believed—was going to fund Jihadist activities. NGOs explicitly set up to collect funds for welfare in Afghanistan and Pakistan were also closed down.

LEBANON

After the Lebanese Civil War, which began in 1975 and continued until the Taif agreement in 1990, the country was essentially run by its Muslim population, which compromised the traditional balance between Muslims and Christians. Though the unofficial National Charter was maintained, where the country's president was always a Christian and the prime minister a Sunni Muslim, seats in the parliament were evenly divided between the two communities instead of the previous preponderance of Christian deputies. Lebanon's postwar president was Elias Hrawi, and billionaire Rafiq Hariri presided as prime minister over the country's reconstruction.

President Emile Lahoud, who took office in 1998, though a Christian, was close to the Syrian government, whose troops continued to maintain the commanding presence that they had taken during the civil war. In this situation, the Islamist movements discovered that they had more scope to develop their political and social activities. These movements were frequently closely linked to the interests of the government, as well as to those of Syria. In the twenty-first century, the Islamist movements, both Sunni and Shi'ite, have been able to act with greater freedom in Lebanon than anywhere else in the Arab states of the region.

On February 14, 2005, the status quo in Lebanon began to collapse with the assassination of the country's former prime minister, Rafiq Hariri. Hariri had opposed the constitutional amendment backed by Syria under which Lahoud's tenure of office would be extended to a further full term. No responsibility for Hariri's death has ever been admitted, but it would appear to have suited Syria's purposes. The result was the so-called Cedar Revolution. On February 28, a large demonstration in Martyrs' Square in the center of Beirut led to the resignation of the government of Omar Karami. Hezbollah, the Lebanese Shi'ite militia and political party, organized a counterdemonstration, where hundreds of thousands of people again attended. On March 14, a vast demonstration in Beirut, again attended by many hundreds of thousands of people, demanded a real investigation into Hariri's death and—importantly—the end of Syrian domination of Lebanon. Under international pressure, Syria withdrew its forces, and by April 26, the last Syrian troops had left Lebanon. Elections were held in May 2005, resulting in a majority of anti-Syrian members. The new majority nominated Fuad Siniora, a former finance minister, to be prime minister.

A year later, on July 12, 2006, Israel once again invaded Lebanon, this time in response to the abduction by Hezbollah of two Israeli soldiers, following a border attack in which three other Israeli soldiers died. Israel's invasion lasted thirty-four days, during which Lebanon's infrastructure was once more destroyed. Israel pulled out of Lebanon without recovering its lost soldiers, and the Shi'ite militant movement Hezbollah was left in a powerful position in the country.

Harakat al-Tawhid al-Islami (Movement for Islamic Unity) (MIU)

The Harakat al-Tawhid al-Islami is a Lebanese movement based principally in the northern Lebanese city of Tripoli. Its novel feature was that it was a conservative Sunni movement that acknowledged Shi'ite inspiration. Its founder, Said Shaaban, who had been trained in Iran, was a follower of Ayatollah Khomeni. The movement was strongly anti-Syrian, regarding the regime in Damascus as anti-religious. It clashed violently with various Syrian proxies in Tripoli, such as the Syrian National Party and the Alawite militias, which it regarded as un-Islamic. The Syrian army was not able to deploy in Tripoli until 1985, after Said Shaaban decided to compromise with Damascus. Some factions of the MIU remained strongly anti-Syrian; however, in December 1986, the MIU clashed directly with the Syrian army. After the deaths of a number of Syrian soldiers, the Syrian forces, together with pro-Syrian militias, made a sweep of the Tripoli region arresting MIU members. Some two hundred were reported killed. A number of prominent individuals were arrested, and some were held for a long period. This put a stop to the movement's anti-Syrian activity. Sheikh Hashim Minqara was held until September 2000. Said Shaaban died in 2003, but, under his son Bilal Shaaban, Harakat al-Tawhid al-Islami continues to be an anti-Syrian presence in Tripoli. It is now said to receive a subsidy from the Lebanese Hezbollah.

Hezbollah (Lebanon)

Hezbollah in Lebanon first came into existence in 1982. It emerged from the coalition of three factions. The first of these was the Party for Islamic Da'wa, which was an Islamist Shi'ite party, originating in Iraq, whose founder was Imam Mohammed Baqer al-Sadr. The second faction consisted of Islamists from the Amal movement, which underwent a split in 1982; the third group was made up of sympathetic militants from the Lebanese Left. Hezbollah also had close links with the Iranian Revolutionary Guards, the Pasdaran. It placed itself in the front line against the Israeli occupying forces in the south of Lebanon, and its program was the establishment of an Islamic Republic on the lines laid down by Ayatollah Khomeini. It identified the United States and Israel as its principal enemies and set itself to expunge all evidence of the Westernization of Muslim societies.

Men of religion occupied a dominant role within Hezbollah, unlike the secular Shi'ite movement Amal. The fatwas issued by its spiritual guide, Mohammed Hussein Fadlallah, were regarded as binding and were seen as based on the inspiration of the thought of Ayatollah Khomeini himself. The armed wing of Hezbollah, known as the Islamic resistance, soon had almost three thousand fighters, who were well trained, and armed by Iran thanks to the good offices of Syria. At the time, in the early 1980s, the strategic alliance between Damascus and Teheran against Iraq was a basic feature of the foreign policy of these two countries. Hezbollah's obdurate resistance to the Israeli occupying forces in southern Lebanon appears to have been the major factor in bringing about the Israeli withdrawal. That decision was taken on the basis of the unacceptability to the Israeli public of the steady toll of casualties inflicted on the Israeli army, much of which was composed of young conscripts and reservists, when measured against the contribution made by the occupation to Israel's national security. After the decision of the Lebanese and Syrian authorities not to deploy the Lebanese army in the south of the country after the rapid withdrawal of the Israeli army from southern Lebanon in May 2000, Hezbollah became the dominant force there. This aroused concern among Lebanese Christians. However, there was no intercommunal strife. Hezbollah began to appear as nothing less than a state within a state, with its own health services, businesses, fuel supplies, building industry, and public works department, among other functions.

Hezbollah's popularity among the Lebanese people and in the Arab world at large could be measured by the success of its TV station, Al-Manar (The Minaret), which began transmitting in September 2000, with the onset of the violent confrontation between Israel and the Palestinians known as the Second Intifada. Hezbollah's official broadcasting station has had no difficulty in reaching audiences beyond Lebanon's frontiers, in neighboring Arab countries, in Palestine, and even as far afield as Algeria, where it is available by satellite. Its coverage of attacks on Israel has riveted its viewers. Hezbollah also has a multiplicity of print media, such as Al-Sabil, al-Bilad, al-Had, and Nur al-Islam. In addition, it controls several radio stations (including Al-Salam, the Voice of the Poor, and the Voice of Light). Lebanese Hezbollah has also been active abroad. On October 16, 2000, for example, it succeeded in kidnapping an Israeli reserve air force officer, Elchanan Tannenbaum, working as a consultant in electronics and military communications, who was abducted either in Lausanne or (as Hezbollah claims) at Beirut airport.

Hezbollah's first leader was Ibrahim al-Sayyed, who became a member of the Lebanese parliament. His successor, Abbasi Moussawi, was assassinated, after which Sobhi Tufail occupied the position for a few months. Since 1992, the leader of Hezbollah has been Sheikh Sayyed Hassan Nasrallah, born in 1960, a former Amal member who studied Shi'ite theology and jurisprudence at a Shi'ite seminary in Najaf, in southern Iraq, the site of a major Shi'ite shrine. Sheikh Nasrallah was principally responsible for the transformation of Hezbollah from a clandestine movement into a respected political party taking part in Lebanon's political and parliamentary life. Hezbollah went into an alliance with Amal in the parliamentary elections in Lebanon in 2000. Lebanon's electoral system is based on multimember territorial constituencies together with a system to ensure the representation of all religious groups. This meant that the Hezbollah-Amal alliance was able to secure a group of twelve deputies in the Lebanese parliament and was able to present itself as a national party. Once elected, Hezbollah's parliamentarians went into the opposition against Prime Minister Rafiq Hariri. They were able to exercise considerable influence, thanks to the general awareness of Hezbollah's strength on the ground.

In February 2005, Prime Minister Rafiq Hariri was assassinated, and, in April 2005, the Syrian troops who had been in Lebanon since 1976 finally withdrew, in response to demands from anti-Syrian groups in Lebanon and international pressure. The so-called Cedar Revolution, when anti-Syrian Lebanese demonstrated for a government free of Syrian influence, succeeded only in further polarizing Lebanon. A new parliament was elected in May 2005, in which the Hezbollah-Amal alliance took 35 seats out of the total of 128. The new prime minister was Fouad Siniora. This time, Hezbollah parliamentarians agreed to become cabinet ministers and took five ministerial portfolios. In July 2006, however, the Hezbollah guerrilla organization found itself engaged in a border clash with Israel, which escalated into a full-scale war. Some 1,500 died, most of them Lebanese civilians. In the aftermath of the war, some international parties demanded that Hezbollah should be disarmed. Hezbollah regarded itself as having fought for Lebanon and appeared to have no intention of disarming itself. On the political front, it demanded the formation of a national government in which it would play a bigger part. In November 2006, Hezbollah mounted a major demonstration in Beirut, against what it said was the undemocratic nature of Lebanon's current political situation. Hezbollah claims that the number of seats Shi'ite parties are able to obtain in parliament is not commensurate with their current 40 percent share of Lebanon's population.

Al-Jama'a al-Islamiya (JI) (The Islamic Association) (Lebanon)

Al-Jama'a al-Islamiya is the longest-established Islamist group in Lebanon, where it operates principally in Tripoli. It is in effect the Lebanese branch of the Muslim Brotherhood. In the 1950s and early 1960s, the principal organization within which the Lebanese Muslim Brothers came together was a prayer group called "A'bad ar-Rahman" (Worshipppers of the Merciful). In 1964, however, the political ambitions of the brotherhood led them to set up Al-Jama'a al-Islamiya. The founders were all from a political and intellectual background. They included Faisal Mawlawi, who had cofounded the Union of Islamic Organizations in France in 1985. Other founding members were Fathi Yakan, a former parliamentarian and an acquaintance of Sayyed Qotb, Zuheir Obeidi, another former parliamentarian, and Ibrahim Misri.

The JI maintained close links with the Syrian Muslim Brotherhood. In 1972, it began to publish the monthly magazine "Al-Chihab," which was noted for its diatribes against the left-wing and Arab nationalist movements. Al-Jama'a al-Islamiya made its entry into the political arena thanks to the general rise of Islamist movements and in particular of Hezbollah after the Israeli invasion of Lebanon in 1982. The Jama'a al-Islamiya gradually gained ground in the face of opposition from competing movements. The Ahbach were hostile, as was Hizb al-Tahrir. The greatest antagonism came from "Harakat al-Tawhid al-Islami" (Movement for Islamic Unification), the Tripoli-based movement led by Said Chaabane, supported initially by Fatah and Iran but subsequently, targeted and crushed by Syrian and Lebanese troops between 1983 and 1985.

The JI did not demand an Islamic state in Lebanon. Its platform was coexistence between Muslims and Christians, and it demanded to be involved at the highest levels of policy. In a document issued by its political office, the JI called for the revision of the constitution and the abolition of Lebanon's confessionally based political system. (Lebanon still has a system that ensures equal numbers of parliamentary seats are held by the different faiths and an unofficial National Pact that lays down to what faith the president, prime minister, and speaker of parliament shall belong to.) In 2003, it claimed a membership of 2000, and it publishes a periodical named *Al-Jinan*. In addition to Faisal Mawlawi and Fathi Yakan, its effective leaders include Ali Sheikh Ammar from Saida and Salaheddine Arqadan from Tripoli. In the elections of 1992, the JI won three seats and one in 1996. In 2000 and 2005, however, it failed to win a single seat.

The JI maintains a strong relationship with the international arm of the Muslim Brotherhood and with Saudi Arabia, while also carefully juggling its relationship with Syria and its alliance with Hezbollah. Formerly of little importance in Lebanon, Sunni Islam has been experiencing a degree of resurgence, accompanied by the sharp radicalization of some of its adherents.

Takfir wa-l-Hijra (Lebanon)

This is a Sunni movement of Wahhabi inclinations that could be regarded as an agency
of Al-Qaida in Lebanon. Its leader is Bassam
Ahmad Kanj, known as Abu Aisha. Kanj
studied in the United States before going
to Peshawar in 1988. From 1990 to 1996, he
appears to have been in the United States.
In 1996, he returned to Lebanon to set up
Takfir wa-l-Hijra. He named his group in
this way to link it to other Salafi groups
such as Takfir wa-l-Hijra in Egypt, which
was instrumental in the assassination in 1981
of Egypt's President Anwar Sadat. Takfir in
Lebanon initially selected Christian targets,
including churches, and in 1994 it launched
an unsuccessful operation against the synod
of Maronite bishops. It also targeted liquor
stores. At its high point, Takfir was thought
to have around three hundred activists. After
a failed attempt at an uprising in 2000, Lebanese troops with Syrian backing crushed
Takfir's stronghold in northern Lebanon, at
Dinniyeh. Fourteen soldiers and twenty-five
militants were killed.

Takfir appears to have had an operational
linkage to another group known as "Osbat
al-Ansar" (The League of Supporters),
which is also on the list of terror organizations drawn up by the U.S. administration
after September 11, 2001. Osbat is based in
the Ain al-Hilweh Palestinian refugee camp
in southern Lebanon, with branches in other
refugee communities. This was established
during the Lebanese Civil War by Hisham
Shreidi, a Palestinian activist. Shreidi was
assassinated in 1991 by agents linked to the
secular Palestinian movement, Fatah. He was
succeeded by Ahmed Abdel-Karim al-Saadi
(known as Abu Mohjen). Mohjen is wanted
by the Lebanese authorities in connection
with a number of incidents, including the
murder in 1995 of Nizar Halabi, leader of Al-
Ahbash. He appears to have taken refuge in
Ain el-Hilweh camp. Suspected members of

Osbat al-Ansar have since been responsible
for a number of attacks, but Abu Mohjen
has disappeared from view.

LIBYA

In Libya, the emergence and growth of the
Islamist movements have been held back
since the Libyan Revolution in 1969 by
the existence of a kind of official fundamentalism established by the state itself, at
the initiative of Colonel Gaddafi, Libya's
leader and guide. There were highly symbolic demonstrations, such as the smashing
of musical instruments on the pavements
and the prohibition of alcoholic drinks.
In addition, Shari'a law has been extended
into ever wider fields and has included the
imposition of the most severe punishments,
including amputations and flogging. Since
1995, the death penalty has been applicable
in cases of heresy.

In 1979, however, the guide of the Libyan
Jamahiriya found himself in confrontation
with the Islamists for the first time. He also
clashed with the Ulema, in their role as the
guardians of orthodox Islam, by expressing
reservations on the Sunna, which he referred
to as a "human artifact" whose credibility
may have been compromised by involuntary distortions. He decreed the Quran as
the sole source of social law. However, it was
the guide's attitude to women's rights that
raised the hackles of the most radical fundamentalists. While polygamy was not entirely
forbidden, it was strictly controlled by the
law. On divorce, the legislation enacted in
1984 gave more rights to wives, who had the
right to a settlement after an Islamic divorce
(a repudiation), which was not the case previously. Colonel Gaddafi also made constant efforts to facilitate women's entry into
professional life.

Through his assumption of the right to
interpret the Quran and by undermining

deep-seated social conservatism, Gaddafi invited the emergence of an Islamist challenge. During this period, mosques were closed and arrests were made in religious circles of those suspected of conspiracy against the regime. In the 1980s, a number of clandestine groups and organizations took shape, sometimes simply to further the interests of tribes that were in conflict with the central government. The most influential of these organizations were Islamic Jihad, Takfir wa-l-Hijra, and the Islamic Liberation Party (ILP). Various groups claiming to be in the tradition of the Muslim Brotherhood also made their appearance. These organizations soon came to be seen as constituting the sole opposition force that had a real basis in society. Some of them set up offices abroad, such as Al-Gamaa al-Islamiya al-Libiya (Libyan Islamic Group), founded in 1979.

In 1983, eight individuals presumed to be members of the ILP were accused of conspiracy and were executed after a hurried trial. Four years later, it was Hezbollah members that were hanged in the public squares. Widespread arrests were carried out throughout the country, and 1,500 people described as heretics and traitors were locked up over the space of a few weeks. Nonetheless, Colonel Gaddafi's policies were not entirely unambiguous. The guide wished to present himself as an important actor within the international community and as an indispensable mediator. Conscious of the international impact of Islamism as an ideological and religious tendency, he financed a number of organizations abroad, such as the Egyptian "Workers' Party." In addition, in Tripoli itself, a very influential organization known as the "Islamic Call Society" (Jami'at al-Da'wa al-Islamiya) developed under the protection of the regime with the remit of propagating the message of Islam in black Africa.

Internal trouble broke out in Libya in the 1990s when the standards of living of the people began to decline, largely due to the fall in oil revenues, together with the economic embargo imposed by the United Nations in April 1992, after pressure by the United States, Britain, and France. In addition, the bullying attitude of the revolutionary committees contributed to the radicalization of the Islamist movements. They formed armed groups that based themselves in Cyrenaica, also the stronghold of the Sanusiya Brotherhood. Some organizations developed operational armed units and political wings, such as Al-Jamaa al-Islamiya al-Muqatila (Islamic Combatant Group, ICG), the Ansar Allah (Partisans of God), and the Harakat al-Shuhada al-Islamiya (Islamic Martyrs' Movement, IMM).

On April 23, 1995, the Islamic Combatant Group, led by its emir, Abdallah Sadek, issued a communiqué announcing its establishment and appealing for support. "The abolition of the apostate regime and the salvation of the Muslim people of Libya from its ordeal cannot be achieved without wounds, suffering, sacrifices and the expenditure of resources. The Islamic Combatant Group appeals to all Muslims to take their places in this battle alongside the Mujahidin." In March 1996, the same group claimed responsibility for an attempt to assassinate Colonel Gaddafi by bombing his motorcade during his visit to the city of Sirte. The ICG's spokesman, Abu Bakr al-Sharif, said, "No compromise can be made with our secular adversary. Democratic ideas can never represent Libyan society." In the same period, Libyan military aircraft bombed the area of Jebel Akhdar, in the northeast of Libya, where most of the ICG cells were hiding out. In this region, in the hinterland of the coastal city of Derna, the Islamist rebels enjoyed the active support of the tribes.

On August 8, 1996, the creation of the group calling itself Ansar Allah was announced. This was a Salafi group, dedicated to the objective of the restoration of the caliphate. As with the ICG, its activists were based in Cyrenaica. However, among the armed Islamic factions, the Islamic Martyrs' Movement, led by Mohammed al-Hami, occupied a unique position, rejecting all collaboration with other organizations. From 1996, it claimed responsibility for many operations against military installations and inside the towns, for example in Benghazi, Sebha, and Tobruk.

From 1997, Colonel Gaddafi began to represent himself to foreign states as an opponent of Islamism. In particular, he instituted collaboration with the Algerian intelligence services. In addition, he had some success in involving the tribes of Libya in his security strategy. In January 2000, he set up a new system of internal administration, criticizing the inadequacies of the present system and attacking the activities of the revolutionary committees. He set up instead a decentralized system of administration based on new institutions to be called "Sha'abiat" (Popular Councils), and in effect handed over a good deal of power to the tribal leaders, thus to some extent retreating from his revolutionary principles.

The armed Islamic movements found themselves facing a security operation better grounded in the local territory and were unable to export their Jihadist activities beyond the confines of Cyrenaica. The result was that they faced significant problems. There has been little activity in the twenty-first century. Nevertheless, there was still no durable relationship between the regime and the tribes of Cyrenaica and no economic policy in place that was capable of halting the decline in the standard of living of ordinary Libyans. The infrastructure for Islamist opposition seems likely to continue to exist, enjoying as it does the undeniable sympathy of significant sections of the population.

In 2006, Islamist opposition to Gaddafi seemed once more to be emerging in Derna, according to observers. A Web site monitored in April 2006, claiming to represent the "Mujahidin of Libya," called for all supporters of Jihad to make their way to Libya to join the struggle against Gaddafi's regime. Another communiqué was signed by a militant calling himself Abu Baraa al-Libi, who claimed the title of leader of Al-Qaida in Libya. Libi—a pseudonym—has been taking an increasingly visible public position. Libya has been reducing the size of its armed forces, and the unemployed ex-soldiers may have provided a pool of recruits for Islamist organizations. The rapid urbanization of Derna and other towns may also have increased the available manpower for Islamism by increasing the proportion of the population who live outside tribal and conservative control. Finally, it may be that Gaddafi's continuing hostility to all manifestations of Islamism may itself be fostering hostility that boosts the very phenomenon it seeks to crush.

LINDH, JOHN WALKER

John Walker Lindh is an American citizen who was captured fighting with the Taliban after the Northern Alliance supported by U.S. special forces attacked the Taliban regime in 2001. He was captured in November 2001, briefly escaped from custody during the uprising in the prison at Mazar-i Sharif, but was then recaptured after being wounded. He was born in Washington DC in February 1981 and grew up in California, where he was mainly educated at home. By his own account, he became interested in Islam after seeing a film about Malcolm X. In 1997, he officially converted to Islam. In 1998, he went to Yemen where he spent almost a year learning Arabic. After some eight months back in the United States, he went to Pakistan in 2000 to study at a madrasa. He went to Afghanistan early in 2001 where he joined a group of Arab fighters. He was trained at a camp not far from Kandahar.

After his capture he was interrogated on board a U.S. warship in the Arabian Sea and was then flown back to Kandahar and then on to the United States. He was sent for trial on a number of terrorist charges, and his case came to court on February 13, 2001. He pleaded guilty to two charges. The issue was complicated by allegations that Lindh had been mistreated in various ways while in U.S. custody. He was sentence to twenty years imprisonment, but could be released in 2018. He apparently continues to study Arabic and Islamic subjects in prison.

LOISEAU, HERVÉ DJAMEL

Hervé Djamel Loiseau was typical of European recruits to Islamism whose enthusiasm for Islam was based on an uncertainty about their own identity. He was born in Paris in March 1973, but spent twenty years in the Kabylie district of Algeria after the separation of his parents. As a French citizen, he returned to France at the age of eighteen to do his military service. He was recalled to Islam by the missionaries of Tablighi Jamaat and rapidly became involved in religious activities. In Paris, he was a regular at the Abu Bakr mosque at 39 boulevard de Belleville, a center of Tabligh activity. In Colmar, in Alsace, he habitually visited the Al-Nasiha mosque. In July 1998, by now living in Paris, he was questioned by the police on suspicion of association with known miscreants connected with terrorist activity. On his release, his enthusiasm for Islam then took him to Saudi Arabia where he wished to deepen his religious knowledge and to become an imam. In March 2000, he traveled from London to Pakistan before going on to Afghanistan. His body was found by villagers from nearby Tandor on the frontier between Pakistan and Aghanistan, near the Tora Bora mountains, where he appeared to have died of exposure.

MADANI, ABASSI (ALGERIA)

Abassi Madani was born in 1931 at Sidi Okba, a small settlement in the Wilaya of Biskra. As an adolescent, he joined Messali Hadj's Algerian People's Party, an independent organization based on Islamic values. On November 1, 1954, at the age of twenty-three, he participated in the anti-French disturbances. On November 17, he was arrested by the French authorities and imprisoned. He was not to be released until Algeria achieved its independence in 1962, eight years later.

Once he was a free man, he enrolled in the faculty of humanities at the University of Algiers, where militant Marxists were at the time in a dominant position. He became a teacher of sociology, but never abandoned his quest to improve his theological awareness. From 1975 to 1978 he was in London, where he completed a Ph.D. in educational studies. After returning to Algiers, he took part in various demonstrations and frequented several mosques, such as the Abdelhamid Chentli mosque in Constantine, where the influential Sheikh Mohammed Salah Abed was to be found. In 1979, the Islamic Revolution in Iran stiffened the resolve of the radical Algerian Islamists. In November 1982, Abassi Madani signed a petition, together with Sheikh Abdellatif Soltani and Sheikh Mohammed Sahnoun, that demanded the introduction of Shari'a law and in the short term called for an end to coeducation in schools and a ban on the consumption of alcohol in university campuses.

On November 27, 1982, Abassi Madani was arrested by the military security forces and was once more imprisoned. He was released in 1984, when the state made an attempt to reconcile the Islamic opposition, and was able to resume his professional activities. Together with a number of others, he participated in the foundation of the Da'wa League, which he then helped to run. This was a coalition of various factions, each of which wanted to take control of the Islamic movement. On February 18, 1989, he was involved in the inauguration of the FIS (Front Islamique de Salut) (Islamic Salvation Front) at the Al-Sunna mosque in Bab el-Oued, of which he became president. His preferred policy was to operate within the law, since the party was granted official recognition, and decided to take the FIS into the electoral process.

In June 1990, in the regional and municipal local government elections, the FIS emerged as Algeria's leading party. Abassi Madani indicated that he was ready for government, but would cooperate with coalition partners. He also indicated that he wanted better relations with Algeria's Maghreb neighbors and was received by King Hassan II of Morocco.

MASSOUD, AHMED SHAH

Massoud was a hero of the resistance against the Soviets in Afghanistan. He was an ethnic Tajik from Panshir, and his ferocity in the struggle against communist regime and the Russians earned him the nickname "The Lion of Panjshir"—in Dari (the local dialect of Persian) this was "Shir-i Panjshir." Later, he was seen as presenting the most serious challenge to the Taliban in Afghanistan. During his career, he also achieved the stature of an authentic statesman. He died at the hands of assassins in September 2001. In 2002, he was posthumously awarded the title of National Hero of Afghanistan, by order of President Hamid Karzai. He was not only a military commander, but was also a cultured man, fluent in French as well as his native Dari, Pushtu, and Urdu. He was a sportsman and an accomplished rider, as well as a devotee of chess and poetry. He particularly admired the Persian poet Hafiz.

His upbringing in Kabul and his education at the French-founded Istiqlal High School gave him an awareness of the outside world that appealed to Westerners. He was also the first Afghan commander to appreciate the importance of the media. He knew how to turn them to his advantage, and his courtesy quickly made him popular with journalists. His sense of humor and ease of manner were in sharp contrast with the other Afghan leaders. His was a determined but flexible nationalist, and he was one of the first to react against foreign invasion of his country. He was the son of a senior police official and studied at the Kabul Polytechnic Institute for Engineering and Architecture. He was at the same time always pious, studied the Quran with the Mullahs, and often led his troops in prayer. His wife, with whom he had five children, lived in the village of his birth, Bazarak, in Panjshir, his power base, where the women wore the "burqa"—the Afghan-style all-enveloping veil. This was not forced, as in Kabul where the women took the veil after the arrival of the Taliban, but a matter of local tradition in a region sequestered from any trace of modernity. Only thanks to a Swedish charitable association were schools for girls ever set up there.

Massoud soon became embroiled in politics, joining the "Jamiyat-i Islami-yi Afghanistan" ("Islamic Movement"). This was led by a theology teacher, Burhanuddin Rabbani. Massoud joined at the same time as another future resistance fighter, Gulbuddin Hekmatyar. In 1974, after the movement criticized Daoud's government for being soft on the communists, Daoud cracked down on it and Burhanuddin, Hekmatyar, and Massoud were obliged to flee to Pakistan. Massoud was able to return after the Taraki coup of 1978. From 1980, back in Panjshir, he organized the resistance to the communists. Six Soviet offensives in the area failed to crush him. A truce was declared in 1983, but it was breached in 1984 by the Soviets, who launched a final but unsuccessful attack. During his entire campaign, he never left his own region, in contrast to other major Afghan leaders who set up their headquarters either in Peshawar or in Iran. The Soviets left Afghanistan in 1989, and Massoud and the other Mujahidin leaders fought on to rid the country of the pro-communist government of Najibullah.

On April 29, 1992, he laid siege to Kabul. Ten days later, he was appointed minister of defense. The disparate coalition of which he was a member fell apart, and the former allies fought each other in the capital. The conflict resolved itself into an ethnic clash. Massoud, as a Tajik, was supported by those from his own background, including former leftists and even ex-communists. In 1993, as part of the factional struggle, Massoud razed the Shi'ite quarter of Kabul, with the death of thousands of people. He left Kabul in 1996, after the capital was taken by the advancing Taliban forces, and returned to Panjshir. He became one of the leading figures of the United Front (known in the West as the Northern Alliance) against the Taliban. He was never to see Kabul freed from the Taliban, as he was murdered on September 9, 2001, by two Arabs from North Africa posing as journalists who detonated a bomb during a purported interview with the Jamiyat leader. Massoud was killed instantly.

The assassination had been organized with great precision. The two killers had provided themselves with false Belgian passports. On July 27, 2001, in Islamabad, they obtained visas to enter Afghanistan. On July 28, they arrived in Kabul and began to solicit an interview with Massoud, whose security failed to spot them as imposters. On August 31, Massoud authorized them to see him. It was noticed that they appeared to pay little attention to their surroundings and constantly read their Qurans. When Massoud was told this, he said that any one who kept the Quran next to his heart was incapable of a bad action. He agreed to give them an interview on September 8, which was delayed by twenty-four hours after a Taliban attack on the United Front. When the interview was set to take place on September 9, the guards failed to search the murderers, who were able to enter with their bomb. Massoud's death devastated and demoralized his supporters.

MAURITANIA

Mauritania's population of just over 3 million people consists virtually entirely of Sunni Muslims. Mauritania was declared an Islamic Republic at its independence from France on 28 November, 1960. Subsequent constitutional amendments have specified Islam as the religion of the state. Mauritanian sources describe the legal system as a combi-

nation of Shari'a law and French legislation. The country was first Islamized as long as one thousand years ago by the Almoravids, and by the seventeenth century, Islam was entirely dominant. The principal language is Arabic, which the Mauritanians call Hassaniya. French colonization began in the early nineteenth century, and the French named the country Mauritania in 1904. In 1920, it became part of what was henceforth called French West Africa. The French administered Mauritania from Senegal, but Nouakchott became the country's capital in 1957. In recent times, the country's Muslims have virtually all been members of the Qadiriya and Tijaniya Islamic Brotherhoods, which are intrinsically conservative. Other smaller Brotherhoods including the Shadhiliya and the local Qudifiya are represented. Only in relatively recent years have Islamist movements gained any ground, though they have been rigorously suppressed.

The country's first leader after independence was Mukhtar Oud Daddah, who was elected president in 1961. There has been a degree of tension between black Mauritanians from the south of the country and the Arabs and Berber speakers. Ould Daddah was overthrown in 1978, and a sequence of military coups in the following years brought rapid changes of government. In 1984, Colonel Muawiya Ould Sidi Ahmed Taya took over. Under his administration, there was a resurgence of hostility between Arabic-speaking Mauritanians and black Africans. Many migrant workers were expelled to Senegal. His decision to establish diplomatic relations with Israel and improve Mauritania's relations with the United States apparently alienated a wide section of the population. In 2005, dozens of Islamist and other opposition leaders were arrested. Nonetheless, President Taya was reelected at a number of elections and survived an attempted coup in 2003. In November 2003, he was again reelected by a large margin, but there seem to have been further attempted coups in 2004. Finally in August 2005, another military officer, Colonel Ely Ould Mohammed Vall, mounted a successful coup. President Vall appears to have honored a commitment to respect democratic institutions. There were parliamentary elections in November 2006, and presidential elections were due in 2007.

Umma Party

The Umma Party of Mauritania came into existence in 1991, comprising various earlier groups that wished to see the immediate and exclusive application of the Shari'a. Its leaders were imams in the capital Nouakshott, who, nevertheless, failed to get official recognition for the new formation. On November 18, 1991, the authorities officially rejected the movement on the grounds that it did not conform to the legislation governing political parties. Despite the ban, its program was widely publicized. Among its demands were the application of the Shari'a in all aspects of society, the establishment of the principal of "Shura" ("Consultation"), and the encouragement of a spirit of unity to combat all manifestations of what it called racism, tribalism, and regionalism. Among significant figures in the political Islamist movement have been Mohammed Jemil Ould Mansour and Mokhtar Ould Mohammed Moussa.

The Umma Party recognized the principle of political pluralism and appeared to adopt a doctrinal position that leaned more toward moderation and less to conservatism than most contemporary Islamist organizations. In its 1992 program, it explicitly recognized that the role of women was "indispensable and irreplaceable." It also declared that the spread of other languages in Mauritania, and particularly of French, was not a derogation of national or religious identity (French had been the colonial tongue). It maintained good relations with sister organizations in Sudan, including Hassan al-Turabi's "National Islamic Front." In September 1994, several members of the party including its president, Ould Sidi Yahya, were arrested on the grounds of preparing to engage in subversive activities. The government interrogated a number of foreigners it suspected of providing funds for the party, including Egyptians, Saudis, and Sudanese. A few days later, they were given a presidential pardon.

The leaders of the Umma Party have been accused by their political opponents of having links with Pakistani and Afghan Islamist networks. During 2001, the Umma Party attempted to organize a demonstration against the policy of normalization of relations with Israel adopted by the current government. The party had strong support in the urban environment and particularly in the slums that surrounded the capital. However, it hesitated to precipitate a confrontation with the authorities. The policy of maintaining normalization with Israel continued to be the policy of both the candidates of the presidential elections of March 2007. The candidates were Ahmed Ould Daddah (the brother of the country's former long-serving president Mokhtar Ould Daddah) and his opponent Sidi Mohammed Ould Sheikh Abdallahi, who is regarded as a modernizer. Abdallahi emerged victorious from the election. Meanwhile, the Islamist movement continues to complain that its wishes are disregarded. Though no Islamist party is officially allowed to take part in politics, the government has allowed Islamists to campaign for election as independents.

In addition to the political Islamists in Mauritania, there are also Salafi and Da'wa movements, though the numbers involved are small. A movement known as Salafiya Ilmiya ("Scientific Salafism") has criticized the government and has issued Fatwas condemning the relations between Mauritania and Israel. Prominent radical figures include

Taki Ould Mohammed Abdellahi and Mohammed el-Hassan Ould Dedew. The latter has been particularly critical of Mauritania's importation of American consumer goods. Tablighi Jamaat is also active in Mauritania. Finally, there is a very small number of would-be violent Islamists who adopt a "Takfiri" style activism, arguing that attacks on foreign targets and what are regarded as apostate Muslims are justifiable. There have been very few incidents, however.

MAWDUDI, ABUL ALA

Abul Ala Mawdudi was one of the leading theologians of twentieth-century Islam. A household name in Pakistan and India, and the expatriate communities from the Indian subcontinent, he is also regarded by those knowledgeable about Islam as a leading theorist of Islamist political theory. His aim—like Karl Marx—was not to understand the world as it existed, but to change it. He was born in 1903 in India, then under British colonial domination. He embarked in due course on a career as a journalist and editor, as well as a theologian. He was self-taught, and did not belong to the class of established clerics, conservative and traditionalist, who served as the repository of Islamic knowledge. In 1927, he began to publish his first major book, *Jihad in Islam,* in serial form in the Urdu language. It was published as a book in 1930. This was the first step in a career that led him to the status of a major theologian on a global level. Mawdudi placed the concept of Jihad at the center of his thinking and elevated it to the status of a permanent strategy for Muslims.

Aptly, in the context of colonial India, Mawdudi's novel concept in his early writings was that of sovereignty—"Hakimiya"—which is nowhere mentioned in the basic texts of Islam. Beginning with the assumption that sovereignty cannot be anything other than divine in character, he reached the conclusion that the present rulers of Muslim countries were usurpers of the absolute sovereignty of God. Any acknowledgment of their authority partakes of the character of "Shirk"—the error of believing that there can be some other power than that of God. In truth, they can aspire only to be the representatives of God, whose sovereignty, being absolute, cannot be divided. In 1933, Mawdudi became editor of *Tarjuman al-Quran* ("Interpreter of the Quran"). Here, he further developed the theory of the Islamic reaction to colonialism and Western domination. Together with the Muslim scholar Muhammad Iqbal, Mawdudi set up an academic institute known simply as the "Dar ul-Islam" ("House of Islam") in the Indian province of Punjab to train scholars in the political philosophy of Islam. His aim was to enable his pupils to understand and counter what he saw as the insidious and dangerous Western conceptual framework imposed on those who accepted education in the English language.

In 1941, he founded the "Jamaat-i Islami" movement, which opposed the Muslim League presided over by Mohammed Ali Jinnah, the architect of Pakistan's independence. On August 14, 1947, after the departure of the British, Pakistan became an independent state separate from India, for India's Muslims. Mawdudi migrated to Pakistan as soon as the state was formed. In 1957, Jamaat-i Islami became a fully fledged political party in Pakistan. In opposition to the government of the day, Mawdudi agitated for an Islamic government and continued to expound his ideas in *Tarjuman al-Quran*. He also produced a list of other publications. *Tafhim al-Quran* ("Understanding the Quran") was his masterpiece. He also wrote *The Political Theory of Islam* and *The Muslims and the Present Political Conflict*.

His criticism of the martial law government of Pakistan led to his arrest in 1953 on the charge of sedition. He was sentenced to death, but was then released. Between then and the mid-1970s, he spent much time outside the country traveling widely in the Middle East, North Africa, Europe, and North America, both in Muslim countries and in the West. His prowess as a theologian was well recognized in Saudi Arabia. His travels and his participation in lectures, conferences, and other academic and religious events contributed to his international reputation.

In 1970, he stepped down from the leadership of Jamaat-i Islami for reasons of ill health. In 1977, two years before his death, Mawdudi had the satisfaction of seeing General Zia ul Haq come to power in Pakistan, who took measures to re-Islamize the country and instituted the Shari'a as the source of law. By the time of his death in 1979 his reputation was firmly established as one of the foremost scholars of fundamentalist Islam. Many regarded him as on par with Sayyed Qotb, the Egyptian ideologue of the Muslim Brotherhood, as the intellectual inspiration of the Islamist movement. In 1979, he went to the United States for medical treatment for a life-threatening kidney condition and died there on September 22, 1979, aged seventy-six.

MERROUN, KHALIL

Khalil Merroun, today the rector of the mosque in Evry, in the southern fringes of Paris, is a Moroccan citizen, born in the Spanish enclave of Ceuta, who migrated to France in 1968. Journalists describe him as affable and personable. He lived first in eastern France and then moved to Evry, where he obtained a position as a technician with "Snecma" ("Société Nationale d'Etude et de Construction de Moteurs d'Aviation") ("National Corporation for the Development and Construction of Avia-

tion Engines"). He immersed himself in local associations and groups in the area, eventually becoming a community leader. The turning point in his life seemed to have come in 1967, before he left Morocco, when he came under the influence of members of Jamaat al-Tabligh and began to travel with them on their proselytizing voyages.

In 1981, he set up the "Association Culturelle des Musulmans d'Ile de France" ("Cultural Association for Muslims in the Paris Region"). By this time, he was an active member of the World Islamic League. He became a regular attender at the mosque at the workers' hostel in Corbeil run by the local housing project for migrant workers and was very keen to set up a venue for prayer in Evry. In 1985, he was among the founders of the National Federation of Muslims in France (FNMF), which is seen as being under Moroccan influence. Thanks to his efforts, and with the help of local government officials in Evry, the project for a prayer room in Evry became more ambitious. The objective was no longer limited to a prayer room and a place for Arabic classes, but was now nothing less than an Islamic center. In 1986, when another Moroccan, Abderrahmane Ammari, became director of the World Islamic League in France, Merroun became assistant director, which greatly assisted his plans. Funds from Saudi Arabia became available for the first time for the cultural association, enabling building land to be bought.

A crucial factor was the involvement of such figures as Omar Nassif, the secretary-general of the World Islamic League and, later, speaker of Saudi Arabia's Majis al-Shura (Consultative Council). Together with a former Saudi information minister, Abduh Yamani, Omar Nassif established a support group in Saudi Arabia to raise funds in Saudi Arabia and Kuwait for the planned Evry mosque. The association also raised a loan from the Islamic Development

Bank. When a sum of 5 million dollars had been raised, work began. The involvement of Saudi Arabia and Kuwait in the project was not entirely disinterested. The key factor was to challenge the influence of Algeria over the Muslim community in France. Critics of Khalil Merroun claim that when Saudi funds have been accepted, the Saudi religious establishment claims the right to dictate policy and limit free speech in the mosque. Morocco also took an interest for the same reason, though unofficially and without making a financial contribution, and the mosque has since been under Moroccan influence. The municipality of Evry appeared happy with the situation. The center would serve some seventy thousand Muslims in the southern suburbs of Paris and both in the size of its premises and the extent of its endowment it was well placed to rival the Grand Mosque in Paris.

The new cultural center included not only a mosque, but also a conventional school with a full syllabus with the addition of Arabic tuition. The intention was that the school should be in a position to apply for the status of a state-recognized private establishment. Cultural activities included debates about Islam open to both Muslims and non-Muslims intended to avoid "misunderstanding of religion." In the words of Khalil Merroun, "the main thing is to make contacts with the other side, with the goal of peaceful coexistence and to foster a spirit of tolerance." Merroun clearly wished to rid himself of the fundamentalist label attached to him for some years. To this end, he kept the Tabligh out of the mosque. Friday prayers and the religious festivals were the backbone of religious activity at Evry, whose Islam had more to do with moral behavior than politics.

In 1996, while Merroun was temporarily absent, a group of Muslims took control of the mosque, complaining of its authoritarianism and arbitrary power and claiming

that it had monopolized Islamic teaching in the area. Merroun claimed that they represented the Grand Mosque in Paris, which is controlled by the Algerian Embassy. Merroun describes the incident as unpleasant. He went to court to reestablish his right to occupation of the mosque and took possession once more in January 1997. His opponents argued that this breached the rule that the imam of a mosque should be chosen by the congregation. He has since played a part in the national politics of Islam in France and became a committee member of the CFCM—the "French Council for the Muslim Faith," set up by the French government in 2003 after a long period of consultation. Though the FNMF is a majority within this institution, it is still controlled by the Grand Mosque and its Algerian backers, which is a source of some tension.

During the controversy over whether Muslim girls in France should be permitted to wear head coverings while at school, he took the view that the issue should be one of good behavior at school and not of dress. In 2005, after the outbreak of rioting by disaffected youths in deprived areas of French cities, Khalil Merroun said there were divisions in Islam in France, but his aim was the construction of a homegrown Islamic community not dependent on patronage from abroad.

MILITANT VANGUARD (MV) (AL-TALI'A AL MUQATILA) (SYRIA)

This movement split off from the Muslim Brotherhood in 1972, as a result of the secession from the Brotherhood of Marwan Hadid, who was joined later by Adnan Oqla. Effectively a hard-line splinter group of the Muslim Brotherhood, it was set up as a clandestine paramilitary group, whose brief was to "counter the violence of the Baathist regime." Before Hafez al-Assad's accession to power, the movement allied itself with the Palestinian Fatah movement in Jordan and made use of the ongoing military training it was able to provide. The confrontation in 1975–1976 between Syria and Lebanon and the PLO (Palestine Liberation Organization) provided an opportunity for a number of operations carried out by Hadid's groups, which fought under various names, including the Youth of Mohammed and the Battalions of God. Hadid paid a high price for his efforts, dying under torture in 1976.

Nevertheless, the Militant Vanguard continued under the leadership of Adnan Oqla and declared its support for the Iranian Revolution. Ayatollah Khomeini, however, naturally preferred to make a strategic alliance with President Assad against Saddam Hussein during the Iran–Iraq War. After 1985, the movement fizzled out, with the mysterious disappearance of Oqla and the arrests of dozens of his fighters. The struggle could, henceforth, only be carried on in exile. One of the MV's remaining leaders, Adnan Saadeddin, fled to Iraq; others scattered throughout Europe. The MV did not struggle on for long, however, and its remaining members reentered the Muslim Brotherhood.

MOHAMMED, KHALID SHEIKH

Khalid Sheikh Mohammed was by 2007 being held by the U.S. authorities at the American base at Guantanamo Bay in Cuba. His trial on terrorist charges opened in March 2007. He is of Baluchi ancestry, but claims to have been born in Kuwait in 1965. Others say he was actually born in the Baluchistan region of Pakistan. He is the nephew of Ramzi Youssef, who was involved in the first attempt to attack the World Trade Center in 1993. He is said to have joined the Muslim Brotherhood at the age of sixteen. His earlier years were appar-

ently spent in both Kuwait and Pakistan. He studied in the United States from 1983 and completed a degree in mechanical engineering at North Carolina University in 1986. He then went to Afghanistan where he fought in the Mujahidin struggle against the communist government and the Soviet forces. He claims that in these years he met Osama bin Laden. Afterward, he took a job with an electronics company. In the 1990s, he went to Qatar to work in a government position as an engineer for the Qatari electricity authority, a job he held until 1996.

He also claims to have fought with the Muslims in Bosnia-Herzegovina against the Serb force and to have spent time in the Philippines, where he claimed to be a Saudi or Qatari businessman. His cousin, Ramzi Youssef, was apparently also in the Philippines in the early 1990s. He is also said to have attempted to mount a plot to blow up a large number of U.S. commercial airliners, traveling between Southeast Asia and the United States. He was allegedly in the Philippines while this plot was being planned. Bombs were to be secreted on planes, timed to explode simultaneously some days later. This became known as the "Bojinka" plot, which was uncovered by the Philippine authorities in 1995. In 1995, Khalid Sheikh Mohammed is said to have traveled to Sudan, Yemen, and Malaysia. No explanation has been offered of how he was able to spend long periods traveling the world posing as a businessman while also holding his government service position in Qatar. By January 1996, his activities had attracted the attention of the U.S. intelligence forces and a request was passed to the Qatari government to detain him. He then fled back to Afghanistan. He claims, at this stage, to have put to bin Laden the outlines of the plan that eventually became the attack of September 11, 2001. He also claims to have taken part in meetings with bin Laden to choose the hijackers. In March

2003, the Pakistani ISI announced that they had captured Khalid Sheikh Mohammed in Rawalpindi, in Pakistan. He was immediately handed over into U.S. jurisdiction and taken to Guantanamo Bay.

At the opening of his trial in March 2007, Khalid Sheikh Mohammed listed an astonishing catalogue of terrorist actions in which he had been implicated. These included not only the Bojinka plot and the September 11 attacks, where there was evidence that he was involved in the shape of information on computers seized from detainees. He also claimed to have carried out many other attacks, including the Bali bombing, a plot against President Musharraf of Pakistan, the beheading of Daniel Pearl, and a long list of other incidents. He also claimed to have planned many terrorist actions that did not come to fruition. In addition, he made grandiose claims for his position inside Al-Qaida, variously claiming to be the number three man, the head of the so-called military council, and to have held various other positions. At the time the trial began, analysts suggested that Khalid Sheikh Mohammed was a fantasist who derived satisfaction from exaggerating his own exploits and also attempted to derail the process of further investigation into other incidents by making false claims.

MOROCCO

The Moroccan monarchy is unique in regarding itself as divine in nature. The king, who claims descent from the Prophet Muhammad, adopts the title of "Commander of the Faithful" ("Amir al-Mu'minin"), thus claiming for himself the leadership of the Muslim community. His person is constitutionally defined as "inviolable and sacred." The Moroccan monarchy cannot in any way be described as constitutional. The king defines the boundaries of the fields of religion and politics and their rules of engagement. His powers extend to the executive, legislative, and judicial areas, and there is no concept of the separation of powers. With an arsenal of judicial powers at the king's disposal for the regulation of political life, he is able at any time to assume plenary powers. In Article 19 of the first Moroccan constitution, promulgated on December 7, 1962, six years after the country regained its independence, the nature of royal authority is defined. "The Commander of the Faithful is the supreme representative of the nation, the symbol of its unity and the guarantee of the continued and continuing existence of the state. He ensures that Islam and the Constitution receive the respect to which they are due. He protects the rights and liberties of the citizens, of social groups and communities."

Since the king is the guardian of Islam, any purportedly Islamist movement in Morocco is regarded by those who accept the king's authority as a deviation and a contradiction in terms. The principle is that none may claim better to represent Islam in Morocco than the king himself. Nonetheless, rebellious preachers who challenged the monarchy's monopoly in the religious sphere began to make their appearance. In January 1980, the late King Hassan II called for the establishment of a "High Council of Ulema in Morocco," of which he acted as president. The role of this body was to define orthodoxy and to monitor the conformity of preachers and imams. The king, in his wisdom, had always tolerated a measure of controlled dissidence, and even took action to cultivate it. However, the establishment of a supervisory body had become necessary for the limitation of behavior that had become overly independent. For example, when war broke out in 1990 between Iraq and Kuwait, the League of Ulema—a competing body—issued a Fatwa forbidding Muslims from allying themselves with "miscreants" to fight another Muslim country (i.e. Iraq).

For many years, however, the ever-present sense of the king's religious legitimacy was enough to inhibit the establishment and restrict the growth of Islamist movements. Another factor was that nationalism and Islam had always been linked in Morocco. The nationalist leader Allal al-Fasi, the founding head of the "Istiqlal" ("Independence") Party, who died in 1973, was a pious and observant man and had been a student of Salafi ideas. Others within Morocco's historic national movement were also religious men, and a Salafi group remained within the Istiqlal. Since the nationalists had already laid claim to religious legitimacy, it was difficult for Islamist movements to establish a place in the Moroccan political spectrum.

Nonetheless, from the early 1970s, King Hassan was well aware of the danger the regime could face from the proliferation of clandestine groups purporting to be inspired by Islamist ideas. Opponents of the regime in exile soon began to form small clandestine groups ready to take part in propaganda against the regime, or even to commit terrorist actions. Among such groups have been "Al-Mujahidun al –Maghariba" ("Moroccan Holy Warriors"), "Al-Jihad" ("Holy War"), "Harakat al-Thawara al-Islamiya" ("Movement of the Islamic Revolution"), and "Majlis al-Tansiq al-Islamiya" ("Committee for Islamic Coordination"). None of these movements represented more than a handful of activists and they had no real operational resources inside Morocco. Their existence was consequently often short-lived. Despite this, their pragmatic alliances with small groups of Islamists of other nationalities with whom they made contact helped them to mount operations against the Moroccan regime and its representatives.

King Hassan continued to attempt to hold back the tide of the emergent Islamic movement through the prohibition of Islamist organizations and energetic police work against clandestine groups. Nevertheless,

religious groups with political ambitions increased in number. Some of these were developing in practice into opposition political parties. Though their political rhetoric was often simplistic and stereotyped, such groups were easily able to recruit new supporters, especially on the urban scene and most of all among students. In the 1990s, bearing in mind the limited effectiveness of his previous policies, King Hassan decided to take a different tack. Instead of banning all Islamist activities, he invited moderate Islamists to play a role in politics. The intention was to provide a safety valve for Islamic activity. The regime's task was complicated by the activities of international proselytizing religious associations such as Jamaat al-Tabligh. In addition, as the international Islamist movement took shape, Morocco was also threatened by non-Moroccan militants. In 1994, two Algerian-born terrorists resident in France carried out an attack against a tourist hotel in Marrakesh, killing two Spanish visitors.

In practice, King Hassan's initial step was to concede a limited level of authorization to the "Hizb al-Adl wa-l-Inma" ("Party of Justice and Development") (PJD), seen by the authorities as the movement most likely to react favorably to the new dispensation. The PJD was able to become a conventional traditional political party, recognized by the authorities and subject to the law. In the elections of 1997, the PJD took nine seats. Since 2002, however, the PJD has been the third largest party in Morocco's parliament, with forty-two seats. The PJD was careful in 2002 not to upset the authorities by scoring successes in elections on too great a scale. It agreed to stand in only 20 percent of the constituencies so as not to cause too great a political upheaval. Nonetheless, it looks set to improve its position further at the election due in September 2007. Another smaller Islamist party, "Al-Badli al-Hadari" ("The Cultural Alternative"), was legalized in 2005. However, votes cast for the legal Islamist parties would probably have been claimed by another movement, Hizb al-Adl wa-l-Ihsan ("Justice and Charity"), if the latter had been able to operate within the law.

Meanwhile, though King Mohammed VI, who succeeded to the throne in July 1999, initiated a process of reform in Morocco, he disappointed those who hoped his regime would be more liberal by continuing to use his security services to suppress Islamist movements. As had his father, his aim was to halt or at least reduce the level of the activities of organizations that rejected the political system and in certain cases he was prepared to use violence. In the early years of the twenty-first century, police attention was focused on the radical fringe of the Salafi movement, known under the general term "Salafiya Jihadiya" (Jihadi Salafism). On May 2, 2002, a young preacher, Mohammed Abdel Wahhab Rqiqi, known as Abu Hafs, was arrested in Fes. Abu Hafs was well known for his incendiary sermons and his statements in favor of Osama bin Laden. He was specifically accused of being behind the formation of religious militias that operated in deprived areas to maintain morals and combat delinquent behavior.

"Al-Adl wa'-l Ihsan" was an increasingly bold movement with widespread support in Morocco that has for some time represented the principal political challenge to the regime. The movement's leader is Abdessalam Yacine, originally an educationist by profession. He was placed under house arrest in 1989 and the movement's publication, *Risalat al-Futuwa* ("The Message to Youth") was banned. During this period, Yacine's daughter, Nadia Yassin, became the movement's spokesperson. When King Mohammed VI came to power in 1999, Yacine wrote an open letter to the king on how he and the government should comport themselves. Despite this, Mohammed VI released him in 2000, clearly hoping to

find a way to include him in the political process. Constant discussion had taken place over the space of a number of years on the possible legalization of the activities of "Al-Adl wa'-l Ihsan."

On September 18, 2001, a week after the attacks in the United States, a group of Moroccan Ulema issued an Anti-American Fatwa. This criticized the policy of the United States in the Arab world and its support for Israel and condemned Moroccan participation in any coalition led by the United States against Afghanistan. The moving force behind this stratagem was Driss Kettani, a founding member of the League of Ulema, notorious for his anti-Western pronouncements, who on this occasion had taken it upon himself to challenge the authority of the king. The Fatwa aroused virulent responses from mainstream politicians.

In 2003, the government found itself faced by more serious problems after an unexpected spate of terrorist attacks in Casablanca. On the night of May 16, bombs were detonated at a Spanish restaurant and at the Belgian consulate. Other targets appeared to be Jewish-related. One bomb went off at a hotel thought to be patronized by Jewish tourists, and others went off at a Jewish community center and a Jewish-owned Italian restaurant. A bomb that seemed destined for the city's Jewish cemetery went off in the street. In all, twelve bombers died together with thirty-three victims. More than a hundred were injured. Two bombers who failed to activate their device were arrested. The perpetrators were linked to Salafiya Jihadia, an offshoot of an apparently recently formed terrorist organization, "Al-Jama'a al-Islamiya al-Muqatila" ("Islamic Fighting Group") (IFG). Most were connected with a deprived suburb of Casablanca called Sidi Moumen. In March 2004, a suspect connected with the incidents was arrested in Belgium. In December 2004, a Moroccan charged in Spain in connection with the 2004 Madrid bombings was questioned in Morocco over whether he had any connection with the Casabalanca incidents. On March 4, 2007, it was reported that eight Islamist sympathizers were sentenced in a Moroccan court for planning terror attacks across Europe and in Morocco. On March 11, 2007, a further suicide bombing took place in Casablanca. The bomb was detonated at an Internet café. Police believe the bomber and his accomplice, who was later arrested, were intending to access further instructions regarding their mission. Newspapers conjectured that the security services were the intended target. Again, both bombers were from Sidi Moumen.

In June 2005, Nadia Yacine, of "Al-Adl wa'-l Ihsan," was arrested for suggesting in a newspaper article that Morocco would be better off as a republic. After a number of court sessions, her trial was deferred until April 2007. In February 2007, a number of "Al-Adl wa'-l Ihsan" activists were arrested in various locations across Morocco as a large number of suspects presumed to have links with various Islamist terror organizations were detained for interrogation. Once again, "Salafiya Jihadiya" appeared to be in focus as airports, sea ports, and the land frontiers with Algeria were subjected to close scrutiny to prevent the flight of suspects.

Association of Islamic Youth (Association de la Jeunesse Islamique: AJI) (Jamiyyat Ash-Shabiba al-Islamiyya) (Morocco)

The AJI, the first organization in the Maghreb explicitly formed with the aim of furthering Islamic political goals, was established in 1969. Its principal leader was Abdelkarim Mouti', a national education inspector and a former militant against the French colonial regime. With the assistance of Kamal Ibrahim, a teacher who took the position of vice president, Mouti' set up the move-

ment's first networks among university and high school students.

The declared aim of the organization was to oppose all influence by Marxist-Leninist organizations, which it viewed as pernicious, while promoting the Islamization of Moroccan society. The AJI, seen as following the line of the Muslim Brotherhood, was recognized officially in November 1972. It ran vacation camps and trained its militants in the techniques of propaganda and agitation.

The Moroccan authorities have accused the AJI of responsibility for the murder on December 18, 1975, of Omar Benjelloun, an official of the USFP ("Union Socialiste des Forces de Progrès") ("Socialist Union for the Forces of Progress"). Another incident for which they were blamed is an attack on Abderrahim Meniaoui, a member of the secretariat of the PPS ("Parti du Progresse et Socialisme") ("Party for Progress and Socialism"). After the arrest of one of the attackers, the subsequent investigation disclosed the existence of an armed branch, run by Abdelaziz Naamani, a law student, which operated under the name of "Al-Mujahidun al-Maghariba" (The Moroccan Combatants).

On December 23, 1975, Kamal Ibrahim was arrested. Abderrahim Mouti' fled to Saudi Arabia, and then spent time in Libya and in Europe. He was appointed a permanent member of the secretariat general of the World Association of Muslim Youth and continued to exercise a degree of influence, though of a limited nature, over the Moroccan Islamist movement. The magazine *Al-Mujahid* (The Combatant), published in Belgium, displayed over a period of some years the tenacity within Europe of small groups professing adherence to the AJI, which was gradually undermined by a series of splits. Subsequently, claims to have inherited the mantle of the AJI, the longest-established Islamist movement in the Maghreb, have been made by a number of diverse movements. These included the violent, sectarian Al-Jihad ("The Struggle") and, in contrast to it, the "Islah wa'l Tajdid" ("Parti de la Réforme et du Renouveau") ("Party of Reform and Renewal"), which advocates a return to conventional political activity.

Adl wa-l Ihsan, Al- (Morocco)

Al-Adl wa-l Ihsan (Justice and Benevolence), a clandestine movement with political and religious aims, came into existence in 1985 and enjoys considerable support, especially in the large cities of northern Morocco. The movement was established and is directed by Sheikh Abdessalam Yacine, a former teacher and religious adept, born in 1928, who is the overall leader of the association. Sheikh Yacine is a prolific author and campaigner, who spent a period in close contact with a religious Brotherhood in the 1960s. Sheikh Yacine has led a troubled life of constant conflict with the Moroccan authorities. In 1974, he sent a critical open letter to King Hassan II, which cost him four years confinement. Al-Adl wa-l-Ihsan recognizes in its manifesto the principle of pluralism and officially repudiates the use of violence for political purposes. At the same time, its ultimate objective continues to be the installation of a new Islamic order. Sheikh Yacine continued to be regarded as a potential troublemaker by the Moroccan government and the late King Hassan II and was again imprisoned for his views in the 1980s. In 1989, he was placed under house arrest in the city of Salé, adjacent to Rabat, a confinement that was not relaxed until May 2000 when he was released by King Mohammed VI.

Following internal discussions, the movement has up to now rejected the idea of participation to a greater extent in Moroccan political life. In the view of Sheikh Yacine and the movement's members, the conventions of politics laid down by Morocco's constitution ruled out any real change. However regular contacts with representatives of other groups have been maintained, especially those who are sympathetic to Islamist views. Meetings on issues concerned with the relationship between religion and politics have over a period of some years brought together members of the leftist establishment and representatives of the Islamist groups.

Al-Adl wa-l Ihsan differs in certain ways from other Maghrebi Islamist groups. The adoption of the expression "Ihsan"—meaning "the performance of good deeds"—is an explicit reference to Sufi tradition and reflects Yacine's background. Each militant is also an adept and a disciple and is subjected to real religious asceticism and is obliged from his entry into the organization to follow an extremely strict training program that combines spiritual education with classical political techniques of agitation and propaganda. His life is strictly supervised, and to this end he is provided with the writings of Sheikh Yacine and his manual of guidance, *Al-Minhaj al-Nabawi* (the Prophetic Path). Basic cells—"usra," literally "families"—operate both in the towns and in the Moroccan countryside.

Al-Adl wa-l Ihsan is organized hierarchically and is divided strictly into cells. Periods of prayer and Sufi practices such as the "Dhikr"—the repetition of the name of God—bring a mystic dimension to the commitment of each militant. Sheikh Yacine has created the basis of a real alternative society, while awaiting historical conditions conducive to the Islamization of the political authority. The rank and file member does not enjoy freedom of opinion, and the party line is not challenged by those who aspire to initiation. While the organization is largely conducted according to the ideas of Sheikh Yacine, around whom a powerful mystique has grown up, the General Council for Orientation and Management is an important body that defines strategic objectives and political positions.

After the expulsion in 1998 of Mohammed Bachiri, one of Al-Adl wa-l Ihsan's leading activists, for having criticized Yacine's leadership, the general council was composed in 2002 of five members. These were Fathallah Arsalane, (secretary-general), Mohammed Ali Suleimani (the longest-standing member and the movement's head in Marrakesh), Mohammed Abbadi, Abdelwahid Muttawakkil, and Abdallah Chibani. Sheikh Yacine's successor will probably be selected from one of these five figures. Paradoxically, in spite of the movement's opposition to the relaxation of the law that restricts the status of women, Sheikh Yacine's daughter, Nadia Yacine, plays a substantial role in running the movement. In response to particular events, such as the Gulf War or the American bombing of Afghanistan, officials were swiftly able to mobilize the entire political machine and to bring out several hundred thousand people.

In order to recruit new members and to open up new sources of funds, Sheikh Yacine and the movement's leadership opted to set up subsidiary organizations whose field of action lay in social and cultural affairs. There are more than two hundred such organizations whose mode of operation is in general to supplement the deficiencies of state provision for the most deprived, in particular in the shanty towns that surround Morocco's principal cities where they supply educational requisites, medical assistance, burial fees, and so on. In spite of significant efforts made by King Mohammed VI in the sphere of social policy and appropriate spending, the influence of the Islamist networks continues to be very strong.

Al-Adl wa-l Ihsan also sponsors its own trade union, Al-Rabita al-Niqabiyya, which appears to be most widespread among railway workers. However, the militants/disciples are for the most part recruited from among the student population and from a number of high schools where indoctrination campaigns are conducted, especially in Casablanca. For several years, the movement has controlled the workings of the main union active in the Moroccan university sector, the National Union of Moroccan Students (UNEM, "Union Nationale des Etudiants Marocains"), which had been the principal vehicle for the Marxist challenge in the 1970s. Taking advantage of the tolerance extended to them by the security forces, the Islamists, who resorted often to violence, substantially diminished the influence of the Moroccan Left, which is today very slight if not actually nonexistent in the universities.

The movement derives the greater part of its funding from donations, which are sometimes of considerable size, as well as from its membership and from a range of lucrative commercial activities. The markets of the communes of Nador and Ksar el-Kebir are under its control. Seaside holiday camps also contributed to the organization's finances, but the government, which was very concerned over the proliferation of makeshift camps on the beaches, acted against the opposition of the Islamists to put an end to this enterprise. Though there are persistent suggestions that there are subventions from the Gulf monarchies, the extent of any such funding remains unknown up to the present.

In 1999, when Mohammed VI came to the throne, Sheikh Yacine sent a memorandum to the palace criticizing the profligate way of life of the sovereign, with the apparent intention of presenting himself to public opinion as the authentic and principal adversary of the monarchical system. Mobilization against the reform of the "mudawana," the personal legal code that in particular restricts the rights of Moroccan women, allowed the movement to demonstrate its ability to mobilize and act, with a substantial demonstration taking place in March 2000. This did not, however, prevent a substantial revision of the status of women backed by

King Mohammed VI from becoming law in Morocco on January 16, 2004.

While adherents of Al-Adl wa-l Ihsan are to be found in many European cities, they seem uninterested in making links with international Islamist activists, preferring to keep themselves aloof. The Moroccan authorities banned a protest march organized by the movement against the bombing of Afghanistan in October 2001. However, since then, the movement may have begun to change its political line, and to be moving away from confrontation with the authorities. In May 2003, some forty-five people died in five virtually simultaneous suicide bombings in Casablanca, but Al-Adl wa-l Ihsan distanced itself from responsibility and the bombings were claimed by a clandestine movement calling itself the Salafi Jihad. Sheikh Yacine had in the past spoken out against violence and said that Morocco would not follow the violent path of Algeria. The movement was reported in February 2004 to be departing from its previous position by considering whether to attempt seek recognition as a conventional political party.

Groupe Islamique Combattant (GIC)
(Islamic Fighting Group)

From 1996, the GIC published a periodical in London entitled *Sada al-Maghreb* (The Echo of Morocco), and in June 1997, it issued a manifesto. It is a clandestine Moroccan movement professing Salafi principles, whose earliest adherents seem to have been Moroccan expatriates in the United Kingdom. They appear to have obtained help and encouragement from Abu Qatada, a Jordanian Islamist based in London with experience of Afghanistan. Its goal was to overthrow the Moroccan regime, which it attacked as irreligious and tyrannical. GIC members have also expressed support for the establishment of a world caliphate, and spoke out in favor of forming the inter-

national "Islamist Brigades." They seem to have attempted to make contact with other organizations that shared their position.

MOUVEMENT POPULAIRE DEMOCRATIQUE ET CONSTUTIONNEL (MPDC) (DEMOCRATIC AND CONSTITUTIONAL POPULAR MOVEMENT)

The MPDC, founded on May 11, 1967, was not originally an Islamist movement. Its founding leader was Dr. Al-Khatib, who was on good terms with the palace and had acted as an international emissary on behalf of the Moroccan monarchical regime. Its membership tended to consist of government officials. It was more of a pressure group than a political party and made only occasional appearances on the political scene. On June 2, 1996, after the negotiations carried out with the blessing of King Hassan II, the Islamist members of the organization "Al-Islah wa-l Tajdid" became members of the MPDC at an extraordinary party congress. Subsequently, many new members were signed up and the MPDC's committees and other organs reflected an increased number of Islamists in its ranks. For instance, after June 2 four of the seven members of its management committee were former members of Islah of the Islamist persuasion.

Dr. Al-Khatib continued to lead the organization, but opposed MPDC participation in the local government elections of 1997. In the wake of the ensuing controversy, action was taken to avoid a split in the party by three former Islah officials, Ahmed Raissouni, Abdelilah Benkirane, and Mohammed Yatim. While declaring their adherence to democratic principles and condemning violence, they encouraged those who wished to stand for election to run as independents. For the Islamists of Islah, however, the establishment of an officially recognized political movement was only the first stage of a transitional phase that would lead to the establishment of an Islamic state governed by the Shari'a. As part of this strategy, the PPDC, now seen as an Islamist movement set up with the blessings of the palace, ran many candidates in the parliamentary elections of 1997, especially in urban working class areas. After an election campaign based on the struggle against corruption, and with a puritanical tone, nine Islamist candidates were elected in six towns (Agadir, Casablanca, Fes, Oujda, Tangier, and Tetouan).

The newly elected MPDC deputies concentrated on the issues of concern to the Islamist movement, such as individual rights and education. From the first, they attempted to build alliances with other parliamentarians who appeared likely to be sympathetic to their views on social issues. On October 4, 1998, at an extraordinary meeting, the MPDC transformed itself into the "Hizb al-Adel wa-l-Inma"—the Party of Justice and Development.

Islah wa-l-Tajdid (Reform and Renewal)

This group was founded in 1982 by former supporters of Abdelkarim Mouti'. Islah was a clandestine Islamist organization also known as Al-Jamaa al-Islamiya. Its leaders, Mohammed Yatim and Abdlelilah Benkirane, were inclined toward a compromise with the palace and to abandon ideas of a revolution. In the movement's two publications, *Al-Islah* and *Al-Furqan,* distributed with the acquiescence of the palace, the leadership adopted a conciliatory tone, opting to condemn "Western decadence" rather than to challenge the monarchy. The Islah leadership, stressing the cultural aspect of their position and avoiding mention of their political objectives, attempted to identify interlocutors and intermediaries. In the light of their aspiration for official recogni-

tion, they avoided anything that could have inflamed the anger of the demonstrators in the hunger riots of 1984.

The rhetoric of the movement's leadership, expressed through demonstrations and statements, concentrated on international issues, such as the Gulf War and the Palestinian question, and on the social field, including such issues as personal rights and the teaching of foreign languages. A number of attempts to set up a new political group with official recognition met with no success. The main setback came in 1992, even though the legal niceties had been observed and an application in due form had been lodged with the Ministry of the Interior. In 1996, however, the palace decided that the time had come to make a gesture toward the Islamists, contriving their entry into the official sphere of political life in Morocco by sanctioning their merger with the hitherto relatively insignificant MPCD.

MOSCOW THEATER SIEGE

On October 23, 2002, a group of Chechen Islamist militants seized a theater in Moscow in mid-performance, capturing 850 hostages including the audience, the performers, and the theater staff. Their demand was the cessation of hostilities in Chechnya and the immediate withdrawal of Russian forces. The threat was that the hostages would be killed if the demands were not met. Around half of the group of thirty-three hostage-takers were women. The police were quickly informed by a number of performers who had escaped from behind the stage and by cell-phone calls from audience members. During the fist two days, the Muslims among the hostages were released and two civilians who tried to enter the theater were killed in stray incidents. The siege came to an end on October 26, when Russian special forces stormed the building after a narcotic gas known as Fentanyl (a morphine derivative) was introduced through the air-conditioning system. One hundred and twenty-nine hostages were killed. According to a later report, all but one died as a result of overdosing on Fentanyl. Most of the dead were children who were unable to tolerate the adult dosage.

Responsibility for the incident was claimed by Shamil Basayev, the Chechen rebel military commander. The Chechen president, Alsan Maskhadov, seems not to have been told in advance of the planned attack. In 1995, Besayev had been responsible for a murderous attack on a Russian hospital in Budyonnovsk in southern Russia and also claimed authorship of the Beslan school siege in 2004. Since April 2002, the Russians had claimed that the Chechen conflict was virtually over. The attack gave the lie to this assertion. This may have been one reason why the Russian authorities attempted to restrict media coverage of the siege. Paradoxically, the Russians reacted with a crackdown in Chechnya. In a battle near Grozny on October 28, thirty rebel fighters died. The Chechens rebels also stepped up their anti-Russian activity. The effect of the siege was to draw international attention to the continuing conflict in Chechnya and the Russian failure to control the situation.

MOUSSAOUI, ZACARIAS

Zacarias Moussaoui, a French citizen from Narbonne in southwest France, is serving a life sentence in the United States for complicity in the plot that led to the attack on the World Trade Center on September 11, 2001. He was said to have been the twentieth man in the terrorist group that carried out the attacks, though this was denied years later by Osama bin Laden. A French citizen of North African ancestry, he took the terrorist route after a process of re-Islamization in Britain at the hands of radical preachers.

He was born on May 30, 1968, at Saint-Jean-de-Luz, between Biarritz and the Spanish border at Hendaye. His parents were Moroccan residents in France. His father was in the building trade, and he was the youngest of four children. When he was four, his parents divorced. His mother Aicha took the children to Mulhouse, in the eastern French province of Alsace, where she put the children into a care home. After a year, when she found a job, she retrieved her children and took them to live in a housing project in the district of Bourtzwiller. She was by this time living with another Moroccan man and discouraged her children from attempting to see their father. Aicha Moussaoui claims not to have given her children any religious education and to have spoken little to them about Morocco. Despite his deprived background, Moussaoui went on to achieve respectable results at school and university.

From the age of four until he reached twelve, Zacarias Moussaoui passed his childhood in Alsace. He obtained unexceptional grades at school, but was good at basketball and hoped to follow a course in sports studies. When he was twelve, the family moved to Narbonne in southwest France, where they lived in a socially difficult area. At school in Narbonne, he kept rough company, but was careful to stay out of trouble as he wanted to go to college. His relations with his mother were bad, and he moved into a studio flat in Narbonne with his brother Abdul Samad. His school record was good, and he passed his technical high-school leaving examination (the French baccalaureat), going on to college in Perpignan to study for a technical diploma. He then signed up at the University of Montpellier, where he took a degree in social and economic administration, before returning to Perpignan to follow a course in applied English language. On campus, he began to associate with young Islamists.

In the spring of 1992, he went to Britain to further improve his English, as a preparation for a career in international trade in the Middle East. He had little money and lived in a hostel for the homeless, working illegally to support himself. Again, his academic record was good, and he succeeded in passing the entry tests at the University of the South Bank to study for an MBA degree. He enrolled at the university in 1993 and took his MBA in international business in 1995. While he was studying in London, he returned regularly to Montpellier to see his brother and his sister. In 1994, his name first appeared in the context of an inquiry into Islamist groups. The name "Zacarias" was found in the address book of an Islamist arrested in France. The French authorities asked to question him, but the British Home Office refused permission.

At this time, Moussaoui began to mix more and more in Islamist circles. His brother Abdul Samad became involved with the group known as Al-Ahbash. In 1995, he was a regular visitor to a number of mosques regarded as the preserve of extremists, including the Finsbury Park mosque in North London. There, the extremist preacher Abu Hamza al-Masri was at the time delivering incendiary sermons. He also studied with Abu Qatada. When his business studies were completed, he returned to Montpellier, but went back to London for the conferment of his degree and stayed for a further year. This time, when he returned to France, he was—as his friends and family saw him—a changed man. He spoke of different subjects and he dressed in the Pakistani style, which caused a stir at the mosque in Narbonne. Between 1996 and 1998, he traveled to various countries, regularly touching base in London. The French security authorities began to keep a file on him where his activities were classified as "sensitive."

Everything on record about him was sent to the American authorities in two reports sent on August 29 and 30, 2001, just eleven days before the attacks in the United States. Here, it was disclosed that Moussaoui spent time in 1999 in Afghanistan, where he was trained for guerrilla fighting in Al-Qaida camps. He stayed at the Algerian hostel in Jalalabad. In London, he had begun to go to the Baker Street mosque, known as a Salafi hotbed. According to the French security forces, he also recruited an old school friend from Narbonne, Shahid Massoud al Benin, a citizen of Benin who converted to Islam and died in Chechnya in April 2000 while attacking a Russian position.

In December 2000, Moussaoui left London for Pakistan. Between February 26 and May 29, 2001, he was in the United States, where he took flying lessons at Airman Flight School in Norman, Oklahoma. However, he failed to gain his pilot's license. His visa expired in May but he remained in the United States. On July 10, 2001, an FBI agent reported the presence of suspect students from the Middle East in a number of flying schools in the United States. In August, he went to the Pan Am International Flight Academy in Eagan Minnesota, where he paid his fees of 6,800 dollars in cash to train to fly a Boeing 747-400. His cash fees and his lack of technical knowledge alerted his instructors to the fact that something might be amiss. On August 16, 2001, Moussaoui was arrested by the FBI and was held initially on a violation of immigration regulations. On December 11, 2001, he was indicted on six felony charges: conspiracy to commit acts of terrorism transcending national boundaries, conspiracy to commit aircraft piracy, conspiracy to destroy aircraft, conspiracy to use weapons of mass destruction, conspiracy to murder U.S. employees, and conspiracy to destroy property. His trial opened in 2002. Moussaoui opted to conduct his own defense. The case was increasingly beset with confusion owing to Moussaoui's contradictory statements.

On April 22, 2005, after protracted legal proceedings, Moussaoui pleaded guilty to all the charges while at the same time denying he ever had any intention of committing the kind of mass killing seen on September 11, 2001. His claim appeared to be that he was training for some other operation. On May 3, 2006, Moussaoui was sentenced to life imprisonment. On May 23, 2006, in a tape supposedly issued by Osama bin Laden, the Al-Qaida leader said that Moussaoui, to whom he referred as Brother Zacarias, had no connection with the September 11 plot.

MUHAJIROUN, AL-

Al-Muhajiroun ("The Emigrants") was banned in Britain in August 2005. It had been operative in Britain since 1986, led by Omar Bakri Muhammed, a Syrian-born activist who had also been connected with Hizb al-Tahrir. Bakri was born in 1958 and joined the Syrian Muslim Brotherhood. He moved to Lebanon in 1977 and then went to Cairo in 1979 to study at Al-Azhar University, where he failed to graduate. He then went on to Saudi Arabia, where he founded Al-Muhajiroun in 1983. The name of the organization is significant, as it refers to the departure of the Prophet Muhammad from Mecca to Yathrib, later to be known as Madina, to escape the unbelievers in Mecca.

He was expelled from Saudi Arabia in 1986. Bakri was supportive of Islamist causes, but was not directly involved in Jihadist activity. He advocated re-Islamization and adherence to Islamic law. However, he was never anything but sweeping and ambitious in his pronouncements. He claimed he wanted to see Islam established as a universal religion, in the West as well as in the Muslim world. In his view, all societies should be run under the Shari'a. Until 1996, he was also a member of Hizb al-Tahrir, which had as its ultimate aim the restoration of the caliphate,

which would become a world government. His uncompromising philosophy meant that his organization was highly popular with students. British universities and student organizations had already taken action to ban Al-Muhajiroun because of the anti-Semitic nature of its propaganda. Bakri had gained legal permanent residence in Britain in 1993, and in 1996, he applied for British citizenship.

After September 11, 2001, his attitude appeared to change. He spoke out in favor of the actions of the terrorists and appeared to have swung toward a Salafi position. He joined Abu Hamza al-Masri's Islamic Council of Britain and praised the September 11 hijackers' bravery. He began to support Jihadist organizations, which led to criticism from British politicians, the press, and mainstream British Muslim organizations. He described the Madrid bombings of 2004 as justifiable revenge attacks. In October 2004, he officially disbanded Al-Muhajiroun, apparently to deflect the unfavorable attention of the authorities. In January 2005, he made public statements advocating Jihad in the West. In August 2005, he left the United Kingdom, apparently ahead of what he believed would be a hostile investigation by the police, returning to Lebanon. The British authorities promptly banned him from returning to Britain. The Muslim Council of Britain, which represents a current of mainstream Muslim opinion in Britain, said his departure would be welcome to the majority of British Muslims. Caught up in the Israeli invasion of Lebanon in August 2006, he asked for repatriation to Britain, which the British authorities refused.

MUQRIN, ABDULAZIZ

Abdulaziz Muqrin was a radical Saudi Islamist who led a group that carried out violent actions against expatriate Westerners and against the authorities inside Saudi Arabia. He was killed by Saudi security forces in a shootout in the Saudi capital Riyadh on June 18, 2004. He is said to have trained with Osama bin Laden's organization in Afghanistan and has also been reported as fighting in Bosnia and as present in Somalia. He claimed to be the leader of Al-Qaida in Saudi Arabia, though it is unclear what connection his group had with Al-Qaida and indeed what the status of Al-Qaida might have been after 2003. So-called Al-Qaida groups appear to have become independent operations, in the spirit of the original movement—in the expression used by some security experts, "franchises."

He apparently succeeded to the leadership of his faction when Yusuf Salih Fahad al-Ayiri was killed by the security forces a year earlier, in May 2003. His earliest involvement with terrorism in the Middle East was his alleged connection with the plot to assassinate Egypt's President Mubarak at the 1996 Organization of Africa Unity summit in the Ethiopian capital Addis Ababa in 1996. In 2004, his group claimed responsibility for attacks on Western expatriates, including the kidnapping and beheading of an American contractor, Paul Johnson. They also killed three Saudis and nineteen foreign civilians in a siege at a residential facility at Khobar in May 2004. Security experts estimate the number of individuals involved in the group's activities as less than hundred.

Muqrin's death did not halt Salafi extremism in Saudi Arabia. Between May 2003 and September 2005, 140 people were killed in terrorist incidents in the kingdom. In June 2004, the BBC correspondent Frank Gardner and a colleague were shot while filming in Saudi Arabia. In August 2005, another ranking figure who claimed to be attached to Al-Qaida, Saleh Mohammed al-A'ufi, was killed during clashes in the holy city of Medina. In September 2005, Saudi security forces fought a battle over several days with a group of militants besieged in a safe house in Dammam. In February 2007, Osama bin Laden was reported in an Islamist Web site called "Voice of Jihad" as exhorting terrorists inside Saudi Arabia to attack any oil facility that supplies the United States.

MURIDS, THE

The Murids, also known as the Muridiya, are a West African Islamic Brotherhood founded by Amadou Bamba (Sheikh Ahmadu Bamba Mbakke) in 1883 and mainly found in Senegal. The word "Murid" means "seeker" (in Arabic). The sheikh was born around 1854 in the village of Mbakke Bawol, southwest of the capital, where the language is Wolof. He is sometimes referred to in the Wolof language as Setin Tuubaa—the Holy Man of Touba, the seat of the Brotherhood, where the great mosque he founded is situated. Touba has become the second largest city in Senegal.

Amadou Bamba's father was a Sufi sheikh of the Qadiriya Brotherhood, one of the most ancient Islamic Brotherhoods, founded in Baghdad in the twelfth century. Sheikh Amadou was himself a religious scholar and a Muslim mystic, who lived through the French conquest of West Africa. He was initiated into the Qadiriya by his father, but believed it was his vocation to found a new order that would be of practical service to the lives of the people of Senegal. He did not advocate war against the French, but instead preached the Jihad al-Akbar (the so-called Greater Jihad)—the mental struggle that employed not arms but piety and the knowledge of God to achieve its objectives. He was known by his followers as a "Mujaddid"—a renewer of Islam. This was a common claim in Senegal for Muslim mystics, following a local tradition—purportedly based on a Hadith—that every century a holy man will arise to rejuvenate the faith.

Sheikh Amadou was exiled by the French—first to Gabon from 1895 to 1902 and then to Mauritania from 1903 to 1907. There are many apocryphal stories about his resistance to the French occupiers, but the French authorities later came to see him more as a force for stability in the country. He died in 1927 and has been succeeded by his descendants. He is buried at the great mosque at Touba, which he built. He is venerated in Senegal to an extent regarded by some Muslims as excessive. The present sheikh, Saliou Mbakke, born in 1918, has led the Brotherhood since 1990.

The Brotherhood was initially strongly African in character. There is a subgroup known as the Baye Fall after its founder, Ibra Fall, who wear colorful rags and wear their hair in a version of dreadlocks. These men claim to substitute labor for piety as evidence of their devotion to Islam and are much in evidence in the streets of Senegal asking for alms. By the early years of the twenty-first century, the Brotherhood was under strong pressure from conservative clerics to become more conventionally Islamic. For example, those of its members accustomed to reciting verses from the Quran in the Wolof version are now being asked to adopt Arabic, the language of the Prophet. Saudi-funded institutions are active in this direction.

In common with other Brotherhoods in Senegal, the Murids have often been accused in the past by social revolutionaries of colluding with the secular authorities. However, as the organization has become more urbanized, it has perceptibly changed, falling further under the influence of brasher interpretations of Islam that are less compatible with the traditional positions and hierarchical structure of the Sufi Brotherhoods. The Murids have also made a successful bid to dominate politics in Senegal. President Abdoulaye Wade of Senegal is a member of the Murids. His political opponent, Abdou Diouf, is a member of an alternative Brotherhood, the Tijaniya.

The Murids are well developed in the expatriate Senegalese community, especially in France and the United States. The Brotherhood maintains meetinghouses in many major Western cities. Its pan-Islamic message is especially attractive with uprooted Senegalese abroad. The Senegalese Murids in the United States, many of whom are small merchants, send substantial subventions back to the Murid leadership in Touba. The singer Youssou N'dour is a Murid devotee, and his recent album *Egypt* is an explicit tribute to the Murid Brotherhood.

MUS'AB, ABU

Syrian by origin, Abu Mus'ab is also known as Omar Abdul Hakim al-Suri. In Syria, he was a radical member of the Muslim Brotherhood and wrote a text entitled *The Islamic Revolutionary Struggle in Syria*. In the 1980s, he was based in London and in Spain, where he married a Spanish citizen. He frequented mosques in London, and then went to Afghanistan where he took charge of training camps near Khost, in the east of the country. In Afghanistan, he is said to have become a senior official within Al-Qaida. In July 2000, persistent reports said he had attempted to lead a split within Al-Qaida. With the alleged support of sixty senior Arab combatants from Algeria, Jordan, Saudi Arabia, Egypt, and Syria, he apparently attempted to bring about a closer merger between the 1,200 Arab fighters in Afghanistan and the Taliban. At this point, bin Laden's position in Afghanistan had begun to seem shaky, as the Afghan government took steps to take closer control of Al-Qaida's activities, closing bin Laden's camps and cutting off his communications. The Taliban, meanwhile, maintained their links with Abu Musab's faction. There were also reports that Pakistan had decided to withdraw support from bin Laden and to hand him over to the United States, and that Abu Musab had been asked to carry out this plan. However, in an interview he gave to Al-Jazeera television in August 2000, Abu Musab denied all these reports.

MUSLIM BROTHERHOOD

The Muslim Brotherhood was founded in Egypt in 1928, just four years after Mustafa Kemal abolished the caliphate in Turkey. Its founder was Hassan al-Banna, an elementary schoolteacher from Ismailiya, a town situated on the Suez Canal. It is the most long-standing Sunni movement, and the movement most strongly identified with Sunni Islam. The central plank of its religious doctrine is the idea of "Tawhid." This is the idea of God's uniqueness, which is key to Islamic thought. Its total identification of religion and politics is the core of Islamist social ideology. The history of the Brotherhood illuminates the Brotherhood's conception of the Islamic state as a theocracy whose ideology is in some aspects totalitarian, and which brothers should strive to see established throughout the world.

The Brotherhood, together with the subsidiary organizations to which it has given rise, adheres to five central commandments. These are: God is our objective; The Prophet is our example; the Quran is our law; the Jihad is our life; Martyrdom is our goal. These maxims are cited from a Brotherhood document dating from 1935. They guided the Brotherhood in its cautious cohabitation with the Egyptian monarchy, before it rushed into a clash with the Egyptian authorities over the Palestinian question. The Brotherhood had its reformist aspect, but at the same time it did not shrink from terrorist action, and oscillated between violent opposition to the Egyptian government and cooperation with it.

Hassan al-Banna, summed up his program as follows: "Power resides with the Caliph, the nation is the whole of the Dar al-Islam. Parliamentary democracy and freedom of the press are superfluous, and non-Muslims occupy a subsidiary position." The program of the Muslim Brotherhood was completed by Sayyed Qutb (1906–1966), also an educationist, who had returned to Egypt after a course of training as a teacher in the United States. His theory of the sovereignty of God came to be adopted by the majority of both Sunni and Shi'ite Islamist movements, and Ayatollah Khomeini acknowledged on a number of occasions his debt to Qutb, whom he called the "great Egyptian brother."

In 1954, Qutb was arrested and tortured. In prison he wrote a will, in the form of a program for the movement, entitled *In the Shadow of God*. This showed the strong influence of Mawdudi, the Indian Islamic reformer, who had in 1941 founded the movement known as Jamaat-i Islami. From this time, there was interaction between the Pakistani and Arab Islamic movements. Mawdudi's publications were translated into Arabic, and those of Qutb were translated into Urdu. Qutb's works were also translated into Pushtun, Turkish, and Bahasa Malaysia.

Under the guise of social action and proselytization, the Brotherhood's objective was the establishment of an Islamic state. This was to be modeled on the government put in place by the Prophet at Medina and that presided over by the first four Caliphs. It was to follow as far as possible the example of the "salaf" (the forebears) and was to be a radical departure from the forms of government imposed by foreigners, which were seen as a corrupting influence imposed on the Muslims. On December 28, 1948, the Brotherhood claimed responsibility for the assassination of the prime minister, Noqrashi Pasha. By this time, it had a million members. In 1949, it was dissolved by the order of the Egyptian government and Hassan al-Banna himself was murdered in circumstances that have remained unclear. Hassan al-Banna's succesor as leader of the Brotherhood (the "Guide General," or "Murshid al-Am" as he was known) was Hassan al-Hudeiby.

The Brotherhood's influence was widespread. Some of the so-called Free Officers, who mounted the Egyptian Revolution, were drawn from its ranks. Gamal Abdel Nasser himself, in his earlier days, appears to have anonymously attended meetings of the Brotherhood, as also did Anwar Sadat, destined to be Nasser's successor. From 1954, however, convinced that the Egyptian Revolution was not going to result in the kind of state they had hoped for, the Brotherhood began to attempt to overthrow Nasser. Nasser hanged one of the movement's leaders, Abdelqadir Awdah, which checked the development of the organization.

The Brotherhood was, nevertheless, able to carry out a wide-ranging program of infiltration and subversion of the Egyptian Revolution. Nasser, as Egypt's new leader, repressed them ferociously between 1954 and 1970. They were arrested in their thousands. Those who evaded imprisonment were obliged to go into hiding, where, as members of a clandestine opposition movement, they were constantly hunted by the security forces. Nasser's regime made a connection between the Muslim Brotherhood and the machinations of Britain, Egypt's former colonial power. The link later established between the Brotherhood and the American administration was very badly viewed by the nationalist Egyptian government. Egyptian officials believed that the CIA had decided to exploit the anticommunist sentiment of the Brotherhood for their own ends. From 1956, the Brotherhood received regular financial and military support from the CIA. This was the year when Nasser broke off relations with the United States after President Eisenhower and John Foster Dulles, his secretary of state, refused American aid to build the Aswan High Dam.

The American refusal prompted Nasser to nationalize the Suez Canal, which was the first stage in his rapprochement with the Soviet bloc.

Under the presidency of Anwar Sadat, from 1970 to 1981, the Muslim Brotherhood once more made its appearance in Egypt's social and political scene, appointing themselves as the arbiters of morality in Egypt's public and private life. At this time, Sadat was attempting to eliminate Nasser's leftist followers, especially from the universities and the labor unions. He restored some freedom of action to the Brotherhood, and in 1971 declared a general amnesty, after which it was allowed to operate openly in Egypt. Umar al Tilmisani became the organization's third guide general in 1973. Though the Brotherhood was not entitled under the constitution to become a political party, it was, nevertheless, permitted to operate as a pressure group. The Brotherhood, nevertheless, contrived to get forty members elected to Egypt's parliament, standing on the tickets of authorized parties, such as the Neo-Wafd, the Labor Party, and the Liberal Party. It also wielded an influence over the various labor organizations that had hitherto advocated moderate and pragmatic Islam.

The Muslim Brotherhood at first limited its scope to what was permitted by the law. One stratagem was the initiation of legal cases against individuals or organizations, drawing attention to pronouncements or actions it claimed were contrary to Islam. However, certain small groups claiming affiliation to the Brotherhood soon began to resort to terrorist action. This radicalization was to a considerable extent a reaction to President Sadat's change of direction in 1977, when he initiated the rapprochement with Israel that led to the peace treaty between Israel and Egypt. These groups were backed by Sudanese extremists. Their targets were the Egyptian regime and its police force, and the Egyptian government and its army, as well as the West in general and Western tourists in particular. A number of writers and filmmakers, declared to be bad Muslims by radical groups, were murdered. The Brotherhood failed to issue a swift and explicit condemnation of its wayward members and their terrorist attacks. In 1981, Sadat paid for his foreign policy with his life, when he was killed by a number of former Muslim Brothers who had set up new radical organizations.

The 1980s saw an internal power struggle between Muhammad Abu al-Nasr and Saif al-Islam al-Banna, the son of the founder. Muhammad Hamid Abu al-Nasr emerged the victor and succeeded Umar al-Tilmisani when he died in 1986, aged eighty-two. However, Abu al-Nasr was unable for health reasons to operate effectively as leader and the Brotherhood was effectively run by his deputy, Muhammad al-Mashhour, who in turn succeeded as the Brotherhood's fifth guide general in 1996. Mashhour's history in the Muslim Brotherhood lay within its militant activities. As long ago as the 1940s, the Brotherhood had established a clandestine armed wing known simply as the "Secret Organization," or "Nizam al-Khas." In 1947, The Egyptian police discovered quantities of arms belonging to the "Secret Structure" and trials ensued, but the Brotherhood argued that its activities were linked only to preparations for the impending war in Palestine. It also began to spread its activities beyond the confines of Egypt. Offices were set up outside the Middle East, in Munich, Berlin, and Geneva, bringing into existence the "International Organization" ("Al-Tanzim al-Dawli"). The Brotherhood also began to organize opposition groups in Iraq, Jordan, Libya, Tunisia, and Algeria. Muhammad Mashhour was the point of reference for all these activities. In the 1980s, Mashhour threw the resources of the Brotherhood into providing Arab volunteers to fight in the Afghan war. A former member

of the organization gives this account: "At the time, he saw the struggle in Afghanistan as the precursor of the establishment of a future Islamic state in Central Asia. Afghanistan was seen by the Brotherhood as the first stage towards the re-establishment of the Caliphate, the only political structure conducive to the eventual reunification of all Muslims." Until his death, Mashhour was regarded by the Egyptian security services as a radical activist who continued to foster the Brotherhood's armed wing. It was he who maintained contacts with such militant groups as Gamaa Islamiya and Jihad.

In 1995, President Sadat's successor, President Husni Mubarak, also narrowly escaped an assassination attempt. Admittedly, the Muslim Brotherhood was not directly involved in the terrorist movement. However, the leadership of the Brotherhood, which had been the breeding ground of the various radical movements, never saw fit to condemn the militants or to repudiate them. The proof of this lay in the repeated attacks on foreign tourists and in particular the incident at Luxor in November 1997. It should be borne in mind that, at the time, tourism earned Egypt almost 5 billion dollars a year. The attacks cut a billion dollars from the country's tourist income and threatened to bring it to an end. The aim of the extremists was no longer merely to infiltrate the Egyptian state, but to destabilize it ahead of bringing it down entirely. This accounts for the savage repression practiced by the regime against the Brotherhood after 1997. The government proscribed all political parties that mixed politics with religion. Meanwhile, within the Brotherhood, the senior leadership fell into conflict with the younger more intransigent members. In 1996, a group of these, led by Abu Ala al Madi, formed a new political party, Hizb al-Wasat (Party of the Center), whose aim was to adapt the Brotherhood to contemporary Egyptian circumstances. Even Christian Copts were prepared to associate themselves with this new political formation. The authorities, however, continued to suspect that the Muslim Brotherhood was acting as a cover for such extremist groups as Gamaa Islamiya, Jihad, Takfir wa-l Hijra, and a relatively new group, Tanzim al-Wa'd (Organization of the Pledge), which espoused a return to violent action.

After the attacks of September 11, 2001, American hostility toward the Brotherhood deepened, despite the Brotherhood's condemnation of the attacks and its efforts to distance itself from Osama bin Laden. U.S. sanctions were put in place against the Taqwa Bank, closely linked to the Brotherhood's international organization through the relationship between the Egyptian cleric Sheikh Yusuf Qaradawi and the banker Yusuf Nada, another Egyptian, both residents in Qatar. A Brotherhood member of Egypt's parliament attempted to explain the Brotherhood's position to the American Embassy in Cairo, but to no avail. Washington froze 43 million dollars of the Brotherhood's assets in the United States.

As the twenty-first century began, the Brotherhood was undergoing a real crisis in several fields, in a development indicative of the problems facing Islamist movements. The succession to Mohammed Mashhour was one of these. Muhammad al-Mashhour died in 2002 at the age of eighty-three, and his deputy, Muhammad Mamoun al-Hodeiby, the son of the Brotherhood's second guide general, succeeded him. However, he faced opposition from other factions within the movement, including candidates from the Egyptian professional organizations representing the lawyers and the medical profession and the recently formed Hizb al-Wasat. Another difficulty for the Brotherhood was a move against it by the authorities of Al-Azhar University, the supreme institution of Egyptian Islam, when, with government backing, al-Azhar took steps to counter the Brotherhood's program to Islamize Egyptian society. This had in the first place been facilitated by President Sadat himself, when he lifted the restrictions on the Brotherhood's activities. It must be said, however, that this was originally a purely political stratagem intended to act as a balance against the remaining influence of the Nasserists and other left-wing movements.

By this time the Muslim Brotherhood had spread throughout the world from its base in Egypt. However, the international movement, which was unofficial and only informally organized, showed itself to be open to both disruption and dissension from within. After 2001, it began to suffer ill effects from the so-called War on Terror promoted by the United States, which prompted it to revise its strategies. Rifaat Said, a left-wing Egyptian parliamentarian, who draws attention to the Brotherhood's economic, commercial, and banking wings, commented on Mashhour's strategy: "Having taken control of the Secret Organization, Mashhour also took charge of the international structure. Naturally, this gave Mashhour and his friends access to financial resources." A front of small business and social activities conceals assets of many millions of dollars, according to informed opinion. The Brotherhood's funds, the driving force of their influence and of the Jihad, are the real source of their hidden power.

Of course, any attempt to investigate the Brotherhood's financial activities meets a wall of silence. Nevertheless, as long ago as the 1920s, it brought into existence what can only be called a parallel economy. In Cairo, it maintains a chain of highly visible supermarkets under the brand name "Al Tawhid," as well as many other businesses, such as butchers' shops, dye-works, and the motor trade. These are only the visible tip of the Brotherhood's diverse and widespread economic activities. However, in 2006, the Brotherhood continued to experience organizational problems, arising from its ideological stand. It is out of sympathy with the international climate generated by the war on terror, and places it in conflict with the Egyptian government.

The Brotherhood in Egypt is reluctant to abandon its strict adherence to the line laid down by the movement's early leadership, though it faces challenges from its younger members. Some of these want to adopt a radical and militant line, while others envisage further compromise with Egypt's existing society. A related difficulty is the Brotherhood's difficulty in replacing its first generation of leaders. It continues to seek its leading figures from among its earliest adherents. When Muhammad Mamoun al-Hodeiby died after only two years in 2004, aged eighty-three, the next guide general chosen by the Brotherhood was Muhammad al-Mahdi Akef, who became the Brotherhood's seventh leader in 2004. Akef was aged seventy-six at the time of his appointment. He was trained within the Secret Organization in his early days in the Brotherhood. Though he is a member of the old school, like his predecessors, Akef has been described as politically aware and open to new ideas.

MUSLIM BROTHERHOOD (EUROPE)

In August 1995, the guide general of the Muslim Brotherhood, Mustafa Mashhour, explicitly recognized for the first time in the Brotherhood's history the existence of the organization's international wing: "We have branches aboard: in London, in Germany, and elsewhere in Europe. Each one of our militants—Brothers who have left Egypt— has set up a branch in his host country and maintains contact with the central organization." The primary objective of the Muslim Brotherhood was to take control of these associated subsidiaries, which have mul-

tiplied thanks to the liberalization of laws governing the establishment of associations in a number of European countries. Rivalry is fierce. They face a number of challenges: they need to absorb the Turks, who have recent presence in France, to combat the proselytism of Tablighi Jamaat—the India and Pakistan-based pious organization— and finally to counter the efforts of the Saudi-sponsored "wahhabis," de facto allies of the Moroccans.

As is their practice elsewhere, the Brotherhood seeks the application of the Shari'a law for Muslim minorities. Their strategy is to struggle for their rights wherever a Muslim association or organization or any group of believers seem to be discriminated against. In the words of a spokesman, "Why not take advantage of western law when it gives us the means to pursue our demands?" In France, the Muslim Brotherhood is strongly represented by the "Union des Organisations Islamiques de France" (UOIF), one of the largest confederations of Islamic Associations. The UOIF also supports the Tunisian Ennahda, led by Rachid Ghannouchi—the Tunisian Islamic leader who lives in exile in London—who recognizes the debt his organization owes to the Muslim Brotherhood.

MUSLIM BROTHERHOOD (JORDAN)

The Jordanian wing of the Muslim Brotherhood was established up secretly in Amman in 1936. In 1945, under the reign of the Hashemite sovereign King Abdullah I (who was assassinated by Palestinian nationalists in 1951), the Muslim Brotherhood began their activities with the acquiescence of the authorities. In 1948, they gained recognition as a charitable organization. The Brotherhood achieved a special relationship with King Hussein, partly because of his antagonism toward regional powers that were hostile to the Brotherhood, namely President Nasser of Egypt, the champion of Arab nationalism, and the Arab socialist Ba'th Party, which was active in both Syria and Iraq. The Brotherhood made their mark in Jordanian politics and was strongly represented in the Ministries of Religious Affairs and Education. Their commitment to the Hashemites survived the clashes of 1970–1971 between the Jordanian government and the Palestinian organizations. Various groups of extremists emerged on the margins of the Brotherhood; however, this did not at first disturb the relationship between the Brotherhood and the palace.

From 1945 to 1985, the interests of the Jordanian government and the Brotherhood coincided, especially regarding the refuge given to Syrian Brothers who were fleeing Ba'thist repression. However, when diplomatic relations between Amman and Damascus began to improve in the mid-1980s, this led to deterioration in relations between the Brotherhood and King Hussein, especially over their differing approaches to the Palestinian question. In 1987–1988, the Palestinian movement "Hamas" was established. The official recognition accorded to Hamas by the Jordanian government posed a problem for the Jordanian Muslim Brotherhood, which saw Hamas as a substantial political adversary, despite the fact that it was in essence an offshoot of the Brotherhood itself. However, the king's new policy of democratization gave the Brotherhood the opportunity it had eagerly awaited to demonstrate its political power. In the event, they were the principal victors of the 1989 elections in Jordan. In 1992, the Brotherhood set up the Islamic Action Front (IAF), which became their legal political party, whose slogan was: "Crush the imperialist and Zionist challenge." Nevertheless, in the 1993 elections, they lost most of their parliamentary seats, while the government appeared irritated

both by their political influence within Jordan and by their support for Saddam Hussein.

In 1999, after King Hussein's death, the situation underwent significant changes. The Al-Aqsa Intifada began in September 2000, and in 2001, King Abdullah II of Jordan expelled three Hamas leaders. They were Khaled Mish'al, Musa Abu Marzuq, and Ibrahim Ghosheh, who committed himself to undertake no further activity on behalf of Hamas. This, however, did not affect the relationship between the Jordanian government and the Muslim Brotherhood. In February 2002, the Jordanian Muslim Brotherhood appointed new leaders for the IAF. Abdul Majid Zanaibat, a moderate figure of Jordanian rather than Palestinian origin, who had a good relationship with the palace, became the new guide. The radical candidate, Hama Said, obtained only seventeen votes from the members of the Brotherhood's Consultative Council (the Majlis al-Shura) as against Zanaibat's twenty. Four members of the forty-one-member council abstained. This relatively narrow majority was, nevertheless, a success for the king, whose aim was to rebuild Jordan's political landscape on the basis of a new elite whose origins were not in the West Bank. In practice, the emergence of this moderate tendency in the Brotherhood lay behind the renewal of the Brotherhood's dialogue with the U.S. Embassy in Jordan in early 2002.

The new Jordanian king, like his father, was wary of the Palestinians, fearing that they could represent a threat to his kingdom. This lay behind the hardening of his attitude to Hamas and the closing of Jordan's frontiers with the West Bank, a move intended to counter the idea that Jordan was an alternative country for the Palestinians. This attitude of the king was shared by the historic leaders of the Muslim Brotherhood in Jordan, such as Ishaq al-Farhan or Abdullatif Arabiyat, a former speaker of the Jordanian parliament. Among the IAF's influential members of the Jordanian parliament, Ahmed al-Qafarin advocated a middle way between alliance with the Hashemite throne and entrenched opposition. Another influential figure was Laith Shbeilat, a former member of parliament and a one-time president of the Engineers' Syndicate. Shbeilat had a good relationship with the Muslim Brotherhood and was a member of the Shadhiliya religious fraternity (tariqa). Shbeilat was imprisoned a number of times by King Hussein, with whom he, nevertheless, had a working understanding. Shbeilat has frequently been in Lebanon in the course of his work as a leading civil engineer and was a founding member of an association called the Arab Nationalist and Islamic Congress in Beirut. This brought together under the aegis of Hizbollah both Shi'ite and Sunni Islamist movements, together with representatives of the old Arab nationalist parties.

MUSLIM BROTHERHOOD (SYRIA)

The Muslim Brotherhood first made its influence felt in Syria in the city of Homs in 1938. Syria was the first country outside Egypt to pay heed to the preaching (Da'wa) of the Muslim Brotherhood, through the intermediary of Syrian students returning from Egyptian universities. In 1947, one of these students, Mustafa al-Siba'i, known even as a young man for his fervor and eloquence, set up a formal branch of the Muslim Brotherhood in Homs, on the model of the Egyptian organization. In the later 1940s and into the 1950s, the Syrian Brotherhood found itself in competition for membership with the Ba'th Party and the Communist Party. They, nevertheless, succeeded in making inroads into the major cities, finding members among working people as well as among committed believers. However,

they were unable to arouse any real interest in the intellectual and trade union circles.

In the period from 1958 to 1961, during the experiment of political union with Egypt, when the two countries became the United Arab Republic, under the presidency of Egypt's charismatic leader, Gamal Abdel Nasser, the Muslim Brotherhood was obliged to tread carefully. Ostensibly, they approved the policy of Syria's President Shukri Quwatli, while behind the scenes they worked to encourage Syrian opposition to Egypt's domination of Syria, especially in the field of agrarian reform. Led by Issam al-Attar, the Brotherhood in due course became a key element in the popular movement to separate Syria from Egypt (the Infisal), which succeeded in ending the unity experiment in 1961. Everything changed, however, with the Ba'thist coup of 1963. This called a halt to the rise of the Brotherhood, which then found itself cast in the role of a radical opposition movement. At this time, in addition to its presence in Homs, Issam al-Attar had also set up a branch of the Brotherhood in Damascus. It also existed in Hama, where Marwan Hadid had set up the movement known as the Militant Vanguard, as well as in Aleppo, where it was led by two notable figures, Abdelfatah Abu Ghida and Adnan Saadeddin. Adnan Saadeddin stood as a candidate in the Syrian parliamentary elections of 1973, organized by President Assad, who assumed power in 1971. Adnan Saad al-Din then became the Brotherhood's leader, or "Muraqib al-Am" (General Supervisor) in Syria.

Despite this, antagonism between the Brotherhood and the Syrian government mounted under Syria's President Assad. From 1976, there was open hostility between the Brotherhood and the government, which was dominated by adherents of the president's heterodox Alawite faith. The Muslim Brotherhood was officially banned in 1980. Muslim Brothers had launched a number of attacks on President Assad's regime, including an attempt to assassinate Assad himself.

This reached its peak in 1982, with the clash between the authorities and the Muslim Brotherhood in Hama. The Brotherhood declared that Hama was a free city, no longer under Ba'thist rule. In retaliation, government forces shelled the quarter of the city the Islamists had made their stronghold. Estimates of the number of deaths are hard to make as many fled the city, but apparently between 10,000 and 30,000 died. The Syrian regime attempted to root out the Muslim Brotherhood from Syria's territory and pursued its leaders even in Europe and elsewhere. Some of the Brotherhood's leaders were imprisoned, while others took refuge in Jordan, Iraq, Saudi Arabia, Germany, Austria, and even the United States. Nevertheless, the leadership maintained contact with the Syrian Brotherhood's activists and were able to keep it alive. The activity of leading figures in the Brotherhood such as Said Hawa, Ziad Hashem, and Abu Raudeh was important, as was that of the group led by Issam al-Attar in exile in Aix-la-Chapelle and Baden-Baden.

From the mid-1990s, there were contacts between the Syrian authorities and the exiled leadership of the Brotherhood, especially between Al-Attar's group based in Germany and the former head of Syrian military intelligence, Ali Duba. The aim was to open a new phase in relations, but the details of the envisaged rapprochement proved to be a stumbling block. The government insisted that the exiles should return as individuals, forswearing further activity, while the Brotherhood wished to negotiate collective permission to return, with a general amnesty and authority to resume their charitable activities. Syria's new president, Bashar al-Assad, who followed the line laid down by his father, offered individual amnesty to those held as prisoners, but repudiated the suggestion of collective negotiation with the Brotherhood. Meanwhile, Ali Sadr al-Din al-Bayanouni, the Syrian Brotherhood's present general supervisor, who was by this time resident in London, began to make an effort to create a unified Syrian opposition in exile. The improvement in relations between Syria and Iraq, together with the crackdown on Syrian members of the Muslim Brotherhood in Jordan rendered the Syrian Brotherhood inoperative in those countries, which enabled him to take control of the Syrian Brotherhood through its exiled membership in Germany and Saudi Arabia.

In 2001, the Syrian Brothers adopted a moderate program advocating nonviolence, calling for unity among those elements calling for change within Syria. As leader, Bayanouni has maintained contacts with the regime. Despite the events at Hama in 1982, and the difficulties faced by the international Islamist movement, the Syrian Muslim Brotherhood continued to be an influential influence in Syrian social and political life and continues to look forward to a post-Alawite period in Syria. In 2005, the Muslim Brotherhood signed the so-called Damascus Declaration, a document in which various opposition groups called for the establishment of genuine representative democracy in Syria. In 2006, Bayanouni met the former Syrian Vice President Abdul Halim Khaddam, now in exile, who is also attempting to organize an opposition coalition. As a Sunni organization, the Muslim Brotherhood would potentially be sympathetic with Sunni insurgents in Iraq.

NAMANGANI, JUMA

Juma Namangani was born in Uzbekistan on June 12, 1969, at Namangan in the province of Ferghana. By 1987, he was in Afghanistan, fighting against the Russian elite forces. He rediscovered his Islamic roots through his contacts with the Afghan Mujahidin and completely took on board their way of thinking. In the early 1990s, back in his home town of Namangan, he and Tahir Yuldashev set up the Adalat (Justice) movement, which took control of part of the town during the winter of 1991–1992, challenging the power of the government. In March, the authorities took tough action to regain control, driving the Islamists out.

Though Namangani's knowledge of religion was limited, his commitment to Islamist militancy was unquestionable, and he believed his Islamist vocation extended beyond Uzbekistan to other countries of the region. He was fluent in Tajik (a language related to Persian) and Russian as well as his own Turkic Uzbek language. When Uzbekistan became too hot for him, Namangani fled to Tajikistan, where the Tajik Islamists were for the time being in control of the capital, Dushanbe. In November, the Tajik authorities retook Dushanbe and Namangana joined the guerrillas in the Tajik region of Tahvildara. In 1997, the Tajik Islamists came to an agreement with their head

of state, Imamali Rahmanov. Namangana was opposed to any compromise and therefore retired to Afghanistan, together with Tahir Yuldashev. There, they established the Islamic Movement of Uzbekistan to carry on the fight in their homeland.

At the time, Namangani was in charge of the Uzbek contingent in Afghanistan. Some Uzbeks reached Kyrgyzstan during the summer months of 1999 and 2000, by way of Tajik territory, and mounted operations against the Uzbek government from there. In the spring of 2001, the informal pact between the Uzbeks and Massoud's Tajiks collapsed, and the Uzbek battalion attacked Panjshir. Everything changed, however, after the American-led attack in Afghanistan in October 2001, when the United States began to assist the United Front. Namangani and his men were driven back into Mazar-Sheif and Namangani was killed when the coalition forces attacked the town. His death signaled a substantial impairment of the IMU's fighting strength.

NATION OF ISLAM (UNITED STATES)

The Nation of Islam is an African-American political and social organization whose goal is the promotion of a separatist agenda, through conversion to a form of radical Islam and its practice. Its ultimate goal is the construction of a separate state, exclusively African American and Islamic. The Nation of Islam was founded in Detroit in the 1930s by an itinerant preacher, Wallace Ford, whose origins are subject to dispute. FBI records suggest that Ford was born in 1891. Ford called himself "Fard" for the purposes of his mission, which was to preach to the African-American population a messianic message of which the burden was "to recover the Nation of Islam, lost amidst the savagery of America." He had been in Chicago and Detroit prior to his declaration of the new faith and had been involved with other para-Islamic ventures. He was a member of a group called the Moorish Science Temple of America and then founded the Allah Temple of Islam. He later signed himself Wallace Fard Muhammad. Wallace Fard disappeared in 1934.

Wallace Fard, later aided by his principal disciple Elijah Mohammed, born Elijah Poole, constructed a cosmogony for the specific use of his fellow African Americans. Elijah Muhammad took on the leadership of the Nation of Islam after Fard's disappearance. According to Elijah Muhammad, writing in 1965, the "Black Race" represents the descendants of the original race of mankind, while white people were the results of a bizarre scientific experiment in ancient times. Elijah Muhammad was the author of the movement's basic text, *Message to the Blackman in America*. In 1963, Malcolm X asserted that "thoughtful white people know they are inferior to black people." According to Wallace Fard's original teaching, 85 percent of the world's population consists of the easily led masses, 10 percent of those who are referred to as "rich slave makers" and 5 percent of "poor righteous teachers." Together with these ideas about the origins of the black and white races, the Nation of Islam claimed to accept all the pillars of Islam, but certain added features rendered them heretical in the eyes of orthodox Muslims. Central among these was Elijah Muhhamad's insistence that Wallace Fard enjoyed the status of prophethood, a claim entirely in contradiction to orthodox Islam.

Under Elijah Muhammad, the Nation of Islam converted new members in large numbers. Their Islam—so far as it was orthodox—was strict, with prayer and fasting at Ramadan, as well as dietary rules and modest dress for women, as well as the establishment of a chain of Islamic schools. The movement strenuously opposed all integration with the white community and took the opposite direction of Martin Luther King's civil rights movement. Elijah Muhammad opposed all interbreeding and asserted that the violation of black women slaves by their white masters had been intended to produce a race of slaves. It was at this time that the movement had its greatest success, partly due to the charisma and high profile of Malcolm X. A problem for the Nation of Islam arose in 1964 when Malcolm X split from the organization over a personal difference with Elijah Muhammad. In 1965, Malcolm X was murdered by other Nation of Islam members.

From the early 1970s, the Nation of Islam seems to have made tentative approaches to the world Islamic movement, funded and under the patronage of Saudi Arabia. It did not, however, abandon its own beliefs. The movement also came under the influence of one of its leading members, Louis Farrakhan, in effect the movement's new strong man, who had joined the Nation of Islam in 1955. In social terms, the Nation of Islam turned to rap performers such as Public Enemy and Ice-T. Farrakhan and his lieutenants embarked on propaganda missions in prisons and correctional institutions, aiming to Islamize the black American community from the grass roots. The Nation of Islam also launched itself into efforts to stem the spread of Aids, which it called a "white conspiracy." Nation of Islam militias, known as the "Fruit of Islam," acted as vigilantes, driving drug dealers and other miscreants out of the African-American areas in the cities, often with the approval of local government.

In 1975, when Elijah Muhammad died, the official leadership of the movement descended to the son of Wallace Fard, known as Wallace Deen Muhammad, who later called himself Imam Warith Deen Muhammad. He renamed the organization the Muslim American Society and moved to bring it closer to Sunni Islam. Many of his followers underwent formal conversions under the guidance of Sunni imams and became mainstream Muslims. Some Nation of Islam devotees, however, were discontented with the new regime. In 1976, Louis Farrakhan quit the reformed organization and began to organize the reestablishment of a renewed Nation of Islam on its original lines. He officially declared the refoundation of the Nation of Islam in 1981. Perhaps the most spectacular manifestation of the new organization was the so-called Million Man March in Washington, DC in 1995, when a figure close to 800,000 Nation of Islam members demonstrated in the American capital.

In 2000, the two wings of the movement announced their reunification and Louis Farrakhan has since been reconciled with Warith Deen Muhammad. In 2005, Louis Farrakhan presided over an anniversary march in Washington, DC, attended this time by around 300,000 participants. The gathering was addressed by many leading African Americans, not limited to the Nation of Islam's own leadership. In August 2006, due to ill health, Louis Farrakhan—now aged seventy-three—handed the management of the Nation of Islam over to a committee. In March 2007, Farrakhan gave a speech in Detroit in which he criticized the American military involvement in Iraq and the policies of President George W. Bush.

However, he also announced his imminent retirement, raising questions as to the future viability of the organization. No charismatic figure able to replace Farrakhan appeared to be likely to come forward. Some members of the organization said it would need to turn more toward mainstream Islam in order to survive, abandoning some of its idiosyncratic beliefs.

NETHERLANDS

By 2007, the Muslim population of the Netherlands had grown to around a million, in an overall population of some 15 million. Probably two thirds of this figure has acquired Dutch citizenship. The earliest Muslims in the country were from the Dutch colony in Indonesia, but today the largest communities are from Turkey and Morocco. The period of immigration began in the 1960s and continued until 1974. Even after a halt was put to primary immigration, however, family consolidation meant that the Muslim community continued to grow. More recently, a number of Muslims have come from Surinam, together with asylum seekers from Iraq, Afghanistan, and Somalia, among other places.

The policy of the Netherlands has traditionally laid stress on multiculturalism—including respect for the cultural specificities of immigrants together with a program favoring integration of migrants into Dutch society. Great stress is laid on human rights and the need for migrants to accept Dutch values in such areas. The foremost issue is what is known as the "woman question"—namely the need for immigrant women to enjoy equal rights and the same level of respect as Dutch citizens. It has been relatively easy for foreign residents to obtain Dutch citizenship, and there have been, at different times, a number of members of the Dutch parliament who are of Muslim origin. Recently, tension has arisen between the Dutch population and the Muslim migrants due to the backlash from a number of incidents.

Radical Islamic groups have been known to be active in the Netherlands since the mid-1990s. The Dutch security services have identified a substantial level of Saudi influence, with funding of Muslim groups and activities from all the usual Saudi sources and NGOs. For example, the Amsterdam "Tawheed" mosque (a name characteristic of Salafi activity) has been linked to the Saudi Al-Haramein Foundation. A number of other mosques receive Saudi funds through one channel or another. On December 23, 2004, the Dutch Ministry of the Interior published a report under the title, *From Dawa to Jihad*. An estimate of the number of Muslims sympathetic to radical ideas puts the figure at 50,000 (5 percent of the total), but adds that the attraction of radical groups for young Muslims appears to be a consistent trend. An estimate in 2005 suggested that a few hundred Muslims at most would be prepared to engage themselves in radical activity. They included a small group of veteran fighters who had returned from Afghanistan and Chechnya. Intelligence sources recommended that the activities of Muslim groups should be monitored.

Salafi groups are particularly active among the Moroccan community. A number of young Moroccans were detained in 2004, on suspicion of association with the planning of violent acts. Self-styled Salafi imams whose sermons are of an intolerant nature have attracted the attention of the Dutch security services, as has the activity of Tablighi Jamaat, an organization that is itself nonpolitical but attracts elements most susceptible to radicalization. Concern about the activities of radicals has been most evident since the Madrid bombings of March 2004. Possible links with the Moroccan Islamic Combatant Group have been carefully monitored, as have links with radical Salafi groups still active in Algeria.

The incident that has given rise to the most concern in the Netherlands, however, was the murder in November 2004 of the filmmaker Theo Van Gogh, well known as a critic of Islam. Theo Van Gogh had cooperated with a former Somali citizen, Ayaan Hirsi Ali, to make a film about the allegedly degrading treatment meted out to Muslim women. Hirsi Ali, an ethnic Somali who had renounced Islam, was a public figure in the Netherlands. The film involved the use of quotations from the text of the Quran, displayed as if written on the bodies of women. A Dutch citizen of Moroccan origin, Mohammed Bouyeri, shot and knifed to death Van Gogh in the street in Amsterdam. He is serving a life sentence without parole for the killing, which he claims to have committed in the name of Islam. The intelligence services linked him with a known terrorist suspect, Samir Azouz. Bouyeri was an attender at the Tawheed mosque and had recently taken up wearing Moroccan dress. Paradoxically, his farewell message, indicating he wished to be a martyr and found on him at his arrest, after an exchange of shots, was written in Dutch rather than Arabic.

Ayaan Hirsi Ali, a Somali citizen born in 1969, came to the Netherlands from Kenya, where she had been living with her family. She settled in the Netherlands in 1992 and in due course acquired Dutch citizenship. She studied political science at Leiden University and graduated with a master's degree in 2000. She became a member of the Dutch parliament in 2003 as a member of a libertarian party, the Volkspartij voor Vrijheid en Democratie (VVD). She originally entered the Netherlands as an asylum seeker, though the circumstances in which she was granted asylum are unclear. She admits having told falsehoods in her asylum application and as a result her status as a Dutch national was thrown into question. She left the country in 2006 and went to work for a conservative think tank in the United States, the American Enterprise Institute.

NIGERIA

Nigeria is one of the largest states of Africa, with a population of 131 million people in 2007. Half the population is Muslim, 40 percent Christian, and 10 percent follow indigenous African beliefs. It was formerly under British colonial rule until its independence in 1960. It has a federal constitution and is officially secular, though Islam plays a legal and administrative role in some of the country's northern states, whose political leaderships have—controversially—incorporated Shari'a law into their legal systems. Since 1960, various regimes, many of them military, have succeeded each other as rulers of Nigeria. All have adopted a repressive policy toward the Islamic movements, seen as threats to public order because of their attacks on deviant Muslims and the Christian community. In 2007, Nigeria's president was Olusegun Obasanjo, elected in 1999 to the country's presidency and reelected in 2003. New presidential elections were set for April 14 and 21, 2007. President Obasanjo is a Christian and a former army chief of staff who had been Nigeria's military ruler from 1976 to 1979. Islam was long established in northern Nigeria. The first Muslims appeared in Nigeria in the fourteenth century, following which various rulers consolidated or extended the Muslim domains. The Jihad led by Uthman Dan Fodio, from 1804 to 1810, established the Sultanate of Sokoto and extended the political authority of Islam over northern Nigeria. In Sokoto, Katsina, and Kano Islam predominates today, with up to 95 percent of the population being Muslims.

For several decades, Nigeria has faced problems linked to ethnic and religious tensions. Severe clashes of religious sensibilities have arisen in Nigeria since independence, to greater or lesser extent finding expression in political activities. There is a Mahdist tradition in the country where prophets emerge and proclaim their own vocation, for instance in the case of Muhammad Marwa (known as Maitatsine) who attracted mass support and incited violent disturbances, but was killed in clashes with the authorities in 1980. Maitatsine made claims for his own powers going far beyond the proprieties of orthodox Islam, verging into heresy. Various manifestations of what might be called Mahdism—the anticipation that a prophet may arise—are seen spasmodically. Other influential movements include the Sunni Yan Izala. The movement's name "Izala" is an abbreviation of an Arabic name, "Jama'at Izalat il-Bid'a wa-l-Iqamat us-Sunna" ("Society for the Abolition of Innovation and the Upholding of Orthodoxy"), which takes a Salafi line and attracts support from NGOs that derive funds from Saudi Arabia. There is a significant Da'wa movement, preaching Islam to those falling away from the faith, with a strongly orthodox Sunni Tabligh-i Jamaat presence that occasionally manifests itself. Many different Muslim groups and sects exist today. The Qadiriya and Tijaniya Sufi Brotherhoods, which have always been well entrenched in Nigeria, are well represented. There are also other local Brotherhood-style organizations that command significant support and membership. The Islamists deplore the existence of the secular state, believing that it is the vehicle of corruption and decadence that will lead back to a state of barbarism—the "Jahiliya" that prevailed before the advent of Islam. The presence of a Christian as president of Nigeria is seen as an omen of disaster.

Of the more extremist Islamist groups within the Sunni community, the Yan Izala is foremost. It was founded at the instance of a conservative cleric, Sheikh Abubakar Gumi, and opposes the activities of the Sufi Brotherhoods. Increasingly significant, however is the so-called Shi'ite movement led by Sheikh Ibrahim Zakzaky, which has common roots with the local Sunni Islamist movements. Local Islamists have for some time been receiving funds from foreign Muslim states, including Saudi Arabia, Sudan, and Libya, who have favored Sunni groups. Iran, however, has also been a donor and has sought a Shi'ite partner or at least an interlocutor with sympathy for Shi'ism. There is traditionally little or no Shi'ite presence in Nigeria, and until the Islamic Revolution in Iran there were very few Shi'ites, with the Shi'ite branch of the faith represented only by a handful of Lebanese emigrant traders and a small number of Ismailis, also mainly merchants. Sheikh Zakzaky was the head of a group calling itself the "Islamic Movement," a radical group that aimed to transform Nigeria entirely into an Islamic state. In the early 1990s, he was adamant he was not a Shi'ite, but made no secret of the inspiration he drew from the Islamic Revolution in Iran.

Zakzaky, born in 1953, studied Arabic and Islamic subjects at school and was an economics student at Ahmadu Bello University in Zaria in the 1970s, where he aligned himself with the Muslim Brotherhood and took his inspiration from Sayyed Qutb, the Egyptian ideologue of the Brotherhood. He was secretary-general of the Muslim Students Society. He was expelled from the university without his degree after he organized a number of demonstrations. This coincided with the Islamic Revolution in Iran, and funds became available for the Islamist students to travel to Iran. The movement led by Zakzaky soon acquired the appellation "Yan Shi'a" (The Shi'ite Community). It had links with the student movement and was strong in the university towns of Zaria, Kano, and Sokoto. Zakzaky soon began to allow himself to be seen as having actually adopted Shi'ism, which led to some dissent within his movement. In 1981, Zakzaky was detained for the first time and was held until 1984. Then in 1987, after the federal government set up special tribunals to deal with

civil disturbances, he was held for another two years. In all, including his later periods of detention, he spent nine years in prison. Zakzaky and his associates continued throughout the 1990s to hold intermittent demonstrations condemning the Nigerian constitution and calling for an Islamic state.

In the 1990s, the activities of the "Shi'ites" began to take an anti-Christian turn. In 1991, in the northern Nigerian city of Katsina, alleged blasphemy by a Christian publication led to major disturbances in which the demonstrators burned down the offices of a newspaper called *The Fun Times,* which was alleged to have libeled Prophet Muhammad. In 1994, the "Shi'ites" condemned to death—but later pardoned—a group of lecturers at Bayero University in Kano who had gone on strike, thus allegedly leaving students free time to commit immoral acts. Matters took a more serious turn later in 1994 when a Christian merchant was beheaded after supposedly desecrating the Quran. The military governor ordered the execution of those responsible, which was to be carried out in secret in the hope of avoiding a violent reaction. In 1996, after attempting to set up a clandestine radio station to propagate Islamic ideas, Zakzaky was arrested again for spreading sedition. The regime of Sani Abacha arrested some 150 Islamists. Riots across northern Nigeria followed. In 1998, there were further disturbances as the "Shi'ites" demanded the observance of Shi'ite customs relating to the end of the fasting month of Ramadan. Despite adopting certain Shi'ite practices and customs, the adherents of the movement continue on a personal basis to be Sunni Muslims and the movement itself resembles the Muslim Brotherhood rather than a Shi'ite organization. Later in 1998, the "Shi'ites" launched a major campaign to have Zakzaky freed. He was released in December 1998 along with other political prisoners by the interim regime in Nigeria of Abdussalami Abubakr.

Since 1999, though the federal government has expressed its entrenched opposition to Shari'a law, twelve states from the northern part of the country have adopted judicial systems based on the Muslim legal system. The introduction of the Shari'a has certainly been encouraged by radical Islamist movements, which have been active in the region for many years. However, the actual instigators of this series of moves have been the President's political opponents. The governor of the state of Zamfara, Ahmed Sani, for example, is an influential official in the opposition All People's Party (APP), which has never been an Islamist movement. He decided to adopt a religious stance and back a programme of re-Islamization for opportunistic reasons, in order to destabilize the central government, with the backing of part of the senior military establishment. Morality in public life is a strong electoral card to play in the Muslim regions where the Muslim Hausa community is for the most part in the majority. Nigeria's President Obasanjo strongly opposed the introduction of Shari'a, declaring that it contradicts the constitution. Religious dissidence has given rise to violent intercommunal strife that is intermittently violent, setting Muslims and Christians against one another.

Under British colonial rule, the Shari'a had been partially applied, but only in civil matters. In the twelve Nigerian states concerned, it was now in criminal cases that the Shari'a was to be applied, though those citizens who were of other religious persuasions were to have their own laws. From the introduction of Islamic tribunals at the end of 1999, many severe penalties have been imposed. These have included amputation of the right hand for thieves and beating or stoning in cases of adultery. These have sometimes caused controversy, and the authorities were accused of courting popularity with the Muslim masses by imposing these severe penalties, rather than

doing it for religious reasons. A distinction has been drawn by analysts between Islamism and neo-Islamism. Islamist ideas, both of the Sunni and Shi'a traditions, call for a wholesale reshaping of society to an Islamic model, after which the application of the full panoply of Islamic law becomes appropriate. Neo-Islamism begins with the strict application of Shari'a in all domains and the crude elimination of Western influences. Such groups as the Sunni Yan Izala and Ibrahim Zakzaky's "Shi'ite" movement have been critical of the actions of politicians with little or no record of Islamic activism jumping on the Shari'a bandwagon.

In 2001, Sheikh Zakzaky was freed and now bases himself in Zaria. Interviewed after September 11, he said the retaliation of the United States for the attacks on New York and Washington, DC constituted a war not on terrorism but on Islam. This contrasted with the federal government, which at the behest of the United States froze assets identified as associated with Osama bin Laden. Zakzaky still has a large following, especially among the deprived urban Muslim youth and claims he could easily field a million people in any demonstration he might choose to call. However, he now faces competition. Splinter groups have been formed by Aminu Aliya Gusau in Zamfara, Ahmed Shuaibu in Kano, and Abubakar Mujahid in Zaria. Abubakar Mujahid calls his faction "Jama'at al-Tajdid al-Islami" ("The Society for Islamic Renewal"). One of the principal bones of contention of these leaders, all self-professed Sunnis, is what appears to be Zakzaky's increasing personal commitment to Shi'ism.

In 2002, the introduction of Shari'a by politicians in the northern states precipitated a constitutional crisis when a young woman was sentenced to death for adultery in Katsina state. She was eventually released by an appeal court. In 2004, there were widespread anti-Christian demonstrations accompanied by violent incidents across northern Nigeria. In July 2006, Sheikh Zakzaky was the prime mover of a large-scale anti-American and anti-Israel demonstration in northern Nigeria when large numbers took to the streets in protest against the Israeli attack on southern Lebanon. Meanwhile, Sheikh Zakzaky's espousal of the Shi'ite faith became ever more evident and considerable numbers of his followers began to observe the Shi'ite ritual and festivals and even to proclaim themselves Shi'ites. In January 2007, Zakzaky visited Iran and went to the Shi'ite spiritual center at Qom, where he met leading Iranian Shi'ite clerics. He also gave a public address on the occasion of Ashura, the Shi'ite day of mourning for the death of Imam Hussein in battle in Karbala. The Ashura processions in Zaria, Kano, and other northern Nigerian cities were attended by thousands of Shi'ite converts. Zakzaky continues to speak out, however, against the introduction of Shari'a in a state that is not fully Islamized, which he believes is premature and leads to injustice.

On the other hand, militant Sunni groups are also active. One group calls itself the "Taliban." Such militants have received funds from groups associated with the official Saudi aid agencies, including the Muslim World League, the World Assembly of Muslim Youth, the International Islamic Relief Organization, and the Al-Haramein Foundation. There are said to be Sudanese and Middle Eastern Islamists inside Nigeria and one report speaks of Pakistanis who have associated themselves with Sunni groups inciting violence. There are allegations that Sunni militias in the pay of state governments in northern Nigeria have been used to harass Shi'ites and the Yan Shi'a movement. Government spokesmen in northern states, themselves Muslims, have said that the Yan Shia phenomenon is beginning to resemble the Maitatsine movement and have claimed to see signs of a Mahdist movement around Sheikh Zakzaky that represents a threat to Nigeria's security.

Jama'at Izalat il-Bid'a wa-l-Iqamat us-Sunna (Society for the Abolition of Innovation and the Upholding of Orthodoxy)

This is a movement of a Salafi type founded in 1978 by the Grand Qadi of Nigeria, Sheikh Abubakar Gumi, who lived from 1922 to 1992. The society is also simply known by an abbreviation of its Arabic name, "Izala." It is less hostile to the Christian community than are most of the Nigerian Islamists. Its leaders prefer to direct their hostility at the major Islamic Brotherhoods present in the country, the Qadiriya and the Tijaniya, whose influence they believe is harmful. There have been in practice significant tensions and some violent confrontations between the supporters of Izala and the members of these brotherhoods. The clashes have led to the deaths of some who were involved and to the arrest of Izala activists. From 1985 to 1993, under the regime of General Babangida, Izala enjoyed better relations with the regime, thanks to the efforts of Sheikh Gumi, and were able to develop their activities in the states of northern Nigeria.

There were a number of factions within the movement, and it underwent a split in 1986. A further faction, calling itself the Ahl as-Sunna ("The People of Orthodoxy"), emerged as a result. This fell largely under the influence of Saudi Arabia and is still led by Yakuibu Musa. Despite efforts by the police to curtail its activities, it appears to have substantial groups of militants at its command in Kano and Kaduna states.

Yan Shia

Yan Shi'a ("The Shi'a Community") is a Nigerian sectarian movement that advocates the establishment of an Islamic Republic and the application of the Shari'a throughout the entire country. It is based in northern Nigeria and is especially well represented in Zaria. It was in the first instance a movement of Sunni Muslims supported by the Shi'ite Islamic Republic of Iran. As the years have passed, however, it has actually become more Shi'ite in character. Yan Shi'a runs charitable networks and publishes a magazine called *The Witness*. Its leader Sheikh Ibrahim el-Zakzaky, one of the country's first political prisoners, has been detained on a number of occasions for conspiracy. Under the regime of President Abacha, he was held from September 1996 to December 1998 and then released when Olusegun Basanjo (a Christian) became president.

Zakzaky does not recognize the multiconfessional nature of the Nigerian federal state. He is suspected of fomenting interconfessional clashes, particularly in Kaduna, where hundreds of people have become the victims of violence. A number of militants have been arrested on charges of destroying shops selling alcoholic drink and have also been accused of involvement of burning down Christian buildings. On October 12, 2001, Yan Shi'a organized a major demonstration in support of Osama bin Laden in Kano, after which trouble broke out that culminated in the deaths of more than two hundred people.

Yan Shi'a also maintains good relations with the Islamic Republic of Iran. Sheikh Zakzaky travels to Iran from time to time, and as long ago as the 1980s he began to celebrate Shi'a festivals. His followers, however, are drawn from Nigeria's Sunni community, as there are virtually no native Shi'ites in Nigeria. In recent years, more of them have been practicing Shi'a rituals and have claimed to be converted to Shi'ism, so that there is now an Ashura procession, for example, in Zaria and other northern Nigerian cities in which several thousand people participate.

In 1994, a small group broke off from Yan Shi'a and called itself the Movement for the Renewal of Islam ("Jama'at ul-Tajdid ul-Islami"). This somewhat undermined the main movement at first, but Sheikh Zakzaky is now once more the undisputed leader of what has become an influential movement that unsettles the Nigerian authorities and challenges the authority of the conventional Islamic structure based in the mosques.

OMAR, MULLAH

Mullah Omar is the leader of the Afghan Taliban. His full name is Omar Abdurrahman Akhunzadeh. He is an ethnic Pushtun, born in 1959 near Mewand, close to Kandahar, into a family of small farmers of the Hotaki tribe, a part of the Ghilzai tribal confederation. His family roots lay in the Arghandeb Valley in the province of Oruzgan, close to Helmand. Relatively little is known about him. While the Taliban was in power, he remained mainly in his residence in Kandahar. He may now be in hiding in the tribal areas of northern Pakistan, close to Peshawar. No Western journalist has ever met Mullah Omar, but those Afghans who have seen him speak of him as a relatively young-looking man in his forties, with a black beard and wearing a black turban. He is said to have studied Islamic subjects in Pakistan before becoming an imam in the village of Singesar, near Kandahar. During the war against the Soviets, he joined one of the movements favored by Pushtun recruits, most of whom adhered either to the faction of Hezb-i Islami led by Younus Khales, a conservative fundamentalist, or the Harakat-i Enqelab-i Islami. He was wounded a number of times and lost the sight of an eye. After the Soviets departed in 1989, Mullah Omar set up his own madrasa in Singesar. Meanwhile, the Najibullah regime fell in

1992, and conflict broke out among the warlords for control of Afghanistan.

Mullah Omar is said to have formed the nucleus of the Taliban movement in 1994. His first action was a raid carried out by just thirty men to rescue two young women held hostage by a renegade commander. He executed Daro Khan, a former mujahidin commander, who extorted ransom money from those traveling on the roads under his control, and afterward made an appeal for the reestablishment of law and order under the Shari'a. This set the seal on his future career. Henceforth, he engaged in a relentless struggle against former comrades that he deemed had fallen short of expectations. He set up a small militia, whose nucleus consisted of the students (the "Taliban") of his madrasa at Singesar, together with veterans of the Jihad against the Soviets, whose goal was to end the tyranny and put a stop of the exactions of the former Mujahidin. His goal was initially limited to the restoration of some kind of calm in his local region, and his movement was primarily concerned with security. At the outset, the Taliban movement was no more than sixty strong, but thousands more volunteers soon joined it. Political and military developments in Afghanistan favored its expansion. Gulbuddin Hekmatyar, the leader of Hizb-i Islami, had hitherto been the best hope of the Islamists, but, after his failure to hold Kabul against other factions,

Pakistan decided to back the Taliban instead. Soon, with the support of the ISI (the Pakistani intelligence services), religious students trained in the Pakistani madrasas—more radical than those in Afghanistan—joined up in large numbers. The movement moved from limited and regional goals to objectives on a national scale and of a political kind. In due course, it stepped up to the international level, under the influence of Osama bin Laden.

From his origins as a simple village imam, Mullah Omar transformed himself into the "Commander of the Faithful"—a title conferred on him by a gathering of several hundred Ulema. This new aura of legitimacy was reinforced by stories that began to be told about him. His mission to liberate his country was said to have come to him in the shape of a divine commandment. It was said he had a vision of a man who asked him to pacify Afghanistan in the name of Islam. God is supposed to have promised him in a dream that he would have victory at Mazar-e Sherif if he rebuilt the tomb in Kabul of Sheikh Fadhel Omar Mujaddedi, the leader of the Naqshbandiya Brotherhood. It was only later that he met Osama bin Laden.

In June 1996, bin Laden settled in Jalalabad, a town held by the supporters of President Rabbani, after his expulsion from Sudan in 1996. Bin Laden, a Saudi multimillionaire, had known the mountains of southeastern Afghanistan since the war of the 1980s against the Soviets, so it was natural that that he should go there to rejoin his former comrades, the commanders Mahmoud, Fazil Haq, and Zainur. All of these had allied themselves with the Taliban. On September 11, 1996, the Taliban took Jalalabad. Osama bin Laden was unknown to the Afghan factions, but in 1997, he met Mullah Omar for the first time. Bin Laden's idea of a strict Islam, voluntarily espoused, serving as a unifying ideology, brought the two together. The Taliban admired his uni-

versalizing vision of a conquering religion confronting the world's primary atheist power, but with some reservations given the limitation of Mullah Omar's horizons to the supremacy of the Pushtuns inside Afghanistan. Mullah Omar rejected as absurd two instruments utilized by bin Laden, the computer and the use of television and video. The country Mullah was, nonetheless, increasingly impressed by bin Laden's charisma and education.

In August 1998, bin Laden played a part in the Taliban recapture of Mazar-e Sherif, less than two weeks before the United States bombed bin Laden's training camps in Afghanistan. Kabul fell to the Taliban at the same time. On October 14, 1998, Mullah Omar met the UN special envoy Lakhdar Brahimi. The United States was bringing pressure to bear to do something about bin Laden. Mullah Omar later told the newspaper *Sharq al-Awsat* that he sought the advice of independent Ulema at this point concerning the question of whether it was legal or not in Shari'a terms to hand bin Laden over. He would repeat this exercise in 2001, after the events of September 11. The Taliban's position was that the Pushtun tribal code, the Pushtunwall, said that dishonor would follow if they were to give up bin Laden, who was their guest. Meetings between the Taliban and the American intelligence services were fruitless, as Mullah Omar sought guarantees from them that they would not give.

Sanctions imposed by the United States and the international community increased the isolation of Afghanistan, where the Taliban government was recognized only by Pakistan, Saudi Arabia, and the United Arab Emirates. However, the economic and military difficulties faced by the country only served to reinforce the position of bin Laden. His contacts, his money, and his Arab fighters gave the regime crucial help that made him indispensable. For whatever reasons, Mollah Omar refused to abandon bin Laden. The religious regime was in any case trapped in the relationship. Al-Qaida had strengthened its position by bringing the Arab combatants together in carefully organized military camps, with a hierarchical structure. A military clash with such well-trained fighters would have been suicidal. Even if the Taliban were to emerge victorious from such a confrontation, which was by no means a certainty, the losses they would certainly sustain would weaken them in relation to the forces at the disposal of Commander Massoud.

The alliance between Mullah Omar and bin Laden, not explicable solely in terms of pan-Islamic solidarity, would in due course bring the Taliban down. Their plan to reconstruct Afghanistan on the basis of the Shari'a and the Pushtun tribes was sacrificed in favor of the objectives of bin Laden, who dragged them after him into his own ventures. In July 2000, Mullah Omar evidently had another dream. This time he saw that the drought suffered by Afghanistan was a plague sent by God in retribution for the country's involvement in the drug trade. (According to his former doctor, speaking to a British newspaper, the *Daily Telegraph,* his propensity to have visions was prompted by a piece of shrapnel in his head, from a mortar bomb.) Whatever the reason, Mullah Omar immediately declared a total prohibition on cultivation of poppy. His orders were not open to discussion, and despite the loss of revenue the farmers did not dare defy the Taliban's orders.

Mullah Omar, in addition to being the spiritual leader of the Taliban, was also the military leader of the Taliban regime's armed forces. In theory, he commanded his forces through a chief of staff and assistant chiefs. In reality, there was no military hierarchy. Mullah Omar maintained direct and permanent contact with his commanders, laying out funds and deciding strategy as he chose. Mullah Omar never met non-Muslims, with a very few exceptions that included representatives of the International Red Cross and the United Nations. Despite his public profile, he was reserved, mystical, and knew little of the outside world. He avoided public appearances and showed little interest in the administration of affairs of state. He remains a somewhat mysterious figure, who never in practice became the political leader that his earlier career seemed to promise. At heart, he has stayed no more than a simple country mullah.

Mullah Omar remained in hiding for some years after his flight from Afghanistan as the result of the attack mounted by the U.S.-backed forces of the Northern Alliance in 2001. However, by 2004, he was reported to have visited Taliban positions in remote areas of Afghanistan's Pushtun territories. He had responded to some messages conveyed to him through intermediaries and claimed in January 2007 that he had not seen Osama bin Laden since his departure from Kabul. In March 2007, he appears to have entered into direct communication with the resurgent Taliban forces in Helmand province in southern Afghanistan. It is said to be due to his influence that the Taliban, led by their new military commander Mullah Dadullah, is once more fighting fiercely against NATO troops in Helmand. Dadullah claimed in March 2007 to have 6,000 fighters under arms and an estimated thirty commanders serve under him. Expert observers of the Taliban predicted that 2007 was set to be a difficult year. On the other hand, a Pakistan-based Taliban leader, Mullah Obaidullah Akhund, was arrested by the Pakistani authorities in March 2007.

ORGANIZATION OF THE ISLAMIC CONFERENCE (OIC)

Between 1963 and 1966, Saudi Arabia strove to implement a plan to bring into being an international organization to include the

Muslim states of the Middle East that would be complementary to the World Islamic League. These years represented the apex of President Nasser's career in Egypt, and Saudi Arabia's hope was that such an organization could serve as a counterbalance to the spreading influence of Arab nationalism. The Saudi scheme was not initially a success, but events soon presented another opportunity. On August 21, 1969, Jewish zealots staged an arson attack on the Al-Aqsa mosque in Jerusalem. The wave of anger and revulsion that spread through the Islamic world offered Saudi Arabia the opportunity to relaunch its scheme plan on a wider basis, aiming at worldwide Islamic solidarity. In September 1969, the new Saudi venture became a reality after an Islamic Summit Conference was held in Rabat. On September 25, 1969, the participating states created a permanent organization to represent the Islamic states. Twenty-four countries immediately became founding members. The organization called itself the Organization of the Islamic Conference (OIC), and it constituted the first international organization whose criterion of membership was religious. From 1971, the OCI maintained a permanent secretariat based in Jeddah.

The OIC became, in effect, a kind of Muslim United Nations. It now includes fifty-seven states and is inclined to show more sympathy to Saudi positions than the Arab League normally does. The OIC presently defines its goals as follows:

> The Organization of the Islamic Conference is an international organization which includes 57 states which have decided to pool their resources, to concert their efforts and to speak with a single voice in order to defend the interests as well as to ensure the progress and well being of their own population as well as of all Muslims throughout the world.

Its Charter appeals for the employment of all political and military means necessary for the liberation of Jerusalem from Israeli occupation. From the outset, the scale of action on which the OIC was to operate was clearly that of the "Umma" as a whole, and not that of its member states.

Other subsidiary organizations are attached to the OIC. These are all based in Jeddah, apart from the Islamic Solidarity Sports Federation, which is based in Riyadh. They include the Academy of Islamic Jurisprudence, the Islamic Solidarity Fund, the International Islamic News Agency, the Islamic States Broadcasting Organization, the International Association of Islamic Banks, the Islamic Committee of the Red Crescent, the Organization of Islamic Cities and Capitals, and the Islamic Shipowners' Association.

The OIC's members and their official date of accession are as follows: Afghanistan (1969), Albania (1992), Algeria (1969), Azerbaijan (1991), Bahrain (1970), Bangladesh (1974), Benin (1982), Brunei (1984), Burkina Faso (1975), Cameroon (1975), Chad (1969), Comoros (1976), Cote d'Ivoire (2001), Djibouti (1978), Egypt (1969), Gabon (1974), Gambia (1974), Guinea (1969), Guinea-Bissau (1974), Guyana (1998), Indonesia (1969), Iran (1969), Iraq (1976), Jordan (1969), Kazakhstan (1995), Kuwait (1969), Kyrghyzistan (1992), Lebanon (1969), Libya (1969), Malaysia (1969), Maldives (1976) Mali (1969), Mauritania (1969), Morocco (1969), Mozambique (1994), Niger (1969), Nigeria (1986), Oman (1970), Pakistan (1969), Palestine (1969), Qatar (1970), Saudi Arabia (1969), Senegal (1969), Sierra Leone (1972), Somalia (1969), Sudan (1969), Surinam (1996), Syria (1970), Tajikistan (1992), Togo (1997), Tunisia (1969), Turkey (1969), Turkmenistan (1992), Uganda (1974), United Arab Emirates (1970), Uzbekistan (1995), Yemen (1969).

The OIC continues to function as an international forum for the Islamic world. In March 2007, the current secretary-general, Professor Ekmeleddin Ihsanoglu, attended the Arab summit meeting in Riyadh on March 28 and discussed the future of the Palestinian areas with the senior Hamas official, Khaled Mish'al. His special envoy Ezzat Kamel Mufti visited Kashmir, and Professor Ihsanoglu participated in the UN Human Rights Council meeting in Geneva. A group of ambassadors from the OIC countries to Washington, DC held an inaugural meeting of a standing OIC group, attended by a senior U.S. State Department representative, and OIC delegations took part in a variety of international discussion groups and working committees.

PADILLA, JOSÉ

José Padilla, who wishes now to be known as Adbullah al-Muhajir, is a citizen of the United States who is accused of plotting to commit terrorist acts. He was arrested in May 2002 and in June 2002 he was declared to be an enemy combatant and was confined in a military prison. At the time of his arrest, he was widely reported in the media to have been involved in a plot to explode a so-called dirty bomb in the United States. A dirty bomb is a device in which conventional explosive would be used to spread radioactive material in a population center. (No such weapon has ever been used or identified.) It was said that he had been assigned the project by Abu Zubayda, an associate of Osama bin Laden. In January 2006, thanks to his status as a citizen, he was moved to the criminal justice system and faced conspiracy charges under the criminal law of the United States.

Padilla was born in New York in 1970 to parents of Puerto Rican origin, but soon moved to Chicago with his parents. Later, after his family moved to Florida, he ran into trouble with the law, spending some time in prison. He became interested in Islam in around 1992, apparently under the influence of a Muslim employer and attended mosques in Florida, some of which had a reputation as centers of extremism. He made a formal conversion to Islam in 1994, initially taking the name Ibrahim. He claims he wanted to learn Arabic and improve his knowledge of Islam. In 2002, he traveled to Middle Eastern countries, including Egypt, Saudi Arabia, and Iraq, and also went to Pakistan and Afghanistan. He had said his travels were funded by friends who wished to help his education. The American authorities were suspicious about his activities and detained him on May 8, 2002, at the international airport in Chicago on his return to the United States. In November 2005, José Padilla was charged with conspiracy to murder, kidnap, and maim victims outside the United States. In spite of the rumors that Padilla had been involved in a plot to use a "dirty bomb," no mention of this was made in the indictment. In August 2006, a federal court in Miami dismissed the charge of conspiracy to murder, but this was reinstated by an appeal court in January 2007.

PAKISTAN

The political evolution of Pakistan has taken a complex path. Its founders intended it to be a democratic country, founded on the principles of Islam. The question that must be answered is why has it evolved in practice into the heartland of an apparently vindictive and intolerant Islamism? The idea of a separate Muslim state to be known as Pakistan—which means the "land of the pure"—was first conceived by the great Indian Muslim writer, Muhammad Iqbal. Pakistan was intended to be a haven for the Muslims of India.

The state of Pakistan actually came into existence in 1947, when India became independent from Britain. The founder of Pakistan, Mohammed Ali Jinnah, had been a political campaigner for Muslim causes within India all his life and was the leader of the All India Muslim League since 1934. In 1940, the league passed a resolution pledging itself to achieve Muslim independence. After the elections of 1946 to India's State Assemblies, when 90 percent of the seats gained by Muslims went to members of his party, he attracted the attention of the British viceroy of India, Lord Mountbatten, with his plan for a separate Muslim state. In 1947, when independence came, Pakistan became a state cut into two by the territory of India. In the east was East Pakistan whose people were Bengalis and who were culturally and linguistically distinct from the larger part of the country situated to the west of India. West Pakistan's population was composed of Punjabis, Pushtuns, Sindhis, and Baluchis, as well as an important component known as the Muhajirs—those who had fled from India after independence.

In the course of its history, the state of Pakistan, founded on the basis of its Islamic nature and its opposition to the Indian adversary, has experienced vicissitudes, including three wars with India, repeated coups d'état, and political instability. The prime minister, Ali Khan, was assassinated in 1951 and General Ayyub came to power in a coup in 1958. In 1969, General Yahya Khan imposed martial law, lasting until the partition of the country in 1971. East Pakistan, which became Bangladesh, was able to break away with the assistance of the Indian military, which inflicted a resounding defeat on Pakistan's armed forces. In the wake of the trauma, Zulfikar Ali Bhutto came to power, installing a left-wing dictatorship. He was overthrown in July 1977 by his chief of staff, General Zia ul Haq, who had him executed two years later. Zia was a convinced Islamist who set up Shari'a courts in Pakistan at the federal level. The international outcry that followed isolated the country until December 1979, when Soviet troops entered Afghanistan. The United States placed Pakistan at the center of its containment strategy and made it the rear base for the Afghan resistance. In exchange, Pakistan got financial aid and sophisticated weapons, as well as the green light to continue with its nuclear program. The death of Zia ul Haq in a mysterious plane crash in August 1988 was the signal for a return to democracy and for Benazir Bhutto, Zulfikar Ali Bhutto's daughter, to take the reins. Nawaz Sharif and Benzir Bhutto would succeed each other in power a number of times, plunging the country into repeated crises. After the Soviet withdrawal from Afghanistan, the Americans canceled all civil and military aid to Pakistan.

Many factors undermined Nawaz Sharif's government. These included endemic corruption and the critical economic situation of a country crippled by debts, as well as clashes between Sunni and Shi'ite extremists, and violence between Sindhis and Muhajirs. There was chronic insecurity in the streets of the large cities and the disaster of the U.S.-imposed withdrawal of Pakistani troops from Kashmir. The government sought unlikely allies in religious circles, leading to an attempt to impose the Shari'a and to a terminal breach with the country's liberals. When Nawaz Sharif sacked General Pervez Musharraf as defense chief, he sparked Musharraf's bloodless coup, which took place on October 12, 1999. This was the fourth time in Pakistan that the military had overturned an elected government, but this time they had the backing of the streets.

General Musharraf at first took the title of chief executive and then in 2001 declared himself to be president.

Pakistan's internal situation was conditioned by its external policies, dominated by the looming presence of India. Since the bloody separation between the two countries, on the basis of religion, hostility between the two states had grown over the issue of Indian Kashmir, a province with a population for the most part Muslim that was claimed in its entirety by Pakistan. On the one hand, the Pakistani army supported Islamic groups who had begun as guerrilla fighters and were by now practicing terrorism. On the other hand, the Indians took tough repressive action. Pakistan had been the chosen ally of the United States and China through the Cold War and then during the Soviet invasion of Afghanistan. After 1990, however, Pakistan retained only China's backing. Washington ostentatiously backed democratic India, which was not only a regional counterbalance against the Chinese, but also offered a major and growing market. As a demonstration of this new orientation, two meetings took place in 2000 between the president of the United States and the prime minister of India, much to the irritation of Pakistan. Pakistan felt increasingly insecure, prompting it to look for new allies and alternative policies.

After its humiliating defeat in the war of 1971, Pakistan threw itself into the development of nuclear weapons, in pursuit of India. In 1980, China, which wished to undermine its Indian rival, gave Pakistan the plans for a nuclear bomb together with other equipment, including M-11 missiles with a range of 300 kilometers. Ghauri-1 missiles with a theoretical range of 1,000 kilometers were developed in cooperation with North Korea. In May 1998, India and Pakistan both carried out nuclear tests. From then on, the conflict took a different turn. Two Third-World powers, both relatively poor and with large populations—150 million Pakistanis and a billion Indians—faced each other. The Kashmir crisis in the spring of 2002 heightened the vigilance of outside powers and especially that of the United States, which used its presence in the region and the country to avert the temptation for either side to turn to the nuclear option.

At the time, Pakistan had at least twenty nuclear devices, which alarmed the Western intelligence services. Catastrophic scenarios sprang readily to the imagination. One possibility was that of a rebellion with an army sensitive to the ideas of the Islamists, in which control could be taken of the nuclear weapons. Another might be the theft of nuclear material that could be used by terrorists. These risks prompted the Americans to send a mission at the end of September 2001 to reinforce security and control of the Pakistani nuclear devices.

In terms of Pakistan's foreign policy in the region, Islam came strongly into play. The other major factor for Pakistan besides India was its relationship with the Muslim states lying broadly to the north. Pakistan had a strong interest in Afghanistan, where there was a common language between northern Pakistan and the Pushtu-speaking regions of Afghanistan. Pakistan's influence dwindled toward the north of Afghanistan, among the Uzbeks and Tajiks. In the Central Asian states, Pakistan may have had ambitions at one time to establish an Islamic zone of influence. These states were geographically quite close. Dushanbe, the capital of Tajikistan, was a mere 450 kilometers north of Peshawar, and the Uzbek capital Tashkent was only 150 kilometers further.

In the 1980s, Zia ul-Haq's plan, which he shared with the ISI, was that once Afghanistan lay under Pakistani influence in a post-Soviet era, Pakistan could secure its oil supplies and build a sphere of influence in the Central Asian states. This was not to be. The two poles of interest for the

Central Asian states continued to be Russia to the north, essentially the former colonial power, and Turkey to the west, where there was a sense of cultural community. Pakistan and Saudi Arabia both extended discreet encouragement to Islamist movements in Uzbekistan, Kyrgizstan, Kazakhstan, Turkmenistan, and Tajikistan. However, in these countries, there was very little sense of commonality with Pakistan, owing in part to the Turkic language and culture of all the Central Asian states save Tajikistan, where the language was closely related to Persian.

Pakistan's ultra-Islamic phase had begun under the presidency of Zia ul-Haq. The United States took the decision to make use of religion to combat the atheist power of the Soviets, thus launching an appeal to the whole world's Muslims. More and more madrasas, many drawing financial support from Saudi Arabia, sprang up in Pakistan. Many of the students from these schools—the "Taliban," literally "students"—were sent north to fight in Afghanistan. They were educated in a faith that admitted of no doubts. They learned that divine truth was the only truth, and that any rebellion against the clergy was a revolt against God. Tens of thousands of students were uprooted from their families and turned into fanatical supporters of an artificial Islamic solidarity. The war in Afghanistan threatened Pakistan's stability, cutting off communications by road with the former Soviet republics and Iran and endangering gas supplies from Turkmenistan. Benzir Bhutto's government gave the green light to a proposal by the Jami'at Ulama-i Islami (JUI), who had set up the first network of madrasas in Pakistan, to send their Taliban into Afghanistan with the backing of the Pakistani intelligence services (ISI) and Saudi money.

The American CIA looked favorably at first at the rise of the Taliban, which was a thorn in the flesh of Russia on its Asian frontiers and opposed Sunni Islam to Iran's Shi'ism. There were also economic considerations. This was of interest to the American oil company Unocal, for which the victory of the Taliban represented a potential means to transfer oil from Central Asia to the Indian Ocean through pacified territory, while avoiding Iran. There was also a further regional consideration that could serve as an explanation for Pakistan's encouragement of the Taliban offensive. This was to obviate Islamist complaints from the Pushtuns against the Pakistani government through unleashing them instead on Afghanistan.

There remained the risk of a backlash on Pakistani soil. Estimates suggest that some 2,500 madrasas had turned out more than 25,000 fanatical fighters, blindly obedient to their religious leaders and ready to kill and die at their command. Some were certainly used on the Pakistani side of the frontier against other Muslims said to have fallen away from the faith. The capture of Kabul in 1996, which established the superiority of the Taliban and entrenched the influence of Pakistan, led to the partial opening of the roads to Pakistani traffic, but failed to open up the way for the movement of oil and gas because of persistent instability.

The attacks of September 11 in the United States furnished India with a further means of isolating Pakistan. The Indian government quickly pointed out that the Pakistani and Taliban nexus that supported the attackers also backed the guerrilla struggle against India in Kashmir. The Indian authorities quickly passed to the FBI videos of guerrilla training camps and details of their locations. On September 14, 2001, India's prime minister, Atal Bihari Vajpayee, gave President George W. Bush his assurance of total cooperation and offered joint action and the use of Indian territory for military operations. The United States lifted the sanctions that had been imposed on India at the time of its nuclear tests, but did not take up India's offer of logistic support. It served American interests better to put the Pakistani regime in the front line against Osama bin Laden. Pakistan was obliged to be subservient to the requirements of the United States. The message to Pakistan was clear. Anything less than full cooperation would isolate Pakistan and place it at a permanent disadvantage as regards India. The threat by the United States to punish the state that helped terrorists also helped to concentrate the minds of the Pakistani leadership.

It remained only for the substantial price to be paid. Pakistan was virtually bankrupt, with 45 percent of the budget devoted to servicing $38 billion of external debt. The drought in Baluchistan had led to a massive movement of population to the towns, which had given rise to political difficulties and mounting social problems. The 2 or 3 million displaced persons potentially further destabilized the situation. Economic aid was urgently needed. General Musharraf obtained the lifting of all sanctions that had ensued from the coup that had brought him to power as well as those that still lingered from the nuclear tests. The United States proposed that Pakistan's debt be rescheduled and partially written off and showed willingness with a credit of $275 million on September 24. More assistance came in at once from the International Monetary Fund, the World Bank, the Asian Development Bank, Japan, and the European Union as well as the United States. The Americans undertook to provide a billion dollars in direct aid and promised to obtain several billion more from international organizations. Within three months, more than $6 billion was received. Washington indicated that it was open to a resumption of military cooperation, which meant new arms sales and the training of officers. Pakistan also tried to bring the United States into the settlement of the Kashmir issue and to ensure the recognition of the "just cause" of the Kashmiri militants.

On October 15, the U.S. Secretary of State Colin Powell said that Kashmir was a central issue in India–Pakistan relations. The Pakistanis wished to present this as the first step toward an internationalization of the issue. However, the Indian response was uncompromising. "We have no need of any mediation over relations between India and Pakistan." In order to avoid a war that could bring down the Taliban, President Musharraf twice sent General Mahmood Ahmad, head of the ISI, to Kandahar. On both occasions, he failed to persuade Mullah Omar, the leader of the Taliban, to hand over Osama bin Laden and to dismantle his organization.

Pakistan also asked for a voice in decisions over what shape Afghanistan's future government might take. "The Northern Alliance should be restrained, to avoid a further period of anarchy," said President Musharraf. "We think only a broadly based government which pays due attention to the realities of Afghanistan's ethnic make-up has any chance of succeeding in Afghanistan." The United States appeared to pay some heed to Pakistan's demands, holding the Northern Alliance back from advancing on Kabul. The requirement for Pushtun representation that would reflect the Taliban movement was a complicating factor in the formation of a post-Taliban government. Pakistan wanted to see no more than a third of the posts in the new government go to the Northern Alliance, which included the Uzbek and Tajik minorities, with the other two thirds going to the Taliban and the Pushtun tribes. The idea of Taliban participation in the government, which was also rejected by both Russia and Iran, also prompted a debate in the American administration. Donald Rumsfeld ruled it out. Colin Powell appeared not to exclude it entirely.

Pakistani concessions were forthcoming as a quid pro quo for U.S. backing. Pakistan closely cooperated with the Americans and offered its bases for the use of the American forces. Meanwhile, Pakistan severed its links with the Taliban, breaking diplomatic relations, closing their embassy, and handing their ambassador over to the Americans. Mullah Omar publicly denounced Pakistan's change of allegiance. On November 1, 2001, in a letter addressed to the Muslims of Pakistan, Osama bin Laden spoke of a crusade against Islam declared that "The government of Pakistan has seen fit to put itself under the banner of the Cross." The post-September 11 era was detrimental to Pakistan because its loss of influence over Afghanistan. Though it was consulted over the formation of a new government in Afghanistan, Pakistan could not avert a certain level of hostility. The presence in the new government of the United Front, as the Northern Alliance had become known, was in itself enough to have that effect. Russia and Iran, which had always assisted the anti-Taliban opposition, became more influential in the region, not least because Pakistan needed to reach agreement with Iran on Afghanistan's future if further problems were to be avoided. The question was: could such powers impose their will on the local actors and their own allies in Afghanistan?

The United Front was able to make political capital out of its military success. Its victorious campaign over the Taliban sowed the seeds of trouble. Despite all the promises of the Americans, United Front's troops occupied Kabul. General Musharraf said he would have preferred to see Kabul demilitarized. On November 14, a spokesman for the Pakistani foreign ministry took the same line, as if rhetoric could change the reality on the ground, remarking that "Pakistan's view is that the Northern Alliance should not occupy Kabul." Once more the Pakistanis felt they had been let down by the Americans. Pictures abounded of American advisers helping the United Front's

forces. The United Front's spokesman at the United Nations claimed that the Front had "indications from the United States that they should enter Kabul." All this gave the impression, as a senior Pakistan official said in a newspaper interview, that "American military might has placed Afghanistan in the hands of Pakistan's worst enemies."

Pakistan had lost out right across the board. It had been obliged to abandon its Taliban allies, and even to assist in their decline. It had failed to present a Pushtun alternative. And now its worst enemies, some of whom were even on good terms with India, had taken possession of Kabul. Realities had to be recognized, however, and Pakistan knuckled under the new situation. On November 27, 2001, in a startling volte-face, General Musharraf announced Pakistan's recognition of the Northern Alliance government in Afghanistan. He pointed out, however, that Afghanistan's landlocked geography implied that any Afghan government would be wise to maintain good relations with its neighbor, only through whose territory could it gain access to the sea. Pakistan was very conscious that India was preparing to offer aid to Afghanistan.

In short, this was the basis of the bilateral relationship between Pakistan and Afghanistan. Afghanistan could achieve no stability unless the Pushtun regions of Pakistan were secure. No development was attainable unless passage through Pakistan was available, especially for the exportation of Central Asia's oil and gas resources. Afghanistan's former president Rabbani, in negotiation with Pakistan, was disposed to forget what he called the "mistakes" of the past. He declared that Afghanistan was mindful of the assistance given it by the people of Pakistan and the Pakistani government during the anti-Soviet struggle, and that Pakistan and Afghanistan were linked by common interests. The reinforcement of these links, he added, was crucial.

The later appointment of Hamid Karzai, a Pushtun with ties to Pakistan and the ISI, was intended by the United States as a reward for Pakistan's President Musharraf. Hamid Karzai's appointment served as a guarantee to Pakistan that Afghanistan would not swing toward India, which was providing aid on a substantial scale. This was the minimal goal of Pakistani diplomacy. In January 2002, the promise of $100 million of aid from Pakistan to Afghanistan over five years—matching India's offer—gave the Pakistani authorities further leverage over Karzai. The war was not yet over, however. The rout of the Taliban brought with it a direct threat to the security of Pakistan. The 1,700 kilometers of shared frontiers, in a mountainous and inaccessible region, could not be impermeable. Low-level activity by the ISI, which had always collaborated with the Taliban, was also likely. Taliban fighters fled into Pakistan's tribal regions where the special administrative status, together with ethnic solidarity, made it difficult to take steps to drive them out. The religious parties continued to mobilize religious students. President Musharraf was accused of having sold out the country's interests, giving away everything while getting nothing in return.

A secret agreement gave the Americans the right of hot pursuit of Taliban elements and their Al-Qaida supporters across the frontier from Afghanistan into Pakistan. Meanwhile, in an unprecedented move, Pakistan deployed its forces in strength in the tribal frontier zones to prevent infiltration from Afghanistan. Army units were helicoptered into inaccessible valleys on the fringes of the country, such as the Tira valley where no soldier had set foot since the British-Afghan War of 1878. The pessimistic predictions were not fulfilled. Most of the tribesmen were cooperative. The tribal chiefs, who had perceived that the Americans were the more powerful, saw no interest in aiding the losers only to be dragged into the war themselves in their turn. None of these tribes were identified with the Taliban, and some were openly antagonistic to them, such as the Shi'ite majority in the Kurram region. The Taliban concept of unifying Muslims around their faith, while struggling against any divisive factor, was a threat to the tribal order, which was founded on other ideas of solidarity. Nevertheless, the idea spread by Mullah Omar and Osama bin Laden that a war was being waged against Islam struck a chord. The first victims were Pakistan's Christians, of whom there were some 2 million spread about the country. Intermittent acts of violence took place, as for example on October 28, 2001, when seventeen were killed in a massacre at a church in Bhawalpur.

In pursuit of its war against the Soviet Union in Afghanistan and against India in Kashmir, Pakistan had allowed the proliferation of dozens of extremist organizations. But the question now had to be asked: to what extent were these a threat to the regime and the state? It seemed that with American help, there was still time to stamp them out. A swift halt was put to the uncontrolled spread of Islamist activities. Pakistan now took official control of the spread of Islamism and obstructed the politicization of religion through obligatory registration of madrasas and mosques, and by taking charge of religious instruction and the delivery of sermons. Prior authorization was, henceforth, demanded for foreign students and teachers.

The United States was ever vigilant owing to the fragile nature of the peace agreement, dismantling the terrorist networks in Afghanistan and not relying on the Pakistani mobilization across the border to control the situation. In Afghanistan, as in Indian-controlled Kashmir, however, Pakistan continued to promote Islamist activities to further its own regional interests. Various incidents illuminate the duplicity of the

ISI. American special forces in an operation against a refuge used by Mullah Omar found themselves under strong Taliban fire, as if the Taliban had been forewarned. The capture and execution by the Taliban of the Afghan commander Abdul Haq, a hero of the war against the Soviets, was even more suggestive. Abdul Haq was on a mission in Afghanistan at the behest of the exiled King Zahir to attempt to rally Pushtun tribal leaders to resist the Taliban. In such an extensive and mountainous area no surveillance could have tracked him down, even by using the most sophisticated devices, which the Taliban did not have, unless he had been betrayed by the ISI.

All in all, Pakistan's position was highly contentious. While it lay at the heart of the American strategic deployment, it faced an accumulation of risks of instability from its ethnic minorities, its Islamist organizations, and the uncertain loyalty of its armed forces, as well as from the presence of nuclear weapons and its conflict with India. The suicide attack on the Indian federal parliament on December 13, 2001 brought the two countries once more to the brink of confrontation. Next day, the Indian minister of foreign affairs said he had proof that the operation was the work of terror organizations based in Pakistan and threatened that India would liquidate such terrorists and their sponsor "whoever they are and wherever they may be." Pakistan's military spokesman responded that India would pay dearly for any such adventure.

The tough response of the Indian Prime Minister Atal Bihari Vajpayee was the consequence of the proximity of elections, where he counted on gaining an advantage through a display of patriotism. America's war on terror also provided scope for propaganda by offering the opportunity to present the issues at stake in the Kashmir conflict as a clash over Islamist terrorism, disregarding the UN resolutions that called for self-determination for a territory annexed by India in 1947 in circumstances of dubious legality. Exchanges of fire in Kashmir, the deployment of medium-range missiles that were nuclear-capable, and the mobilization of troops on the frontiers all ratcheted up the tension, evoking the threat of a conflict of a different order of magnitude.

American pressure obliged President Musharraf to take measures against belligerent movements both in Kashmir and in Afghanistan. On January 12, 2002, he banned five Islamist groups and arrested more than 1,500 militants. The move related to the two organizations most active in Kashmir, Lashkar-i Tayba, and Jaish-i Mohammed, but two other movements were also banned. These were Sepah-i Sehaba and Tehrik-i Nefaz-i Shariat-i Mohammedi. He also proscribed a Shi'ite organization, Tehrik-i Jafria, founded in 1984, whose purpose was to ensure respect for Shi'ite law in a Sunni country. All these movements reappeared with different names. To expect President Musharraf to silence the Kashmiri separatists entirely, however, would have been an unrealistic demand that would have threatened his position. The credibility of Pakistan as a state, in the eyes of its citizens, was ineluctably bound up with Kashmir. Any abandonment of the policy pursued since the country's inception, part of Pakistan's founding mythology, would lead inexorably to a rebellion. There was a tricky balance between, on the one hand, the necessity for compromise with India, achievable by imposing limitations on the Islamist groups and, on the other hand, the obligation to preserve the unity of the nation. The Islamists had hitherto a free hand, with the Pakistani government's blessing, or even its help. Any move to constrain their activities could lead to a shift in public opinion and the destabilization of a government already facing external problems, no doubt to the benefit of some more nationalist regimes.

In the end, with no sustained action to take down the Islamist networks, these Islamist networks seemed capable of gaining in strength. For President Musharraf, the reappearance of banned movements under new designations undermined his attempt to settle the problem. If the Islamist issue were no more than displaced from Afghanistan to Kashmir, nothing would be resolved. Sooner or later, the problem would need to be tackled at the root. Meanwhile, an apparently new movement in Pakistan, Tarjuman al-Qanoon ("The Interpreter of the Law"), carried out an attack at the embassy of the United States in Karachi on June 14, 2002, with eleven dead and forty-six wounded. A communiqué averred that the attack "was only the beginning of a Jihad against the United States, and its ally and puppet, the government of Pakistan."

Since then, the atmosphere between India and Pakistan has markedly improved, as a result of systematic measures taken by the two sides to reduce tension and build confidence, reducing the scope for Islamist ventures in Kashmir. Nonetheless, Islamist ideas have the active support of a minority estimated at up to a quarter of Pakistan's population, while many more approve them to some extent. At the same time, running the risk of arousing popular antagonism, Pakistan's armed forces have continued their attacks on Taliban targets and militant targets inside Pakistan's frontiers. In March 2007, clashes broke out between tribesmen and a group of over a thousand Islamist Uzbek fighters led by Tahir Yuldashev who had been allies of Osama bin Laden and the Taliban, but fled into Pakistan in 2001. However, the situation was not clear-cut. The Uzbeks were under attack by a young local commander known as Maulvi Nazir, who was said also to be leading groups of Taliban inside Afghanistan fighting the NATO peacekeeping forces. The clashes seem, therefore, to have been more a local quarrel than evidence that the tribal population was turning against the Islamists. In April 2007, American intelligence officials revealed their suspicion that there is a group of former Al-Qaida fighters of Arab origin in the tribal areas of Pakistan who are working with the Taliban and are trying to organize international terrorist plots.

General Pervez Musharraf

General Musharraf is a former artillery officer whose political career has displayed a highly developed ability to seize the main chance and a thirst for power. He was born in 1943 in India, in the area of Daryaganj, an unpretentious area of Old Delhi, into a middle-class family of "Seyyeds" (descendants of the Prophet Muhammad). When he was four, his father, a civil servant, migrated to the new country of Pakistan after Indian independence from Britain led to the partition of the Indian subcontinent into two states. Musharraf's father joined Pakistan's foreign service and was posted in due course in Ankara, so that from six until thirteen Musharraf lived in Turkey, where he learned the language. From that period, he retained an admiration for the secularism of Kemal Ataturk and is said to have acquired a belief that religion should be confined to the private sphere. On the other hand, paradoxically, he has said that Pakistan should be an Islamic republic.

On his return to Pakistan, he was educated at Christian schools in Karachi and Lahore and entered the military academy in 1961. He fought in the war with India over the independence of Bangladesh in 1971 and then in Kashmir in 1987. He rose rapidly through the ranks to become a brigadier, the rank he held in 1990 when he attended the Royal Military Academy in Britain, from which he graduated with a master's degree. He was promoted to the rank of general on his return to Pakistan in 1991. In 1998, he became chief of staff under Prime Minister Nawaz Sharif. Nawaz Sharif attempted to dismiss him the following year, but Musharraf immediately displaced him in a bloodless coup. Musharraf sentenced Nawaz Sharif to life imprisonment, but later allowed him to go into exile in Saudi Arabia.

General Musharraf took over on October 11, 1999, giving himself the title of chief executive of Pakistan. Those close to him said he had been reluctant to act, as he had no political ambitions. The United States supported him. General Anthony Zinni said that Musharraf "may be America's last hope in Pakistan, and if he fails the fundamentalists would get hold of the atomic bomb." His relationship with Islam was from the first ambiguous. Immediately after the coup d'état that brought him to power, he asked the Islamic clergy to clamp down on "elements seeking to exploit religion for their own ends." His reputation as a liberal thinker had already earned him the mistrust of the Islamists. However, he quickly changed his attitudes. He appears to have intended to reform the blasphemy law, but drew back because of the reluctance of his colleagues in arms. He campaigned against corruption, but excused the army and the religious establishment from investigation. And, though he had asked for moderation, he emulated his predecessor in proclaiming Jihad in Kashmir and by supporting the madrasas. In a landmark speech on January 12, 2002, Musharraf condemned what he called Islamic terrorism.

In his early days, Musharraf was anxious to maintain the proprieties. The Supreme Court ruled that he must hand the country back to civilian rule before October 2002, so in June 20, 2001, after the retirement of Pakistan's President Rafiq Tarar, he appointed himself president. After the parliamentary elections in 2002, President Musharraf appointed a civilian prime minister, Shaukat Aziz, while retaining his own status as unelected president. On December 14, 2003, he survived the most serious assassination attempt he had faced, when a bomb failed to detonate as his motorcade passed over a bridge. On January 1, 2004, he declared himself to have been elected president when he obtained a majority of votes in an indirect election by the Electoral College of Pakistan (consisting of both houses of parliament and the four provincial assemblies). However, many Islamic deputies cast their votes against him.

His diplomatic rapprochement with India following the summit of 2001 and the success he achieved in defusing the confrontation with Pakistan's powerful neighbor were entirely at his own initiative and were carried out without the blessing of his army colleagues. These trends continued up to 2007. He astutely avoided negative consequences by continuing to pay strict lip service to the rectitude of Pakistan's case in the dispute over Kashmir, which guaranteed him a certain level of approval. Under pressure from the Americans, he got rid of the generals who had brought him to power. He took the opportunity to purge the ISI and the army of all elements suspected of sympathy toward Islamism. Though regarded internationally as a pariah when he first came to power, he succeeded in becoming indispensable, above all to the Americans.

In early 2007, having been Pakistan's leader for eight years, he indicated that he intended to continue in office. In April 2007, he took steps to curb the power of Pakistan's judiciary, finding himself as a result in confrontation with a coalition of opposition groups. Some of these groups were explicitly Islamist in nature, exposing the continued existence of Islamist opposition to President Musharraf. President Musharraf's ongoing problem in 2007 was to find a way of suppressing the Islamists to an extent that would satisfy the Americans, who have poured by now large sums of money into supporting his government, while at the same time not antagonizing the population.

Da'wat wal-Irshad, Al-

Da'wat wal-Irshad was set up in 1987 by Hafiz Mohammed Saeed and Dr. Zafar Iqbal, both former students in Medina. It is linked to the Pakistani group Ahl-i Hadith and like Ahl-i Hadith it is a wahhabi movement, which derives support from Saudi sources. The financial support it receives from Saudi Arabia gives it a security its rivals do not enjoy. Its twin emphases are Jihad and Da'wat (struggle and preaching). However, its originality lies in the development of a highly specialized system of education, of a more modern kind than that in Pakistan's traditional madrasas. Da'wat's school system was set up in 1994 and gives modern teaching in sciences and in English. Its pupils come from backgrounds wider than Ahl-i Hadith's sympathizers.

The movement's headquarters, which is also an educational center, is at Murdike, near Lahore, in a complex built on a site donated by General Zia ul-Haq, Pakistan's former president—killed in an aviation accident—who played a central part in the Islamic radicalization of the country. Major gatherings of jihadists from the region are regularly held there. Da'wat presents itself as a link between movements accepted in the political sphere and the extremists, a philosophy which accounts for its support for the Taliban. In the context of jihad, the movement has set up an armed wing, "Lashkar-i Tayba." Its combination of a respectable public façade with a radical and military branch is a feature it shares with many Pakistani movements.

Deoband (Pakistan and India)

The school of Islam known as Deoband derives its name from a madrasa founded close to the Indian capital of New Delhi in 1867. The teaching given there is grounded in the reformist ideas of the school established by Shah Waliullah, the great Islamic reformist who lived from 1702 to 1763, who was a student of the Hadith and a practitioner of Ijtihad—the reinterpretation of the Sunna. He laid stress on the defence of Islam against other religions, especially the Hindu faith, and advocated the use of the Urdu language, which served as a common link between all Indian Muslims. Deoband was founded by disciples of Shah Waliullah, trained in his own madrasa, which was destroyed by the British-occupying power in 1857. The Deobandis prioritize "da'wat" (preaching) before "jihad" (struggle) and stress the primacy of education. To this end, they developed a network of madrasas, especially in northern India in the days of the British Empire. After the partition of India, however, many Deobandi ulema relocated to Pakistan, where, somewhat unusually in twentieth century Islam, Deoband was a rural phenomenon, which developed in mosques in the countryside. In a further development particular to Pakistan, the Deobandi movement set up a political wing, the Jamiat Ulema-i Islami, led by Mawlawi Fazl ur-Rahman, who had links with Zulfikar Ali Bhutto's Pakistani People's Party (PPP).

Deoband in itself was, therefore, neither politically radical nor wahhabi in its sympathies, but it served as a fertile soil for such movements, to the extent that it drew attention to the threats that faced Islam, and stressed the importance of international solidarity. In addition, the system of schools that it developed and the content of their curriculum were not specifically Deobandi, but became broadly "wahhabized" from the 1980s onward, under Saudi influence, exercised though the provision of funding, of scholarships, and the supply of teachers. It propagated an Islam less linked to traditional culture and much more militant, and Deobandi students took part in the jihad in Afghanistan.

In the wake of the process of militarization that ensued from the war in Afghanistan, military training became part of the regular program at many madrasas that professed Deobandi Islam. Another factor was the explosion of violence between Shi'ites and Sunnis in Pakistan. Certain of the madrasas—for example that of Senator Sami ul-Haqq at Akora Khattak—systematically sent their students to fight in Afghanistan, especially in 2000 and 2001, during the campaigns against Massud. Gradually, jihad became the dominant note in these schools, just as their numbers were growing because of the failure of the public school system. There was no centralized administration, but to build one was seen by the young mullahs as a way of establishing a personal power base, taking the form of a political-military organization. This reduced the length of the curriculum and in consequence the young "Taliban" (students)—who were trained only in religion—saw in Islamization their only route into active life. This increased the demands on the religious movements and prompted violent competition among students as well as among the political-religious movements themselves. From 1998 onward, Prime Minister Nawaz Sharif's government tried, without success, to impose its control over the madrasas.

The events of September 11, 2001 prompted his successor General Musharraf to initiate a reform of the teaching system and to bring it under the control of the government. However, while the public school system fails to offer a good level of teaching, there will continue to be a demand for the madrasas. They provide education for at least one and a half million pupils and cannot quickly be replaced. However, President Musharraf's decision under U.S. pressure after 2001 to clamp down on the activities of foreigners in Pakistan, and especially any with apparent links to Al-Qaida or the Taliban, has at least temporarily minimized the role of Pakistan as a training ground for Islamist extremists. Western donors have agreed in effect to support Pakistan's military system in exchange for such assistance as Pakistan has been prepared to give in what President Bush calls the "War on Terrorism." In September, President Musharraf came under Western criticism for policies of noninterference in the north of the country, especially close to Afghanistan, which some said could create a safe haven for Al-Qaida and Taliban sympathizers. This risks a future popular backlash in a strongly religious country. In October 2006, Pakistani forces used helicopters to attack a madrasa near the Afghan border allegedly run by a Taliban sympathizer, killing eighty students and teachers.

Harakat ul Ansar/Harakat ul Mujahidin (Pakistan)

The "Harakat ul Ansar" (Movement of the Ansar) was established in Pakistan in 1991 by Fazlur Rehman Khalil and Masood Azhar, who was arrested in 1994 in Kashmir by Indian troops. Masood Azhar appears to have been known to the Pakistani military intelligence service, the ISI (Inter-Services Intelligence). "Ansar" was the name given to those who originally supported the Prophet Mohammed's movement in Medina. It was originally a splinter group that broke off from the movement known as "Harakat ul Jihad," whose Pakistani adherents were the first to fight alongside the Afghan mujahidin, often traveling to Pakistan as individuals. It had its own training camps in Afghanistan in the days of the Taliban. Another adherent of Harakat ul-Ansar was Ahmed Omar Saeed al-Sheikh, a young Pakistani brought up in Britain, who left the London School of Economics to become an Islamist activist. Pakistan's President Musharraf claims he was a double agent originally sent to spy on Muslim activists by Western intelligence. In 1994, Sheikh kidnapped a number of British nationals in India, but was captured by the Indian security services and given a prison sentence.

"Harakat ul Ansar" changed its name to "Harakat al-Mujahidin" in 1998, after being declared a terrorist organization by the United States. It continued to provide support for Afghan and Kashmiri majuhidin. The camp at Zawar bombed by the Americans in reprisal for the 1998 attacks on the U.S. embassies in East Africa belonged to "Harakat ul Mujahidin." In December 1999, activists hijacked an Indian airliner in Afghanistan with 155 passengers, demanding the release of Masood Azhar and Ahmed Omar Saeed al-Sheikh, as well as a third man, Mushtaq Ahmed Zargar. All three were released and took refuge in Pakistan. The faction of Harakat ul-Mujahidin controlled by Masood Azhar changed its name again to Jaish-i Mohammed in February 2000.

ISI (Inter-Services Intelligence)

The Pakistani intelligence services, the ISI, have been of crucial importance in the Islamist project in Pakistan. Since its establishment in 1971, the ISI has exceeded its original brief, which was to gather intelligence and undertake clandestine operations. Instead, it has come to exercise an influence on Pakistan's foreign policy in India (over Punjab and Kashmir) and in Afghanistan. A part of the Pakistani armed forces, the ISI has come over time to resemble a state within the state, to the extent that it opposed Benazir's policy of liberalization between 1988 and 1990, though it failed to make her fall into line. During the Soviet occupation of Afghanistan, the head of the ISI, General Hamid Gul, received substantial funds from the CIA and from Saudi Arabia, as well as a billion dollars was earmarked for the Afghan resistance. The

ISI also arranged for the training of Jihadist fighters, arming them and providing them with instructors. After the withdrawal of the Soviet troops, the ISI continued its policy of influence and involvement in Afghanistan. It armed the Taliban, putting aircraft at their disposal with pilots and mechanics, set up NGOs that its agents could use as cover, and took revenue from the drug trade.

The extreme Islamization of Pakistan began under General Zia ul Haq. Zia gave the ISI the monopoly over logistic support for the Afghan and Kashmiri guerrillas. It became the initiator and overseer of Pakistan's entire regional policy, at the expense of the Ministry of Foreign Affairs. The ISI's leadership was not necessarily made up of Islamists, with the exception of General Hamid Gul, who was its head from 1988 to 1991. However, it made systematic use of Islamism, reserving its support for the most radical movements, in particular Sepah-i Sehaba, Jaish-i Mohammed, Hizb-i Islami, and the Taliban.

The American intelligence services also made use of religion in their fight against the atheistic ideology of the Soviets and appealed to Muslims around the world. A substantial network of madrasas funded by Saudi Arabia sprang up that provided tens of thousands of militants willing to fight for Islam. In Peshawar, close to the Afghan border, the Maktab al-Khidmat ("Service Office") took care of recruitment and training for Jihad volunteers to fight against the Soviets. All this took place under the auspices of the ISI with the blessing of the CIA and Saudi funding. This organization was set up by a leading figure from the Muslim Brotherhood in Jordan, the Palestinian-born Abdullah Azzam, who was soon to be joined by one of his former pupils from Jeddah, Osama bin Laden. Its role was to arrange for recruitment across a range of countries, including the West, and to run charitable and media operations.

In 1984, with the assistance of the ISI and the CIA, bin Laden opened his first reception center for foreigners in Peshawar. After Azzam's death in 1989 in a violent incident, bin Laden took charge of the "Service Office." After the Soviets withdrew from Afghanistan, the United States cut off its funds for the "Office" and the Pakistani authorities closed it down in 1995 after an attack on the Egyptian embassy in Islamabad. President Musharraf promised the United States full cooperation, adding that Pakistan "saw terrorism as a threat to the global community." He kept his word. Pakistan cooperated closely with the United States and made its bases available to the American forces. The head of the ISI, General Mahmoud Ahmad, and his deputy in Afghanistan, General Mohammed Aziz Khan, were both too hostile to the United States and too close to the Taliban, with the result that both were dismissed.

The appointment of General Ehsan ul-Haq to lead the ISI opened the way to better cooperation with the CIA against the Taliban. Nonetheless, there was much reluctance within the ISI, which was being asked to destroy what it had created. Lower-level functionaries of the ISI and the armed forces, of whom up to 40 percent were ethnic Pushtuns, had been educated at exactly the same madrasas as the Taliban. Their loyalty became dependent on Pakistan's policy in Kashmir. For Pakistani nationalists, this was the key issue.

Jaish-i Mohammed (See Harakat ul Ansar)

Jaish-i Mohammed was established in Pakistan by Masood Azhar in February 2000. Among its targets were Pakistan's political class, anything linked to the United States, and the Shi'ite community. It seeks recruits in the Deobandi madrasas in Pakistan and is also active in the Pakistani migrant community in Britain. From the outset, suicide bombing has been one among its tactics.

Its goal was to free Kashmir from Indian control. Some of its members were also affiliated to Sepah-i Sehaba, to which it was ideologically close. Masood Azhar was born in 1968 in Bhawalpur, into a religious family. He was a former student at the Deobandi madrasa in Binori Town, close to Karachi. He joined the "Harakat ul Ansar" and fought in Afghanistan and Kashmir, where he was captured by the Indian army in 1995 and imprisoned in India.

He was released from prison after his freedom was demanded by hijackers who seized an Air India passenger airliner and grounded it in Kandahar in December 1999. The Taliban helped to negotiate his release. Shortly afterward, Masood Azhar appeared in public in Pakistan and undertook a speaking tour where his theme was the need to destroy India and the United States. The Pakistani intelligence services, the ISI, appears to have assisted him to set up Jaish-i Mohammed. Masood's lieutenant, the British-educated Ahmed Omar Saeed al-Sheikh, also became involved in the new movement.

In December 2001, Jaish-i Mohammed mounted an attack on the Indian parliament building. Fourteen people died, including the five attackers. India identified Jaish-i Mohammed as the faction responsible for the attacks, and under strong diplomatic pressure Pakistan placed Masood Azhar under arrest. In January 2002, Pakistan's President Pervez Musharraf addressed the nation on the dangers of terrorism and initiated a clampdown on militant groups, with some 2,000 arrests. Only a month later, however, most of them were released. Jaish-i Mohammed was one of the militant organizations that was banned, but it continued to operate as Khuddam ul-Islam. This was banned in November 2003.

On January 23, 2002, the British expatriate Ahmed Omar Saeed al-Sheikh kidnapped the American journalist Daniel Pearl in Karachi, ostensibly demanding the release of prisoners at Guantanamo Bay. Pearl was murdered on February 1, 2002. There were allegations that Masood Azhar was implicated. However, even though Jaish-i Mohammed was declared illegal by Pakistan in January 2002, Masood Azhar was still apparently receiving some assistance from the ISI. Saeed was arrested on February 12, 2002 and was charged with the murder. He was sentenced to death on July 15, 2002. In September 2002, the Pakistani government refused to agree to an American request to interrogate Masood Azhar on his links with Saeed and Al-Qaida. There have been persistent rumors that Sheikh's actual killer was Khaled Sheikh Mohammed, a key Al-Qaida activist. Masood Azhar was released in January 2003. Masood Azhar has subsequently maintained a low profile. In November 2006, his name featured in a list of wanted men handed to Pakistan by India's foreign minister at a meeting in New Delhi.

Jamaat-i Islami (Pakistan)

Jamaat-i Islami in Pakistan is the descendant of an all-India Islamic movement founded in 1941 by the theologian Abul Ala Mawdudi. After the partition of India, the party split along national lines. The Pakistani branch was led by Mawdudi himself until his death in 1979, when he was succeeded by Myan Tufail until 1987, and then by Qazi Hussein Ahmed. In the parliamentary elections of October 2002, Jamaat-i Islami won just over 11 percent of the vote and took 53 seats out of 272. Qazi Ahmed Hussein is an ethnic Pushtun of Pakistani nationality. The party's platform is the creation of an Islamic state, with an Islamic constitution and appropriate institutions. Jamaat-i Islami is a conventional Islamist party, which seeks to make a political ideology out of Islam. It has always adopted a policy of working within the political system, and is an elitist institution that does not seek mass participation.

It has always aimed at extending its membership among the Pakistani elite, whom it seeks to convert to its ideas. Its members, known in Pakistan as "Jamaatis," seek to exercise their influence in all branches of Pakistani society.

During the years when Zia ul Haq was in power, from 1977 to his death in an engineered air crash in 1988, Jamaat-i Islami played a very important role, even though it never won more than 5 percent of the vote in the elections. It chose instead to infiltrate decision-making circles and to cultivate senior military officers, in particular those of the Inter-Services Intelligence (ISI), the powerful Pakistani secret service. Jamaat-i Islami wanted to present itself as a possible option in case of a political crisis. It was never seen as a terrorist organization, though its student wing, Jamaat Tulaba, had been involved in violent actions on university campuses. In 1989, it set up an armed branch, the Hizb al-Mujahidin, which was intended to fight in Kashmir. Hizb al-Mujahidin proved in practice to be less radical than other Jihadist groups involved in Kashmir and accepted the truce in 1997.

After the end of the First Afghan War against the Soviet-dominated Afghan government, the influence of Jamaat-i Islami declined. In the field of political radicalism, it was overtaken by Deobandi groups and the various Taliban movements. Without the same kind of popular base, Jamaat-i Islami was seen by the new fundamentalists as too moderate. Pakistan's secular politicians, nevertheless, continued to regard it as a radical phenomenon.

Jami'at Ulama-i Islam (Jui) (Pakistan/India)

Jami'at Ulama-i Islam is a movement that gives political representation to the Deobandi school of Islam. It was founded in Calcutta on October 26, 1945 as a splinter group of Jami'at Ulama-i Hind, which opposed the partition of India. In its early years, it remained to a considerable extent aloof from politics, but in the 1970s and 1980s it threw itself into political activity in opposition to Jama'at-i Islami. JUI attracted limited electoral support, however, and under its leader Maulana Fazlur Rahman it won only two parliamentary seats. In terms of Pakistani politics, it somewhat surprisingly lent its support to Zulfikar Ali Bhutto and then, in the 1990s, to his daughter Benazir Bhutto.

JUI's relaunch as a radical group is of relatively recent date and took place only in the early 1980s with the creation of Sepah-i Sehaba, which was effectively its armed wing even though there was no formal link between the two organizations. JUI has over the years split into three factions. The first of these, that came into existence when Maulana Abdullah Darkhwasti split off from the parent organization, came into existence in 1982 and maintained good relations with Ahl-i Hadith and the Wahhabi ulema. The third faction arose from a further split in 1991 when a group known as JUI-Sami was created by Pakistani Senator Sami ul-Haq, a Pushtun who was the director of the Haqqanya madrasa in Akora Khattak, near Peshawar. This wing gave very active support to the Afghan mujahidin, initially through the Afghan Pushtun religious leaders in the tribal zone, such as Jallaludin Haqqani, who had studied at the madrasa, and then to the Taliban themselves.

The JUI became progressively closer to the Taliban, and the two leaders embarked on appeals to take part in the Jihad and in direct attacks against the Americans. The students at JUI madrasas were encouraged to fight in Afghanistan side by side with the Taliban. The JUI's trajectory was a perfect example of the way in which conservative clerical circles became increasingly radicalized in the direction of support for Jihadism. However, because of the influence it wielded in the arena of Pakistani politics, it was never listed by the Americans as a terrorist organization.

Jami'at Ulama-i Pakistan

In contrast to the Deobandi orientation of the Jami'at Ulama-i Islam, Jami'at Ulama-i Pakistan (JUP) represents the traditionalist Barelvi school of Islam, which is perfused by Sufi practices, in particular the veneration of saints and of the person of the Prophet. For this reason, it is deprecated by the puritanical and strict Muslims of the Deobandi persuasion. Jami'at Ulama-i Pakistan was founded in 1948. The JUP power base is in Sind and a part of Punjab. It has been led since the 1970s by Mawlana Shah Ahmed Noorani. A separate faction split off in 1988 under the leadership of Maulana Sattar Khan Niazi, who had links with one of the major national organizations, Nawaz Sharif's Muslim League. Other factions also defected, including a Punjabi group led by Sahabzada Anisul Hassnian.

The JUP has played its part in mainstream politics in Pakistan, but was also affected by the prevalent radicalization of Islamic movements and set up its own armed wing, the Tehrik Islami. The Barelvi community is not exempt from the influence of radical ideas, and it should not be forgotten that it was the Barelvi community that initiated the Salman Rushdie affair in Britain in 1989. They were particularly incensed by the book *The Satanic Verses,* as they saw in it a direct attack on the person of the Prophet. Though the Barelvis were very hostile to the Wahhabism of the Deobandis, they could still take common cause with them against the West. In 1994, Niazi became a senator in the national government of Pakistan. He died in May 2001 (at the age of eighty-six). In 2003, there was a move toward reunification of the various branches. Noorani died in December 2003, aged seventy-eight.

Before his death, he persuaded Pakistan's Islamic parties to form a coalition known as the Muttahida Majlis-e Amal (United Action Council). This is now seen as the major Islamic party in Pakistan and includes a spread of factions, including the JUP, two sections of the JUI, Jamaat-i Islami, and the Shi'ite Tehrik Jafaria Pakistan.

Lashkar-i Jhangvi

Lashkar-i Jhangvi (LIJ) ("The Army of Jhangvi") is a Pakistani terrorist organization that split off from the Sepah-i Sahaba in 1994. It is a militant Sunni group that has specialized in the assassination of Shi'ites. It is named after the founder of Sepah-i Sehaba, Maulana Haq Nawaz Jhangvi, who was arrested by the Pakistani authorities in 1994 and executed in February 2001. LIJ regarded the Sepah-i Sehaba as having become institutionalized, while it operated underground, almost certainly with no more than a few hundred militants. LIJ's leader was Riaz Basra, originally from Sargodha. Basra had previously been a member not only of the Sepah-i Sahaba, but also of Jamiat Ulama Islami, indicating that there is a link between the three movements. In 1999, it was responsible for an attempt to murder the prime minister of Pakistan, Nawaz Sharif.

In 2000, the movement split between a group led by Riaz Basra, based in Peshawar, and another group based in Karachi led by Qari Asadullah. Asadullah's group was apparently implicated in the kidnapping of the American journalist Daniel Pearl in early 2002. In March 2002, LIJ members bombed the International Protestant Church in Islamabad during a religious service, killing five and injuring forty. Riaz Basra was killed in a shoot-out with police at Multan in May 2002. His successor was Muhammad Ajmal, whose nom de guerre is Akram Lahori. Lahori was arrested in June 2002. Since then, LIJ

activities have continued under a succession of acting leaders. Akram Lahori's conviction was set aside by an appeal court in March 2006. In the same month, the U.S. consulate in Karachi was attacked, apparently by LIJ activists. In October 2006, LIJ was reported to have carried out a recruitment drive.

Lashkar-i Tayba

Lashkar-i Tayba (LIT) (Soldiers of Purity) is the armed wing of Da'wat wa-l-Irshad in Pakistan. It focuses its activities primarily on Kashmir. There, with the assistance of the Pakistani army, it has replaced the conventional guerrilla movements, which had proved too attached to nationalist ideas and were—from Pakistan's point of view—too difficult to control. LIT has been responsible for savage attacks on Indian army units and also carried out the attack on the Indian parliament building in Delhi on December 13, 2001. It takes strong stands on international issues, though its membership is entirely Pakistani. It does not explicitly advocate suicide bombing, but has developed a cult of martyrdom. Its militants, who have passed through training camps in Afghanistan, are renowned in Kashmir for their toughness. They do not shrink from attacking the civilian population, including Hindus, Sikhs, and even moderate Muslims, and since 1999 they have been responsible for most attacks on the Indian army. A ritual has developed around those who are martyred. Their families refuse to mourn and the lives of the deceased combatants are celebrated. On January 12, 2002, President Musharraf declared a ban on the movement.

Sepah-i Mohammed (Army of Mohammed)

Sepah-i Mohammed is a violent Shi'ite organization that split off from Tehrik-i Jafriya Pakistan (Pakistani Movement for Jaafari Law). In 1987, it transformed itself into a political party. After the assassination in August 1988 of its leader, Allama Husseini, a Pushtun from Parachinar, it moderated its policies. In 1994, two young radical clerics trained at Qom, Ghulam Raza Naqvi and Murid Abbaṣ Yazdani, set up another more radical branch. Sepah-i Mohammed undertook armed attacks on Sepah-i Sehaba, which retaliated in kind.

After 1998, Sepah-i Mohammed virtually disintegrated. Most of its activists were either in prison or had fled to Iran or southern Lebanon. Only a few members remained, without organization or command, who, nevertheless, continued to take violent action in reprisal against anti-Shi'ite attacks. Sipah-i Mohammed was formally banned in August 2001.

Sepah-i Sehaba (Army of the Companions of the Prophet)

Sepah-i Sehaba is a radical Sunni group in Pakistan whose origins lie in the Jami'at Ulama Islam, whose ideology it shares. It is the armed branch of Jami'at Ulama Islam, though this is denied by Jami'at itself. Sepah-i Sehaba was set up in September 1985 in Jhang, with the approval of the military authorities, to counter the rising power of the Shi'ites. In addition to being violently anti-Shi'ite, it also condemns the Barelwi sect of Sunni Islam, which practices the cult of "Pirs" ("Saints"), who are supposed by devotees to be able to intercede with God. It demanded there should be legal sanctions on any attack on the honor of the companions of the Prophet and on the Prophet's last wife Aisha. This would effectively outlaw Shi'ism, which is critical of those they see as responsible for the deaths of Hassan and Hussein, the Prophet's grandsons and the sons of Ali.

Its founder, Maulana Haq Nawaz Jhangvi, was murdered in February 1990, which set off a sequence of incidents between Sunnis and Shi'ites that culminated in December 1990 with the assassination in Lahore of the consul general of Iran, Sadqi Ganji. Ganji's assassin, who had adopted the name of Haq Nawaz, was hanged in February 2001. Those who succeeded Haq Nawaz Jhanbvi as leaders of Sepah-i Sehaba were also killed. Maulana Esar ul-Qasmi was murdered in 1991 and Zia ul-Rehman Farooqi in 1997. In February 1997, Sepah-i Sehaba murdered five Iranian cadets who were visiting Pakistan. Its leader, until it was banned by the government of Pervez Musharraf, was Maulana Azam Tariq, a Muhajir by origin (a person born in India who had migrated to Pakistan).

Outside Jhang itself, the strongholds of Sepah-i Sehaba are in Faisalabad, in the center of the country, and in southern Punjab (Bhawalpur, Multan, Muzaffargarh, and Rahim Yar Khan). In these areas, it mobilized the Sunni peasantry against the Shi'ite landowners, thus combining a social movement with one based on religious solidarity. Sepah-i Sehaba was not only a violent movement, but it was also active in politics and took part in the elections of 1992. It won seats in the Punjab Provincial Assembly, representing Jhang, its place of origin. Under Benazir Bhutto's second government, from 1993 to 1996, it allied itself with her Pakistan People's Party in Punjab and had a minister in the provincial government.

Sepah-i Sehaba claimed to have around 300,000 members, mainly in Punjab and in Punjabi circles in Karachi. It found its members in the Deobandi madrasas of Punjab (for example at Faqirwali and Faisalabad), and had also begun to develop in Sindh. It maintained offices outside the country, in the United Arab Emirates and Saudi Arabia, in Britain, and in Canada. The office in Bangladesh was closed in 2002. In January 2001, Azam Tariq traveled to France. On February 27, 2001, after his return, he was once more arrested after the disturbances that followed the hanging of Haq Nawaz. The movement's funds came from private Saudi sources and elsewhere in the Middle East, from Punjabi businessmen in Europe, and perhaps even from the proceeds of drug trafficking. It was linked to the support of the Taliban and set up some units that may have been implicated in the massacres of Afghan Shi'ites and Iranian diplomats at Mazar-i Sharif in 1998.

The movement was banned in August 2002. Azam Tarqi was placed under house arrest, but stood for parliament in the October 2002 election and was elected. He also filed a petition to have the ban on Sepah-i Sehaba lifted, on the grounds that it was a religious and political organization with no link to violence. Sepah-i Sehaba re-formed under the anme Millat-i Islamiya ("Party of the Islamic Nation"). In April 2003, Azam Tariq appealed to the Lahore High Court to get the party's funding unfrozen.

Sunni Tehrik (Sunni Movement)

The Sunni Tehrik is an ultraradical Barelvi movement in Pakistan that emerged in 1990 from the Jami'at Ulama Pakistan, the main Barelvi political party. The Barelvi school of Islam in Pakistan represents traditional Pakistani Islam as distinct from the puritanical Deobandi school and includes traditional beliefs and practices including the cult of "Pirs" ("Saints") who are held to be able to intercede with God. It is anti-Deobandi, anti-Shi'ite, and anti-Christian and represents the radicalization of traditional and conservative circles. It is very far from the ideas of Saudi Wahhabism regarding Sunni Islam. It draws its membership from radical elements within Jami'at Ulama Pakistan and from the Barelvi madrasas. It is strongly represented in Karachi and the Punjab and clashes with Sepah-i Sehaba for control of the region and its mosques. Its director, Maulana Saleem Qadri, was murdered in

Karachi in May 2001. Sunni Tehrik accused Sepah-i Sehaba of responsibility. It does not appear to receive support or funding from abroad, but gets substantial support from the Pakistani diaspora.

Tehrik-i Nefazi Shariat-i Mohammed (Movement for the Application of the Law of Mohammed) (TNSM)

The TNSM was established in 1994 at Malakand in the North-West Frontier Province of Pakistan by a dissident from Jamaiat-i Islami, Sufi Mohammed. A Wahhabi tribal faction active in its own province, the TSNM's goal was the installation of the Shari'a. It was based on a combination of tribal and Islamist solidarity of the kind that was also characteristic of the Taliban in Afghanistan. It supported the Taliban fiercely and was badly affected by their defeat. However, the Pakistani government dealt with it tactfully so as not to provoke tribal revolts. The tribes in these frontier regions of Pakistan were effectively beyond the reach of Pakistan's national jurisdiction and gave refuge to the fleeing remnants of the Taliban and Al-Qaida.

PALESTINE

The territory of Mandatory Palestine, which was entrusted to British administration after World War I, was divided between Arab Palestine and the new state of Israel by the United Nations resolution in 1947. The Arab inhabitants, with the support of the surrounding Arab states, rejected the partition, and when the British forces withdrew after the end of the UN mandate on May 15, 1948, war between the two sides broke out as the Arabs attempted to destroy the new Jewish state. The Arab forces were incompetent and Israel was determined and well supplied. Israel proved to be the victor, taking a greater part of Palestine than had been assigned to it by the United Nations. The Palestinians held on only to the West Bank of the River Jordan, which was soon annexed by the Hashemite Kingdom of Jordan, and the Gaza Strip, which came under Egyptian administration. In 1967, war broke out once more when Israel launched a preemptive strike on the Arabs after months of threats from the champions of Arab nationalism, led by President Nasser of Egypt. This time, the West Bank and Gaza also fell to the Israelis. Rather than annexing these new areas, however, with their substantial Arab populations, they chose to administer them as occupied territories. This was the origin of the Palestinian problem.

Since 1967, the Palestinians have sought to obtain the return of their land to Palestinian control. Successive Israeli governments have vacillated over whether to hand back the occupied territory, and if so how much of it, and to whom. The situation was confused and Israel's options were narrowed as determined Zionists began to create settlements in the West Bank and Gaza, with the acquiescence of the Israeli authorities, especially at periods when Israel had a right-wing government. The Palestinian movement initially took the form of nationalist resistance and coalesced into the Palestine Liberation Organization, led by Yasser Arafat, the head of its largest faction, Fatah. Grass roots resistance to the Israeli occupation began with the first Intifada, which started in December 1987, which was essentially nonviolent, restricting itself to demonstrations, noncooperation, and stone-throwing.

Peace talks began in Madrid in October 1991 and led on to negotiations in Washington, DC. In 1993, Israeli and Palestinian delegations met secretly in Norway and elsewhere, concluding an agreement known as the Oslo Accords that was intended to lead to Palestinian self-government in the occupied territories. As soon as 1994, the accords began to unravel over the impossibility of reaching agreement on implementation of the details and such unresolved questions as the status of Jerusalem and the right of refugees to return to their original homes. In 1995, the assassination of Israel's Labor prime minister, Yitzhak Rabin, struck a blow at the peace process. Subsequent attempts to reach agreement failed, up to the final collapse of talks at Taba in January 2001 between Yasser Arafat and Israel's Labor prime minister, Ehud Barak. Little progress seems likely under right-wing administrations in Israel, despite the Israeli decision to pull its settlers out of Gaza. In September 2000, a renewed Palestinian resistance movement got under way, which had become known as the Second Intifada, or the Al-Aqsa Intifada.

The Muslim Brotherhood had begun early to take root in the occupied territories, and the militant Palestinian Islamist movement known as Hamas, an offshoot of the brotherhood, made its appearance as soon as the first Intifada got under way in 1987. Hamas is very emphatically a Sunni organization, but over the years it has not refused various forms of assistance and moral support from the Shi'ite government of the Islamic Republic of Iran. It gradually became more influential in the occupied territories through the familiar Islamist trajectory of combining charitable organizations with militancy.

Its strength was boosted by the apparent failure of the Palestinian nationalists to achieve the desired independence for Palestine, as the achievement of the Oslo Accords—which had at first seemed to the Palestinian people as the dawn of a new era—trickled away into the sand. For the people, Islam now seemed to be their only remaining choice, and the Hamas leadership presented itself as the only Palestinian body that has not offered territorial compromise with Israel. By the close of the 1990s, Hamas was becoming the most influential Palestinian movement. At this time, the campaign of suicide bombings within Israel had become a serious problem for Israel. The constant threat of bombing on buses, in cafés, and other public places has constituted a permanent threat to Israel. Besides the distress caused by the casualties, the bombs have disturbed the normal fabric of life in Israel, creating a permanent sense of unease.

Hamas formed a government in the Palestinian territories in January 2006, under Prime Minister Ismail Haniyeh, who has never been able to govern satisfactorily due to obstruction from the Palestinian president, Mahmoud Abbas, the leader of Fatah. But more damagingly, Israel's prime minister, Ehud Olmert, has refused to recognize Hamas as the ruling party, withholding funds it should have paid over to the Palestinian authority and taking other steps to impede its activities. Israel says it cannot accept Hamas as a partner, while Hamas continues to refuse to recognize Israel's legitimacy as a state and apparently condones violence. Hamas will not recognize Israel, but has offered a truce that could be protracted indefinitely.

In March 2006, a Hamas delegation went to Saudi Arabia to look for support. Hamas's ultimate objective is the recovery of the entire territory of historic Palestine. Meanwhile, the United States and the European Union have also refused to accept the Hamas administration, creating difficulties for it on the international front. In December 2006, armed clashes broke out between Hamas's supporters and those of Fatah. In January 2007, Saudi Arabia offered talks to try to settle the dispute. In February, the talks began in Mecca, with the involvement of King Abdullah and other senior Saudi officials. On March 17, 2007, Hamas and Fatah announced the formation of a joint Palestinian administration, which Israel also refused to recognize. In April 2007, there were allegations that Hamas had given money recently received from Saudi donors to the Izzeddin al-Qassem Brigades, its armed wing. Cooperation between Hamas and Fatah broke down in June 2007, with fierce armed clashes between them.

Hezbollah (Influence in the Palestinian Territories)

The Second Intifada in Palestine, which began in 2000, was obviously of a more Islamist character than the first Intifada, which originated in 1987. Undoubtedly, the precedent of Lebanon's Hezbollah had some influence on it. The strategy of suicide bombing, for example, clearly imitated the practice of Lebanese Hezbollah, which was gaining in strength. It should not be forgotten that in the eyes of the Islamists—and indeed of the Palestinians in general—the Israeli withdrawal from Lebanon was a victory for Islamism and a step toward the liberation of Jerusalem and the Holy Places. Such radical Islamic forces as Hamas and Islamic Jihad in Palestine look up not only to Al-Qaida, but also to the Lebanese Hezbollah, whose success on the ground is palpable and whose techniques are more applicable in Palestine. In the recent events of 2006, it seems clear that the abductions of Israeli soldiers by both Hamas and Hezbollah were prearranged as a concerted effort. The late Yasser Arafat's Fatah movement made its attempt in the mid-1970s to build bridges with the Arab Shi'ite community. A particular Fatah official, Imad Mughnieh, was put in charge of these efforts. Now that Fatah no longer forms the government of Palestine, it has other concerns. For the new Islamist Palestinian government formed by Hamas, the Lebanese Hezbollah is an ally in the sense that it travels in the same direction of confrontation with Israel, but, nonetheless, is an ally, of which Hamas, which is essentially a Sunni movement linked to the Muslim Brotherhood, remains wary.

In recent years, Hezbollah flags have been displayed in the Haram al-Sherif, on the Aqsa Mosque, and the Dome of the Rock. Before September 2000, such a thing was never seen. Today, it is not only students, intellectuals, and militants who call for the Palestinian leadership to follow Hezbollah's example, but also many others who have never previously showed sympathy for political Islam. Especially after Israel's failure to impose its will in Lebanon in July 2006, Hezbollah is seen as the giant-killer who has vanquished the mighty Israeli armed forces. The present upheavals in the Palestinian territories stem from the actions of Israel, but the Islamic radicalization of the Palestinian political landscape also bears some responsibility.

Islamic Jihad

Islamic Jihad in Palestine came into being in 1980, as the result of a move by militant members of the Islamic Liberation Party to embark on a clandestine campaign of violence. This group had no real link with a small organization linked to Yasser Arafat's Fatah, which was active in Gaza in the late 1970s. The founders of Islamic Jihad were Sheikh Abdel Aziz Odeh, Sayyed Baraka, Ramadan Shalah, and Fateh Shikaki, the movement's effective leader. Jihad was influenced by the ideas of Iran's new leader, Ayatollah Khomeini, and was a radical and fundamentalist group, which adopted a pro-Iranian position.

Gradually, Fateh Shikaki positioned Islamic Jihad in opposition to Arafat and adopted Iranian ideas more explicitly. Jihad thus became the first Islamic Palestinian organization to advocate armed struggle as the means to recover "Sacred Palestine" in its entirety. It was very active during the first Intifada, rejecting the Oslo Accords and all other moves to make peace with Israel. Fateh Shikaki was murdered by Mossad agents in Malta in 1995 as he was returning to Pales-

tine after a visit to Libya. Jihad's new leader was Ramadan Abdallah Shalah, born in Gaza in 1955 and known as Rashid Qassem, who was based in Damascus at the head of a force of several hundred Palestinian fighters. His right-hand man, Abdallah Shami, was based in Gaza. Though its popular base was limited, Islamic Jihad had the backing of Iran and Syria, which provided logistic and financial support. It began to plan and carry out suicide attacks, a policy later imitated by Hamas and the Al Aqsa Martyrs Brigade.

Islamic Jihad features on the lists of terrorist organizations drawn up by the United Nations and the European Union. Its military wing, Saraya al-Quds (The Battalions of Jerusalem), which is well entrenched in Gaza, has played a leading role in the militarization of the Second Intifada.

PARIS MOSQUE

The Grand Mosque of Paris was opened in 1926. It was built at the expense of the French state. Its current rector is Dr. Dalil Boubakeur, who was appointed 1992. Dr. Boubakeur's father, Sheikh Hamza Boubakeur, an Algerian Quranic scholar, was the previous rector of the mosque, from 1957 to 1982. Dalil Boubakeur was educated in France and in Egypt, where he studied Arabic literature, and is a medical doctor. The mosque is financially supported by the Algerian government and is regarded by Muslims in France as a manifestation of official Algerian Islam. Moroccan Muslims in France in particular regard the official position of the mosque as giving excessive emphasis to Algeria. Dr. Boubakeur's position is one of studied moderation. He has gone on record as saying that young French Muslims should regard themselves as entirely French.

The Algerian government effectively took full control of the mosque in 1982, with the appointment as rector of an Algerian citizen, Sheikh Abbas ben Sheikh el-Hocine, who was the rector from 1982 to 1989. The mosque began to make efforts at this time to make itself the spokesman of an increasingly diverse spread of organizations in France. Sheikh Abbas attempted to set up regional federations of Muslim associations. When the French government began to set up institutions for the official expression of Islamic opinion in France, the Mosque was quick to step in. In the 1990s, it played a role in CORIF, the French-government sponsored consultation body. In 2003, Dr. Dalil Boubakeur became chairman of the CFCM (French Council for Muslim Worship), a position he has retained despite the faction directly supporting the mosque having obtained relatively few seats in the council.

PEARL, DANIEL

Daniel Pearl was an American journalist of Jewish origin, who was murdered in Karachi in Pakistan on February 22, 2002. At the time of his death, he was working for the *Wall Street Journal,* investigating links between Al-Qaida and Richard Reid, the so-called shoe bomber, who apparently attempted to blow up an aircraft bound for the United States from Paris on December 22, 2001. He had become bureau chief for the paper's South Asia office in the Indian city of Mumbai in 2000. He was temporarily in Karachi trying to arrange interviews with contacts that might have helped his investigation. He was known to be anxious to meet several people, including Mubarak Ali Shah Gilani, leader of a terror group known as Jamaat al-Fuqara that apparently had contacts in the United States and the Caribbean. Ahmed Omar

Saeed al-Sheikh, a British national educated at the London School of Economics, operating under a pseudonym, who was linked to Jaish-i Mohammed, had been one of Pearl's prior contacts before coming to Pakistan. He was able to abduct Pearl, apparently by telling him he would be taken to meet one of the individuals he wished to interview.

Pearl was abducted on January 23, and three days later a ransom note accused him of being a CIA agent and demanded the release of Pakistanis from Guantanamo Bay as well as the delivery of American fighter planes to Pakistan. Photographs were sent of Pearl with a pistol held to his head. On February 5, Saeed surrendered to the Pakistani ISI. He had been identified through a computer from which emails had been sent. He was handed over to the police on February 12. He told police he thought Daniel Pearl was probably dead. Saeed's role appears to have been to arrange the abduction, after which he handed Pearl over to another individual named Amjad Farooqi. Members of Jaish-i Mohammed also appeared to be involved. Pakistan's President Musharraf blamed Jaish-i Mohammed for the killing. Pictures of Daniel Pearl's death were placed on the Internet, but his body was not immediately recovered. On May 16, his remains were discovered and identified. Ahmed Omar Saeed al-Sheikh was condemned to death for the murder and three Pakistani citizens were given life imprisonment. They were Salman Saqib, Fahad Naseem, and Shaikh Adil. In March 2007, responsibility for the murder was claimed by Mohammed Khaled al-Sheikh, a Pakistani militant with links to Osama bin Laden and Al-Qaida. At Sheikh's trial in Guantanamo Bay, he claimed personally to have beheaded Pearl.

AL-QAIDA

Following the attacks on the twin towers of the World Trade Center in New York and on the Pentagon in Washington, DC, the term "Al-Qaida" became known around the world as the name of the terrorist organization led by Osama bin Laden and established by him in Afghanistan in 1987. The literal meaning of the Arabic word "Al-Qaida" is the "base" or the "headquarters." It is a word that has previously been used in the military context to designate a headquarters. (In the Arab Legion in Jordan, for example, the office from which the British commanding officer Glubb Pasha ran the Jordanian armed forces was known to both Arab and British officers as "Al-Qaida.") In the first instance, the word was quite generally used and included the entirety of the Islamist movement that had come to train in Afghanistan through bin Laden's network, without signifying any established structure.

The name Al-Qaida was first applied to a camp close to the Afghan city of Jalalabad, where an Egyptian aide of bin Laden's known as Abu Ubeida al-Banshiri organized the training of newly arrived volunteers before they were sent to fight. The camp had no specific geographical name and was therefore known simply as "The Base"—"Al-Qaida." On the ground, what existed was much more of a group of like-minded people than a structured party with a defined membership. Relationships within it gradually became more formalized, and an embryonic organization that was recognizably the ancestor of Al-Qaida took shape toward the end of 1987. This took the form of a group of acolytes who were in contact with bin Laden and were directly loyal to him and a nebulous larger group of a varying number of followers. At this time, bin Laden first began to reach out to make contacts with other Islamist organizations in the Middle East and elsewhere.

By 1990, Al-Qaida's membership was made up of two generations. The first consisted of volunteers who had come directly from the Middle East to fight in Afghanistan against the Russians, aiming both to fight the Jihad and to undertake "Da'wa" ("Preaching") with the aim of bringing lapsed Muslims back to Islam. Some of them went back to their countries of origin after the end of the war with the Soviets, setting up radical groups in their own countries, such as Algeria and the Philippines. These volunteers constituted the second generation. The links between the various groups of militants were characteristically based on personal relationships. Between 1991 and 1992, bin Laden consciously strove to internationalize his field of action. He himself returned to Saudi Arabia and then went to Sudan, where he observed the defeat of the U.S.

marines in Somalia in 1992. The first operation linked to Al-Qaida outside Afghanistan was mounted in the United States in February 1993 by Sheikh Omar Abderrahman and Yusuf Ramzi, when they carried out the first attack on the World Trade Center. The FBI inquiry that led to the arrest of the perpetrators revealed bin Laden for the first time as the head of a terrorist network.

Bin Laden first began to apply himself to Saudi and Middle Eastern affairs in 1994, when he linked up with a group of Saudi dissidents calling themselves the Committee for Advice and Reform (CAR). This group sought the violent overthrow of the Saudi regime and its replacement by a theocratic government. The CAR's definition of its mission was "the application of God's teaching to all aspects of life." Its approach to social and political transformation was founded on a precise interpretation of Islam, the Quran and the Sunna of the Prophet, as it had been interpreted by the Sunni forefathers. Bin Laden was apparently making a claim to be the legitimate heir of Muhammad Ibn Abdel Wahhab, the religious progenitor of the Saudi state. CAR defined four objectives for itself. These were the application of God's teaching in all spheres, the establishment of the Shari'a, the reform of the Saudi political system, and the expurgation of all forms of corruption from Saudi Arabia. They wanted the citizens of Saudi Arabia to be able to criticize their rulers, while the latter abided by the dictates of the Ulema.

On August 3, 1995, bin Laden addressed what he described as an open letter to King Fahd. In it he accused the regime of falling short of the teaching of Muhammad Ibn Abdel Wahhab. He also said that the country's rulers were incapable of ensuring Saudi Arabia's defense, instead bringing in foreign troops for the purpose, and added that they were wasting public funds and squandering the oil revenues. He concluded his letter

by calling on King Fahd to step down. Bin Laden also attacked the leading Ulema of the state and criticized their Fatwas, in particular those that justified the reliance on foreign forces during the Gulf War and others that appeared to justify reconciliation between the Arabs and Israel. Bin Laden's picture of the world embodied the concept of the weakness of a Muslim culture threatened by hostile western maneuvers and in need of protection. His concept of the Jihad was one of combat against non-Muslims. Bin Laden extended the struggle of the Muslims against Soviet "atheism" in Afghanistan to a wider war on "Crusaders" and Jews.

In 1996, Al-Qaida got into its stride as an organization when bin Laden returned to Afghanistan and was entrusted by the Taliban with sole charge of all foreign fighters present on Afghan soil, except the Pakistanis. He surrounded himself with an operational general staff that included Ayman al-Zawahiri, Mohammed Atef, and Abu Zubeida, all of them Egyptians. Abu Zubeida's responsibility was the selection of volunteers from those who flooded into the training camps in Afghanistan. Some were those destined to be foot soldiers, who fought in Afghanistan at the side of the Taliban. Another group consisted of those who had a good knowledge of the West and were sent back there after training to set up terrorist cells. There was also a new generation of militants—young men who had no experience of the Jihad against the Soviets. In general they had no political or religious experience. Among these were agents who were recruited individually in the West through contacts and who would later carry out attacks in the West. They included Mohammed Atta, Zacarias Moussaoui, Ahmed Ressam, and Richard Reid. Their assignments were decided on and planned during their stay in Afghanistan, but they were given wide latitude in the sphere of practical organization. There do not seem to have been any intermediary command structures between the headquarters in Afghanistan and the operational level. Al-Qaida set its sights on westernized circles as a field for its recruitment. The young people it targeted had identified Islam as a means to challenge the established order and, especially, to contest the globalization sponsored by the United States. The major targets struck in Al-Qaida's operations have been linked to the United States—the embassies, the USS *Cole,* and the World Trade Center, and have not directly touched the Arab regimes, despite the vituperation with which bin Laden speaks about them.

Al-Qaida's militants have come mainly from three countries, Saudi Arabia, Egypt, and Algeria. However, the organizational links between Al-Qaida and the movements that are operational inside those countries do not seem strong. No attack in Saudi Arabia or Egypt followed Al-Qaida's final defeat in Afghanistan in 2003. The geographical area in which it has operated tends, rather, to be on the periphery of the Arab world—Afghanistan, Bosnia, Chechnya, Kashmir, the Philippines, East Africa, the United States, and Europe. Al-Qaida is more like a sect than a revolutionary movement. It does not maintain legal organizations that serve as cover and has no subsidiary movements such as political parties, youth groups, or women's movements. It produces no publications and has no sympathizers. Meanwhile, it seems quite logical, in view of its tendency to recruit among a rootless younger generation, that it attracts converts to Islam. Al-Qaida's ideology is wholly based on the concept of Jihad together with the idea of the "Umma" (the "Muslim Nation") while it also adopts a traditional anti-imperialist rhetoric and anti-imperialist targets. Its goal is to mobilize the entire world against the United States, without itself taking up nationalism, even an Islamic nationalism. It deplores the nationalism of Islamic Iran, which it believes has

made the error of attempting to construct Islamism in one country. Al-Qaida is a resolutely internationalist movement.

Jihad is seen as the better means to mobilize the masses, in comparison with Da'wa—such as is preached by other groups, especially the Salafis. Though Al-Qaida did not invent the concept of suicide bombing, it is its favorite tactic, of which the attacks of September 11 were the ultimate examples. Suicide bombing conduces to the infliction of the maximum number of casualties by a small nucleus of determined militants. On the other hand, Al-Qaida has developed no concrete plans for the establishment of a wholly Islamic society. Its style is, above all, one of activism.

Al-Qaida signaled its intentions with a communiqué issued on February 23, 1998, by the so-called "World Islamic Front for Jihad against Jews and Crusaders." The text of the communiqué reads as follows:

> Since God created the Arabian Peninsula, with its deserts and seas, it has never been subjected to a trial to compare with that inflicted by the crusader forces who are deployed on this land like locusts, devouring it riches and its crops. All this has come as the various nations have allied themselves like people squabbling over a dish of food. Given the gravity of the situation, and our lack of support, we should examine together the significance of present developments and reach agreement on how to assess them and deal with them. No one today disputes three proven and unarguable facts. Let us list them, so that all may recall them, so that both those who live and those who die may be aware of these truths:
>
> 1. The United States occupies the most holy part of the land of Islam—the Arabian Peninsula—pillaging its wealth, imposing its law on its rulers, humiliating its inhabitants, terrorizing its neighbors, and making it[s] bases in the Peninsula the spearhead for attacks on the neighboring Muslim peoples.

In the past, some have questioned whether this occupation exists. Now, all the inhabitants of the Arabian Peninsula accept that the reality of the occupation. When the Americans insisted in using the Arabian Peninsula as a base for its continuing aggression against the Iraqi people, despite the refusal of all its rulers, they were forced to agree.

2. Despite the enormous devastation inflicted on the Iraqi people by the Crusader-Zionist alliance and the vast number of casualties, exceeding a million, the Americans are preparing once more to commit appalling massacres. It appears that they are no longer content either with the protracted embargo that has followed the violence of the war, or with the destruction and devastation of the country. They are preparing to commit genocide on what remains of the Iraqi people and to humiliate Iraq's Muslim neighbors.

3. The objectives of the United States in these wars are religious and economic, but they also serve to deflect attention from the occupation of Al-Quds ("The Sanctuary"—i.e. Jerusalem) and from the slaughter of Muslims by Israel. The actions of the United States demonstrate their wish to destroy Iraq, as well as other powerful Muslim states, and to destroy all such countries in the region as Iraq, Saudi Arabia, Egypt and Sudan by splitting them into weak and powerless mini-states. Their intention is to ensure Israel's survival and the continuation of the evil occupation of the Arabian Peninsula by the Crusaders.

All these crimes and depredations committed by the American[s] are an open declaration of war against God, his Prophet, and the Muslim people. All the "Ulema," both in the past and through all Muslim eras, agree that the Jihad is an obligation if an enemy attacks the lands of the Muslims, and that it is the sixth pillar of Islam. ...

We therefore, in accordance with God's commandments, proclaim the following Fatwa, for the attention of all Muslims, exhorting them to:

kill the Americans and their civil and military allies, which is an individual duty for every Muslim, who may do so wherever possible, until the Aqsa Mosque and the Holy Places are free from their domination. Drive their armies out of the lands of Islam, until they are conquered, humiliated and unable to threaten any Muslim. ... We call on the Ulema and the loyal rulers of Muslim states, and on our faithful young men and our soldiers, to launch attacks on the soldiers of Satan, on the Americans and their allies, Satan's assistants ...

The Fatwa was signed by Osama bin Laden and by a number of his associates, including Ayman al-Zawahiri, Abu Yasser Rifai Ahmed Taha (an Egyptian cleric), Mawlana Mir Hamza (Association of Uleama, Pakistan), Mawlana Fazl ur-Rahman Khalil (Amsar Movement, Pakistan), and Sheikh Abdel Salam Mohammed (Jihad Movement, Bangladesh).

In August 1998, this was followed by the simultaneous attacks on the U.S. embassies in Dar es Salaam and Nairobi, which caused hundreds of deaths and left thousands injured. This was the true declaration of war against the United States. The American reprisal attacks ordered by President Clinton prompted the organization to close ranks. There followed a number of operations directly or indirectly attributed to Al-Qaida. These included the "Millennium Operation," where attacks would have been launched in Jordan and the United States on January 1, 2000, to coincide with the celebration of the Millennium of the Christian era. This was foiled by the arrest of an activist group in Jordan and the detention of Ahmed Ressam on the U.S. frontier with Canada. Other incidents included the successful attack on the USS *Cole* in harbor at the Port of Aden in October 2000. Further attacks were forestalled. A planned attack on the cathedral at Strasbourg was prevented by the dismantling of the Melliani network in Europe by operations in Germany in December 2000 and in Italy in April 2001. Meanwhile, an attack on the U.S. embassy in Paris was foiled by the arrest of Djamel Beghal in Dubai in July 2001 followed by the destruction of his network of contacts in Europe.

By 2000, Al-Qaida was undeniably a structured organization. Osama bin Laden was its leader, and presided over a Consultative Council ("Majlis al-Shura") made up of his senior officials. This presided over national groups in different countries that made up its structure. Answerable to the Majlis al-Shura were four committees that were responsible for military affairs, financial administration, religious and legal issues, and public relations. In the interests of security, secrecy and clandestinity were obligatory. The inner circle of Al-Qaida included the following figures: Ayman al-Zawahiri, Mohammed Atef Ahmed, Ibrahim al-Najjar, Osma Khaled Samman, Ahmed Mustafa Nawwa, Osma Ali Ayub, Aslam al-Ghoumri, Mustafa Hamza, Hussein Shmeit, Adel Said Abdel Quddus, Yasser Tawfiq al-Sirri, and Osama Rushdy al-Khalifa.

Al-Qaida's most spectacular achievement was of course the attack on the World Trade Center in New York on September 11, 2001. Many millions of words have been devoted to this incident. Here, it will suffice to cite the account given at the military hearing at Guantanamo Bay of the crimes committed by Khaled Mohammed Sheikh. (Sheikh claims to have conceived the idea of the attacks and to have put the proposition to Osama bin Laden that a team should be recruited to carry them out):

On the morning of 11 September 2001, four airliners traveling over the United States were hijacked. The flights hijacked were: American Airlines Flight 11, United Airlines Flight 175, American Airlines Flight 77, and United Airlines Flight 93. At approximately 8:46 a.m., American Airlines Flight 11 crashed into the North Tower of the World Trade Center, resulting in the collapse of the tower at approximately 10:25 a.m. At approximately 9:05 a.m., United Airlines Flight 175 crashed into the South Tower of the World Trade Center, resulting in the collapse of the tower at approximately 9:55 a.m. At approximately 9:37 a.m., American Airlines Flight 77 crashed into the southwest side of the Pentagon in Arlington, Virginia. At approximately 10:03 a.m., United Airlines Flight 93 crashed in Stoney Creek Township, Pennsylvania. These crashes and subsequent damage to the World Trade Center and the Pentagon resulted in the deaths of 2,972 persons in New York, Virginia, and Pennsylvania.

In the wake of the attacks, the United States took the decision in 2001 to support a Northern Alliance attack on the Taliban in Kabul and to provide Special Forces assistance to the new Afghan government to track down the remnants of Al-Qaida. Osama bin Laden soon fled to the distant regions of Afghanistan on the Pakistani border, where he is presumed still to be in hiding. Al-Qaida in Afghanistan was destroyed in practical terms. Nonetheless, it has continued to exist as an idea. Perhaps Al-Qaida would still continue even if bin Laden were to die. However, his continued existence and the stream of video and audio tapes he has released and has contrived to convey to the international Arab media have kept the concept of Al-Qaida alive.

Al-Qaida, in the post-Afghan era, has become more of an idea than an institution. Around the world, Islamist militants proclaim their affiliation to Al-Qaida, though there appears to be no pyramid of command. In the Philippines, Jemaa Islamiya proclaims that it is an Al-Qaida affiliate. In Iraq, a group of Islamist militants fighting the American and coalition forces claims to be Al-Qaida, and in 2006 in Algeria the erstwhile Salafi Groupe Salafite pour la Prédication et le Combat (GSPC) renamed itself "Al-Qaida in the Islamic Maghreb." Meanwhile, Al-Qaida is resurgent even in Afghanistan. Under the umbrella of the reemergent Taliban movement that is challenging the Afghan government and the NATO forces, new Al-Qaida training camps are said to have been set up on the border between Afghanistan and Pakistan where Afghans, Pakistanis, and Arabs train and indoctrinate recruits. Leading figures linked to bin Laden in the past have been tracked down and killed, but this has not halted the organization as a whole. In April 2007, suicide bombers in Algiers claiming to be affiliated to Al-Qaida targeted the prime minister's office, and in the Moroccan city of Casablanca, a number of suicide bombers detonated their weapons when targeted by the police.

Security analysts have suggested that what might be called the new Al-Qaida may be more dangerous to western states than the old. Groups in different countries appear to be making contact with each other and may be sharing resources and techniques. On the other hand, there is general agreement that there is no hierarchical chain of command. Al-Qaida is more a concept than a formal organization. Those who act in what they believe to be its spirit declare their loyalty to it. There also seems to be little, if any, sharing of funds. Al-Qaida's big operation, September 11, required expenditure, but current actions are conducted on a modest scale susceptible to local funding on the basis of contributions and the proceeds of black market operations or petty crime. Meanwhile, thanks to international developments, Al-Qaida's ideology seems to be more attractive to disaffected young Muslims than ever before. Justifications that are consistently cited by Islamist militants in vindication of their actions include the American-led military presence in Iraq and the large and growing number of casualties there. Others include Israel's control over Jerusalem and the continued presence of American troops in Saudi Arabia and the Gulf.

QARADAWI, YUSUF ABDULLAH

Yusuf Abdullah al-Qaradawi was born on September 9, 1926, at Saft el-Turab in the Gharbiya province of western Egypt. He was left an orphan at the age of two and was brought up by an uncle's family. He attended the village Quranic school and appeared to be destined for a village trade. However, he memorized the Quran by the age of ten, after which his family began to call him the "Sheikh." He studied at the Al Azhar religious institute at Tanta and then took his degree at Al Azhar in Cairo. He came first in his class in the faculty of "Usul ad-Din" ("Foundations of Religion") in 1953.

Qaradawi was influenced by Ibn Taymiya, Ibn al-Qayyim, and Sheikh Rashi Rida and was a great admirer of Hassan al-Banna. His thinking was also affected by Abu Hamid Mohammed al-Ghazali (1917–1966), an Egyptian Azhar graduate of 1941 who taught in Saudi Arabia, Qatar, and Algeria, where he played a part in the political Islamization of Algeria. Between 1953 and 1960, Qaradawi continued his studies at the Faculty of Letters, but eventually he prioritized his activities as a militant in the Muslim Brotherhood and abandoned his studies. In the 1960s, Nasser clamped down hard on the Muslim Brotherhood's activities, and it was not until 1973, after Anwar al-Sadat had become President of Egypt, that he was able to present his thesis: "Fiqh al-Zakat" ("Zakat and its role in the solution of social problems"). This got him his doctorate in Islamic Sciences. In addition to his abilities as an Islamic jurist, he also had a talent for the composition of poetry on Islamic subjects.

Throughout the 1950s in Egypt, Qaradawi had combined his theoretical studies with militant activity. He was jailed four times between 1949 and 1962. He first preached in Cairo mosques in 1956. As early as 1959, however, he was banned from further preaching and was transferred to the department of Islamic cultural studies at Al-Azhar. From the late 1970s, it was evident that he was the rising star in the Muslim Brotherhood's international department. His supporters regarded him as the scholar of the Islamic reawakening. In 1977, Qaradawi transferred to Qatar, where he founded the Department of Islamic Studies at the University of Qatar, which he continues to head. From the mid-1980s, he became the prime mover of the Union of Islamic Organizations in France (UOIF) and the Union of Islamic Organizations in Europe, based in London. He is associated with the Oxford Center for Islamic Studies in Britain and the World Islamic League's Center for Shari'a Studies in Mecca. He teaches at the UOIF's Islamic Center in France and is the president of the European High Council for Fatwa and Research. Among his many published works are his doctoral theses "Fiqh al-Zakat" and "Al-Hilal wa-l-Haram" ("The permitted and the forbidden"). He has also written a significant work on what he has called the "Islamic Renaissance."

Qaradawi has not confined himself to preaching in the mosques and to his study and teaching in the university world. He also used the medium of television to become the most renowned preacher in the Arab world. His weekly program under the title "Shari'a and Life" on the Qatar-based channel Al-Jazeera has been widely watched—his regular audience is estimated at 40 million. The issue of Fatwas and opinions on contemporary Muslim affairs represented for Qaradawi the best way to pursue his personal Jihad. He believes in the use of modern media, and as early as 1997 he set up his own Internet site to publicize his ideas. In the international field, he maintained a close relationship with Hassan al-Turabi in Sudan. He has also taken care to develop a relationship with the Islamic republic of Iran while keeping up his links with Saudi Arabia. He travels regularly to Britain where he preaches to enthusiastic audiences. Western statesmen have sought his help in resolving problems in the Muslim world.

Though a conservative Islamic scholar, Qaradawi has presented himself as a force for moderation. He has riled Islamist extremists by criticizing terrorist attacks. He has also been unrestrained in his criticism of the governments of Muslim countries when he believes such criticism is necessary. However, he did not unambiguously condemn the Taliban's execution of their opponents, nor has he condemned without reserve terrorist incidents in Egypt and Algeria. On the other hand, he distances himself from Osama bin Laden, and, in particular, he is adamant that bin Laden has no religious status and is not in a position to issue Fatwas or declare Jihad. He also heads an organization known as "I'tilaf al-Kheir" ("Coalition for Welfare"), which collects funds for Palestinian causes. This is an organization that includes representatives of Islamist organizations from around the world. He says that ordinary Muslims should donate to Palestine rather than spend their money on luxuries. He has also justified the use of suicide attacks by Palestinians against Israel. However, he argues that suicide attacks are only justified in extreme circumstances, and that in the circumstances of Palestine and Israel they were carried out in self-defense. He condemns suicide attacks carried out by Muslims in the West.

Qaradawi has been severely criticized in Europe for his attitude on a number of issues such as the rights of women and homosexuality. He has been accused of justifying the mistreatment of women within marriage. Of his seven children, three daughters have Ph.D. degrees from British universities. However, his position is that he is frankly unable to understand the western tolerance of homosexual practices.

QUTB, SAYYED

Sayyed Qutb, who later become one of the most influential Islamist thinkers of his day, was born in 1906 in the village of Musha in upper Egypt. He was a graduate of the secular Dar ul-Ulum college in the Egyptian capital, Cairo, and became a teacher afterward. He never married, and his health was always delicate. During the 1930s and 1940s, he also lived the life a typical Cairo intellectual, writing literary criticism and novels. He was instrumental in promoting the early career of Naguib Mahfouz, the Nobel Prize–winning Egyptian novelist. In 1939, he became an official in the Ministry of Education, and this eventually to the upheaval that changed his life. In 1948, he won a scholarship to go to the United States to study the American educational system. He was already turning toward Islam, but during his American trip he was, by his own account, alarmed and disgusted by what he saw as the licentious way of life of the country, which reaffirmed his commitment to the Islamic faith. In 1950, when he returned to Egypt, he resigned from his government post and joined the Muslim Brotherhood, becoming an official of the organization and the editor of the Muslim Brotherhood's weekly publication "Al-Ikhwan al-Muslimin."

Sayyed Qutb was acquainted with the Brotherhood's General Guide Hassan el-Hudeiby and rose rapidly through the ranks to take charge of publication and propaganda. During the short period of alliance between the Egyptian "Free Officers," who carried out the revolution in 1952,

Qutb preached justice and socialism, vindicating the policies of Egypt's new rulers on Islamic grounds. The Brotherhood was soon disillusioned, however, when the new regime refused to implement any aspect of the Shari'a, failing even to ban the sale of alcohol. The mistrust was mutual. The revolutionary leader Gamal Abdul Nasser suspected the Brotherhood of intending to infiltrate and subvert the revolution, and on January 21, 1954, he decreed its dissolution. Along with many other Muslim Brothers, Qutb was arrested in 1954 and spent ten years in prison. Though Qutb was at first ill-treated, in his later years in jail he was allowed to write. In 1964, he was released, but was then rounded up again in 1965, just eight months later, after an attempt by Muslim Brothers on President Nasser's life. He was questioned, put on trial, and then on August 29, 1966, he was hanged.

Qutb's first book on Islamic subjects was published in 1949, during his time in the United States. This was "Al-'Adala al-Ijtima'iya fi-l-Islam" ("Social Justice in Islam"). His two most important books were written while he was in prison, after 1954. One of these, destined to become his most influential book, was "Ma'alim fi-l-Tariq" ("Milestones," the title by which it has become known in English—which literally means "Signposts along the Road"). The other book was his major work, a commentary on the Quran entitled "Fi Zilal al-Qur'an" ("In the Shade of the Quran"). In his philosophy, Qutb sharply contrasted the world of Islam with all that was not enlightened by Islam, which he called the "Jahiliya" ("Ignorance")—the word used to signify the condition in which the world of humankind existed before the revelation of the Quran. If the Shari'a was not being applied, then societies—even if they imagined they were Muslim—lapsed back to the state of Jahiliya. For Qutb, democracy is not compatible with Islam, while freedom is to be found only under the Shari'a. Qutb followed Ibn Taymiya in justifying opposition to rulers who supposed themselves to be Islamic but failed in their duty to manage all things according to the Shari'a. Such were to be declared to be apostates—the process known as "Takfir"—and the good Muslim should withdraw himself from them and their society.

Qutb is a powerful influence in Islam today, and his works are much revered by young radical Muslims of a Salafi inclination. However, they are also read by other Muslims and have their resonance throughout Muslim society. Qutb is, in particular, the spiritual father of those groups that call themselves "Takfir wa-l-Hijra" ("Rejection and Withdrawal"). Other Muslims argue vigorously that the condemnation of fellow Muslims as falling short of the faith is not what a Muslim should do.

RAMADAN, HANI

Hani Ramadan is the fourth son of Said Ramadan and Wafa Hassan al-Banna, the daughter of the founder of the Muslim Brotherhood, Hassan el-Banna. He was born in 1959 in Geneva and is of Swiss nationality. He studied humanities and embarked on a career as a teacher. He is a teacher of French within the Swiss school system. Soon, he became involved with the outreach activities of the Eaux-Vives mosque in Geneva, though continuing to teach. He maintains a lower profile than his brother Tariq and is less influential in intellectual and university circles but is nevertheless seen as the spokesman of the family, because of his frequent media appearances. He sends large numbers of letters to newspapers and writes frequent op-ed articles, all of which put forward the concepts of the "right to a difference of identity," the "debate between civilizations," and the need for an "honest dialogue with the West." He is also a prolific lecturer.

The Islamic Center at Eaux-Vives has held numerous demonstrations and open-air prayer gatherings in support of various Islamist causes. On March 11, 1995, Hani Ramadan led a meeting of ex-members of the Algerian FIS (Islamic Salvation Front) at the Place des Nations in Geneva, in front of the European headquarters of the United Nations. A number of activists from FIDA (the Islamic Front for Armed Jihad) participated in this demonstration, together with representatives of Anouar Haddad, now based in Washington, DC, and European supporters of the Algerian GIA (Armed Islamic Groups). In his closing address, Hani Ramadan spoke of the need for what he called an "international struggle against the impious." "The advantage of being in Europe is that we can take advantage of the freedom provided by democratic political systems."

The Islamic Center has guest rooms for twenty visitors and is the meeting point for the European representatives of various Islamist organizations. Hani Ramadan has frequently been invited to visit sister organizations but was banned from visiting France on February 1, 1995. On March 1, 1997, the French government justified its ban, which was later lifted, on the following grounds:

Mr Ramadan is the director of the Islamic Center in Geneva, known to the special services of the police as a meeting place for leading European Islamists and a junction point for financial networks. Mr Ramadan is the grandson of the founder of the Muslim Brotherhood in Egypt. Like his brother, Tariq Ramadan, Hani Ramadan is a significant figure in the European Islamist movement and has close relations with the UOIF in France. This association has participated in demonstrations in favor of the wearing of Islamic head-coverings and has sympathies with the Palestinian Hamas movement.

Upon the death of Said Ramadan in 1992, the Ramadan brothers had found themselves in control of substantial funds that their father had administered on behalf of the Egyptian Muslim Brotherhood. There were some minor disagreements between the two over the use of the funds, which were soon reconciled. Hani Ramadan stressed to interviewers that intellectually he and his brother were "two sides of the same coin," though he takes an apparently less subtle view on doctrinal questions than Tariq. However, the more serious issue appeared to be that the Egyptian Brotherhood wished their funds to be returned, whereas the Ramadan brothers intended to use the money to fund their activities in Europe. They expanded their activities in the French city of Lyon and stepped up the activities of the "Al-Tawhid" bookshop and Islamic publishing business they maintained there.

Apart from ideological and militant considerations, the strategy of the Ramadan brothers appeared to be to convince wealthy Arab Muslim donors of their ability to exercise influence in intellectual, media, and university circles in France, Switzerland, and elsewhere in Europe, in order to attract further funding. They had become well known in cultural and humanitarian circles in Switzerland, but they had so far failed to make a wider impact. They therefore threw themselves into Islamic activities in France, especially in Lyon and Grenoble. A number of ill-judged statements earned a ban on Tariq Ramadan from entering France and a restriction of his freedom of expression in Switzerland. To continue to impress potential donors in Saudi Arabia and the Gulf, Hani stood in for his younger brother, while the latter spent a sabbatical year in London. In 2003, Hani Ramadan lost his teaching job

in Switzerland after stating that he approved of the stoning of women for adultery. He was reinstated in 2005 by a Swiss court of appeal. Women's organizations in France protested against his presence in the country and disrupted his lectures. On April 14, 2007, he addressed a UOIF (Union of Islamic Organizations in France) conference at Le Bourget.

RAMADAN, SAID

Said Ramadan was one of the principal organizers of the deployment of the Muslim Brotherhood overseas after the clamp down by President Nasser in 1954 on the organization's activities in Egypt. He was the heir and disciple of his father-in-law, Hassan el-Banna, the founder of the Muslim Brotherhood. After his flight from Egypt, he spent time in Saudi Arabia and then in Pakistan, where he studied with Sunni Shari'a scholars. In the late 1950s, he persuaded Saudi sources to contribute to a Da'wa campaign in Europe and was able in the first instance to open an Islamic Center in Munich. He chose Germany, as it was a preferred destination for Egyptian students and there was a growing Turkish community. There had also been contacts in the 1930s between the Muslim Brotherhood and Nazi Germany. The contributions of Turkish adherents facilitated the establishment of the Brotherhood's international existence. The Munich Islamic Center prospered, to the satisfaction not merely of Said Ramadan but also of his Saudi backers.

During his time in Germany, Said Ramadan presented a doctoral thesis at the University of Cologne. The thesis, entitled "Islamic Law, its Scope and Equity," was indicative of the Muslim Brotherhood's procedures. The means of proselytization were adapted to the circumstances. He also took the position that only believers can achieve true knowledge of Islam—an important point for those who wish to understand the religion. The thesis laid stress on a central concept of the Brotherhood's ideology, that an Islamic state is a divine necessity and deprecated the influence of Western historiography on Muslim authors. Said Ramadan also asserted that Islam was obliged to be totalitarian in its ambitions, because all religious concepts that seek to define the range and content of human thought must be totalitarian, in practice or at least in principle. As he argued, religion must necessarily "seek to impose its own values and rules on all human activities and social institutions, for primary schools up to the law and the government."

Said Ramadan then began to look at the prospects of launching further developments from the Munich Islamic Center, which had been intended to serve as the base for other such centers in European countries. His Saudi patrons urged him to go to Switzerland, for a number of reasons, both political and financial. Switzerland had not merely been the repository of choice for Saudi petrodollars since World War II; it was also where the Algerian Islamists had placed their resources. Said Ramadan envisaged a possible role for the Muslim Brotherhood in Algeria. He therefore set himself up in Geneva, where Saudi assistance enabled him to develop the Brotherhood's international wing. In 1961, he set up the Islamic Center at Eaux-Vives, now run by his son Hani. Hani Ramadan refuses to say whether he adheres to the Muslim Brotherhood, answering only that Hassan el-Banna established his society according to nothing more and nothing less than the laws of Islam. Hani Ramadan therefore sees no necessity to admit to being anything other than a Muslim. It is a rule of the Muslim Brotherhood that no Brother admits to membership.

RAMADAN, TARIQ

In 2003, the young Muslim intellectual and academic Tariq Ramadan achieved notoriety in France when he engaged in a live television debate with French interior minister Nicolas Sarkozy on the position of France's Muslim community. As a result of that encounter, and his participation in the European Social Forum, he has come to be regarded as a leading spokesman for Muslims in France. He certainly wields much influence over French Muslim attitudes. He has been accused in the United States of links with known terrorists. He has also been accused of anti-Semitism, because of his hostile remarks about the support given by French Jews to Israel. The French media have identified him with the views of the UOIF (Union of Islamic Organizations in France), which is regarded as extreme in its views. He first became widely known in 1994, with the publication of a book *Muslims in a Secular Society* (*Les Musulmans dans la laïcité*). On the basis of his writings, he has made a reputation as a leading Muslim intellectual and an exponent of Islamic ideas, especially as they relate to the presence of a Muslim community in Europe. He is widely regarded as a spokesman for moderation, though some disagree with that view. Tariq Ramadan was offered an academic post in the United States in 2003, which he was unable to take because the American administration did not grant him a visa. He has been a visiting fellow at St. Antony's College, Oxford, since 2005 and continues his academic work in Europe.

Tariq Ramadan is a Swiss national of Egyptian descent, who was born in Geneva in 1962. His father, Said Ramadan, a leading member of the Muslim Brotherhood, was exiled by Egypt's President Nasser in 1954. In 1961, Said Ramadan established the Islamic Center in Geneva, which is now run by Tariq Ramadan's brother Hani. Tariq

Ramadan's mother was Wafa al-Banna, the eldest daughter of Hassan al-Banna, the Egyptian founder of the Muslim Brotherhood. He studied at the University of Geneva, where he took a degree in philosophy and French literature and a doctorate in Islamic studies. He currently teaches Islamic studies at the University of Freiburg and philosophy at the College of Geneva. The mistrust with which he is viewed in the United States apparently relates to meetings he is said to have arranged between Ayman al-Zawahiri, the number two in Al-Qaida, and Omar Abdel Rahman, who masterminded the 1993 attack on the World Trade Center. Tariq Ramadan denies having met either man. He is also accused of having associations with Algerian Islamists linked to violent groups, which he also denies. U.S. authorities later said that he had been denied a visa because of donations he had given to charities that had links with Palestinian terror organizations. His brother Hani Ramadan continues to run the Islamic Center in Geneva but denies that it is an extremist organization. Saudi Arabia initially funded the Center, but it now depends on private donations. Its staff members deny that any money comes from fundamentalist groups. Hani Ramadan lost his job as a teacher of French in the Swiss state education system after publishing articles in which he justified the stoning of women adulterers.

In 1995, Tariq Ramadan was banned from France for several months by the Ministry of the Interior. Equally at home in Arabic, French, and English, he fascinated the media. He had already been an ever-present press and television interviewee. After he was banned from entering France, many intellectuals, media personalities, and religious figures sprang to his support. This was the apogee of his career. He gave increasing numbers of lectures, wrote more articles, and began to seem omnipresent. He was the fashionable preacher and the "big brother" of the young people of France's Muslim ghettos. He was invited to many European and African countries. His pronouncements were increasingly respected in a wide range of spiritual and political circles. His critics saw him as no more than the latest Muslim media star, but he began to regard himself as the representative of the Muslims of Europe, expressing a political stance, closely linked with a moral standpoint and a spiritual position. Media coverage encouraged this development. Meanwhile, a number of recognized experts on Islam began to question the honesty of his rhetoric of moderation. Some called him a contemporary neofundamentalist, whereas others queried whether he was merely presenting old Islamic positions in a new guise. One thoughtful commentator queried whether his constant criticism of Western society could serve as a basis for the integration of young Muslims into the West.

The constant theme of his oratory is the need for a dialogue of cultures, but with no compromises. The intention is always the same—to assert the superiority of Islam over other monotheistic religions. According to Tariq Ramadan, the concept of the separation between politics and religion, prevalent in France, can be traced back to the triumph of the eighteenth-century enlightenment philosophers over a Catholic Church that was at the time obscurantist. As he puts it:

> In the 15th century, the initial outburst of humanism was a rebellion. There had been such stultifying oppression for centuries that it had begun to appear obvious to many thinkers that a man could realize himself as a human being outside the Church.

In Islam, meanwhile, there was "no conflict between faith, based on dogma, and reason, which is an aspect of human freedom." For Tariq Ramadan, as the ideology of the Muslim Brotherhood teaches, Islam is more than a religion. It is universal and encompasses every aspect of social life. The issue of secularism, therefore, does not arise in the Muslim world. Symptomatically of his contradictory logic, Tariq Ramadan writes as follows on the subject of education: "Biology classes may include teaching that is not consistent with the principles of Islam. The same is true of history or philosophy.... But what is at issue is not placing a ban on such courses." Instead, he argues, young Muslims must be given the opportunity to follow, in parallel, other courses that will provide them with the Islamic responses. On several occasions, his recommendation of Islamic teaching of biology, history, philosophy, and, even, gymnastics aroused hostile responses from his teaching colleagues and from the Swiss authorities.

A further dimension of Tariq Ramadan's oratorical preconceptions is the development of a virulent criticism of the West, which he sees as a global monolith. He also attacks Western culture and the westernization of the world. "God, duty, morality and modesty are absent from everyday speech and life. The passing moment is for liberty and gratification.... Far removed from ethical and moral preoccupations, the world goes on its way and loses its coherence." Given a trend toward decadence, experienced as deprivation and a loss of direction, Islam provides the solution. "The re-awakening of Islam can provide an as yet unsuspected contribution to a genuine renaissance of the spirituality of the men and women of our world." The bankruptcy of the West had already been a long-standing theme of the preaching of Hassan el-Banna and Said Ramadan. In the view of the Muslim Brotherhood's founder, the West ought soon to fall "under the sway of the East."

In Tariq Ramadan's thesis, which he devoted to the reformist strand of Muslim thought, he recapitulates the arguments of his grandfather. "Everything leads us to the identical conclusion: the future belongs to Islam." When his critics point out the ways in which Tariq Ramadan's thought resembles earlier formulations and is derived from them, his reaction is hostile. Like all preachers, the grandson of Hassan el-Banna does not appreciate contradiction. "What must be retained from the legacy of El-Banna is the methodology and the interpretative effort. I would never deny my debt, but I nonetheless claim the right to develop my own thought and approach."

Tariq Ramadan has been involved in the various controversies in France relating to the wearing by women of Islamic head coverings. In the context of his role as an educator, he has often advised his young pupils to choose the veil, while denying that he is indulging in proselytization. Like his brother Hani, he rejects any suggestion that he has any connection with the Muslim Brotherhood, although at the same time recognizing his debt to their theology. Behind his traditional rhetoric, Tariq Ramadan adopts political positions that clearly tend toward the recognition of the rights of Muslims as a community—as the British are reputed to do. According to his sympathizers, this is a logical position for him to take up, because "it is only in such a context that he can truly become the representative of the Muslims of Europe."

REID, RICHARD

On December 22, 2001, Richard Colvin Reid attempted to blow up an American Airlines flight from Paris to Miami by detonating an explosive charge concealed in his shoe. On January 30, 2003, he was found guilty of terrorism charges by an American Federal Court in Boston. He claimed that his motive was his devotion to Islam and repeatedly declared that he hated the United States because it had murdered innocent people. He was given multiple life sentences and a number of sentences of twenty- and thirty-year imprisonment, to be served consecutively. He is presently held in a maximum-security prison in Colorado. He has been linked to Al-Qaida in a number of ways. An alleged Al-Qaida adherent captured in Oman in 2003 said that Khaled Sheikh Mohammed, a known Al-Qaida associate, suggested the shoe bomb mission to Reid. Ahmed Ressam says he saw Reid in Afghanistan in 1998. In 2006, Zacarias Moussaoui claimed that he and Reid were to be the fifth hijacking team on September 11, 2001, but this appears to have been groundless boasting on the part of Moussawi.

Reid was born in the London suburb of Bromley in 1973. His father was Jamaican and his mother English. His father was in prison for most of Reid's childhood and adolescence. Reid was jailed himself in the 1990s for a series of muggings and apparently converted to Islam while he was held in a young offenders' institution in Feltham in west London. (His father, too, had separately converted to Islam at an earlier date.) After his release, he began to attend Brixton mosque in south London. He called himself Abdel Rahim and showed a willingness to help at the mosque and to learn Arabic. It is possible that he met Zacarias Moussaoui at Brixton. He appears to have encountered a number of extremists when he started to attend another mosque in Finsbury Park in north London, where more militant preachers including Abu Hamza al-Masri wielded influence. Takfir wa-l-Hijra groups were operative at the mosque. In 1998, he went to Pakistan and may have visited a training camp in Afghanistan. In 2001, he visited Israel, where he was kept under surveillance and seemed to be showing a strong interest in potential terrorist targets. He then seems to have gone to Egypt and Turkey before returning to Pakistan. He then visited Amsterdam (where he sent many e-mails to Pakistan from Internet cafés) and Brussels before going to Paris to take a flight and put his plan into action.

RUSHDIE, SALMAN

Salman Rushdie is the Indian-born British writer who was the subject of a Fatwa issued on February 14, 1998, by Ayatollah Khomeini, the supreme leader of Iran, effectively condemning him to death by declaring it lawful for Muslims to kill him. His transgression was the publication of a book entitled *The Satanic Verses*. The book is indubitably insulting to Islam in a number of ways and, from the day of its publication, had caused a hostile reaction among Muslims in a number of countries, though this was mainly in English-speaking countries. There were demonstrations in the north of England, mainly by Deobandi groups, and the book was banned in South Africa and sparked riots in India and Pakistan. However, it appears to have been brought to Ayatollah Khomeini's attention by a British Islamist, Kalim Siddiqui, the founder of Britain's so-called Muslim Parliament, who was visiting Iran and persuaded intermediaries to tell Khomeini about it.

The reason for the international resonance of the affair was Rushdie's standing as a writer. Rushdie was born in Bombay (now Mumbai) in 1947, and his wealthy Muslim parents migrated to Pakistan in 1964. Rushdie was educated at a well-known private school in England (Rugby School) and then at Cambridge University. After a stopgap career as an advertising copywriter and a period of apprenticeship that resulted in the publication of a first novel, he achieved fame with his novel *Midnight's Children*, about the independence and partition of British India as seen through they eyes of a number of protagonists. This won numerous literary prizes. A later novel, entitled *Shame*, caused considerable offence in Pakistan because of its disobliging portrayal of a fictionalized version of the Bhutto family. *The Satanic Verses* was his fourth novel. After its publication and the resulting furor, many liberal commentators sprang to his defense and both the British government and the European Union have extended their support. Rushdie was given British police protection, on a permanent basis. He has, however, been obliged to lead a semi-clandestine life because of the refusal of the Iranian authorities to rescind the Fatwa after Ayatollah Khomeini's death. They argue that it can only be withdrawn by the authority who issued it, and of course Ayatollah Khomeini is dead. Others suggest that even if it were not withdrawn, it could be overruled by a Fatwa from a current "Marja'"—a Shi'ite Ayatollah of sufficient authority to be emulated.

RUSSIA

Though the Russian leadership keeps a wary eye on Islam inside the country, there is nonetheless a view that Russia should instrumentalize Islam as part of its strategy to maintain its position as a world power and, in particular, as a counterbalance to the influence of the United States. It is estimated that as many as 10 percent of Russia's population may be Muslims, after the break up of the Soviet Union. The Russian Empire of the Tsars began to absorb Muslim areas as early as the sixteenth century. In modern times, swayed by the concept of Russia as a "Eurasian" power, with a foot in both continents, the leadership has reinstated an Islamic policy in Russia's list of priorities. The rationale is that the independence of Russia should go hand in hand with continuing Russian hegemony over the Muslim peoples to the south. In nationalist circles in Russia, there are pragmatic pro-Islamic currents that regard Islam as a resource available to Russia in its efforts to resist the hegemony of the United States.

The philosophy was summed up in part by the extreme right-wing Russian politician

Vladimir Jirinovsky, leader of Russia's Liberal Democratic Party (LDP), as follows:

> We need not fear Islamic fundamentalism, which is no more than the establishment of a social order and traditions connected with the peoples of the South. What harm can we Russians suffer from polygamy, respect for older people, social order, traditional crafts, and the Quran? The Turkish choice of modernizing democracy, which has enabled the Turks to spread throughout Europe, would be much worse for us.

In a publication in 1993, Jirinovsky distanced himself from classic "Eurasian" thinking on the partition of the world when he wrote:

> If we compete for territory we mutually disadvantage each other. But there can be agreement on how to divide the planet. The Japanese and Chinese will take responsibility for South-East Asia, the Philippines. Malaysia, Indonesia and Australia. Russia will manage Afghanistan, Iran and Turkey. Western Europe will have Africa, and the United States will control Latin America.

On February 17, 1993, Zhuganov, the leader of the Communist Party, said in an interview with Pravda, "Our country, from time immemorial, has been a union of Slavs and Muslims." The neo-Eurasian tendency influences the broad lines of Russia's foreign policy by providing an ideological basis for post-Soviet imperialism, of which Russia's rapprochement with Iran, its mistrust of Turkey, and its alliance with Germany are all aspects.

On the other hand, Russian ultranationalist circles utterly reject what they regard as Eurasian fantasies concerning the country's future, which in their view fail to take into account Russia's national interests and would lead not to a Russian renaissance but to a profound distortion of its national, cultural, and historic consciousness. The ultranationalists maintain that Eurasianism would lead as surely to the destruction of Russia's essential nature as would its opposite, the Atlantic idea. Their unease rests in part on the apparently ineluctable demographic decline of the Slavs in comparison with the burgeoning Muslims, for the most part Turks. Since 1991, among the Slav population of Russia, the annual preponderance of deaths over births has run at a figure of several hundred thousand. The fear of Islamization from within has led the nationalists to advocate the isolation of Russia from the Islamic world, beginning with the granting of independence to the peoples of the northern Caucasus. This idea was developed by Alexander Solzhenitsyn in his book *Rebuilding Russia*.

Another ultranationalist politician, the leader of the National Republican Party, Nicholas Lysenko, has spoken out both against Islam and the alleged incursions of the Turks:

> It would be either unacceptable romanticism or criminal short-sightedness not to be concerned over the activities of our brothers the Turks, whose rampant expansion is overrunning our towns and villages. I would be the first to declare my friendship for the Azeris, the Chechens, the Turkmens and the Uzbeks, were they to direct their expansion toward the South. They could go to Afghanistan, Turkey, Pakistan, or wherever they will, but not to the North. If they fail to understand this, the Russian response will be pitiless. Turkey is interfering impudently in Russian affairs. In reply we should crush them, politically and militarily.

Any pragmatic agreement between such views and those of the "Eurasians" might occur over the issue of how to deal with the Turkic peoples. There are large numbers of speakers of Turkic languages within Russia's national territory and consequent fears that they may demand recognition as a separate community, or even autonomy. It is unclear, however, whether such demands would be based on Islam, or whether they would be on ethnic grounds. The reaction of the Russian political class would depend on which was perceived as the more dangerous: Islamic fundamentalism or pan-Turkism. Russian policy would tend to respond to whichever seemed the more serious threat.

Islamic Renaissance Party (Russia—Soviet Union)

The Islamic Renaissance Party (IRP) of the Soviet Union was founded June 1990 at Astrakhan. Its founding leaders were Ahmedzay Akhtaev and Valiahmed Saddour. Its stated goal was the unity of the Muslim community of the country. Its ambition was to supplant the country's official Islam and win political power as the leadership of the Muslim community—hitherto powerless in political and social life in the Soviet Union. The Soviet IRP, less explicitly, also wished to position itself as a key player in the Islamic world, given the large number of Soviet Muslims, of whom there were some 60 million. In December 1992, the first issue of the IRP's political newspaper, *Al-Wahdat* (*Unity*), defined the party's basic principles: "Our aim is to be an intellectual organization that will develop the Muslim political leadership that will be required within a true Muslim state."

Nevertheless, the IRP failed to reach out to the Muslim mass in the Soviet Union and remained on the margins, failing to develop a coherent political philosophy. Within it, there were four main factions:

1. The pro-Saudi Wahhabi group, typified by the brothers Abbas and Bahaeddine Kebedov, who attracted attention in the 1970s and 1980s for their militant activities in Daghestan.

2. The group close to the Muslim Brotherhood, headed by Adam Diniev, also the leader of the Chechen IRP, whose policy was to aim at a takeover of power through parliamentary means and a process of compromise.
3. The pro-Iranian minority headed by Gaidar Jemal.
4. The pro-Turkish tendency, hampered by the antagonism of Turkey itself to the IRP. Nonetheless, links had been established with Necmettin Erbakan's Refah Party.

The leaders and activists of the Soviet IRP for the most part lacked a definite ideology, reacting ad hoc to circumstances and the current balance of power. Few IRP members backed either the pro-Iranian or the pro-Saudi factions, though there was a groundswell of support for the pro-Saudi group, thanks to the financial support promised by Saudi Arabia. The IRP supported the continuing existence of the Soviet Union inside its current frontiers but opposed its current political structure. The dismemberment of the Soviet state prompted a debate in Moscow over the issue of whether the IRP branches in the new Republics should be subsidiaries of a central party or whether they should be independent, with full freedom of action. The arguments were different in Central Asia, in part because foreign political parties were banned in some of the new Republics, and partly because the local IRP officials did not wish to appear to be under the thumb of the Russian IRP, as happened in Tajikistan.

In practice, any possibility of unity foundered on the existence of ethnic divisions. Competition between Persian and Turkic speakers resulted in a failure to agree between the Uzbek IRP and that in Tajikistan, which were attached to their respective countries. There was also a clash between the Moscow IRP, run by Turkic speakers, and the Persian-speaking Tajik IRP. Other divisions sprang up between the national groups, as in Kyrgyzstan, where the party initially split and then halted its activities entirely after clashes broke out in Osh, where the Kyrgyz came into conflict with the Uzbeks who were active in the local movement. There had been up to one thousand activists, of whom most were Uzbeks, with a few of the Dargins exiled from Daghestan by Stalin. Clashes between the Uzbeks and the Tajiks in Osh split the IRP, which ceased to function.

After the IRP in Tajikistan was crushed by the government, other IRP wings were suppressed by the respective national governments in Kyrgyzstan and elsewhere. IRP activists were demoralized by the civil war in Tajikistan, for which the media put the blame entirely on the Islamists. Though the party took a less high-profile line in Uzbekistan, it was nonetheless banned, and the same thing happened in Kazakhstan. The leadership was closely watched by the police and was forbidden to communicate with the Russian IRP. In Kyrgyzstan, it proved impossible to hold a national founding congress, and only small local groups were able to function.

In other areas of the former Soviet Union, the IRP—despite its popularity—had difficulties. It was refused recognition in Chechnya in 1993 because of its differences with the official local Mullahs preferred by Dudaiev. From a membership of four or five thousand, it slumped to less than a thousand activists. In Azerbaijan, the IRP never got off the ground despite attempts to negotiate with the Azeri Islamic Party and the Tawbah movement. Islam in Azerbaijan did not have deep popular roots, and the real opposition to the government was the Popular Front, an anti-communist and democratic movement. Even in Moscow itself, the activities of the IRP tailed off, with its activists drifting away toward other parties.

SADR, MOHAMMED BAQR AL-

Mohammed Baqr al-Sadr was born in 1932 in Kazimein, a Shi'ite sanctuary close to Baghdad. His family were Shi'ite ulema who were involved in the politics of the Iraqi constitutional monarchy. His uncle, Sayyed Mohammed al-Sadr, was Iraq's prime minister in 1948. From 1945, he studied in Najaf with Ayatollah Qasim al-Khoei, acquiring a solid foundation in theology. Writing in Al-Adwa, a religious publication, he criticized the allies of colonialism and deplored the existence of divisions in the Islamic Umma. From 1955, he became involved in editing works on law, Islamic economics, and education. By the late 1950s, Mohammed Baqr al-Sadr had become concerned about the growing influence of communist ideas on deprived young Shi'ites, and in 1958 he became involved in the launch of the Da'wa party, Iraq's principal Shi'ite Islamist organization. In his book, Our Philosophy, he condemned the ideas of Marxism and historical materialism and called instead for the resurgence of Islam.

Though he took no official post in Al-Da'wa, he was the association's leading ideologue. He took part in the campaign of protest against the regime of the brothers Aref (1963–1968), whom he attacked for their secularism. In 1964, he met Ayatollah Khomeini and also developed relationships with other key political figures in the region in the course of his travels. These included Sheikh Hussein Fadlallah in Lebanon. He supported Ayatollah Khomeini's concept of Velayat al-Faqih and was a supporter of the overthrow of the Islamic Revolution in Iran in 1979. He took the view that the Islamic Revolution should be spread and threw himself into direct confrontation with the regime in Iraq by calling for an uprising. He issued a fatwa declaring members of the Ba'th Party to be non-Muslims and attempted, though without much success, to attract Sunni support. Disturbances broke out in several of Iraq's major cities.

In June 1979, he was detained and put under house arrest. Some weeks later, Saddam Hussein became head of state and crushed the Shi'ite rebellion. On April 5, 1980, there was a large-scale security operation and Mohammed Baqr al-Sadr was arrested at his home and then taken to Baghdad. Several days later, he was executed. He continues to be regarded as a major Islamic thinker, whose influence extended beyond the frontiers of Iraq.

SAID, MOHAMMED (1947–1995) (ALGERIA)

Mohammed Said, whose birth name was Lounis Belkacem, was of Kabyle origin. He

was born in the village of Zaknoun, in the Wilaya of Tizi Ouzou. He studied at the faculty of letters at the University of Algiers. He took his degree in 1976 and then studied theology while also beginning work as a teacher. He attended the university mosque, which was also frequented by radical Islamists. At that time, Mohammed Said (still known as Belkacem) came into contact with a number of francophone intellectuals, many with a background in the sciences, whose goal was to combat what they saw as the pernicious influence of socialist ideas at the highest level of the state. He became a teacher at the Higher Institute for Religious Studies at the University of Algeria and imam at the Dar al-Arqam mosque and found himself as the leading light of a group dedicated to the establishment of what they called "Algerian Islam."

In November 1982, he participated in the publication of a fourteen-point manifesto, also signed by Sheikh Abassi Madani, whose central point was the application of the Shari'a. He was soon arrested and imprisoned, but was set free once more in 1984. Together with his reputation as a scholar, this period of detention contributed to his standing among the Islamists. He took the name Mohammed Said in memory of an ANL officer who had fought in Wilaya III (Kabylie) during the war of liberation, who had been famous for his piety. In October 1988, counseled against Ali Belhadj's decision to hold a protest gathering, in which, in the event, several dozen demonstrators died.

In 1989, when he was approached during the negotiations that led to the founding of the FIS (Islamic Salvation Front), Mohammed Said was reluctant on the grounds that the move would be premature before the adoption of a new constitution. He was, therefore, not among the FIS's fifteen founder members. He joined the FIS in October 1990, however, when he saw the popular enthusiasm it aroused and its spectacular results in the local elections. He became one of the organization's leading figures and took on the role of spokesman for the "Algerianist" tendency. On December 6, 1990, he participated in a rally held in support of the Palestinian Intifada.

On April 1, 1991, the government's planned changes in the electoral law and the distribution of constituencies were passed by the National Assembly in preparation for the parliamentary elections. The Algerianists argued for a general strike leading to confrontation with the authorities on the grounds that the government's proposals would favor the FLN (National Liberation Front) and its allies. Mohammed Said also believed that this would conduce to the success of the Algerianist scheme to take control of the FIS. On May 23, a strike was called by the FIS leadership. On June 30, 1991, after violent clashes with the security forces and an official ultimatum, seven members of the FIS "Majlis al-Shura" (Consultative Council) were arrested. This placed Mohammed Said and his supporters, at least temporarily, in control of the FIS.

At the beginning of July 1991, Mohammed Said then became the official spokesman of the FIS. This alarmed the government, and on July 7 he was arrested. He was soon freed, however, and resumed his role in the FIS. After the cancellation of the elections, he was able for a time to elude the general trawl of FIS members. He became part of a small group made up of members of the FIS executive office and the Majlis al-Shura, which attempted to draw up a new strategy. In the face of continued operations by the security forces to dismantle the FIS, the working group soon decided that armed struggle was the sole option. Mohammed Said went into hiding, while maintaining his contacts with a number of key members of the Algerianist group.

On September 18, 1993, a FIS political office was established in Europe, known as the Executive Office of the FIS in Europe (Instance Exécutive du FIS à l'Etranger) (IEFE). Exile beckoned, but Mohammed Said decided—without consultation with his FIS colleagues—to join the radical GIA when its leader Chérif Gousmi (a man of only twenty-six at the time), also known as Abou Abdallah Ahmed, opened up his organization to incorporate other tendencies. Mohammed Said's objective from the start was to gain control of the GIA. On May 13, 1994, a number of GIA leaders published a statement entitled "Concerning Union, Jihad, and the respect for the Book and the Sunna." This declaration, which established an alliance between a number of ideological tendencies, was signed by Chérif Gousmi, Said Mekhloufi of the "Movement for an Islamic State," and Abderrazaq Redjam. Mohammed Said was the organization's spiritual leader and headed its political committee. In this capacity, he laid down the lines of the GIA's strategy in Kabylie, where he had the help of Abdelwahhab Lamara, who joined the GIA after the publication of the declaration. Meanwhile, the AIS (Islamic Salvation Army), the FIS's armed wing, opposed the GIA's strategy of violence and Said's political ambitions.

In October 1994, after Gousmi's death, the influence of the Salafis seemed to be on the increase. In the competition to succeed him, Mohammed Said supported one of his associates, Mahfoud Tadjine, also known as Abou Khalil Mahfouz, also of Kabyle origin. Abou Khalil Mahfouz was appointed, but he was quickly pushed aside in favor of a Salafi, Djamel Zitouni, alias Abderrahman Amin. Dissent within the GIA became more bitter, and Zitouni organized a purge. In November 1995, Mohammed Said was killed in an ambush near Medea, apparently by GIA members. Persistent rumors also suggest, however, that government special forces might have been responsible for his death. His intellectual ability and his charisma made him a tough opponent for the military.

SAUDI ARABIA

The oil-rich Kingdom of Saudi Arabia, with a quarter of the world's known petroleum reserves, is a desert and sparsely populated country. Perhaps significantly, this petroleum-based monarchy is the only state in the world to be known by the name of its ruling family. According to the most recent estimates—dating from July 2006—Saudi Arabia's population is 27 million, including over 21 million Saudi citizens and more than 5 million foreigners. After the attacks of September 11, 2001, Saudi Arabia's position began to look profoundly contradictory. The difficulty was that investigations of the terrorist networks and their sources of finance appeared to lead inexorably back to individuals in Saudi Arabia. At the same time, the Saudi regime was an ally of the United States and sought to play a part in the action taken by the United States against terror groups.

Saudi Arabia has been described as "the epicenter of the Islamist earthquake." At the same time, with the apparent blessing of the United States, it has played a significant role both locally, within the Arabian Peninsula, and internationally in the Arab and Islamic world as a whole. Thanks to its oil wealth and to the influence it gains from its management of the Holy Places of Islam, it has been able to preserve itself from regional threats. In the latter half of the twentieth century, it fended off the Arab nationalism inspired by Egypt's late President Nasser, which threatened to undermine it from within. Since 1979, it has also withstood the Shi'ite challenge of the Islamic Republic of Iran for regional hegemony. In fact, it has made its own successful counterbid for influence within the Islamic world.

Following the creation of the "Organization of the Islamic Conference" (OIC), the kingdom undertook the global promotion of Sunni Islam by underwriting pietist and fundamentalist movements throughout the world on a massive scale. It reached out into the entire Arab and Islamic world, including the diasporas in the West. Saudi Arabia financed every possible means to transmit its official Islamic philosophy of Wahhabism, Sunni fundamentalist Islam as preached by Mohammed Ibn Abdul Wahhab (1720–1792). These included mosques, Quranic schools, cultural centers, and hospitals. Such financial subventions were made either directly, through the agency of princes of the royal household, or through a network of international Islamic institutions. Such organizations were affiliated to the OIC (officially an international institution) or to the Saudi-sponsored World Islamic League. Various NGOs with cultural or pious objectives were also involved, as well as the World Assembly of Muslim Youth (WAMY) (which is very active in America, the Caribbean, and in the Comoros). Humanitarian and charitable organizations such as Islamic Relief also took part, as well as Saudi private banks.

The "Dar al-Mal al-Islami" (DMI) (Islamic Finance House), which was set up in Geneva in 1981, had a significant role in financing such charitable organizations. Following the Gulf War of 1990–1991, during which Islamist movements had tended to side with Saddam Hussein, official Saudi aid was cut back in favor of private funding. However, the influence of the Islamic institutions, which by 2002 were worth $230 billion—forty times as much as in 1982—meant that they were still highly important to the American economy, for which they were represented significant trading opportunities.

Saudi Arabia's alliance with Washington was crucial to the protection of the autocratic Saudi regime, whose existence contradicted all the principles officially espoused by the West. A historic meeting took place on February 14, 1945, between President Roosevelt and Saudi Arabia's leader Ibn Saud (King Abdulaziz ibn Abdulrahman Al Faisal Al Saud) on board the USS Quincy, moored in the Suez Canal's Great Bitter Lake. Ibn Saud was given an important assurance of American support. After this, the U.S.-Saudi alliance gained strength, especially in terms of military cooperation. In exchange for American diplomatic and military protection, which guaranteed the flow of oil, the United States was granted a quasi-monopoly of the exploitation of Saudi petroleum resources by the concession accorded to Aramco, which has today become "Saudi Aramco."

The Gulf War of 1990–1991, precipitated by the invasion of Kuwait by the Iraqi leader Saddam Hussein, further institutionalized American protection of Saudi Arabia. Saudi Arabia signed some $35 billion of arms deals with the United States, and after the war ended a substantial American garrison remained on Saudi soil, together with some families and civilian support, in addition to oil personnel living in Aramco compounds. (The bulk of America's armed forces were, however, withdrawn from Saudi Arabia in 2002.) The U.S. commitment to Saudi Arabia was accompanied by a tacit convention of noninterference in the interior affairs of the kingdom. The United States maintained its vigilance to ensure that no issue related to Saudi Arabia was raised at the UN Human Rights Commission at Geneva. In 2001, the humanitarian organization Amnesty International listed seventy instances of capital punishment in the country, noting that China, Iran, and Saudi Arabia were responsible for 90 percent of all known executions.

The close relations between the kingdom and the United States aroused growing antagonism among the Saudi public as well as among members of the country's elites.

Two attacks on American interests in the country were attributed to Islamists. One of these, in November 1995, at a center for National Guard instructors in Riyadh killed five American military advisers; another on the base at Al-Khobar near Dhahran in June 1996 killed nineteen American soldiers and wounded sixty-four. Islamist militants were also suspected of being behind a further series of bomb attacks against Western interests throughout the kingdom. It was unclear whether anti-American feeling was confined to a minority of committed fundamentalists. Or was it a sentiment to which a substantial part of the opposition was committed, strong enough to serve as a rallying point for factions within the kingdom's new elites that no longer felt confident that the status quo would continue?

The consensus on which the kingdom depends is rooted historically in the royal family and its affiliated tribes. The number of princes of the royal household is 4,300. These feature in a confidential civil list that consumes 20 percent of the total budget of the state. The state has been at pains to give itself a modern facade of ministers and administrators, to which it has now added the Consultative Council, or "Majlis al-Shura," consisting of ninety members appointed by the king. What holds Saudi Arabia together, however, has continued to be the consensus of the tribes, which has become less and less appropriate for a modern and expanding state.

In this context, the demographic structure is significant. More than 50 percent of the population consists of people under twenty, while a quarter is made up of immigrants, including 780,000 Pakistanis and 1,230,000 Indians, who hold half the jobs. Meanwhile, the population, much of which had during the 1960s continued to be nomadic, had by 2000 become 80 percent sedentarized. The unemployment rate is around 25 percent. Sixty percent of the

unemployed are Saudi citizens. Each year 100,000 young Saudis come to the labor market. The attempt to cope with this has resulted in the obligatory "Saudi-ization" of jobs and has pushed up wages considerably. The state has experienced growing cash flow problems, but the program of restructuring launched by King Abdullah in 1998 (when he was crown prince) has begun to show significant results. From 1983, the Saudi budget had been in deficit, but in 2004 the budget surged into surplus on the sharp increase in oil prices. The Saudi budget was in surplus by $70 billion in 2006 and was projected to be $20 billion in surplus in 2007. Growth was over 4 percent per annum. Public sector debt in 2006 had fallen to the equivalent to 35 percent of GDP. On the other hand, brighter state finances have not translated into halt to the decline in personal standards of living in Saudi Arabia. The average income per inhabitant has fallen from 22,500 USD in 1980 to 12,000 USD in 2006. At the same time, the state has no longer been able to provide its citizens with all the services they had formerly been accustomed to. This relative impoverishment has brought with it a feeling of injustice that has fed the mounting hostility toward the ruling family.

Meanwhile, by the 1990s, Saudi Arabia was in the paradoxical position of facing criticism both from those who believed it was too liberal and from those who did not consider it was liberal enough. This became evident when the Islamist opposition from within, which had formerly been careful not to draw attention to itself, now began expressing its criticism of the regime. Fundamentalist ulema from the interior of the country were especially likely to be critical of the authorities. From its base in London, the "Committee for the Defense of Legitimate Rights" led by Mohammed Mas'ari strove to organize international Islamist resistance to the Al Saud. At the same time, there has been pressure from the country's new elites for modernization of the country's political system and even for liberalization. Enlargement of the Majlis al-Shura was demanded, together with an extension of its powers, and there was pressure for a change in the legal status of women. The self-styled Wahhabi regime of the Al Saud is attacked both by Islamists who demand greater rigor and greater effort in the fight against corruption and by modernists who seek to reform the machinery of state.

The Saudi regime regularly draws attention to its stand on the Arab-Israeli conflict in an effort to reinforce its standing in Arab and Muslim eyes. On February 17, 2002, Crown Prince Abdullah, by now in charge of Saudi policy, suggested what he called a "comprehensive Arab peace plan." This would involve a return by Israel to the pre-1967 frontiers, including withdrawal from East Jerusalem in exchange for which its existence would be recognized by the Arab states. In addition, after September 11, 2001, Saudi Arabia set about giving the impression that it had embarked on a process of internal reform. The kingdom was faced by four principal problems. The first of these was the unsatisfactory position at the highest levels of power, where the ailing King Fahd was unable to rule, but had not completely handed over power to Crown Prince Abdullah. The second was the issue of the kingdom's relations with the United States. The third was the need to make new arrangements for the exploitation of oil resources. The fourth, but not least, was the issue of social change in a kingdom where people under twenty make up more than half the population.

In the short term, despite its problems, the stability of the kingdom and its institutions appeared secure, so long as it was not destabilized by some aspect of the U.S. response to the attacks of September 11, 2001. The American-led invasion of Iraq in March 2003 may have had just such an effect, by reducing an important neighbor of Saudi Arabia to a state of chaos. It was increasingly difficult for the Saudi Arabian regime's allies in the West to maintain that it was appropriate for Saudi Arabia to eschew democracy while the claim was being made that the installation of democracy was the reason for the overthrow of Saddam Hussein's tyranny in Iraq. In the longer term, structural reforms will be unavoidable and Saudi Arabia's institutions will be obliged to evolve toward a less rigid form of government.

In view of the long-term requirements of domestic finance, it is perhaps rash of Saudi Arabia to continue its present style of international sponsorship of Sunni Muslim communities not only within the Arab world, but also in the diasporas in the United States and in Europe. The financing of Islamist groups in Europe may well be an inappropriate use of the kingdom's money, given the opposition of certain Islamists to the regime in Saudi Arabia. Faced with the multiplication of Islamist groups, however, and the growth of their influence, the Saudis have decided that it is safer to pay up. Saudi Arabia views itself as the most Islamic country and its people as the best of Muslims; therefore—in the Saudi view—any Muslim should logically choose the Saudi path, including the Islamists. Islamist parties in the Arab and Islamic world, and in Europe, have not been reluctant to profit from this financial largesse.

Saudi Arabia has numerous institutions through which its funds are disbursed and its influence exercised. These tend to fall under a number of different umbrella organizations:

The first of these is "Al-Rabita al-Islamiya al-Alamiya" (the World Islamic League). This is a theoretically nongovernmental organization established in 1962 in Mecca at the behest of the crown prince, Faisal ibn Abdulaziz, later to be King Faisal. The Arab world was at that time experiencing the peak of Nasserism, and the

Saudi aim was to create a counterweight. Rabita was to be an organization that would militate against "dangerous associations where the enemies of Islam aim to arouse Muslims to rebel against their religion, destroying their unity and their fraternity." Al-Rabita also has the remit of protecting Muslim minorities in non-Muslim countries. It is a tightly organized institution, whose activities are coordinated by a secretary-general in Mecca, assisted by an executive council of fifty-three members, delegated by each of the Islamic countries. The council meets once a year, with the effect that the secretary-general, who is always of Saudi nationality, in reality exercises sole authority. He appoints regional Islamic councils for each continent. The council for Europe has its headquarters in London, where it coordinates the activities of organizations funded by the League.

The secretary-general also appoints the members of the World Council of Mosques, whose brief is to coordinate, manage, and finance the construction of places of worship. The European wing of this organization is in Brussels. In each country, the secretary-general establishes an office of the "Organization of the World Islamic League." Through this structure, built up over the last forty years, Saudi Arabia finances Islamist organizations in Europe. The office in France is run by two French nationals of Moroccan origin. A number of large-scale projects in Europe have come to fruition under the League's aegis. These include the Islamic Center in Brussels, mosques in Madrid, Rome, London, and Copenhagen, the construction in France of the mosque at Mantes-la-Jolie and that of Evry, which has cost the League almost 5 million euros.

The second of the three principal channels for Saudi aid is the Organization of the Islamic Conference (OIC), with which the activities of the League are not to be confused. The OIC is an international organization of Muslim states that collectively represents them. The OIC was also founded at Saudi Arabia's initiative, subsequently to the World Islamic League, and serves as a kind of United Nations for the Muslim world that provides a forum for the discussion of international issues. The OIC makes finance available for projects in the Islamic organizations through the Islamic Development Bank (IDB), an arm of the OIC set up in 1973. Islamic banking is the third umbrella organization through which Saudi Arabia exercises its influence. Its remit is to finance infrastructure and development projects in Islamic countries, but since the majority of its shareholders are Saudis it inclines toward projects favored by Saudi Arabia and the World Islamic League.

In its early days, the World Islamic League was conceived of as a war machine against Arab socialism and the secular concept of Islamic unity that prevailed in the 1960s and early 1970s. Today, however, the World Islamic League attempts to combat those it characterizes as extremists, the "mutatarifin," toward whose creation, paradoxically, it has itself largely contributed. The Afghan war and the Bosnian conflict offered Saudi Arabia an opportunity to widen its field of action, whereupon Saudi diplomacy took up the cause of Islamization, in order to "assist the Afghan fighters to struggle against the atheist Soviet invader." Prince Turki Al Faisal, the son of King Faisal, who founded the World Islamic League, was for twenty-five years, until August 2001, the head of the country's external intelligence services. In the days of the first Afghan war, there was a level of cooperation between Saudi Arabia and Pakistan. From 1979, when Pakistan's President Zia ul-Haq stepped up the process of Islamization, Pakistan could be regarded as an Islamic state. Prior to this date, though Pakistan was a state consciously established as redoubt for India's Muslims, it was not in practice a confessional state.

The expense of the Afghan war proved to be immense. The World Islamic League and the OIC provided what funds they were able to, but the cost of the Afghan war was a bottomless pit. This was when the private Saudi banks stepped in to become part of the third plank of Saudi Arabia's financial support for Islamism. In 1981, as the Islamic summit at Taif was held, Muslim investors, rallied by Prince Muhammad Al Faisal, Prince Turki's brother, launched a private Islamic bank, the "Dar al-Mal al-Islami" (Islamic Treasury), with its headquarters at Geneva. The bank helped in financing Afghan networks and their connections in Europe. This was not the only such effort. In 1982, as King Fahd acceded to the Saudi throne, he also involved the banking arm of the Saudi conglomerate "Dallah al-Baraka," founded in 1969 by Saleh Abdullah Kamel. Thanks to these private networks, the Islamic League and the OIC were able to set up some twenty Islamic NGOs, mainly based in Pakistan but with offices in Europe and the United States. The two largest of these were the International Islamic Relief Organization (IIRO) and the Islamic Relief Agency (ISRA). The staff of these organizations, all speaking excellent English, came principally from the Middle East. The NGOs raised funds from Muslim businessmen across the Islamic world, but especially from Saudi or Kuwaiti merchant families. Funds also went to Europe, where London became the heart of a network, as the seat of the "Islamic Mission for the United Kingdom," run by two leading members of the Saudi intelligence service.

Educational establishments constituted another channel for the dissemination of Islamist ideas. Saudi Arabia, through the agency of the OIC, helped to fund the Islamic University of Islamabad. This was established in 1980, the date of the invasion of Afghanistan by Soviet troops. Many Arab Islamists continued their education there. The Saudis also funded the institute for the training of imams in Europe at Saint-Etienne-de Fougeret, which was run by Muslim Brothers belonging to the "Union of Islamic Organizations in France" (UOIF). Saudi Arabia also backed other groups, including Palestinian Hamas, the FIS in Algeria, and the Jordanian and Syrian Muslim Brothers. It supported the installation of Saudi and Pakistani imams in Europe and also of Moroccan imams in mosques in France. One of the principal aims of the World Islamic League was to further the process of conversion to Islam in Europe. The numbers of converts are difficult to estimate, but it seems likely that there are 40,000 in France and a similar number in Great Britain. Converts, however, play little part in contemporary Muslim politics in Europe. After the end of the first Afghan war, the funding institutions supported by Saudi Arabia broadly transferred their activities to Bosnia.

Saudi Arabia has struggled with the contradictions it has faced since September 11, 2001. The kingdom has been energetic in its condemnation of Osama bin Laden and Al-Qaida. Bin Laden had, of course, been stripped of his Saudi citizenship long before, in April 1994. At the same time, it is hard for the Saudi authorities to disengage from the worldwide program of funding Muslim institutions on which they long ago embarked. An inquisition into whether any given channel of funding might lead to some body with which terrorists are or have been involved would seem invidious and would be extremely difficult to carry out. Western governments and it must be said the so-called antiterrorist experts place great emphasis on the perception that suspect groups and individuals have "links" with other organizations known to be frequented by terrorists. However, in a complex and interdependent world, it is almost always possible to discover such "links." The fact that a terrorist has been a member of some organization, or had frequented some mosque, does not necessarily mean that all members of the organization or the mosque are sympathizers with terrorism, let alone that they are terrorist suspects. However, Saudi Arabia does want to maintain its good relations with the United States, and sometimes takes actions at the behest of the United States that it would not have undertaken on its own initiative. Saudi Arabia wishes to be a friend of the Western community of nations, but without betraying the commitment it believes it has to further Islamic (rather than Islamist) causes. There is also, after a spate of incidents within the kingdom, the suspicion that Saudi Arabia itself is not as secure as it was in the past.

Spokesmen for the kingdom have acknowledged that there is an upsurge of criticism within Saudi Arabia, but stress that the moving spirit of this criticism is a conservatism strictly related to Saudi internal conditions, unrelated to revolutionary or Jihadist Islamism elsewhere in the world. Claims are also made that in the new circumstances Saudi Arabia has acted to halt any funding that might flow toward terrorist organizations. The United States has been anxious to underline that the official view of Saudi Arabia in Washington is that it remains a strong ally in the Middle East.

Saudi Arabia: King Abdullah

As crown prince, Prince Abdullah ibn Abdulaziz was in de facto control of the affairs of Saudi Arabia from 1996, presiding over a difficult period in the history of the country. He is the successor of King Fahd, who was born in 1921 and came to the throne in 1982, but never recovered from a cerebral embolism he suffered in 1995. He did not abdicate, but continued to enjoy the title of Servant of the Two Holy Places (Mecca and Medina), a title he took on October 26, 1986 partly to counter a bid by Iran to interna-

tionalize the administration of the Islamic shrines.

The Saudi law of succession as laid down in 1992 by King Fahd provides that the king is chosen by the Family Council of the Al Saud (the royal clan), and his succession is then endorsed by the Council of Ulema. In principle, under the rules of succession announced in 1992, the succession to the throne was open to both the sons and the grandsons of the founder of modern Saudi Arabia (King Abdulaziz ibn Abdulrahman Al Faisal Al Saud, known as "Ibn Saud," who established the kingdom in 1932). Though the succession of King Abdullah seemed assured, the issue was technically not settled until the Family Council had met. Most experts on the Saudi monarchy consider that now that Prince Abdullah has succeeded King Fahd he will be the last of Ibn Saud's sons to occupy the Saudi throne and that the succession will now pass to the next generation.

King Abdullah was born in Riyadh in 1923, the thirteenth son of Ibn Saud. Abdullah's mother came from the Shammar tribe, a powerful Bedouin tribe from Nejd, in the center of the country, which Ibn Saud had long fought, but had failed to overcome. Among Abdullah's numerous half brothers, the four oldest had already succeeded to the throne: these were King Saud (who reigned from 1953 to 1964), King Faisal (1964–1975), King Khaled (1975–1982) and King Fahd (1982–2005). Among the other half brothers is a group only a few years younger than Abdullah himself who were very influential during Fahd's lifetime. These were the group known as the Sudairi seven, the sons of Hassa bint Ahmed Al Sudairi, Ibn Saud's favorite wife, who were King Fahd's full brothers. These are, in descending order of age, Fahd himself, Prince Sultan, Prince Abdul Rahman, Prince Nayef, Prince Turki, Prince Salman, and finally Prince Ahmed. These men all hold key positions of ministerial rank. (It should be noted that the Prince

Turki mentioned here is not the Prince Turki mentioned earlier, the former head of intelligence, later ambassador to London, who is a grandson of Ibn Saud.) Prince Nayef is thought to be a religious conservative, more sympathetic than others to radical views.

After a religious education, Abdullah had military training, which enabled him to succeed Prince Khaled as the commander of the National Guard. This is separate from the main body of the Saudi armed forces and is the monarch's personal defence force. It is principally recruited from the tribes closest to the royal family and only those completely trusted by the royal family hold posts of responsibility. Abdullah is genuinely a pious man, though he does not ostentatiously display his faith. He is respected by the religious establishment for his integrity and correctness. He can, therefore, count on the support of both the religious oligarchy and the tribes linked to the Al Saud, two of the most important pillars of the regime.

By comparison with Fahd and Sultan, who were regarded relatively as "modernizers," to the extent that such categories may be applied to the Saudi royal family, Abdullah is regarded as a traditionalist. He is said to have given much thought to the potential consequences of economic development on Saudi society. In imposing a regime of economic austerity on Saudi Arabia, notwithstanding its position as the world's leading oil state, Abdullah has set himself the objective of balancing the kingdom's budget and of persuading Saudi Arabia to live within its resources. He had already taken measures that met with the approval of ordinary Saudis, who were asked to live within their means. In 1997, he cut the spending power of the junior royal princes, which had hitherto been excessive. He even put restrictions on the number of free tickets to which they were entitled on the Saudi national airline and set a limit to the size of telephone and electricity bills that the state would be prepared to meet.

In regional terms, he is conscious of the value of stability, and in 1999 he engineered a dramatic rapprochement between Saudi Arabia and Iran, sealed by the visit of Iran's President Mohammed Khatami to the kingdom in May 1999. He is known to favor the establishment of a formal security pact between Saudi Arabia and Iran. At the Arab Summit in Beirut in March 2002, he made significant overtures to Saddam Hussein's Iraq, warmly greeting Iraq's deputy leader Ezzat Ibrahim. Before the American invasion of Iraq, Prince Abdullah—who did not want to see regional conflict—predicted that there would be no war. When war broke out, Saudi Arabia refused to permit American forces to operate from the kingdom. However, he later agreed with the United States that Saudi Arabia would set aside a substantial part of Iraq's debt to the kingdom when Iraq once more has a sovereign government, in order to assist Iraq's recovery. As the protagonist of the "Comprehensive Arab Peace Proposal" for the Middle East, he aimed to give a new direction to the kingdom's foreign policy, militating for a "just" settlement of the Arab-Israeli conflict. On 25 April, 2002, he once more put this proposal to President George W. Bush during a visit to the President's ranch at Crawford, Texas.

Finally, it could well be that King Abdullah will initiate a change in the U.S.-Saudi alliance, which has survived since the end of World War II. In February 2002, the Pentagon initiated a transfer to Qatar and Oman of troops and equipment from the Prince Sultan airbase near Riyadh. The transfer accelerated in the spring of 2002 when Abdullah indicated his opposition to the possibility of conflict in Iraq and to the redeployment of some 75,000 U.S. troops. The U.S. command set up in Saudi Arabia on October 7, 2001 to coordinate the operations of the antiterrorist coalition was transferred to the Al-Udeid base in Qatar, while other units were repositioned in Kuwait, Oman, Bahrain, and the UAE.

In April 2002, Prince Abdullah told President Bush that Saudi Arabia would not be used as a base for any new attack on Iraq. This reconfiguration of the U.S.-Saudi alliance, for which Prince Abdullah was principally responsible, was the most significant change in the kingdom since the end of World War II. After the U.S. attack on Iraq in March 2003, the remaining 5,000 American troops were pulled out of Saudi Arabia. Only a few hundred advisers to the National Guard were left behind, in a move glossed by Washington as a concession to the Saudi leadership. King Abdullah did not wish further to antagonize Islamist opponents inside the kingdom who were already enraged by the U.S. attack on Iraq. In July 2003, U.S.-Saudi relations were put under further strain when a section of the U.S. congressional report on the attacks of September 11, 2001, apparently related to allegations concerning the involvement of Saudi Arabian citizens in planning the attacks, was withheld from the Saudi government.

In October 2005, soon after becoming king, Abdullah gave an interview to American TV in which clarified his position on many international issues in which the United States takes an interest. He said:

Yes, the Saudi people have some disagreements with the United States, in particular when it comes to the issue of the Palestinian question, the war in Afghanistan and the war with Iraq. I believe this may have influenced the opinion of the Saudi public towards the United States ... What we ask for is that justice and equity prevail among all of the ethnic groups in Iraq. We believe that all Iraq is one country in which all Iraqis live in peace and justice. The Kingdom of Saudi Arabia until today has not interfered in Iraq's affairs. We have not done so because we don't want to open ourselves up to charges or accusations that we ... have a hand in the disintegration of ... of Iraq. We also have been accused in the past of having a hand in what happened in Iraq, in particular with regards to terrorism and the violence, and we are innocent of these charges. And we have remained neutral in spite of the injustices that we see currently going on.

In February 2007, King Abdullah launched a major effort to resolve the internal clashes between Palestinians that were threatening a severe crisis in Gaza. Representatives of Hamas and the Fatah party were invited to Mecca after a rebuke issued to them by King Abdullah over the fighting. This was part of a new flurry of diplomatic activity on the part of Saudi Arabia, which had previously been inclined toward a low profile. Saudi Arabia has been concerned over a number of issues. The continuing chaos in Iraq is cause for alarm. Another is the growing influence of Iran in the region, visible in Iraq, Lebanon, and Palestine. Iran has been giving Hamas its support in the Occupied Palestinian Territories. Saudi Arabia does not wish to see increasing polarization in the region between Sunni Muslims and the Shi'ites. King Abdullah had held a meeting with Ali Larijani, the Islamic Republic of Iran's international negotiator on nuclear affairs. Observers say Saudi Arabia wishes to be seen by the United States as a force for regional stability.

Saudi Arabia: International Organizations

Islamic Development Bank (IDB)

The Islamic Development Bank (IDB) was formally opened on October 20, 1975, following a declaration by a conference of OIC finance ministers in Jeddah in December 1973. It is the OIC's principal banking institution. The IDB was set up originally both to finance infrastructure projects in Islamic countries and to fund economic and social development. Its headquarters is in the Saudi city of Jeddah, with branch offices in countries that are members of the OIC.

The Saudi monarchy holds 25 percent of its capital and controls its activities closely. Other major investors are Kuwait and Libya. Requests for funding from projects initiated by the World Islamic League are always favorably received, even when such requests relate more to proselytization than to the development of infrastructure. The IDB helped to frustrate American foreign policy by compensating Pakistan for the economic sanctions imposed after its 1998 nuclear tests, raising the ceiling of its loans to Pakistan from $150 to $400 million.

In 2005, the bank's authorized capital was $22 billion. It funds extensive aid operations and capital projects in Africa, and in November 2004 a conference was held in Istanbul on investment in Muslim countries. It made a substantial contribution to relief after the Asian tsunami in 2005. It continues to finance trade and export guarantees. The bank is currently following the lines of a strategic plan developed in 2004, which in the words of IDB documents is based on a "commitment to assist member countries in their pursuit of the achievement of economic development and social progress." Bank literature stresses the use of capital from wealthy Muslim nations to further the development of the less wealthy. In January 2007, the bank's current president, Dr. Ahmed Mohammed Ali, stressed the bank's ongoing commitment to the development of Muslim countries.

Islamic Educational Scientific and Cultural Organization (ISESCO)

The founding conference of this organization, set up at the behest of the OIC foreign ministers, was held in the Moroccan city of Fes in 1982. ISESCO has its headquarters in Morocco's capital, Rabat. Its charter proclaims its goal as Muslim cooperation in the fields of "education, science, culture and communication." ISESCO's current director general is Dr. Abdulaziz Othamn Altwaijiri.

Membership of the organization, which is conditional on membership of the OIC, currently includes forty-eight member states and the self-declared state of Palestine. Just as the OIC is intended to be an Islamic United Nations, ISESCO presents itself as an Islamic UNESCO. On the one hand, it openly avows the goal of proselytization, while it also aims to develop the scientific and cultural independence of the Islamic countries in order to preserve them from non-Islamic influences, in other words, from the influence of the West. As part of its activities, ISESCO manages the Federation of Universities in the Islamic World (FUIW). Other subsidiaries are IBEST (the Islamic Body on the Ethics of Science and Technology), which examines research developments in light of the Shari'a, and ICPSR (the ISESCO Center for the Promotion of Scientific Research).

Recent actions of ISESCO have included a criticism of Israel's announced intention to conduct further works in the neighborhood of the Aqsa Mosque in Jerusalem and a plea to the Palestinian factions in Gaza to halt their internecine struggle. ISESCO also cooperates with other bodies such as the Council of Europe on international cultural understanding.

The Organization of the Islamic Conference (OIC) see separate entry

The World Assembly of Muslim Youth (WAMY)

WAMY was set up in 1972, at the instance of Saudi Arabia, and has its headquarters in Riyadh. It is active in at least fifty-five countries and includes more than five hundred Muslim youth organizations across the world. Among its principal stated objectives are "the preservation of the Muslim identity of the young" and "the establishment of relations with the non-Muslim world to further awareness of Islam as a comprehensive system and a way of life." The Muslim identity of young people is preserved through activities enabling young Muslims to remain at all times within a Muslim framework, in order to avoid contact with other cultures. WAMY encourages Muslim sporting, leisure, and educational activities. WAMY also directly controls a significant number of schools throughout the world and participates in the construction of mosques, which serve as meeting points and places of education. By 2002, WAMY had built more than a hundred mosques and a further hundred were under construction.

Other fields in which WAMY is active include the care of orphans, the building of hospitals, the publication of Islamic literature targeted both at Muslims an non-Muslims, participation in conferences, support for Muslim organizations, and the organization of study tours and pilgrimages. In contrast to the World Islamic League, WAMY seldom involves itself in politics, but sticks closely to its long-term aim of re-Islamizing young people along Wahhabi lines.

The World Islamic League (WIL) ("Al-Rabita al-Islamiya al-'Alamiya")

The World Islamic League was inaugurated on December 15, 1962, by King Faisal. It was intended to be a counterweight to the Arab League (the League of Arab States), which had become the mouthpiece of Nasserist and Arab nationalist ideas. The WIL, however, was a very different body. It does not have national members but is a Saudi NGO dedicated to the propagation and support of Islam around the world. As early as 1956, Saudi Arabia's Prince Salman had stated that "Islam should be at the heart of the Kingdom's foreign policy." The World Islamic League is based in Mecca and the majority of its senior officials are Saudis. It presents itself as a religious organization whose goal is the propagation of the Islamic message. By reason of its Saudi inspiration, the version of

Islam it upholds is closely based on Wahhabi precepts.

One focus of the WIL's activities is the provision of spiritual support to Muslim minorities around the world. This support includes the training of imams, the provision of funds to mosques, and the distribution of copies of the Quran. The annual pilgrimage to Mecca, the Hajj, offers the occasion to recruit preachers from many nationalities. The WIL's interventions sometimes venture into political affairs. These have included a request made to France in 1970 for the independence of Djibouti, the denunciation of the Soviet intervention in Afghanistan in 1980, an offer of assistance to the Turkish Cypriots in 1982, and support offered to the Bosnian and Chechen Muslims between 1993 and 1995. It has also served as the vehicle for overtures that have preceded official Saudi diplomatic action, for example when it opened an office in Beijing two years before the establishment of diplomatic relations between China and Saudi Arabia.

The WIL, however, has also been the object of discreet but persistent complaints on the part of a number of countries including Algeria, Egypt, and France, which have charged it with the provision of financial assistance to Islamist groups under the cover of support for preaching activities. The WIL has, in its defense, reaffirmed its adherence to the principle of noninterference in the internal affairs of third countries and reiterated in June 1993 its condemnation of terrorism, while also drawing attention to the impossibility of controlling the provision of private finance.

Saudi Arabia: Islamist Opposition

The Islamist opposition in Saudi Arabia comes broadly from those who regard themselves as the guardians of Wahhabi doctrine against modifications that they believe are being made by the authorities. Their goal is to remind the Saudi monarchy that its obligation is respect for the strict precepts of Islam, rather than the pursuit of political goals.

The opposition is religiously based and has flourished since the arrival in Saudi Arabia of American forces during the Gulf War, which was seen as a threat to Islam. Sermons preached by younger ulema, such as Safar al-Hawali, Awad al-Qarni, Salman al-Awda, and Nasir al-Omar, expressed opposition ideas and were rapidly distributed throughout the kingdom on audio cassettes. In the first instance, these sermons restricted themselves to calling on the king and the High Council of Ulema to be vigilant against "secular" tendencies and to reinforce the authority of Islam. Later, the sermons became the basis of two crucial documents issued by the Islamic opposition in Saudi Arabia. These were the "Letter of Request" drafted by Saudi Arabia's then grand mufti, the late sheikh Abdulaziz bin Baz, and the "Advisory Memorandum," a more ambitious document that was signed by four hundred religious figures but disowned by bin Baz.

The "Advisory Memorandum" purports to be the consensus (ijma') of the leading ulema on reforms expected from the regime. It is in fact signed by 109 ulema, of whom most are from the province of Nejd. It is regarded as an embodiment of the reforms demanded by the Islamists in ten major areas. Its aim is to elevate the standing and independence of the religious establishment in relation to the political authorities, who were tainted by the suspicion of compromise with the West and of prioritizing secular interests first. The ten themes addressed are as follows:

1. The standing of the ulema and the imams;
2. The issue of laws and regulations;
3. The judicial system;
4. The rights of Muslims;
5. The conduct of public administration;
6. The economy and financial matters;
7. Social institutions;
8. The army;
9. Information;
10. Foreign policy.

Together, the propositions put forward constitute the foundations of a society that respects the Shari'a, which is able to serve as a model for the Umma, particularly as regards Islamic finance, scientific education, the development of a defense industry, the and the creation of world-class media under Islamic censorship.

Following the issue of these two documents, which were in effect the manifesto of the Islamist opposition to the regime of the Al Saud, other individuals and groups broke ranks to express their own positions regarding the regime in different ways. Many of these were linked to the movement known as the "Sahwa al-Islamiya" ("The Islamic Awakening"), which made its first appearance as early as the 1960s. These included Safar al-Hawali and Salman al-Awda, as well as some new voices. These included Mohammed al-Mas'ari, the founder of the Committee for the Defense of Legitimate Rights (CDLR), and Saad al-Faqih with his Movement for Islamic Reform (MIR). Though not an Islamic cleric, Osama bin Laden also joined the chorus of criticism, setting up his Committee for Advice and Reform (CAR) before his expulsion from Saudi Arabia in 1994.

Saudi Arabia: Islamist Opposition

Salman al-Awda

Salman Awda was born in 1955 in Al-Basr, near Buraydah, in the Qasim province of Nejd. His family background was modest but respectable. He studied at the Al-Buraydah institute and then at the Imam Mohammed bin Saud University in Riyadh. He then taught at Buraydah and in Riyadh at his former university.

Salman al-Awda was part of the clerical movement known as the "Sahwa al-Islamiya." The Sahwa originated in the 1960s as a radical group of ulema whose thinking was, nevertheless, held in some esteem. The younger generation of Sahwa thinkers turned to Islamist opposition after the Gulf crisis of 1990–1991 appeared to put the country under a great degree of American control. Salman al-Awda was imprisoned in 1994 after a demonstration and subsequent riots at Buraydah two days after he refused to sign a document undertaking not to criticize Saudi policy. He was finally set free in 1999, at the same time as Safar al-Hawali.

He both signed and helped to draft the "Letter of Request" and the "Advisory Memorandum," and between 1990 and 1994 he was regarded as one of the leading figures in the Islamist opposition to the regime, largely owing to the wide diffusion of the audio cassettes of his sermons. Gradually, he began to go beyond the purely religious field to express his views on political issues, both internal and external to Saudi Arabia. His views changed over time. At first, he maintained that Saudi Arabia was destined to remain an oasis of peace, but later he suggested it had a violent future ahead, on the lines of Algeria and Egypt. On the whole, he did not express discontent with the regime in power, calling only for a greater role for Islam in its policies. He even expressed admiration for some aspects of the states of the West. These included the respect shown for public opinion, the independent power of the press, and freedom of expression. All these were part of what he said he wished to see in Saudi Arabia, with the proviso that such freedoms should be subject to the Shari'a.

He did not hesitate to point out that the present regime in Saudi Arabia was originally based on an alliance between religion and politics. Its sole aim, in its early days, was the propagation of Islam. He therefore concluded that that any attack on the position of the "ulema," or on the centrality of religion in politics, would undermine the authority of the royal family. He insisted that the royal family should always consult the religious authorities. Salman Awda has never been the object of any official criticism by the official religious authorities. The kingdom's High Council of Ulema has at most noted what it said were his errors. He was in fact a member of the conservative religious establishment to which the official ulema look for support against the more radical reformists.

He has written little. His pronouncements, particularly on the Palestinian issue, are found in cassettes of his sermons, which are circulated mainly by the Committee for the Defense of Legitimate Rights (CDLR). Fundamentally, Salman al-Awada expounds a theory of the superiority of the Saudi nation, which he considers is obliged by its position to promulgate its views, and above all its religion, to the rest of the world.

Saad al-Faqih and the Movement for Islamic Reform (MIR)

Saad al-Faqih is a doctor by profession, who was born in 1958 in the Iraqi town of Al-Zubair, into a conservative religious family from the central Saudi Arabian province of Nejd that was related by marriage to the Al Saud. He lived in Iraq until the age of sixteen. He studied at the Al-Najat school of medicine in Riyadh and became professor of surgery at King Saud University in Riyadh, a post he held until 1994. His family was not regarded as particularly influential, which diminished the impact of his criticism of the royal family, especially after he had left the country. He was, nevertheless, socially superior to Mohammed al-Mas'ari due to the latter's nontribal origin.

As a young man, under the influence of his elder brother Salah, he moved in Muslim Brotherhood circles, especially while he was a medical student. He became acquainted with the works of Sayyed Qutb. He was a founding member of the CDLR and initiated the 1996 split that led to the establishment of the MIR, of which he became leader. He rejected the internationalist direction given to the CDLR by Mas'ari, preferring to concentrate on Saudi Arabia's internal problems. He presented himself as the authentic heir of the original "Sahwa" protest movement inaugurated by Salman al-Awda and Safar al-Hawali, which had led to the publication of the "Letter of Request" and the "Advisory Memorandum." The MIR followed Al-Awda and Hawali's ideological line and distributed the tracts they drafted during their period of imprisonment from 1994 to 1999. However, the MIR's focus on Saudi issues led Saad al-Faqih to prefer the approach of Salman al-Awad to that of Safar al-Hawali. Politics, in his view, should be the implementation of the decisions of the ulema.

In its manifesto of 1997, the MIR described itself as "Salafi," but emphasized its Saudi orientation. Saad al-Faqih placed particular attention to the role of the Saudi royal family, especially in his Arabic work "The Saudi System according to Islamic Values," published in London in 1998. In his view, the Al Saud has distorted the political situation through the maintenance of its monopoly of power. It leaves no scope either for men of religion to express their views or for able individuals to gain access to positions of authority. He also criticized the High Council of Ulema, and in particular Sheikh Abdelaziz bin Baz, and Mohammmed bin Utheimin. He accused these senior clerics of blindly serving the authorities, issuing fatwas to justify Saudi Arabia's reliance on American forces during the Gulf War and condemning the "Advisory Memorandum." He also accused them of support for the idea of compromise with Israel.

Safar al-Hawali

Safar al-Hawali is a significant figure in the Saudi Islamic opposition. Together with Salman al-Awda, he was a figure identified with the clerical movement known as the "Sahwa" (Awakening). The Sahwa originated in the 1960s as a radical but respected group of ulema, but veered into opposition after the Gulf crisis of 1990–1991 brought American troops into the country.

Hawali was born in 1950 in the Al-Baha region south of Taif. He studied at the Buraydah institute and then pursued his higher studies at the Islamic University of Medina. He continued his studies at Umm al-Qura University in Mecca, where he took a master's degree followed by a doctorate in 1986, with a thesis on the topic of secularism. He then accepted a teaching position in the university's department of "aqidah" (doctrine). The central theme of his teaching was the defense of Islam against Western attempts to introduce secularization, prominent among which was the policy of the United States in the Middle East.

Hawali went beyond purely theological opposition to the Saudi regime and began to write as a geopolitical theorist. When he postulated the existence of what he called a "clash of civilizations" in his 1991 tract "Realities behind the Gulf Crisis" he became, in a sense, the Muslim counterpart of the American theorist Samuel Huntington. In another work, "Palestine between the True Promise and the False," he examines what he sees as a de facto alliance between Christians and Jews, arguing that this is especially evident in the context of the Israeli-Palestinian conflict. More recently, he has looked at the causes and consequences of the Al-Aqsa Intifada of 2000, in a tract entitled "The Day of Wrath: Is the Rajab Intifada only the Beginning?" He calls for the Muslim countries to strengthen themselves and emphasize their autonomy from the West, arguing that the military dependence of the Arab states on the

West that was revealed by the Gulf War can only lead to economic and cultural subjugation. He was one of the originators of the "Advisory Memorandum" whose proposals include the unification of the "umma," the spread of Islam in the non-Muslim countries, withdrawal by the Muslims from the Western financial system, and the construction of a Muslim financial system in its stead.

The primary objective of his strategy is to combat "the enemy within," namely the quasi-secular or nonreligious Muslim states. He violently criticizes Muslim states where the law is based primarily on Western codes, seeing this as an error imported from the West, to the detriment of the Shari'a. On this basis, he endorses the "Salafi Revolution" in Algeria as the salutary awakening of a people long subjected to Western influence, first by French colonialism and then from within by the secular FLN. He refrains from criticism of the Saudi system, however, as it is the government that most closely approaches what an authentic Islamic power should be. On the other hand, he does attack the monarchy's apparent inability to change and to withstand Western pressure and at the apparent submission of Saudi Arabia to the United States, which he sees as a longer-term threat to the Muslim Umma as a whole.

Though it is difficult to assess exactly what effect Hawali's message may have had on the Saudi population, his writings and his cassettes have certainly been widely disseminated. There has apparently been some sympathy for his advice to the king, due to his standing in the religious establishment and respect for his tribal background. At the time of the Gulf War, his message was heard only by a small minority. However, he has gradually reached a wider audience. In 1994, together with Salman al-Awda, he was arrested and imprisoned by the regime after a demonstration in Buraydah, Salman Al-Awda's home town, against government corruption. This led to riots in Buraydah that were crushed by the authorities. In July 1999, both clerics were released and placed under legal supervision.

Hawali's more recent expressions of opinion are "The Day of Wrath," on the Aqsa Intifada (mentioned above), and his "Open Letter" to President Bush of October 15, 2001. In the latter, he set out his view of relations between the Muslim world and the United States, urging moderation on President Bush following the latter's warlike statements. However, after September 11, 2002, Hawali appears to have changed his direction, modifying his critical view of the Saudi authorities and distancing himself from Jihadist factions. First, he denounced Al-Qaida when it became clear that they were linked with the American atrocity. After the attack on targets linked to the Americans in Riyadh on May 12, 2003, Hawali condemned the action. In December 2004, he denounced Mohammed al-Mas'ari for attempting to organize demonstrations and civil disobedience in Saudi Arabia. In 2005, Hawali reportedly issued a fatwa against resistance to the regime in Saudi Arabia, but said that it was lawful to travel to Iraq to join the insurgency there.

Mohammed al-Mas'ari and the Committee for the Defense of Legitimate Rights (CDLR)

The CDLR was founded on May 3, 1993, and it is still the leading Sunni Islamist opposition organization in Saudi Arabia. Its inaugural communiqué was signed by five eminent Saudi figures who lent the organization their credibility. These were, Hamid al-Sulaifa (an educationist), Abdullah bin Suleiman al Mas'ari (a retired judge and former president of the Supreme Court), Abdullah bin Abdulrahman al-Jibrin (a member of the Fatwa committee), Abdullah al-Hamid (a professor at King Saud University), and Abdullah al-Tuwaijiri (professor at Imam bin Saud University in Riyadh).

In practice, the activities of the group were initially led by a group of younger Saudi Islamists: Mohammed al-Mas'ari, Muhsin al-Awaji, Khalid al-Humeidh, Abdelaziz al-Qasim, Abdel Wahhab al-Turairi, and Saad al-Faqih. Though the groups that set up the CDLR were among those responsible for the Letter of Request and the Advisory Memorandum, they asked for registration as an officially recognized organization after the submission of these two documents. No sooner had the committee come into being than it was denounced as contrary to Islam by the High Council of Ulema, in a memorandum of May 12, 1993. Mohammed al-Mas'ari (Abdullah al-Mas'ari's son) was imprisoned for six months, after which he went into exile in London, which had by then become the hub of the Arab press and a center for opposition movements and Islamists. In its communiqué of April 20, 1994, issued in London, the CDLR officially announced its intention to become a real opposition political party.

In the West, the CDLR was at first misunderstood. The Western media reported it widely, but took it to be a group defending human rights in the Western sense of the term, though the term "legitimate" was in fact intended to refer to rights embodied in the Shari'a. The name of the organization in Arabic is "Lijnat al-Difa' 'an al-Huquq al-Shari'a" (Committee for the Defence of the Rights of the Shari'a). The impact of the establishment of the CDLR was better understood in the Muslim world, where it was also widely commented on. Mohammed al-Mas'ari had in fact become the de facto spokesman for the group thanks to the accident that his father deputed him to speak in an interview with the Arabic Service of the BBC. Though Mohammed Mas'ari was personable, a number of factors, nevertheless, limited the impact his message had on the Saudi public. One was that he lacked high-level religious qualifications. He also had known links with the West. He had studied mainly in Germany, before moving to the United States, where he married an American. But a big problem lay with his family origins. Though he was from the Al-Dawasir tribe, a significant tribe from Nejd which was linked to the Al Saud by marriage, both his mother and his grandmother were foreigners, which placed him in the category of nontribal citizens and effectively excluded him from political responsibility. On the other hand, however, a plus point was the reputation of his grandfather, Abdelaziz, also a signatory of the first CDLR communiqué, who had been a contemporary of Ibn Saud and had been to school with the then grand mufti, Abdelaziz bin Baz.

One of Mohammed Mas'ari's main themes was that the ulema could, if they chose, oppose the royal family. He drew attention to a number of occasions when bin Baz had dared to do precisely this, though his courage seemed to have abandoned him after he became grand mufti. Similarly, he cited the example of his own father, who as a religious scholar had, on a number of occasions, disagreed with Ibn Saud and King Faisal on points of law. From the vantage point of his exile in London, Mohammed al-Mas'ari was able to take full advantage of the media, spoke at academic conferences, and was even received by British parliamentarians at the House of Commons. Pressure brought to bear by the Saudi authorities to have him expelled resulted only in his obtaining refugee status and also brought him further publicity. The CDLR had also quickly grasped how anxious the media were to publicize its views and quickly developed a presence on the Internet, in both Arabic and English. In 1995, the CDLR expressed its support for Crown Prince Abdullah, whom it had not criticized as much as it had other members of the royal family. Gradually, however, the audience for the CDLR's views dissipated, as the group lost its monopoly on expressing the views of the Saudi Islamic opposition. In addition, Mohammed al-Mas'ari made the strategic mistake of getting too close to the Syrian Omar al-Bakri, a notorious radical Islamist based in London who was the leader of the Muhajirun. This cost him some of his supporters.

In terms of internal Saudi affairs, the CDLR's criticism of the Saudi government was targeted at economic management, differences of opinion over the Shari'a, and problems within the royal family. Mas'ari took the view that the cement of Saudi society should be Islam and Islamic awareness, rather than tribal affiliation—no doubt thanks to his own origins outside the tribal aristocracy. He took the view that discrimination on tribal grounds contradicted the principle of equality between Muslims within the Umma. As regards Saudi regional policy, Mas'ari spoke out against the alignment of Saudi policy with American policies, which prevented Saudi Arabia assisting Muslim combatants in Palestine and in Afghanistan, except in support of the United States and when the Americans permitted. Finally, in international politics, the CDLR attempted to discredit Saudi Arabia in the eyes of the West, emphasizing human rights issues and inequalities in development and wealth. He especially condemned Saudi Arabia's participation in the United Nations and the Gulf Cooperation Council (GCC). Mas'ari regarded this as un-Islamic, particularly because it appeared to endorse the idea of the nation state as distinct from the Umma and because the United Nations Charter embodied provisions that were contrary to the Shari'a.

In his book Evidence for the un-Islamic nature of the Saudi State, Mohammed al-Mas'ari attacked the very foundations of the regime, the alliance between the founder of Wahhabism, Mohhamed ibn Abdelwahhab, and the Al Saud, refusing to accept that the concept of "da'wa" (proselytization) be limited to a local ideology calculated to serve the political interests of a single family. On March 4, 1996, a split within the CDLR led to the creation of the Movement for Islamic Reform (MIR) led by Saad al-Faqih. Following this, Mohammed al-Mas'ari moved closer to Omar Bakri's Muhajirun and increasingly concerned himself with non-Saudi issues and the immigrant communities in London. He thus lost the sympathy of the Saudi population, and especially the opposition. In addition, he neglected his Internet site, as the CDLR merged into London's Islamist circles.

Saudi Arabia: Middle East Peace Plan

On February 17, 2001, Crown Prince Abdullah used an article in The New York Times to launch a peace proposal that provided for "full normalization" between the Arab world and Israel, in exchange for Israel's "complete withdrawal from all the occupied territories, in according with the United Nations resolutions, including Jerusalem. This initiative was reminiscent of the "Fahd plan" of 1982, which proposed, without further clarification, "the recognition of the right of all states in the region to live in peace." In the end, after talks held in March 2002 at the Arab League headquarters in Cairo, Saudi Arabia agreed to accept a Syrian demand to replace the expression "full normalization" by "comprehensive peace": a formulation that relates to diplomatic relations between governments, rather than to relationships between peoples. This Saudi peace initiative, leaving aside semantic issues and changes of wording, invites a number of comments.

First, the crown prince's initiative was an attempt to rebut any insinuation that the kingdom had played any role in relation to terrorist attacks, whether in terms of financing such attacks or of their sponsorship. Second, it put pressure on Washington to not only take Saudi Arabia under its political wing, but also to provide physical security for Crown Prince Abdullah. The United States had no desire to see Abdullah meet the same tragic fate as Egypt's President Anwar Sadat. In this sense, the United States henceforth became responsible for the survival of the crown prince. In addition, the United States was obliged to guarantee the political future of the crown prince. Third, the Saudi initiative increased Iran's diplomatic isolation, which henceforth appeared in the world's eyes, and particularly to the United States, as the last obstacle to a comprehensive peace agreement. Finally, the proposal of a peace plan placed Saudi Arabia in the forefront of political and diplomatic efforts in the region, a position that had traditionally been occupied by Egypt. As crown prince, King Abdullah was making a bid to be seen as a major actor on the regional and international scene.

Saudi Arabia: Nongovernmental Organizations

Three NGOs particularly stand out because of the scale of their funds and their international penetration. These are the IIRO, Al-Haramein, and the Saudi Red Crescent. The interdependence between the Saudi state and the NGOs is still very strong, as is shown by the establishment by the state itself of two coordinating bodies at the local level of NGO action, namely the Saudi High Commission for Relief (SHCR) and the Saudi Joint Relief Committee (SJRC).

Al Haramein

The Al-Haramein Foundation (named after the two holy shrines), with its seat at Riyadh, is active in fifty-five countries. It has religious objectives in relation to existing Muslims—to reinforce their faith and to increase their awareness of the Sunna, as well as the humanitarian aim of assisting Muslims who have been the victims of various disasters. However, its central aim is active proselytization, especially to attract non-Muslims to Islam, and to confront ideological and atheistic tendencies. Al-Haramein is organized into nine general committees: the permanent Charity Committee, the Committee for Ad Hoc Projects, Committees for Africa, Asia, Europe, America, and Committees for the Call to Islam (Da'wa), Mosques, Medical Affairs, and the Internet. Its main practical activities are in the religious field. These have included the construction and renovation of well over 1,000 mosques, as well as schools providing education for more than 30,000 pupils, and the sponsorship of around 4,000 preachers and imams. The organization also distributes Islamic dress for the use of women, as well as donating sheep for sacrifice in Muslim festivals. In addition, it publishes leaflets on Islam—some 10 million copies to date—and maintains Internet sites. In the humanitarian field, it supports medical care, the construction of housing and distribution of food to the needy, aid for refugees, and the care of some 6,000 orphans.

The International Islamic Relief Organization (IIRO)

This Saudi NGO, set up in 1978 at the behest of King Fahd and based in Jeddah, is affiliated to the World Islamic League. Its secretary-general is Dr. Adnan Khalil Basha. Its brief is to offer humanitarian support to Muslim populations that fall victim to natural catastrophes or wars. Its funding is provided by "zakat" as well as by individual gifts from wealthy Saudis, including members of the royal family. The IIRO has established the "Sanabil al-Khair Foundation" (The Seed-Corn of Welfare) to manage its financial resources. The IIRO is judged to be the largest of the Islamic NGOs and functions principally through its "Department for Urgent Relief and Refugees," which operates in many countries, in the Balkans, the

Caucasus, and sub-Saharan Africa. It also works with educational causes, funding many teachers and schools, as well as working with the World Islamic League and the Islamic University in Medina to train preachers.

The Saudi Red Crescent

The Saudi Red Crescent is the national branch of the International Red Crescent, which is itself affiliated to the International Red Cross Committee. It is responsible for the management of the health and care system during the pilgrimage. Outside the country, it mainly operates through the "Saudi Joint Relief Committee of Kosovo," in addition to the "Islamic Council of Pehsawar," which was active during the Afghan war.

Saudi Arabia Nongovernmental Organizations (Conflict Specific)

Increasing unease over the precise role of the Wahhabi, and especially Saudi, NGOs in certain countries has led to close vigilance over their activities by various countries in which they operate. The Saudi leadership has been asked to account for the apparently close relationship between these NGOs and the Saudi state. Apparently, radical Islamic movements have operated as they did in Afghanistan, by setting up ad hoc NGOs in particular conflict zones. This has enabled them to enjoy logistic support in their principal areas of activity, while benefiting from the cover offered by NGO status. At the same time, they have avoided compromising the work of the large charitable organizations. Such ad hoc organizations include the following.

Omega Relief Foundation

The Omega Relief Foundation, (ORF), used to raise funds for the jihad in Chechnya, is a "virtual" organization with no physical existence. It first appeared in March 2000 as an Internet site (www.omegarelief.org), but its existence appears to have been registered nowhere. The Internet domain name is traceable only to an accommodation address in the Philippine capital, Manila. The site itself represents an apparently respectable NGO carrying out various charitable and religious projects across the world, though it appears in no NGO handbook, and the Internet site provides no address or telephone number. At the same time, however, the defunct site www.qoqazfr.tripod.com, a mouthpiece for the jihad in Chechnya, was very informative, describing the ORF as "the sole benevolent organization we would recommend for conveying donations to Chechnya. We do not claim that is the sole benevolent association involved in the provision of assistance for Chechnya, but the others are not worthy of trust. We would say only that it is the only organization to which we would recommend contributions be given." This eloquent recommendation was issued by the spokesmen for the Chechen commander Khattab. The ORF, however, had only an ephemeral existence, and its site disappeared in the spring of 2001, after some months.

Al-Wafa

This NGO first came to light after September 11, 2001, when it was listed among twenty-seven organizations and individuals whose funds had been frozen by the American authorities. It was described in the listing as follows: "Wafa Humanitarian Organization, a Saudi NGO whose particular brief was to distribute food and has built a hospital in Kabul." This organization was also quite active in Bosnia at the time of the war of 1992–1995. Nothing further is known about it. According to Abdullah bin Saleh al-Obeid, a member of the Saudi Shura and secretary-general of the World Islamic League, Wafa has not operated at least since 1996 and there is no proof that it is run from

Saudi Arabia. Mr. Al-Obeid has asked the United States to provide proof of its allegations. Meanwhile, American investigators allege that an inactive NGO that was not under suspicion had been used to provide logistical provision for the Taliban and for Al-Qaida in Afghanistan without attracting attention.

Saudi Arabia Nongovernmental Organizations (Coordination Bodies)

Saudi High Commission for the Collection of Donations for Bosnia and Herzegovina

Founded in 1993 by Prince Salman bin Abdul Aziz, this body operates in the field of religious and educational projects. It promotes the re-Islamization of the Bosnian people, with a special focus on children. In 2000, Prince Salman visited Sarajevo to open the King Fahd Islamic Center and Mosque.

Saudi Joint Relief Committee for Kosovo and Chechnya (SJRC)

This organization coordinated the activity of the principle NGOs in Kosovo and in Chechnya, looking after social projects such as care centers, schools, and orphanages, as well as religious ventures, such as mosques and Islamic centers.

Saudi Nongovernmental Organizations (Fields of Activity)

Saudi state and Wahhabi agencies are subject to limitations because of their governmental status. In contrast, non-state actors are much less restricted. In addition, they operate in different fields. Action by the state is in general directed toward the political and financial support of populations (normally Muslims), undertaken over a relatively short term.

The aim of non-state action, on the other hand, is the re-Islamization of Muslim societies on Wahhabi lines, over the longer term. Their preferred fields of action lie in education and other aspects of childhood, such as orphanages and schools, aiming to influence future generations. They also involve themselves in health, development aid, and emergency assistance. They offer an Islamist model to a variety of Muslim societies, discouraging them from seeking assistance elsewhere, particularly from the West. The non-state agencies are not entirely independent, however. Close links may well exist between the non-state organizations and the Saudi regime.

On occasions, this places the Saudi authorities in delicate situations. If non-state organizations exceed their brief, the Saudi regime can hardly disown them and finds itself obliged to defend their actions as if they had been the responsibility of the Saudi state itself. Sometimes, however, such non-state organizations may act as officially as local intermediaries for Saudi foreign policy and diplomacy. Saudi NGOs regularly step up the level of aid they provide if they find a Shi'ite Iranian organization in the same region. The goal is to counter the attraction of the Islamic Republic, which has made efforts to extend its influence even among Sunnis.

The Saudi NGOs have faced criticism over their imposition of their particular vision of Islam on the populations to whose aid they have come. Excesses fall into two major categories. First, there has been a tendency to destroy the local religious and historic heritage. For example, architectural and decorative features have been stripped from Ottoman mosques in favor of Wahhabi-style austerity. The idea is to remove the local accretions from Islam, replacing it with an "original" Islam that the Wahhabis see as universal. Second, they have pressurized local populations to behave in a more "Islamic" and, therefore, more religious way. This has included the wearing of the veil by women and beards by men, attendance by children at Quranic schools, and abstention from alcohol. The Saudi NGOs generally offer incentives to achieve their objectives. For example, after an initial period when assistance is unconditional, they gradually begin to offer additional aid in the form of cash gifts or food supplies to individuals or groups that accept their standards of religious observance. Cases have even been reported where aid has become entirely dependent on these criteria, thus leaving target populations little choice. By these means, the Saudi NGOs are an effective instrument for the re-Islamization of Muslim societies on the Wahhabi model—at least according to Wahhabi criteria—at least superficially.

SALAFISM

In modern terms, Salafism is a word that has become in practice a little more than a synonym for "fundamentalism," though it has many other connotations. Salafis claim to make a direct appeal to the Quran and the Sunna, and thus insist that they attain moral superiority. The Sunna is the tradition relating to the acts and sayings of the Prophet Muhammad as related by those who were present, passed down to later generations in the form of "Hadith" (Arabic: "hadith," plural "ahadith") collected by Muslim scholars and quoted with the chain of transmission that confers authenticity. The word "Salafi" in Arabic has become a slogan adopted by groups of young men who feel the impulse to purify society, to overturn old governments that they believe are impious and tainted by the ideas of the West, and to expunge corruption and sin from society. Such groups often turn to violence, which they seek to justify on the basis of religion. Here, the idea of Salafism suits their purposes.

As they claim to appeal directly to the original sources of Islam, Salafis are able to follow the "Fatwas" (Arabic "fatwa," plural

"fatawa") issued by their own self-appointed religious leaders, untrammeled by the weight of traditional interpretation that might otherwise stand in their way. A Fatwa is a ruling on a matter of religious law, issued in Sunni Islam by a "mufti," who is a cleric recognized by the community as fit to issue such rulings. Salafis, who purport to refer only to the Quran and the Sunna, reach their own interpretations, often in defiance and frequently in ignorance of the weight of Muslim scholarship. Such "fatwas" are sometimes issued to provide a form of religious justification for acts of extremist violence.

Theologically, a Salafi is one who claims to draw his religious doctrine directly from the "Salaf al-Salih"—the ancestors. These are the first three generations of Muslims: the companions, the followers, and those who succeeded the followers. A Salafi claims to take his interpretation of Islamic doctrine directly from the Quran and the Sunna as they were understood and practised by the Salaf. In practice, Salafis recognize a list of approved interpreters of the Quran and the Sunna over the years. These notably include Ibn Taymiya, from the thirteenth century, who justified war against corrupt Muslim rulers in the interests of fighting the Mongols, Muhammad ibn Abdul Wahhab, the founder of the Wahhabi sect in the eighteenth century, and certain modern Saudi clerics.

Conventional Islamic scholars criticize self-styled Salafi theologians on the grounds that by claiming to derive rulings on matters of Islamic law from the original sources they set themselves up as equivalent in learning and stature to the recognized authorities of Islam. The Quran and the Sunna do not explicitly provide the rules needed for all the eventualities of modern life, which the Shari'a must cover. They were, therefore, subjected by the early theologians to the process known as "Ijtihad"—intellectual struggle, applied to the four "Usul" (foundations)—in order to derive suitable rulings.

The four fundamentals are the Quran, the Sunna, and the processes of "Ijma" (consensus of the clerics) and "Qiyas" (analogy). The Salafis spurn Ijma and Qiyas, which they see as having introduced extraneous elements into the faith. Salafis clearly arrogate to themselves the ability to apply their own Ijtihad in order to reach their own decisions on theological matters. This has major consequences for their actions and the way they justify them. A paradox is that the reformist theologians of the nineteenth century such as Muhammad Abduh, who claimed to be bringing Islam into modern times by the practice of Ijtihad, also described themselves as "Salafi."

From the sociological point of view, radical Salafis have been identified with a policy of subversion of supposedly impious government in the Islamic world, while refraining from all involvement with political society in Europe. Salafism has an appeal to the poorer and more deprived segments of society. It offers a direct root to "authenticity" for those disillusioned with contemporary structures, including those of Islam. Some Salafis are quietist and take the view that Muslims—especially those in the West—should concern themselves with spiritual affairs. Others adopt a more active philosophy. Salafis are not necessarily committed to Jihad, but there is a school of radical Salafism that argues for violent Jihad as route to the reconstruction of society.

SENEGAL

Muslims make up more than 90 percent of the population of Senegal, where there are a number of Muslim organizations whose differences arise from their origins and social function. They fall into three groups— "reformist" movements, those which openly admit to be Islamist, and finally more traditional organizations based on the Islamic Brotherhoods. The reformists preach a return to the early days of Islam, on the model of the life of the Prophet. The longest established movement of this type in Senegal is the Muslim Cultural Union ("Union Culturelle Musulmane") (MCU) founded in 1953 in Dakar by Sheikh Touré. The MCU strongly opposed the colonial regime and struggled vigorously against the pre-Islamic animist local religion. Later, it went into partnership with the Socialist Party, which retained power in Senegal until 2001.

The Islamist tendency, made its appearance at the start of the 1960s, in the shape of the "Al-Falah" movement, which was ideologically inspired by Wahhabi ideas. Saudi Arabia gave money for mosque building and related ventures in the capital Dakar and elsewhere. Al-Falah's founder, Mahmoud Baa, had studied in Saudi Arabia. Al-Falah's doctrine was that Senegalese Islam should rid itself of popular superstitions in order to return to a purified and rigorous religious practice. It maintained a number of centers for Quranic teaching and also sponsored Arabic language teaching. An organization known as "Jamaatou Ibadou Rahmane" (Servants of the Merciful) operated in Dakar. In the words of its manifesto, its goal was to "inform the Senegalese Muslim public of the reality of Islam, so that it may the better live up to its responsibilities, become authentically Islamic, and choose suitable leaders." Especially active among students, its aim was to participate in Senegal's multiparty political scene.

Finally, there is a specifically Senegalese flavor to the local Brotherhoods. These have sprung up in the context of the "Daira" (local circles), which assemble Muslims in local groups for the purposes of mutual aid. The two main Senegalese Brotherhoods are the Tijaniya (originally founded in Morocco at the end of the eighteenth century) and the "Mourides" (a prosperous local order established by Sheikh Amadou Bamba, who lived in Senegal from 1850 to 1927). These orders currently follow the teachings of their respective religious leaders, Ahmad Sy and Abdoulaye Sarr. The ancient order of the Qadiriya is also represented. This was founded in Baghdad by the Sufi mystic saint Abdel Qadir al-Jilani in the twelfth century and is now represented across the entire Muslim world. It spread to Senegal from North Africa in the eighteenth century. Since the early 1980s, the brotherhoods have sought to expand their membership among the student population, especially in Dakar, seeking to establish a bridgehead among Senegal's future elite. Islamist tendencies have been added on to the secrecy and selectivity, which are the traditional characteristics of the brotherhoods.

SHARI'A

The Shari'a is the religious law that governs the life of Muslim societies. It regulates matters in the sphere of religion and in the daily lives, private and public, of Muslims. Modern Shari'a courts in countries where there is also state law tend to cover the personal domains of marriage, divorce, and inheritance as well as financial affairs. In its full form, however, the Shari'a extends to all issues, whether these be private or public, personal or political.

The Shari'a is based on the Quran and the Sunna of the Prophet Mohammed—that which is known of his life and practice as recorded in the Hadith, passed down to later generations by those who observed them and collected in recognized anthologies. For Muslims, the Quran represents the word of God, transmitted to Mohammed by the Archangel Gabriel. The Sunna consists of the ensemble of the additional rules governing religious and moral life, as derived from the deeds and words of the Prophet. All Muslims regard the Sunna as a completion and exegesis of the Quran. It

complements the Quran in the sense that though the Quran asserts that "nothing has been omitted from the text" (Quran: Sura VI, Verse 38), there are issues unmentioned in the text and passages that are obscure. In this case, the source of authority is the Sunna of the Prophet, which may be searched for an example or a ruling.

The Sunna is in essence known to us by way of collections of stories about the life of the Prophet—the Hadith. A Hadith is a saying attributed to the Prophet or a description of his practice on some occasion from which practice may be justified or confirmed. The Hadith were transmitted down the generations until the ninth century of the Christian era, when the first efforts were made to classify them and to gather them into anthologies. The most celebrated collection is that of Ahmed Ibn Hanbal, who gathered some 30,000 Hadith originating from seven hundred original sources in a volume of 2,885 pages. Subsequent collections took a thematic approach, rather than classifying Hadith according to their originators, making them easier to consult by scholars. In the end, six collections of Hadith were compiled that were seen as worthy of consultation by theologians. The two principal collections are that of Bukhari, a pupil of Ibn Hanbal, and that of the scholar known as "Muslim" (who died in 874).

The expansion of Islam outside the Arabian Peninsula and the establishment of the caliphate led to the development of the science of "Fiqh," defined as the knowledge and formulation of divine and human law. The subject matter of Fiqh was the practice that the Shari'a imposed on the believer. From the theological point of view, Fiqh was revealed law, whose sources were the Quran and the Sunna. In practice, however, it was necessary to rely on various logical stratagems in order to legislate for cases not foreseen by the Quran, even with its complement in the Sunna. These were "Ijma"—consensus—and

"Qiyas"—reasoning by analogy. "Ijma" was initially meant to represent the consensus of the community of believers, but for obvious practical reasons tended to become the consensus of a group of Ulema seeking the approval of their colleagues. The "Ijma" of earlier generations became binding on those that followed. Meanwhile "Qiyas"—reasoning by analogy—was bounded only by the limits set by the Quran, the Sunna, and the process of "Ijma."

The process of deriving legal rulings from these four recognized sources to suit changing circumstances not originally envisaged was known as "Ijtihad." This was defined as the critical study of the four bases of the faith, the Quran, the Sunna, "Ijma," and "Qiyas." It implied the right to go beyond established opinions and the authorities of the past and to conceive and promulgate new opinions based on a better understanding of the Quran and of the content of the Sunna. This led to a difficulty. It began to appear that while the Shari'a should flow primarily from the Quran and the Sunna in preference to other sources, the conventional interpretation of these texts by the jurists had begun to take precedence over the letter of the text itself. (This was the problem perceived by the Salafis.) From the eleventh century onward, many within the Sunni community—though not the Shi'ites—declared that the "gate of Ijtihad" ("Bab al-Ijtihad") was closed, in other words that no further Ijtihad was legitimate. This obliged scholars and believers to follow "Taqlid" (tradition) and to submit entirely to the rulings of one or other of the four great schools of law that had come into existence: the "madhhab." The gate of Ijtihad was never truly closed, however, and in practice continued in the Sunni world. A key theologian who rejected the idea that "Ijtihad" was no longer permissible was Ibn Taymiya in the thirteenth century—a hero of the Salafis. Reformist

Muslims in the nineteenth century such as Muhammad Abduh openly practiced a form of "neo-Ijtihad."

The schools of law in Sunni Islam were the Hanbali, Shafi'i, Hanafi, and Maliki schools. Each was based on the work of a single scholar as developed by his disciples and presented essentially a body of established fiqh that enabled jurists and scholars to reach decisions in legal matters. Each school has tended to predominate in a particular area of the world. The areas that formed part of the Ottoman Empire as well as the Indian subcontinent are broadly faithful to the Hanafi school, while East Africa, Arabia, and Southeast Asia are Shafi'i zones. The Maliki school predominates in North and West Africa, and the strict Hanbali school prevails in Saudi Arabia. Shi'ites have their own body of "Hadith," their own fiqh, and their own legal schools—the mainstream Shi'ite "Ja'afari school and the Za'idi school". For the Shi'ites, "Ijtihad" has never ceased. The Shi'ite Ayatollahs are regarded as "Mujtahids" (capable of exercising Ijtihad), and their rulings are binding on Shi'ites.

Today, the Shari'a is the basis of the legal systems of many Muslim countries. Others draw on it to a greater or lesser extent as the inspiration for their legislation. With the emergence of Islamism, the insistent demand for the application of Shari'a has taken on a new meaning. What is at issue is no longer solely the application of the religious law based on the Quran. The Islamist objective is to read the Quran afresh in such a way as to obstruct all unwanted social and political change and to create a barrier against any Western penetration into Muslim countries and the Muslim world. Shari'a then acquires political and adversarial connotations and serves political rather than religious or social interests.

Pronouncements by prominent Islamists make their position clear. In 1994, in a speech made at the Popular Arab and Islamic

Conference (PAIC), Hassan al-Turabi, then the leader of Sudan's National Islamic Front, spoke as follows: "The Muslims have taken the decision to launch themselves today on the road towards re-awakening, basing their new life on the solid foundation of belief in God, on the Shari'a, and on the lessons of history. The renaissance of civilization is founded on the renaissance of religion, and for the masses of the people religion encompasses every aspect of life. This will halt the process of disintegration which opens the way for the western cultural invasion."

Fatwa

A "Fatwa" (Arabic plural "Fatawa") is nothing more or less than the answer to a question on a matter of religion put to a person qualified to deliver answers to such questions, who is known as a mufti. It is a statement of how the Shari'a is to be interpreted and applied to some specific issue. In Sunni Islam, the status of a Fatwa very much depends on by whom it is issued. In a non-hierarchical context, the validity of a Fatwa is rather like the validity of a monetary currency—its value depends on who issues it and their reputation for reliability. In Sunni Islam, it could be argued that a Fatwa issued by an individual, no matter whom, would need to be validated by a Shari'a court. On the other hand, there would be little argument about a Fatwa issued by a mufti at Al-Azhar University. In Shi'ite Islam, the ability of clerics of particular ranks to issue Fatwas and to demand "emulation" is conventionally more codified.

It is a vulgar error to suppose that a Fatwa is a "sentence of death," or some such thing, as Western journalists sometimes imply. This notion gained currency at the time of the Fatwa pronounced in February 1989 by the Ayatollah Khomeini regarding Salman Rushdie, when it was declared lawful for a

Muslim to bring about the death of Rushdie. In the Ayatollah's words: "The author of the book entitled 'The Satanic Verses,' which has been compiled printed and published in opposition to Islam, the Prophet and the Quran, as well as those publishers who were aware of its contents, have been sentenced to death." In light of these words, the mistake about the concept of a "Fatwa" is understandable. For example, the Somali apostate Ayaan Hirsi Ali, whose artistic collaborator Theo Van Gogh was murdered by a Moroccan Islamist in Amsterdam in November 2004, has been said to be "under Fatwa." However, it is important to remember that Fatwas can and almost always do concern mundane matters, religious niceties, points of law, and new situations. (For instance, in what direction should a Muslim astronaut point when he prays?)

In Shi'ite Islam, a definitive Fatwa is one pronounced by a grand ayatollah, who is recognized as such by his peers and is therefore worthy of emulation. In Sunni Islam, a Fatwa must be issued by a cleric of standing with profound knowledge of the Shari'a. Other clerics may well disagree with any particular Fatwa, so that obedience depends on the respect in which the issuing authority is held. The custom grew up in historical times that a particular cleric in any given city was accepted as the "mufti." This status was accredited by the mufti's peers and often endorsed by the civil authorities. Today, Muslim states often appoint a mufti—for example Saudi Arabia and Egypt. Among the Islamists, those who regard themselves as Salafis tend to claim that their own religious leaders have the power to issue binding Fatwas. Even such figures as Osama bin Laden, with no background in conventional religious scholarship, have had the temerity to issue what they have described as "Fatwas." These have little or no merit in law. Salafis, who believe themselves to be following the original sources of the law—the Quran and the Sunna—appear to consider that zeal and sincerity are sufficient qualifications for the issue of "Fatwas."

SHI'ISM

The Shi'a and the Sunni faiths are the two major organized sects of Islam; however, the Shi'ites are the minority. There is mistrust between the two. Shi'ites feel they are the victims of oppression, while Sunnis view Shi'ite practices with suspicion. Almost 90 percent of Muslims are Sunnis, and the Shi'ites are somewhat over 10 percent. Shi'ism is the faith of the Islamic Republic of Iran and has thus in the last quarter of a century taken on a high profile, attracting the spotlight to other Shi'ite groups. The achievement of Ayatollah Khomeini and his successors in overthrowing the former regime of the shah and installing in its place an Islamic state inspired admiration around the Muslim world. The success of the Islamic Republic encouraged Islamists to greater efforts to overthrow what they saw as their own impious governments and to defy the West. There is also a major Shi'ite population in Iraq, which represents in fact a majority of the population and significant Shi'ite communities in Lebanon and Bahrain.

The public role of Shi'ism is a new phenomenon. Until relatively recent times, Shi'ites have always tended to reticence about their faith. Shi'ites have felt themselves to be in the position of a vulnerable minority. There is a word in Arabic for this secretiveness—"Taqiya,"—which means precisely the act of dissimulating the real nature of one's faith. The need to conceal an allegiance to Shi'ism dates back to the early days of Islam and the wars between Sunnis and Shi'ites. Sunni Arab armies fought those who rejected the orthodox version of Islam and clung to the idea of the right of succession of Ali's sons Hassan and Hussein

to the mantle of the Prophet. The Shi'ites believe that twelve rightful imams, or Khalifas (Caliphs) ruled the community, starting with Ali, and that the twelfth, Muhammad al-Muntazar, disappeared from view (was "occulted"), but will in due course return to restore the Islamic community to its rightful balance.

The distinction between Sunni and Shi'ite Muslims has its origin in the disagreement over who should be the successor of the Prophet Muhammad as the leader of the Muslim community as a whole. Mainstream Muslims believed that Muhammad did not establish a fixed system for the selection of his successor. The decision of the early community was that the best qualified person should lead, and therefore they asked Abu Bakr, a close companion of the Prophet and Muhammad's father-in-law, to succeed after the death of Muhammad in 632. Abu Bakr was succeeded by Umar. Some felt that Muhammad's cousin and son-in-law Ali should have been selected. In 656, however, when Ali succeeded eventually to the leadership of the early Muslim community after the murder of the third Khalifa (or Caliph) Uthman, the community was fatally split. In 661, Ali himself was murdered by a religious fanatic from a group known as the Kharijites ("Al-Khawarij"). The fate of Ali and his sons—Hassan, who was pushed aside, and Hussein, who died in battle on October 19, in 681—became a cause of indignation for their supporters, who began to call themselves the Shi'at Ali. Meanwhile Mu'awiyah, a member of Uthman's family, took on the leadership of the mainstream Sunni community.

Over the intervening centuries, the Shi'a has developed into a community different in many ways from the body of Sunni Muslims. The Shi'a has always felt itself to be persecuted and in a minority and has placed the notion of martyrdom on a pedestal. It has developed its own rituals and its own cultural flavor. The death of Hussein at the battle of Karbala is celebrated each year at "Ashura," when Shi'ites flagellate themselves in an orgy of misery at the memory of his death. Shi'ism continued to flourish in the eastern part of the Muslim world, corresponding to southern Iraq and Iran—the majority lands of Shi'ism today. The most important development came in 1502 when Shah Ismail of Persia, the first of the Safavid dynasty, made Shi'ism the official faith of Persia. Persia had also culturally resisted the Arab invasion to the extent of keeping its own language after its people converted to Islam. The combination of cultural separateness and religious difference meant that Persia became a sanctuary for the Shi'ite sect and serves as its heartland. Shi'ism also spread eastward into India, down into the Gulf, and elsewhere in the Muslim world. A particular community developed in Lebanon, from which Shi'ites have traveled all over the world as Lebanese migrants.

Shi'ites developed their own version of Muslim religious law and their own way of organizing the faith. Though there are variant collections of "Hadiths" and specifically Shi'ite schools of law, they differ in practice from the Sunni faith only in detail. The lives and doctrines of the twelve Caliphs are in theory seen as sources of law. The clergy became a much more formalized institution than in Sunni Islam and the notion of a hierarchy of religious scholars culminating in the ayatollahs and grand ayatollahs took shape. The Shi'ites regard their ayatollahs as "Mujtahids," scholars capable of adding new interpretations to the scriptures and therefore of extending Shari'a law. However, thanks to the Iranian Islamic Revolution, Shi'ite Islam is today a force in the world.

SOMALIA

Somalia became independent in 1960, when the former British and Italian colonies amalgamated. In 1969, a military coup toppled the civilian regime and General Mohammed Siad Barre became president. In 1977, Somalia attacked Ethiopia, its Christian-led neighbor, with the aim of recovering the Somali-speaking province of Ogaden, but failed to make good its goal. Ethiopia obtained help from the Soviet Union and Cuba. After Somalia's defeat in 1978, Siad Barre's government became increasingly dictatorial. Finally, in 1991, civil war broke out between the warring factions and rival warlords, with the result that the country fell apart and civil authority disintegrated. In May 1991, tribal groups in the north declared an independent Republic of Somaliland. In December 1992, a United Nations force led by U.S. troops, together with contingents from other states including Muslim troops from Pakistan and Malaysia, entered the country to keep the peace. After a U.S. helicopter was downed with the loss of nineteen men in May 1993, the force was withdrawn.

Throughout the 1990s, competition between warlords continued, with the country effectively carved up into a number of autonomous zones. The warlords were more concerned with the maintenance of their power and with personal profit than with the administration of the country. In 1998, another area, known as Puntland, also declared its autonomy. This was followed by a declaration of autonomy in 2002 in the southwest of the country. In August 2004, a Transitional Federal Government (TFG) for Somalia was declared in Kenya, with international support and particular encouragement from the United States. In February 2006, the TFG's parliament met inside Somalia for the first time, at the Somali city of Baidoa, 260 kilometers from the traditional capital, Mogadishu. The TFG was relatively powerless, however, and depended on international support, principally from Ethiopia, which acted as a local surrogate for the United States. The U.S. interest in the situation was partly to counter the spread of fundamentalist Islam and partly its suspicion that the Union of Islamic Courts had links with Al-Qaida.

The Islamist bodies known as the Islamic Courts had made their first appearance in Somalia in the 1990s. The courts were identified with a particular Somali clan, the Hawiye', dominant in Mogadishu and the south of the country. Their stated aim was to extend the use of Islamic Shari'a law over the country, which had become anarchic due to the declining power of the warlords and their increasing fragmentation. They had the support of Somalia's business community and were popular with ordinary people who were fatigued by the constant factional fighting of the warlords. They dealt with crime and enforced civil law and business contracts. In the first instance, however, they were relatively apolitical. They, nevertheless, developed a police operation to enforce their jurisdiction and a youth-based militia, known as the Shabab. In 2000, the separate institutions formed the Union of Islamic Courts (UIC) to coordinate their action across Somalia. This brought them increasingly into conflict with the various warlords identified with other clans and led to mounting tension.

In January 2006, conflict between the UIC and the warlords broke out when a warlord faction clashed with the principal financial backer of the courts, Abu Bakr Omar. In May 2006, forces loyal to the UIC clashed with the warlords in Mogadishu and by June 2006 the UIC claimed to have extended its control over most of the country. Their initial victories over the warlords left the UIC in control of much military material and enabled them to continue to expand. A key factor was the relative popularity of the UIC, in a context in which the brutality of the warlords and the chaotic situation of the country had largely alienated the population. The UIC began to take steps toward the normalization of the country. In July 2006, the UIC opened Mogadishu airport for the first time since 1995. The TFG in Baidoa, however, refused to accept the UIC's authority, and in September 2006 an attempt at a compromise failed. By December 8, Ethiopia was supporting a Somali force described as troops of the Transitional Federal Government. On December 21, a force of 15,000 Ethiopian troops invaded Somalia. The United States denied giving direct assistance to Ethiopia, but certainly approved the Ethiopian action. Between 2002 and 2006, Ethiopia received $20 million in U.S. military aid and some hundred U.S. military advisers were working in the country, according to U.S. sources. The United States was concerned over the spread of Islamist control in Somalia through the activities of the UIC, though the U.S. administration wanted to see action against terrorism, not Islam. In order to attract American support, the TFG has presented itself as defending Somalia against radical Islamists. Washington was also specifically said to be alarmed that the UIC were sheltering Al-Qaida activists who had been implicated in the attacks on the U.S. embassies in Kenya and Tanzania. The UIC made little attempt at resistance against the Ehtiopian forces, and its supporters stood down rather than fighting. The Shabab appear to have withdrawn in good order, and estimates have been made that a hard core of 3,000 activists remains, with their weapons, which could take up arms again at a future date.

On December 27, 2006, the senior leaders of the UIC, Sheikh Hassan Aweys and Sharif Sheikh Ahmed, made a statement in which they claimed that the unity of Somalia had always been their priority and apparently acknowledged their defeat by the invading troops. The prime minister of the TFG, Ali Mohammed Gedi, took power. The United States had been particularly suspicious of

Sheikh Aweys, an influential figure within the UIC, who was on the State Department's list of terrorist suspects. He was the former head of a group called "Al-Ittihad al-Islamiya," alleged by the Americans to be connected to Al-Qaida. Al-Ittihad al-Islamiya was a Salafi organization maintaining a network of mosques, schools, and charitable ventures that gained the support of the people in a war-torn and otherwise chaotic country. Links have been alleged between other senior members of the UIC and the Afghan insurgency. On the other hand, there is little history of Islamic extremism in Somalia. The UIC chairman, Sharif Sheikh Ahmed, has a reputation as a moderate and always insisted that his aim was no more than the restoration of stability to Somalia after fifteen years of violence.

By December 31, the UIC forces had been driven from their last refuge in the town of Kismayo close to the Kenyan border, and the TFG asked Kenya to close its borders to fleeing Islamists. A TFG spokesman claimed that foreign Islamist fighters, who were supposed to have come to Somalia to aid the UIC, made up a majority of the Islamists' strength. However, intelligence estimates suggested that a few hundred foreign fighters at most had joined the UIC movement. Most of these were from Yemen, with others from Eritrea and a few from further afield, such as Pakistan. An early result of the ousting of the UIC was the return of the stimulant drug Qat to the streets of Mogadishu. In June 2006, the Islamists had banned Qat, used mainly in Yemen and Somalia and widely regarded as a social problem. Analysts said in January 2007 that unless Ethiopian troops remain, the TFG may need to seek help from the warlords to maintain its authority and to prevent factional fighting from restarting. The security situation continued to deteriorate in the absence of the control exercised by the UIC. There were some indications that the UIC might initiate a new insurgency. Kenya pre-

vented refugees from crossing the border as the search continued for suspected Islamists, and especially Al-Qaida supporters, while U.S. naval ships patrolled in the vicinity. Nevertheless, according to Yemen's foreign minister speaking in January 2007, senior members of the UIC leadership succeeded in reaching Yemen, where they have been given refuge. In mid-January 2007, reports said that Sheikh Ahmed had been arrested at a refugee camp on the Kenyan border.

Islamic Union (al-Ittihad al-Islami)

Beginning in the early 1990s, Somalia fell into a state of anarchy, accompanied by territorial and ethnic fragmentation. Against this background, various Islamic movements, all calling for the installation of Shari'a law, began to play a part in Somali affairs. They were particularly present in the coastal regions and in the outskirts of Mogadishu, Somalia's capital. The most sizeable of these was the Islamic Union ("Ittihad al-Islami"), which came into being in the later 1990s, thanks to the union of a number of smaller groups. Led by Ali Warsama, its objective was the establishment of an Islamic Republic in Somalia. Its military wing was led by Colonel Hassan Maher Aweys. Its presence was strong in Mogadishu and in the south of the country, close to the Kenyan frontier. It also attracted some support in the north of the country in the coastal towns abutting on the Gulf of Aden. It enjoyed a degree of backing from Sudan and maintained a territorial claim to the Ethiopian province of Ogaden. From time to time, it received aid from foreign Islamists. It also enjoyed the patronage of Saudi Arabia.

In 1996 and 1997, the Ethiopian regime launched a number of armed operations against the Islamic Union, which, however, was itself well armed. The leaders of the Islamic Union faced the accusation that they would welcome Al-Qaida militants in their camps. They were also suspected of having provided the explosives used in the attacks on the U.S. embassies in Kenya and Tanzania in 1998. The Islamic Union was included in the U.S. administration's blacklist of organizations and individuals linked to Al-Qaida. Its destruction would have been an objective of military intervention in Somalia. Thanks to its links with international business and the collection of funds abroad for the Jihad, the Islamic Union became a highly important actor in Somalia, presenting itself as able to use its ideological basis to transcend the ancestral divisions between the country's various clans.

After 2000, the Islamic Union allied itself with the leader of the Transitional National Government (TNG), President Salah Hassan. The TNG was set up in the wake of the Arta Conference, held in Djibouti in April and May 2000. It joined the TNG militias in fighting against various movements supporting tribal and clan interests that opposed the attempt to install a government. A leading Islamic Union member, Omar Maalim Nur, headed the movement that became known as the Islamic Courts of Mogadishu.

SOUTHEAST ASIAN ISLAMISM

Indonesia has the world's largest Muslim population, estimated in 2005 at 195 million, 90 percent of the inhabitants of the country. Half of Malaysia's population of just over 20 million people are Muslims. There are also significant Muslim minorities in other countries, including Thailand, where there are over 8 million Muslims among the country's estimated population of 60 million. The Philippines has 10 million Muslims out of almost 75 million inhabitants. Islam began to spread in the region some five hundred years ago, carried by traders and missionaries from the Middle East and soon became the majority religion, though much of the local culture also survived. There are a number of Islamist and separatist organizations in the region, which target both regional governments and targets identified with the West.

Indonesia

Indonesia is a secular state. However, Islamist Muslims have always represented a challenge to the authorities in postindependence Indonesia. The original Islamist movement in Indonesia was Darul Islam, founded by a radical political figure, Sekarmadji Maridjan Kartosuwiryo, born in 1905. Darul Islam emerged from Muslim movements that had taken shape in Indonesia during World War II. During the Japanese occupation, the Japanese made use of Muslim groups as the nucleus of an anti-Dutch opposition. Muslim groups were merged into an umbrella organization called Masyumi. Masyumi cooperated with postwar Indonesian governments. Darul Islam, however, was opposed to the authorities and was formally set up in 1948, with the aim of creating an Islamic state in independent Indonesia. After independence, it clashed with the government of Indonesia. Kartosuwiryo was captured and executed in 1962. The group was allied to other Islamist groups in South Sulawesi, led by Kahar Muzakkar, who died in 1965, and also had links with a group in the province of Aceh.

Most current Islamist groups have roots in either Masyumi or Darul Islam. Masyumi fell under the influence of the Muslim Brotherhood, and the Jamaat-i Islami movement in Pakistan, but contained groups and tendencies from a wide spectrum of positions, from political Islamists to quietist conservative groups. The Darul Islam network survived the destruction of its leadership in 1962, and in the 1970s and early 1980s antigovernment actions were attributed to its former members. A group calling itself Kommando Jihad proved to be made up of former Darul

Islam members. In the 1980s, Islamist activism began to be fashionable in Indonesia's universities and Da'wa groups were active in re-Islamizing students. The works of such Middle Eastern and South Asian theorists as Sayyed Qutb and Abul Ala Mawdudi were highly influential. By the 1990s, groups calling themselves Salafis had begun to appear. In the 1990s, a prominent organization was KISDI (Indonesian Committee for Solidarity with the World of Islam). Since 2000, notable groups have been Majelis Mujahidin—made up of former Darul Islam members—and Laskar Jihad, which emerged from the student milieux. Both opposed Indonesia's regime, and indeed the process of democracy, but eschewed armed action. However, the Majelis Mujahedin elected as its leader Abu Bakar Ba'asyir (Bashir), a Kommando Jihad veteran, who had been in exile in Malaysia. Ba'asyir had set up an international network in a number of countries in the region, including Malaysia and the Philippines as well as Indonesia. This began to be referred to as Jamaah Islamiyah and is presumed to have several thousand active members.

From 2001, when the focus was turned on Al-Qaida, regional security authorities began to regard Ba'asyir as the local Al-Qaida commander. When a nightclub was bombed on October 12, 2002, in the Indonesian island of Bali, where many Westerners holiday, Jamaah Islamiyah was the natural suspect. Two hundred and two people died, including 164 foreign nationals. Ba'asyir and two others were arrested. Ba'asyir was convicted of lesser charges and was finally released in June 2006. All those interviewed by the police have been either given short sentences or acquitted on technicalities. Another Jamaah Islamiyah activist known as Hambali has been taken into custody by the United States, which is thought to be reluctant to hand him over to the Indonesian authorities because of the light sentences

given to other suspects. It is unclear whether linking Southeast Asian organizations with Al-Qaida throws much light. It seems likely that there is sympathy for Al-Qaida's goals and emulation of its philosophy, but no operational link. However, there are persistent reports that there have been transfers of funds for Jamaah Islamiyah from Al-Qaida or Gulf sources. A hard core of activists will certainly have seen Al-Qaida in action in Afghanistan, though most Southeast Asian Mujahidin fought there against the Soviets and left before the second Afghan war between the Northern Alliance and the Taliban began.

Malaysia

The party that now serves as the Islamist opposition party in Malaysia, PAS (Parti Islam Se Malaysia) (Islamic Party of Malaysia), had its origins in an Islamic conference held in 1947. A leading figure was Dr. Burhanuddin al-Helmy. The conference established a permanent body known as MATA (Majlis Agana Tertinggi) (Supreme Religious Council). MATA was a comprehensive body that included conservative Muslims and those with radical tendencies. At its conference in 1948, differences began to emerge between UMNO (the United Malay National Organization) and the more radical elements. On March 17, 1948, the Hizbul Muslimin was formed, only to be banned by the British colonial authorities, who claimed it had links with the Malayan communist party. In due course, activists who had avoided the attentions of the authorities set up PAS.

Radical Islam took a new turn in Malaysia after independence in 1957. In 1969, a Muslim youth organization known as Angatan Belia Islam Malaysia (ABIM) was founded at the University of Malaya. Anwar Ibrahim, later to be deputy prime minister, became its leader in the mid-1970s. At this time, an active Da'wa movement began to emerge in student circles. This was a period of tension in Malaysia, with bloody race riots between Malays and Chinese. The Islamic opposition and the student Da'wa movement rattled the UNMO-led Barisan Nasional (National Coalition) government, which attempted to placate Islamist feelings by taking a more radical stand on Islamic issues. The government sponsored Da'wa groups and set up an Islamic University and also underwrote Muslim charitable ventures. In 1982, Anwar Ibrahim joined UNMO, and under his influence the administration moved further toward the support of radical causes. The influence of ABIM was evident in the direction the government was taking.

Dr. Mahathir Mohammed became prime minister in 1991 and attempted to halt the drift toward Islamization of policy. In 1994, he banned the sect known as Al-Arqam, a radical Muslim movement formed in 1967 by Ashaari Mohammed. Arqam had built up a substantial capital through trading activities and donations. Its stated aim was to re-Islamize the population and combat Western influence. It also began to influence neighboring countries, including Thailand, and the regional association of states, ASEAN, became concerned. Reports had begun to suggest that Ashaari's ultimate aim was the overthrow of regional governments and the establishment of an Islamic state. Finally, he was accused of heresy.

In 1998, Mahathir Mohammed acted against Anwar Ibrahim, his activist deputy prime minister. Anwar Ibrahim was dismissed, and bizarre charges were brought against him. In 1999, he was convicted of corruption and sentenced to six years imprisonment, and in 2000 he was convicted of sodomy. In 2004, an appeals court set aside the second conviction, and he was released. (In November 2006, Anwar Ibrahim declared that he intended to run for parliament once more in 2008, after the expiry of a

disqualification.) Meanwhile, during Anwar Ibrahim's troubles, PAS seemed to find new strength. It allied itself pragmatically with the Democratic Action Party, dominated by Malaysia's Chinese population, and with Keadilan, a new party formed by Anwar Ibrahim's wife, Wan Azizah. The resulting alliance is known as the Barisan Alternatif. However, in the 2004 election, PAS's parliamentary representation fell from twenty-seven seats to only seven. It has also narrowly retained control of only one provincial assembly, in Kelantan.

At the same time, there has been mounting evidence of illegal Islamist activity. The most serious group is Jamaah Islamiyah (JI), estimated to have thousands of active members across the region, where it seeks a pan-Islamic state in the territory of Indonesia, Malaysia, and the Philippines. The Bali bombing was its most spectacular success. Malaysia has declared it an illegal organization and a number of its members are in detention. Singapore has also acted against JI. A plot to bomb the U.S., British, and Israeli Embassies in Singapore was infiltrated and broken.

Kumpulan Mujahidin Malaysia is a small local group founded in 1995 by a group of individuals led by Zainon Ismail—a veteran of the struggle against the Soviets in Afghanistan in the 1980s. Its program is the overthrow of the government and the installation of an Islamic state. It has regional ambitions and would also like to topple the existing regimes in Indonesia and the Philippines. In its literature, it condemns the existing governments as tools of imperialism. It appears to have regional networks and apparently has links and shares members with JI. It is thought to be self-financing, on the basis of local criminal activities. It apparently has something of the order of hundred active members.

In June 2006, the Malaysian government announced that it had arrested twelve dissidents belonging to the Darul Islam organization who had been plotting to bomb targets in Malaysia. The twelve, who were detained in Sabah, were from a number of regional states—with four Indonesians and two Filipinos as well as twelve Malaysians. According to police sources, their role was to aid Indonesian militants to reach the southern Philippines, to undergo training, and obtain weapons. The Malaysian government has stepped up surveillance in the maritime regions among the three states.

Philippines

The Moro Islamic Liberation Front is a political and military movement that seeks the establishment of an Islamic state in the southern part of the Philippines, comprising broadly the island of Mindanao, together with the Sulu archipelago, Palawan, Basilan, and neighboring islands. The area has a deep-rooted Muslim presence, dating from as long ago as the thirteenth century. The MILF is a spin-off of the Moro National Liberation Front, set up in 1968. By mid-1972, violent conflict, on broadly religious lines, was widespread in Mindanao and the Sulu archipelago. In late 1976, the Organization of the Islamic Conference brokered peace talks between the MNLF and the authorities, which proved abortive.

Discontented with the MNLF's reluctance to embark on a full-scale campaign against the government, a faction of the MNLF under the leadership of Hashim Salamat began to operate separately and in 1981 renamed itself the Moro Islamic Liberation Front. Hashim Salamat, who had joined the struggle in 1972, was a graduate in Islamic sciences from Al-Azhar University in Egypt and a disciple of Sayyed Qutb. His power base lay particularly in Mindanao and the neighboring islands. He attempted to set up areas independent of the government, where Shari'a law and Islamic taxation were applied. Under Hashim Salamat,

the MILF took a radical line and dissociated itself from any move toward peace talks or agreements between the government and the guerrilla movements. Nevertheless, by 1997, the MILF was ready to accept a general cessation of hostilities with the government.

This agreement was broken by the government in 2000, when the government of Joseph Estrada launched a sweeping operation in the areas controlled by the MILF, in which many guerrilla fighters were killed. The result was the surrender of large parts of the rebel organization, and the reestablishment of government control in areas hitherto held by the rebels. Negotiations between the rebellious Muslims and the government began again under the auspices of Libya. Peace conferences were held in Kuala Lumpur and in the Libyan capital, Tripoli, and in 2001, an agreement was signed by the MILF and Philippine President Gloria Arroyo in the presence of Seif al-Islam, the son of the Libyan leader, Colonel Gaddafi. The resulting ceasefire lasted for some two years. In 2003, the MILF leader Hashim Salamat died. His successor was Al Haj Murad Ibrahim.

In late 2004, the MILF and the Philippine government announced that they intended to cooperate against more radical Muslim groups, including that led by Abu Sayyaf and the Jemaah Islamiyah (JI), both of which were seen as linked in some way to Al-Qaida. Discord, nevertheless, rumbled on, in an area in which no leader could claim to be in full control, and the MILF was obliged to reject accusations that it was sheltering JI fighters. A peacekeeping force was supplied by Malaysia, Brunei, and Libya. A further attempt to reach a definitive peace agreement in September 2006 ended in partial failure. Al Haj Murad Ibrahim put the blame for the breakdown on the government, suggesting that their aim was still to crush the Islamist movement and their participation in talks was insincere. The situation was further confused by government action against Abu Sayyaf and JI groups. In November 2006, talks were continuing. A decision by the government to drop charges against Al Haj Murad Ibrahim in connection with bombings in central Mandanoa in October 2006 was seen as improving the atmosphere for talks.

The Abu Sayyaf group is an armed Islamic movement, sympathetic to Al-Qaida, which operates in the southern part of the Philippines. A clandestine organization practicing jihad, it was set up in 1990 by Abdurajak Janjalani, a student of Islamic law who had studied in Saudi Arabia, Syria, and Libya and then fought in Afghanistan. Particularly well represented in the island of Basilan, it has directed its attacks not only at the Philippine security forces, but has also from time to time perpetrated indiscriminate massacres against the Christian population. On April 4, 1995, a large-scale armed operation was mounted by factions connected to the Abu Sayyaf organization in the region of Ipil, in the Mandanao archipelago, resulting in some fifty deaths. The organization has also repeatedly burned and pillaged churches.

The movement seeks international recognition and has on a number of occasions demanded the liberation of those convicted of the abortive attack on the World Trade Center in New York in 1993. In its pronouncements, it makes reference to geopolitical factors and appeals for jihad. It also appears to maintain contacts through intermediaries with Islamist organizations in various countries, such as Afghanistan, Pakistan, and Libya, which share its aspirations and objectives.

After the death of Abdurajak Janjalani, who was killed by police on December 18, 1998, there was factional conflict within the movement. A split developed between the supporters of Abdurajak's younger brother, Kadhafi Janjalani, who had experience of combat in Pakistan, and a faction based in Jolo led by Nadzmi Saadullah—known as Commander Global—who had studied criminology and was known for his ruthlessness. The younger Janjalani was able to keep control. In 2000–2001, a group claiming to be attached to the Abu Sayyaf organization carried out a number of kidnappings, of which the most high profile were of foreign tourists, as part of a plan to raise funds. Following large-scale operations bet the army, Abu Sayyaf cells were dismantled. However, its capacity to act remained significant. A number of Abu Sayyaf commanders were killed or captured in 2002 and 2003. A bomb attack on a Philippine army military base in February 2006 was seen by the Philippine military as the work of Abu Sayyaf. In September 2006, a Philippine army force launched an operation to flush out Abu Sayyaf fighters in Jolo.

Thailand

On January 4, 2004, Muslim militants launched an attack on a military facility in southern Thailand that was the signal for a campaign of violence, which has continued since. More than 1,800 people have lost their lives. The population of this part of southern Thailand is ethnically Malay and Muslim by religion. It was annexed by Thailand in 1902, having previously been the independent Sultanate of Pattani. After World War II, there were intermittent uprisings, inspired by the progress toward independence of the neighboring Muslim states of Indonesia and Malaya. Disturbances continued up to the 1980s under the auspices of Pattani United Liberation Organization (PULO), an Islamic movement. The government abandoned a policy of assimilating Muslims and attempted to conciliate Muslims by promoting local culture, as well as through cooperation with the government of Malaysia to improve security.

Radical groups of local Muslims, nevertheless, appeared to have adopted a policy of violence in pursuit of their political goal of autonomy or independence. The "Movement of Islamic Mujahidin of Pattani" was set up in 1995 by an Afghan veteran, Nasoree Saesang. Saesang made contact with other regional radical Islamist organizations, and his group affiliated itself to Rabibat ul-Mujahidin, formed by Jamaah Islamiyah to coordinate regional activity. The movement seemed to lose some of its impetus, but after the events of September 11, 2001, Muslim irredentism seemed to be reenergized. Some Thais were ready to see the reason for the renewed militancy in the unofficial system of Muslim education in the south of country, where Arabic was taught and a form of Salafi Islam was promoted. One of the leading Muslim educational establishments is Yala Islamic College, where the principal in 2004 was Dr. Ismail Lutfi, a Thai citizen who graduated from the Ibn Saud University in the Saudi capital, Riyadh. His student body learns Arabic and the Wahhabi version of Shari'a law.

By the close of 2004, the provinces of Pattani, Narathiwat, and Yala were racked by terrorist violence. Immediately before the tsunami of December 26, 2004, U.S. observers had begun to comment that the border areas with Malaysia were becoming a potential base for terrorist operations. The prime minister, Thaksin Shinawatra, declared martial law. Amid increasing confusion, the military pushed Thaksin aside in September 2006 and installed its own candidate, Surayud Chulanont. The military strongman behind the coup was Sonthi Boonyaratglin, himself a Muslim, and conciliatory tactics seemed once more to be the government's tactic of choice. On December 31, 2006, there were bomb explosions in the capital, Bangkok, for which the government initially refused to blame Muslim dissidents. However, in February 2007, a government spokesman in charge of the investigation said the Islamists appeared to be responsible.

Islamism in Spain

Islam has a long history in Spain. From 711 to 1512, waves of Arabized Berbers moved northward into Spain, establishing Muslim states and dynasties. These in due course disappeared, but left behind the rich heritage of the Andalusian civilization, which has exercised its influence over the foreign policy of Spain toward the Muslim world up to the present day. In the twenty-first century, Spain has a population of at least a million Muslims. The modern Muslim population started to arrive in significant numbers in the 1970s. Many were Moroccans who came to work in the tourism industry, and subsequent growth came when their families joined them. The state recognizes Islam, affording it a number of privileges including the teaching of Islam in schools and religious holidays. There have been some reports of tension toward Muslim immigrants. Spain was shaken in 2004 when terror attacks by suspected radical Islamists killed 191 people on commuter trains near the capital Madrid.

The existence of an Islamic community was officially recognized in Spain in 1989, with the establishment of FEERI (Spanish Federation of Islamic Religious Groups). This made an unsuccessful attempt to set itself up as an official spokesman for the Muslims and to give them legal representation. The Muslim community in Spain was not exempt from the inroads of Islamism. Of a hundred or so societies, only thirty-one were officially registered with the Ministry of Justice. The others formed part of the Islamist movement and were divided between adherence to Tabligh and the Muslim Brotherhood. In addition, in the 1970s, Morocco maintained control over its own citizens through its diplomatic representation. By the 1980s, and especially after the Gulf War, the Tablighis and the Muslim Brotherhood were challenging Morocco for its monopoly of control over those of Moroccan origin.

The Iberian Peninsula was a strategic location for Islamists from all quarters. In the early 1990s, Algerians were prominent, and by 1996 international Islamists had begun to appear. Spain became the favorite route for contraband, replacing the French city of Marseille, which had played this role for the Maghreb, and particularly for Algeria, up to 1993. The Spanish ports became the channel for what the mujahidin wanted to move in and out of Europe. The Islamists imposed their own tax on the import of counterfeit designer clothes, watches, and jewelry and spread this type of merchandise through Europe's population centers. The proximity of Gibraltar, where there were associations that acted as a cover for the Islamist organizations, was an added incentive for the Islamists to make use of Spain.

Both Saudi Islamists and the Saudi royal family participated in the general interest in Spain for the Islamists. King Fahd and his entourage regularly spent vacations in Spain, and financial aid was provided by the World Islamic League and the Saudi government in support of the main Islamic associations in Spain. These included the Islamic Commission, the Grand Mosque of Madrid, and the Abu Bakr Islamic Center. In 1991, Prince Salman Bin Abdelaziz inaugurated the European Muslim Cultural Center in Madrid, the largest such institution in Europe. This occupied a site 20,000 square meters in extent, which was made available by the municipality of Madrid for the symbolic price of one peseta and financed by King Fahd, who provided $13 million for its construction. This was carried out by the Muslim Association of Spain, which also owned Madrid's Tetuan Mosque.

On March 11, 2004, bombs were detonated on four commuter trains traveling to the Spanish capital of Madrid in the morning rush hour, killing 191 people and wounding more than 1,700. The result was a sharp change of political direction in Spain. The bombings took place just three days before a scheduled general election. José Maria Aznar, Spain's previous prime minister, lost the election, and his successor, José Luis Rodriguez Zapatero, took Spanish troops out of Iraq. An inquiry into the bombings, which reported in March 2006, concluded that the Islamic terrorists who planted the bombs acted independently. They were Moroccan, Tunisian, and Syrian immigrants to Spain, and though they appeared to have been inspired by Al-Qaida propaganda they had no direct link with any organization outside the country. Nonetheless, it is undoubtedly true that there are networks of individuals in the country, predominantly of Moroccan and Algerian origin, who are influenced by Islamist ideas and are willing to carry out attacks in order to further the aims of other Islamist groups in the Middle East and elsewhere. A key event appears to have been a video released by Osama bin Laden on October 18, 2003, in which he said that Spain should be a target for terror attacks, because it had sent troops to Iraq. The use of cell phones to detonate the bombs appears to have been learned from extremist sites on the Internet.

SUDAN

Sudan was technically an Anglo-Egyptian condominium, in practice administered by the British, until its independence in 1956. It first came under Egyptian rule in 1820. In 1885, an Islamist revolt led by a local religious leader, Muhammad ibn Abdullah, known as the Mahdi, overthrew the colonial regime. Britain reconquered Sudan in a two-year campaign in the 1890s, culminating in the battle of Omdurman in 1898. In 1899, the Anglo-Egyptian Sudan was established. Power in independent Sudan was contested by two factions, the descendants of the Mahdi, known as the Ansar, and a powerful tribal Islamic brotherhood called the Khatmiya. These identified themselves with two political parties, the Umma, representing the Ansar, and the Democratic Unionist Party (DUP) ("Al-Hizb al-Ittihadi al-Dimuqrati"), representing the Khatmiya. The two parties sat in the constituent assembly, which failed to develop a final form for Sudan's constitution. In 1958, a military coup was mounted by General Ibrahim Abboud. In 1964, Abboud stepped down and the political parties formed a coalition government under Mohammed Mahjoub.

In 1969, Colonel Jaafar Nimeiri took power in a second coup. At first, he was opposed to Islam in politics and the Muslim Brotherhood, led by the lawyer and academic Hassan Turabi, was dissolved. Nimeiri's main task was to attempt to quell the civil war that had plagued Sudan since its independence. Sudan, a vast African country, consists of an Islamic and Arabized north together with a Christian and animist south. In 1972, peace was restored under the terms of the Addis Ababa agreement. In 1970, the Mahdist Ansar attempted to defy Nimeiri's authority, but were unsuccessful, and Nimeiri also survived an attempted communist coup in 1971. In 1976, the Ansar attempted a further coup, but once again failed. This sparked a change of direction on the part of President Nimeiri. In 1977, Hassan Turabi became his adviser, and in 1983 Nimeiri introduced Shari'a law. Civil war broke out once more in southern Sudan, and the current principal opposition movement, the "Sudan People's Liberation Movement," was formed in 1983 by John Garang. Nimeiri was overthrown by a transitional military government in 1985, partly because of his introduction of

the Shari'a and partly due to the worsening situation in the south. The military government held elections in 1986, which returned the Ansar leader Sadeq al-Mahdi to power with ninety-nine seats in Parliament. The DUP took sixty-eight seats.

Hassan Turabi's organization, now known as the National Islamic Front, took third place in the 1986 elections with fifty-one seats, representing only a fifth of the seats in Parliament. However, on this basis, Turabi began to lay the groundwork for the installation of an Islamist state in Sudan. In 1989, General Omar Hassan al-Bashir took power in a coup, with Hassan Turabi as his right-hand man and adviser. Bashir reimposed Shari'a law in Sudan, banned political parties, and reorganized his administration to give a bigger role to the Islamists. In 1991, Turabi set up an international African association called the Popular Arab Islamic Conference (PAIC), intended to consolidate African opinion behind opposition to American policy in the world. Turabi was also instrumental in opening up Sudan to international Islamists, including Osama bin Laden, who made the country his base in the 1990s. In 1993, Bashir announced a return to civilian government with himself as president, and was elected with 75 percent of the votes in an election in 1996. Nonpartisan elections were also held in 1996 to a new Sudanese parliament. Turabi was elected as a member of Parliament and became speaker.

In 1999, President Bashir decided to reintroduce political parties to Sudan, and he and Hassan Turabi set up the National Congress Party. Bashir and Turabi soon quarreled, however, and Turabi urged the electorate not to reelect Bashir as president. Bashir won with 86 percent of the votes, and in 2000, Sudan ceased to host the PAIC. In February 2001, Turabi was arrested on charges of attempting to overthrow the government. Turabi was released in October 2003, rearrested in March 2004, and released again in

June 2005. Now in his seventies, he says he has no further interest in public office.

African Islamic Centre/African Islamic University

The African Islamic Center was established in Khartoum in 1967. It was initially funded by Saudi Arabia. At that time, the conflict between Egypt's President Nasser and the Arab conservative monarchies was in full swing, and the Gulf monarchies were anxious to contain Nasserism, which had explicitly defined Africa as one of its three "circles of influence." In 1969, President Nimeiri closed the center when he came to power, just as Gaddafi took power in Libya.

The center reopened in 1977, as the Nimeiri regime turned toward Islamism. Hassan al-Turabi was minister of Justice, and later brought in a legal system based on the Shari'a. In 1992, the center was refounded as the African Islamic University. It became the principal means for the regime of President Omar al-Bashir to disseminate its political message in Africa. Nigeria was a particular target of Sudan's Islamic propaganda.

Darfur

The conflict in Darfur is conventionally said to have begun in February 2003 when a local rebel group, the Darfur Liberation Front, attacked government targets, though there had been some earlier incidents. In April 2003, a rebel force inflicted serious damage on government installations and troops at Al-Fasher. The complaint of the rebels is that Darfur is neglected by the authorities. Oil prospecting had been taking place in Darfur, and local movements feared that the government in Khartoum had no intention of allowing local interests to share the profits. Studies undertaken in Darfur had doubled the estimate of Sudan's oil resources to half a billion barrels.

In response to the rebel actions, groups of marauders referred to as "Janjaweed" (Spirit Riders), drawn from nomadic Arabic-speaking tribes, attacked settled villagers from the Fur, Massaleet, and Zagawa tribes. Both tribesmen and villagers are Muslims, and the villagers speak Arabic as well as local languages. The inhabitants of Darfur have previously been regarded as Muslim northern Sudanese. The conflict has seen them redefined as "black" African. The Sudanese government claims it is not responsible for any armed attacks in Darfur. However, large numbers of the inhabitants have been displaced and NGOs estimate that hundreds of thousands have been killed. Sudanese Islamists have said that they would regard a United Nations intervention in Darfur as an assault on Islam.

Popular Arab Islamic Conference

In April 1991, less than two years after the coup d'état in Sudan known as the "Revolution of Salvation," Hassan al-Turabi, the leader of the National Islamic Front and the government's strong man, founded the "Popular Islamic Conference" in Khartoum. The invitees to the opening session included not only Islamists, but also Palestinians of all persuasions, including even the PFLP (Popular Front for the Liberation of Palestine) and the Democratic Front for the Liberation of Palestine, led respectively by two Christian figures, George Habash and Nayef Hawatmeh. The participants also included Egypt's Sheikh Qaradawi, as well as Abdellatif Arabiyat, the former speaker of the Jordanian parliament, and Abdel Majid Zandani, the former president of Yemen's Consultative Council.

This Islamic "International" served as a meeting place for the Shi'ite Iranian Islamic movement and its disciples and the Sunni Muslim Brotherhood, together with various radicals and intellectuals. It became Turabi's flaghsip, and he took the position of its secretary-general. Khartoum, henceforth, became an obligatory port of call for Islamists. What Turabi had in mind was to make Sudan the spearhead of an international Islamist project. In 1996, the conference changed its title to the Popular Arab Islamic Conference, but its star soon waned. Its leading activist, Ibrahim el-Senoussi, was exiled in February 1999 and the Sudanese government ceased to host its meetings in 2000. Turabi's imprisonment in 2001 effectively ended his influence.

SUNNI ISLAM

Sunni Islam is the mainstream Islam of the vast majority of the Muslim community. By 2007, there were at least 1.5 billion Muslims in the world, of whom almost 90 percent were Sunni Muslims. The only serious dissenters from Sunni Islam are the adherents of the Shi'a (the "Faction"), though Shi'ites—it must be stressed—share all the basic tenets of Islam with the Sunni faith. The original difference between the Shi'a and the Sunni majority was political. In the seventh century, the Shi'a were those who wanted Ali, the Prophet Muhammad's cousin and son-in-law to succeed him as leader of the community. The Sunni majority took a different view: that the consensus of the community should prevail on the issue of who would be the best leader. Over the years, the difference became doctrinal and cultural. In modern Iraq, the Sunni minority and the Shi'ite majority are locked in a conflict that has grown ever more bitter since the bombing of the great Shi'ite mosque at Samarra in February 2006. The two sides can recognize each other by their names, where they live, aspects of their behavior, and the symbols in their houses.

Sunni Muslims are so-called because of the Sunna, the "way" of the Prophet as reported in the Hadith, which together with the Quran is the basis of all Muslim faith. The Prophet Muhammad is the messenger of Islam, as it was to him that the Book was revealed. Islam means "submission" (i.e. to God) and a Muslim is one who has submitted himself. The Prophet Muhammad is said to be the "seal" of the prophets ("Khatam al-Nabiyyin")—there were not and will not be any further Prophets after him. Sunni Muslims accept the Shari'a law, derived from the Quran and the Sunna according to the tenets of one or other of the four great schools of Islamic law developed by the scholars. Their practice is defined by what are known as the five pillars of Islam. These are as follows:

1. The "Shahada": This is the profession of faith—that there is no God but God and Muhammad is his Prophet. Muslims believe that the sincere pronunciation of this formula allows a person to become a Muslim.
2. "Salat": These are the prayers that must be said by Muslims five times a day, beginning at dawn. Prayers should be said facing Mecca.
3. "Zakat": These are the alms that must be given according to Muslim law. In some Muslim countries, the money is raised as a tax. Other Muslims should give privately and without publicity.
4. "Sawm": This is the fast that takes place in the month of Ramadan. Adult Muslims should fast from dawn to dusk, and refrain at the same time from malign thoughts or behavior. The old and the ill are exempted. Those who are traveling are excused, but must fast later in compensation.
5. The "Hajj": This is the pilgrimage to Mecca that every Muslim should undertake at least once in his lifetime, if possible. During the five days of the Hajj, ritual actions must be undertaken, each at the right place and right time.

In addition to these formal requirements, there are many customs and usages. Friday prayer is held at the mosque, and those who can reach a mosque should do so. The end of Ramadan and the day of the sacrifice during the pilgrimage are observed as festivals. There are many ways in which the behavior of Sunni Muslims identifies them to each other.

An important way in which Sunni Islam differs from the Shi'ite faith (and from the way Christian confessions are in general structured) is its lack of hierarchy. As has often been said, there is no pope in Islam. Those who are regarded as learned and authoritative are so seen because of the respect of their peers and not because of their occupancy of any particular position. Naturally, to be the mufti (legal expert) or qadi (Judge) of a country or city is a key position to which the occupant has risen because of his ability and reputation. The pinnacle of authority in the Sunni Muslim world is often said to be Al-Azhar Mosque and University in Egypt. Muslims from India and Pakistan revere the authority of the seminary at Deoband or the Barelvi institutions. However, the authority of such positions is moral rather than hierarchical. These attitudes have transferred into the Muslim populations in European countries and elsewhere in the world, so that no one speaks with unchallenged authority for Islam in such countries as Britain or France, much to the distress of European authorities in search of a partner for dialogue on religious issues.

Within such a vast community and in the absence of hierarchical authority, it goes without saying that there is a great deal of local variation and coloration within Islam. Depending on the influences they have come under, Muslims adopt a spectrum of views on the relationship of Islam to the state and the role of the faith in political life. There are many organizations that have attracted the loyalty of Muslims such as the Muslim Brotherhood, founded in Egypt and now worldwide, that takes an activist and ascetic view of Sunni Islam. The Deobandi school attracts many adherents from India and Pakistan. As a total contrast, Barelvi practices, with music, festivals, and the veneration of holy men, are also influential. In Saudi Arabia, the Wahhabi school, flowing from the ideas of Muhammad ibn Abdelwahhab in the eighteenth century, though based on the Hanbali school of law, also claims that access may be gained through Ijtihad to the original ideas of Islam. The Salafism of Jihadist groups is a different phenomenon, claiming to reject all traditional Islamic lore except what can be derived directly from the Quran and the Sunna. The so-called Sufi orders are widespread and are not seen as incompatible with the Sunni faith. These are membership organizations of Muslims who follow rites laid down by their founders that promote the performance of mystic rituals devoted to the "Dhikr" (remembrance) of God. But for most Muslims, Islam is an everyday and almost prosaic matter of prayer, attendance, and the mosque and the presence of religious ideas in daily life. For any Muslim, Sunni or Shi'ite, God is ever present in speech and thought in a way that is almost never the case in the West.

SWEDEN

Sweden's Muslim population is at least 300,000, though precise figures are hard to obtain. This is 3 percent of the population of just over 9 million—the second highest percentage in Europe after France, though still numerically small in comparison to France's Muslim population of up to 6 million and Britain's 1.6 million. Sweden's Muslims are from diverse origins, including primarily Turkey and Bosnia. There are also Muslims from many other origins, including North Africa, Iraq, Iran, Lebanon, Syria, and other Middle Eastern countries. There is a growing contingent from Somalia. The number of Muslims in the country has increased sharply in recent years. In the late 1980s there were 100,000 Muslims, including many from Algeria and Morocco. By 1996, there were around 200,000. Though the largest numbers of asylum seekers arrived in the 1980s, there has also been a new surge in recent times. The annual number of asylum seekers doubled in 2006 to 40,000, of whom half were from Iraq. Sweden keeps a relatively open door to asylum seekers and is permissive regarding access to its liberal social benefits. It has therefore become a destination of choice for Muslims wishing to leave their countries of origin. In all, over a million Swedish residents are of foreign origin. Nationality is simple to acquire, after five years residence (four for an asylum seeker).

In Stockholm, the Muslim presence was acknowledged with the opening of a new mosque inaugurated in 2000 in a converted former electric power station. The controversial Egyptian cleric Yusuf al-Qaradawi and the exiled Tunisian Islamist leader Rashid al-Ghannouchi attended a conference at the mosque in July 2003. There are five official mosques in Sweden and there are said to be 150 small prayer centers. Though Swedish policy is to disperse asylum seekers throughout the country, most gravitate back to the major cities after an initial period. The Swedish population is undoubtedly becoming more concerned about the Muslim presence. Such issues as female genital mutilation, the wearing of Islamic dress, "Halal" slaughter, and religious education have become the subject of debate in Sweden as elsewhere in Europe. Some Swedes undoubtedly regard the Muslim presence as detrimental. The areas of Sweden's large cities where Muslims live are increasingly being seen as recruiting grounds for Islamist activists, for example the Malmö suburb of Rosengaard. Malmö, close to the Danish border, has the highest proportion of Mus-

lims of any city in Europe. While there is a mainstream mosque, which was attacked by arsonists in 2003, small groups of radicals have their own prayer gatherings in houses and other venues. In September 2005, a small group calling itself Ansar al-Sunnah in Sweden claimed on an Islamist Web site to have established a guerrilla training camp in Skane, a region of southern Sweden near Malmö, though no evidence of any such camp has been found. The Web site also threatened a Swedish Christian preacher who had criticized the personal life of the Prophet Muhammad.

Since 2000, state aid has been distributed to Muslim organizations on an equal basis with the Lutheran church, which has been disestablished from the state. There is complete religious freedom in Sweden. There are three national Muslim associations in Sweden that receive government support. The "Förenade Islamiska Församingar i Sverige" (FIFS) (United Islamic Communities in Sweden) was established in 1974 to provide an umbrella organization for smaller local Muslim groups. Groups falling under the FIFS include a Shi'ite association as well as Sunni organizations of various persuasions. The Sveriges Förenade Muslimska Församlingar (SMF) (Swedish United Muslim Communities) split off from the FIFS in 1982. This is primarily an Arab and Sunni organization. In 1990, as the result of another split, the Islamiska Kulturcenterunionen was formed (IKUS) (Islamic Culture Center Union), which is identified with the Kurds. The main groups cooperated in 1990 to form the Sveriges Muslimska Råd (SMR) (Swedish Muslim Council) whose remit was to promote relations with Swedish society. The SMR is ideologically aligned with the Muslim Brotherhood and is active in disseminating information about Islam, as well as setting up mosques and schools. Islamic schools in Sweden receive state support.

Since September 11, 2001, Sweden has controlled immigration by Muslims more closely and has adopted antiterrorist measures. Nonetheless, Sweden continues to monitor complaints carefully for evidence of discrimination against Muslims. Muslims maintain a relatively low profile in the media. Only two Muslim publications are distributed at the national level, Minaret and Salaam. A radio station in Stockholm, "Radio Islam," broadcasts locally. Among the Algerian refugee population, members of the GIA and the GSPC have found Sweden a convenient retreat. A GIA publication, Al-Ansar, has been printed in Sweden. The French authorities have been concerned that some activists wanted by French justice have found refuge in Sweden. In 1995, a suspected GIA leader in Europe, Abdelkarim Deneche, wanted for questioning in connection with the attacks of July 25 that year, was arrested in Stockholm, but was release on October 31.

TABLIGHI JAMAAT (SOCIETY FOR THE PROPAGATION OF ISLAM) (in Arabic: JAMAAT AL-TABLIGH)

Tablighi Jamaat, often simply called Tabligh, is a Sunni movement devoted to Da'wa (preaching), established in 1926 in India by Mawlana Mohammed Ilyas. Ilyas liked to call the movement Tahrik-i Iman ("The Faith Movement"). The motive of this initially unremarkable Islamic cleric, from the Deobandi school of Islam, was the defense of Islam, a minority religion in the part of colonial India, where his movement had its origin. His goal was to struggle against the influence of Hinduism, in the context of an India under British colonial rule, where Hindus were socially predominant. In its origins, it was a movement quite different from the conventional idea of Islamism, as the West conceives it. Tabligh aimed to inculcate piety into the hearts of Muslims. Mohammed Ilyas was himself a member of an Indian Islamic Brotherhood, or "Tariqa," namely, the Sabiriya branch of the Chishtiya order, and his ways of engendering piety were derived from the order's ideas. Initiates into Tabligh did not automatically join the Chishtiya, but membership was open to them if they so desired. Tabligh has spread throughout the world into more than a hundred countries where Muslims live and is still spreading. Tabligh claims that it is nonpolitical and does not preach to non-Muslims.

Its sole aim is to bring back Muslims into the fold of the proper practice of Islam.

At the end of the 1920s, the Indian subcontinent was under British rule, and Pakistan had not yet come into existence. Muslims were a minority in the country, among a Hindu majority. In these circumstances, the aim of Tabligh was to rid Islam of all popular and customary accretions, and especially of any Hindu ideas, making it easy to understand and simple to practice. This would be an Islam for ordinary people. On the basis of this premise, a number of straightforward concepts emerge from the teaching of Mohammed Ilyas and the principles of Tabligh. Essentially, Muslims must at all times follow the example of the Prophet Muhammad, because what better example can there be but he who has received the word of God. Every action, even the most trivial, should find its roots in the life, the practice, and the sayings of the Prophet. Mohammed Ilyas' strong adherence to this principle led him to lay down seven basic principles that should guide, direct, and control the lives of all Muslims. These were the profession of faith, prayer, remembrance of God, sincere intention, respect for Muslims, the donation of time, and abstinence from idle chatter.

1. From the profession of faith flows the submission of each Muslim to God, which is the literal meaning of the word "Islam." All that

happens in his life or in the world originate with the will of God. Without God's will, nothing can happen in a Muslim's life or in this world. A Muslim must therefore make himself heard by God, and for that reason it is his duty to pray.

2. Prayer is also one of the five pillars of Islam. The principle is that every Muslim must say his prayers five times each day. Conventionally, he may pray alone, at home, at work, or in any other place. In contrast, the Friday prayers must be said collectively at the mosque, to remind the Muslim that he belongs to his local community and to the Muslim community as a whole. Ilyas did not agree with this principle. In his view, all prayers should be collective where possible, because there is no salvation outside the Umma (the Muslim community). On this issue, Ilyas refers to the Prophet, who says, "A prayer said in the mosque is twenty-seven times better than one said alone." This consecration of the group is the key to Ilyas's thought. All his life, he never ceased to stress that Muslims should always be together, and he used to cite a "hadith" of the Prophet, saying, "A Muslim cannot be a good Muslim if he is alone."

3. In order to pray to God, a Muslim must know God, through the remembrance of God's name, his qualities, and his greatness, at every moment of his life. This is what Tabligh refers to as "Dhikr," literally "remembrance." Every Muslim should say three prayers in Arabic—the language of the Quran—each morning and each evening. Dhikr, however, is constant. Through coming to know God, one comes to love him. It is in the love of God that a Muslim's faith blossoms. This principle, obligatory for every adept of Tabligh, leads to the infiltration of Islam into every corner of everyday life.

4. The fourth principle, sincere intention, is intended to discriminate between the authenticity of the faith of the true believer, while drawing attention to the hypocrisy of certain "Ulema" and other Islamic clerics. Sincerity of intention conduces to solidarity within the group, because the faith and devotion of all are above suspicion.

5. The fifth principle—respect for fellow Muslims—is also intended to reinforce the solidarity of the community. It comes into its own in countries where Muslims, who are mainly of modest means, find themselves isolated within society. Thanks to Tabligh, Muslims can feel that they belong to a community whose members are supportive of one another. Each man feels respected and honored because of the Islamic faith he shares with the group and believes that as a Muslim he is close to God and enjoys his love. This principle is highly effective in mobilizing believers, who feel valued in diverse ways: social, economic, and personal, in the family and among the social circle. The believer is asked no more than to be a good Muslim, which will make him the equal of the wealthy, the cultured, and those who exercise power.

6. The sixth principle, the donation of time, is to set aside time to bring the message to others. In the view of Mohammed Ilyas, the master should not wait for his pupils to come to him. His duty is rather to seek out his future disciples. Tablighis take this injunction very seriously and travel together constantly. A Tablighi's duty is to travel with a small group of friends to another town or city in the country where he lives, or even to another country, to spread the word to lax Muslims and bring them back to the fold. Mosques sympathetic to the movement or Tablighi friends provide accommodation to those away from home. Such travels deepen their faith, teaching them to live together and to show a good example to prospective new recruits. Missionary expeditions from every country travel the world in groups of ten, or smaller groups if they are less far afield, to knock on the doors of Muslims who have fallen away from regular observance and to pray in the mosques and prayer rooms they find.

7. The final principle was abstention from worldly and useless talk. Tablighis are not meant to gossip but should talk of serious matters and of God. Ilyas made this the pillar of his movement. Those who were distracted from God were not able to do his work.

Tabligh is not violent but can be seen as centered on the Muslim community and opposed to interaction with non-Muslims. Its concept of Islam is that of a return to strict orthodoxy and to the Quran and the Hadith. In this respect, it is not far from Salafi ideas. However, strict Wahhabis have some reservations over its practices. Its essence is its missionary character and the simplicity and directness of its injunctions, which have seen it spread to the four corners of the planet. It organizes the daily life of the believer and takes upon itself the position of a moral arbiter in the community.

Tabligh is still very active in the Indian subcontinent. It holds an annual meeting, one of the world's largest religious gatherings, at Bhopal, India. In November 2006, more than half a million people came from almost sixty countries. Tabligh is also widespread in Western Europe, where there are Pakistani and Indian migrants. It is also strongly represented in North Africa, where it is known as Jamaat al-Tabligh, as well as in Saudi Arabia, despite the theological misgivings of the Saudi establishment. It is also present in the countries of Africa's eastern coast. It has, in addition, spread to Southeast Asia and to migrant communities in Australia, Canada, and the United States. It holds an annual meeting, for example, at Al-Falah Mosque in Corona in the New York Borough of Queens, which is normally attended by around two hundred people. In Britain, Tabligh currently plans to build a huge mosque adjacent to the site of the 2012 Olympic Games, at an estimated cost of $600 million. The movement's accounts at the British government agency that monitors

charities show that Tablighi Jamaat's charitable arm, Anjuman-e Islahul Muslimeen, receives donations of as much as a billion dollars a year. However, questions have been raised about how the new London mosque is to be funded. Some conjecture is that Saudi Arabia must inevitably be involved through the agency of World Muslim League.

Tablighi Jamaat and Violence

Tabligh has never been linked to violent actions or political initiatives. However, it has served as an entry point by which young people become involved in active Jihad and may join more radical movements. Tabligh attracts many who wish to deepen and strengthen their relationship with the Muslim faith, and although the vast majority of these are interested only in religion, a few may be drawn to violent movements. Certainly, many of the young European Islamists who have attracted the attention of the media or the courts have had a connection with Tabligh. Some may have been sent to Pakistan at Tabligh's expense for courses in Quran studies or other forms of training, whereas others may have gone to Pakistan at their own initiative to attend madrasas. This may have brought them into contact with the men of violence.

A few such students move on to Peshawar, on the Afghan frontier, where they may attend training camps in the hills surrounding the town. Their passports are in general taken away by their new friends, and with a new *nom de guerre,* they effectively become different individuals. (The sequestered passports were seldom returned, and European consulates in Islamabad registered in the 1990s a sharp increase in reports from their nationals of stolen passports.) The individuals themselves seem to have been pressed into service for occasional operations, where it was prudent to use young militants whose identities are not known. Afterward, most are sent back to Europe. A stay in Peshawar undoubtedly confers a patina of religious prestige on young Tablighis. Once in their home countries, young Tablighis may well be approached and possibly recruited by some radical Islamic group.

French intelligence services have concluded that Tabligh is in some sense the "gateway" to Al-Qaida and like-minded movements, and this view seems to be shared by the United States. It is undeniable that violent Islamists have passed through Tabligh and Tabligh-oriented mosques. They are centers for Islamic enthusiasm and inevitably attract young men interested in religion, whether peaceful or violent. But Tabligh does not itself promote terrorism, and it should be remembered that the vast majority of Tablighis are interested only in the dissemination of the faith.

TAJIKISTAN

Islamic Renaissance Party

The Islamic Renaissance Party (IRP) in Tajikistan was a highly structured and disciplined political organization that had some ten thousand members at the time of the civil war that began in 1992, in which it was defeated a year later in 1993. Its supporters put the figure of its adherents considerably higher. It was established in 1991 as a branch of the Soviet IRP. But it broke away because of excessive tendency of the Moscow movements to identify themselves with Turkic nationalism, which was anathema to the Persian-speaking Tajiks. The IRP's objective was to bring about a renaissance of Islam that—in its view—represented Tajikistan's way back to prosperity. They did not call for the departure of the Russians or for ethnic homogeneity in Tajikistan. For the IRP, Islam was a way to transcend regionalism and the emphasis on ethnic communi-

ties. The IRP was frequently misrepresented in the official Russian and Tajik media. It was presented as an extremist movement that threatened the security of Central Asia as a whole. In 1992, the media declared that training camps for Tajik Islamists had been set up in Afghanistan, in the areas of Kunduz and Shirkan. During the civil war, the Russian frontier force often reiterated that the Tajiks were armed and trained by the Afghans.

Three of IRP's leading figures were in particular accused by the Russians of being fundamentalist extremists. The first of these was Said Abdullah Nuri, an Islamic cleric. Another was Mohammed Sharif Himatzoda, the IRP's former president. The third was Akbar Turajunzade, an Islamic judge or "Qadi," who had never in fact been a party member. None of these in fact are in favor of the establishment of an Islamic Republic, which they rejected because the necessary social basis on which it could be constructed did not exist. Mohammed Sharif Himatodza said that "Islamic democracy is the highest form of democracy" but would only press ahead toward an Islamic state if this was what the people chose:

> We hope—as all Muslims dream—that Islam will achieve recognition as the religion of the state, and that we shall live in accordance with the laws of Islam. However, the people have to be ready. An Islamic state can only be created in a peaceful way.

The same language was heard throughout the IRP. For example, a deputy leader, Said Ibrahim, said that the IRP's goal should be a "popular and democratic state where political liberty and freedom of religion would be respected." Qadi Turajunzade stressed in all his public statements that at least twenty-five years would be needed for the construction of an Islamic Republic. In September 1991, when he was urged to stand in the presidential election, he justified his refusal by saying that "the clergy has no place in politics."

Geopolitics played a part in limiting the activities of a movement such as the IRP, which had national pretensions. In a mountainous country such as Tajikistan, the ties between different regions are not strong. As a result, regional cultures flourished. Each province developed its own loyalties, which hindered the establishment of a central authority and has been a barrier to national domination by the IRP. However, the IRP's reluctance to press for an Islamic Republic did not mean it had abandoned its values. Its predominance in certain areas led to limitations on freedom of expression, in the Western sense. In the words of Mohammed Himatzoda in 1991:

> The publication of articles that are critical of Islam, depraved, or not conducive to good morals cannot be permitted in the name of press freedom. For example, the book by the author Salman Rushdie cannot be tolerated. However, we respect other religions and we do not insist that our women should cover their heads.

The conflict in Tajikistan in 1992–1993, which ostensibly took the form of a struggle between communists and Islamists, in fact set the various Persian-speaking Muslim tribes of Tajik identity in opposition to each other and was more complex than it seemed. The fierce independence of each tribe was the result of a deep-rooted regional consciousness that had persisted in the absence of a fully developed national identity. The IRP was in a minority in the regions of Leninabad and Kouliab. It was seen not so much as a religious party, but as a group that instrumentalized religion to strengthen its domination in its stronghold of Gharm. Its principal antagonists were for the most part not atheist communists but other Muslims who—though sometimes profoundly religious—were prepared to fight to preserve

their position in the existing state. For example, at the wake held for the anti-Islamist fighter Faisali Salidov, second to none in his fierce hostility to the IRP, there was a fervently religious atmosphere among the mourners, wearing battle dress while reciting Quranic passages and prayers. The pro-communists, when they destroyed villages in Gharm, generally spared the mosque, unless the Mullah had been particularly active in the opposition.

Typical of the religious figures who militated against the IRP was Mullah Khaidar Sharifzade. The head of the local religious establishment in Kouliab, he did not accept the IRP's claim to hegemony, and in June 1992, he repudiated the authority of Qadi Akbar Turajunzade, whom he regarded as the ideological chief of the Islamists. Sharifzade was attacked by the IRP as the inspiration of Sangak Safarov's "Popular Front," a tough militia that backed the communist regime and was ultimately responsible for the IRP's downfall. Sharifzade was from a new generation of Mullahs that had emerged in the 1970s, who had found favor with the Soviet authorities, even though their approach and their ideas about Islam seemed radical to the ordinary people. For their part, the Soviets aimed to back an Islamic elite that would be acceptable in the eyes of other Islamic countries. Sharifzade had imposed strict Islamic rules in Kouliab, including obligatory prayers, and respect for the whole range of Islamic practices. He underlined his religiosity by beginning every utterance with the formula "Bismillah ar-Rahman ar-Rahim" ("In the name of God the merciful and the compassionate").

Meanwhile, on the other side, among the IRP supporters who eventually fled to Afghanistan, there were former Communist Party and KGB officials who had helped to run armed self-defense groups for the IRP. As may be seen, to suppose that the battle lines were drawn between communists supporting Safarov and Islamists backing the IRP was too simplistic. For instance, the Upper Badakhchan region, which backed the opposition, was opposed to any kind of Islamic state because of the minority Ismaili faith of the majority of its inhabitants. Even the inhabitants of Gharm, although giving their political support to the IRP as the only credible opposition force, did not for the most part want to see the establishment of an Islamic Republic.

In the spring of 1993, after the Islamist opposition had fled into Afghanistan, its members set up a government in exile on the basis of a new Islamic movement established as the successor to the IRP. It also attracted members from among former adherents of the Tajik Democratic Party and the democratic Rastakhez movement. Qadi Turajunzade refused to lead the new movement; hence, Said Abdullah Nuri became the president of the government in exile and the supreme commander of its armed forces, with a political program that still eschewed the formation of an Islamic Republic. Three administrative structures were formed: a Jihad committee, a supreme council, and an executive committee. With a radio station of their own, known as the "Tajik Voice," the Islamists succeeded in setting up an effective military force, with help from the Islamic countries, on the basis of recruitment from the Tajik refugee camps in Afghanistan. The Russians were obliged to accept that the Tajik regime in Dushanbe could not survive without their acquiescence.

The Tajiks of Afghanistan in fact helped create a powerfully armed and well-trained opposition movement. Iran took the stance of a regional power interested in stability and played only a marginal role, opting to be the honest broker recognized by all the Tajik parties, including the communists. Teheran studiously took a line that followed the Russian position and avoided direct involvement. Iran was in fact one of the first countries to give recognition to the post–civil war neocommunist government in Dushanbe. It was obliged to show solidarity with the Islamists, while other Islamic states were doing so, but kept this in practice to a minimum.

From 1996, inside Afghanistan, the IRP was faced by a choice, as the Taliban attacked Kabul and gained control of the Kunduz enclave. The IRP was obliged either to back the Taliban, thus opting for the principle of international Islamic militancy, or to keep faith with Tajik national identity, represented by Commander Massoud, who wanted to see a stable Tajikistan. The IRP chose the latter option, of Tajik nationalism at the expense of Islamic solidarity. In June 1997, the Tajik IRP signed an agreement in Moscow with the neocommunist administration to come into a coalition government in Tajikistan more inclined toward nationalism than Islamism. It set aside any residual ambition to create an Islamic state and forged international ties on the basis of interest rather than ideology. Under the banner of the Unified Tajik Opposition, the IRP allied itself with the democratic Rastakhez movement and the Ismaili minority from Pamir, both of them secular movements.

In October 1997, the Taliban reacted by intercepting an aircraft taking Said Abdullah Nuri from Teheran to Dushanbe. They attempted to persuade Nuri to resume the Jihad, but Nuri rejected their approach. The militants of the Unified Tajik Opposition returned to Tajikistan, where they continued to uphold the principle of Tajik national identity. This went in tandem with the developments in Dushanbe, where from 1995 the government found itself up against a revolt initiated by the Uzbek commanders, initiated by Mahmoud Khadaberdaiev and discreetly backed by Tashkent. Once again, ethnic ties proved more powerful than ideological solidarity.

Some of the IRP commanders, based in the Upper Gharm Valley, carried on the armed struggle for a while and gave shelter to the Uzbek militants. However, their support for the Uzbek Islamists soon ended. With the new closer links between the Tajik IRP and the Tajik government, with Mullah Nuri as vice president and another leading member as a minister, it gradually dissociated itself from the activities of local armed commanders. Some of these then relapsed to the status of small-scale local chieftains, whereas others, like Rahman "Gitler" Muakkal, were wiped out.

TAKFIR WA-L-HIJRA (EGYPT)

Takfir wa-l-Hijra was founded in the early 1970s. Its leader was Shukri Ahmed Mustafa, an agricultural engineer in his thirties, who had been a member of the Muslim Brotherhood. It based itself on the ideas of Sayyed Qutb and advocated a break with modern society and all its values. In his pamphlet "Al Khilafa," Shukri Ahmed Mustafa stressed the apostasy of Muslim society in Egypt, which had in his view lapsed from its principles. He conceived of Takfir as the elite community ("Al-Firqa al-Najiya"), whose members were blessed with knowledge of the true state of affairs and whose Jihad was destined to take them to Paradise. To that end, the Takfir had twin objectives—to distance itself from a sinful world and to replace it with a pure ("Salafi") society, based on the true precepts of Islam. Takfiris practiced an austere way of life and rejected all interpretation of the foundations of the religion that might distance them from the pure faith. Its members refused to seek employment from the state, to perform military service, or to attend state schools. Their rejection of society also meant that they refused to pray in the public mosques. As an organization, they preserve their confidentiality by organizing themselves in a classic revolutionary manner, with cells of six or seven militants led by an "Emir."

Following the path trodden by Islamic Jihad and Gamaa Islamiya, the Takfiris soon sought to put their doctrine of the rejection of society into practice. In July 1977, they kidnapped and then killed the former minister of religious affairs in Egypt, Sheikh Mohammed Hussein al-Dahabi. This provoked proportionally severe action against the movement, and in March 1978, Shukri Ahmed Mustafa was sentenced to death and hanged, together with four associates. The decease of Shukri Ahmed Mustafa, however, did not halt the movement. There are suggestions that former Takfiris may have been involved in the assassination of Egypt's President Anwar Sadat on October 6, 1981. Takfir in Egypt inspired numerous imitative groups across the Middle East as well as in North Africa and Europe. Following the Afghan Jihad and the growth of Islamist radicalism in the 1980s and 1990s, Takfir became the most radical and bloodthirsty group in Algeria and Lebanon as well as in Central Asia and France. In recent times, the organization has apparently been less active in Egypt, but there is every indication that its underground groups still exist.

TALIBAN

The Taliban—literally "Students of Religion"—was a movement originally formed of former students of the Deobandi "madrasas" on one side or the other of the frontier between Afghanistan and Pakistan. They formed themselves into a political and religious movement that burst on the Afghan scene in 1994. Students who completed their courses in Pakistan returned to Afghanistan to set up their own schools, where the same syllabus was followed. The Taliban recruited mainly among the poorer peasants from Pushtun tribal society in southern Afghanistan, between Kandahar and Ghazni. However, the effect of the war with the Soviets was that after young men became caught up in the Jihad, they never completed their studies. Though they were too inexperienced and not sufficiently qualified to become Islamic clerics, they nevertheless continued to call themselves "students," or Taliban.

The links of patronage between the Pakistani and Afghan madrasas served as channels for financial aid that came from Pakistan and the Arab countries. This established a connection between the Taliban and international fundamentalist circles, and especially the Saudi Wahhabis, who both funded students and sent religious teachers. Saudi influence gradually spread over the teaching itself, which gradually became more "Wahhabized." During the war with the Soviets, the Taliban did not set up their own separate organization, instead joining other groups, especially Harakat-i Inqilab, led by Nabi Mohammed, and Younes Khales's Hizb-i Islami. However, local groups forming within the madrasas were already known as the "Taliban Front." It was in 1994, at the instigation of Mullah Omar, that the Taliban established their own political and military movement. The importance they achieved was the result of three factors. First, the stage was set by the state of anarchy that prevailed in Afghanistan after the fall of the communist regime. Second, the Pakistanis were looking for a new instrument to further their political aims in Afghanistan. Third, the Pushtun tribesmen were furious over their exclusion from the new government in Kabul.

The Taliban took Kabul from the Tajik commander Massoud in 1996, with the support of the Pakistanis. Although at first the Taliban had an understanding with the United States, their leader Mullah Omar gradually took them down a more radical path. They refused to hand over Osama Bin Laden to the Americans, either after the anti-American attacks of August 1998 or after the attack on the World Trade Center on September 11, 2001. In February 2001, they defied international opinion by destroying the Buddha statues of Bamyan, and in August 2001, they detained some Christian missionaries. Within the country, all cultural activities unrelated to the practice of religion were banned, and women were forbidden to work or go to school.

Historically, theological students such as these had always been attached to the network of religious schools of the Deobandi persuasion that first came into existence in the later nineteenth century in the northeastern territory of the British-ruled Indian Empire. On their return from Pakistan, Afghan students from these schools set up their own madrasas, both in the rural areas of the Pushtun tribal zone in the south of the country and in the region of Badakhshan in the north. An international network thus came into being, based especially on the linguistic affinities of Pushtu speakers. The Taliban recruited in the tribal areas but transcended the traditional tribal divisions. This cross-tribalism was given a boost by the process of emigration. Young Pushtuns who went to Pakistan joined "mother" madrasas, where they were fed and lodged, while the Mujahidin came for periods of rest between battles. In Afghanistan, interpretation of scriptural texts replaced all other cultural activities, and the Persian language fell into disuse in favor of Pushtu.

Until 1991, the Pakistanis had utilized Gulbuddin Hekmatyar's Hizb-i Islami—a Pushtun and Islamist organization—as their agent in Afghanistan. This was accepted by both the Americans and the Saudis. In 1990, however, Hekmatyar ruled himself out of further cooperation when he expressed his support for Saddam Hussein at the time of the Gulf War. In 1992, Massoud took possession of Kabul but, as the country fell into anarchy, was unable to establish a stable regime. In 1994, a new situation emerged when the Pakistan People's Party of Benazir Bhutto won the elections of 1993 and began to look for a new partner in Afghanistan, with the proviso that it should be Pushtun and fundamentalist. In August 1994, a young Talib from the region of Kandahar, Mullah Omar, brought in the Shari'a law in regions under his control, reined in the warlords, and reopened the main roads to traffic. This immediately won him the support of the truck drivers, a key group. The Jami'at Ulema Pakistan proposed him to the Pakistani Interior Minister, General Babar, who at once gave his backing and advised the Americans to do likewise. Mullah Omar soon took delivery of a major arms shipment from the Pakistani armed forces. In the process, the Taliban became an effective political and military movement, operating independently both of the Mujahidin parties and of Pakistan.

The Taliban movement was therefore based on two principles. First, it presented itself as a religion-based and puritanical movement that was fundamentalist and rigorous but with no political motive other than the installation of the Shari'a—"the Shari'a, the entire Shari'a, and nothing but the Shari'a." The Taliban's creed derived both from the ideas of Wahhabism, imported from Saudi Arabia, and from the Sunni school of Deoband. In addition, they preached the principle of the restoration of the Caliphate, as in the early days of Islam, with the Shari'a as the basis of all social relations, internal and external. In practice, they were also as observant of the Pushtun tribal law, which separated girls from boys at the age of seven. Any glimpse of the flesh or hair of a woman was regarded as a devilish incitement. To obviate the prevalence of sin, women were confined to their houses and beaten, when necessary, to ensure their morality, and when they left the house—which should be as little as possible—they were obliged to cover themselves from head to foot. In addition, all the prohibitions and requirements characteristic of fundamentalism were applied, including the compulsion to wear beards and go regularly to the mosque and a ban on music and other forms of entertainment. Art was entirely alien to the Taliban scheme, and all its manifestations were eradicated. In 1998, the Taliban burned the 55,000 books from the Pol-i Khomsi library, some of which dated back to the Middle Ages. The destruction of the giant Buddha statues at Bamyan at the end of 2000 gave the appearance of a deliberate challenge to the international community but was fully consistent with the religious motivation of the Taliban. The extremism of the Taliban Mullahs met with the disapproval of both the Sunni Sheikhs of Al-Azhar in Cairo and the Shi'ite theologians of Qom.

The second principle, based on the Taliban's tribal origins, was that of Pushtun nationalism, whose goal was the reconstruction of the Afghan state as it had formerly been, as the traditional fief of the Pushtuns that had been "stolen" from them in 1992 by the Northern Alliance led by Massoud. The Shari'a was a state-building tool, as it allowed the bridging over of tribal divisions and even—though to a lesser extent—ethnic splits, hence the considerable efforts on the part of the Taliban to obtain international recognition, although they were aware that they were failing in this respect.

Neither of these two principles in itself put the Taliban into opposition with the Western world. In addition, the initial response of the Americans, the agencies of the United Nations, and nongovernmental organizations (NGOs) was to recognize the Taliban, in the hope of bringing them round to a more flexible attitude, especially over women's rights. After September 11, 2001, however, everything changed. Mullah Omar's support for Osama Bin Laden resulted in the reversal of the policy of recognition of the Taliban and, soon, in their anathematization by the West.

TANZANIA

The rise of Islamist movements in the Horn of Africa has had its repercussions on this traditionally peaceable country of 38 million people, of whom around 14 million are Muslims. Tanzania consists of the former mainland country of Tanganyika, a German colony before World War I, and the former Sultanate of Zanzibar. In particular, the million or so Muslims who make up the population of the almost wholly Muslim island of Zanzibar have flirted with Islamist extremist movements. Zanzibar has partial autonomy from mainland Tanzania, and Arabic has been declared one of its official languages. Muslims came in numbers to the Indian Ocean area of Tanzania in the fourteenth century, though there are some signs of earlier Muslim civilization. Most of Tanzania's Muslims are Sunni, but there is also a community of Shi'ites of Asian descent. Among these are both mainstream "twelver" Shi'ites ("Ithna Asheri") and Ismailis. During the pre–World War I German colonial era, Islam expanded into the interior of the country because of the presence of Muslims in the armed forces and the German administration. Other Muslims were opposed to the German occupation. In particular, the Islamic Brotherhoods, especially the Qadiriya and the Shadhiliya, were opposed to the colonial regime and provided the backbone of the 1905 rising against the Germans.

It has been estimated that 80 percent of Tanzania's Muslims are affiliated to an Islamic Brotherhood. The strength of the Qadiriya Brotherhood is attributed to the influence of a Somali Sheikh, Uways bin Muhammad, known as Shehu Awesu, who came to Zanzibar at the invitation of the Sultan in the 1880s. Knowledge of Arabic, however, is limited in Tanzania, and many practices and rituals have taken on a local tinge. The Shadhiliya spread to Tanzania from the Comoros Islands. Under the British colonial system that followed the defeat of the Germans in World War I, Christians tended to play the dominant role. However, in the 1950s, Da'wa movements from India and Pakistan began to visit Tanzania, and Tablighi Jamaat played its customary part. In 1954, the Tanganyika African National Union was founded to promote independence, and Muslims took a significant role within it. Only the Shi'ite Muslims remained aloof from Tanzania's independence movement. In 1945, the Agha Khan had founded a separate organization, the East African Muslim Welfare Society (EAMWS), which was led by Shi'ites but attempted to attract a broader membership.

The mainstream national Muslim organization known as BAKWATA ("Baraza Kuu la Waislam wa Tanzania") ("Tanzania Muslim Council") was set up in 1968 after EAMWS and other Muslim organizations were dissolved by official decree. It was closely connected with the Tanzanian government. In 1987, BAKWATA called for the reinstatement of Shari'a courts such as had existed in precolonial times in Tanzania. Arab countries including Saudi Arabia have financed the building of schools, mosques, clinics, and pharmacies. Islamic schools have also been established. The World Council of Mosques, an organization based in Jeddah, has opened an office in Tanzania. The Iranian Islamic Republic has also offered aid. When Zanzibar took the step of joining the Organization of the Islamic Conference, secular leaders in Tanzania argued that this was a breach of the country's constitution.

Other Muslim organizations have also made their appearance. BALUKTA ("Baraza la Uendelazaji Koran Tanzania") ("Tanzania

Quranic Council") was founded in 1987 for religious and educational purposes. In 1993, however, members of BALUKTA attacked shops selling pork products in the capital, Dodoma, with the result that the organization was shut down by the government. An educational association, the Dares-Salaam University Muslim Trusteeship, has attempted to promote increased participation by Muslims in higher education and government. Another organization, "Baraza Kuu la Jumuia Taasis za Kiislam" ("The Supreme Council of Islamic Organizations"), made an attempt to take over the leadership role from BAKWATA. However, it was in 1998 that the Tanzanian Islamists really began to attract attention. It has been established that the attack on August 7, 1998, against the American embassy in Tanzania, carried out by militants linked to Al-Qaida, benefited from local logistical support. Two small Islamist groups known as Al-Mahdi and Ansar al-Sunna appeared to be involved. These had already been implicated in a number of anti-Christian actions.

In 2001, legislation was passed that gave the government control over the Muslim community, with an officially recognized Mufti who, in theory, controls Muslim affairs. Muslim associations are obliged to register with the interior ministry, and the Mufti may approve or reject the request. Zanzibar has its own separate Mufti. The Mosques in Tanzania are administered by BAKWATA. BAKWATA also chooses the Mufti, who is technically not a government servant. In 2005, there were demands from some part of the Muslim community for the resignation of the Mufti as he was not genuinely independent of the government. On another issue, some Muslim groups have spoken out against the antiterrorism legislation passed by the Tanzanian government in 2002 in the wake of September 11, 2001. They claim that the powers of search and arrest conferred by the act are disproportionately used against Muslims. In 2004, an umbrella group known as Uamsho (Revival), claiming to represent Islamist organizations, held demonstrations both on the mainland and in Zanzibar. Arrests were made after a number of small bomb explosions intended to unsettle the authorities.

Some Tanzanian students now go abroad to study Islam, and there have been instances of attempts by radicalized groups to take over mosques. There are two societies in Zanzibar, "Imam Majlis" ("Society of Imams") and "Da'awa Islamiya" ("Islamic Preaching"), that challenge the more conservative existing Islamic leadership. More students from all parts of Tanzania are studying in Saudi Arabia. However, there is little evidence of extreme militancy, and an Islamist campaign against Western targets or the existing authorities seems unlikely. In April 2007, BAKWATA's deputy leader, Sheikh Abubakar Zubeir, spoke out against a political plan for Tanzania to join other East African countries in an East African federation and also announced the construction of a new national mosque in Dar es-Salaam.

TUNISIA

Since the mid-1990s, Tunisia has relied mainly on a security policy based on tough and effective suppression to maintain its control over the Islamist movement. The Islamic faction in the country came into existence partially as a reaction to the uncompromisingly secular policies adopted by President Bourguiba and drew some of its impetus from the failure of Bourguiba's socialist economic experiment. It has always been dominated by a single organization, inspired by the ideas of the Muslim Brotherhood, that has adopted different titles according to the political circumstances. This movement originated as "Islamic Action," then became the "Movement of the Islamic Tendency" ["Mouvement de la Tendance Islamique" (MTI)], and finally "Ennahda."

From its first inception, this movement accepted the principle of political pluralism and chose the route of legal activity, but in its quest for recognition by the authorities, it met with repeated refusals. Bourguiba's regime regularly swept up and arrested its members, holding mass trials. The regime of President Ben Ali has followed the same policy. At the same time, a number of small radical groups (including Jihad, the Party of Islamic Liberation, and the Tunisian Islamic Front) attempted to bring into being a popular uprising that stubbornly refused to materialize. From time to time, the authorities seemed briefly to adopt a more flexible policy, embarking on dialogue and offering limited concessions to some Islamist figures. Such moves toward compromise were made at least partly at the initiative of Prime Minister Mohammed Mzali, who held office under President Bourguiba from 1980 to 1986 and was able to exercise a limited influence on policy. After Bourguiba was deposed by President Zine el-Abdine Ben Ali, in the context of an atmosphere that was at first apparently more liberal, policies were at first adopted that gave some reason to expect a complete restructuring of politics in Tunisia. The operation of the Tunisian students' union ["Union Générale Tunisienne des Etudiants" (UGTE)], considered to have connections with the MTI, was legalized. More significantly, in 1989, representatives of the Islamist movement were permitted to stand as independent candidates in the parliamentary elections, and for several months in 1990, restrictions were lifted on the publication of Ennahda's publication El Fajr ("The Dawn").

From the end of 1990, however, the Ben Ali regime reverted to a policy of repression, whose apparent aim was to destroy all the Islamist organizations. In May 1991 alone, more than three hundred activists accused of membership of Ennahda were arrested and accused of terrorist conspiracy. The UGTE was officially banned, and the security services interrogated several hundred students. Many supporters of the Islamist cause fled to Libya or Algeria to evade police pursuit. Mass trials were mounted, and all those linked to those arrested were carefully investigated. From this point on, the regime's policy continued unchanged. This was not enough, however, to prevent Islamist groups from launching a number of attacks on Jewish synagogues in Tunisia in March and April 2002. Two bombs in Sfax and the Tunis suburb of La Marsa caused no damage, but on April 11, 2002, an attack on the historic synagogue at El-Ghriba on the southern island of Djerba left twenty-one people dead, including seventeen tourists. An Islamist organization was identified as culpable by the authorities, and a self-styled Al-Qaida spokesman claimed responsibility. President Ben Ali dismissed several of his security officials. The incident supported the theory that dormant Islamist networks continued to exist.

As Ennahda continued its efforts to unify the opposition in exile through sustained contacts with Islamist personalities in exile in Europe, the Djerba incident threatened to reawaken internal tensions between those who wanted to take the route of activity within the law and those who sought a violent confrontation with the regime. New Jihadist movements regularly cropped up, such as the Tunisian Islamic Front, based on organizations set up in European countries. The Tunisian intelligence services were aware of this tendency and established closer contacts with their European counterparts. Meanwhile, Tunisian militants began to become involved with various international groups, such as the overseas wing of the Algerian GSPC, whose objective was to target American interests around the world.

Many Islamists were still held in Tunisian prisons. In 2003, according to some estimates, there were still as many as a thousand in detention, though others set the figure lower. On March 23, 2003, an imprisoned Islamic militant, Abdelouahab Boussa, died after a hunger strike lasting four months. Human rights lawyers say that known Islamists are systematically harassed, and even those who pray too often are sometimes questioned. In June 2005, six young men were imprisoned for long terms for alleged terrorist activity. In February 2006, however, seventy imprisoned members of Ennahda were released as part of a broader amnesty. Meanwhile, the government continued to attempt to exclude Islamist influences. Ennahda's Web pages were prohibited in Tunisia, and access to them became impossible. In September 2006, as the educational year began, the government of President Zine el-Abdine Ben Ali resuscitated a law, brought in initially by President Bourguiba in 1981 and strengthened by later amendments, to ban the wearing of the Islamic veil in government offices and educational establishments. Islamists and human rights activists voiced concern in case women were barred from educational opportunities as a result. In a bizarre development, the authorities also attempted to ban the sale of an Islamic doll known as "Fulla"—an Islamic response to the Western Barbie doll—and many dolls were confiscated from shops. Traders complained that they were harassed by police for what they had presumed were legitimate activities and had lost money as a result.

In December 2006, with no prior hint of trouble, there were exchanges of fire in Tunisia in various locations between security forces and a group described by informed sources as an Islamist group of a Salafi character. Apparently, the police obtained information about the existence of the group and launched a preemptive attack on its members. Some twenty people appeared to have been killed, including the supposed leader of the group, Lassaad Sassi, a former policeman, from Hammam-Lif, who is said to have had combat experience in Afghanistan and Algeria. Since the American invasion of Iraq in 2003, several hundred Tunisian militants are said to have gone to Algeria. On December 30, 2006, Algerian authorities claimed that two Tunisians had been arrested, who they said were linked to an "international terrorist network." The group active in Tunisia was said to have been formed of Algerians and Mauritanians as well as Tunisians. Their base was reported to be in the Djebel Ressas region, near Hammam-Lif.

Ennahda

Ennahda ("Al-Nahda," in Arabic: "rebirth") was the new name adopted in 1989 by the MTI in Tunisia. Its goal was to seek official recognition and to obtain official exemption from the provision of law governing political organizations, which specified that "no party shall make either religion or language the basis of its principles, its objectives, its activities or its program."

The new organization nevertheless drew its central political principles from the MTI and, thanks to a period of political liberalization inaugurated by President Ben Ali—and especially because of a helping hand from the prime minister—obtained de facto recognition. Ennahda successfully negotiated the right to participate in elections, though it was refused official recognition as a party. However, the principle that its candidates would be permitted to stand as independents in the parliamentary elections of April 2, 1989, was not contested, at a time when various opposition lists were put forward, including that headed by the Democratic Socialist Movement of Ahmed Mestiri. Ennahda's activists and officials felt encouraged to take part in large numbers in the electoral process and emerged with the second largest vote, though they won no seats. Nevertheless, Ennahda's leader, Rachid Ghannouchi, decided to leave

Tunisia in May 1989, fearing renewed government repression. He went first to Paris and then to London in 1991, where he was given political asylum in 1993 after being sentenced in absentia to life imprisonment.

Ennahda's candidates were from relatively privileged backgrounds, with connections with conservative religious figures. They had no links with political organizations. The polls in 1989 were marred by fraud and led to a polarization of the Tunisian political scene. The independent Islamic candidates took 13 percent of the vote. As the Islamists saw it, the results of the elections were a simultaneous demonstration both of their strength in the country and of the futility of the socialist platforms of the other opposition candidates. Ennahda also maintained its close links with the UGTE (General Union of Tunisian Students), which, once it had obtained official recognition, swiftly became the leading student organization on the university campuses. In January 1990, official permission was given for the publication of the official Ennahda newspaper El Fajr ("The Dawn"), which was widely distributed.

Nevertheless, Ennahda's repeated applications for official recognition in 1989 and in 1990 were fruitless. The movement was apprehensive of a further period of repression and made changes in its internal organization, protecting its clandestine networks with enhanced security. It whipped up political agitation against the United States at the time of the Gulf War of 1990–1991, in the hope of strengthening its popular base. On November 29, 1990, President Ben Ali ordered internal investigations into the highest levels of Tunisia's machinery of state, announcing afterward that an Islamic network had been dismantled that had included members of the security services. The period that had been called the "Tunisian Spring," in which there had undoubtedly been some political liberalization, appeared to be at an end. On December 26, 1990, two hundred

Ennahda activists were arrested and charged with plotting to overthrow the regime.

Some months later, other officials said that Ennahda's policies could not be permitted. Lawyer Abdelfatah Mourou accused the movement of resorting to violence to impose its will. The UGTE was suppressed, and many students were arrested. Publication of the periodical "El Fajr" was banned, and Ennahda's organization was largely dismantled. Several hundred Ennahda members fled, to Algeria or to Libya, taking advantage of the porous frontiers between the neighboring countries. In a series of trials organized throughout the country in 1992, draconian penalties were often imposed, and dozens of those accused were sentenced to lifetime imprisonment. At the end of 1992, Ennahda's leadership announced its decision to quit the country. In exile, Ennahda's activists associated themselves with human rights organizations and strengthened their ties with Islamists of other nationalities. In France, they joined the Union of Islamic Organizations in France (UOIF), which had ideological sympathies with the Muslim Brotherhood. In exile, by maintaining links with secular Tunisian opposition groups, as well as by steering clear of involvement with the more violent Islamic factions, Ennahda's intention has appeared to be to safeguard its political future, while waiting for more favorable circumstances in Tunisia.

Ghannouchi, Rashid

Rashid Ghannouchi was born in 1941 in the district of Gabès in southern Tunisia, into a large family. Thanks to family support, he was able to go to Tunis at the age of eighteen to study Islamic subjects at the Al-Zaytuna school from 1959 to 1962. On graduation from Al-Zaytuna, he briefly worked as a primary school teacher but was unhappy with the situation in Tunisia under the regime of President Bourguiba. As a young man, he was inspired by the ideas of Arab nationalism and Nasserism and decided to go to Cairo. In 1964, he enrolled at the faculty of agriculture at Cairo University, but after a few months, following an accord between the Egyptian government and Bourguiba on the treatment of Tunisian political dissidents, he was expelled from Egypt as an undesirable. Ghannouchi then went to Syria, where he embarked on a course in philosophy and social sciences. In Damascus, he fell under the influence of Islamist thinkers from the Muslim Brotherhood. He was strongly influenced by the writings of Hassan al-Banna and Sayyed Qutb, becoming determined to pursue his religious studies to a high level. He took part in advanced discussion groups at the mosques and at the same time took a passionate interest in politics. In 1965, he spent a period in Europe, traveling to Germany by way of Turkey, Yugoslavia, and Bulgaria. He spent time in Germany, France, Belgium, and the Netherlands. He was appalled by what he saw as Western decadence and also began to become disillusioned with Arab nationalism. By 1966, Ghannouchi began to proclaim his adherence to Islamist ideas and began to move in Salafi circles. He graduated in Damascus in 1968 and went to Paris, where he enrolled as a student for a master's degree in philosophy. In France, he encountered activists from Tablighi Jamaat and became general secretary of a student Islamic society.

At the end of 1969, he returned to Tunisia, where he embarked on a career as a teacher in Tunis, where he met fundamentalist Muslims who, like himself, rejected the current ascendancy of the socialist intellectuals. He took up journalism and joined an Islamist magazine, Al-Ma'rifa. Writing as a religious commentator propagating the ideals of the Muslim Brotherhood, he criticized the collapse of morals in the West and advocated the Islamization of Tunisian society. He dealt with political themes while avoiding head-on clashes with political authorities. From 1977, he was editor of Al-Ma'rifa." He also moved in university circles in Tunis, seeking to counter the influence of Marxist student groups. Together with other Islamists, he began to set up a political network, "Islamic Action." In August 1979, Islamic Action set up a new publication, Al-Mujtama'. Rachid Ghannouchi and his colleagues now saw the transition to politics as a realistic objective. At a time when the Arab states were beginning to be concerned over the effects of the Iranian revolution, "Al-Mujtama" was banned after a few months. Ghannouchi was arrested on December 21, 1979, accused of spreading false information and encouraging subversion. He was imprisoned, but a few days later, on January 5, 1980, he was freed.

Nevertheless, the experience decided him to change his way of life, and he determined that he must dedicate himself to political action, even if this brought him into conflict with authorities. After a period traveling abroad, he returned to Tunisia to set up his Islamist organization, the MTI—"Mouvement de la Tendance Islamique" (Movement of the Islamic Tendency). A founding conference was held, and he was confirmed as leader. He attempted in vain, however, to get legal recognition for the MTI. In July 1981, the regime set in train a campaign of arrests against Islamist figures. Ghannouchi was again arrested, together with most of the other members of the MTI's leadership. After a trial, he was given an unexpectedly severe sentence. He was to serve eleven years in prison on a number of charges, including belonging to an unrecognized organization. He was held at Bordj Erroumi and then transferred to a prison in Tunis. On August 31, 1984, he was again freed, this time as a result of an amnesty from which other MTI leaders also benefited.

Once more installed as leader of the MTI, Ghannouchi continued his activities. He rebuilt the organization's clandestine networks and opened negotiations with Tunisia's Prime Minister Mohammed Mzali. In 1985, a student branch of the MTI was set up, which was to become the UGTE. He was still seen as a leading opponent of the regime and was arrested again on March 13, 1987. At a collective trial of a large number of MTI militants and officials, he was sentenced to penal servitude for life. President Bourguiba wanted to go further and ordered a new trial with the intention of condemning him to death. However, Bourguiba's fall on November 7, 1987, opened the way for a new policy of reconciliation on the part of President Ben Ali. In May 1988, Ghannouchi was pardoned, and on this occasion, he decided to adopt a highly conciliatory attitude toward the new regime. Attracted once more by the possibility of legal operation, he agreed to participate on behalf of his organization in talks on a proposed "National Pact." At the parliamentary elections of April 2, 1989, Islamist candidates were permitted to stand as independents. After the vote, the movement, which had by now adopted its new title, "Ennahda," appeared to be the only opposition group that had any real following in the country. However, after public discussion of what status Islamists should be allowed to occupy in Tunisian politics, Ghannouchi began to suspect the direction government thinking was taking. Fearing a new wave of repression, he decided to leave the country.

Ghannouchi had good connections in Europe and had good relations with the Islamic Republic in Iran. However, he went initially to Sudan, where he received a friendly welcome from Hassan al-Turabi and took up residence for a period. During the Gulf War of 1990–1991, he took a belligerent stand, calling for a Jihad against the coalition forces in Iraq. With a Sudanese passport, he traveled to London in 1991 with the agreement of the British authorities.

President Ben Ali's conciliatory mood did not persist, as Ghannouchi had suspected, and in 1992, as a result of his activities and statements abroad, Ghannouchi was sentenced to life imprisonment in absentia in Tunisia for plotting to overthrow the government. In 1993, he was granted political asylum in Britain. From London, he cultivated his European links and was able to wield considerable religious and political influence over the Muslim community in Britain.

In his writings, he has sometimes sought to justify the use of violence as a means of political action in certain contexts, whereas at other times advocating the principles of democracy and human rights. Always the pragmatist, Ghannouchi established connections with Tunisian opposition groups, including those whose views diverged from his own, and took care not to compromise himself by being seen to have links with radical groups practicing violence in the West. However, he has largely concentrated on theoretical and abstract studies of Islam in politics. In international affairs, he has taken a strongly anti-American stand and has condemned the Middle East peace process as one of surrender to Israel. He won damages in 2003 in the British courts against publications that claimed he had links with Al-Qaida. Since then he has taken a relatively high profile in the United Kingdom, taking part in conferences and lecturing at reputable academic institutions. In February 2006, President Ben Ali pardoned and released some seventy-five Ennahda activists still imprisoned in Tunisia, though no pardon has been extended to Ghannouchi, whose sentence of life imprisonment still stands.

Hizb al-Tahrir al-Islami (Party of Islamic Liberation) Tunisia

The Tunisian branch of Hizb al-Tahrir appeared to have been set up in 1982, initially as a subsidiary of the Jordanian organization of the same name. It shares the same goals, namely, the reestablishment of the Caliphate and the overthrow by force of impious regimes in Muslim countries. Its founding leader was Mohammed Djerbi. It attracted little support among the student population but made inroads into the civil service and the army. It based itself on the precepts of the Jordanian Sheikh Takieddine Nabhani. It was secretive and was able to count on the support of only a few hundred activists. It made an attempt to infiltrate the army to help create circumstances for a popular uprising, but this was discovered and foiled by security forces. In August 1983, thirty-four of its activists were sentenced by a military tribunal in Tunis. In a second trial two years later, in March 1985, more of its members were convicted, though they were handed down less severe sentences than those given to the MTI. After this, Hizb al-Tahrir in Tunisia strove in vain to reorganize. Subsequent to the implementation of repressive policies of President Ben Ali in 1990–1991, it no longer appeared to have any real presence in Tunisia.

Islamic Jihad

Islamic Jihad is a name common to Islamist groups across the Arab world. In Tunisia, it was the name taken by an armed group established in 1984 that was made up mainly of radical adherents of the MTI (Mouvement de la Tendance Islamique). Its objective was to overthrow the Tunisian regime by precipitating a revolutionary situation. In August 1986, following the discovery of one of its clandestine cells, three of its members, described as leaders of the movement, were condemned to death and executed. A year later, other groups that were still active were responsible for a series of bomb attacks on hotels in Sousse and Monastir. These operations were intended to weaken the national

economy by undermining tourism. However, Islamic Jihad was to expand its membership and was therefore unable to carry out further operations on any substantial scale in Tunisia. The MTI adopted the name Ennahda in 1989 and sought recognition as a political party. Following major operations by security forces in Tunisia between 1990 and 1991, a number of MTI's former activists chose to leave the country.

Mouvement de la Tendance Islamique (Movement of the Islamic Tendency)

The MTI was set up as a clandestine Islamist group in October 1979. It acknowledged the influence of the Muslim Brotherhood, and its aim was to achieve the status of a legally recognized political organization in Tunisia. It had its origins in small and relatively disorganized groups in universities, and its members were, on the whole, intellectuals whose objective was to manipulate the political process in Tunisia to bring into existence, in due course, an Islamic Republic. The organization's leader was Rashid Ghannouchi, who was appointed president at its founding conference. Abdelfattah Mourou, a lawyer, became secretary-general. From its earliest days, though its core membership was made up of intellectuals in the country's capital, the MTI deliberately built up its structure in towns and villages throughout Tunisia.

In April 1981, another conference was held in Sousse to discuss how best to achieve official recognition. The conference framed new policies to enable the organization to operate within the law. Individual activists were instructed to make cautious contact with other opposition groups, especially the Movement for Popular Unity and the Democratic Socialists. They were also encouraged to join the national trade union, the "Union Générale des Travailleurs Tunisiens" (UGTT). The MTI's agreement to open low-level relations with the left wing, which it had formerly vilified, appeared to set aside its ideological antagonism against secular factions in favor of the overriding goal of achieving recognition by the authorities. The leadership of the MTI succeeded in making contact with a number of well-placed officials in the administration who appeared receptive to Islamist ideas.

On June 6, 1981, the MTI leadership launched the movement officially at a press conference and asked explicitly for recognition from the government. Though the prime minister, Mohammed Mzali, was well disposed toward the MTI, President Bourguiba and his security chief Zine el-Abdine Ben Ali (later to be minister of the interior and then president) were antagonistic. Rather than achieving recognition, the movement was henceforth banned, and its request for recognition was officially refused. In July, members of the MTI began to be arrested, and some officials prudently left the country. The senior leadership was interrogated by the police. At the first group trial of MTI members, heavy sentences were imposed both on officials and on rank and file members.

As president of the MTI, Rashid Ghannouchi was the key figure in the movement. Meanwhile, the ultimate decision-making body was the national consultative council. Day-to-day control, however, was exercised by the executive office. As the organization's central decision-making body, it was the executive committee that was targeted by the security services. After all its key members were jailed, replacements were appointed. Meanwhile, there were two rival minority groups attempting to drag the movement's policy to opposite extremes. Some thought that the moment had come for armed struggle. Others, whose ideas were close to the Progressive Islamists (PI), waned the movement to stand aloof from all politi-

cal action—including operation as a legal political party—restricting itself to cultural and social activities and thus avoiding the attention of the authorities.

The president and minister of the interior, Driss Guiga, were well aware of the internal tensions and differences of opinion within the MTI and lost no opportunity to exacerbate them. However, the organization was helped by the current economic crisis, whose devastating effects on ordinary people assisted it to attract members from among students and the middle class. In the summer of 1984, Prime Minister Mzali, alarmed by the mounting popular discontent, persuaded President Bourguiba to agree to substantial changes that would indicate a will on the part of the government to embark on political liberalization. Bourguiba announced a wide-ranging amnesty that covered the Islamist detainees. For their part, the MTI leaders, including Rashid Ghannouchi, were prolific in their conciliatory gestures, declaring they were ready to participate in democratic politics and accepted the principle that sovereignty lay with the people. The prime minister saw the leader of the main Tunisian trade union [the UGTT (Tunisian Workers' General Union)], Habib Achour, as a political rival and therefore sought to limit the union's power and influence, in part by encouraging the Islamists. In 1985, he backed the establishment of an Islamist union in universities, known as the UGTE (General Union of Students), which rapidly became very powerful.

At the same time, taking its inspiration from the practice of the Muslim Brotherhood in the countries of the Middle East, the MTI attempted to use young people who sympathized with its ideas to infiltrate the institutions of the state, especially the army and the police. In July 1986, after Mohammed Mzali was replaced as prime minister by Rashid Sfar, the possibility that an Islamist organization could become part of the political system was once more off the agenda. Parliamentary elections of November 1986 consolidated the presidential party as the sole political formation with seats in Parliament. President Bourguiba once again cracked down on the opposition, including the Islamists, and in February and March 1987, many MTI leaders and activists were once more arrested. However, the president was beginning to seem increasingly isolated. In these circumstances, those MTI leaders who had escaped arrest began to think of the overthrow of the regime. Thanks to their earlier policies, there were by now many MTI sympathizers in the armed forces. Demonstrations took place in towns across the country.

It was not, however, the Islamists who were to depose President Bourguiba. On November 7, 1987, he was removed from his positions by Zine el-Abdine Ben Ali, who had been prime minister since October 1. For some time, Ben Ali had been Bourguiba's designated successor. He justified his action on the basis of constitutional provisions stipulating that the president could be replaced if he proved incapable of proper exercise of his functions. Over the days that followed his constitutional coup, he arrested a number of people who were accused of plotting against Bourguiba. Nevertheless, in December 1987, he embarked on a process of reconciliation. Both the Tunisian communist party and a number of independent candidates were allowed to take part in a partial parliamentary election. In May 1988, many MTI members were set free, and Rashid Ghannouchi was pardoned to mark the Id al-Fitr (the Islamic festival at the end of Ramadan). He responded by acknowledging Ben Ali's seizure of power as a "historic development" and called for dialogue.

In order to assist it to achieve recognition, the party decided to demonstrate its willingness to make a break with the past.

It changed its name to Ennahda ("Renaissance") and declared itself willing to conform to the legal regulations governing the activity of political parties. Nevertheless, Ghannouchi felt it would be prudent to leave the country. In May 1989, he went into voluntary exile. After France and Germany both refused him residence, he eventually found asylum in Britain, where, in 2007, he still makes his home.

Al-Islamiyun al-Taqadumiyun (The Progressive Islamists)

This movement represents a unique school of Islamic ideas specific to Tunisia. Also known as the "Islamic Left," it derives from the ideas of the Egyptian philosopher Hassan Hanafi. The PI rejected confrontation with the regime and advocated a modified approach on the part of Muslims instead. The movement's origin can be traced back to 1982, when a number of Tunisian intellectuals, mainly with a background in "Islamic Action," set up a new group opposed to the policies and ideas of the MTI (which later became Ennahda). Leading figures in the movement included Ahmida Enneifer and Salaheddine Jourchi.

They opted not to set up a political party, and on the ideological front, they began to question the intellectual legacy of the Muslim Brotherhood. Instead, they set themselves the task of constructing what they described as a society "adapted to Tunisia's social needs." Members of what became known as the Progressive Islamists joined trade unions and associations, in particular the UGTE. Within the Islamic movement as a whole, they ensured that their ideas were kept in the public eye through their publication, La Revue 15/21. Following President Ben Ali's measures to eliminate Islamism from Tunisia, they seem—in common with other Islamic groups—to have effectively been closed down.

TURABI, HASSAN AL-

Hassan Turabi was born into a religious family on February 1, 1932, in Kassala Province, in northeastern Sudan, close to the Eritrean frontier. His grandfather was the leader of a small Islamic Brotherhood and was Turabi's first teacher. From 1954, he was an activist in the Muslim Brotherhood. He graduated in law from the University of Khartoum in 1955 and took his MA at London University in 1957. He then moved to Paris, and in 1964 he took a doctoral degree in legal studies at the Sorbonne. His thesis was entitled "Emergency powers in Anglo-Saxon and French Law." While he was in France, he founded the Association of Islamic Students in France (AEIF), which, when he left, he handed over to an academic of Indian origin, Mohammed Hamidullah. Turabi is multilingual, speaking English and Arabic perfectly and expressing himself well in both French and German. He is well connected and is married to Wisal al-Mahdi, the sister of Sadiq al-Mahdi, the leader of the Mahdi family (descendants of the Mahdi who fought General Gordon and presided over the period of Sudanese independence from 1885 to 1898). Sadiq was the leader of the Ansar, the social movement formed by the Mahdi's supporters and the Umma Party, their political dimension.

In 1964, after the completion of his studies and his return to Sudan, Turabi took a post in the department of law at the University of Khartoum, where he rapidly rose to become Dean of the Faculty. In October 1964, he established the Islamic Charter Front (ICF) ("Jabhat al-Mithaq"), in effect an offshoot of the Muslim Brotherhood. His goal was ambitious—to use the ICF as a springboard for his project to construct nothing less than a new kind of Islamic society. His aim was a rejuvenated Muslim world, able to face challenges presented by modernity and global competition. He was an early advocate of a peaceful settlement of the conflict in southern Sudan. From 1965 to 1968, the ICF cooperated with Sadiq al-Mahdi's Umma Party to militate for an Islamic constitution for Sudan, which had still not—post independence in 1956—settled its constitutional arrangements.

In May 1969, everything changed. A relatively unknown solider, Colonel Jaafar Nimeiri, took power in a military coup, and Turabi was arrested. Nimeiri's government was at first resolutely secular, and Turabi spent much of the 1970s either in prison or in exile. As Nimeiri began to be more persuaded of the virtues of Islamism, Turabi finally made up his differences with Nimeiri. In 1979, he returned to public life, becoming Attorney General. He used his position to influence the government's direction, and in September 1983, Nimeiri's government introduced the Shari'a. When Nimeiri was deposed in 1985 by a transitional government headed by General Suwar al-Dhahhab, Turabi transformed the ICF into the National Islamic Front (NIF), which he deployed as a political party. By this stage, he had left the Muslim Brotherhood behind, describing it as "too rigid, and unable to envisage alternative ideas."

At the parliamentary elections of 1986 held by the transitional government, the NIF failed to make an impression against Sadiq al-Mahdi's Umma and the Democratic Unionist Party, which represented the other great Islamic Brotherhood in Sudan, the Khatmiya, led by the Mirghani family. Sadiq al-Mahdi formed a government, and the NIF came third, with only 51 seats out of 264. However, Turabi skillfully maximized the influence of his relatively restricted number of seats in Parliament by playing each of the main parties off against the other. Behind the scenes, he was already developing other ideas. In due course, he took the plunge and began to make clandestine approaches to the country's military leadership. On June 30, 1989, the army mounted a coup against Sadiq's government. This so-called National Salvation Revolution was conducted by the military but with Turabi's NIF pulling the strings behind the scenes. The ostensible leader of the coup was General Omar Hassan al-Bashir, as the head of the Revolutionary Command Council for National Salvation (RCC-NS), but the real decision maker was Turabi, who liked to call himself the "Guide."

His concept in these years was to use Sudan as a laboratory for his revolutionary ideas and his plans for social transformation. He established durable links with the Islamic Republic of Iran, bridging to a certain extent the Sunni–Shi'a gap, and at the same time, he built connections with Sunni Islamists. Among Turabi's friends abroad were the Egyptian scholar Sheikh Yusuf Qaradawi, Abdul Majid al-Zandani (in Yemen), and Tariq Ramadan, the European Islamist scholar. His trump card was the creation in 1991 of the Popular Arab Islamic Conference (PAIC), whose opening conference drew more than two hundred foreign delegates from forty-five countries, with the objective of countering the growing hegemony of the United States in the Middle East and the influence of Israel. This enhanced his standing, both abroad and inside Sudan. In 1991, he invited Osama Bin Laden to come to Sudan, after Bin Laden decided it was prudent to leave Afghanistan. Another visitor to Sudan in 1991 was Iran's President Rafsanjani, who offered aid and commended Turabi's Sudan as the "vanguard of the Islamic revolution in Africa."

During the 1990s, Turabi attempted to transform Sudanese policy on several fronts. He made good use of his personal sophistication and command of languages to cultivate foreign diplomats and the Western media. On the other hand, his regime was anathema to some. Egypt's President Mubarak regarded him as a threat and a destabilizing

factor. Turabi's critics accused him of turning Sudan into a haven for terrorists, though he raised no objection to the seizure in 1994 of the terrorist suspect "Carlos" (Ilich Ramirez Sanchez) by French agents acting on Sudanese soil. He also showed no hesitation in expelling Osama Bin Laden in 1996, when the Saudi Islamist's presence in Sudan began to embarrass the regime. On the internal front, the war between the Khartoum government and the rebel movement in southern Sudan demanded all of Turabi's skills. He opted to attempt to reach a federal solution with the South, but the application of the Shari'a was a knotty problem. A reason for Turabi's eagerness to settle with the South was his belief in the need to develop Sudan's oil resources to ensure the security of the regime. Finally, Turabi forged novel foreign contacts for Sudan, for instance with France, China, and Malaysia.

In 1993, the RCC-NS was abolished, and Turabi was instrumental in restructuring Sudan's government. The RCC-NS was replaced by the Transitional National Assembly, and in March 1996, a new parliament was elected, though still without political parties. Turabi consolidated his position by taking the post of Speaker of the Sudanese parliament from 1996 to 1998. However, Turabi's weakness from the beginning was his ambiguous relationship with General Omar Hassan al-Bashir, who increasingly began to chafe under Turabi's assumption that it was his prerogative to decide Sudan's policy. Turabi also began to experience friction with former NIF colleagues who had become more identified with Bashir's government, including Osman Ali Taha, who had become vice president, and Ghazi Salaheddin, a powerful figure in the Islamist establishment who had become a presidential adviser. In 1998, Turabi reconstructed the NIF as a political party under the name of "National Congress." In December 1999, relations between Turabi and Bashir reached breaking point because of differences over policy issues. Turabi had to concede the leadership of the National Congress to President Bashir, who dissolved Parliament. The constitution was suspended, and the president ruled by decree. In 1999, Turabi set up his own splinter movement, the Popular National Congress, but boycotted elections that were held that year.

In 2000, Turabi's political career began to falter, despite his continuing popularity and his reputation in Sudan as a redoubtable Islamist leader. President Bashir ceased to host the regular meetings of Turabi's PAIC, thus severing some of Turabi's international connections and depriving him of part of his power base. Parliament was reinstated in February 2001, but Turabi was arrested for having signed an agreement in January 2001 with the southern rebel movement, the Sudan People's Liberation Army. He was placed under house arrest on February 21, 2001. After the events of September 11, 2001, in New York, Turabi made a statement denying that there was a clash of civilizations between Islam and the West, but he called on the West, nonetheless, to abandon its pretensions to hegemony in the Middle East and elsewhere. Rumors circulated that he was linked to a failed coup attempt in 2003, which he denied. In 2004, he was once more arrested, though he was released in June 2005, and a ban on his Popular National Congress was lifted. Turabi's more recent activities have been difficult to assess. Despite persistent rumors, he denies all connection with an Islamist group known as the "Justice and Equality Movement" (JEM) that forms part of the rebel Darfur movement against the Khartoum government. JEM is headed by Dr. Khalil Ibrahim, said to be a protégé of Turabi, who has sought political asylum in the Netherlands. In January 2006, Turabi said that the presence of foreign troops in Sudan compromised the country's independence. However, in September 2006, he criticized the Sudanese government for creating what he called a catastrophic situation in Darfur.

TURKEY

The groundbreaking figure in the Islamist movement in Turkey was Necmettin Erbakan. He enjoys the distinction of being the first Islamist leader in Turkey to have become prime minister, which he achieved in July 1996, in coalition with a former antagonist, Mrs. Tansu Çiller, who had earlier herself been prime minister. One thing that has been consistent in the policy of Turkey's Islamists is their pragmatism and willingness to compromise. On the other hand, they regard themselves as the natural heirs of the Caliphate, abolished in 1924 after the fall of the Ottoman Empire. In the longer term, they believe that their destiny is to lead the "Umma," the Islamic community in the world. They do not accept that either the Arabs or the Islamic Republic of Iran, the only regional power large enough to rival Turkey, could play this role.

Mustafa Kemal Ataturk's Turkey, the successor state to the Ottoman Empire, was the first Muslim state completely to separate state from religion, and for more than four hundred years the Ottoman Empire taught all its provinces, and especially the Arabs, the meaning of the concepts of state and government. The vast majority of the Turks are Sunni Muslim, in common with 90 percent of the world's Muslim population. They are Hanafis, as are half of the Muslims of the world. In the days of the Ottoman Empire, there was no debate over the relationship between the "Umma" and the Turkish authorities, whose supremacy was taken for granted. Even though Turkey is now secular, the ministry of religion has never ceased to exist, and it controls important aspects of the lives of Turkey's Muslim citizens. It appoints imams and approves the syllabus for religious education in the schools. Religion is still specified, given on every citizen's identity card. Paradoxically, the control of religion by the secular state has enabled Turkey to flourish.

The re-Islamization of Turkish society is not a recent phenomenon. From the 1950s onward, the constraints and limitations imposed on religion have been alleviated. Gradually, Islam has been recognized as the vital element binding the nation together. It is no longer dismissed, as it was in the early days of the Turkish Republic, as an unfortunate legacy from the past that has caused all the afflictions of the nation and the people. Islam has become an instrument of the state in Turkey, despite the country's secular constitution. The result has been tension between Islamic governments and the military, which regards itself as the guarantor of the country's secular heritage, first created by the creator of Turkey as a modern nation, Mustafa Kemal Ataturk.

Nonetheless, the centrality of Turkish Islamism in Turkey's political life contrasts with the other preoccupation of Turkish politics, that of relations with the West. After World War II, those who desired integration into the West as their primary objective encountered the fierce opposition of the mass of the newly urbanized Turkish peasantry, driven to towns by the relative economic decline of the countryside, who were reluctant to see the westernization of society. Although new Western-style civilian and military schools produced a class of secularized junior and middle-ranking officials, social groups of rural origin remained outside this evolution and turned instead to the religious schools. Confrontation between a modernizing elite and a supposedly backward peasantry became a theme of Turkish society. The originality of Turkey's Islamists is that they have tried to reconcile these opposites.

Since 1980, however, the number and quality of the available Islamic schools have greatly increased. Although they have no official standing, these schools have offered their pupils a way to advance themselves. Graduates of Islamic schools have in more recent years entered the professions and all branches of the higher administration, except for the military. One commentator has offered this analysis:

> Re-Islamization from below has also been intensified by the proliferation of universities throughout the country, which has enabled the religious sector to gain control over some of them, thus creating an entire career structure. While continuing to teach technical subjects and social sciences, this educational strand attempts to adapt them to a religious position, emphasizing their repudiation of what are supposed to be western thought and the western way of life.

For some Islamists, the debate is certainly not so much about the relationship with the West as the means by which the West can be overcome. The most radical have no faith in the reformist strategy of using the very process of westernization as a means of facing up to western supremacy. In their view, western values such as humanism, democracy, and human rights are an affront to the unity of God, from who all wisdom flows. These issues are not specific to Turkey: the entire Islamic world is preoccupied with the same questions. The Islamists believe that Islamic faith must regain its place as a basic element of Muslim identity. As one Muslim thinker has put it: "It is not a question of catching up with or equaling the West, but of being superior to it. The supremacy of the Muslim faith over other religions must necessarily imply supremacy over the West."

Turkish Islamism of this kind is characterized by a radical hostility toward the West. It advocates a return to the moral values of Islam as well as a struggle against "licentiousness and debauchery." Women must once more wear modest dress, and the values of the patriarchal family should be respected. This kind of radical Islam opposes capitalism and is antagonistic to monopolies and the cosmopolitan bourgeoisie. On the other hand, it seeks to support peasant farmers crushed by debts and to encourage small businesses in the countryside. Some radicals go as far as to believe that nothing in the political and social spheres can be independent of Islam.

AK Party

Turkey's ruling AK Party (Adalet ve Kalkinma Partisi) ("Justice and Development Party") was established by Turkey's veteran Islamist leader Recep Tayyip Erdogan on August 14, 2001. AK is a center-right party based on Islamist ideas but asserts that religion is not its basis. It claims to be pragmatic in its approach and committed to democratic pluralism. Meanwhile, on July 20, 2001, those members of the former Fazilet Party who were not enthusiastic over Erdogan's move toward moderation and who continued to support the ideas of Necmettin Erbakan, Erdogan's predecessor and the doyen of Turkey's Islamist movement, formed the Saadet ("Felicity") Party. Saadet is now led by Recai Kutan, a former senior figure in Fazilet. AK is in many ways the successor to previous Islamic parties, the old Refah ("Welfare") Party and the more recent Fazilet ("Virtue") Party, dissolved on June 22, 2001, at the behest of Turkey's National Security Council. This powerful body, chaired by the president and containing members from the military leadership and the government, has been enshrined in the constitution since 1961. It regards itself as the guardian of Turkey's democratic ideals. The military component of the National Security Council consists of the Chief of Staff and four senior armed forces commanders. The prime minister and the ministers of the interior, defense and foreign affairs also sit on the Council.

The AK Party came to power in parliamentary elections on November 3, 2002, in a landslide victory, when it took 353 of the 550 seats in the Turkish parliament, wiping out a number of older parties. Support for Turkey's Islamist parties has historically been based in rural areas and in less privileged parts of towns. AK's support, however, has clearly gone beyond this constituency. When elected, AK pledged to respect the secular basis of the Turkish constitution. It was initially led by Abdullah Gül, because Recep Tayyip Erdogan was barred from sitting in Parliament after an incident in which he allegedly disrespected Turkey's secular principles on a public occasion. (In the course of a speech he recited a religious verse that was regarded by the judiciary as seditious.) In February 2003, Parliament amended the constitution opening the way for Erdogan's return in a by-election. On March 1, 2003, the AK Party survived a political crisis after a rebellion by its parliamentarians blocked its intention to allow the U.S.-led coalition against Iraq from launching an attack on Iraq from Turkish soil. On March 9, 2003, Erdogan was reelected to Parliament, resuming the post of prime minister on March 14. Abdulah Gül, who became Erdogan's foreign minister, is now the AK Party's candidate for the presidency. Erdogan's leading concern since then has been to press forward Turkey's bid for membership of the European Union. He also engineered a reduction of tension with Turkey's old adversary, Greece, when he visited Greece in 2004 and enlisted the support of Athens for Turkey's European bid. AK won renewed support from the electorate in 2004 when it scored 34 percent of the vote in local elections, making gains from other parties.

During 2006, Recep Tayyip Erdogan's ambition to become president of Turkey in the 2007 presidential election gave rise to a degree of strain between the AK Party and the military leadership. The AK Party attempted to prevent the appointment of a diehard secularist, General Yasar Buyukanit, as Chief of Staff, which would give him a key position on the National Security Council. Meanwhile it was clear that General Buyukanit, who became Chief of Staff despite the government's opposition, was determined to block Erdogan from being a candidate for the presidency. The objection was that the three great offices of state, the presidency, the office of prime minister, and the post of speaker of parliament should not all be held by Islamists. A minor issue that, however, looms large in the conceptions of Turkish secularists is that the wives of both Recep Tayyip Erdogan and Abdullah Gül wear Islamic head-coverings. Mustafa Kemal Ataturk was deeply opposed to Islamic dress, and it is a convention in Turkey that it is not worn in Parliament, government offices, universities, and schools. In addition, the wives of military officers may not wear Islamic dress. On the other hand, in the country at large, a 2006 survey reported that 64 percent of women cover their heads.

By April 2007, it appeared as if the impasse had been resolved, when Erdogan agreed to put forward his close colleague Abdullah Gül, a former prime minister and foreign minister (who had initially been slated to replace Erdogan as prime minister), as the AK Party candidate for president. Gül's democratic and secular credentials were apparently more acceptable to the military than those of Recep Tayyip Erdogan himself, who seemed set to remain prime minister. However, the military questioned whether Abdullah Gül's past connections with Islamism might rule him out from the presidency, which involves a commitment to uphold the country's secular constitution.

If elected, Gül would chair the National Security Council. The current President, Ahmet Necdet Sezer, an avowed secularist has used his chairmanship of the National Security Council to veto many of the AK Party's legislative initiatives. On Saturday 28 April, a demonstration hundreds of thousands strong protested in Istanbul against Erdogan's presidential ambitions. On the other hand, this may have represented a mainly urban constituency, whereas the AK Party's support still comes mainly from the small towns and the rural areas.

Hilafet Devleti (Kalifatstaat) (The State of the Caliphate)

The "State of the Caliphate," also known as the Union of Islamic Associations and Communities, was a clandestine Islamist movement set up by Turkish expatriates in the German city of Cologne in 1998. Its aim is the restoration of the Ottoman State. Its original members, who were mainly supporters of Necmettin Erbakan, were disciples of Cemaleddin Kaplan, a former Mufti from Adana who had come to Cologne as a refugee in 1983. Together with his son Metin Kaplan, he established an important Muslim network in Europe that became known as the Hilafet Devleti (in German, Kalifatstaat) which translates as the State of the Caliphate.

The Kalifatstaat set up an Islamic Center in Cologne, which was closed in 1987 by the German authorities. Kaplan professed his belief in the use of violence by Islamists to achieve their aims and sent his supporters to be trained in Afghanistan, Bosnia, and Chechnya. Metin Kaplan became leader on his father's death in 1995. In 1996, he was accused of murdering a rival, Ibrahim Sofu, and in 2000, he was jailed for four years in Germany for conspiracy to cause Sofu's death. In 2001, the Kalifatstaat was banned in Germany. In 2004, Kaplan lost his refugee status and faced extradition to Turkey, where he was wanted for offences against the Turkish state. In October 2004, he was sent to Turkey, where he was arrested. In June 2005, he was sentenced to life imprisonment. Kaplan makes no secret of his total rejection of democracy and democratic pluralism. He is said to have sent emissaries to Afghanistan to ask Osama Bin Laden if he would assume the Caliphate.

Islamic Brotherhoods in Turkey

The Islamic Brotherhoods, or Sufi Orders— semi-clandestine and therefore relatively little known—is an important element within Turkish Islamism. Virtually every Turkish adult male has belonged, at one time or another, to an Islamic Brotherhood. The four most important that operate today all have branches in Europe. These are

- The "Suleymanciya," which favors the restoration of the Caliphate.
- The "NurÁu," set up by a Kurdish mystic at the beginning of the twentieth century, struggles against the Kemalist secular ideal. At present, this Brotherhood has more than a million members and proselytizes vigorously.
- The "Naqshbandiya"—an older Order— which aims at the installation of Islamic Law (Shari'a). When necessary its members practice "Taqiya" (the concealment of their religious affiliation). This group receives most of the donations given by Saudi Arabia to the Turkish Islamists.
- The "Qadiriya"—another of the long established Orders, who follow the teachings of the twelfth century Iraqi saint, Abd al-Qadir al-Jilani.

These Turkish Orders have been able to inculcate a highly active Islam social life in Europe among immigrant workers of Turkish origin. The activities connected to this manifestation of Islam, which has concentrated on the strengthening of community solidarity, have tended fall into three principal categories. These are the construction of mosques, the provision of Quranic instruction, and the reinforcement of the old values of the Ottoman Empire. This last point, in particular, has helped restore lost pride to members of a community whose sense of identity had been undermined.

In the 1920s, Mustafa Kemal Ataturk, the founder of the Turkish Republic, peremptorily suppressed the Islamic Brotherhoods. However, they have today reestablished their presence in Turkey, both in the countryside and in the major towns. Mehmet Zahid Kotku, the leader of the Islamic Brotherhood in which Necmettin Erbakan grew up, encouraged him to establish his first political organization, the Party of National Order, in January 1970, and then in October 1972 to set up the National Salvation Party (NSP)—"Milli Selamet Partisi" (MSP). However, the Sheikhs who led the Brotherhoods did not lend their support exclusively to religious parties but often also struck up agreements with the major lay political parties. The strength of the Brotherhoods was that they permeated large swathes of society with their mosques, schools, foundations, investments, and TV channels, in spite of the efforts of the military to promote the secularization of Turkey.

Following the end of World War I and Turkey's struggle for independence, the Kurdish Naqshbandi Sheikh Said Piran led a revolt in the eastern part of the country which seriously challenged the foundations of the new Turkish Republic. The leaders of the Kurdish revolt were young Naqshbandi or Qadiri Sheikhs (belonging to the Qadiriya order), many of whom were redoubtable tribal and military leaders in their own right. The revolt was an illustration of the strength of the religious orders in those former Ottoman lands that now formed part of Turkey and an indication of the support they enjoyed. The uprising demonstrated the ability of the Brotherhoods to mobilize their support. Mustafa Kemal Ataturk was obliged to crushing the revolt by force of arms, and the threat it had represented prompted him to attempt to eradicate the Brotherhoods, which had been strong enough to threaten his authority.

On November 30, 1925, Ataturk banned the Brotherhoods under Law 677 of the Turkish Republic, confiscating their assets and forbidding the use of religious appellations such as "Sheikh." As he puts it, "Turkey cannot be the country of Sheikhs, Dervishes and adepts of the Brotherhoods." The strict enforcement of this law, with the arrest of the powerful Sheikhs—who had been highly influential in the Ottoman Empire—as well as the nationalization of the Islamic endowments known as "Vakif" (Arabic: "Waqf"), deprived the Brotherhoods of their financial power and therefore of their social influence. Ataturk's motive was fundamentally political: his intention was to suppress the influence of the religious establishment, which questioned the legitimacy of the new republican government, and to establish the dominance of the central administration over local sources of authority.

The ban on the Brotherhoods continued through successive Turkish constitutions, until, in 1960, it was declared irreversible. It is still in force. However, there continues to be ample visible evidence of the presence of religious devotees of the Brotherhoods in Istanbul and Turkey's other cities. In the Fatih quarter of Istanbul, for example, next to the Golden Horn, there is what can only be described as a "sacred zone," in which are found the Naqshbandi "tekke" of Ismail Aga, the "Dergah" (Sufi centre) of Karagümrük, and the mosque of Fatih. Virtually all the buildings in the area are occupied by mosques, religious schools, Sufi institutions, or the seats of religious foundations. In the streets there is to be seen an unusually large proportion of veiled women, together with men in green or black turbans, indicating their religious affiliation. The residences of the Brotherhoods are full, and their ceremonies are openly conducted. Such a figure as the Nurçu leader Fertullah Gülen even heads a media conglomerate and has become a television personality in his own right. The fact is that, up to the present day, those on whom the mantle of the great "Dervish" leaders of the Ottoman Empire has fallen continue to turn their backs on legal restrictions to maintain their traditions. They have adapted themselves to Turkey's changing circumstances and have flouted the letter of the law to reestablish their dominance over Turkish society. Presently a fact of life in Turkey which cannot be disregarded, the Brotherhoods have been able—despite Ataturk's ban—to continue their activities and preserve their influence under a veneer of secrecy.

In 1950, Turkey's transformation from a one-party state into a multiparty democracy meant that the parties vied for the support of the Brotherhoods in their quest for electoral support. Once in government, these parties in turn began to dilute the state's anti-Brotherhood policies. A second significant opportunity which the Sheikhs eagerly seized was the liberalization of the law relating to the "Vakif." This culminated in a law passed in 1967 that reestablished certain elements of Ottoman law. The Brotherhoods were quick to take advantage, setting up new charitable foundations which gave them social leverage.

The "Vakif," under whose cover the Brotherhoods were thinly concealed, were of different varieties. They sometimes took the form of associations for the restoration of a historic monument on the site of a former place of worship or for the preservation of some form of sufi music or dancing used at the sessions of the adepts (known as "zikr" or remembrance, suitably "folklorized" for the sake of appearances). For example, the Khalwati-Cerrahi "tekke," or chapter-house, in Karagümrük, up to 1987 headed by Sheikh Muzaffer Özak, presently has a recognized existence as a "Foundation for research into the Sufi Lore and Music of Turkey." Certain Brotherhoods expanded their activities into the social sphere, concentrating in particular on educational projects for young people. A classic example of this was the Haykol Vakif, founded by the Naqshbandi Sheikh Zahid Kotku (who died in 1980 at the age of eighty-three), who was the imam of the Iskander Pasha Mosque. This Vakif operated as a publisher of books and magazines as well as running schools. Its savings bank, its cooperative enterprises, and its benevolent fund became private companies after the establishment of a parent company known as "Server Holding." The financial weight of this body was highly instrumental in the success of the Iskender Pasa group, which has become the largest Naqshabandiya subsidiary in Turkey. Other groups, similar to the Brotherhoods in their aims and organization, which were set up after the 1925 ban, have followed the same path. For example, the Suleymanci Sheikh, Süleyman Hilmi Tunahan, who died in 1959, did his bit to hold back the tide of state-sponsored secularism by organizing widespread Quran-reading classes. The Suleymancis today run a network of private schools. The Nurçu, or "Jemaat Nurçu (the Community of the Disciples of Light)," were originally the followers of Said Nursi (1876–1960), who wrote the "Risale-i Nur" (The Treatise on Light).

The spearhead of the Brotherhoods' strategy was to construct solid bastions in the schools and the universities, through providing student residences and endowing scholarships and by setting up private schools and courses at the university level. The Brotherhoods were thus able to infiltrate a new class of educated young people into the Turkish elite, whose background lay in the countryside or the popular quarters of the towns. The Brotherhoods, whose initiation rites had become less forbidding and exclusive, expanded their recruitment into the more precarious classes, whom they helped to rise within Turkish society. Those concerned were the second generation of the rural exodus, the children of migrants whose goal was to claim a position for themselves in urban society in a way their parents may have failed to do. The support networks provided by the Brotherhoods, by offering financial support, played a key part in attracting streams of young people from the economically backward countryside to the medium-sized towns. These young people were thus able to complete their university studies, rather than being obliged to swell the floods of unassimilable internal migrants to Istanbul.

A convergence of interests and ideological affinities enabled the Brotherhoods—whose traditional milieu had been among small tradesmen and skilled workmen—to attract the sympathy of a new class of businessmen, engineers, and members of the professions who sought to distinguish themselves from the Kemalist middle classes. This new class was able to prosper thanks to the policies of President Turgut Özal, well acquainted with the Brotherhoods and sympathetic toward them, who allowed them to flourish in the 1980s. The strength accrued by the Brotherhoods in President Özal's decade (1983–1993) was exemplified by the financial and media empires they established. The Islamic banking system also gained a foothold, in the form of companies associated with Naqshbandi groups connected with the Özal family, providing an invaluable resource for the Sheikhs and the Dervishes.

"Server Holding" was not the only such institution established by the Brotherhoods. The son-in-law of the of the founder of the Naqshbandi Isikcilar community set up "Ihlas Holding," linked to the daily newspaper Türkiye. Meanwhile, "Asya Holding," itself sizeable, was only part of the business interests owned or controlled more or less directly by the Nurçus. Each of these "Holdings" characteristically owns newspapers and media organizations, as well as a cluster of private religious or nonreligious schools. The Naqshbandiya was the first of the Brotherhoods to attempt to utilize its social presence to acquire political influence. In the 1970s, Sheikh Mehmet Zayid Kotku made a bid for power. His project, intended, as he expressed it, to "safeguard the faith" from the constraints imposed on it by the official system and ideology, would increasingly be involved in the social and economic affairs and would also become involved in the arena of politics.

It was on Sheikh Kotku's advice that Necmettin Erbakan—one of his disciples—first embarked on the creation of an Islamist political party. As an engineer, Erbakan had worked for small companies in provincial Turkey. He began as a member of the Justice Party, which was politically on the centre-right, and the predecessor of the True Path Party of Tansu Çiller. However, against the wishes of the party leaders, Erbakan attempted to make himself the spokesman of the provincial lower middle class, where the Brotherhoods found most of their members. Expelled by the Justice Party, he was elected to Parliament as an independent for the town of Konya, a bastion of traditional Islam in central Anatolia. When he set up the NSP, Naqshbandi support enabled him to attract broad support across the country. The NSP's useful electoral success led on several occasions to Erbakan being offered posts in coalition governments, including governments led by the Left.

Another Brotherhood grouping that found itself in a position to play a part in politics was the Nurçu, which adopted a different strategy. The Nurçu refrained from participating directly in the struggle for power but attempted to consolidate a social base from which they could negotiate with the secular governing parties. The alliance made in the 1950s between Said Nursi and the leaders of the Democratic Party was succeeded by another with the Justice Party, which in 1965 allocated five parliamentary seats to representatives of the Nurçu. Later, they established a similar link with the True Path Party. After the military coup of September 12, 1980, an increasing number of politicians opted to turn to the Brotherhoods for support, appearing—as they did—more stable than the parties, which frequently broke up or ceased to operate. Another consideration in the renewed rise of the Brotherhoods is that the civil government, which for many years had been obliged to coexist with the military authorities, attempted discreetly to cultivate any source of influence which could serve as a counterbalance to the military. The Brotherhoods were the only institution in Turkey that existed throughout civil society.

The death of Sheikh Kotku on November 13, 1980, caused problems. Not only was there a serious issue over who would succeed him as the Naqshabandi leader, the Naqshbandiya had begun to have misgivings over the extent of his political involvement and needed to decide on its future stance. Sheikh Kotku's spiritual successor was his son-in-law, Mahmut Esat Cosan. He took the view that the Naqshbandiya to take the form of a pressure group rather than the political party headed by Erbakan. Erbakan therefore sought the support of an alternative Naqshbandi group. On July 19, 1983, with the backing of Sheikh Mahmut Ustaosmanoglu of the Ismail Aga "tekke," who was also the imam of the Çarsamba mosque in Fatih, he set up the Refah Party ("Welfare Party"). This attracted the support of other smaller groups affiliated to the Naqshbandiya. These were the

Sultanbabcilar, through which the party attracted support from women, the Yahya Dergah, based in the Kayseri region, and a section of Sheikh Mahmut Sami Ramazanoglu's Erenköy—the most powerful group after that of Iskender Pasa.

The Iskender Pasa group itself, although it did not go into politics directly, exercised substantial influence within ANAP (the Motherland Party) and within the government of Turgut Özal, with his Naqshandi links. The Naqshbandi wing of ANAP won a majority of the seats in the party's central committee, and its leader, Mehmet Kereciler, became a member of the prime minister's private office. After Özal died in 1993, the Iskender Pasa group continued to support ANAP but, in 1997, swung over to the New Party founded by Özal's brothers, who split off from ANAP. Other Naqshbandi groups have more recently become associated with a party first set up in 1992, the BBP (Grand Union Party), which espouses an explicit Islamic nationalism. One of these was the group known as "Menzil," which is especially well represented in eastern Turkey. Tansu Çiller also attempted to attract the votes of this group for her own DYP. For its part, the Qadiriya originally supported Erbakan's NSP, but later swung round behind Tansu Çiller. The Trabzon-based businessman Haydar Bas, a leading figure in the Naqshbandiya, became an adviser in the government formed by Tansu Çiller.

Meanwhile, Suleyman Demirel, who led the DYP before becoming president of Turkey, maintained the same kind of relationship with Fetullah Gülen, the leading Nurçu, as had his predecessors in the Democratic Party with Said Nursi. The steady progress of the Refah Party toward power, as it won the municipal elections of 1994 and the parliamentary elections of December 24, 1995, was only one symptom among others of the resurgent influence of the Brotherhoods. These were operative across the spectrum, in the spiritual, educational, social, and economic fields. Politically, the Sheikhs prudently diversified their commitments, and the leaderships of the Qadiriya, the Nurçu, the Suleymanciya, and even the powerful Naqshbandi groups, such as that of Iskender Pasa, supported the supposedly lay parties, some the Motherland Party and others the True Path. The Sufi and the Islamist constituencies—or to be more precise, the segments of the population that supported the Naqshbandi Order and the Refah Party—were only partly identical.

In due course, either willfully or through misfortune, the Islamist municipalities lost the support of the Dervishes. For example, some municipalities adopted positions too extreme for the Sufi Brotherhoods to accept, prompted perhaps by Salafism and by subsidies from the Gulf States. Such positions were also distant from the normal line of Erbakan's party. Other Refah supporters claimed to see in the veneration of the Prophet Mohammed's nephew and son-in-law Ali characteristic of most of the Sufi Orders—with the noteworthy exception of the Naqshbandiya—an unacceptable deviation from Sunni orthodoxy reminiscent of Turkey's Alevi minority (and similar to the Alawites in Syria).

In general terms, there is an underlying rivalry between three manifestations of organized Islam in Turkey. These are the militant Islam of the Refah Party, the official Islam of the "Diyanet" (the government's administrative office for Religious Affairs), and the major Brotherhoods that are politically active. In broad terms, Refah and the Brotherhoods seem to have been in de facto alliance throughout the period of Erbakan's government, from June 1996 to June 1997. Some 61 percent of Brotherhood members are said to have voted for Refah in the parliamentary elections of December 24, 1995. The Motherland Party took only 14 percent of Brotherhood votes, the True

Path 9 percent, and the Nationalist Party 8 percent. Once Refah was in charge of the government and the municipalities in the large towns, all the Brotherhoods and other Islamic movements were able to establish more "Vakif" and religious schools—some five hundred per year, as against two hundred per year under the previous government. This unprecedented penetration of Turkish society by the Sheikhs, however, spurred the army leadership into action to protect the secularist spirit of Kemalism, of which it regarded itself as the guardian. The generals were determined in the longer term to halt the process of Islamization of Turkey and took steps to block the movement of religious movements, including both the Islamists and the Brotherhoods.

The existence of armed radical Islamist groups such as the IBDA-C (Islamic Great Eastern Raiders Front)—a Sunni Salafi group—or Hizbollah, said to be linked to the "Menzil" organization of the Naqshbandiya in eastern Turkey, prompted the military to develop a new strategic priority. The internal menace represented by "reaction" was rated as a threat even greater than Kurdish separatism, and the deployment of force against this "obscurantism" was henceforth legitimized. The secular revolution was not to be permitted to be diluted and thus not to degenerate into a long twilight for the ideals of Kemalism. The task was not easy, and constant vigilance needed to be combined with occasional sharp crackdowns. This was the moral that the Turkish army appeared to have drawn from the developments of the previous decades. In early 1997, the military general staff submitted to the National Security Council a report on "reactionary activities" which gave an account of the links among the Brotherhoods, the worlds of economics and politics, and terrorist circles. In the words of the report: "At a certain point, the Brotherhoods which were linked to the Tekke, the Zaviya and the

Dergah abandoned their spiritual vocation and became institutions which served the purposes of reactionary circles. These institutions were closed down in the early years of the Republic. Today, however, institutions which claim to be their heirs are still in operation." The military insisted on legislation that immediately returned responsibility for religious teaching to the state. A law prescribing eight years of compulsory secular education targeted the schools run by imams and preachers, to which pupils had previously been able to go after five years of primary school. In June 1997, the policy of putting religious teaching once more under the control of the Ministry of Education led to Erbakan's resignation.

The new legislation raised the prospect of a polarization within the state apparatus between the secular Ministries—on this occasion the Ministry of Education—and the Ministry for Religious Affairs, responsible for the administration of the Vakif, which was more or less regarded as under the influence of Islamist ideas. This antagonism led to disagreements over the supervision of the content of courses in the private schools. However, the Brotherhoods were expert at turning this kind of controversy to their own advantage. The extension of the period of compulsory education and the confrontation which ensued between the military authorities and the Refah Party—which continued until Refah's dissolution in February 1998 and its replacement by the Fazilet (Virtue) Party—did not necessarily damage the Brotherhoods. The reform did not in practice affect the Vakif controlled by the Dervishes, who either already had at their disposal or were able swiftly to set up, and primary schools that were able to give the teaching required by the law, in addition to their own curriculum.

However, the military general staff's 1997 report also provided for state control over the Vakif and the reapplication of Turkey's "revolutionary" laws which specified the closure of the Tekke as well as legal steps to be taken against any who might oppose such measures. Erbakan's party was the primary target of the military, but they were not reluctant also to take measures against the Brotherhoods. At the behest of the army general staff and the National Security Council, an inquiry was opened into the Vakif, with the intention of subjecting them to stricter control and of punishing any dissident activity. Scandals erupted over the property owned by the great Brotherhood Vakif, such as the Fetih Islamic complex built by a member of the Ismail Aga "Tekke" at Beykoz, and the private property owned by certain of the Sheikhs, such as Esat Cosan's villa. Finally, a number of highly visible raids were carried out in the Fetih quarter, targeting any institutions displaying sporting religious symbols, although no serious action was taken. However, it was sufficient to remind the Brotherhoods that they owed their success only to the temporary disregard of a law which could at any moment be brought once more into play with all due force.

Fazilet Partisi (The Virtue Party)

The Virtue Party was founded in December 1997, as the successor to the Refah Party, subsequent to legal proceedings that led eventually to an official ban on Refah imposed on January 13, 1998. Fazilet laid stress on its rejection of any use of violence for political ends and on its support for democratic pluralism. Refah was popular and by early 1998 had already attracted 4 million members, according to its leadership. Despite its commitment to democracy, its stated objective was the re-Islamization of Turkey. The leaders of the Virtue Party were all associates of Necmettin Erbakan. Its first head was Ismail Alptekin, a lawyer, who was succeeded by Recai Kutan, one of the leaders of the NSP who had also served as a member of parliament for the party. However, it was subject to severe internal strains, with the "old guard" criticized for its conservatism by a faction of reformists who wished to reconcile Islam with modern ideas. This faction's leaders were the former Mayor of Istanbul, Tayyip Recep Erdogan, and the Party's deputy president, Abdullah Gül, an economist (who would later found the AK Party.

At the parliamentary elections of April 1999, Fazilet suffered a setback. It lost ground in its strongholds in central Anatolia to the extreme right wing Milliyetçi Hareket Partisi (MHP) (the Nationalist Action Party), led by Devlet Bahçeli. Meanwhile, in the Kurdish region in southeast Turkey, there was a surge in the popularity of the Halkin Democrasi Partisi (HADEP) (the Popular Democracy Party). This movement specifically sought to promote Kurdish interests. Nationally, Fazilet took only 15.2 percent of the votes and came third, trailing the Democratic Left Party (DSP) of Bulent Ecevit and the MHP. This poor performance occurred at a politically difficult time, when the army, which expressed its intention of taking action against "reactionary religious movements," had already initiated a series of legal measures in the courts against the Islamic movement. The principal sufferer was Tayyip Erdogan, who was arrested following a speech he made at Siirt, in southeast Turkey, and on September 25, 1988 was given a ten-month prison sentence for "arousing religious hatred."

In May 1999, woman newly elected as a Fazilet member of parliament, Merve Kavakci, was barred from the chamber after attempting to be sworn in while wearing her Islamic head-covering, an act illegal under Turkey's secular constitution. When it was revealed that she had also become a citizen of the United States she was stripped of her Turkish nationality. In due course, broader judicial procedures were brought against

Fazilet, as they had been against its predecessor Islamist parties, apparently at the initiative of the all-powerful National Security Council, a constitutionally important body in Turkey composed of both military leaders and politicians that enjoys the power of veto over legislation and appointments. Fazilet was officially dissolved on June 22, 2001, because of what were described as its "anti-secular" activities. This new legal episode in the history of Turkish Islamism led to a break between the two factions, the old guard and the reformists. Neither faction abandoned the policy of operating within the law, and set in train measures to set up two competing organizations. Erbakan set up the so-called Felicity Party, or Saadet, whereas on August 14, 2001, Erdogan and his supporters set up the Justice and Development Party (AK Party: the word "Ak" means "clean" or "unblemished" in Turkish).

Milli Selamet Partisi (National Salvation Party)

The NSP was founded in 1972, declaring its objective to be the political expression of Islamic principles. Its program also displayed populist and nationalist overtones. The party deplored what it called Turkey's "moral decadence," calling for the reestablishment of the Shari'a and for the legal protection for the profession of the Muslim faith. Its founding leader was a lawyer, Suleyman Arif Emre, who was succeeded in May 1973 by Necmettin Erbakan, an engineer by profession. With most of its officials drawn from the civil service, the universities, or the professions, the NSP was a populist organization run by intellectuals.

By declaring their support for nationalism, the Islamists were able on this occasion to gain the approval of the military high command. The party's leadership backed the military intervention in Cyprus in July 1974 and subsequently solicited the support of Muslim powers for the Turkish intervention. The NSP published its own periodical, the "Milli Gazete" ("The National Newspaper") and maintained a youth branch. It also succeeded in attracting support from Islamist sources outside Turkey. After the 1973 elections, it became a key party, with 12 percent of the votes and forty-eight seats in Parliament. It took part in a number of coalition governments, most notably with Bulent Ecevit's Republican People's Party, under Ecevit as Prime Minister, from January 1974 to January 1978.

Refah Party

The Refah Party was an Islamist organization created in 1983 by former members of the NSP that was very influential in Turkish politics in the 1990s, particularly during its period as part of a coalition government. The party's final dissolution on January 13, 1998, signaled the end of a historic compromise with the military high command. In its early days, under its founding leader, Ali Turkmen, Refah benefited from a relatively propitious political atmosphere, as Prime Minister Turgut Ozal, the leader of the Motherland Party, introduced a series of parliamentary measures to reestablish a place for Islam in Turkey's secular society. However, the party remained marginalized within Turkey's political spectrum, taking only 4.4 percent of the votes cast in the 1984 election. In 1985, however, Necmettin Erbakan became leader of the party. Erbakan's energy and personality enabled him to boost the party's appeal and greatly expand its membership. Its most impressive electoral results came in the Kurdish regions of Bingol and Diyarbakir, where the Islamic Brotherhoods were most influential.

The party deployed various strategies to strengthen its position. The town of Konya is renowned in Turkey for its religious conservatism, and Refah made great efforts to capture its parliamentary and local government seats, which would symbolize the party's claim to be the authentic representation of Islam. In 1990, in another key stratagem to strengthen its support, Refah established an association of business leaders sympathetic to its ideas, to be known as "Musiad." From the outset, this body, made of the leaders of small and medium businesses, spoke a different language from the directors and managers of the large national industrial concerns. They advocated an "Islamic common market" to comprise Turkey's Muslim neighbors, and Refah spoke about what it called the "Asian model of development." Boosted by the faithful support of Turkish small businessmen, Refah enjoyed solid financial support throughout the 1990s. One way in which Refah was different from most other contemporary Islamist organizations was the size and activity of its women's branch. This made a major contribution to its electoral success, especially in the large cities. The party published a magazine for women, "Mektup," and claimed to have developed a synthesis of women's liberation with Islam and modernity.

In 1991, Refah went into alliance with the extreme right-wing party MHP ("Party of National Action") and made its entry for the first time into Parliament with forty seats. This provisional alliance had its roots in goals shared by the two parties, especially in foreign policy. During the first Chechen war, from 1993 to 1996, the paramilitary wing of the MHP, known as the "Bozkurlar" ("The Grey Wolves")—in honor of Kemal Ataturk—had sent men to fight with the Chechen rebels. At the same time, Necmettin Erbakan made an appeal for the liberation through Jihad of what he called "occupied Chechen territory." With its ultranationalist supporters, Refah was also able to ensure its immediate political survival for the time being by coming to an accommodation with the military high command.

Since 1989, Refah already had been in control of a number of town councils in south-eastern Turkey and in central Anatolia, including Van and Kahraman-Maras. However, on March 27, 1994, Refah gained its first real electoral breakthrough by taking the majority of the seats in a number of large municipalities. Two party officials, Recep Tayyip Erdogan and Melih Gökçek, were elected as mayors of Istanbul and Ankara respectively. Once elected to power, the Islamists aimed to install a new moral order that would combine puritanism with social justice. In Ankara, they attracted support by subsidizing the prices of essential products including bread and coal. In the parliamentary elections of 1995, Refah became the leading political formation in the country with over 21 percent of the votes, partly due to the reputation it had gained for fighting corruption and racketeering in business. It then adopted a very risky strategy by going into coalition with the True Path Party of Tansu Çiller, although this party had lost support due to recurrent accusations over alleged links with criminal elements. The resulting "Refahyol" coalition, led by Necmettin Erbakan as prime minister, was short-lived. In June 1997, there was a political crisis leading to the resignation of Necmettin Erbakan as prime minister and the withdrawal of Refah from the government.

Although Refah was a master of political pragmatism, and even though it made a number of painful concessions, its major policy successes had been limited to the field of foreign policy. Refah was antagonistic to the major institutions of the international community, which it saw as "in thrall to the western powers" as become apparent over the issue of Turkey's adhesion to the European Union. Its response was to initiate a new Muslim economic organization, the so-called D8 group, made up of eight major Muslim states: Bangladesh, Egypt, Iran, Indonesia, Malaysia, Nigeria, Pakistan, and Turkey itself. As the Refah leadership saw it, this initiative was the first political step on the road to the establishment of novel institutions that would lead to a new world order. The plan, which was highly ambitious, failed to come to fruition because of a lack of solidarity within Turkey's political class. Instead, the military leadership set up an alliance with Israel. After the collapse of the coalition, linked partly to financial scandals implicating Mrs. Çiller, the army leadership initiated a process intended to halt Refah's activities. On January 13, 1998, the Refah Party was officially dissolved.

TURKMENISTAN

Turkmenistan appears to be the most stable and homogeneous state in Central Asia, despite the residual possibility of disturbances originating with the Uzbek minority. Of its population of just over 5 million (estimated in 2006), 85 percent are Turkmens, with 5 percent Uzbek and 4 percent Russian. Turkmenistan has substantial energy resources. Its foreign policy is based on safeguarding its independence from Russia, while cultivating good relations with its neighbors, including Afghanistan. Turkmenistan implements bilateral agreements, more conducive to maintaining its freedom of action, rather than entering multinational pacts that might pull it unwillingly into regional conflicts.

Turkmenistan has an 1100 kilometer border with Iran and shares 600 kilometers of frontier with Afghanistan, with which it maintains good relations despite the difficulties that have intermittently arisen due to political anarchy in the country. On the other hand, Turkmenistan is geographically relatively distant from Russia, which helps it to maintain its political distance. It refused to assist in Russian peace-keeping operations in Tajikistan, and in July 1993, it withheld

permission for Russian aircraft supplying the Russian forces in Tajikistan to stop over in Turkmen territory. Its discreet support for the Taliban, at the time when Russia was arming and giving financial support to the Northern Alliance, contributed to the cooling of relations between the two countries. This policy, adopted in view of the Taliban's strength and prospects of victory, ensured the integrity of Turkmenistan's Afghan frontier and kept alive the possibility of realizing Turkmenistan's project of an eventual pipeline to the Indian Ocean across Afghanistan and Pakistan. Turkmenistan's cultural link with Turkey has facilitated a level of practical cooperation between the two countries, but exchanges with Shi'ite Iran have remained limited owing to the barrier of language and religion—the population of Turkmenistan is 89 percent Sunni Muslim.

Turkmenistan claims there are a million Turkmens in Afghanistan and at least 2 million in Iran—although other estimates put the figures lower, at 300,000 and 800,000 respectively. These minorities are a factor in Turkmen relations with neighboring states. Throughout the twentieth century, there has been antagonism between the Sunni Turkmen minority in Iran and the Shi'ite Persian state. During the Islamic Revolution in 1979, the Iranian Turkmens set up a cultural and political organization that called for the redistribution of land and a greater degree of autonomy. The response of Khomeini's regime was a severe clamp down on their activities. From the point of view of the government of Turkmenistan, however, the presence of the Turkmen minority in Iran is a mixed blessing. The Turkmens in the Iranian provinces of Kharasan and Mazandaran belong to the Yomut tribe, whose representatives within Turkmenistan regard themselves as oppressed by the dominant Tekke tribe. Any claim they might make for autonomy might well be taken to apply to both sides of the frontier and has the potential to destabilize both countries. Teheran and Ashqabat therefore have a mutual interest in reaching an understanding.

Islam arrived late in Turkmenistan and, broadly speaking, manifests itself more as a cultural preference than as a deeper commitment to religion. Although virtually all Turkmens would claim to be Muslims, few attend the mosques. Although the Muslim population is relatively unreligious, the government has taken some steps since the end of the Soviet Union to accommodate Muslim predilections. Alcohol has been banned, and polygamous marriages are recognized, although no more than 5 percent of the male population is involved in the latter phenomenon. The Uzbek mionority is more religious, but there is relatively little contact between the communities. The people of the towns are marginally less committed to religion than those in the countryside. During the communist era, 8 percent in the towns were estimated to be practicing Muslims and 10 percent in the villages. The most observant regions are in the province of Dashoguz, close to the Uzbek frontier, and Ahal on the Iranian frontier. The most ostentatiously pious Turkmen tribe is that of the Nohur, whereas it has been said that the village of Bagir, inhabited by part of the tiny Kurdish minority within Turkmenistan, is perhaps the most pious community.

Turkmenistan's constitution, adopted on May 18, 1992, lays down the principle that the country is a secular republic, in which the state guarantees the freedom of religion. At the same time, however, religion is precluded from all involvement in education or state affairs. The law on religious affairs, promulgated on April 12, 1993, takes up the same theme of the separation of the state from religion, the equality of treatment of religious communities, and the separation of religion from the educational system. It established the institution known as the "Kaziat" for the management of religious affairs, which is subject to the authority of the Mufti of Tashkent. The law also provides for various means of control over the religious activities of foreigners. The financing of mosques by foreign donors is prohibited, and proselytization by foreign preachers is banned without prior authorization from the authorities.

In the period 1991–1992, Islamic preachers came from Saudi Arabia, Pakistan, and India, who were at first permitted to preach in the mosques and used their sermons to press for the establishment of an Islamic Republic and the introduction of the Shari'a. The government lost no time in suppressing the phenomenon and expelling what it regarded as trouble makers. The Kaziat and the president's religious advisory council have since enabled the government to keep effective control of religious affairs. More recently, there has been a modest increase in the numbers of fundamentalist Islamists antagonistic to the secular government. Their spokesmen, although unable to operate openly, are better educated, more eloquent, and therefore more persuasive than the traditional religious establishment. However, conclusions may be drawn concerning the persistent lack of strength of religious sentiment in Turkmenistan from the failure of an attempt by the Central Asian Islamic Renaissance Party to set up a branch in Ashqabat, which attracted only two hundred or three hundred members.

Under Turkmenistan's President Saparmurat Niyazov, the conscious relegation of Islam to the level of a traditional practice has helped to ensure that Islamist activities have made little inroad into Turkmen society. The Turkmens have created an amalgam between the practices of the Islamic Brotherhoods, which arrived in the region from the tenth century onward, and the tribal loyalties and practices. The modern phenomenon of Salafi preachers, who exhort the faithful to change their ways of life and demanding worship in anonymous city mosques, has little appeal. In addition, the state has swiftly clamped down on any sign of religious enthusiasm. There have been arrests, and infrequent attempts at subversion have been swiftly dealt with. After an assassination attempt against the president on November 25, 2002, apparently for political reasons, repression against all potential opposition factions was increased, having its effect on Islamist groups. The laws on secularism are strictly enforced, and unauthorized religious congregations may not meet. The president—"Turkmenbashi," as he calls himself—has organized a society in which military service, social projects, and even his idiosyncratic laws against the growing of beards and certain forms of dress conspire to leave little scope for Islamists to recruit to their cause.

UDUGOV, MOVLADI

According to the Russians, Movladi Udugov, the former minister of culture in Chechnya under Dudaiev, was the country's leading exponent of Islamism. In fact he has always taken a practical view of Chechnya's situation. Now living in exile, Udugov's opinion is simply that the West can be of no assistance to Chechnya in its struggle for independence, but he deems it preferable that Chechnya place its faith in the Muslim countries and in Islamic organizations. He calculates his rhetoric to the goal of gaining access to funds from such sources. His Internet site, known sometimes as "Chechnya Online," may therefore be less than wholly faithful to the facts.

UGANDA

Over the last decade and before, violent Islamist movements have made their appearance in this African state where 16 percent of the country's population of 27 million consists of Muslims. The first Muslims to make their appearance in Uganda modern times arrived in the 1840s. The influence of Islam grew, and after the accession to the throne of King Mutesa I, the "Kabaka" of Uganda, in 1856, he went through a formal conversion to Islam and actively promoted the religion. In the 1970s, there was a marked increase in the number of converts to Islam, but in the end, the Christianity brought by missionaries became dominant in the country. This was encouraged by the British colonial regime. The remaining Muslims were mainly from the less privileged class of small traders and blue-collar workers.

In more recent times, Islam has taken a more central role. The "National Association for the Advancement of Muslims" was founded in 1965, with the support of the government of President Milton Obote. There were also other Muslim factions. In 1971, when Idi Amin, himself a Muslim from a typically Muslim background, overthrew Milton Obote's government, he established and funded the Uganda Muslim Supreme Council (UMSC), to take the place of previous Muslim organizations. Under Idi Amin, the standing of Islam in Uganda rose. In 1974, Uganda became a member of the Organization of the Islamic Conference (OIC) and began to receive help from the international Sunni Muslim community. In the 1970s and 1980s, a number of Ugandans were educated in Saudi Arabia and came under the influence of the Wahhabi version of Salafi thinking. The mosques they established in Uganda appealed to younger Muslims in the country. In 1979, Idi Amin was overthrown, and in 1986, President Yoweri Museveni came to power. He maintained

Uganda's membership of the OIC despite the minority status of Islam in the country.

In the 1970s and 1980s, the international Sunni preaching movement Tablighi Jamaat, or "Tabligh" (sometimes also locally written "Tabliq"), also became active in Uganda. Though Tabligh is essentially nonpolitical, in Uganda it took a political turn in the hands of local enthusiasts. For example, Sheikh Suleiman Kakeeto began as a Tablighi missionary and then set up his own organization. Another leading Salafi linked to Tabligh was Jamil Mukulu. In 1991, the Museveni government confirmed the conservative Sheikh Ibrahim Luwemba in the post of Mufti of Uganda. This led the younger Salafis, many of whom were by now associated with Tabligh, to challenge the government and the UMSC. On March 22, 1991, a Salafi group occupied the UMSC headquarters in the old Kampala mosque, leading to a clash in which a number of policemen were killed. Hundreds of Muslim activists were arrested and jailed. In the aftermath, Jamil Mukulu went to prison, whereas Sheikh Kakeeto assumed the leadership of the Tabligh movement, explicitly renouncing further violence.

In August 1992, after his release from prison, Jamil Mukulu established a more radical wing of Tablighi Jamaat that he dubbed the "Salaf Foundation." Many of his followers were those who had earlier clashed with the authorities. His mode of operation was through the customary Salafi program of welfare activities, undertaken as an intermediate step on the way to building a new social order based on the Shari'a. Jamil Mukulu preached at the Masjid Noor Mosque, where his sermons followed a markedly political agenda. By 1995, Mukulu's explicit defiance of the government had reached the point where he decided to flee the country for his own safety, retiring to Sudan. Sheikh Kakeeto's more moderate Tabligh faction, however, was left relatively unmolested by the authorities.

A new movement made its appearance in the 1990s, calling itself the Allied Democratic Front (ADF), whose objective was the violent overthrow of President Museveni. This consisted of a number of dissident groups, but prominent among them was the hard core of Mukulu's radical Tabligh group. By 1995, Jamil Mukulu is said to have made contact with Osama bin Laden in Sudan. It is possible that ADF members went to Sudan for training, and some have claimed that ADF elements later went to Afghanistan. Sudan's Islamist ideologue Hassan al-Turabi backed the ADF and may have seen the Islamization of Uganda as a step toward his goal of spreading Islam throughout Africa. Sudan is said to have supplied the ADF with arms and material support. In 1997, the ADF attacked Ugandan army units on the Congolese border. They were responsible in the 1990s for a spate of bomb attacks and have abducted civilians. By 2004, however, the ADF had been largely contained by the Ugandan armed forces, known as the Ugandan People's Defence Force (UPDF). Tabligh missionaries from Pakistan and India have since been denied access to Uganda, though there is no suggestion that they have taken any direct part in violence. The use of the name of Tabligh by groups dedicated to violence runs directly counter to Tabligh's basic ideology.

ULEMA

The Arabic word "Ulema" is the plural of the word "Alim," which means "learned man." It is used to refer to Islamic clerics, who may be preachers, imams, judges, muftis, jurists, or teachers. In general, "Ulema" refers to the class of Muslim clerics, who are regarded as the guardians of knowledge and wisdom relating to the Islamic faith and the only reliable source of information about it. A difficulty, however, is that in Sunni Islam there is no hierarchy. The "Ulema" acquire respect and achieve their position on the basis of their reputation and standing with their peers and with the Muslim community in general, rather than from any hierarchical appointment. Historically, the rulers of countries and cities often appointed their own muftis (jurists), qadis (judges), and imams (prayer leaders) at mosques in their domain. The authority these enjoyed came only partly from their appointments, however. There was an equally important sense in which rulers attempted to bolster their own authority by appointing respected figures to such posts, thus associating their secular authority with the religious standing of the figures they had been able to associate with the state.

It has always been the case, nevertheless, that there are some sources of authority that automatically command respect. The Sheikhs of Al-Azhar, the ancient mosque and university in Cairo, are regarded as authoritative throughout the Sunni world. Graduates and honorands of Al-Azhar enjoy real prestige. The senior clerics of Saudi Arabia wield authority over those who subscribe to the Wahhabi doctrine. Among the Muslims of India and Pakistan, the school at Deoband is regarded as the source of religious orthodoxy and authoritative rulings. Senior figures within such organization as Tablighi Jamaat and the Islamic Brotherhoods also enjoy great respect. Only "Ulema" of standing may issue "Fatwas" worthy of respect and emulation. Nothing, of course, prevents any person from promulgating a Fatwa, but it will not be respected by the community. This has not prevented Osama bin Laden, who has no religious standing, from purporting to originate Fatwas (though he has attempted to associate Ulema of standing with his pronouncements). In Europe, the Egyptian cleric Sheikh Qaradawi has founded the European Council for Fatwa and Research and commands a substantial audience among European Muslims. The late Zaki Badawi, formerly principal of the Muslim College, was widely regarded as an authority in Britain and was awarded an honorary knighthood by the British government in recognition of his efforts in the field of community relations. In France, Dr. Dalil Boubakeur, rector of the Paris Mosque, enjoys great respect among the Muslim community.

Within the Salafi school, less attention is paid to the traditional sources of judgment within the structure of Islamic society. There is an assumption that the preferable case is that religious judgment be exercised by the individual Muslim. Salafis accord a hearing only to would-be authorities whose pronouncements they find acceptable. In historical terms, respect is accorded to certain figures, including notably the thirteenth century cleric Ibn Taymiya—especially venerated by Salafis—who is seen as endorsing rebellion against Muslim leaders who have allegedly fallen away from the observance of the true faith. More orthodox Muslims take the view that the Salafis are setting themselves up as their own sources of "Ijtihad"— the interpretation of the basic sources of the faith—in a way their scholarship and standing does not justify.

The situation is different in Shi'ite Islam. Within the Shi'ite faith, religious scholars pass through a hierarchy of ranks—Hojateleslam, Ayatollah, and Grand Ayatollah—depending on the consensus of their peers that they be so recognized. However, the rank, once achieved, has a permanent and quasi-official status within the hierarchy. The ranking of religious authorities and jurists is therefore much more formally structured than in Sunni Islam. Grand Ayatollahs have always been accepted as the authorities within Shi'ite Islam. With the establishment of the Islamic Republic of Iran and in the context of the constitution devised by Ayatollah Khomeini, recognition as the ultimate authority within Islam, at least inside Iran, has been accorded to the "Faqih" (often known as the Supreme Leader). Even here, however, Grand Ayatollahs of similar standing would in some circumstances claim comparable authority.

UNITED STATES

There is a substantial Muslim community of American citizens within the domestic United States, whose origins are very diverse. Recent estimates of the number of Muslims in the United States vary wildly, ranging from 3 million up to 6 million. The true figure seems likely to be in this bracket. An estimate of the proportions in which various Muslim communities are represented has been made by the "Council on American–Islamic Relations" (CAIR), set up in 1994, to represent the interests of Muslims in the United States. According to CAIR, working from records of those who actively attend mosques, one-third of the Muslims in the United States are from the Indian subcontinent (India, Pakistan, and Bangladesh), 30 percent are African Americans, and a quarter are of Arab origin. The remainder comes from many backgrounds, including Turkey and Southeast Asia. The true proportions within the Muslim community as a whole, where many are nonobservant, may be different.

CAIR has received funding from Middle Eastern sources including the Islamic Development Bank and the World Association for Muslim Youth (WAMY), as well as from wealthy individuals such as Prince Walid bin Talal of Saudi Arabia and the deputy ruler of Dubai, Sheikh Hamdan Al Maktoum. After September 11, 2001, CAIR helped to arrange the promulgation of a Fatwa by the Fiqh Council of North American condemning extremism. Nonetheless, CAIR has been the object of frequent criticism and of accusations by those wary of the activities of Muslims in the United States that it fosters violence and extremism. There are many other Islamic societies and associations in the United States including the Islamic Society of North America (ISNA) and the Islamic Circle of North America. The Islamic Supreme Council of America is a body coordinating the efforts of Muslim groups that attempt to practice Islam within the American context. The Islamic Assembly of North America promotes "Da'wa" (preaching) and Islamic orthodoxy. Among the African-American community in particular, the Islamic Society of Muslims is a successor to the Nation of Islam. There are also Muslim student organizations, many of whose members are not U.S. citizens. An important educational institution is the Al-Zaytuna Institute in California. In addition to these largely Sunni bodies, there are Shi'ite organizations, including North American Shi'a Ithna-Asheri Muslim Communities (NASIMCO) and a branch of the Al-Khoei Foundation. The American Society for Muslim Advancement (ASMA) promotes interfaith understanding. The Muslim Public Affairs Council lobbies on Muslim issues in Washington, DC. Many other specialized and small Muslim associations represent the particular interests within the Muslim community in the United States in a variety of ways.

In the post–September 11, 2001 **era**, the position of Muslims in the United States has become more difficult. Many have been living lives that are either secular or at least do not include ostentatious religious observance. Some such people have found themselves for the first time singled out as objects of hostility, even though young Muslims from such backgrounds are serving in the armed forces of the United States. Arab Muslims in particular, identifiable because of their names, have been subjected to unusual surveillance when traveling. A very small number of Muslims in the United States seems to have become radicalized, after the pattern of some Muslims in Europe. Some have developed hostility to the United States, and at least nine Muslim individuals have been given long prison sentences for support to organizations including Al-Qa'ida. However, the overwhelming majority of millions of American citizens of Muslim origin are unshaken in their determination to be patriotic citizens of their country.

Guanatanamo Bay

Guantanamo Bay is a U.S. naval base situated at the eastern end of the island of Cuba. It was ceded to the United States by treaty in 1903. The present Cuban government contends that the treaty has been abrogated and that the base is now held illegally by the United States. Since late 2001, it has been used by the American authorities for the detention of prisoners apprehended in various countries around the world who are suspected of terrorist activity and hostile intentions toward the United States. The first prisoners arrived from Afghanistan on January 11, 2002. The facility in which they were held was named Camp X-Ray. Conditions were extremely basic. By March 27, 2002, the facility held three hundred prisoners of some thirty-three different nationalities. On April 29, 2002, Camp X-Ray was closed, and the prisoners were transferred to Camp Delta, a permanent facility. The U.S. government classified the prisoners as "illegal combatants," because they were not members of a regular army. This is not a category recognized by the Geneva Conventions on prisoners of war, but on June 29, 2006, the Supreme Court ruled that the Geneva Conventions in fact apply to the prisoners.

By November 7, 2005, the five hundred or so prisoners included one hundred from Saudi Arabia, eighty from Yemen, sixty-five from Pakistan, and fifty from Afghanistan.

Prisoners had been apprehended in a variety of circumstances, including a number detained by the security forces in Pakistan and handed over to American custody. By November 2006, approximately 775 prisoners had been brought to Guantanamo, of whom 340 had been released, leaving 435 in custody. Of these, 70 are likely to be tried, 110 are ready to be released if a country can be found to accommodate them, and the fate of 255 remains uncertain. These may apparently be held indefinitely. Varying allegations have been made about the level of involvement in terrorism of the detainees. Some are indubitably culpable, whereas others appear to have been the victims of circumstances. A senior American officer in 2003 claimed that three-quarters of those held had some terrorist connection. In September 2006, a number of prisoners were transferred to Guantanamo who had been held in previously unacknowledged prisons in various locations. Allegations of various forms of torture at Camp Delta have been made by prisoners who have been released. Undoubtedly, the prisoners are subjected to constraints and discomforts. The U.S. administration has ruled that prisoners at Guantanamo will be tried before military tribunals and has expressed the hope that trials, convictions, and releases into the custody of other countries will eventually permit the closure of Camp Delta.

Among prisoners who have been at Guantanamo Bay, some are of European origin. All the British citizens held have now been released. In May 2004, after being held for two years, Jamal al-Harith, Tariq Dergul, Asif Iqbal, Ruhel Ahmed, and Shafiq Rasul were set free. In January 2005, Martin Mubanga, Feroz Abbassi, Richard Belmar, and Moazzam Beg were released. No evidence was produced against any of these. A long-term British resident, Bisher al-Rawi (of Iraqi nationality), arrested while on a business trip to the Gambia, was released in April 2007. Seven other British residents were still held by May 2007. These were Jamil el-Banna (originally from Jordan), Shaker Aamer (Saudi), Omar Deghayes (Libyan), Ahmed Errachidid (Moroccan), Ahmed Belbacha (Algerian), and Abdelnour Sameur (Algerian), against none of whom allegations have been made and Binyam Mohammed (Ethiopian) has been accused of involvement in a so-called dirty bomb plot.

Of the French citizens held, Nizar Sassi is of Tunisian antecedents, born in 1979 and a resident of Venissieux in the Lyon region. He was captured in Afghanistan by U.S. forces and taken to Guantanamo Bay under suspicion of belonging to Al-Qaida. Seven other French citizens have also been transferred to Guantanamo Bay. These were Mourad Benchallali, born in 1982, from Venissieux; Brahim Yadel, 1972, Seine-Saint-Denis; Moustapha Abdel Rahman Hawari, 1980, Paris; Khaled Radouane, 1967, Seine-Saint-Denis; Jean Baptiste Milhoud, 1980, Paris; Khaled bin Moustapha, 1972, Lyon; and Olivier Bazart, 1956, Bordeaux.

Islamism and the United States

Relations between the U.S. government and the world of Islam go back to the early twentieth century. The first interlocutors for the Americans in the Near East and Middle East were the Saudis, the new masters of Arabia. The relationship sprang up in the context of oil prospecting by American companies in Arabia in the 1920s and 1930s and the emergence of the United States as the new great world power after World War II. For the understanding of this strong but informal relationship, a historical perspective is needed.

In more recent times, the origin of the supremacy of the United States in the Middle East was Britain and France's ill-judged Suez venture in 1956, when the two European states invaded the Suez Canal Zone, while Israel, in collusion with them, launched a simultaneous attack on the Sinai Peninsula. Under joint pressure from the United States and the Soviet Union, the victorious invaders were obliged to withdraw from Egypt's territory, with the result that Britain and France surrendered what remained of their hegemonic standing in the Middle East to the new nuclear superpowers. In effect, the United States and the Soviet Union became the new power brokers of the Arab and Muslim Middle East. The Arab world emerged from the experience split into two parts. On the one hand, those countries that regarded themselves as progressive clustered around the leadership of Egypt's President Gamal Abdel Nasser, whereas the conservatives lined up behind Saudi Arabia.

The decision of the United States to extend its patronage to the petroleum monarchies was not an accident. The United States, as the British had done before, prioritized their own interests by seeking control of the oil and gas fields, exploitation, refineries, and transportation. It was scarcely surprising, therefore, that Saudi Arabia became a key element of American strategy, at the expense of Egypt, not an oil power, whose ruler had shown arrogance and hostility toward the West. Arabia was not the only interlocutor to be singled out in this way. Good relations with Iran, despite the internal troubles that threatened that country's vast oil reserves, also became a diplomatic target for the United States. Meanwhile, for strategic reasons, Turkey chose to ally itself with America and made itself become a valuable bulwark against the Soviets. After the war of 1967, Israel also became a close ally of the United States.

At the same time, the United States was reluctant to enter into relationships with organized groups of states, though the Arab countries had formed themselves into a unified organization by setting up the Arab League. Washington wanted only bilateral relations with the states of its choosing and, following the principle of divide and rule, actually aimed to prize the Arab League apart. In 1972, however, the change of direction by Egypt's President Anwar Sadat, who abruptly sent home some 18,000 Soviet advisers, furnished American diplomacy with a unique opportunity to reconstruct the balance of power in the region. From this point on, it was easier for Washington to reconcile its economy with its strategic interests in the region. The West promoted itself as the sponsor of peace in the region, which made it all the easier to establish good relations with Egypt, which wanted an equitable resolution of its conflict with Egypt and the return of its territory.

Henry Kissinger's strategy as National Security Advisor and then as Secretary of State in fact had four main objectives. These were:

1. The fragmentation of the Middle East.
2. U.S. involvement in all regional problems, where the United States would present itself as an interlocutor impossible to ignore.
3. The control of oil and other major economic sectors, including air transport, telecommunications, and IT industries.
4. The suppression of all manifestations of Arab unity, which in Washington's view could only be hostile.

To achieve these objectives, three principle strategies were brought to bear. These were:

1. Weakening and undermining hostile regimes.
2. Instrumentalization of Islam and Islamism.
3. Management by proxy of a fluid and unstable region.

The Lebanese war, usually referred to as a "civil war," was a focus for all the contradictions and paradoxes of the Middle East. From 1975 to 1983, during the first eight years of the conflict, foreign actors were involved in every aspect of the Lebanese war, including the Palestinian organizations, Syria, such outside nations as Libya and Sudan, and Israel. The only fully "civil" phase of the conflict took place from September 1983, when the Christians clashed with the Druzes. It should be noted that, from the moment the first shot was fired in Lebanon, there were no further conflicts, coups, or revolutions elsewhere in the Arab world. Seen in this light, the Lebanese conflict seems to have been an early success of the Kissinger strategy. The Camp David accords, agreed in 1978, with the subsequent peace treaty between Egypt and Israel, seemed to be a further manifestation, dividing Egypt from the Arab world so that in future the Arabs would lack Egypt's leadership. All the hyperbole of the "Rejectionist Front" countries and any acts of violence they might instigate were to be of little avail. The Arab world was henceforth powerless.

In 1979, the Islamic Revolution took place in Iran. Its consequences included the seizure of the U.S. Embassy in Tehran and the holding hostage of its diplomatic staff. However, the United States was not the only country threatened by the Islamic Republic of Iran. It was also a threat within the region, perhaps especially to Saudi Arabia, America's leading ally in the region. Iran is a Shi'ite country in a Sunni world and a lone Persian state with a population of some 70 million (40 million in 1979) amid an Arab population of hundreds of millions. It was in a sense a natural frontier between Arab and non-Arab Islam. It was also the strongest regional power in the Persian Gulf and therefore controlled the transit route for 35 percent of the oil supplies of the West. The emergence of a newly powerful Iran looked to the United States like a threat. However, it was Iran's immediate Arab neighbor Iraq that had become a source of concern owing to its military power, industrial development, growing economy, and belligerent attitude. Iraq also represented a serious challenge to Saudi Arabia.

In the event, Saddam Hussein and his military establishment took upon themselves the new mission—that of defending the region and the West against Iran's Ayatollahs. On September 22, 1980, as the Soviets were moving into Afghanistan, Saddam Hussein invaded Iran. The resulting war was to last eight years, weakening both countries and in the end bringing no change on the ground. During the war, Saddam received financial assistance from the Arab oil states and tacit help of various kinds from Western countries that were technically neutral. The sole benefit was to Saudi Arabia and the Gulf, which profited from the temporary distraction of its two regional rivals. When the war was over, however, Saddam Hussein sought recognition of his country's "sacrifice" on behalf of the Gulf States. In particular, a quarrel with Kuwait was quick to develop.

Saudi Arabia forgave Iraq's debt, but Saddam Hussein demanded that debts incurred by Iraq to Kuwait during the Iran–Iraq War should also be revoked. Acrimonious discussions took place over this issue. Saddam also claimed that Kuwait was overproducing oil, thus driving down the international price, and that it was exploiting oil in fields close to the border that truly belonged to Iraq. He also renewed the Iraqi demand that Kuwait cede the Gulf islands of Bubiyan and Warbah, which would provide better access for Iraq to the Gulf. Finally, he also revived the long-standing territorial claim by Iraq to Kuwait's territory that all Iraqi rulers since General Qassem had reiterated. Saddam wished to secure Iraq's position by adding Kuwait's oil resources to Iraq's own. In July 1990, when Saddam held his last talk with the American ambassador in Iraq, April Glaspie, she said that the United States had "no opinion on the Arab–Arab conflicts, like Iraq's border dispute with Kuwait." This may have given the Iraqi leader the impression that Washington would not object to any moves against Kuwait he might choose to make.

However, when Iraqi forces occupied Kuwait on August 2, 1990, the result was the U.S.-led operation known as "Desert Storm." Twenty-nine countries from around the world came together under the leadership of President Bush to eject the Iraqi invaders. These included Arab states such as Syria and Morocco. The outcome was the destruction of the Iraqi army, purported by the Americans at the time to have been the fourth strongest armed force in the world. Saudi Arabia had every reason to believe itself restored to security. Many unpredictable consequences flowed from President Bush's "crusade" against Iraq. First, there was further fragmentation of the Arab world into those against Iraq and those for it. Another consequence was the visible defeat of the secular concept of Arab nationalism, opening the way to an ideological victory for Islamism. In addition, each Arab state was obliged to look to its own security, which undermined solidarity between states and further weakened Arab nationalism. These new concerns were reflected in the policies of the Arab states toward outside powers. Each state sought to safeguard its position by striking up links with powers outside the region, enabling such powers to increase their regional influence. Meanwhile, there was a risk that Iraq might fall apart, thus setting a precedent for frontier change in the region as a whole. The outcome was that Syria, Iran, and Turkey were all henceforth on their guard against any move that might result in alterations in Iraq's frontiers.

A further result of the crisis was to enhance the regional influence of Israel as a major player in the region. The threats to Israel within the region were diluted for a number of reasons, resulting in a reinforcement of its position. Iraq's disappearance as a regional power was the most significant of these. Iraq's implicit and explicit threats to take action against Israel had begun to loom large. In addition, the decision by the United States to restrain Iran, the disunity between the Arab states, the financial crisis of the oil monarchies, and the collapse of the Soviet Union, which supervened immediately after the Gulf War, all played their part. Israel's superiority was evident in the fields of security, military strength, economics, and technology.

Finally, the American policy toward Arab and Muslim countries accentuated the divisions between regional states. The United States singled out particular powers to act on its behalf in each region. These were Saudi Arabia for the Arabian Peninsula, Egypt for the Nile Valley, and Israel for the Levant. In North Africa, the United States believed it could operate through Algeria. Algeria had won its freedom from France and held large oil and gas resources. Before becoming a client of the United States, which backed the Algerian authorities, it had faced the threat of destabilization following the rise of an Islamist movement whose goal was to overthrow the government.

In the closing years of the twentieth century, the Arab world continued to be politically disunited and technologically backward. The gap between rich and poor states was such that Arab wealth served only to highlight the problems of backwardness in other countries rather than to ameliorate them. In this situation of disarray, the region lay broadly under American hegemony, with U.S. bases in the Gulf and in ten Arab states including Egypt and Saudi Arabia. Those Arab states that rejected American supremacy were faced hostile propaganda and were characterized as pariah states or states that supported terrorism. The first group comprised Libya and Sudan as well as Iraq, though the threat from Iraq was countered by the American-led invasion in 2003 after

which Libya opted for reconciliation with the United States. The most prominent member of the second group was Syria, accused by the United States of sponsoring terrorist activities.

In the prevailing situation in the Middle East, the Islamists took the lead in the denunciation of the region's decline. In the mosques and madrasas across the region, the Islamist viewpoint became dominant, and the United States seized the chance to instrumentalize it, obliging those states that refused to align themselves with American policy to face the threat of destabilization. The *de facto* part played by the United States in the expansion of Islamism was part of a widespread strategy that operated in Central Asia and the Indian subcontinent as well as in the Middle East. In 1977, the ambition of the Saudis and their new ally, Pakistan, under the leadership of Zia ul-Haq, was to establish a Sunni Muslim entity between the Soviet Union, India, and Iran. This was almost realized when the Jihadists overthrew Afghanistan's communist regime and drove the Soviet Union to withdraw from Afghanistan.

The goal of Pakistan and Saudi Arabia in Central Asia and in Afghanistan was the spread of re-Islamization, which they believed would bring to power conservative Muslim regimes. The United States also saw Saudi Arabia as a counterbalance to Iranian influence, which had great wealth at its disposal. Its role was to provide finance, through private or semipublic channels, for Islamic projects. These included the construction of mosques, the distribution of copies of the Quran, the endowment of scholarships, and the provision of religious teachers. As regards the Afghan conflict, the United States became more directly involved. Before the Soviet withdrawal from Afghanistan, the CIA financed the Afghan mujahidin, according to a Congressional report, to the extent of $150 and $300 million a year, paid through accounts run by the Pakistani secret services (the ISI).

Until September 11, 2001, it never struck the Americans that Wahhabi-inspired Salafi Islam could be a danger to the United States itself, on its own soil. After September 11, 2001, FBI investigators began to realize the extent of the wealth of Osama bin Laden, who had received a vast personal fortune as part of his share of the family fortune. His father, Mohammed Awad bin Laden, who died in 1967, was the founder of the civil engineering conglomerate, the Saudi Bin Laden Group (SBLG). With financial subsidiaries in Europe and the United States, the family business had even bought a stake in the Carlyle Group, an American investment management company of which the elder President George Bush was a prominent shareholder, though this was later sold. The SBLG also took substantial holdings in other American investment funds. At Mohammed Awad bin Laden's death in 1967, when the group was worth an estimated $2 billion, control of the SBLG passed to Salem bin Laden, the eldest son, who pursued the goal of establishing close relations with American business leaders. There appear, fortuitously, to have been business links with the family of President Bush and his associates. Osama bin Laden's personal fortune, however, was apparently based entirely on his personal inheritance and did not depend on the family firm. In the 1970s, Osama bin Laden progressively distanced himself from his family and became a radical Islamist. During the 1979–1989 Afghan war against the Soviets and their allies in Afghanistan, he raised money and provided engineering services for the Islamists. He also became directly involved in the fighting. At this stage, he was continuing to receive help from the United States through various channels.

In 1991, Osama bin Laden broke with the United States. He had returned to Saudi Arabia, but was obliged by the Saudi authorities to leave the country after the Gulf War because of his criticism of the Saudi regime and his anti-American statements. In 1994, he was stripped of his Saudi nationality. In 1997, he declared that the continued presence of American troops in Arabia amounted to an occupation of the Muslim holy places. The strain that developed between bin Laden and the United States during the 1990s exemplified the gradual divorce between American policy and radical Islamism. On August 20, 1998, the breach became overt, when President Clinton ordered an air strike on bin Laden's training camps in Afghanistan in retaliation for the attacks on the U.S. embassies in Kenya and Tanzania. It was not until a year later that the United States imposed sanctions on the Taliban. The United Nations brought in its own sanctions a year later, in December 2000. Until this time, however, the United States carefully refrained from questioning the assistance given by the Pakistani ISI and Saudi Arabia to the Taliban and to bin Laden's Arab fighters, the so-called "Afghans."

By 1998, the United States had seen that complete victory for the Taliban would, for various reasons, be opposed by Russia, Iran, and India. The Americans then began to bring pressure to bear on the sponsors of the various Afghan factions to obtain an agreement between all the parties involved that would save some position for the Taliban. The United States asked the Taliban to extradite bin Laden and to compromise with the Northern Alliance, their principal internal enemies. In return, the United States would recognize the Taliban regime and would ensure that it received international aid while it completed the gas pipeline project planned by Unocal from Central Asia through Afghanistan to Pakistan. In order to bring pressure to bear on the Taliban regime, the United States sponsored UN Security Council resolution 1267, passed on October 15, 1999, which imposed sanctions on the Taliban. At the same time, it set up the negotiating group known as the six plus two, which comprised the six states bordering on Afghanistan, together with Russia and the United States.

President George W. Bush's electoral victory in 2000 led to a fresh look at the relationship between the United States and the ·Taliban. Like Bush himself, most of his staff had links to the oil companies. The overall strategy of the Americans was dictated by oil interests in the region. Hitherto, the Caspian countries had been obliged to use the Russian oil pipelines to transport their oil and gas output, with the payment of large premiums. President Bush's close aide was the National Security Advisor, Condoleezza Rice, who had advised his father on Soviet Affairs, had been since 1991 a member of the Board of Directors of Chevron Oil, and had advised the Board on Central Asia. Her own adviser on Afghanistan was Zalmay Khalilzad—later U.S. ambassador to post-conflict Iraq and then the United Nations—who between 1995 and 1998 negotiated the line of the Unocal oil pipeline with the Taliban. Many other members of the Bush administration had links with oil companies, not least the Vice President, Dick Cheney, former CEO of Halliburton, the leading company providing services to the oil industry. Throughout 2001, the Bush administration attempted to persuade the Taliban to hold a "Loya Jirga" (a grand council of tribes and factions). The Bush administration judged this an authentic and moderate Muslim procedure. It was also the option favored by Zalmay Khalilzad, who was still negotiating with the Taliban over the expulsion of bin Laden.

The Bush administration also withheld support from the Northern Alliance, which renamed itself the United Front at the beginning of 2001. The Northern Alliance had at its disposal 5,000 men loyal to Massoud and Sayyaf in the northwest of the country, with 15,000 others who could be called on, as well as Rashid Dostum's force which was at most 5,000 men and an indeterminate number of Shi'ite Hazaras. They were vastly outnumbered by the Taliban and their allies, who had 15,000 men and another 70,000 who could be summoned from the tribal hinterland. The Taliban also had the support of the 5,000 or so Arab "Afghans" loyal to bin Laden who could be called on to fight, which gave them a substantial advantage. The main advantage enjoyed by the Taliban, however, was the Northern Alliance's lack of unity.

American interests in the oil sector have continued to dictate developments. In spite of the events of September 11, 2001, and their consequences, and the proven links of those responsible with Saudi Arabia, the United States continued to protect Saudi Arabia and its 100 billion barrels of proven reserves. American actions against Islamists have continued to be selective. The Bush administration has apparently chosen to deal with Islamists who serve their interests and fight only against those implacably hostile to the United States. One thing which is certain, however, is that the consequences of the events of September 11 have encouraged and even helped the United States to extend the "Americanization" of the entire Middle East and Central Asia, begun at the time of the Gulf War in 1991.

The American attitude toward Islamists displays some contradictory features. Though the Saudi regime itself comes under attack from Salafi factions which believe it has deviated from the true path of Islam, the contradiction inherent in the close relations between Saudi Arabia and the United States remains blatant. Secondly, the United States took the decision to identify as a part of the Islamist threat the explicitly secular regime of Saddam Hussein in Iraq, which seems highly unlikely in fact to have had any connection with Islamic extremism. Thirdly, while the United States has been extremely anxious to promote a campaign to win over hearts and minds in the Middle East, its actions have had other effects. The security measures targeted at Arabs and Muslims within the United States, and the hostility of attitudes toward them inside the United States and on the part of Americans abroad, have alienated the Islamic world. The result has been increasingly to drive a wedge between the United States on the one hand and the Arab world and Muslim Umma on the other. On September 20, 2001, President George W. Bush spoke of what he called a "War on Terror" against Al-Qaida and its sympathizers and allies in the world. This has since to great extent colored and directed relations between the United States and Islam. There is real hostility to the United States, even in countries and among social groups where previously the attitude to the United States was positive, or at worst neutral, based on reports of American actions against those it identifies as Muslim terrorists.

Saudi Arabia and the United States

The pragmatic but apparently impregnable alliance between the United States and Saudi Arabia has its origins in a historic meeting at the close of World War II between President Franklin D. Roosevelt and the King of Saudi Arabia, King Abdulaziz, known as Ibn Saud. In 1945, three days after the end of the Yalta conference, President Roosevelt stopped over in Egypt, where he had asked the U.S. consulate in Jeddah to arrange a meeting with the King. This took place on February 14, 1945, on board a cruiser of the U.S. Navy, the USS Quincy, which lay at anchor in the Great Bitter Lake, south of Ismailiya, on the Suez Canal. President Roosevelt was joined on board by Ibn Saud, who was brought from Jeddah aboard the USS Murphy, the Quincy's escorting destroyer. This was no small matter for the King, who had never previously left the confines of Saudi Arabia.

When the two met, Roosevelt expressed his pleasure at meeting the King and went on to ask what he could do for the Saudi ruler. Ibn Saud responded that as Roosevelt had requested the meeting he imagined the president wanted something from him. The two men talked for several hours, in the shade of the naval guns on the Quincy's upper deck. King Saud remained inflexible on Palestine and the fate of the Jews. "What injury have the Arabs done to the Jews of Europe?" he asked, "It is the Christian Germans who stole their homes and lives. Let the Jews pay." Roosevelt gave the King a guarantee that the United States would take no action on Palestine without taking Arab interests into account. The president then went on to the need of the United States for harbor facilities in the Gulf. The King was accommodating but in exchange demanded a guarantee that there would never be an U.S. military presence on the ground within the Kingdom of Saudi Arabia. Finally, Roosevelt embarked on the issue of oil—the key topic, which he had kept to the end. What the president wanted was no less than the exclusive right for the United States to exploit Saudi Arabia's oil resources in their entirety. Again, the King's terms were exacting, but he responded positively. Throughout, Ibn Saud, who had assiduously prepared for the meeting, responded with wary acuity to all the American demands.

Finally, the talks came round to the question of the wording of an agreement between the two leaders. A number of issues were at stake. The United States declared that the stability of the Kingdom of Saudi Arabia would henceforth form part of the "vital interests" of the United States. The Kingdom today contains 26 percent of the world's known oil reserves, and its potential was already evident. Its significance as a potentially indispensable source of oil had already become clear to the Americans during World War II, when other oil resources were cut off by Japanese occupation. Though Saudi Arabia had so far relatively little oil in production, the Kingdom already seemed likely to be able in the future to guarantee the energy needs of the United States. In return for rights to Saudi oil, the United States would undertake unconditionally to protect the Kingdom against any threat that might arise. Ibn Saud would not need to give up an inch of territory, because the oil companies would be merely tenants of their concessions.

The King bargained hard for practical concessions, and it was agreed that the premium paid to him would rise from eighteen cents to twenty-one cents on each barrel of oil exported from Saudi Arabia. The two sides agreed that the duration of the concessions would be sixty years and would be expanded to 1.5 million square kilometers. On the expiry of the oil contracts in 2005, all wells, installations, and equipment would revert in their entirety to the monarchy. (In practice, after Roosevelt's death in April 1945, Ibn Saud did not regard himself as bound by the agreement and threatened to nationalize Aramco in 1950. Thereafter the Kingdom acquired control of the company in stages, taking full control in 1980.)

The United States also declared that the stability of the Arabian Peninsula as a whole would also form part of its "vital interests." In practice, American support for the Kingdom in future would relate not only to its role as a supplier of moderately priced oil but also to the Kingdom's position as the dominant power in the Arabian Peninsula. The United States therefore agreed to take joint responsibility for the maintenance of the stability of the Arabian Peninsula and more generally of the Gulf region, the principal objective of Ibn Saud's foreign policy. As soon as the oil began to come on stream, an oil analyst has noted, Aramco gave the Kingdom every kind of assistance in any case where the Saudis were in conflict with any other state in Arabia.

An economic, commercial, and financial partnership was also agreed between the two countries. This has continued into modern times, with the United States increasing its oil purchases while concluding arms contracts that grow constantly larger (from 1993 to 2000, $28 billion of arms were sold to the Kingdom). Meanwhile, economists estimate that today at least $500 billion of Saudi funds, taking public and private investment together, are invested in the United States, much of it in Treasury bonds, whereas the investment in Saudi Arabia by multinational companies based in the United States exceeds $5 billion. It may easily be seen that Kingdom regards its relationship with the United States as a form of insurance policy. Noninterference with Saudi Arabia's internal politics is the quid pro quo for Saudi Arabia's policy of preference for the United States. Washington never raises issues connected with human rights in Saudi Arabia, a position increasingly difficult to maintain after September 11, 2001. Public opinion in the United States increasingly demands an examination of Saudi Arabia's internal affairs. Only over Palestine was it impossible for the two leaders to reach agreement.

Both the president and the king seemed satisfied with the outcome of their meeting. After the meeting was over, a memorandum setting out what had been agreed was prepared in both Arabic and English texts by the U.S. consul in Jedda, William Eddy, and Yusuf Yasin, a Syrian citizen who was serving as Ibn Saud's foreign minister. The King, who had gone ashore in Egypt, immediately signed his copy, and President Roosevelt signed the next day in Alexandria, to which the USS Quincy had by then sailed. The memorandum was kept confidential and never passed through the State Department's formal channels. Ibn Saud, for his part, regarded his copies of the documents, in Arabic and English, as private records of a confidential meeting between himself and

President Roosevelt. They were evidence of the good faith between the two men. Though the main lines of the agreement survived Roosevelt's death, the King did not expect them to be enforceable, as they did not form part of an international treaty. Mutual confidence persisted, however, and in 1951, a further agreement was made enabling the United States to open the Dhahran air base. In the years that followed, successive U.S. presidents have given their own assurances to the Saudi state of continued support.

The agreement made between Ibn Saud and Roosevelt in 1945 was a new departure in international relations in the Middle East in the postwar era. Ousting the influence of Britain, the agreement positioned the United States as the dominant element in the political balance in the region at the expense of the European states. It also set the seal on a new kind of deal—oil for security—that would later become the model for other agreements of the same kind made by the United States, especially in Central Asia. This historic deal had many consequences. Not only did it exchange the promise of oil against the guarantee of security, it also ensured the continuation of one of the most conservative religious dynasties in the world, which was the guardian of the Holy Places of Islam. This had a surprising consequence. It enshrined the power of Saudi Arabia and thereby curtailed the ambitions of the secular Arab nationalists. Thus, it enhanced the security of the State of Israel. This might have seemed contradictory. On the contrary, however, the phenomena were the two sides of the same process, joined at the hip by Islamic fundamentalism. Aboard the USS Quincy, the American and Saudi leaders concluded an agreement that would make each of them, in different ways, the guardians of Islamism.

Only today, in the new circumstances that prevail after the events of September 11, are questions sometimes raised about the *de facto* alliance between the United States and Saudi Arabia. The lineup in the global war on terror declared by President George W. Bush still places Saudi Arabia on the side of the United States. Washington's determination to maintain American links with Saudi Arabia is based on the Kingdom's status as the oil supplier of last resort to the United States. American oil imports from the Middle East are so far something over 20 percent of the total oil imports of United States and therefore 12 percent of the total oil use of the United States. Most oil imports to America are from Venezuela, Mexico, and Canada. Nevertheless, as western hemisphere oil supplies increasingly fall under the control of unfriendly left-wing regimes, and as domestic sources dwindle toward zero, the importance of Middle East oil in the medium to longer term may well continue to grow, unless deliberate action is taken. Subsidiary considerations linking the two countries are the size of American investment in Saudi Arabia, and the scale of Saudi investment in the American economy, as well as the importance to American industry of arms sales to the Gulf. Nevertheless, the linkage between Saudi Arabia and violent Islamist activity is hard to ignore.

The Saudi government is itself harassed by Salafi extremists, who are responsible for violent incidents inside the Kingdom. The arch-exponent of international Islamist terror, Osama bin Laden, is himself by origin a Saudi grandee, and fifteen of those of who carried out the attacks of September 11, 2001 were Saudi citizens. But despite the groundswell of Islamist feeling in the Kingdom opposed to the current dynasty, the Saudi royal family and many close to them continue to support, in one way or another, international Islamic organizations. In turn, some such organizations are suspected of endorsing, or at least not discouraging, Islamist activities round the world. Such activities may be more extreme than the funding persons or bodies would consciously countenance, and King Abdullah certainly stresses that Saudi Arabia does not support terrorism in any shape or context. In April 2007, the Saudi government claimed it had broadly overcome the problem of internal terrorism and was reeducating terrorist detainees to enable them to rejoin civil society. Another problem for the West, however, is that human rights issues in the Kingdom are increasingly hard to ignore. Nonetheless, no serious question has so far been raised on either side about the continuation of the partnership between Saudi Arabia and the United States. Salafi attacks within the Kingdom have enabled the regime to claim it is itself a victim of terror. At the same time, however, it can be argued that Saudi funding around the world—whether deliberately or not—creates a climate in which Islamist violence can flourish.

UZBEKISTAN

Some 92 percent of the population of Uzbekistan is Muslim. The vast majority are Uzbek Sunni Muslims, with 5 percent of Shi'ite Tajiks and some other small minorities. The remainder is made up of Orthodox Christians and a shrinking Jewish minority of tens of thousands. There is a variety of Islamic traditions. Under the Soviets there were around 65 official mosques and some 3,000 Muslim clerics. The Soviet institution that oversaw Islam in Central Asia—the Muslim Spiritual Administration of Central Asia—was based in Tashkent and headed by a senior cleric whose title was the Grand Mufti. The first postindependence Mufti was Muhammad-Sodiq Muhammad Yusuf, who had by 2007 become in many ways the unofficial Islamic leader of Uzbekistan. He was removed from office in 1993 and went into exile first in Libya and then in Saudi

Arabia, where he obtained a position with "Rabita" (World Muslim League). He returned to Uzbekistan in 2000, where he maintains a position of critical coexistence with the government.

The preindependence attitude of the Soviet authorities toward Islam was ambiguous. The official policy of the Soviet Union was opposed to religion, but nonetheless the authorities were aware that religion could be instrumentalized in the control of a Muslim population. Uzbeks are earnest in their profession of Islam, though they lack the sophistication of Muslim practice in the Middle East or Pakistan. In August 1991, Uzbekistan became independent. Islam Karimov was elected President in December 1991. By 1999, radical Muslims had begun to make their presence known. In February 1999, President Karimov narrowly escaped an attempt on his life. The government blamed the Islamic Movement of Uzbekistan (IMU). After the government of Uzbekistan committed itself to the so-called war on terror launched by the United States in 2001, there was further violence. In March 2004, another outbreak of bomb attacks was blamed by President Karimov on the international organization, Hizb ut-Tahrir. Independent analysts queried this attribution. Twenty people were killed in two suicide bombings in the market at Tashkent. In July 2004, attacks on the embassies of Israel and the United States in Tashkent killed three. Responsibility was claimed by a little known Jihadist group. On May 13, 2005, government troops opened fire on thousands of opposition demonstrators, killing dozens. Hundreds lost their lives in the ensuing disturbances. The severe repression by the Uzbek government of all opposition, including that of Islamists, has earned it a reputation for the neglect of human rights. In October 2006, the Uzbek government proposed a new law imposing draconian controls on Islamic activities outside the official mosques. The international Islamic cultural organization ISESCO named Tashkent as the world capital of Islamic culture for 2007 in recognition of what ISESCO described as Uzbekistan's contribution to Islamic culture. President Karimov has set up a number of Islamic institutions including the Tashkent Islamic University.

Islamic Movement of Uzbekistan

The Islamic Movement of Uzbekistan (IMU) was established toward the end of 1997 by militants formerly belonging to such movements as Adolat, Lashkar-i Islami (The Islamic Army), and especially to the Uzbek Islamic Renaissance Party (IRP). Subsequent to the fall of the Soviet Union, Salafi activity began to intensify in the Ferghana Valley. The IRP, a Sunni movement, first made its appearance in Uzbekistan in 1991, but an attempt to hold a gathering in Tashkent was dispersed by the police. In 1992, all religious parties were banned following President Karimov's election in 1991. Many IRP members fled to Tajikistan or Afghanistan, but a faction remained in Uzbekistan to form the IMU under the leadership of Jima Namangani and Tahir Yuldeshev.

The IMU launched itself into armed struggle against government targets in December 1997, when a senior police official was assassinated. On February 16, 1998, the Uzbek Minister of Foreign Affairs, Abdulaziz Kamilov, criticized the role played by Pakistan in training and supporting Islamic activists. Exactly a year later, on February 16, 1999, matters came to a head with an attempt on the life of President Karimov that was immediately blamed on the Islamists. In August 1999, and again in the summer of 2000, the IMU launched operations against Uzbekistan from bases in Tajikistan and Kyrghizstan, seeking once more to gain a foothold in the Ferghana Valley. By this time, the IMU was based

in Afghanistan under the protection of the Taliban. IMU militants succeeded in reaching Tashkent, where some were arrested. Though it was at first concerned only with Uzbkeistan and had personal links with the commanders of the Tajik wing of the IRP, the IMU became within two years completely identified with the Taliban. In June 2001, Uzbeks of the IMU fought against Massoud in Afghanistan, and in October 2001, they fought shoulder to shoulder with Al-Qaida against the Northern Alliance. Juma Namangana was killed, which was a severe setback. Afterwards, its activists began to disperse.

Islamic Renaissance Party (Uzbekistan)

The Uzbek IRP was founded in January 1991, at the initiative of the IRP in the Soviet Union. It essentially played the part of a moderate Islamic group. Its first leader was Abdullah Otaiev. At its founding conference in Tashkent, the Uzbek security forces arrested the four hundred activists present, of whom 75 percent were Uzbeks. However, soon after its foundation the IRP was able to muster 4,000 militants, not only in Tashkent but also in Namangan, Indigan, and Koukant. The Uzbek IRP took a moderate line and was careful to stay on good terms with the government. It associated itself with the Birlik party in advocating secular government and declared its intention to respect all faiths, though a central place in society was to be taken by Islam. The IRP refused to ally itself with Adolat, which it regarded as extremist.

Its moderation was detrimental to its image in the eyes of the Islamic world. In contrast to the Tajik IRP, it received no international Islamic aid. The representatives of Saudi Arabia ostentatiously turned their backs on it, preferring to make a direct approach to the established local religious officials and to the mosques. In February 1991, an Uzbek law on public organizations forbade the formation of parties on the basis of religion. This provided a justification for the IRP to be suppressed and for its leadership to be imprisoned. There was little public reaction, even in areas where the IRP was at its strongest, which indicated that its influence on society was limited.

Tawbah Movement

In the early months of 1992, a group of some two hundred Islamic activists, discontented with the relatively quietist views of the existing Islamist organizations in Uzbekistan, set up the Tawbah organization, whose goal was radical political activity. "Tawbah" means "repentance" and is the name of a Surah in the Quran. The members of Tawbah began to mete out their own justice to those they deemed unworthy, kidnapping their adversaries and setting fire to cars. They demanded the establishment of an Islamic Republic and took up violently nationalist and anti-Russian positions. They were especially anxious to separate the education of boys from that of girls. The movement was eventually broken up, and its leaders were either imprisoned or exiled.

VELAYET-E FAQIH (IRAN)

The principle of Velayet-e Faqih, adopted by Ayatollah Khomeini before the foundation of the Islamic Republic of Iran, is that the "Faqih"—the most learned and able theologian and Islamic jurist—shall act as the representative of the Twelfth and final "occulted" Imam of Shi'ism. In theory, only when the Twelfth Imam returns can the perfect Islamic state be created. In the meantime, however, the most learned jurist should rule. Khomeini's argument was that God would not have created the Quran and allowed the Sunna to develop had He not wished the Shari'a to be implemented. According to this principle, therefore, in modern circumstances the Faqih is the repository of the power conferred by God upon the Prophet and the subsequent imams. Thus, although the Faqih lays no claim to divine status, logic and expediency demand that he should rule.

In the absence of the Twelfth Imam, authority within society and the state devolves upon the Faqih. His position endows upon him the authority to take charge of the religious, social, and political affairs of the Umma. The theory of Velayet-e Faqih—the spiritual and temporal authority of the *marja'-e taqlid* ("antecedent for emulation")—is the logical outcome of an evolution within the Shi'ite clergy that began centuries ago and reached

its culmination in the eighteenth century under the reign of Fath Ali Shah Qajar. The concept of *marja'-e taqlid* refers to the status achieved by a cleric after a long process of development that begins with the recognition of his capacity to exercise the power of "ijtihad."

According to Mullah Ahmad Naraghi, a prominent theoretician of the concept:

> [I]n a similar fashion and for the same reasons that the Prophet and the Imams have exercised the Velayet, and have held sway over the lives and activities of the people, the Faqih, by virtue of that which has come down to him from the Prophet and the Imams, exercises the same prerogatives.

Mullah Ahmad Naraghi concludes that "government, in the sense of political leadership and the management of the affairs of the country, is by definition the prerogative of the Faqih." The concept had long been a topic solely for theological discussions. In 1970, however, Imam Khomeini made the theory of the Velayet-e Faqih the themes of the lectures he gave to his students in the Shi'ite holy city of Najaf in Iraq. For the first time, a major cleric lodged a claim to both temporal and spiritual power on behalf of the ulema, the Islamic clergy.

When the constitution of 1979 was drafted by Council of Experts, Velayet-e

Faqih became the basis of the law, bestowing upon the Faqih powers comparable to those of the sovereign in a constitutional monarchy. Ten years later, however, Khomeini approved constitutional amendments that gave autonomous status to the Velayet-e Faqih, bringing together the entire range of powers of both the government and the state. Under this disposition, the Faqih was regarded as appointed by God himself, and the duty of the Council of Experts was to "discover" who was God's chosen one. In this, Khomeini had the invaluable support of another Shi'ite *marja'-e taqlid,* Imam Mohammed Baqer al-Sadr, the leading personality in Iraqi Shi'ite Islam, who would meet his death at the hands of the Iraqi regime in 1980. On February 4, 1979, a week before Khomeini took power, Mohammed Baqer al-Sadr was consulted by Lebanese Shi'ite clergy, who asked for his views on the draft constitution Khomeini had drawn up, based on the concept of Velayet-e Faqih, for the Islamic Republic of Iran. He took the occasion to endorse the theory of Velayet-e Faqih, affirming that the *marja'-e taqlid,* in the absence of the Twelfth Imam, was best able to lead the faithful.

At this point, Shahpour Bakhtiari was still prime minister of Iran and the Islamic Revolution was yet to achieve victory. It was not until February 11, 1979, that the old regime was finally swept away. The concept of the Islamic Republic had not yet taken its final shape and Khomeini's theory of the Velayete Faqih, which was to be its basis, had so far provided the future Islamic government only with general ideas. Baqer al-Sadr gave precise shape to what had up to now been little more than a rallying point. Baqer al-Sadr's response to the Lebanese clerics was exceptional from a number of points of view. In the first place, it was unusual in the form it took, because it was nothing less than a political prospectus. It made reference to conceptual categories such as the role of the state and the separation of the executive, legislative, and judicial powers as well as the place of the military in society, which are normally more the object of contemporary political science than of traditional religious rhetoric. It was also original in its content, where, with its detailed account of how an Islamic Republic would function, it institutionalized for the first time the direct exercise of political power by the Islamic clergy.

In contemporary circumstances, the emergence of such ideas was in tune with the prevalent rise of the Islamic movement. It was also, as particularly regards Shi'ism, the logical culmination of a process of evolution embarked on some nine centuries ago. Since that time, the Shi'ite clergy, through a process of exegesis and innovative interpretation, has laid down a solid theoretical basis for its increasing power.

WAHHABISM

Wahhabism takes its name from its founder, Muhammad ibn Abd el-Wahhab (1703–1792), who was inspired by Ibn Taymiyya (1263–1328), whose interpretations of Islamic doctrine were based on the the Hanbali school of "fiqh"—one of the four schools of interpretation of Islamic law. Wahhabism was a conservative school of interpretation characterized by its literal reading of Islam and its rigorous and puritanical aspect. Muhammad ibn Abd el-Wahhab, a member of the Bani Tamim tribe, was born in the southern part of Nejd, the central region of Saudi Arabia, into a family that was religious but not especially wealthy. He pursued a course of religious studies in Medina and then traveled first to Basra and Baghdad, and then to Persia where he studied and taught in Isfahan and Qom. In 1799, he returned to Uyaynah, in Nejd, where his father was a judge.

After his return to Nejd, he published three books that sum up his religious philosophy. His chief work was the Kitab al-Tawhid (The Treatise on Unity). In his teaching, Abd el-Wahhab stressed the imperative of a return to the sacred texts and the importance of setting limits to human involvement in the process of religious reasoning. On the basis of these ideas, Abd el-Wahhab prioritized the orthodox theological concept of "tawhid"—the absolute unity of God—and the doctrine that the essence of Islam is its repudiation of false Gods and idols and, therefore, of "shirk"—the fallacy of associating any other concept with God. "Shirk" may consist of the inappropriate veneration of "a king, a prophet, a tree, or a tomb."

Such customs, which he characterized as barbarous and impious, needed to be replaced by the Shari'a, in order to facilitate the return to the Islam of the pious forebears—the Salaf as-Salih: the term that designates companions of the Prophet Mohammed and those who followed them. Abd el-Wahhab and his disciples, who were called the Wahhabis by their enemies, called themselves the "muwahidun"—those whose guiding principle was unity. Upholding a radical and puritanical Islam, he suppressed all beliefs reminiscent of polytheism and idolatry, such as the worship of saints and pilgrimages to their tombs, as well as tobacco, alcohol, prayer beads, music, and singing. He also called for major reforms within an Islam that had come to embody certain elements left behind from pre-Islamic days.

In practice, his ideas demanded a return to the literal interpretation of the Quran, and he rejected any innovation not sanctioned by the original teaching of the Quran and the Sunna. All that is contrary to orthodox Islam is to be repudiated and struggled against, so that Sufism, mysticism of all kinds, and the Shi'ite sect are all to be rejected. The state should follow the Shari'a to the exclusion of other legal principles. In the field of politics, Abd el-Wahhab put forward a model of society based on the principle of absolute obedience of the faithful to their sovereign. In turn, the ruler was to display complete observance of the principles of Islam, on pain of being deposed. Supervision of the sovereign's observance of Islamic principles was to be the responsibility of a body of religious dignitaries. Abd el-Wahhab thus took up the ruling of Ibn Taymiya regarding the repudiation of any sovereign who might have strayed from the paths of Islam.

Muhammad Ibn Abd el-Wahhab then embarked on a campaign to spread his call for a reformist and puritanical Islam, attacking both Shi'ites and the prevalent pagan practices. Leading his disciples, he attacked pagan places of worship and destroyed trees and tombs. He quickly clashed not only with the Shi'ites, but also with the local Sunnis, who refused to accept his ideas, which they deemed contrary to local Muslim tradition. He was, therefore, obliged to go once more into exile. In the end, he found sanctuary in the village of Dir'iya, in the heart of Nejd, where the local chieftain, Muhammad Ibn Sa'ud, accepted his ideas. In 1744, the two men made a pact aimed at the establishment of an Islamic state to be governed by the Al Sa'ud and based on the theological and political ideas of Abd el-Wahhab. The union between the two families was formalized by the marriage of one of Ibn Sa'ud's sons to the daughter of Abd el-Wahhab.

Through his pact with Muhammad Ibn Sa'ud, Abd el-Wahhab gave a practical dimension to his ideas, ensuring that they would henceforth be spread by force of arms. In practice, owing to the extreme rigor of his teaching, it had hitherto been accepted voluntarily hardly at all in other regions. In religious terms, Wahhabism was definable as

the wish to take as a model the original Islam, as practiced by Muhammad and his companions, repudiating all authorities other than the Quran and the Sunna, except for "ijma" (the consensus of the clergy) in certain circumstances. The rejection of innovation, including legal principles derived from "ijtihad," lay at the heart of the doctrine. Only principles dating from the era of the pious forebears would be acceptable.

In this respect, the more conservative element within the Salafi trend may be assimilated to Wahhabism, namely the school of Salafi thought that postulates the eradication of "ijtihad" in favor of sole reliance on the pious forebears. Those Salafis who envisage the reinterpretation of the Quran and the Sunna on new bases, on the other hand, are irreconcilable with Wahhabi ideas. The principal distinction between Wahhabism and Salafism schools relates to their conception of the Islamic state. Wahhabism accepted local rulers, given that they respect and impose the Shari'a, while Salafism desires the return of the caliphate—a single ruler for the entire "umma." Nonetheless, most current Salafi movements accept that the first stage on the way to this ultimate goal is in practice the Wahhabi solution of a local "emir" of the believers.

The Saudi system has no counterpart anywhere in the world. What is at issue is an absolute Islamic monarchy based on coexistence between the political power of the Al Sa'ud and the Wahhabi religious dogma, which teaches the necessity of the "bay'a"— the oath of absolute and unconditional allegiance to the sovereign. The only limitation on the sovereign's absolute power is his own respect for the law of God in his conduct of the affairs of state, which gives the clergy an institutional role. The history of the Al Sa'ud dynasty is, therefore, one of political expansion based on the Wahhabi doctrine. After the conclusion of the pact of 1744, Muhammad Ibn Sa'ud, who at the time ruled only in the Nejd village of Dir'iya, embarked on the conquest of neighboring settlements, destroying idols and obliging his new subjects to submit to Wahhabi Islam. At the time of Muhammad Ibn Sa'ud's death in 1765, he controlled most of Nejd, henceforth ruled according to the ideas of Abd el-Wahhab, who died in 1792. After Muhammad Ibn Sa'ud's death, the pact of 1744 was maintained by his successors.

By 1801, Abdelaziz Ibn Muhammad was making forays outside the Arabian Peninsula in search of plunder, and his army sacked the town of Karbala (in modern-day Iraq). Karbala is one of the holy cities of the Shi'ites and the site of the tomb of Hussein, one of the sons of Ali, the Prophet's son-in-law, and the Saudi incursion greatly angered the Shi'ites. In 1803, Abdelaziz's forces pressed on southward and westward to the Hejaz, where after the massacre of the male population of Ta'if they captured Mecca and Medina. There they destroyed the tombs of saints and votive shrines, which they condemned as idolatrous and polytheist. By this stage, the Wahhabi realm included much of the Arabian Peninsula. The Saudi possessions were governed by Saud Ibn Abdelaziz, the son of Abdelaziz Ibn Muhammad, who was murdered in 1803 by Shi'ites in revenge for the destruction of Karbala.

After the Saudi seizure of Mecca and Medina, the Ottoman sultan deputed his vassal Mohammed Ali, the khedive of Egypt, to recover the Muslim Holy Places. In a campaign between 1816 and 1818, an army commanded by Mohammed Ali's son Ibrahim Pasha recovered the Hejaz and challenged the Al Sa'ud in their home territory of Nejd. In 1818, the Saudi capital of Dir'iya was razed and plundered, and Sa'ud Ibn Abdelaziz's successor, Abdullah Ibn Sa'ud, was sent to Istanbul and beheaded on the orders of the sultan. Believing that the Wahhabis had been destroyed, the Egyptian forces withdrew from Nejd in 1819, basing

themselves in Hejaz where they mounted guard over the Holy Places and the pilgrimage caravans. However, a member of the Al Sa'ud, Abdullah's great-uncle Turki, had escaped the Ottoman siege. He embarked on the reoccupation of the Al Sa'ud's erstwhile territory. He recovered Dir'iya in 1824 and then reconquered the region around Riyadh, which became the Al Sa'ud's new base.

At his death, in 1834, Turki controlled Nejd and Hasa, which comprised the eastern coastal region of the Arabian Peninsula, and had made an alliance with Abdullah Ibn Rashid, who ruled Jebel Shammar. However, the Al Sa'ud had difficulty in holding their own against the Al Rashid and the Egyptian forces. The Al Rashid, in effect, became the masters of the Arabian Peninsula, driving the Al Sa'ud even from Riyadh. What remained of the Saudi dynasty took refuge in Kuwait. Little changed until 1902 when Abdelaziz Ibn Abderrahman Al Sa'ud, better known as Ibn Saud, returned from Kuwait with a raiding party of just forty men to begin the reconquest of the Al Sa'ud's domains. On January 15, they attacked and took the Rashidi stronghold in Riyadh. Ibn Sa'ud went on to consolidate his success, and by 1906 he was once more in control of Nejd. From 1912, Ibn Saud began to organize the bedouin tribesmen into groups he called the "Ikhwan"—"Brothers"—settling each in an agricultural village known as a "hijra (plural "hujar"). Their loyalty was henceforth to the Wahhabi doctrine and not to tribal law. In May 1913, he took advantage of the weakness of the Ottoman Empire and sent the Ikhwan to conquer Hasa, which he took virtually without a fight.

During World War I, Ibn Saud won the support of the British, with whom he entered into a treaty in 1915. This favored the Al Sa'ud against the Al Rashid, whom the British were unable to wean away from their good relations with the Ottoman Empire.

Under the treaty with the British, the Al Sa'ud were recognized as the rulers of Nejd, and the eastern region of Hasa, together with Qatif and Jubail, and all the ports and towns in those areas. In exchange they undertook not to enter into relations with other foreign countries without the prior permission of the British. The British took the decision to weight the scales in favor of the Al Sa'ud by giving them crucial military aid.

After World War I, Ibn Sa'ud sent his son Faisal to conquer Asir, then part of Yemen. In 1921, he attacked the remaining Rashidi stronghold of Jebel Shammar, where they quickly gained control thanks to support from the inhabitants of Hail and divided loyalties in the opposing camp. The remaining obstacle for the Al Sa'ud was the Hejaz and the Hashemite family, who had traditionally ruled the Holy Places on behalf of the Ottoman Empire. In March 1924, when the caliphate was abolished by Mustafa Kemal, the postwar nationalist ruler of Turkey, the Hashemite ruler of Mecca, Sherif Hussein, declared himself to be caliph. The move was seen by the Al Sa'ud as a challenge. In September 1924, an army of 3,000 Ikhwan took Taif and then recaptured Mecca, completing the conquest of the Hejaz in 1925. This victory gave a boost to the Wahhabi interpretation of Islam, which extended its influence into the emirates of the Gulf and whose influence began to make itself felt as far afield as India and Sudan.

In 1932, Ibn Saud declared the establishment of the Kingdom of Saudi Arabia. In 1934, a treaty between Saudi Arabia and Yemen endorsed by the British gave Saudi Arabia the three areas of Asir, Jizan, and Najran, completing the territorial expansion of the kingdom. From then onward, Saudi Arabia concentrated on its internal development, a task facilitated after World War II by the exploitation of the oil resources of Hasa. It established its reputation with the other Arab states as the sole state capable of protecting the Holy Places. At the outset, Ibn Saud experimented with involving the other Arab states in the administration of the Holy Places, despite the fact that they were mainly colonized or supervised under the mandate system. However, owing to their quarrels and rivalries, he finally opted to take sole responsibility.

Ibn Saud had no ancestry he could trace back to the Prophet Muhammad, and he never made the mistake of proclaiming himself caliph or of laying claim to any Islamic distinction other than that of Protector of the Holy Places. In addition, the potential for disagreement in the Muslim community became only too clear to him as the result of disappointments he experienced at conferences held in the 1940s to deal with the issue of the Holy Places. Nevertheless, Ibn Saud never lost sight of the ideal of the establishment of an overarching state incorporating all the Muslims of the world, under the leadership of Saudi Arabia, which he saw as the only truly independent Muslim regime.

The Wahhabi Roots of the Saudi Monarchy

The Ikhwan

Ibn Saud established the Ikhwan—the Brothers—in 1912 to provide himself with a religious fighting force that would be based on the principles of Wahhabism and would devote itself to the dissemination of his message by means of the Jihad. Ibn Saud's policy had a number of different objectives. First, in the political and military field he wanted a fighting force that would be independent of the unstable intertribal alliances and would weld the tribesmen together into a military machine capable of providing training and of making war when required. Second, in religious terms, he wished to make a break with the bedouin ideas of Islam, imbued with superstition that had emerged from the tribal and nomadic way of life. The goal was to open the way toward re-Islamization according to Wahhabi ideas.

Third, however, on the social and economic front, he was aware that Saudi Arabia would never develop and become wealthy while it was founded on the traditional way of life of the nomadic tribes. Settled agriculture was the means of assuring both the exploitation of the land and a self-sufficiency among the population that would serve as a basis for the growth of the population, hitherto limited by the prevalence of war and a propensity toward emigration. The bedouins who became Ikhwan abandoned their nomadic life in order to establish themselves within the "hujar," agricultural colonies constructed for them, where they were supposed to follow a way of life based on religion. They were meant to be courageous in war, devoted to religious observance, and indifferent to worldly advancement. They played a key role in the expansion of the Saudi realm, showing themselves to be the fiercest of warriors in the early decades of the kingdom. The new social structure of the Ikhwan was meant to mark a break with the nomadic era, heralding in a new age truly ordained by God.

The Ikhwan revolt between 1927 and 1929, led by the tribal chieftains of the Ibn Ithlayn and the Al Dawish, was the earliest Islamist opposition to the Al Sa'ud. These leaders rebelled because of allegations that Ibn Saud had abandoned his mission to spread the Wahhabite doctrine in favor of the enhancement of his personal power, thus upsetting the equilibrium between the religious and political bases of the state. Ibn Saud, with the backing of the Ulema of Nejd, crushed the uprising. Today, the Ikhwan rebellion is seen more as a by-product of generalized hostility toward the process of forming the state than as arising from specific hostility toward the legitimacy of the Al Sa'ud. The Ikhwan were opposed to the introduction of all novel technologies, for example

the telegraph. They also refused to accept constraints on their freedom of action, especially regarding punitive operations against individuals or groups they regarded as culpable of moral or religious laxity. The pro-Al Sa'ud position taken by the Ulema of Nejd was based on their apprehension of descent into anarchy and the outbreak of civil war.

The antagonism of the Ikhwan to any move in the direction of modernization would much later, in 1965, give rise to an attack on the TV station in Riyadh by a group of Ikhwan led by a prince of the royal household. Incidents of this type, however, seemed to be not so much as an assault on the government but rather as a signal that the religious authorities should be more fully consulted on prospective changes within the kingdom.

The National Guard

After the defeat of the Ikhwan at Sabilah in 1929, Ibn Saud organized a large section of them into a tribal army known as the "White Army" on account of the color of the robes of the bedouin, who did not wear military uniform. In 1962 it was renamed the "National Guard" and was reorganized by Crown Prince Abdullah Ibn Abdulaziz (Saudi Arabia's present king). It did not fall under the aegis of the Ministry of Defense. In 1967, Prince Badr Ibn Abdulaziz was appointed deputy commander with the brief of modernizing the fighting units (known as mujahidin), thus transforming the guard into a military institution and part of the nation's cultural identity.

This new army, based on the Ikhwan, was absolutely loyal to the Saudi royal family, which made particular use of it to control the regular armed forces, which were occasionally inclined toward mutiny. The guard's principal recruiting center was in Qassim, in the heart of Nejd, where its bedouin troops swore allegiance to the state in the form of a "bay'a," a traditional oath of loyalty to the sovereign, thus placing their traditional bedouin values at the state's service. The National Guard was estimated in 1992 to be 75,000 strong, including 20,000 reserves available for immediate mobilization. Basically, it ensures the regime's internal security. It bases are situated on the periphery of large towns and close to oil installations. The National Guard suppressed the outbreaks of violence by Shi'ites in 1979 and 1980. It also took part in the American-led coalition action against Iraq in 1991. In addition, the National Guard is responsible for the well-being of participants in the annual pilgrimage.

The Mutawa

The Mutawa are religious functionaries, literally "volunteers," whose original role was as missionaries that supported the forces of Muhammad Ibn Sa'ud as they spread the Wahhabi interpretation of Islam. Organized into "Committees for the Prevention of Vice and the Promotion of Virtue," they were the kingdom's religious police. In the early days, they were despatched to suppress the religious practices of the inhabitants of the Hejaz that were deemed incompatible with Wahhabism. In Nejd, they were deployed to encourage the bedouin to settle in the religious encampments known as "hujar," especially in order to control the tribes at times when the Ikhwan rebellion caused concern.

They were originally under the control of the kingdom's grand mufti, but in 1962, as part of King Faisal's reforms, he brought them under the authority of the Council of Ministers. Despite being known as "Volunteers," the Mutawa are today salaried officials of the state. They normally patrol in small groups, with a brief to maintain good morals and ensure the observation of religious duties. Such issues include the closing of shops during the hours of prayer, keeping the fast during Ramadan, and making sure that women are covered, are accompanied by a male family member, and do not drive cars. They enforce the separation of the sexes especially in shopping malls, which serve as a favorite meeting place for the young, and also close restaurants where music is played. They are entitled to enter private residences if they suspect alcohol is being drunk. Finally, they suppress all signs of non-Muslim religious observance, especially during Christian festivals such as Christmas. Their behavior attracts a degree of disapproval, even among religious Saudis. Occasionally, the regular Saudi police find themselves obliged to protect citizens who have become the victims of particularly excessive displays of zeal on their part.

Their function evolved after 1990, with the outbreak of the Gulf crisis and the presence of some 600,000 troops in Saudi Arabia, mainly from Western countries. A senior cleric, Abdelaziz Al Said, became director of the Mutawa, with ministerial rank, and new guidelines were laid down to ensure that the rights of individuals would be more carefully observed. The new regulations had the effect that the Mutawa were no longer supposed to use force to compel the population to conform, and if they made an arrest they were obliged to hand the offender over to the regular police. In practice, however, the new measures seemed only to intensify their activities and Article 37 of the constitution failed to protect the inhabitants from intrusions into their residences.

The Council of Senior Ulema

Abd el-Wahhab's doctrine lays down that people are subject to the absolute authority of the sovereign in return for the sovereign's absolute obedience to the law of God, as derived from the Quran and the Sunna. The sovereign's fidelity to his commitment must therefore be verified by a body of "ulema," whose role is to examine his policies to verify that they conform to the principles of Islam.

In Saudi Arabia this body is the Council of Senior Ulema, established in 1971 by royal decree, which includes the principal ulema of the kingdom, who are appointed by the king, and headed by the Saudi grand mufti, Sheikh Abdulaziz Al Sheikh, who succeeded Sheikh Abdulaziz Bin Baz. According to the terms of the decrees, the council expresses the opinions given by the ulema, in the light of the Shari'a, concerning issues submitted to it by the king. More generally, it advises the king and issues fatwas for the guidance of Muslims in religious and political matters. Though the council is theoretically independent, it must be observed that in practice it virtually never expresses opposition to any proposal from the royal family.

Within the council there is a body known as the Permanent Committee for Islamic Research and Fatwas, whose task is to prepare the council's agenda. The committee also issues fatwas in individual cases. The committee functions as the policymaking organ of the Council of Senior Ulema. Its members are Sheikh Abdelaziz Al Sheikh, Abdullah Ibn Ghudayyan, Abdullah Ibn Qu'ud, Abdullah Ibn Munay, Saleh Ibn Fawzan, and Bakr Abdullah Abu Zayd.

September 11 and After

In the wake of September 11, 2001, Saudi society underwent profound change. Its four elements, the army, the ulema, the bedouins, and the new middle class, have ceased passively to submit to the authorities. The ulema in particular are for the most part supporters of Osama bin Laden, flying in the face of the wishes of the royal family, and despite the fact that bin Laden had been deprived of his Saudi nationality as long ago as 1994. The bedouin also seemed swayed by bin Laden's ideas, especially in relation to the presence of foreigners on Saudi Arabia's "sacred" soil. On the other hand, the army officers, many of them linked to the royal family and its allies, give their unconditional support to the Al Sa'ud. Meanwhile, the middle class was beginning to revolt against the notion that since they made no financial contribution to the kingdom's budget they were not entitled to any say in Saudi policy. After the Gulf conflict of 1990–1991, and especially in the wake of September 11, 2001, the new middle class wanted some input into Saudi policy decisions. The reforms brought in by King Abdullah in his closing years as crown prince tended in this direction. He set up a social and economic advisory council and reestablished the Consultative Council. The greatest challenge to the Saudi leadership, however, was to maintain the link with the United States, as Saudi Arabia became an increasingly troublesome ally.

WORLD TRADE CENTER

The Attack of February 26, 1993

On February 26, 1993, a large bomb was detonated in the underground car park of the North Tower of the World Trade Center. The bomb weighed 600 kilograms and was made of nitroglycerin, urea, and other combustible material. It was brought into the building in a commercial van. The bomb caused extensive damage and six people were killed. However, the building survived. The intention had been to cause the North Tower to topple into the South Tower, thus destroying both. The chief culprit was Ramzi Yousef, a nephew of Khalid Sheikh Mohammed, who was born in Kuwait and is of Baluchi ethnicity and Pakistani descent. He had begun to plan the attack in 1991 after entering the United States on a false Iraqi passport and taking up residence in New Jersey. In all, ten conspirators were identified and accused of the conspiracy to cause the explosion. The blind Islamic cleric Sheikh Omar Abdel Rahman appeared to have conceived the idea of the bomb, and he was sentenced in 1995 to life imprisonment. Ramzi Yousef was sentenced to life imprisonment in 1998. The bomb appeared to have been constructed by Abdul Rahman Yasin, an American citizen of Iraqi descent who had obtained a U.S. passport in Jordan. Yasin was able to flee while on bail and apparently went to Iraq, where his family was living.

The Attack of September 11, 2001

From the indictment of Khaled Sheikh Mohammed: "On the morning of 11 September 2001, four airliners travelling over the United States were hijacked. The flights hijacked were American Airlines Flight 11, United Airlines Flight 175, American Airlines Flight 77, and United Airlines Flight 93. At approximately 8.46 am, American Airlines Flight 11 crashed into the North Tower of the World Trade Centre, resulting in the collapse of the tower at approximately 10.25 am. At approximately 9.05 am, United Airlines Flight 175 crashed into the South Tower of the World Trade Centre, resulting in the collapse of the tower at approximately 9.55 am. At approximately 9.37 am, American Airlines Flight 77 crashed into the southwest side of the Pentagon in Arlington, Virginia. At approximately 10.03 am, United Airlines Flight 93 crashed in Stoney Creek Township, Pennsylvania. These crashes and subsequent damage to the World Trade Centre and the Pentagon resulted in the deaths of 2,972 persons in New York, Virginia, and Pennsylvania." Nineteen hijackers were involved in the hijackings and the subsequent downing of the aircraft involved. Sixteen of them were of Saudi Arabian nationality. The pilots were Mohammed Atta (Egyptian), Mohammed Shehhi (from the United Arab Emirates), Hani Hanjour, (Saudi), and Ziad Jarrah (Lebanese).

MALCOLM X

Malcolm X, whose birth name was Malcolm Little, was the leader of the "Nation of Islam" in the 1950s and 1960s. He was born on May 19, 1925, in Omaha, Nebraska. He was the son of a black Baptist pastor and a woman of mixed race. He was raised in a predominantly black area of Boston. His father died in 1931, when he was six. Later, trouble with the police led to a period in prison, and he served seven years in all. While in jail, he discovered the Nation of Islam and concluded that white society and Christianity were implicated in a racist conspiracy against black people. Released in 1953, he began to work for the Nation of Islam and came into contact with Elijah Muhammad, the then Nation of Islam's principal leader, whom he greatly venerated. This was when he ceased to call himself Malcolm Little and took the name of Malcolm X.

By this time he was an accredited preacher for the Nation of Islam and an advocate for the Black Muslim movement, playing a leading part in spreading the message of complete separation between black and white people in the United States. He became Elijah Muhammad's trusted lieutenant, and under his influence, the movement reached its peak. He succeeded in expanding the Nation of Islam to a quarter of a million members, throughout the United States, on whom he imposed strict discipline. Malcolm X began to concentrate on the ideas of black self-defense and black self-sufficiency, and he is credited as the originator of the idea of "black power." Others who were more militant than he did not shrink from violence and some formed what was known as the Black Panther movement. Under President Kennedy, white leaders and some within the black community thought that a more just society could be created in the United States, but Malcolm X believed this was impossible. He said, "If we don't protect ourselves, no-one else will, certainly not the police." After the death of President Kennedy in 1963, Malcolm X was misreported as saying that the president had "got what he deserved." He had apparently intended to say that the president's death was inevitable in the climate of hatred. Elijah Muhammad banned him temporarily from preaching.

When Malcolm X discovered that Elijah Muhammad had been guilty of sexual misdemeanors, he decided to quit the Nation of Islam and set up his own organization. He visited Mecca to contact the World Islamic League and to seek inspiration and advice, and after his return to the United States he set up his own religious group, known as the "Muslim Mosques," together with a political wing, the "Organization of Afro-American Unity." After his return from Mecca, he began to reproach Eljah Muhammad for the heretical nature of some of his ideas and to preach the adoption of mainstream Sunni Islam by the American black community. By now under the influence of the ideas of the world Muslim community, he said he wished to reach out to all Muslims, across racial, ethnic, and national divides. He visited a number of Arab and African countries and performed the ritual of the pilgrimage to Mecca. At this stage, he began to use the name Malik al Shabbaz.

In 1964, he continued his evolution toward a more reconciliatory stance on racial issues when he met the black champion, Dr. Martin Luther King, who advocated compromise between blacks and whites. The same year, he traveled widely in Europe, Africa, and the Middle East. He visited Saudi Arabia again to seek funds for his organizations, which were not flourishing as much as he wished. In 1965, he was murdered by three black men who shot him at a public meeting at a hotel in New York as he began to give his speech. At least two of the culprits appeared to be Nation of Islam militants and it seems most probable that his death was connected with the internal feud within the Black Muslim movement.

YACINE, ABDESSALAM

Abdessalam Yacine was born in 1928. His family were Berber-speaking agriculturists who claimed Sherifian origin—descent from the Prophet Muhammad. Yacine grew up in Marrakesh, where he was educated at private schools. By the age of nineteen he had graduated from Marrakesh's Institute for Arabic and Islamic Studies, and in 1948 he embarked on a career as a teacher in the state educational system. His first job was as an elementary school teacher in El Jadida. After three years, he returned to Marrakesh, where he taught first in a primary school and then at the Mohammed V High School, where he became a teacher of Arabic. In 1956, he was appointed as a school inspector. His responsibility was initially for primary education, and later for secondary education, in a number of cities in Morocco, including Casablanca, Beni Mellal, Rabat, and Marrakesh.

Yacine was a man of natural piety, and his goals in life were to develop his religious knowledge and to teach the principles of Islam. He traveled abroad on a number of occasions, particularly to the United States. In 1965, at the age of thirty-seven, while undergoing a spiritual crisis, he met a sufi sheikh and joined his "brotherhood," the Boushishiya. This period of spiritual apprenticeship, which lasted until 1973, greatly influenced his later life. He became pro-

foundly convinced that the monarchy had not succeeded in establishing a truly Islamic society, and that the king of Morocco, who designated himself the "Commander of the Faithful," was primarily responsible for this failure. Yacine believed he had a mission to rectify the situation and drafted an open letter more than a hundred pages long to the king. He sent this to King Hassan II and at the same time ensured its publicity by distributing it widely. In the letter, he spelled out the shortcomings of the king and admonished him for his failures, while also setting out what Hassan II needed to do. "You will make a public and explicit acknowledgement of your repentance, and of your intention to revitalize Islam. You will set out your program for the accomplishment of this renovation, and you will ask for forgiveness for the ludicrous spectacle you have referred to as an Islamic renaissance."

In the letter, he wrote at length about the pernicious influence of the West, the spread of atheism, and the dire situation of the underclass. He also sketched out the lines of a political platform that laid down the lines of an Islamic state. This disloyal initiative led to the incarceration of Sheikh Yacine and his subsequent transfer to the psychiatric hospital of Berrechid, south of Casablanca. In March 1978, after he was set free, he began to set up his first political organization with the assistance of another teacher, Mohammed Alaoui. From 1979 to 1983, he published a periodical, Al Jemaa, with a print run of three thousand copies, whose themes were the decline of moral standards and the difficulty experienced by genuine believers in practicing their faith. In a series of articles, he also attacked the Arab states, which he described as despotic, as well as taking to task Westernized Arab intellectuals, as he made out the case for a genuine Islamic rebirth.

He came to the conclusion that in order to achieve his objective of the establishment of an Islamic state, he needed to set up a political party. However, his bid to register such an association at the government's administrative offices in Rabat was frustrated. There had been difficulties in distributing Al Jemaa, which in the end was banned. He then attempted, also without success, to launch two other publications, Al Sobh and Al Khitab. On December 27, 2003, he was arrested, and judicial proceedings were instituted against him. In May 1984, he was sentenced to two years imprisonment, after a trial held as his supporters surrounded the court. He was sent to the prison at Salé. His followers, however, who included many university students, persisted with a plan to set a clandestine political movement, divided into cells and subject to strict discipline. In 1987, with the help of some of Yacine's associates, including Mohammed Bachiri and Fathallah Arsalane, the secret organization known as "Hizb al-'Adl wa'l-Ihsan" came into being. Its objective was to put Yacine's doctrines into practice, and in the long term to overthrow the established order. Abdessalam Yacine was placed under house arrest in 1989 and wrote a number of books that would be much discussed, including Al-Minhaj al-Nabawi (The Prophetic Path) and Islam, Nationalism and Secularism.

Yacine's followers, who were very numerous in the universities, clashed with extreme violence with the Marxist students and also with the activists of another Islamic group, known as "Renewal and Reform" (Al-Islah wa'l-Tajdid), founded by Abdelilah Benkirane. Control of the university faculties and the establishment of subsidiary organizations continued to be the main priority of 'Adl wa'l-Ihsan, which led it to reject all alliances with other factions, even those that were ideologically similar. 'Adl wa'l-Ihsane was officially banned in 1990, amid suspicions that Abdelilah Benkirane's party had conspired with the security forces. Abdessalam Yacine laid the blame for Morocco's misfortunes at the door of other political organizations and wrote a study of the malfunctions of the political system in Morocco under the title "a Dialog with the Good Democrats."

Toward the close of the reign of King Hassan II, the restrictions imposed on Abdessalam Yacine were gradually lifted. After King Mohammed VI's accession to the throne, Yacine addressed an open letter to the new monarch. His aim was to remind the king that he was the Moroccan government's principal adversary. He violently criticized the extravagances of the king and his officials, and reemphasized his objective of the establishment of an Islamic renaissance. Abdessalam Yacine's undoubted charisma has allowed him to continue as the leading figure of the Moroccan Islamist movement. However, his health began to curtail his activities. By the end of 2006, his condition had begun to cause anxiety to his followers. His daughter, Nadia Yacine, has become a leading figure in 'Adl wa'l-Ihsan. However, she was accused in 2005 of insulting the Moroccan monarchy by expressing her preference for a republic in the country, and after many postponements her trial was set to resume on April 19, 2007.

YASSIN, SHEIKH AHMED

Sheikh Ahmed Yassin was the founder and spiritual guide of the Palestinian Hamas movement. He was born in Gaza in 1937, but led a valetudinarian existence, paralyzed and half blind from the age of twelve after a serious accident. Nevertheless, this did not curtail his activities. As a young man, while he was a student in Cairo, he joined the Muslim Brotherhood. On his return to Gaza, he set up an Islamic center. While the Gaza Strip was under Egyptian administration before 1967, Sheikh Yassin was sent to prison for the first time after being accused of subversive activities.

Under the Israeli occupation, Yassin undertook charitable work in Islamic institutions for which he obtained funds from the Arab states of the Gulf. This experience led him to take his first steps in political activity. In the early 1980s, this suited the interests of Israel: at the time it was convenient for Israel to encourage a movement that could serve as an alternative to Yasser Arafat's Palestine Liberation Organization. By 1982, however, Sheikh Yassin had become convinced of the need for violent action, which led him to set up the armed wing of his Islamic movement. In July 1984, Yassin was arrested after being implicated in the activities of an arms smuggling network that was uncovered by the Israeli authorities. After trial, he was sentenced to thirteen years of imprisonment. Thanks to negotiations undertaken by supporters of the Palestinian guerrilla leader Ahmed Jibril for an exchange of prisoners, Yassin was freed in May 1985. In 1987, he participated in the foundation of Hamas and became the spiritual leader of the movement.

On May 18, 1989, during an Israeli military crackdown, Sheikh Yassin was again arrested, and this time a military court gave him a life sentence. He was, nevertheless, able to continue to exercise an influence over political developments in the Palestinian territories. After the signature of the Oslo accords in August 1993, Israel's preferred interlocutor was Yasser Arafat. Yassin, for his part, took a more radical direction and declared his implacable opposition to what he described as the surrender of the Palestinians. In 1997, after Mossad's attempt to murder the Hamas leader Khaled Meshaal in Amman, Israel took various measures to mollify King Hussein of Jordan, who had declared himself humiliated by the attack, which was blatantly carried out on Jordanian territory. On October 6, 1997, Israel once more gave Sheikh Yassin his freedom, as part of its effort to compensate King Hussein.

After a tour of the Middle East and the Gulf, Yassin returned to Gaza in 1998. He was placed under house arrest in November 1998 after an attack on an Israeli school bus for which Hamas claimed responsibility. In March 2000, Hamas survived a major Israeli operation against it in Gaza in which Sheikh Yassin was not directly targeted. From his redoubt in Gaza, he continued to express his determination to liberate the whole of historic Palestine form Israeli occupation and to be the principal adversary of Arafat's Fatah movement. Sheikh Yassin died in an Israeli missile strike on Gaza on March 22, 2004.

YEMEN

Islam came early to Yemen. The country's first mosques, including the mosque in Sanaa, were built during the Prophet's lifetime. The population of 22 million is made up virtually entirely of Muslims, with a small number of Jews and very small numbers of Hindus and Christians. Just over half of Yemen's Muslims are Sunnis, who live mainly in the south and southeast of the country, while somewhat less than half are Shi'ites of an unusual sect. These are the Zaidis, a local group that has developed in isolation from mainstream Shi'ism, who believe that only the Prophet himself and four rightly guided Caliphs have ruled Islam.

Believers of the more usual Shi'ite faith, as found in Iran, recognize twelve Caliphs.

The Zaidis established a dynasty in northern Yemen as early as the ninth century that persisted until the twentieth century, ruling all or part of the country. Yemen had a complex political history, with a variety of rulers, culminating in the Ottoman Turks, who withdrew from Sanaa in 1918 after the end of World War I. The leader of the Zaidis, Imam Yahya, then extended his rule over the whole of North Yemen. The Muta-wakkilite Kingdom of Yemen (as Yahya's imamate was known) became a member of the newly formed Arab League in 1945 and a member of the United Nations in 1947. The Imam was finally overthrown in the Yemeni civil war of the 1960s, and the country became the Yemen Arab Republic after the withdrawal of the Egyptian troops in 1967.

The southern and mainly Sunni part of Yemen, meanwhile, followed a different trajectory. The Port of Aden was annexed by the British in 1832 and became the British Colony of Aden in 1837. Subsequently, by treaty with local rulers, a wide area of southern Yemen became the Aden Protectorate. In 1963, Aden became the State of Aden and the wider British-controlled area was designated the Federation of South Arabia, while other sections under looser British control formed the Protectorate of South Arabia. A local Marxist movement (FLOSY—the Front for Liberation of Occupied South Yemen) was formed to fight the British and seek independence. In 1967, the British left South Yemen, which became independent as the People's Republic of South Yemen. In 1969, this became the People's Democratic Republic of Yemen. In 1990, North and South Yemen formed the Republic of Yemen as a unified state under the leadership of President Ali Abdullah Saleh, the leader of the General People's Congress, who had already ruled in North Yemen for a decade. The unified state sur-

vived a brief civil war in 1994 after southern Yemen attempted to secede. President Ali Abdullah Saleh is said to have made use of Yemeni Islamists returned from Afghanistan as a fighting force to help suppress the attempted secession—a move that enabled them to regroup as a unified body that later threatened state security. The returned fighters were known as the "Afghans" and described themselves as Wahhabi Salafis.

Yemen's constitution establishes Islam as the religion of the state and enshrines the Shari'a as the source of law. Schools teach Islam, and the law forbids the conversion of Muslims to any other faith. The authorities monitor Islamic activities carefully, and sermons are forbidden to incite violence or endanger security. President Ali Abdullah Saleh is aware of the threat to his government from Islamist movements. Analysts have recently described the situation as, "the constant threat of an insurgency led by Yemen's powerful Islamist movement." Ali Abdullah Saleh controls carefully to the best of his ability the activities of the Islamic movements in the country and is conscious of the extent to which it is in his interests to maintain Yemen's good relations with the United States. During the Gulf crisis of 1990–1991, Yemen supported the position of Saddam Hussein and was as a result for some years on poor terms with the United States and with its powerful neighbor, Saudi Arabia.

When the USS *Cole* was bombed in the harbor at Aden on October 12, 2000, with the deaths of seventeen American sailors, relations between Yemen and the United States were badly damaged. Since then, the Yemeni government has processed hundreds of suspects of Islamist terrorism through its penal system. The United States has viewed this process with a degree of satisfaction, but there is a view in Washington that Yemen has let too many potential terrorists go free under deals that offer early release or amnesty to prisoners. President Ali Abdullah Saleh treads a careful path, maintaining good relations with the United States and avoiding confrontation with local factions. In 2004, the U.S. administration identified Sheikh Abdel Majid Zindani of the Islah Party as a supporter of terrorism. President Ali Abdullah Saleh has described Sheikh Zindani as a moderate, however, and refuses to allow him to be pursued, which he says would be "unconstitutional." In April 2006, Sheikh Zindani met the Hamas leader Khaled Meshaal with a view to raising funds for the Hamas government in the Palestinian territories. Ali Abdullah Saleh has tribal connections with another leading member of the Islah Party, Sheikh Abdullah al-Ahmar, of the Hashed tribe, to which the president also belongs.

However, the Yemeni government has indubitably taken real action against suspected terrorists. The Yemeni security forces are harsh, and human rights organizations have alleged that the Yemeni government pays scant attention to the rights of suspects. On November 3, 2002, in an operation in the Yemeni region of Marib, by covert American forces, Ali Qa'ed Senyan al-Harthi, a wanted suspect with links to Al-Qaida, was killed by a missile fired apparently by an unmanned CIA drone, apparently with Yemeni approval. A Saudi-born suspect also liked to Al-Qaida, Mohammed Hamdi al-Ahdal, was arrested in November 2003. A further nineteen men have been charged with planning revenge attacks after the death of Al-Harthi. On April 19, 2006, thirteen Islamists led by Sufyan al-Amari were convicted of various charges connected with planned attacks against the Yemeni authorities. However, the escape of twenty-three Islamist prisoners in Yemen in February 2006—not the first such jail break—led to renewed strain with the United States. There have been allegations that the escape was facilitated by

collusion on the part of the Yemeni intelligence services.

On March 29, 2007, assassins murdered Ali Mahmoud Qasayla, the head of criminal investigation in Al-Marib, who was alleged to have been involved in the killing of Al-Harthi. In May 2007, the Yemeni government offered rewards for the capture of three named suspects. A group calling itself Al-Qaida in Yemen has claimed responsibility for the death of Qasayla. There seems no clear evidence, however, that this group has any connection with the mainstream Al-Qaida organization, and the level of threat it represents to Yemen's stability is uncertain.

Aden-Abyab Islamic Army (AAIA) "Jaish Aden-Abyan al-Islami"

"Jaish Aden-Abyan al-Islami," the AAIA, is a radical Islamist group that made its first public appearance in 1997. It was formed in the early 1990s by some three hundred veterans of the Afghan conflict and was supported by the government of the unified Yemeni state under President Ali Abdullah Saleh. It was a useful source of support for Sanaa against the southern forces of the ex-People's Democratic Republic of Yemen during the Yemeni civil war of 1994. Operating from its stronghold in the southern Yemeni province of Abyan, the group continued to receive Arabs returned from Afghanistan in its training camps. Between 1998 and 1999, apparently in coordination with Al-Qaida, it claimed responsibility for a number of bomb attacks in Yemen, on hotels, on various economic targets, and on installations at the Port of Aden, which caused ten deaths and left eighty wounded.

Its most spectacular action, however, was the kidnap of sixteen Western tourists in December 1998, when the Aden-Abyan Islamic Army called for an end to what they called the Western aggression in Iraq and the withdrawal of American and British forces from the Gulf region. When the Yemeni security forces acted to rescue the hostages, three British and one Australian captive were killed. The leader of the Jaish Aden al-Islami Abyan, Zain al-Abdin Al-Mihdar, also known as Abu al-Hassan, was arrested by the Yemeni authorities. This operation exposed the Aden-Abyan Islamic Army's links with radical Islamists in London and in particular revealed its connection with Abu Hamza al-Masri. Abu Hamza's son was himself involved in the terrorist operation. Zain al-Abdin Al-Mihdar was sentenced to death and executed. In April 2001, his successor Hatem bin Farid was sentenced to seven years imprisonment.

Once President Ali Abdullah Saleh had committed himself to the anti-terrorist struggle after the attacks of September 11, 2001, his son and potential successor General Ahmed Saleh, head of Yemen's special forces, began a campaign against the radical Islamists. Al-Qaida and the Aden Abyan Army were particular targets. However, the Jaish's tribal support together with the mountainous terrain of south Yemen meant he had an uphill task. On May 11, 2002, President Ali Abdullah Saleh acknowledged the presence in Yemen of "forty American experts to support the efforts against terrorism of the Yemeni forces." At the same time, he complained about what he referred to as "certain Arab intelligence services," who were giving Washington the impression that Yemen was a potential sanctuary for terrorists. However, the United States was discontented with what it saw as the policy of the Yemeni government of arresting and releasing potential terrorists, rather than clamping down on them. In December 2002, the murder of three American missionaries, who were working at a hospital, appears to have been the work of another group. The killer was a sole gunman who claimed to be part of Islamic Jihad in Yemen.

Though the Yemeni government claims to have eradicated the Aden-Abyan Army, leadership of the group appears in fact to have been taken over by Khalid Abdel Nabi. Abdel Nabi is a former aide of Al-Mihdar, who had also been in Afghanistan and had fought against the former communists in the Yemeni civil war of 1994. Abdel Nabi was arrested in May 2006 and was released by the government. He has disappeared from view and his fate is mysterious, but the Yemeni government claims that he has agreed to abandon his former militancy. Informed estimates suggest the group may never have had more than a few dozen active members. Nonetheless, despite the government's claim to have stamped out the AAIA, the small size and informality of such an organization mean that it may reappear at the whim of a few individuals.

The Cole Affair

On October 12, 2000, an American guided missile destroyer, the USS Cole, was attacked by terrorists while in the harbor of Aden. A hole ten meters across was blown in the side of the ship by a large bomb after two suicide bombers in a small boat approached the Cole. Seventeen U.S. personnel were killed and thirty-nine injured. Heavy casualties occurred because the bomb exploded next to the galley where lunch was being served to the crew. The Cole was refueling in Aden, where the U.S. Navy's strategic fuel reserve had been located since 1999, when it was transferred from Djibouti. The United States and Yemen had held joint military exercises in 1998, which had given rise to local opposition to military cooperation. Allegations were made by opponents of the government in Yemen that the United States had opened what was virtually a military base in Aden, a claim the American administration denied. Various groups, one calling itself "Jaish Muhammad" and another the "Islamic Deterrence Forces," claimed to have attacked the American naval vessel.

In the aftermath of the Cole incident, the United States sent a detachment of special forces to Yemen to secure military and diplomatic facilities. The American administration also asked Yemen to assist an investigation by the FBI. The Yemeni government detained a number of suspects. However, President Ali Abdullah Saleh was unwilling to permit the interrogation of senior officials and political figures. Cooperation between Yemen and the U.S. authorities improved after September 11, 2001. On the other hand, ten suspects held in the Cole investigation escaped from prison in April 2003. There had been claims that the United States had asked for the trial and sentence of suspects to be delayed so that they could continue to be interrogated. There were persistent rumors that the Cole perpetrators may have been linked to the East Africa bombings of U.S. Embassies in 1998. Six men were eventually tried and two were sentenced to death in 2004, while four others received lengthy prison sentences.

Islah (Al-Tajammu Al-Yamani Li-L-Islah) (Yemeni Assembly for Reform)

In May 1990, North and South Yemen (the former People's Democratic Republic of Yemen) declared the reunification of the country. In September 1990, the Yemeni Assembly for reform (Islah) was established as a political party in the newly unified Republic of Yemen by Islamist sympathizers. The party enjoyed the patronage of the senior tribal chief of the Hashed tribal confederation, Sheikh Abdullah al-Ahmar, a first cousin of the president of Yemen, Ali Abdullah Saleh, the leader of the General People's Congress. The Islah Party was built on the foundation of the existing Muslim Brotherhood branch in North Yemen, which dated from 1947. Islamists of

many persuasions rallied to the banner of the Islah Party. The leader of Islah's militant wing was Abdel Majid Zindani. Zindani, an Afghan veteran with presumed links to Osama bin Laden as well as the Sudanese Islamist leader Hassan al-Turabi, was the head of Al-Iman University, an Islamist institution. By 2000, the Islah Party included a heterogeneous mixture of extremist militants, technocrats, wealthy merchants, and even attracted some supporters of President Ali Abdullah Saleh.

The civil war in Yemen, which broke out in 1994 after an attempted secession by the former communist south, led to a de facto alliance between President Saleh and the Islamists. For a while there was a split in the Islamist ranks when the Islamists in Hadramaut, who had ties with Saudi Arabia, attempted to forge an alliance with the ex-communists of South Yemen against Ali Abdullah Saleh's bid to strengthen and consolidate his government in Sana'a. At this point, Saudi Arabia began to have misgivings over its support for Ali Abdullah Saleh, having begun to see a strong Yemen as a potential rival in the Arabian Peninsula. The Saudis also wanted a favorable settlement of the long-standing territorial dispute between the two countries over the frontier province of Asir. In this confused situation, Islamists from a number of countries, especially Egypt and Saudi Arabia, were able to gain a foothold in Yemen. The United States tacitly continued to back the presidency of Ali Abdullah Saleh, though he had expressed support for Saddam Hussein during the Gulf conflict, as it saw in him a potential ally against the Islamists in case of need.

Meanwhile, Sheikh Abdullah al-Ahmar became Speaker of Yemen's parliament, and as the leader of Islah and a traditional ally of Saudi Arabia, he was faced with the task of remaining on good terms both with his cousin President Ali Abdullah Saleh and the Saudi leadership. However, the rise to power of Crown Prince Abdullah in Saudi Arabia—who has now succeeded King Fahd—facilitated the settlement of the Asir issue in the treaty of 2000, which retains the province for Saudi Arabia while redrawing the border more favorably to Yemen. This also enabled Islah to reconcile its support for Ali Abdullah Saleh on the one hand and its links with Saudi Arabia on the other.

Following his victory in the 1999 presidential election, Ali Abdullah Saleh took steps to limit Islah's influence. Personal propaganda against Al-Ahmar signaled worsening relations between Islah and the President's General People's Congress, and the United States began to ask for a crackdown on the Islamists. From 2000, the relationship between Islah and the government of Ali Abdullah Saleh was increasingly hostile. The government took away Islah's control over a number of religious and teaching institutions, and prevented foreign students from attending Al-Iman University, which was suspected by the Americans of indoctrinating the youth with anti-American opinions and of acting as an agency for Al-Qaida. In October, there was a shoot-out between police and Abdullah Al-Ahmar's guards. Politically, Islah's tactics in opposition have been to keep up its pressure on the government by means of its tribal links and its roots in the religious seminaries. Islah sometimes crosses the border between politics and direct action, as is often the case with movements connected with the Muslim Brotherhood.

The supporters of bin Laden also continued to make their presence felt. On October 12, 2000, suspected Al-Qaida sympathizers attacked the USS *Cole* lying at anchor in Aden, resulting in the deaths of seventeen American sailors. It should not be forgotten that bin Laden is of Yemeni descent, as his father came originally from Hadramaut. Bin Laden's men were able to play on tribal and Islamic solidarity to hamper the plans of the

United States in Yemen. Arabic-speaking FBI agents flew from America to investigate those who were responsible for the accident, and some progress was made in linking the incident to Al-Qaida. However, the Yemeni government was not happy with the presence of American agents and the U.S. Embassy eventually asked for their removal in the interests of good relations. However, President Ali Abdullah Saleh's decision to take up a more pro-American stance after September 11, 2001, which had its origins in the fear of reprisals, meant that the investigation was able to continue.

After 2001, in the light of the president's new more pro-American stance, there was some effort by the Yemeni government to identify and prosecute alleged Islamic extremists accused of terrorist links. In December 2001, the government claimed that Islah was responsible for the murder of Jarallah Omar, a Yemeni socialist leader. Jarallah Omar had actually advocated an alliance between socialists and Islamists against what he alleged to be the corruption of the government. This allegation in effect ended the understanding between Islah and the government. In January 2002, Yemen was rewarded for its change of position by the United States and the Gulf Arab states when it was permitted to join the Gulf Cooperation Council, with observer status. In November 2002, the CIA was allowed to mount an operation in Yemen when a pilotless drone was launched by CIA operatives to kill six suspected Al-Qaida members near Marib. February 2004, the United States specifically named Sheikh Zindani in particular as a terrorist suspect and indicated that it would like to see his extradition to be charged with assisting Al-Qaida. In early 2005, the U.S. Congress praised Yemen as a Middle East state taking an appropriate path, but by October 2005 reports suggested that Washington was becoming less gratified by Yemen's stance.

In September 2006, President Ali Abdullah Saleh, who had been in power for twenty-six years, submitted himself once more for reelection, though not until after a delay of two years from the date prescribed by the constitution. There was little doubt that the president would win, though he was challenged by Faisal bin Shamlan, a candidate representing a coalition known as the Joint Meeting Party, in which Islah played a leading role. Election monitors said the poll was fair though there had been issues over voter registration and some irregularities. Shamlan campaigned on an anti-corruption platform. A claim by President Saleh that some of Shamlan's associates were implicated in Al-Qaida was strongly rejected. President Saleh won the election as expected, but Shamlan took 25 percent of the vote.

After the election, President Saleh continued to accuse the opposition, and in particular the Islamists, of links with terrorist groups. Some reports, however, suggest that the Yemeni government is seeking to distance itself once more from the United States, and it does appear that the Islamists are to some extent allowed to operate in public. In April 2006, Sheikh Zindani, whose extradition is not under consideration, is known to have met Khaled Mishaal, the Palestinian Hamas leader based in Syria, at a fundraising event. In other actions against Islamist supporters, Mohammed Hamdi al-Ahdal, a Saudi citizen, was accused of organizing bomb attacks on U.S. targets, and nineteen Yemenis face similar charges. On April 13, alleged members of Al-Qaida were convicted of attacking government targets and sixty more prisoners were brought to trial. The Yemeni government's attitude retains a certain element of unpredictability, however. Many Islamist prisoners accused of links with terrorism were quickly released back into the community, and in February 2006 twenty-three Islamists badly wanted by the United States escaped with ease from a prison run by the Yemeni security services. Meanwhile, the United States holds over a hundred Yemeni detainees at Guantanamo Bay. One Yemeni prisoner who was formerly a member of the Islah Party's Shura Council is serving a sentence in the United States for financing terrorist activities.

On the political front, Sheikh Abdullah al-Ahmar left Yemen for Saudi Arabia in January, announcing that he was abandoning Yemen to Ali Abdullah Saleh and his family, The move was seen as the preliminary to a possible later bid by Islah to take power in Yemen. One scenario envisaged by observers is an energetic Islah campaign against the president, after which Sheikh Al-Ahmar might return to bring about conciliation and bring to bear his standing as a tribal dignitary and Ali Abdullah Saleh's kinsman to reap the rewards of his standing as a mediator. Sheikh Zindani has warned the president that South Yemen is once more in a mood to secede if given the chance. There is also dissidence among the Shi'ite tribesmen in North Yemen, though this has no connection with Islah or other Sunni movements.

ZAKAT

The payment of "zakat" is a religious obligation. It would be a misnomer to describe it as a religious tax, and it is strictly speaking not a charitable gift. It is one of the five pillars of Islam and is therefore a moral obligation and an absolute duty. The concept of zakat is linked to the idea of purification. Sura 9 of the Quran, verse 103, reads, "Take alms from their wealth, with which to purify them and cleanse them." In most verses where zakat is mentioned, it is linked to the practice of prayer. The two institutions are connected to the extent where prayer, the second pillar of Islam, acquires its value when it is accompanied by the virtuous action of zakat. "Perform the prayers; pay the zakat; bow down with those who bow down" (Sura 2, verse 43). According to the Quran, everything in the world belongs to God, and he created possessions to enable his creatures both to live and to give alms to those who deserve them. The believer is thus returning only a minuscule part of what has been given to him or her by God.

Those who have the right to receive the zakat are listed in the Quran, "The parents, the near of kin, the orphans, the needy and the wayfarer" (Sura 2, verse 215). The Quran also says, "The alms are for the poor, the needy and their representatives, those whose hearts are reconciled, and for the purchase

of captives and the relief of debtors." Those who distribute the zakat retain part of it as their recompense, even if they are rich. Gifts should also be made to those who are likely to convert to Islam. This last condition remains operative today, despite being abandoned by the Caliph Omar (who reigned from 634 to 644) at a time when the number of converts across the Islamic empire became very large.

Those of the Shafi and Hanafi schools of law take the view that the field of application of the zakat in particular and of good works in general may be wider than these specific areas. Material aid may be given in other fields, particularly in those related to Da'wa (the propagation of Islam). This may be undertaken in various styles, from the most moderate to more radical methods. If the donor fails to remember the underlying spiritual reasons for the donation of zakat and forgets its religious nature, he or she, in effect, deprives it of the spirit of generosity and becomes no more than a mechanical reflex. The use of zakat to relieve the sufferings of the poor achieves its spiritual purpose only if it is undertaken in a spirit of brotherhood rather than egotism and if the welfare of the community takes precedence over individual considerations.

The possibility of ambiguity in the use of zakat rests in the concept of community. Its diversion to political channels by Islamists is justified in the name of spirituality and of the advancement of the true faith, which these funds, it is argued, should in the end be used to promote.

ZANZIBAR

Zanzibar is an archipelago of islands off the Tanzanian coast with autonomous internal status within Tanzania. The main island is Zanzibar itself. Its population of a million people is 99 percent Muslim. The ruling party in Zanzibar has always been the Revolutionary Party (CCM) (Chama Che Mapinduzi), whereas the principal Muslim political party in Zanzibar is the Civic United Front (CUF). The CUF has traditionally endeavored to draw a distinction between Zanzibar and the African identity of the federal state of Tanzania of which Zanzibar became a part in 1964 after a year of chaotic independence. The CUF has also been able to strike up links with mainland African Muslims, such as Ibrahim Haruna Lipumba, one of its own leaders, whose original home was Tabora, deep in mainland Tanzania.

The CUF consciously harks back to the former Sultanate of Zanzibar, before the fusion with mainland Tanganyika formed the state of Tanzania. It receives support from several Gulf Arab states. In early 2001, there were bloody clashes between CUF militants and the Tanzanian police and military, often after Friday prayers. After this, the CUF's rhetoric and activity took a markedly radical turn. Re-Islamization of society, based firmly on the demand for separation, already a goal of the CUF, was made the unambiguous priority. Some CUF militants chose to operate in secrecy, apparently seeking to make contacts with Osama bin Laden's movement. One of those convicted in connection with the bombing of the U.S. embassy in Tanzania in 1998 was Khalfan Khamis Muhammad, originally from Zanzibar.

Some Islamist activists have been identified. Sheikh Ponda Issa Ponda is thought to be an instigator of militant activism and has frequently been detained by the security forces. He has been connected with incidents in the Tanzanian mainland as well as with a bombing incident in 2002 in Stone Town. There is also an organization called Uamsho ("Islamic Propagation and Awareness") that appears to receive Saudi funds and apparently has connections with Pakistan. It distributes Jihadi literature and militates for the introduction of Shari'a law. It protests against the influence of tourism and has attacked churches. In March 2003, Uamsho held a major illegal demonstration in Zanzibar and in the following weeks attacked the homes of the Mufti and of a cabinet minister. Uamsho's leader is Sheikh Azzani Khaled Hamdan. He is reported to want the departure of non-Muslims from Zanzibar or their conversion to Islam. However, there is no clear relationship between Uamsho and the CUF. An activist movement that appears to have some connection with Uamsho is Simba wa Mungu ("God's Lion") that singles out supposedly corrupt Muslims and targets foreigners.

On October 30, 2005, the CCM held on to power in elections that had been preceded by several months of clashes with the supporters of the CUF. The CCM leader Amani Abeid Karume was returned to office with over half the vote, and the CUF candidate Seif Sharif Hamad took only 46 percent. The results were immediately challenged by the CUF that demanded a re-run. President Karume resisted the Islamist challenge. Normal political relations were maintained, however, and the CUF continues to function as an accepted opposition party.

ZAWAHIRI, AYMAN AL-

Ayman al-Zawahiri was born on June 19, 1951, in the comfortable middle-class

Cairo suburb of Maadi, into a well-known and prestigious family. Muhammad Rabi' al-Zawahiri, his father, was a professor of pharmacology, and Sheikh Al-Ahmadi Al-Zawahiri, his grandfather, was the imam of the Azhar mosque in Cairo Umayma Azzam, his mother, was the daughter of Abdel Wahhab Azzam, a distinguished literary scholar. Abdel Wahhab, the president of Cairo University and the Egyptian ambassador to Pakistan, was the brother of Abdel Rahman Azzam, the founding secretary-general of the League of Arab States in 1945. At school, Ayman al-Zawahiri was an assiduous student, and as he grew older, he showed an increasing interest in religion. By the age of fourteen, he had joined the Muslim Brotherhood and began to study the works of Hassan al-Banna and Sayyid Qutb. At the age of fifteen, he was arrested because of his Muslim Brotherhood activities.

Nevertheless, he followed his father's footsteps and embarked on a medical career. In 1974, he graduated with high honors from the medical school at Cairo University, afterward signing up for three years as a doctor with the Egyptian Army. At the same time, he led a local Muslim Brotherhood cell. Although continuing on the path of Islamist activism, he specialized in surgery. In 1978, he took a master's degree in surgery and married Azza Ahmad Nuwair, a Cairo University graduate. Meanwhile, he had become a founder member of a more radical group, Islamic Jihad, set up in 1977. Islamic Jihad advocated violent action against political regimes, and individuals deemed to be impious. Zawahiri was fiercely opposed to the 1978 Camp David accords and the subsequent peace treaty made between Egypt and Israel in April 1979.

In 1980, Ayman al-Zawahiri went to Pakistan for the first time, at the suggestion of his contacts in the Muslim Brotherhood. There, he served for four months as a medical officer at the Red Crescent hospital in Peshawar, where international jihadists and local Islamic radicals met and mingled. He seems to have visited Afghanistan also. In early 1981, he spent another two months in Pakistan. While in Pakistan, he may have met Osama bin Laden for the first time. The entire experience of his journey influenced him profoundly. After his return to Egypt, he became involved in the movement against President Anwar Sadat and apparently used his contacts in the Egyptian Army to seek out army officers with Islamist sympathies, with the help of Abboud al-Zumar, an Egyptian Army intelligence officer who was a member of Islamic Jihad. He was among hundreds arrested in the police swoop that followed the murder of President Sadat on October 6, 1981, although he was exonerated of direct involvement. However, he was convicted of illegal possession of arms and sentenced to three years of imprisonment.

He was released in 1984, and in 1985, he traveled to Saudi Arabia and then on to Pakistan. By 1987, he had set up an office for Egyptian jihadists in Peshawar. At this time, he is said to have come into close contact with Osama bin Laden. Osama bin Laden was at the time running the Maktab al-Khadamat (Services Bureau) that provided backup and logistics for Arab volunteers for the jihad against the Soviets in Afghanistan. Both worked at that time under the direction of Abdullah Azzam, bin Laden's Jordanian mentor. When bin Laden broke with Azzam, Zawahiri's influence increased. In 1990, after the end of the war against the Soviets, the Arab fighters left mainly Afghanistan. Zawahiri is said to have visited various countries but may well have been attempting to conceal his true whereabouts.

By 1992, he was with Osama bin Laden in Sudan. While based in Sudan, Zawahiri set up training camps in Yemen and organized a campaign against the Egyptian President Husni Mubarak, Sadat's successor. In 1993, unsuccessful attempts were made to assassinate the Egyptian Prime Minister Atef Sidki and the Interior Minister Hassan al-Alfi. In June 1995, Zawahiri's followers made an attempt on Mubarak's life as he arrived in Addis Ababa to attend an Organization of African Unity summit in Ethiopia. In November 1995, the Egyptian Embassy in Islamabad was bombed. The Egyptians identified Zawahiri as a major threat and are said to have attempted to target him in Sudan. Egyptian intelligence succeeded in penetrating Zawahiri's organization inside the country, and most of Islamic Jihad's activists were rounded up. Zawahiri has apparently sent militant volunteers to Somalia also.

Zawahiri and bin Laden returned to Afghanistan in 1996 after the triumph of the Taliban. It was at this time that Al-Qaida began to establish itself as a redoubtable organization on the international scene. He is also said to have visited the United States in 1996 under an assumed identity, to raise funds and assess the effectiveness of Islamist networks in United States. He appears to have traveled widely in the mid-1950s. According to an article in the *Wall Street Journal,* when he was detained on the Chechen border in December 1996, documents found in his possession indicate he had been in China, Hong Kong, and Malaysia. Bin Laden and Zawahiri effectively declared war on the United States on February 23, 1998, when Zawahiri put his name to the document issued as a fatwa by bin Laden on that date that inaugurated the so-called International Islamic Front Against Jews and Crusaders. In 1999, he was sentenced to death in absentia in Egypt.

After September 11, 2001, Zawahiri was identified as a danger by the U.S. administration. In October 2001, he was named in the FBI list of most wanted terrorists. In November 2001, he said in an interview on Al-Jazeera television that Al-Qaida would strike wherever possible at the United States.

He went into hiding after the beginning of the U.S.-backed attack on the Taliban in Afghanistan by the Northern Alliance. In December 2001, his wife and three children were reported killed in an U.S. air strike on caves near Jalalabad. At the close of 2001, he published a book setting out his views on the need for jihad against the West. In March 2004, his voice was apparently heard on a videotape, urging Pakistanis to rise up against President Musharraf. In February 2005, a videotape of Zawahiri was broadcast by Al-Jazeera. On January 13, 2006, an U.S. air attack at Damadola, a Pakistani village close to the Afghan border, prompted rumors that Zawahiri had been killed. However, messages and interviews with Zawahiri continue to appear at regular intervals. It is said that in May 2007, he poured scorn on the plans of the U.S. administration to maintain their military presence in Iraq.

ZOUABRI, ANTAR

Antar Zouabri was born in 1970 at Boufarik, thirty kilometers south of Algiers. At an early age, he was strongly influenced by his brother Ali Zouabri, an inspector at the town's wholesale food market and a notorious member of the Islamic Salvation Front (FIS). Antar Zouabri left school early and became a political militant under his brother's influence. In 1992, after government action against members of the FIS, Ali Zouabri was among the earliest of the Islamist militants who took to the hills to continue their struggle. Antar Zouabri, who was at the time doing his military service, deserted his unit and secretly joined his brother, who was killed a few months later in an action by the security forces at Larbaa. Antar Zouabri's family suffered in the violence. Achour, another of his brothers, who had been a tax official, was detained on suspicion of subversive activity and sentenced to three years of imprisonment. Militants from another unit killed several other members of the Zouabri family as part of a personal vendetta. Mohammed, his father, aged eighty-two, was murdered outside the home where he had raised his family, on a former colonial estate.

Antar Zouabri joined a cell of the Armed Islamic Group (GIA) and rose to be local commander in the Boufarik region after the security authorities destroyed many units operating in the foothills of the Blidan hills. When Djamel Zitouni became leader of the GIA, Antar Zouabri rose higher in the organization. After the internal purges in the GIA, and the brutal expulsion of the Algerianist tendency that took place between November 1995 and January 1996, he became one of Zitouni's close aides. He was given responsibility for maintaining liaison between Zitouni and the various regional leaders or "emirs." In the context of this task, he became aware of the great potentiality for splits within the GIA. He helped to frustrate the ambitions of such regional leaders as Hassan Hattab and Habbi Miloud, both of whom challenged Zitouni's leadership and accused him of "deviationism." On July 16, 1996, Zitouni was murdered at the hands of fighters linked to the Algerianist tendency and the GIA split into several factions.

Antar Zouabri, by now using the nom de guerre Abou Talha, became Zitouni's successor, thanks to the support of many influential combatants, after he had fought off a challenge from Habbi Miloud. After achieving leadership of the movement, Antar Zouabri took up a position of extreme radicalism. He maintained that jihad was legitimate not only against the representatives of the "apostate" government and their allies but also against private citizens who refused to take part in the conflict. In this light, he initiated a large number of collective massacres that instilled terror in the population and brought them into submission. In some cases, the security services failed to prevent such operations, an issue over which troubling queries have been raised. However, his family once again suffered. In 1997, his mother and his sister were arrested and imprisoned for three years.

In 1997, most of the international Islamists who had supported the GIA withdrew their backing, because of Zouabri's extremism and their inability to endorse either his actions or his religious pronouncements. The publication "Al Ansar" ceased to appear, and the movement failed to recruit new fighters. In 1998, the GIA was weakened when a faction led by Hassan Hattab split off. This undermined Zouabri, who was also accused of being manipulated by the Algerian security services. Zouabri took refuge in his headquarters and only occasionally left the Chrea hills, in the neighborhood of Blida, where his so-called Green Guard protected him. His death had on many occasions been falsely reported, but Zouabri was finally killed—in his birthplace, Boufarik—on February 8, 2002.

Index